6/15/2009

Congratulations!

Thank you for purchasing a new copy of *Designing the User Interface*, Fourth Edition. Your textbook includes six months of prepaid access to the book's Companion Website. This prepaid subscription provides you with full access to all reader resources, including:

- Links to hundreds of HCI resources, examples, and research, which enhance and expand upon the material in each chapter.
- Self-assessment questions.
- Assignments and projects.
- And more!

To access the *Designing the User Interface* Companion Website for the first time:

You will need to register online using a computer with an Internet connection and a Web browser. The process takes just a couple of minutes and only needs to be completed once.

1. Go to **http://www.aw-bc.com/dtui**.
2. Click **General Resources**.
3. Click the **Register** button.
4. Use a coin to scratch off the gray coating below and reveal your student access code*. Do not use a knife or other sharp object, which can damage the code.

5. On the registration page, enter your student access code. Do not type the dashes. You can use lowercase or uppercase.
6. Follow the on-screen instructions. If you need help at any time during the online registration process, simply click the **Need Help?** icon.
7. Once your personal Login Name and Password are confirmed, you can begin using the *Designing the User Interface* Companion Website!

To log into this Web site after you've registered:

You only need to register for this Companion Website once. After that, you can access the site by going to http://www.aw-bc.com/dtui, clicking "General Resources," and providing your Login Name and Password when prompted.

*IMPORTANT: The Access Code on this page can only be used once to establish a subscription to the *Designing the User Interface*, Fourth Edition Companion Website. This subscription is valid for six months upon activation, and is not transferable. If this access code has already been scratched off, it may no longer be valid. If this is the case, you can purchase a subscription by going to http://www.aw-bc.com/dtui and clicking "General Resources."

DESIGNING THE USER INTERFACE

DESIGNING THE USER INTERFACE

FOURTH EDITION STRATEGIES FOR EFFECTIVE HUMAN-COMPUTER INTERACTION

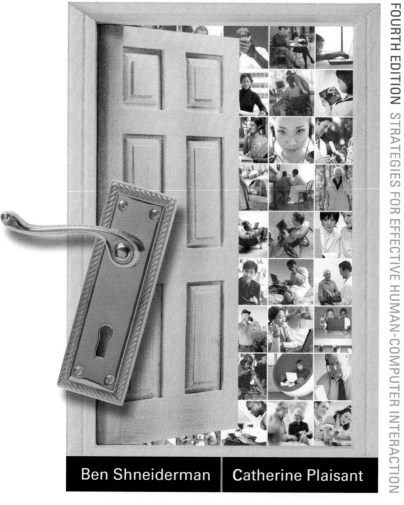

Ben Shneiderman | Catherine Plaisant

University of Maryland, College Park

PEARSON

Addison
Wesley

Boston   San Francisco   New York
London   Toronto   Sydney   Tokyo   Singapore   Madrid
Mexico City   Munich   Paris   Cape Town   Hong Kong   Montreal

Executive Editor	Susan Hartman Sullivan
Senior Acquisitions Editor	Michael Hirsch
Project Editor	Maite Suarez-Rivas
Marketing Manager	Nathan Schultz
Senior Marketing Coordinator	Lesly Hershman
Senior Production Supervisor	Jeffrey Holcomb
Project Management	Edalin Michael, Argosy Publishing
Copyeditor	Rachel Wheeler
Proofreader	Kim Cofer
Indexer	Larry Sweazy
Composition and Art	Argosy Publishing
Cover and Interior Designer	Joyce Cosentino Wells
Cover Photos	© 2004 Getty Images
Prepress and Manufacturing	Caroline Fell

Access the latest information about Addison-Wesley titles from our World Wide Web site:
http://www.aw-bc.com/computing

Many of the designations used by manufacturers and sellers to distinguish their products are claimed as trademarks. Where those designations appear in this book, and Addison-Wesley was aware of a trademark claim, the designations have been printed in initial caps or all caps.

The programs and applications presented in this book have been included for their instructional value. They have been tested with care, but are not guaranteed for any particular purpose. The publisher does not offer any warranties or representations, nor does it accept any liabilities with respect to the programs or applications.

Library of Congress Cataloging-in-Publication Data

Shneiderman, Ben.
    Designing the user interface : strategies for effective human-computer interaction / Ben Shneiderman, Catherine Plaisant.--4th ed.
      p. cm.
    Includes bibliographical references and index.
    ISBN 0-321-19786-0
    1. Human-computer interaction. 2. User interfaces (Computer systems) I. Plaisant, Catherine. II. Title.

QA76.9.H85S54 2004
005.1--dc22
2003068940

ISBN 0-321-19786-0
2 3 4 5 6 7 8 9 10-QWT-08 07 06 05

To Jenny and Peter;
Anna, Sara, and Thomas

Preface

Designing the User Interface is written for students, researchers, designers, managers, and evaluators of interactive systems. It presents a broad survey of how to develop high-quality user interfaces for interactive systems. Readers with backgrounds in computer science, psychology, industrial engineering, information science, information systems, business, education, and communications should all find fresh and valuable material. Our goals are to encourage greater attention to usability issues and to promote further scientific study of human-computer interaction.

Since publication of the first three editions of this book in 1986, 1992, and 1998, practitioners and researchers have grown more numerous and influential. The quality of interfaces has improved greatly, but the community of users and their diversity has grown dramatically. Researchers and designers could claim success, but user expectations are higher, applications are more demanding, and the variety of platforms has grown. In addition to desktop computers, designers must now accommodate web-based services and mobile devices. At the same time, some innovators provoke us with virtual and augmented realities, whereas others offer alluring scenarios for ubiquitous computing, embedded devices, and tangible user interfaces.

These innovations are important, but much work remains to improve the experiences of novice and expert users who still struggle with too many frustrations. These problems must be resolved if we are to achieve the goal of universal usability, enabling all citizens in every country to enjoy the benefits of these new technologies. This book is meant to inspire students, guide designers, and provoke researchers.

Keeping up with the innovations in human-computer interaction is a demanding task. Requests for an update to the third edition began shortly after its publication. The growth of the field has encouraged me (Ben Shneiderman), the author of the first three editions, to work with a co-author (Catherine Plaisant), who has been a long-time valued research partner. We harvested information from books and journals, scanned the World Wide Web, attended conferences, and consulted with colleagues. Then we returned to our keyboards to write. Our first drafts were only a starting point to generate feedback from colleagues, practitioners, and students. The work was intense, but satisfying. We hope you will put these ideas to work and produce innovations for us to report in future editions.

New in the Fourth Edition

Readers will see the dynamism of human-computer interaction reflected in the substantial changes to this fourth edition. The good news is that most universities now offer courses in this area and some require it in computer science or other disciplines. There is still some resistance, but courses and degree programs in human-computer interaction are a growing phenomenon at every level on a worldwide basis. Corporate and government commitment to usability engineering grows stronger daily, although many usability practitioners must still fight to be heard. The business case for usability has been made repeatedly and whole Web sites describe scores of studies demonstrating strong return on investment for usability efforts.

Comments from instructors who used the third edition were influential in our revisions. The main change was to delete the chapter on the World Wide Web and instead describe Web-based, desktop, and mobile device designs throughout. Every chapter is updated with fresh ideas, examples, figures, and references. The opening chapter addresses the growing issue of ensuring universal usability for increasingly diverse users of interactive systems. Then guidelines, principles, and theories are substantially updated to reflect new ways of thinking. Part II covers the refinements to development methodologies, evaluation techniques, and software tools. Part III presents progress in direct manipulation and its extensions such as virtual and augmented reality, as well as changes to menus, form fillin, and command languages brought about by the new platforms, especially consumer electronics devices. Since collaborative interfaces have become so central, this chapter is moved forward in the book. Part IV emphasizes Quality of Service and a series of important design issues. Since user manuals and online help are vital to serve the goal of universal usability, that chapter is thoroughly revised. Finally, information search and visualization get special coverage since we believe that these topics will continue to grow in importance.

We strive to give balanced presentations on controversial topics such as 3D, speech, and natural language interfaces. Philosophical controversies such as the degree of human control and the role of animated characters are treated carefully to present fairly the viewpoints that differ from our own. We gave colleagues a chance to comment on these sections, and made a special effort to provide a balanced presentation while making our opinions clear. Readers will have to judge for themselves whether we succeeded.

Instructors wanted more guidelines and summary tables; these elements are shown in boxes throughout the book. The Practitioner Summaries and Researcher Agendas remain popular; they are updated. The references are expanded and freshened with many new sources, with classic papers still included. Because some of the previously cited works were difficult to find, a much larger percentage of the references now are widely available sources. Figures, especially those showing screen designs, age quickly, so many new user interfaces are shown. The printing in full color makes these figures even more valuable.

Ways to Use This Book

We hope that practitioners and researchers who read this book will want to keep it on their shelves to consult when they are working on a new topic or seeking pointers to the literature.

Instructors may choose to assign the full text in the order that we present it or to make selections from it. The opening chapter is a good starting point for most students, but instructors may take different paths depending on their disciplines. For example, instructors might emphasize the following chapters, listed by area:

- Computer science: 2, 5, 6, 7, 8, 9, 10, 14
- Psychology: 2, 4, 6, 10, 11, 12, 13, 14
- Industrial engineering: 2, 4, 6, 10, 11, 12, 13, 14
- Library and information science: 2, 4, 10, 12, 13, 14
- Business and information systems: 3, 4, 6, 10, 11, 12, 14
- Education technology: 2, 4, 6, 10, 13, 14
- Communication arts and media studies: 4, 6, 10, 12, 13
- Technical writing and graphic design: 3, 4, 6, 12, 13

Companion Web Site (www.aw-bc.com/DTUI)

The presence of the World Wide Web has a profound effect on researchers, designers, educators, and students. We want to encourage intense use of the Web by all these groups and to integrate it into common practice. However, the volatility of the Web is not in harmony with the permanence of printed books. Publishing Web site URLs in the book would have been risky, because changes are made daily. For these and other reasons, we have established a Companion Web site to accompany this book. We hope that every reader will visit the site and send us ideas for improving it.

Supplements

A variety of supplemental materials for this text are available at the book's Companion Web site: www.aw-bc.com/DTUI. The following are accessible to all readers who register using the prepaid access card in the front of this book:

- Links to hundreds of human-computer interaction resources, examples, and research that enhance and expand on the material in each chapter

- Chapter/section summaries
- Self-test questions and discussion questions for each chapter
- Homework assignments and projects

Acknowledgments

Writing is a lonely process; revising is a social one. We are grateful to the many colleagues and students who contributed their suggestions. We appreciate the strong contributions from Jean-Daniel Fekete to Chapter 5 and Jennifer Preece to Chapter 10. Our close daily partners at the University of Maryland have had a great influence on our work: Ben Bederson, Allison Druin, Kent Norman, Anne Rose, and François Guimbretière. We give special thanks to Charles Kreitzberg and Gary Marchionini for their personal and professional support over many years.

Extensive comments from the review panel played a strong role in our revisions. These individuals made numerous constructive suggestions:

Robert St. Amant, *North Carolina State University*

Catherine I. Beaton, *Rochester Institute of Technology*

Richard F. Bellaver, *Ball State University*

William H. Bowers, *Penn State Berks-Lehigh Valley College*

Roger J. Chapman, *Ohio State University*

Andrew Johnson, *University of Illinois at Chicago*

Bill Killam, *User-Centered Design, Inc.*

Alfred Kobsa, *University of California, Irvine*

Adrienne Olnick Kutzschan, *Queen's University, Canada*

Bruce R. Maxim, *University of Michigan-Dearborn*

D. Scott McCrickard, *Virginia Tech*

Jane Webster, *Queen's University, Canada*

In addition, colleagues commented generously on certain chapters or sections for which they were especially knowledgeable: Len Bass, Stephen Brewster, Justine Cassell, Andy Cockburn, Mary Czerwinski, Daniel DeMenthon, Mikael Fernstrom, Evan Golub, Art Graesser, Michael Green, Harry Hochheiser, Bonnie John, Lewis Johnson, Dan Olsen, Judy Olson, Ian Pitt, Theresa-Marie Rhyne, George Robertson, Bernhard Suhm, Alistair Sutcliffe, and Colin Ware. We appreciate Kendra Knudtzon's help with the figures, and the many people and organizations that provided figures are acknowledged at the end of the book. Roger Chapman and Adam Perer played instrumental roles in the development of much of the material on the book's Companion Web site.

The publisher's editorial and production staff was actively involved in this book from the start. We appreciate the contributions of Michael Hirsch, Maite Suarez-Rivas, Joyce Wells, Jennifer Pelland, Jeffrey Holcomb, Lesly Hershman, Meghan James, and others. The copy editor, Rachel Wheeler, taught us a lot about lucid and informative writing. We apologize if we have left out anyone. We also appreciate the students and professionals from around the world who sent comments and suggestions. Their provocative questions about our growing discipline and profession encourage us daily.

Ben Shneiderman (ben@cs.umd.edu)
Catherine Plaisant (plaisant@cs.umd.edu)

Brief Contents

Contents

Introduction

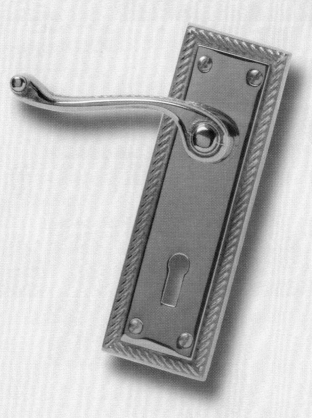

1

Usability of Interactive Systems

Designing an object to be simple and clear takes at least twice as long as the usual way. It requires concentration at the outset on how a clear and simple system would work, followed by the steps required to make it come out that way—steps which are often much harder and more complex than the ordinary ones. It also requires relentless pursuit of that simplicity even when obstacles appear which would seem to stand in the way of that simplicity.

T. H. NELSON
The Home Computer Revolution, 1977

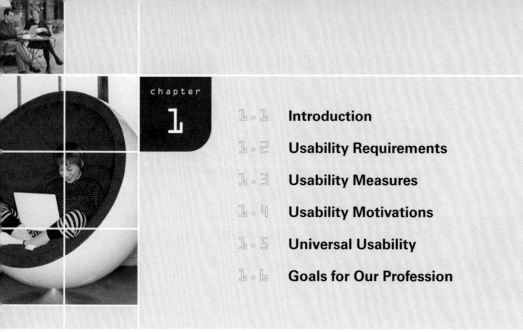

1.1   Introduction

New technologies provide extraordinary—almost supernatural—powers to those people who master them. Networked computers with advanced interfaces are compelling new technologies that are being rapidly disseminated. Great excitement spreads as designers provide remarkable functions in carefully crafted interactive devices and interfaces. The opportunities for rule-breaking innovators and business-focused entrepreneurs are substantial, and the impacts on individuals, organizations, and cultures are profound.

Like early photography equipment or automobiles, early computers were usable only by people who devoted effort to mastering the technology. Harnessing the computer's power is a task for designers who combine an understanding of technology with a sensitivity to human capacities and needs.

Human performance and user experience with computer and information systems will remain a rapidly expanding research and development topic in the coming decades. The interdisciplinary design science of *human-computer interaction* began by combining the data-gathering methods and intellectual framework of experimental psychology with the powerful and widely used tools developed from computer science. Then, contributions accrued from educational and industrial psychologists, instructional and graphic designers, technical writers, experts in human factors or ergonomics, information architects, and adventuresome anthropologists and sociologists. And now, as computers and user interfaces are becoming the basis for increasingly powerful sociotechnical systems, policy analysts, economists, lawyers, privacy advocates, and ethicists are playing a growing role.

User interfaces help produce business success stories and Wall Street sensations. They also produce intense competition, copyright-infringement suits, intellectual-property battles, mega-mergers, and international partnerships. Crusading Internet visionaries promote a world with free access to music, while equally devoted protectors of creative artists argue for fair payments.

User interfaces are also controversial because of their central role in national identification schemes, homeland defense, crime fighting, medical records management, and so on. In the aftermath of the September 11, 2001 terrorist attacks, some members of the U.S. Congress blamed the inadequacies of user interfaces for the failure to detect the terrorists.

At an individual level, user interfaces change many people's lives: effective user interfaces for professionals mean that doctors can make more accurate diagnoses and pilots can fly airplanes more safely; at the same time, children can learn more effectively and graphic artists can explore creative possibilities more fluidly. Some changes, however, are disruptive. Too often, users must cope with frustration, fear, and failure when they encounter excessively complex menus, incomprehensible terminology, or chaotic navigation paths. What user wouldn't be disturbed by receiving a message such as "Illegal Memory Exception: Severe Failure" with no guidance about what to do next?

The steadily growing interest in user-interface design, which spans remarkably diverse communities, stems from a desire to improve the user experience (Figs. 1.1 to 1.3 show some popular operating systems). In business settings, better decision-support and desktop-publishing tools support entrepreneurs, while in home settings digital photos and voice messaging enhance family relationships. A significant number of people take advantage of the World Wide Web's remarkable educational and cultural heritage resources, e-government services, and health-support communities. Access to outstanding art objects from China, music from Indonesia, sports from Brazil, and entertainment from Hollywood enriches daily life for many users, including those with disabilities and limited literacy (Figs. 1.4 to 1.6 show examples of popular web sites). Globalization promoters and dissenters debate the role of technology for international development.

Making these diverse applications successful requires contributions from researchers and practitioners in many fields. Academic and industrial researchers are developing descriptive taxonomies, explanatory theories, predictive models, and prescriptive guidance, while experimenters are collecting empirical data as a basis for new theories. The motor, perceptual, and cognitive foundations are growing firmer, while the social, economic, and ethical impacts are becoming clearer. Designers are using sound (such as music and voice), three-dimensional representations, animation, and video to improve the appeal and information content of interfaces. Techniques such as direct manipulation, telepresence, and

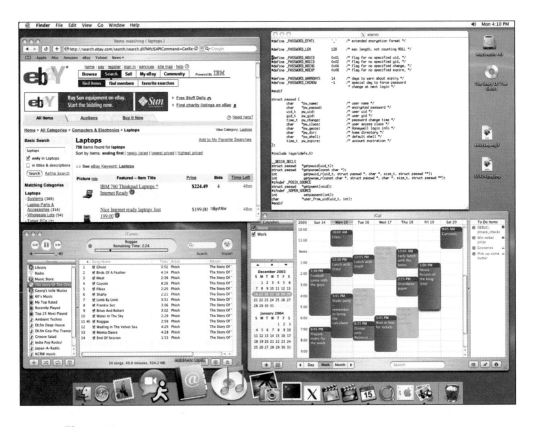

Figure 1.1

Mac OS X. All windows are set to a "metallic" theme. The top-left window shows eBay (http://www.ebay.com), a popular online auction site. The top-right window shows an Xterm window, which gives users direct access into the Unix underpinnings of Mac OS X. ITunes, the built-in music player for Mac, is shown on the bottom left. The bottom-right program is iCal, the built-in calendar program. The bottom of the screen also shows the Dock, the menu of frequently accessed items where selected items grow larger on mouse-over.

virtual reality may change the ways that we interact with technology, think about our work, or relate to our friends.

Sociologists, anthropologists, policymakers, and managers are currently dealing with issues of organizational impact, computer anxiety, job redesign, distributed teamwork, work-at-home schemes, and long-term societal changes. As face-to-face interaction gives way to screen-to-screen, does organizational loyalty and personal trust dissipate?

Designers face the challenge of providing services on small-, wall-, and mall-sized displays, ranging from portable devices such as cell phones or pocket

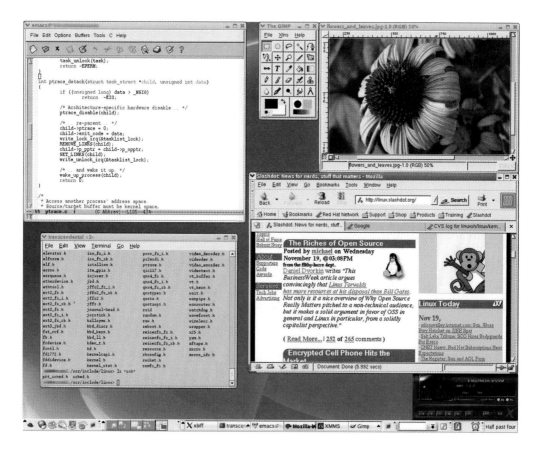

Figure 1.2

Linux RedHat 8 with KDE 3 window manager. The top-left window is GNU Emacs, an editing environment popular for programming. At the bottom left is a terminal window which provides a simple command-line interface for the user. The top-right window is The GIMP, a graphical image manipulation program; below this is the Mozilla browser, displaying Slashdot.org, a popular news web site. At the very bottom is XMMS, for playing music. The taskbar at the bottom controls multiple desktops. All these programs, including the operating system, are free and open source.

computers to large plasma panels and projected displays. The *plasticity* of their designs must ensure smooth conversion across display-size variations, delivery by way of web browsers or the telephone, translation into multiple languages, and compatibility with accessibility-support devices for disabled users.

Some innovators promise that desktop computers and their user interfaces will disappear, only to become ubiquitous, pervasive, invisible, and embedded in the surrounding environment. They believe that novel appliances will be

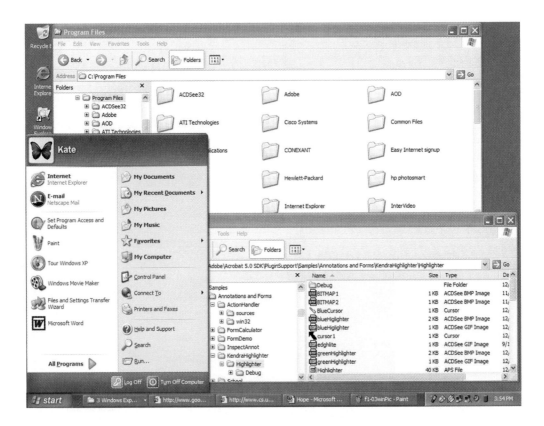

Figure 1.3

Microsoft Windows XP, showing the Program Files directory in the folder view,
a directory in the details view, and the new startup menu.

context-aware, attentive, and perceptive, sensing users' needs and providing
feedback through ambient displays that glow, hum, change shape, or blow air.
Some visionaries focus on advanced mobile devices that are portable, wearable,
or even implanted under the skin. Other designers promote persuasive technologies that change users' behavior, multi-modal or gestural interfaces that
facilitate use, and affective interfaces that respond to the user's emotional state.

We are living in an exciting time for developers of user interfaces. The inspirational pronouncements from technology prophets can be thrilling, but rapid
progress is more likely to come from those who do the hard work of tuning

designs to genuine human needs. These developers will rigorously evaluate actual use with eager early adopters, as well as reluctant late adopters, and seriously study the resistant non-users. The authors believe that the next phase of human-computer interaction will be strongly influenced by those who are

Figure 1.4

Microsoft Internet Explorer showing the NewYorkTimes web site (http://www.nytimes.com).

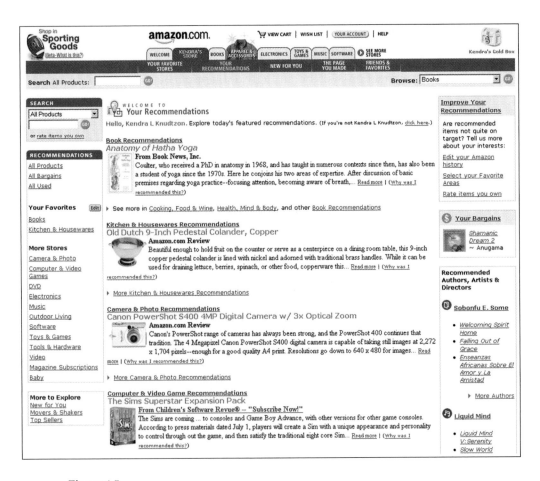

Figure 1.5

Amazon.com web site. Amazon.com will make book and product recommendations based on personal history with the web site. (http://www.amazon.com/)

devoted to broadening the community of users of interfaces and consciously promoting universal usability. The examples in this book address desktop, web, and mobile devices, with applications for novices, intermittent users, and frequent users.

This first chapter gives a broad overview of human-computer interaction from practitioner and research perspectives. It lays out usability requirements, measures, and motivations in Sections 1.2, 1.3, and 1.4, takes on the large topic of universal usability in Section 1.5, and closes with a statement of goals for our profession. Specific references cited in the chapter appear on page 45, and a set of general references begins on page 47. Lists of books, guidelines documents,

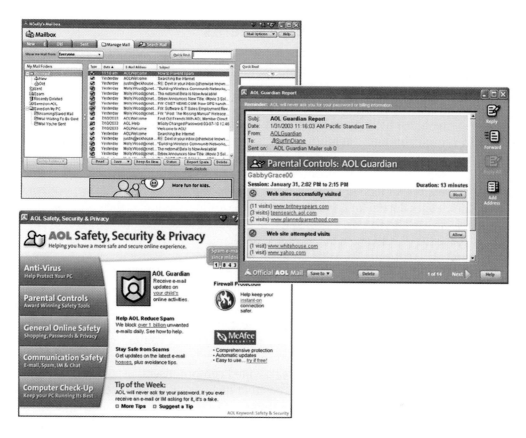

Figure 1.6

AOL 9.0. America Online's popular services include email and tools for parental controls for web browsing.

journals, video collections, and professional organizations give readers starting points for further study.

The second chapter reviews the guidelines, principles, and theories that will be drawn on and refined throughout the book. Chapters 3–5 introduce development processes and software tools, while Chapters 6–10 cover interaction styles that range from graphical direct manipulation to textual commands and their implementation using common interaction devices. Collaboration is included in this part to emphasize the need for every designer to go beyond the personal computer and consider the many forms of social computing. Chapters 11–14 address the critical design decisions that often determine the difference between the success and failure of products and could lead to breakthroughs that open the way to new possibilities. The Afterword reflects on the societal and individual impacts of technology.

1·2   Usability Requirements

Every designer wants to build high-quality interfaces that are admired by colleagues, celebrated by users, and imitated frequently. Appreciation comes not from flamboyant promises or stylish advertising, but rather from inherent quality features such as usability, universality, and usefulness. These goals are achieved through thoughtful planning, sensitivity to user needs, devotion to requirements analysis, and diligent testing.

Managers can promote attention to user-interface design by selection of personnel, preparation of schedules and milestones, construction and application of guidelines documents, and commitment to testing. Designers then propose multiple design alternatives for consideration, and the leading contenders are subjected to further development and testing (see Chapters 3 and 4). User-interface building tools (see Chapter 5) enable rapid implementation and easy revision. Evaluation of designs refines the understanding of appropriateness for each choice.

Successful designers go beyond the vague notion of "user friendliness," probing deeper than simply making a checklist of subjective guidelines. They have a thorough understanding of the diverse community of users and the tasks that must be accomplished. Moreover, they are deeply committed to serving the users, which strengthens their resolve when they face the pressures of short deadlines, tight budgets, and weak-willed compromisers.

Effective interfaces generate positive feelings of success, competence, mastery, and clarity in the user community. The users are not encumbered by the interface and can predict what will happen in response to each of their actions. When an interactive system is well designed, the interface almost disappears, enabling users to concentrate on their work, exploration, or pleasure. Creating an environment in which tasks are carried out almost effortlessly and users are "in the flow" requires a great deal of hard work by the designer.

Setting explicit goals helps designers to achieve those goals. In getting beyond the vague quest for user-friendly systems, managers and designers can focus on specific goals that include well-defined system engineering and measurable human-factors objectives. The U.S. Military Standard for Human Engineering Design Criteria (1999) states these purposes:

- Achieve required performance by operator, control, and maintenance personnel
- Minimize skill and personnel requirements and training time
- Achieve required reliability of personnel–equipment/software combinations
- Foster design standardization within and among systems

These functional purposes are good starting points, but effective interfaces might also enhance the quality of life for users or improve their communities.

Setting such goals is controversial, and the goals vary across cultures. These broader issues are left for the Afterword.

The first goal in requirements analysis (see Box 1.1) is to ascertain the users' needs—that is, what tasks and subtasks must be carried out. The frequent tasks are easy to determine, but the occasional tasks, the exceptional tasks for emergency conditions, and the repair tasks to cope with errors in use of the interface are more difficult to discover. Task analysis is central, because interfaces with inadequate functionality frustrate users and are often rejected or underutilized. If the functionality is inadequate, it does not matter how well the user interface is designed. Providing excessive functionality (which is probably the more common mistake of designers) is also a danger, because the clutter and complexity make implementation, maintenance, learning, and usage more difficult.

A vital second goal is to ensure proper reliability: actions must function as specified, displayed data must reflect the database contents, and updates must be applied correctly. Users' trust of systems is fragile; one experience with misleading data or unexpected results will undermine for a long time a person's willingness to use a system. The software architecture, hardware components, and network support must ensure high availability. If the system is not available or introduces errors, it does not matter how well the interface is designed. Designers also must pay attention to ensuring privacy, security, and data integrity. Protection must be provided from unauthorized access, inadvertent destruction of data, and malicious tampering.

The third set of goals for designers is to consider the context of use and promote appropriate standardization, integration, consistency, and portability. As the number of users and software packages increases, the pressures for and benefits of standardization grow. Slight differences between interfaces not only increase learning times but also can lead to annoying and dangerous errors. Gross differences between interfaces require substantial retraining and burden users in many ways. Incompatible storage formats and hardware and software versions cause frustration, inefficiency, and delay. Designers must decide whether the improvements they offer are useful enough to offset the disruption to the users.

Box 1.1

Goals for requirements analysis.

1. Ascertain the users' needs.
2. Ensure proper reliability.
3. Promote appropriate standardization, integration, consistency, and portability.
4. Complete projects on schedule and within budget.

Standardization refers to common user-interface features across multiple applications. Apple Computers (1992, 2002) successfully developed an early standard that was widely applied by thousands of developers, enabling users to learn multiple applications quickly. When the Microsoft Windows (1999, 2001) interface became standardized, it became a powerful force. Similarly, the standards provided by the World Wide Web Consortium have done much to accelerate adoption of the Web. The International Organization for Standardization (ISO) produces at least two dozen standards related to usability, including the widely read and lengthy ISO 9241, "Ergonomics Requirements for Office Work with Visual Display Terminals," which covers displays, menus, keyboards, work environments, and more.

Integration across application packages and software tools was one of the key design principles of Unix. (Portability across hardware platforms was another.) If file formats are used consistently, users can apply multiple applications to transform, refine, or validate their data.

Consistency primarily refers to common action sequences, terms, units, layouts, colors, typography, and so on within an application program. Consistency is a strong determinant of success of interfaces. It is naturally extended to include compatibility across application programs and compatibility with paper or non-computer-based systems. Compatibility across versions is a troubling demand, since the desire to accommodate novel functionality or improved designs competes with the benefits of consistency.

Portability refers to the potential to convert data and to share user interfaces across multiple software and hardware environments. Arranging for portability is a challenge for designers, who must contend with different display sizes and resolutions, color capabilities, pointing devices, data formats, and so on. Some user-interface building tools help by generating code for Macintosh, Windows, Unix, and other environments, so that the interfaces are similar in each environment or resemble the style in those environments. Standard text files (in ASCII) can be moved easily across environments, but slideshows, spreadsheets, video images, and so on are more difficult to convert.

The fourth goal for interface designers is to complete projects on schedule and within budget. Delayed delivery or cost overruns can threaten an interface project because of the confrontational political atmosphere in a company, or because the competitive market environment contains potentially overwhelming forces. If an in-house system is delivered late, other projects may be affected, and the disruption may cause managers to choose to install an alternative system. If a commercial system is too costly, customer resistance may emerge to prevent widespread acceptance, allowing competitors to capture the market.

Proper attention to usability principles and rigorous testing often lead to reduced cost and rapid development. A carefully tested design generates fewer changes during implementation and avoids costly updates after release. The business case for usability is strong and has been made repeatedly (Landauer, 1995; Norman, 2000), but the strongest case is provided by the many successful products whose advantage lies in their superior user interfaces.

1.3 Usability Measures

If adequate requirements are chosen, reliability is ensured, standardization is addressed, and scheduling and budgetary planning are complete, developers can focus their attention on the design and testing process. Multiple design alternatives must be evaluated for specific user communities and for specific benchmark tasks. A clever design for one community of users may be inappropriate for another community. An efficient design for one class of tasks may be inefficient for another class.

The relativity of design played a central role in the evolution of information services at the U.S. Library of Congress (Fig. 1.7). Two of the major uses of computer systems were cataloging new books and searching the online book catalog. Separate interfaces for these tasks were created that optimized the design for one task but made the complementary task difficult (Marchionini et al., 1993). It was impossible to say which was better, because both were fine interfaces but they were serving different needs—posing such a question would be like asking whether the New York Philharmonic Orchestra is better than the New York Yankees baseball team.

The situation became even more complex when Congressional staffers and then the public were invited to use the search interfaces. Three- to six-hour training courses were appropriate for Congressional staffers, but the first-time public users were overwhelmed by the command language and complex cataloging rules.

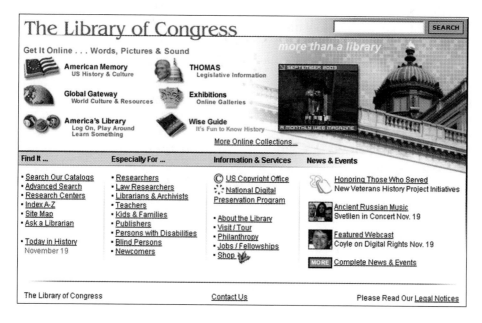

Figure 1.7

Library of Congress web site (http://www.loc.gov).

Eventually a touchscreen interface with reduced functionality and better information presentation was developed and became a big success in the public reading rooms. The next step in evolution was the development of a World Wide Web version of the catalog to allow users anywhere in the world to access the catalog and other databases. These changing user communities and requirements each led to interface revisions, even though the database and services remained similar.

Careful determination of the user community and of the benchmark set of tasks is the basis for establishing usability goals and measures. For each user and each task, precise measurable objectives guide the designer, evaluator, purchaser, or manager. The ISO 9241 standard focuses on admirable goals (*effectiveness*, *efficiency*, and *satisfaction*), but the following usability measures, which focus on the latter two goals, lead more directly to practical evaluation:

1. *Time to learn*. How long does it take for typical members of the user community to learn how to use the actions relevant to a set of tasks?

2. *Speed of performance*. How long does it take to carry out the benchmark tasks?

3. *Rate of errors by users*. How many and what kinds of errors do people make in carrying out the benchmark tasks? Although time to make and correct errors might be incorporated into the speed of performance, error handling is such a critical component of interface usage that it deserves extensive study.

4. *Retention over time*. How well do users maintain their knowledge after an hour, a day, or a week? Retention may be linked closely to time to learn, and frequency of use plays an important role.

5. *Subjective satisfaction*. How much did users like using various aspects of the interface? The answer can be ascertained by interview or by written surveys that include satisfaction scales and space for free-form comments.

Every designer would like to succeed in every category, but there are often forced tradeoffs. If lengthy learning is permitted, task-performance times may be reduced by use of complex abbreviations, macros, and shortcuts. If the rate of errors is to be kept extremely low, speed of performance may have to be sacrificed. In some applications, subjective satisfaction may be the key determinant of success; in others, short learning times or rapid performance may be paramount. Project managers and designers who are aware of the tradeoffs can be more effective in making their choices explicit and public. Requirements documents and marketing brochures that make clear which goals are primary are more likely to be valued.

After multiple design alternatives have been raised, the leading possibilities should be reviewed by designers and users. Low-fidelity paper mockups are useful, but high-fidelity online prototypes create a more realistic environment for expert reviews and usability testing. The user manuals and the online help can be written before the implementation to provide another review and perspective on the design. Next, the implementation can be carried out with proper software tools; this task should be a modest one if the design is complete and precise. Finally, the acceptance test certifies that the delivered interface meets the goals of the designers and customers. The development processes and software tools are described in Chapters 3, 4, and 5.

1.4   Usability Motivations

The enormous interest in interface usability arises from the growing recognition of how poorly designed many current interfaces are and of the benefits elegant interfaces bring to users. This increased motivation emanates from developers of life-critical systems; industrial and commercial systems; office, home, and entertainment applications; exploratory, creative, and collaborative interfaces; and sociotechnical systems.

1.4.1   Life-critical systems

Life-critical systems include those that control air traffic, nuclear reactors, power utilities, police or fire dispatch, military operations, and medical instruments. In these applications high costs are expected, but they should yield high reliability and effectiveness. Lengthy training periods are acceptable to obtain rapid, error-free performance, even when the users are under stress. Subjective satisfaction is less of an issue because the users are well-motivated professionals. Retention is obtained by frequent use of common functions and practice sessions for emergency actions.

1.4.2   Industrial and commercial uses

Typical industrial and commercial uses include banking, insurance, order entry, inventory management, airline and hotel reservations (Fig. 1.8), car rentals, utility billing, credit-card management, and point-of-sales terminals. In these cases, costs shape many judgments. Operator training time is expensive, so ease of learning is important. Since many businesses are international, translation to multiple languages and adaptations to local cultures are necessary. The tradeoffs for speed of performance and error rates are governed by the total cost over the system's lifetime (see Chapter 11). Subjective satisfaction is of modest importance; retention is obtained by frequent use. Speed of performance becomes central for most of these applications because of the high volume of transactions, but operator fatigue, stress, and burnout are legitimate concerns. Trimming 10% off the mean transaction time could mean 10% fewer operators, 10% fewer terminal workstations, and a 10% reduction in hardware costs.

1.4.3   Office, home, and entertainment applications

The rapid expansion of office, home, and entertainment applications is the third source of interest in usability. Personal-computing applications include e-mail, bank machines, games (Fig. 1.9), educational packages, search engines, cell

Figure 1.8

Netscape 7.1 showing http://www.orbitz.com, a site for purchasing airline tickets that has the capacity to display price options for multiple days, as for this trip from Washington, DC to San Francisco, CA on any weekend in January.

Figure 1.9

Tony Hawk Underground.

phones, and mobile devices (Fig. 1.10). For these interfaces, ease of learning, low error rates, and subjective satisfaction are paramount because use is frequently discretionary and competition is fierce. If the users cannot succeed quickly, they will abandon the use of a computer or try a competing package. In cases where use is intermittent, clear, easy-to-remember procedures are important, and if retention is still faulty, comprehensible online help becomes important.

Choosing the right functionality is difficult. Novices are best served by a constrained, simple set of actions, but as users' experience increases, so does their desire for more extensive functionality and rapid performance. A layered or level-structured design is one approach to graceful evolution from novice to expert usage. Users can move up to higher layers when they need additional features or have time to learn. A simple example is the design of search engines, which almost always have a basic and advanced interface. Another approach to winning novice users is to carefully trim the features to make a simple device, such as the highly successful Palm Pilot. Low cost is another important goal because of lively competition.

1.4.4   Exploratory, creative, and collaborative interfaces

An increasing fraction of computer use is dedicated to supporting human intellectual and creative enterprises. Exploratory applications include World Wide Web browsing (Figs. 1.11 to 1.13), search engines, scientific simulation, and

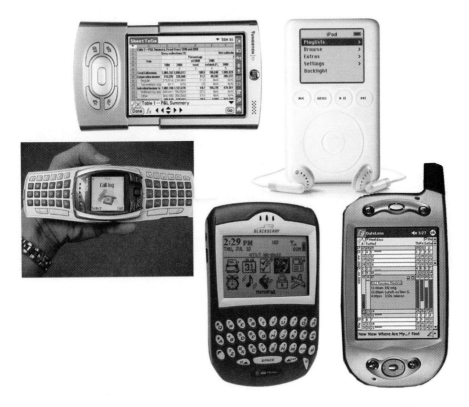

Figure 1.10

A variety of small mobile devices. Palm Tungsten, IPod, the Nokia 6800 phone, Black-berry, and the Microsoft Pocket PC phone displaying the University of Maryland's DateLens program.

business decision making. Creative environments include writing workbenches, architectural design systems (Fig. 1.14), artist or programmer workstations, and music-composition systems. Collaborative interfaces enable two or more people to work together, even if the users are separated by time and space, through use of electronic text, voice, and video mail; through electronic meeting systems that facilitate face-to-face meetings; or through groupware that enables remote collaborators to work concurrently on a document, map, spreadsheet, or image.

In these systems, the users may be knowledgeable in the task domain but novices in the underlying computer concepts. Their motivation is often high, but so are their expectations. Benchmark tasks are more difficult to describe because of the exploratory nature of these applications. Usage can range from occasional to frequent. In short, it is difficult to design and evaluate these

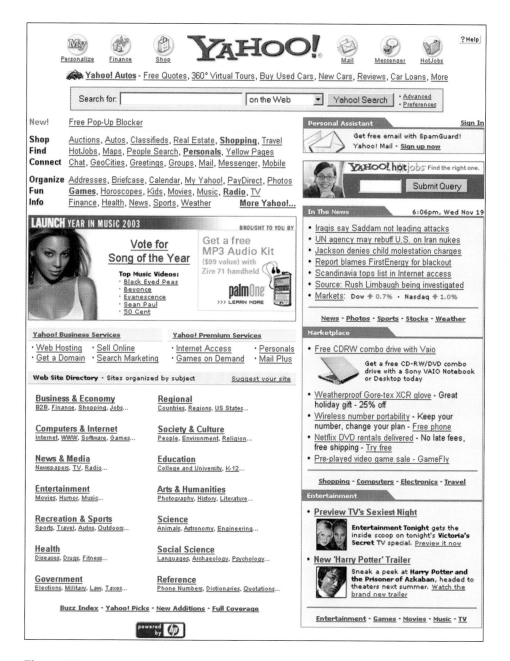

Figure 1.11

The Yahoo portal gives users access to e-mail, weather, healthcare, banking, and personal photo services. It provides a search window (near top, center), 14 categories for browsing (lower left), plus news, shopping, and entertainment links (righthand side).

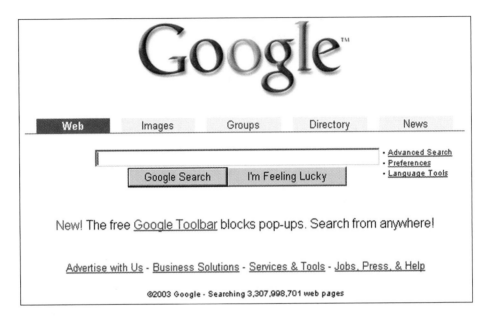

Figure 1.12

The Google search engine (http://www.google.com). This window shows the simple user interface for searching.

systems. At best, designers can pursue the goal of having the computer vanish as users become completely absorbed in their task domains. This goal seems to be met most effectively when the computer provides a direct-manipulation representation of the world of action (see Chapter 6), supplemented by keyboard shortcuts. Then, tasks are carried out by rapid familiar selections or gestures, with immediate feedback and new sets of choices. Users can keep their focus on the task, with minimal distraction in operating the interface.

1.4.5   Sociotechnical systems

A growing domain for usability is in complex systems that involve many people over long time periods, such as systems for voting, health support, identity verification, and crime reporting. Interfaces for these systems, often created by governmental organizations, have to deal with trust, privacy, and responsibility, as well as limiting the harmful effects of malicious tampering, deception, and incorrect information. Users want access to verifiable sources, adequate feedback about their actions, and ways of easily checking status. They will want to know who to turn to when things go wrong, and maybe who to thank when things go right. For example, in electronic voting systems (Bederson et al., 2003) citizens need to have reassuring feedback that their votes were correctly

Figure 1.13

The Google search engine showing the results of a search on "human computer interaction."

recorded, possibly by having a printed receipt. In addition, government officials and professional observers from opposing parties need to have ways of verifying that the votes from each district and regional aggregations are correctly reported. If complaints are registered, investigators need tools to review procedures at every stage.

Designers of sociotechnical systems have to take into consideration the diverse levels of expertise that users with different roles have. Successful designs for the large number of novice and first-time users emphasize ease of

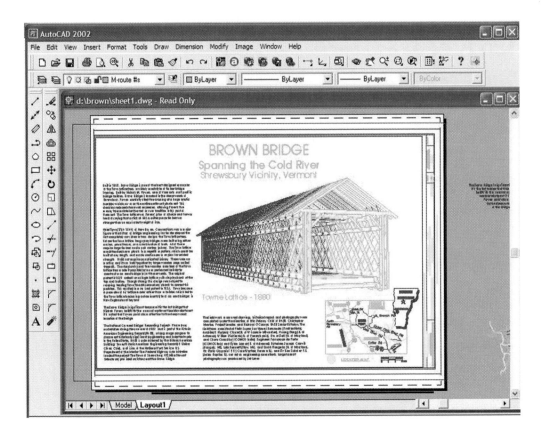

Figure 1.14

AutoCAD for Windows. This design environment gives architects rich facilities for three-dimensional drawing. (Drawn by Kimberly Clauer.)

learning and provide the feedback that builds trust. Designs for the professional administrators and the seasoned investigators will enable rapid performance of complex procedures with visualization tools to spot unusual patterns or detect fraud in usage logs.

1.5   Universal Usability

The remarkable diversity of human abilities, backgrounds, motivations, person-alities, cultures, and work styles challenges interface designers. A right-handed female designer in India with computer training and a desire for rapid interaction using densely packed screens may have a hard time developing a successful interface for left-handed male artists in France with a more leisurely and free-form work style. Understanding the physical, intellectual, and personality differences between users is vital for expanding market share, supporting required government services, and enabling creative participation by the broadest possible set of users. As a profession, we will be remembered for how well we meet our users' needs. That's the ultimate goal—addressing the needs of all users.

While skeptics suggest that accommodating diversity requires dumbing-down or lowest-common-denominator strategies, our experience is that rethinking interface designs for differing situations often results in a better product for all users. Special needs for one group, such as curb cuts in sidewalks for wheelchair users, have payoffs for many groups, such as parents with baby strollers, skateboard riders, travelers with wheeled luggage, and delivery people with handcarts. With this in mind, we address the challenges of physical, cognitive, perceptual, personality, and cultural differences. This section then covers users with disabilities, older adults, and young users, ending with a discussion of hardware and software diversity. The important issues of different usage profiles (novice, intermittent, and expert users), wide-ranging task profiles, and multiple interaction styles are covered in Section 2.3.3. As interest grows in ubiquitous or pervasive computing and as market forces push towards broad consumer appeal, the pressure for designs that are universally usable will rise.

1.5.1   Variations in physical abilities and physical workplaces

Accommodating diverse human perceptual, cognitive, and motor abilities is a challenge to every designer. Fortunately, there is much research and experience from design projects with automobiles, aircraft, typewriters, home appliances, and so on that can be applied to the design of interactive computer systems. In a sense, the presence of a computer is only incidental to the design; human needs and abilities are the guiding forces.

Basic data about human dimensions comes from research in *anthropometry* (Dreyfuss, 1967; Pheasant, 1996). Thousands of measures of hundreds of features of people—male and female, young and adult, European and Asian, underweight and overweight, and tall and short—provide data to construct means and 5- to 95-percentile groupings. Head, mouth, nose, neck, shoulder, chest, arm, hand, finger, leg, and foot sizes have been carefully cataloged for a variety of populations. The great diversity in these static measures reminds us that there can be no image of an "average" user, and that compromises must be made or multiple versions of a system must be constructed.

The choice of keyboard design parameters—in terms of distance between keys, size of keys, and required pressure (see Section 9.2)—evolved to accommodate the differences between the physical abilities of users. People with especially large or small hands may have difficulty in using standard keyboards, but a substantial fraction of the population is well served by one design. On the other hand, since screen-brightness preferences vary substantially, designers customarily provide a knob to enable user control. Controls for chair seat and back heights and for display angles also allow individual adjustment. When a single design cannot accommodate a large fraction of the population, multiple versions or adjustment controls are helpful.

Physical measures of static human dimensions are not enough. Measures of dynamic actions—such as reach distance while seated, speed of finger presses, or strength of lifting—are also necessary (Bailey, 1996).

Since so much of work is related to perception, designers need to be aware of the ranges of human perceptual abilities (Ware, 2004). Vision is especially important and has been thoroughly studied (Wickens and Hollands, 2000). For example, researchers consider human response time to varying visual stimuli, or time to adapt to low or bright light. They examine human capacity to identify an object in context, or to determine the velocity or direction of a moving point. The visual system responds differently to various colors, and some people are color-deficient, either permanently or temporarily (due to illness or medication). People's spectral range and sensitivity vary, and peripheral vision is quite different from perception of images in the fovea (the central part of the retina). Flicker, contrast, and motion sensitivity must be considered, as must the impact of glare and of visual fatigue. Depth perception, which allows three-dimensional viewing, is based on several cues. Some viewing angles and distances make the screen easier to read. Finally, designers must consider the needs of people who have eye disorders, damage, or disease, or who wear corrective lenses.

Other senses are also important: for example, touch for keyboard or touch-screen entry and hearing for audible cues, tones, and speech input or output (see Chapter 9). Pain, temperature sensitivity, taste, and smell are rarely used for input or output in interactive systems, but there is room for imaginative applications.

These physical abilities influence elements of the interactive-system design. They also play a prominent role in the design of the workplace or workstation (or playstation). The draft standard *Human Factors Engineering of Computer Workstations* (2002) lists these concerns:

- Work-surface and display-support height
- Clearance under work surface for legs
- Work-surface width and depth
- Adjustability of heights and angles for chairs and work surfaces
- Posture—seating depth and angle; back-rest height and lumbar support
- Availability of armrests, footrests, and palmrests
- Use of chair casters

Workplace design is important in ensuring high job satisfaction, high performance, and low error rates. Incorrect table heights, uncomfortable chairs, or inadequate space to place documents can substantially impede work. The standard document also addresses such issues as illumination levels (200 to 500 lux); glare reduction (antiglare coatings, baffles, mesh, positioning); luminance balance and flicker; equipment reflectivity; acoustic noise and vibration; air temperature, movement, and humidity; and equipment temperature.

The most elegant screen design can be compromised by a noisy environment, poor lighting, or a stuffy room, and that compromise will eventually lower performance, raise error rates, and discourage even motivated users. Thoughtful designs, such as workstations that provide wheelchair access and good lighting, will be even more appreciated by users with disabilities and older adults.

Another physical-environment consideration involves room layout and the sociology of human interaction. With multiple workstations for a classroom or office, alternate layouts can encourage or limit social interaction, cooperative work, and assistance with problems. Because users can often quickly help one another with minor problems, there may be an advantage to layouts that group several terminals close together or that enable supervisors or teachers to view all screens at once from behind. On the other hand, programmers, reservations clerks, or artists may appreciate the quiet and privacy of their own workspace.

The physical design of workplaces is often discussed under the term *ergonomics*. Anthropometry, sociology, industrial psychology, organizational behavior studies, and anthropology may offer useful insights in this area.

1.5.2   Diverse cognitive and perceptual abilities

A vital foundation for interactive-systems designers is an understanding of the cognitive and perceptual abilities of the users (Wickens and Hollands, 2000; Ashcraft, 2001; Goldstein, 2002). The human ability to interpret sensory input rapidly and to initiate complex actions makes modern computer systems possible. In milliseconds, users recognize slight changes on their displays and begin to issue streams of commands. The journal *Ergonomics Abstracts* offers this classification of human cognitive processes:

- Short-term and working memory
- Long-term and semantic memory
- Problem solving and reasoning
- Decision making and risk assessment
- Language communication and comprehension
- Search, imagery, and sensory memory
- Learning, skill development, knowledge acquisition, and concept attainment

They also suggest this set of factors affecting perceptual and motor performance:

- Arousal and vigilance
- Fatigue and sleep deprivation
- Perceptual (mental) load
- Knowledge of results and feedback
- Monotony and boredom
- Sensory deprivation
- Nutrition and diet
- Fear, anxiety, mood, and emotion
- Drugs, smoking, and alcohol
- Physiological rhythms

These vital issues are not discussed in depth in this book, but they have a profound influence on the quality of the design of most interactive systems. The term *intelligence* is not included in this list, because its nature is controversial and measuring pure intelligence is difficult.

In any application, background experience and knowledge in the task domain and the interface domain (see Section 2.5) play key roles in learning and performance. Task- or computer-skill inventories can be helpful in predicting performance.

1.5.3 Personality differences

Some people dislike computers or are made anxious by them; others are attracted to or are eager to use computers. Often, members of these divergent groups disapprove or are suspicious of members of the other community. Even people who enjoy using computers may have very different preferences for interaction styles, pace of interaction, graphics versus tabular presentations, dense versus sparse data presentation, step-by-step work versus all-at-once work, and so on. These differences are important. A clear understanding of personality and cognitive styles can be helpful in designing interfaces for a specific community of users.

One evident difference is between men and women, but no clear pattern of gender-related preferences in interfaces has been documented. It is often pointed out that the preponderance of video-arcade game players and designers are young males. There are women players of any game, but popular choices among women for early video games were Pacman and its variants, plus a few other games such as Donkey Kong and Tetris. Designers can get into lively debates speculating why women prefer these games, which are distinguished by their less violent action and quieter soundtracks. Also, the board is fully visible, characters have personality, softer color patterns are used, and there is a sense of closure and completeness. Can these informal conjectures be converted to measurable criteria and then validated? While early game designers focused on the needs and desires of men and boys, many newer games are more attractive to women. For example, The Sims and its online version are innovative simulations of families that attract more female players than males.

Turning from games to productivity tools, the largely male designers may not realize the effects on women users when command names require the users to KILL a process or ABORT a program. These and other potential unfortunate mismatches between the user interface and the users might be avoided by more thoughtful attention to individual differences among users. Huff (1987) found a bias when he asked teachers to design educational games for boys or girls. The designers created gamelike challenges when they expected boys as users and used more conversational dialogs when they expected girls as users. When told to design for students, the designers produced boy-style games.

Unfortunately, there is no simple taxonomy of user personality types. A popular, but controversial, technique is to use the Myers-Briggs Type Indicator (MBTI) (Keirsey, 1998), which is based on Carl Jung's theories of personality types. Jung conjectured that there were four dichotomies:

- *Extroversion versus introversion.* Extroverts focus on external stimuli and like variety and action, whereas introverts prefer familiar patterns, rely on their inner ideas, and work alone contentedly.

- *Sensing versus intuition.* Sensing types are attracted to established routines, are good at precise work, and enjoy applying known skills, whereas intuitive types like solving new problems and discovering new relations but dislike taking time for precision.

- *Perceptive versus judging.* Perceptive types like to learn about new situations but may have trouble making decisions, whereas judging types like to make a careful plan and will seek to carry through the plan even if new facts change the goal.

- *Feeling versus thinking.* Feeling types are aware of other people's feelings, seek to please others, and relate well to most people, whereas thinking types are unemotional, may treat people impersonally, and like to put things in logical order.

The theory behind the MBTI provides portraits of the relationships between professions and personality types and between people of different personality types. It has been applied to testing of user communities and has provided guidance for designers, but the linkage between personality types and interface features is weak.

Successors to the MBTI include the Big Five Test, based on the OCEAN model: Openness to Experience/Intellect (closed/open), Conscientiousness (disorganized/organized), Extraversion (introverted/extraverted), Agreeableness (disagreeable/agreeable), and Neuroticism (calm/nervous). In addition, there are hundreds of other psychological scales, including risk taking versus risk avoidance; internal versus external locus of control; reflective versus impulsive behavior; convergent versus divergent thinking; high versus low anxiety; tolerance for stress; tolerance for ambiguity, motivation, or compulsiveness; field dependence versus independence; assertive versus passive personality; and left- versus right-brain orientation. As designers explore computer applications for home, education, art, music, and entertainment, they may benefit from paying greater attention to personality types.

Another approach to personality assessment is by studies of user behavior. For example, some users file thousands of e-mails in a well-organized hierarchy of folders, while others keep them all in the inbox, using search strategies to find what they want later. These distinct approaches may well relate to personality variables, and for the designer the message of dual requirements is clear.

1.5.4   Cultural and international diversity

Another perspective on individual differences has to do with cultural, ethnic, racial, or linguistic background (Fernandes, 1995; Marcus and Gould, 2000). Users who were raised learning to read Japanese or Chinese will scan a screen differently from users who were raised learning to read English or French. Users from reflective or traditional cultures may prefer interfaces with stable displays from which they select a single item, while users from action-oriented or novelty-based cultures may prefer animated screens and multiple clicks. Preferred content of web pages also varies; for example, university home pages in some cultures emphasize their impressive buildings and respected professors, while others highlight students and a lively social life. Mobile device preferences also vary across cultures—for example, from small, brightly colored, unusually shaped forms to large gray boxes.

More and more is being learned about computer users from different cultures, but designers are still struggling to establish guidelines for designing for multiple languages and cultures. The growth of a worldwide computer market (many U.S. companies have more than half of their sales in overseas markets) means that designers must prepare for internationalization. Software architectures that facilitate customization of local versions of user interfaces should be emphasized. For example, all text (instructions, help, error messages, labels, and so on) might be stored in files, so that versions in other languages can be generated with no or little additional programming. Hardware concerns include character sets, keyboards, and special input devices. User-interface design concerns for internationalization include the following:

- Characters, numerals, special characters, and diacriticals
- Left-to-right versus right-to-left versus vertical input and reading
- Date and time formats
- Numeric and currency formats
- Weights and measures

- Telephone numbers and addresses
- Names and titles (Mr., Ms., Mme., M., Dr.)
- Social security, national identification, and passport numbers
- Capitalization and punctuation
- Sorting sequences
- Icons, buttons, and colors
- Pluralization, grammar, and spelling
- Etiquette, policies, tone, formality, and metaphors

The list is long and yet incomplete. Whereas early designers were often excused from cultural and linguistic slips, the current highly competitive atmosphere means that more effective localization may produce a strong advantage. To promote effective designs, companies should run usability studies with users from different countries, cultures, and language communities.

The role of information technology in international development is steadily growing, but much needs to be done to accommodate the diverse needs of users with vastly different language skills and technology access. To promote international efforts to create successful implementation of information technologies, representatives from around the world met for the 2003 United Nations World Summit on the Information Society. They declared

> our common desire and commitment to build a people-centred, inclusive and development-oriented Information Society, where everyone can create, access, utilize and share information and knowledge, enabling individuals, communities and peoples to achieve their full potential in promoting their sustainable development and improving their quality of life, premised on the purposes and principles of the Charter of the United Nations and respecting fully and upholding the Universal Declaration of Human Rights.

The plan called for applications to be "accessible to all, affordable, adapted to local needs in languages and culture, and [to] support sustainable development."

1.5.5   Users with disabilities

The flexibility of desktop and web software makes it possible for designers to provide special services to users who have disabilities (Edwards, 1995; Vanderheiden, 2000; Paciello, 2000; Stephanidis, 2001; Thatcher et al., 2003). In the United States, the 1998 Amendment to Section 508 of the Rehabilitation Act requires Federal agencies to ensure access to information technology, including computers and web sites, by employees and the public (http//:www.access-board.gov/508.htm). The Access Board spells out the implications for vision-impaired, hearing-impaired, and mobility-impaired users, such as keyboard or mouse alternatives, color coding, font-size settings, contrast settings, textual alternatives to images, and web features such as frames, links, and plug-ins.

Screen magnification to enlarge portions of a display or text conversion to Braille or voice output can be done with hardware and software supplied by many vendors (Blenkhorn et al., 2003). Text-to-speech conversion can help blind users to receive electronic mail or to read text files, and speech-recognition devices permit voice-controlled operation of some software. Graphical user interfaces were a setback for vision-impaired users, but technology innovations from commercial tools such as Freedom Scientific's JAWS, GW Micro's Window-Eyes, or Dolphin's HAL screen readers facilitate conversion of spatial information into spoken text (Poll and Waterham, 1995; Thatcher, 1994; Mynatt and Weber, 1994). Similarly IBM's Home Page Reader and Conversa's web browser enable access to web information and services. Speech generation and auditory interfaces are also appreciated by sighted users under difficult conditions, such as when driving an automobile, riding a bicycle, or working in bright sunshine.

Users with hearing impairments generally can use computers with only simple changes (conversion of tones to visual signals is often easy to accomplish) and can benefit from office environments that make heavy use of electronic mail and facsimile transmission (FAX). Telecommunications devices for the deaf (TDD or TTY) enable telephone access to information (such as train or airplane schedules) and services (federal agencies and many companies offer TDD or TTY access). Special input devices for users with physical disabilities will depend on the user's specific impairment; numerous assistive devices are available. Speech recognition, eye-gaze control, head-mounted optical mice, and many other innovative devices (even the telephone) were pioneered for the needs of disabled users (see Chapter 9).

Designers can benefit by planning early to accommodate users who have disabilities, since at this point substantial improvements can be made at low or no cost. For example, moving the on/off switch to the front of a computer adds a minimal charge, if any, to the cost of manufacturing, but it improves ease of use for all users, and especially for the mobility-impaired. Other examples are the addition of closed captions to television programs for deaf viewers, which can be useful for hearing viewers as well, and the use of ALT tags to describe web graphics for blind users, which improves search capabilities for all users.

The motivation to accommodate users who have visual, hearing, and motor disabilities has increased since the enactment of U.S. Public Laws 99–506 and 100–542, which require U.S. government agencies to establish accessible information environments for employees and citizens. Any company wishing to sell products to the U.S. government should adhere to these requirements. Further information about accommodation in workplaces, schools, and the home is available from many sources:

- Private foundations (e.g., the American Foundation for the Blind and the National Federation of the Blind)
- Associations (e.g., the Alexander Graham Bell Association for the Deaf, the National Association for the Deaf, and the Blinded Veterans Association)

- Government agencies (e.g., the National Library Service for the Blind and Physically Handicapped of the Library of Congress and the Center for Technology in Human Disabilities at the Maryland Rehabilitation Center)
- University groups (e.g., the Trace Research and Development Center on Communications and the Control and Computer Access for Handicapped Individuals at the University of Wisconsin)
- Manufacturers (e.g., Apple, IBM, Microsoft, and Sun Microsystems)

Learning-disabled children, including dyslexics, account for at least two percent of the school-age population in the United States. Their education can be positively influenced by design of special courseware with limits on lengthy textual instructions, confusing graphics, extensive typing, and difficult presentation formats (Neuman, 1991). Based on observations of 62 students using 26 packages over 5.5 months, Neuman's advice to designers of courseware for learning-disabled students is applicable to all users:

- Present procedures, directions, and verbal content at levels and in formats that make them accessible even to poor readers.
- Ensure that response requirements do not allow students to complete programs without engaging with target concepts.
- Design feedback sequences that explain the reasons for students' errors and that lead students through the processes necessary for responding correctly.
- Incorporate reinforcement techniques that capitalize on students' sophistication with out-of-school electronic materials.

The potential for benefit to people with disabilities is one of the gifts of computing; it brings dividends in the increased capacity for gainful employment, social participation, and community contribution. In addition, many users are temporarily disabled: they can forget their glasses, be unable to read while driving, or struggle to hear in a noisy environment. The University of Wisconsin TRACE Center and the United Nations Enable web sites provide guidelines and resources for designers who are addressing universal usability.

1.5.6   Older adult users

There are many pleasures and satisfactions to seniority, but aging can also have negative physical, cognitive, and social consequences. Understanding the human factors of aging can lead us to computer designs that will facilitate access by older adult users. The benefits to senior citizens include improved chances for productive employment and opportunities to use writing, accounting, and other computer tools, plus the satisfactions of education, entertainment, social interaction, and challenge (Furlong and Kearsley, 1990). The benefits to society include increased access to seniors for their experience and the emotional support they can provide to others.

The National Research Council's report on Human Factors Research Needs for an Aging Population describes aging as

> A nonuniform set of progressive changes in physiological and psychological functioning.... Average visual and auditory acuity decline considerably with age, as do average strength and speed of response.... [People experience] loss of at least some kinds of memory function, declines in perceptual flexibility, slowing of "stimulus encoding," and increased difficulty in the acquisition of complex mental skills,... visual functions such as static visual acuity, dark adaptation, accommodation, contrast sensitivity, and peripheral vision decline, on average, with age. (Czaja, 1990)

This list has its discouraging side, but many people experience only modest effects and continue participating in many activities, even through their nineties.

The further good news is that interface designers can do much to accommodate older adult users, and thus to give older adults access to the beneficial aspects of computing and network communication. How many young people's lives might be enriched by electronic-mail access to grandparents or great-grandparents? How many businesses might benefit from electronic consultations with experienced senior citizens? How many government agencies, universities, medical centers, or law firms could advance their goals by easily available contact with knowledgeable older adult citizens? As a society, how might we all benefit from the continued creative work of senior citizens in literature, art, music, science, or philosophy?

As the world's population grows older, designers in many fields are adapting their work to serve older adult citizens. Larger street signs, brighter traffic lights, and better nighttime lighting can make driving safer for drivers and pedestrians. Similarly, desktop, web, and mobile devices can be improved for all users by providing users with control over font sizes, display contrast, and audio levels. Interfaces can also be designed with easier-to-use pointing devices, clearer navigation paths, consistent layouts, and simpler command languages to improve access for older adults and every user (Czaja and Lee, 2002). Researchers and system developers are beginning to work on improving interfaces to golden-age software. Let's do it *before* Bill Gates turns 65! In the United States, the AARP's Older Wiser Wired initiatives provide education for older adults and guidance for designers. The European Union also has multiple initiatives and research support for computing for older adults.

Electronic-networking projects, such as the San Francisco–based SeniorNet, are providing adults over the age of 50 with access to and education about computing and the Internet "to enhance their lives and enable them to share their knowledge and wisdom" (http://www.seniornet.org). Computer games are also becoming attractive for older adults, because they stimulate social interaction, provide practice in sensorimotor skills such as eye-hand coordination, enhance dexterity, and improve reaction time. In addition, meeting a challenge and gaining a sense of accomplishment and mastery are helpful in improving self-image for anyone.

In our experiences in bringing computing to two residences for older adults, we also encountered residents' fear of computers and belief that they were incapable of using computers. These fears gave way quickly with a few positive experiences. The older adults, who explored spreadsheets, word processors, and educational games, felt quite satisfied with themselves, were eager to learn more, and transferred their newfound enthusiasm to trying automated bank machines or supermarket touchscreen computers. Suggestions for redesigns to meet the needs of older adults (and possibly other users) also emerged—for example, the appeal of high-precision touchscreens compared with the mouse (see Chapter 9).

In summary, computing for older adults enables them to share in the benefits of technology and enables others to profit from their participation. For more information on this topic, check out the Human Factors & Ergonomics Society, which has an Aging Technical Group that publishes a newsletter and organizes sessions at conferences.

1.5.7   Designing for and with children

Another lively community of users is children, whose uses emphasize entertainment and education. Even pre-readers can use computer-controlled toys, music generators, and art tools (Fig. 1.15). As they mature to begin reading and gain limited keyboard skills, they can use a wider array of portable devices, desktop applications, and web services. When they become teenagers, they may become highly proficient users who often help their parents or other adults. This idealized growth path is followed by many children who have easy access to technology and supportive parents and peers. However, many children without financial resources or supportive learning environments struggle to gain access to technology. They are often frustrated with its use and are endangered by threats surrounding privacy, alienation, pornography, unhelpful peers, and malevolent strangers.

The noble aspirations of developers of children's software include educational acceleration, socialization with peers, and the positive self-image or self-confidence that comes from mastery of skills. Advocates of educational games promote intrinsic motivation and constructive activities as goals, but opponents often complain about the harmful effects of antisocial and violent games (Future of Children, 2000).

For teenagers, the opportunities for empowerment are substantial. They often take the lead in employing new modes of communication and creating cultural or fashion trends that surprise even the developers, such as instant

Figure 1.15

Child using an educational computer game (LeapFrog's LeapPad Learning System) which has books and a pen that children can use for learning to read, learning letter sounds, and playing games.

messaging, text messaging on cell phones, playing with simulations and fantasy games, and exploring web-based virtual worlds.

Appropriate design principles for children's software recognize young people's intense desire for the kind of interactive engagement that gives them control with appropriate feedback and supports their social engagement with peers (Druin and Inkpen, 2001; Bruckman and Bandlow, 2002). Designers also have to find the balance between children's desire for challenge and parents' requirements for safety. Children can deal with some frustrations and with threatening stories, but they also want to know that they can clear the screen, start over, and try again without severe penalties. They don't easily tolerate patronizing comments or inappropriate humor, but they like familiar characters, exploratory environments, and the capacity for repetition. Younger children will sometimes replay a game, reread a story, or replay a music sequence dozens of times, even after adults have tired. Some designers work by observing children and testing software with children, while the innovative approach of "children as our technology-design partners" engages children in a long-term process of cooperative inquiry during which children and adults jointly design novel products and services (Druin et al., 1999) (Fig. 1.16).

Designing for younger children requires attention to their limitations. Their evolving dexterity means that mouse dragging, double-clicking, or small targets

Figure 1.16

Two children using the International Children's Digital Library (ICDL), a digital library for children with 10,000 books in at least 100 languages. Children have partnered with adults to develop interfaces to support children in searching, browsing, reading, and sharing books in electronic form (http://www.icdlbooks.org).

cannot always be used; their emerging literacy means that instructions and error messages are not effective; and their low capacity for abstraction means that complex sequences must be avoided unless an adult is involved. Other concerns are short attention spans and limited capacity to work with multiple concepts simultaneously. Designers of children's software also have a responsibility to attend to dangers, especially in web-based environments, where parental control over access to violent, racist, or pornographic materials is unfortunately necessary. Appropriate education of children about privacy issues and threats from strangers is also a requirement.

The capacity for playful creativity in art, music, and writing, as well as educational activities in science and math, remain potent reasons to pursue children's software. Enabling them to make high-quality images, photos, songs, or poems, and then share them with friends and family, can accelerate children's personal and social development. Offering access to educational materials from libraries, museums, government agencies, schools, and commercial sources enriches their learning experiences and serves as a basis for children to construct their own web resources, participate in collaborative efforts, and contribute to community-service projects. Providing programming and simulation-building tools enables older children to take on complex cognitive challenges and construct ambitious artifacts for others to use (Fig. 1.17).

1.5.8   Accommodating hardware and software diversity

In addition to accommodating different classes of users and skill levels, designers need to support a wide range of hardware and software platforms. The rapid progress of technology means that newer systems may have a hundred or a thousand times greater storage capacity, faster processors, and higher-bandwidth networks. Designers need to accommodate older devices and deal with newer portable devices that may have low-bandwidth connections and small screens.

The challenge of accommodating diverse hardware is coupled with the need to ensure access through many generations of software. New operating systems, web browsers, e-mail clients, and application programs should provide back-

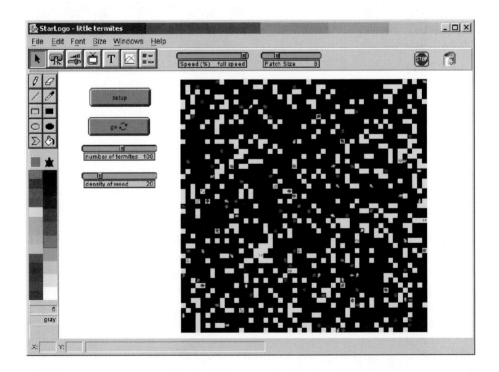

Figure 1.17

StarLogo, a programmable modeling environment for kids (and adults) that explores the workings of decentralized systems.

ward compatibility in user-interface design and file structures. Skeptics will say that this requirement can slow innovation, but designers who plan ahead carefully to support flexible interfaces and self-defining files will be rewarded with larger market shares (Shneiderman, 2000).

For at least the next decade, three of the main technical challenges will be:

- *Producing satisfying and effective Internet interaction on high-speed (broadband) and slower (dial-up and some wireless) connections.* Some technology breakthroughs have already been made in compression algorithms to reduce file sizes for images, music, animations, and even video, but more are needed. New technologies are needed to enable pre-fetching or scheduled downloads. User control of the amount of material downloaded for each request could also prove beneficial (for example, allowing users to specify that a large image should be reduced to a smaller size, sent with fewer colors, converted to a simplified line drawing, or even replaced with just a text description).

- *Enabling access to web services from large displays (1200 × 1600 pixels or larger) and smaller mobile devices (640 × 480 and smaller).* Rewriting each web page for different display sizes may produce the best quality, but this approach is probably too costly and time-consuming for most web providers. New software-tool breakthroughs are needed to allow web-site developers to specify their content in such a way that automatic conversions can be made for an increasing range of display sizes.

- *Supporting easy maintenance of or automatic conversion to multiple languages.* Commercial operators recognize that they can expand their markets if they can provide access in multiple languages and across multiple countries. This means isolating text to allow easy substitution, choosing appropriate metaphors and colors, and addressing the needs of diverse cultures (see Section 1.5.4).

The good news is that rethinking designs to accommodate these diverse needs can improve the quality for all users. As for costs, with appropriate software tools, e-commerce providers are finding that a small additional effort can expand markets by 20% or more.

1.6   Goals for Our Profession

Clear goals are useful not only for interface development but also for educational and professional enterprises. Three broad goals seem attainable: (1) influencing academic and industrial researchers; (2) providing tools, techniques, and knowledge for commercial developers; and (3) raising the computer consciousness of the general public.

1.6.1   Influencing academic and industrial researchers

Early research in human-computer interaction was done largely by introspection and intuition, but this approach suffered from lack of validity, generality, and precision. The techniques of psychologically oriented controlled experimentation can lead to a deeper understanding of the fundamental principles of human interaction with computers. The scientific method for interface research, which is based on controlled experimentation, has this basic outline:

- Understanding of a practical problem and related theory
- Lucid statement of a testable hypothesis
- Manipulation of a small number of independent variables
- Measurement of specific dependent variables
- Careful selection and assignment of subjects
- Control for bias in subjects, procedures, and materials
- Application of statistical tests
- Interpretation of results, refinement of theory, and guidance for experimenters

Materials and methods must be tested by pilot experiments, and results must be validated by replication in variant situations.

Of course, the scientific method based on controlled experimentation has its weaknesses. It may be difficult or expensive to find adequate subjects, and laboratory conditions may distort the situation so much that the conclusions have no application. Controlled experiments typically deal with short-term usage, so understanding long-term consumer behavior or experienced user strategies is difficult. Since controlled experiments emphasize statistical aggregation, extremely good or poor performance by individuals may be overlooked. Furthermore, anecdotal evidence or individual insights may be given too little emphasis because of the authoritative influence of statistics.

Because of these concerns, controlled experimentation is balanced by ethnographic observation methods. Anecdotal experiences and subjective reactions are recorded, thinking aloud or protocol approaches are employed, and field or case studies can be carried out. Other research methods include automated logging of user behavior, surveys, focus groups, and interviews.

Within computer science, there is a growing awareness of the need for greater attention to usability issues. Courses on human-computer interaction are required for some undergraduate degrees, and interface-design issues are being added to many courses. Researchers who propose new programming languages, privacy-protection schemes, or network services are more aware of the need to match human cognitive skills. Developers of advanced graphics systems, agile manufacturing equipment, or consumer products increasingly recognize that the success of their proposals depends on the construction of a suitable human interface.

There is a grand opportunity to apply the knowledge and techniques of traditional psychology (and of subfields such as cognitive psychology) to the study of human-computer interaction. Psychologists are investigating human problem solving and creativity with computers to gain an understanding of cognitive processes. The benefit to psychology is great, but psychologists also have a golden opportunity to influence dramatically an important and widely used technology.

Researchers in information science, business and management, education, sociology, anthropology, and other disciplines are benefiting and contributing by their study of human-computer interaction. There are so many fruitful directions for research that any list can be only a provocative starting point. Here are a few:

- *Reduced anxiety and fear of computer usage.* Although computers are widely used, they still serve only a fraction of the population. Many otherwise competent people resist use of computers. Some older adults avoid helpful computer-based devices, such as bank terminals or word processors, because they are anxious about—or even fearful of—breaking the computer or making an embarrassing mistake. Interviews with nonusers of computers would help us to determine the sources of this anxiety and to formulate design guidelines for alleviating the fear. Tests could be run to determine the effectiveness of the redesigned interfaces and of improved training procedures.

- *Graceful evolution.* Although novices may begin their interactions with a computer by using menu selection, they may wish to evolve to faster or more powerful facilities. Methods are needed to smooth the transition from novice to knowledgeable user to expert. The differing requirements of novices and experts in prompting, error messages, online assistance, display complexity, locus of control, pacing, and informative feedback all need investigation. The design of control panels to support customization is also an open topic.

- *Specification and implementation of interaction.* User-interface building tools (discussed in Chapter 5) reduce implementation times by an order of magnitude when they match the task. There are still many situations in which extensive coding in procedural languages must be added. Advanced research on tools to aid interactive-systems designers and implementers might have substantial payoffs in reducing costs and improving quality. For example, tools for World Wide Web designers to enable automatic conversion for different computers, screen sizes, or modem speeds could be substantially improved, thereby facilitating universal usability.

- *Direct manipulation.* Visual interfaces in which users operate on a representation of the objects of interest are extremely attractive (see Chapter 6). Empirical studies could refine our understanding of appropriate analogical or metaphorical representations and of the role of rapid, incremental, reversible operations. Newer forms of direct manipulation—such as visual languages, information visualization, telepresence, and virtual reality—are further topics for research.

- *Input devices.* The plethora of input devices presents opportunities and challenges to interface designers (see Chapter 6). There are heated discussions about the relative merits of the high-precision touchscreen; stylus, voice, eye-gaze, and gestural input; the mouse; and haptic devices. Such conflicts could be resolved through experimentation with multiple tasks and users. Underlying issues include speed, accuracy, fatigue, error correction, and subjective satisfaction.

- *Online help.* Although many interfaces offer some help or tutorial information online, we have only limited understanding of what constitutes effective design for novices, knowledgeable users, and experts (see Chapter 13). The role of these aids and of online user communities could be studied to assess effects on user success and satisfaction.

- *Information exploration.* As navigation, browsing, and searching of multimedia digital libraries and the World Wide Web become more common, the pressure for more effective strategies and tools will increase (see Chapter 14). Users will want to filter, select, and restructure their information rapidly and with minimum effort, without fear of disorientation or of getting lost. Large databases of text, images, graphics, sound, and scientific data will become easier to explore with emerging information-visualization tools.

1.6.2   Providing tools, techniques, and knowledge for commercial developers

User-interface design and development are hot topics, and international competition is lively. Employers, who used to see usability as a secondary topic, are increasingly hiring user-interface designers, information architects, user-interface implementers, and usability testers. These employers recognize the competitive advantage from high-quality consumer interfaces and from improving the performance of their employees. There is a great thirst for knowledge about software tools, design guidelines, and testing techniques. User-interface building tools (see Chapter 5) provide support for rapid prototyping and interface development while aiding design consistency, supporting universal usability, and simplifying evolutionary refinement.

Guidelines documents have been written for general and specific audiences. Many projects are taking the productive route of writing their own guidelines, which are tied to the problems of their application environments. These guidelines are constructed from experimental results, experience with existing interfaces, and knowledgeable guesswork.

Iterative usability studies and acceptance testing are appropriate during interface development. Once the initial interface is available, refinements can be made on the basis of online or printed surveys, individual or group interviews, or more controlled empirical tests of novel strategies (see Chapter 4).

Feedback from users during the development process and for evolutionary refinement can provide useful insights and guidance. Online electronic-mail facilities allow users to send comments directly to the designers. Online user consultants and fellow users can provide prompt assistance and supportive encouragement.

1.6.3 Raising the computer consciousness of the general public

The media are so filled with stories about computers that raising public consciousness of these tools may seem unnecessary. However, many people are still uncomfortable with computers. When they do finally use a bank machine or word processor, they may be fearful of making mistakes, anxious about damaging the equipment, worried about feeling incompetent, or threatened by the computer "being smarter than I am." These fears are generated, in part, by poor designs that have complex commands, hostile and vague error messages, tortuous and unfamiliar sequences of actions, or a deceptive anthropomorphic style.

One of our goals is to encourage users to translate their internal fears into outraged action (Shneiderman, 2002). Instead of feeling guilty when they get a message such as SYNTAX ERROR, users should express their anger at the interface designer who was so inconsiderate and thoughtless. Instead of feeling inadequate or foolish because they cannot remember a complex sequence of actions, they should complain to the designer who did not provide a more convenient mechanism or should seek another product that does.

Usability ultimately becomes a question of national priorities. Advocates of electronic voting and other services, promoters of e-healthcare, and visionaries of e-learning increasingly recognize the need to influence allocation of government resources and commercial research agendas. Policymakers and industry leaders become heroes when they facilitate access and promote quality, but they become villains when failures threaten children, disrupt travel, or menace consumers.

As examples of successful and satisfying interfaces become more visible, the crude designs will begin to appear archaic and will become commercial failures. As designers improve interactive systems, some users' fears will recede and the positive experiences of their competence, mastery, and satisfaction will flow in. Then, the images of computer scientists and interface designers will change in the public's view. The machine-oriented and technical image will give way to one of personal warmth, sensitivity, and concern for the user.

Practitioner's Summary

If you are designing an interactive system, thorough user and task analyses can provide the information for a proper functional design. A positive outcome is more likely if you pay attention to reliability, availability, security, integrity, standardization, portability, integration, and the administrative issues of schedules and budgets. As design alternatives are proposed, they can be evaluated for their role in providing short learning times, rapid task performance, low error rates, ease of retention, and high user satisfaction. Designs that accommodate the needs of children, older adults, and users with disabilities can improve the quality for all users. As your design is refined and implemented, evaluation by pilot studies, expert reviews, usability tests, user observations, and acceptance tests can accelerate improvement. The rapidly growing literature and sets of design guidelines may be of assistance in developing your project standards and practices and in accommodating the increasingly diverse and growing community of users. The criteria for success in product development are shifting from testimonials by a few enthusiastic users to hard evidence that universal usability is being attained.

Researcher's Agenda

The criteria for success in research are shifting to innovations that work for broad communities of users performing useful tasks over longer time periods. At the same time, researchers are struggling to understand what kinds of imaginative consumer products will attract, engage, and satisfy diverse populations. The opportunities for researchers are unlimited. There are so many interesting, important, and doable projects that it may be hard to choose a direction. The goal of universal usability through plasticity of interface designs will keep researchers busy for years. Getting past vague promises and measuring user performance with alternate interfaces will be central to rapid progress. Each experiment has two parents: the practical problems facing designers, and the fundamental theories based on principles of human behavior and interface design. Begin by proposing a lucid, testable hypothesis. Then consider the appropriate research methodology, conduct the experiment, collect the data, and analyze the results. Each experiment also has three children: specific recommendations for the practical problem, refinements of theories, and guidance to future experimenters. Each chapter of this book ends with specific research proposals.

WORLD WIDE WEB RESOURCES

This book is accompanied by a web site (http://www.aw.com/DTUI/) that includes pointers to additional resources tied to the contents of each chapter. In addition, this web site contains information for instructors, students, practitioners, and researchers. The links for Chapter 1 include general resources on human-computer interaction, such as professional societies, government agencies, companies, bibliographies, and guidelines documents.

Readers seeking references to scientific journals and conferences can consult the online searchable bibliography for human-computer interaction (http://www.hcibib.org/). Built under the heroic leadership of Gary Perlman, it makes available more than 25,000 journal, conference, and book abstracts.

Three wonderful sets of pointers to World Wide Web resources are:

1. HCI Index (http://degraaff.org/hci/)
2. Diamond Bullet Design (http://www.usabilityfirst.com/)
3. Usability and Beyond (http://www15.brinkster.com/stijnscholts/links/default.asp)

Electronic mailing lists for announcements and discussion lists are maintained by ACM SIGCHI (http://www.acm.org/sigchi/) and by the British HCI Group (http://www.bcs-hci.org.uk/).

http://www.aw.com/DTUI

References

Specialized references for this chapter appear here; general information resources are given in the following section.

Bederson, B. B., Lee, B., Sherman, R., Herrnson, P. S., and Niemi, R. G., Electronic voting system usability issues, *CHI 2003 Conference on Human Factors in Computing Systems, CHI Letters*, 5, 1, ACM Press, New York (2003), 145–152.

Blenkhorn, Paul, Evans, Gareth, King, Alasdair, Kurniawan, Sri Hastuti, and Sutcliffe, Alistair, Screen magnifiers: Evolution and evaluation, *IEEE Computer Graphics and Applications*, 23, 5 (Sept/Oct 2003), 54–61.

Bruckman, Amy and Bandlow, Alisa, HCI for Kids, in Jacko, Julie and Sears, Andrew (Editors), *Handbook of Human-Computer Interaction,* Lawrence Erlbaum Associates, Hillsdale, NJ (2002).

Center for Information Technology Accommodation, Section 508: The road to accessibility, General Services Administration, Washington, DC (2002). Available at http://www.section508.gov/index.cfm.

Czaja, S. J. and Lee, C. C., Designing computer systems for older adults, in Jacko, Julie and Sears, Andrew (Editors), *Handbook of Human-Computer Interaction*, Lawrence Erlbaum Associates, Hillsdale, NJ (2002), 413–427.

Czaja, Sara J. (Editor), *Human Factors Research Needs for an Aging Population*, National Academy Press, Washington, DC (1990).

Druin, Allison and Inkpen, Kori, When are personal technologies for children?, *Personal Technologies 5* (3) (2001), 191–194.

Druin, A., Bederson, B., Boltman, A., Miura, A., Knotts-Callahan, D., and Platt, M., Children as our technology design partners, in Druin, Allison (Editor), *The Design of Children's Technology: How We Design and Why*, Morgan Kaufmann Publishers, San Francisco, CA (1999), 51–72.

Edwards, Alistair D.N., *Extra-Ordinary Human-Computer Interaction: Interfaces for Users with Disabilities*, Cambridge University Press, Cambridge, U.K. (1995).

Furlong, Mary and Kearsley, Greg, *Computers for Kids Over 60*, SeniorNet, San Francisco, CA (1990).

Future of Children 10 (2), Special Issue on *Children and Computer Technology*, David and Lucille Packard Foundation, Los Altos, CA (Fall/Winter 2000).

Huff, C. W. and Cooper, J., Sex bias in educational software: The effect of designers' stereotypes on the software they design, *Journal of Applied Social Psychology*, 17, 6 (June 1987), 519–532.

Keirsey, David, *Please Understand Me II: Temperament, Character, Intelligence*, Prometheus Nemesis Books, Del Mar, CA (1998).

Marchionini, Gary, Ashley, Maryle, and Korzendorfer, Lois, ACCESS at the Library of Congress, in Shneiderman, Ben (Editor), *Sparks of Innovation in Human-Computer Interaction*, Ablex, Norwood, NJ (1993), 251–258.

Marcus, Aaron and Gould, Emile West, Cultural dimensions and global user-interface design: What? So What? Now What?, *Proc. 6th Conference on Human Factors and the Web*, (2000). Available at http://www.tri.c.com/hfweb/.

Mynatt, Elizabeth D. and Weber, Gerhard, Nonvisual presentation of graphical user interfaces: Contrasting two approaches, *CHI '94 Human Factors in Computer Systems*, ACM, New York (1994), 166–172.

Neuman, Delia, Learning disabled students' interactions with commercial courseware: A naturalistic study, *Educational Technology Research and Development*, 39, 1 (1991), 31–49.

Poll, Leonard H. D. and Waterham, Ronald P., Graphical user interfaces and visually disabled users, *IEEE Transactions on Rehabilitation Engineering*, 3, 1 (March 1995), 65–69.

Shneiderman, B., Universal Usability: Pushing human-computer interaction research to empower every citizen, *Communications of the ACM 43*, 5 (May 2000), 84–91.

Thatcher, James W., Screen Reader/2: Access to OS/2 and the graphical user interface, *Proc. ACM SIGCAPH: Computers and the Physically Handicapped, ASSETS '94* (1994), 39–47.

Vanderheiden, Greg, Fundamental principles and priority setting for universal usability, *Proc. ACM Conference on Universal Usability*, ACM, New York (2000), 32–38.

Whitcomb, G. Robert, Computer games for the elderly, *Proc. Conference on Computers and the Quality of Life '90*, ACM SIGCAS, New York (1990), 112–115.

General information resources

Primary journals include the following:

ACM CHI Letters (archival designation for key conferences, such as CHI and UIST)

ACM interactions: A Magazine for User Interface Designers, ACM, New York.

ACM Transactions on Computer-Human Interaction, ACM, New York.

Behaviour & Information Technology (BIT), Taylor & Francis Ltd., London, U.K.

Computer Supported Cooperative Work, Kluwer Academic Publishers, Dordecht, The Netherlands.

Human-Computer Interaction, Lawrence Erlbaum Associates, Hillsdale, NJ.

Information Visualization, Palgrave Macmillan, Houndmills, Basingstoke, U.K.

Interacting with Computers, Butterworth Heinemann Ltd., Oxford, U.K.

International Journal of Human-Computer Interaction, Lawrence Erlbaum Associates, Hillsdale, NJ.

International Journal of Human-Computer Studies, formerly *International Journal of Man-Machine Studies (IJMMS)*, Academic Press, London, U.K.

Other journals that regularly carry articles of interest include:

ACM: Communications of the ACM (CACM)

ACM Computers in Entertainment

ACM Computing Surveys

ACM Transactions on Graphics

ACM Transactions on Information Systems

Cognitive Science

Computers in Human Behavior

Ergonomics

Human Factors (HF)

IEEE Computer

IEEE Computer Graphics and Applications

IEEE Multimedia

IEEE Software

IEEE Transactions on Systems, Man, and Cybernetics (IEEE SMC)

Journal of Visual Languages and Computing

Personal and Ubiquitous Computing

Presence

Technical Communication

UMUAI: User Modeling and User-Adapted Interaction

The Association for Computing Machinery (ACM) has a Special Interest Group on Computer & Human Interaction (SIGCHI), which publishes a newsletter and holds regularly scheduled conferences. Other ACM Special Interest Groups, such as Graphics and Interactive Techniques (SIGGRAPH), Computers and the Physically Handicapped (SIGCAPH),

Hypertext, Hypermedia, and Web (SIGWEB), and Multimedia (SIGMM), also produce conferences and newsletters. Other relevant ACM groups are Computers and Society (SIGCAS), Design of Communication (SIGDOC), Groupware (SIGGROUP), and Information Retrieval (SIGIR).

The IEEE Computer Society, through its many conferences, transactions, and magazines, covers user interface issues. The American Society for Information Science & Technology (ASIST) has a Special Interest Group on Human-Computer Interaction (SIGHCI) that publishes a newsletter and organizes sessions at the annual ASIST convention. Similarly, the business-oriented Association for Information Systems (AIS) has a SIGHCI that also publishes a newsletter and runs sessions at several conferences. The long-established Human Factors & Ergonomics Society runs annual conferences and has a Computer Systems Technical Group with a newsletter. Also, the Society for Technical Communications (STC), the American Institute of Graphic Arts (AIGA), the International Ergonomics Association, and the Ergonomics Society increasingly focus on user interfaces.

The International Federation for Information Processing has a Technical Committee and Working Groups on human-computer interaction. The British Computer Society Human-Computer Interaction Group and the French Association Francais pour l'Interaction Homme-Machine (AFIHM) promote development within their countries. Other national and regional groups conduct events in South Africa, Australia/New Zealand, Scandinavia, Asia, and Latin America.

Conferences—such as the ones held by the ACM (especially SIGCHI and SIGGRAPH), IEEE, ASIST, Human Factors & Ergonomics Society, and IFIP—often have relevant papers presented and published in the proceedings. INTERACT, Human-Computer Interaction International, and Work with Display Units are conference series that cover user-interface issues. Several more specialized ACM conferences may also be of interest: User Interfaces Software and Technology, Hypertext, Computer-Supported Cooperative Work, Intelligent User Interfaces, Universal Usability, Computers and Cognition, Designing Interactive Systems, and more.

Brad Myers's brief history of HCI is one starting point for those who want to study the emergence and evolution of this field (*ACM interactions*, March 1998). Another approach is to review key books such as Gerald Weinberg's *The Psychology of Computer Programming* (1971), which remains a continuing inspiration. James Martin provided a thoughtful and useful survey of interactive systems in his 1973 book, *Design of Man-Computer Dialogues*. Ben Shneiderman's 1980 book, *Software Psychology: Human Factors in Computer and Information Systems,* promoted the use of controlled experimental techniques and scientific research methods. Rubinstein and Hersh's *The Human Factor: Designing Computer Systems for People* (1984) offered an appealing introduction to computer-system design and many useful guidelines. The first edition of this book, published in 1987, reviewed critical issues, offered guidelines for designers, and suggested research directions.

Don Norman's 1988 book, *The Psychology of Everyday Things* (reprinted as *The Design of Everyday Things*), is a refreshing look at the psychological issues in the design of the everyday technology that surrounds us. The sections dealing with doors and showers are as provocative as those dealing with computers and calculators. This book has a wonderful blend of levity and great depth of thinking, practical wisdom, and thoughtful theory.

A steady flow of influential books during the 1990s included Hix and Hartson's *Developing User Interfaces* (1993), Nielsen's *Usability Engineering* (1993), Preece et al.'s *Human-Computer Interaction* (1994), and Landauer's *The Trouble with Computers* (1995). Recent recommended books include Nielsen's *Designing Web Usability: The Practice of Simplicity*

(1999); Preece, Rogers, and Sharp's *Interaction Design* (2002); and Norman's *The Invisible Computer* (2000).

An important development for the field was the creation (in 1991) of a professional group, the Usability Professionals Association, and their new magazine, called *User Experience*. 1994 marked the appearance of ACM's professional magazine, entitled *interactions*, and academic journal, *Transactions on Computer-Human Interaction*. As the field matures, specialized topics form their own subgroups and publications, as is happening with mobile computing, web design, online communities, information visualization, virtual environments, and so on.

The following list of guidelines documents and books is a starting point to the large and growing literature in this area.

Guidelines documents

Ahlstrom, Vicki and Longo, Kelly, *The Human Factors Design Standard*, U. S. Federal Aviation Administration, Atlantic City, NJ (June 2003). Available at http://acb220.faa.tc.gov/hfds/.

—Extensive compilation of human-factors standards for contractors to follow, especially relevant to aircraft and air-traffic control.

Apple Aqua Human Interface Guidelines, Apple, Cupertino, CA (2002).

—Explains how to design interfaces for Mac OS X.

Apple Computer, Inc., *Macintosh Human Interface Guidelines*, Addison-Wesley, Reading, MA (1992).

—A beautifully produced color book. A well-designed CD-ROM, *Making it Macintosh*, exemplifies these Mac guidelines (Addison-Wesley, Reading, MA, 1993).

BSR/HFES Human Factors Engineering of Computer Workstations (Draft Standard), Human Factors Society, Santa Monica, CA (March 2002).

—Carefully considered revised standards for the design, installation, and use of computer workstations. Emphasizes ergonomics and anthropometrics.

Human Engineering Design Criteria for Military Systems, Equipment and Facilities, Military Standard MIL-STD–1472F, U.S. Government Printing Office, Washington, DC (1999).

—Covers traditional ergonomic and anthropometric issues. Later editions pay increasing attention to user-computer interfaces. Interesting and thought-provoking reminder of many human-factors issues.

International Organization for Standardization, *ISO 9241 Ergonomic Requirements for Office Work with Visual Display Terminals (VDTs), Part 11: Guidance on Usability*, Geneva, Switzerland (1998); *ISO 16071 Ergonomics of Human-System Interaction—Guidance on Accessibility for Human-Computer Interfaces*, Technical Specification, Geneva, Switzerland (2002). Available from American National Standards Institute, 11 West 42nd Street, New York, NY.

—General introduction, dialog principles, guidance on usability, presentation of information, user guidance, menu dialogs, command dialogs, direct-manipulation dialogs, form-filling dialogs.

Koyani, Sanjay J., Bailey, Robert W., Nall, Janice R., and others, *Reseach-based Web Design & Usability Guidelines*, Dept. of Health & Human Services, National Institutes of Health Publication 03-5424, National Cancer Institute, Washington, DC (Sept 2003). Available at http://www.usability.gov/.

—Authoritative and packed with numerous full-color examples of information-oriented web sites.

Microsoft, Inc., *The Microsoft Windows User Experience*, Microsoft Press, Redmond, WA (1999).

Microsoft, Inc., *Windows XP Visual Guidelines*, Microsoft Press, Redmond, WA (2001).

—These thoughtful analyses of usability principles (user in control, directness, consistency, forgiveness, aesthetics, and simplicity) gives detailed guidance for Windows software developers. The guidelines for Windows XP emphasize simplicity, color, freshness, and excitement.

NASA User-Interface Guidelines, Goddard Space Flight Center-Code 520, Greenbelt, MD (January 1996). Available at http://aaaprod.gsfc.nasa.gov/usability/use/UG_96/.

—The purpose of this document is to present user-interface guidelines that specifically address graphic and object-oriented interfaces operating in either distributed or independent systems environments. Principles and general guidelines are given, with many graphic-interface examples for a variety of platforms.

Smith, Sid L. and Mosier, Jane N., *Guidelines for Designing User Interface Software*, Report ESD-TR–86–278, Electronic Systems Division, MITRE Corporation, Bedford, MA (August 1986). Available from National Technical Information Service, Springfield, VA.

—This thorough document, which has undergone several revisions, begins with a good discussion of human-factors issues in design. It then covers data entry, data display, and sequence control. Guidelines are offered with comments, examples, exceptions, and references.

Sun Microsystems, Inc., *Java Look and Feel Design Guidelines: Second Edition*, Addison-Wesley, Reading, MA (2001). Available at http://java.sun.com/products/jlf/ed2/book/.

—Shows designers how to create visual design and behaviors in a consistent, compatible, and aesthetic manner.

World Wide Web Consortium's Web Accessibility Initiative, *Web content accessibility guidelines 1.0*, Geneva, Switzerland (1999). Available at http://www.w3.org/TR/WAI-WEBCONTENT/.

—Practical, implementable three-level prioritization of web design guidelines for users with disabilities.

World Wide Web Consortium's Web Accessibility Initiative, *Evaluation, repair, and transformation tools for web content accessibility*, Geneva, Switzerland (2002). Available at http://www.w3.org/WAI/ER/existingtools.html.

—An occasionally updated list of software tools related to accessibility; demonstrates lively activity.

Books

Classic books

Bolt, Richard A., *The Human Interface: Where People and Computers Meet*, Lifelong Learning Publications, Belmont, CA (1984).

Brown, C. Marlin "Lin," *Human-Computer Interface Design Guidelines*, Ablex, Norwood, NJ (1988).

Cakir, A., Hart, D. J., and Stewart, T. F. M., *Visual Display Terminals: A Manual Covering Ergonomics, Workplace Design, Health and Safety, Task Organization*, John Wiley & Sons, New York (1980).

Card, Stuart K., Moran, Thomas P., and Newell, Allen, *The Psychology of Human-Computer Interaction*, Lawrence Erlbaum Associates, Hillsdale, NJ (1983).

Carroll, John M., *The Nurnberg Funnel: Designing Minimalist Instruction for Practical Computer Skill*, MIT Press, Cambridge, MA (1990).

Crawford, Chris, *The Art of Computer Game Design: Reflections of a Master Game Designer*, Osborne/McGraw-Hill, Berkeley, CA (1984).

Dreyfus, W., *The Measure of Man: Human Factors in Design, Second Edition*, Whitney Library of Design, New York (1967).

Duffy, Thomas M., Palmer, James E., and Mehlenbacher, Brad, *Online Help: Design and Evaluation*, Ablex, Norwood, NJ (1993).

Eberts, Ray E., *User Interface Design*, Prentice-Hall, Englewood Cliffs, NJ (1993).

Ehrich, R. W. and Williges, R. C., *Human-Computer Dialogue Design*, Elsevier Science Publishers B.V., Amsterdam, The Netherlands (1986).

Foley, James D., van Dam, Andries, Feiner, Steven K., and Hughes, John F., *Computer Graphics: Principles and Practice in C, Second Edition*, Addison-Wesley, Reading, MA (1995).

Hiltz, Starr Roxanne, *Online Communities: A Case Study of the Office of the Future*, Ablex, Norwood, NJ (1984).

Hiltz, Starr Roxanne and Turoff, Murray, *The Network Nation: Human Communication via Computer*, Addison-Wesley, Reading, MA (1978, revised edition 1998).

Hix, Deborah and Hartson, H. Rex, *Developing User Interfaces: Ensuring Usability Through Product and Process*, John Wiley & Sons, New York (1993).

Kantowitz, Barry H. and Sorkin, Robert D., *Human Factors: Understanding People-System Relationships*, John Wiley & Sons, New York (1983).

Kearsley, Greg, *Online Help Systems: Design and Implementation*, Ablex, Norwood, NJ (1988).

Krueger, Myron, *Artificial Reality II*, Addison-Wesley, Reading, MA (1991).

Laurel, Brenda, *Computers as Theater*, Addison-Wesley, Reading, MA (1991).

Marcus, Aaron, *Graphic Design for Electronic Documents and User Interfaces*, ACM Press, New York (1992).

Martin, James, *Design of Man-Computer Dialogues*, Prentice-Hall, Englewood Cliffs, NJ (1973).

Mumford, Enid, *Designing Human Systems for New Technology*, Manchester Business School, Manchester, U.K. (1983).

National Research Council, Committee on Human Factors, *Research Needs for Human Factors*, National Academy Press, Washington, DC (1983).

Nickerson, Raymond S., *Using Computers: Human Factors in Information Systems*, MIT Press, Cambridge, MA (1986).

Nielsen, Jakob, *Usability Engineering*, Academic Press, Boston, MA (1993).

Norman, Donald A., *The Psychology of Everyday Things*, Basic Books, New York (1988).

Norman, Kent, *The Psychology of Menu Selection: Designing Cognitive Control at the Human/Computer Interface*, Ablex, Norwood, NJ (1991).

Pheasant, Stephen, *Bodyspace: Anthropometry, Ergonomics and the Design of the Work, Second Edition*, Taylor & Francis, London, U.K. (1996).

Preece, J., Benyon, D., Davies, G., Keller, L., and Rogers, Y., *A Guide to Usability: Human Factors in Computing*, Addison-Wesley, Reading, MA (1993).

Rubinstein, Richard and Hersh, Harry, *The Human Factor: Designing Computer Systems for People*, Digital Press, Maynard, MA (1984).

Sanders, M. S. and McCormick, Ernest J., *Human Factors in Engineering and Design, Seventh Edition*, McGraw-Hill, New York (1993).

Sheridan, T. B. and Ferrel, W. R., *Man-Machine Systems: Information, Control, and Decision Models of Human Performance*, MIT Press, Cambridge, MA (1974).

Shneiderman, Ben, *Software Psychology: Human Factors in Computer and Information Systems*, Little, Brown, Boston, MA (1980).

Shneiderman, Ben and Kearsley, Greg, *Hypertext Hands-On! An Introduction to a New Way of Organizing and Accessing Information*, Addison-Wesley, Reading, MA (1989).

Thimbleby, Harold, *User Interface Design*, ACM Press, New York (1990).

Thorell, L. G. and Smith, W. J., *Using Computer Color Effectively*, Prentice-Hall, Englewood Cliffs, NJ (1990).

Tognazzini, Bruce, *Tog on Interface*, Addison-Wesley, Reading, MA (1992).

Travis, David, *Effective Color Displays: Theory and Practice*, Academic Press, Harcourt Brace Jovanovich, London, U.K. (1991).

Turkle, Sherry, *The Second Self: Computers and the Human Spirit*, Simon and Schuster, New York (1984).

Vaske, Jerry and Grantham, Charles, *Socializing the Human-Computer Environment*, Ablex, Norwood, NJ (1990).

Weinberg, Gerald M., *The Psychology of Computer Programming*, Van Nostrand Reinhold, New York (1971).

Weizenbaum, Joseph, *Computer Power and Human Reason: From Judgment to Calculation*, W. H. Freeman, San Francisco, CA (1976).

Winograd, Terry and Flores, Fernando, *Understanding Computers and Cognition*, Ablex, Norwood, NJ (1986).

Zuboff, Shoshanna, *In the Age of the Smart Machine: The Future of Work and Power*, Basic Books, New York (1988).

Recent books

Ashcraft, Mark H., *Cognition, Third Edition*, Prentice-Hall, Englewood Cliffs, NJ (2001).

Bailey, Robert W., *Human Performance Engineering: Using Human Factors/Ergonomics to Achieve Computer Usability, Third Edition*, Prentice-Hall, Englewood Cliffs, NJ (1996).

Beaudouin-Lafon, Michel, *Computer Supported Co-operative Work Trends in Software*, John Wiley & Sons, New York (1999).

Beyer, Hugh and Holtzblatt, Karen, *Contextual Design: Defining Customer-Centered Systems*, Morgan Kaufmann Publishers, San Francisco, CA (1998).

Borchers, Jan, *A Pattern Approach to Interaction Design*, John Wiley & Sons, Chichester, U.K. (2001).

Carroll, John M., *Scenario-Based Design: Envisioning Work and Technology in System Development*, John Wiley & Sons, New York (1995).

Carroll, John M., *Making Use: Scenario-Based Design of Human-Computer Interactions*, MIT Press, Cambridge, MA (2000).

Constantine, Larry L. and Lockwood, Lucy A. D., *Software for Use: A Practical Guide to the Models and Methods of Usage-Centered Design*, Addison-Wesley, Reading, MA (1999).

Cooper, Alan, *About Face: The Essentials of User Interface Design, Second Edition*, IDG Books Worldwide, Foster City, CA (2003).

Dix, Alan, Finlay, Janet, Abowd, Gregory, and Beale, Russell, *Human-Computer Interaction, Second Edition*, Prentice-Hall, Englewood, NJ (1998).

Dourish, Paul, *Where the Action Is*, MIT Press, Cambridge, MA (2002).

Druin, Allison and Solomon, Cynthia, *Designing Multimedia Environments for Children: Computers, Creativity, and Kids*, John Wiley & Sons, New York (1996).

Dumas, Joseph S. and Redish, Janice C., *A Practical Guide to Usability Testing*, Ablex, Norwood, NJ (1999, revised edition).

Elmes, David G., Kantowitz, Barry H., and Roediger, Henry L., *Research Methods in Psychology, Seventh Edition*, Wadsworth Publishing, Belmont, CA (2002).

Fernandes, Tony, *Global Interface Design: A Guide to Designing International User Interfaces*, Academic Press Professional, Boston, MA (1995).

Galitz, Wilbert O., *The Essential Guide to User Interface Design: An Introduction to GUI Design Principles and Techniques, Second Edition*, John Wiley & Sons, New York (2003).

Goldstein, E. Bruce, *Sensation and Perception: 6th Edition*, Wadsworth Publishing, Pacific Grove, CA (2002).

Hackos, JoAnn T. and Redish, Janice C., *User and Task Analysis for Interface Design*, John Wiley & Sons, New York (1998).

Horton, William K., *Designing and Writing Online Documentation: Hypermedia for Self-Supporting Products*, John Wiley & Sons, New York (1994).

Isaacs, Ellen and Walendowski, Alan, *Designing from Both Sides of the Screen: How Designers and Engineers Can Collaborate to Build Cooperative Technology*, New Riders Publishing, Indianapolis, IN (2001).

Johnson, Jeff, *GUI Bloopers Don'ts and Do's for Software Developers and Web Designers*, Morgan Kaufmann Publishers, San Francisco, CA (2000).

Landauer, Thomas K., *The Trouble with Computers: Usefulness, Usability, and Productivity*, MIT Press, Cambridge, MA (1995).

Mandell, Theo, *The Elements of User Interface Design*, John Wiley & Sons, New York (1997).

Marchionini, Gary, *Information Seeking in Electronic Environments*, Cambridge University Press, Cambridge, U.K. (1995).

Mayhew, Deborah J., *The Usability Engineering Lifecycle: A Practitioner's Guide to User Interface Design*, Morgan Kaufmann Publishers, San Francisco, CA (1999).

Mullet, Kevin and Sano, Darrell, *Designing Visual Interfaces: Communication Oriented Techniques,* Sunsoft Press, Englewood Cliffs, NJ (1995).

Newman, William M. and Lamming, Michael G., *Interactive Systems Design,* Addison-Wesley, Reading, MA (1995).

Nielsen, Jakob, *Multimedia and Hypertext: The Internet and Beyond,* Academic Press, Cambridge, MA (1995).

Norman, Don, *The Invisible Computer: Why Good Products Can Fail, the Personal Computer Is So Complex, and Information Appliances Are the Solution*, MIT Press, Cambridge, MA (2000).

Olsen, Jr., Dan R., *Developing User Interfaces*, Morgan Kaufmann Publishers, San Francisco, CA (1998).

Preece, Jenny, *Online Communities: Designing Usability and Supporting Sociability*, John Wiley & Sons, New York (2000).

Preece, Jenny, Rogers, Yvonne, Sharp, Helen, Benyon, David, Holland, Simon, and Carey, Tom, *Human-Computer Interaction*, Addison-Wesley, Reading, MA (1994).

Preece, Jenny, Rogers, Yvonne, and Sharp, Helen, *Interaction Design: Beyond Human-Computer Interaction*, John Wiley & Sons, New York, (2002).

Raskin, Jef, *Humane Interface: New Directions for Designing Interactive Systems*, Addison-Wesley, Reading, MA (2000).

Reeves, Byron and Nass, Clifford, *The Media Equation: How People Treat Computers, Television, and New Media Like Real People and Places*, Cambridge University Press, Cambridge, U.K. (1996).

Rubin, Jeffrey, *Handbook of Usability Testing: How to Plan, Design, and Conduct Effective Tests*, John Wiley & Sons, New York (1994).

Schuler, Douglas, *New Community Networks: Wired for Change*, ACM Press, New York, and Addison-Wesley, Reading, MA (1996).

Shneiderman, Ben, *Leonardo's Laptop: Human Needs and the New Computing Technologies*, MIT Press, Cambridge, MA (2002).

Turkle, Sherry, *Life on the Screen: Identity in the Age of the Internet*, Simon and Schuster, New York (1995).

Ware, Colin, *Information Visualization: Perception for Design, Second Edition*, Morgan Kaufmann Publishers, San Francisco, CA (2004).

Wickens, Christopher D. and Hollands, Justin G., *Engineering Psychology and Human Performance*, Prentice-Hall, Englewood Cliffs, NJ (2000).

Web design resources

Alliance for Technology Access, *Computer and Web Resources for People With Disabilities: A Guide to Exploring Today's Assistive Technology*, Hunter House, Alameda, CA (2000).

Brinck, Tom, Gergle, Darren, and Wood, Scott D., *Usability for the Web: Designing Web Sites that Work*, Morgan Kaufmann Publishers, San Francisco, CA (2001).

Cato, John, *User-Centered Web Design*, Addison-Wesley, Reading, MA (2001).

Forsythe, Chris, Grose, Eric, and Ratner, Julie (Editors), *Human Factors and Web Development*, Lawrence Erlbaum Associates, Hillsdale, NJ (1997).

Lazar, Jonathan, *User-Centered Web Development*, Jones & Bartlett Publishers, Boston, MA (2001).

Lynch, Patrick J. and Horton, Sarah, *Web Style Guide: Basic Design Principles for Creating Web Sites*, Yale University Press, New Haven, CT (1999).

Nielsen, Jakob, *Designing Web Usability: The Practice of Simplicity*, New Riders Publishing, Indianapolis, IN (1999).

Nielsen, Jakob and Tahir, Marie, *Homepage Usability: 50 Websites Deconstructed*, New Riders Publishing, Indianapolis, IN (2002).

Paciello, Michael G., *Web Accessibility for People With Disabilities*, CMP Books, Gilroy, CA (2000).

Rosenfeld, Louis and Morville, Peter, *Information Architecture for the World Wide Web, Second Edition*, O'Reilly & Associates, Inc., Sebastopol, CA (2002).

Spool, Jared M., Scanlon, Tara, Schroeder, Will, Snyder, Carolyn, and DeAngelo, Terri, *Web Site Usability: A Designer's Guide*, Morgan Kaufmann Publishers, San Francisco, CA (1999).

Van Duyne, Douglas K., Landay, James A., and Hong, Jason I., *The Design of Sites: Patterns, Principles, and Processes for Crafting a Customer-Centered Web Experience*, Addison-Wesley, Reading, MA (2002).

Collections

Classic collections

Adler, Paul S. and Winograd, Terry (Editors), *Usability: Turning Technologies into Tools*, Oxford University Press, New York (1992).

Badre, Albert and Shneiderman, Ben (Editors), *Directions in Human-Computer Interaction*, Ablex, Norwood, NJ (1980).

Carey, Jane (Editor), *Human Factors in Management Information Systems*, Ablex, Norwood, NJ (1988).

Carroll, John M. (Editor), *Interfacing Thought: Cognitive Aspects of Human-Computer Interaction*, MIT Press, Cambridge, MA (1987).

Carroll, John M. (Editor), *Designing Interaction: Psychology at the Human-Computer Interface*, Cambridge University Press, Cambridge, U.K. (1991).

Durrett, H. John (Editor), *Color and the Computer*, Academic Press, San Diego, CA (1987)

Greenberg, Saul (Editor), *Computer-Supported Cooperative Work and Groupware*, Academic Press, London, U.K. (1991).

Hartson, H. Rex (Editor), *Advances in Human-Computer Interaction, Volume 1*, Ablex, Norwood, NJ (1985).

Helander, Martin (Editor), *Handbook of Human-Computer Interaction*, North-Holland, Amsterdam, The Netherlands (1988).

Laurel, Brenda (Editor), *The Art of Human-Computer Interface Design*, Addison-Wesley, Reading, MA (1990).

Nielsen, Jakob (Editor), *Advances in Human-Computer Interaction, Volume 5*, Ablex, Norwood, NJ (1993).

Norman, Donald A. and Draper, Stephen W. (Editors), *User Centered System Design: New Perspectives on Human-Computer Interaction*, Lawrence Erlbaum Associates, Hillsdale, NJ (1986).

Shackel, Brian and Richardson, Simon (Editors), *Human Factors for Informatics Usability*, Cambridge University Press, Cambridge, U.K. (1991).

Shneiderman, Ben (Editor), *Sparks of Innovation in Human-Computer Interaction*, Ablex, Norwood, NJ (1993).

Thomas, John C. and Schneider, Michael L. (Editors), *Human Factors in Computer Systems*, Ablex, Norwood, NJ (1984).

Van Cott, H. P. and Kinkade, R. G. (Editors), *Human Engineering Guide to Equipment Design*, U.S. Superintendent of Documents, Washington, DC (1972).

Wiener, Earl L. and Nagel, David C. (Editors), *Human Factors in Aviation*, Academic Press, New York (1988).

Recent collections

Baecker, R., Grudin, J., Buxton, W., and Greenberg, S. (Editors), *Readings in Human-Computer Interaction: Towards the Year 2000*, Morgan Kaufmann Publishers, San Francisco, CA (1995).

Bergman, Eric, *Information Appliances and Beyond*, Morgan Kaufmann Publishers, San Francisco, CA (2000).

Bias, Randolph and Mayhew, Deborah (Editors), *Cost-Justifying Usability*, Academic Press, New York (1994).

Carey, Jane (Editor), *Human Factors in Information Systems: Emerging Theoretical Bases*, Ablex, Norwood, NJ (1995).

Carroll, John M. (Editor), *Minimalism Beyond the Nurnberg Funnel*, MIT Press, Cambridge, MA (1998).

Carroll, John M. (Editor), *Human-Computer Interaction in the New Millennium*, Addison-Wesley, Reading, MA (2002).

Carroll, Johh M. (Editor), *HCI Models, Theories, and Frameworks: Toward a Multidisciplinary Science*, Morgan Kaufmann Publishers, San Francisco, CA (2003).

Cassell, Justine and Jenkins, Henry (Editors), *From Barbie to Mortal Kombat*, MIT Press, Cambridge, MA (1998).

Druin, Allison (Editor), *The Design of Children's Software: How We Design, What We Design and Why*, Morgan Kaufmann Publishers, San Francisco, CA (1999).

Earnshaw, Rae, Guedj, Richard, van Dam, Andries, and Vince, John (Editors), *Frontiers in Human-Centred Computing, Online Communities and Virtual Environments*, Springer-Verlag, London, U.K. (2001).

Gardner-Bonneau, Daryle (Editor), *Human Factors and Voice Interactive Systems*, Kluwer Academic Publishers, Boston, MA (1999).

Greenberg, Saul, Hayne, Stephen, and Rada, Roy (Editors), *Groupware for Real Time Drawing: A Designer's Guide*, McGraw-Hill, New York (1995).

Helander, Martin, Landauer, Thomas K., and Prabhu, Prasad V. (Editors), *Handbook of Human-Computer Interaction*, North-Holland Elsevier Science, Amsterdam, The Netherlands (1997).

Jacko, Julie and Sears, Andrew (Editors), *Handbook of Human-Computer Interaction*, Lawrence Erlbaum Associates, Hillsdale, NJ (2003).

MacDonald, Lindsay and Vince, John (Editors), *Interacting with Virtual Environments*, John Wiley & Sons, New York (1994).

Perlman, Gary, Green, Georgia K., and Wogalter, Michael S. (Editors), *Human Factors Perspectives on Human-Computer Interaction: Selections from Proceedings of Human Factors and Ergonomics Society Annual Meetings 1983–1994*, HFES, Santa Monica, CA (1995).

Rudisill, Marianne, Lewis, Clayton, Polson, Peter B., and McKay, Timothy D. (Editors), *Human-Computer Interface Design: Success Stories, Emerging Methods and Real-World Context*, Morgan Kaufmann Publishers, San Francisco, CA (1995).

Salvendy, Gavriel (Editor), *Handbook of Human Factors, Second Edition*, John Wiley & Sons, New York (1997).

Stephanidis, Constantine (Editor), *User Interfaces for All: Concepts, Methods, and Tools*, Lawrence Erlbaum Associates, Hillsdale, NJ (2001)

Thatcher, Jim, Waddell, Cynthia, Henry, Shawn, Swierenga, Sarah, Urban, Mark, and Burks, Michael (Editors), *Constructing Accessible Websites*, Apress, Berkeley, CA (2003).

Trenner, Lesley and Bawa, Joanna (Editors), *The Politics of Usability: A Practical Guide to Designing Usable System in Industry*, Springer-Verlag, Berlin, Germany (1998).

Winograd, Terry (Editor), *Bringing Design to Software*, ACM Press, New York, and Addison-Wesley, Reading, MA (1996).

Videotapes

Video is an effective medium for presenting the dynamic, graphical, interactive nature of modern user interfaces.

The Technical Video Program of the ACM SIGCHI conferences makes it possible to see excellent demonstrations of often-cited but seldom-seen systems. All CHI videos can be ordered directly through ACM at http://www.acm.org/sigchi/video/.

The Human-Computer Interaction Lab at the University of Maryland has produced video reports since 1991 at http://www.cs.umd.edu/hcil/pubs/video-reports.shtml, and a selection are available on the Web from the Open Video project at http://www.open-video.org/.

chapter

2

Guidelines, Principles, and Theories

We want principles, not only developed—the work of the closet—but applied, which is the work of life.

HORACE MANN
Thoughts, 1867

There never comes a point where a theory can be said to be true. The most that anyone can claim for any theory is that it has shared the successes of all its rivals and that it has passed at least one test which they have failed.

A. J. AYER
Philosophy in the Twentieth Century, 1982

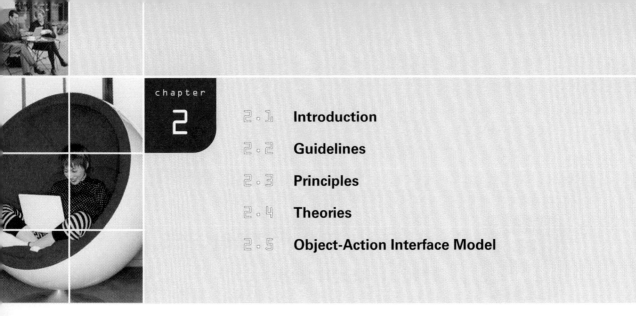

2.1   Introduction

Successful designers of interactive systems know that they can and must go beyond intuitive judgments made hastily when a design problem emerges. Fortunately, guidance for designers is available in the form of (1) specific and practical guidelines, (2) middle-level principles, and (3) high-level theories and models. The practical guidelines prescribe cures for design problems, caution against dangers, and provide helpful reminders based on accumulated wisdom. The middle-level principles help in analyzing and comparing design alternatives. For developers of high-level theories and models, the goal is to describe objects and actions with consistent terminology so that comprehensible explanations can be made to support communication and teaching. Other theories are predictive, such as those for reading, typing, or pointing times.

In many contemporary systems, there is a grand opportunity to improve the user interface. The cluttered displays, complex and tedious procedures, inadequate functionality, inconsistent sequences of actions, and insufficient informative feedback can generate debilitating stress and anxiety. It is perfectly understandable that users whose network connections drop as they are completing lengthy online purchase orders may become frustrated and even angry. These experiences can lead to poor performance, frequent minor slips, and occasional serious errors, all contributing to job dissatisfaction and consumer frustration. Guidelines, principles, and theories—which can provide remedies and preventive medicine for these problems—have matured in recent years. Reliable methods for predicting pointing and input times (Chapter 9), helpful cognitive theories (Chapter 11), and better frameworks for online help (Chapter 13) now shape research and guide design.

This chapter begins with a sampling of guidelines for navigating, organizing displays, getting user attention, and facilitating data entry (Section 2.2). Then Section 2.3 covers some fundamental principles of interface design, such as coping with user skill levels, task profiles, and interaction styles. It offers eight golden rules of interface design, explores ways of preventing user errors, and closes with a section on the controversial strategies for integrating automation with human control. Section 2.4 reviews several theories of interface design, and Section 2.5 concentrates on the object-action interface model.

2.2   Guidelines

From the earliest days, interface designers have tried to write down guidelines to record their insights and guide the efforts of future designers. The early Apple and Microsoft guidelines, which were influential for desktop-interface designers, have been followed by dozens of guidelines documents for the Web and a few for newer mobile devices (see the list at the end of Chapter 1). A guidelines document helps by developing a shared language and then promoting consistency among multiple designers in terminology, appearance, and action sequences. It records best practices derived from practical experience or empirical studies with appropriate examples and counterexamples. The creation of a guidelines document engages the design community in a lively discussion of input or output formats, action sequences, terminology, and hardware devices (see Section 3.3.1). Another source of design guidelines is the work of graphics designers (Mullet and Sano, 1995; Lynch and Horton, 1999; Galitz, 2003), whose dos and don'ts record current styles.

Critics complain that guidelines can be too specific, incomplete, hard to apply, and sometimes wrong. Proponents argue that building on experience from design leaders contributes to steady improvements. Both groups recognize the value of lively discussions in promoting awareness. The following four sections provide examples of guidelines, and Section 3.3 discusses how they can be integrated into the design process. The examples address some key topics, but they merely sample the thousands of guidelines that have been written.

2.2.1   Navigating the interface

Since navigation can be difficult for many users, providing clear rules is helpful. This sample of guidelines comes from the National Cancer Institute's effort to assist government agencies with design of informative web pages, but these guidelines have widespread application (Koyani et al., 2003; http://www.usability.gov). Most are stated positively ("reduce the user's workload"), but some are negative ("do not display unsolicited windows or graphics"). The National Cancer Institute's 388 guidelines, which are backed by research findings, cover the design process, general principles, and specific rules. This sample of the guidelines gives useful advice and a taste of their style:

- *Standardize task sequences.* Allow users to perform tasks in the same sequence and manner across similar conditions.
- *Ensure that embedded links are descriptive.* When using embedded links, the link text should accurately describe the link's destination.
- *Use unique and descriptive headings.* Use headings that are unique from one another and conceptually related to the content they describe.
- *Use check boxes for binary choices.* Provide a check box control for users to make a choice between two clearly distinguishable states, such as "on" or "off."
- *Develop pages that will print properly.* If users are likely to print one or more pages, develop pages with widths that print properly.
- *Use thumbnail images to preview larger images.* When viewing full-size images is not critical, first provide a thumbnail of the image.

These guidelines are clarified by examples and supported by research studies. A goal for guidelines writers is to be clear and comprehensible, using meaningful examples. However, controversies over guidelines are lively, often leading to revisions and the creation of alternatives.

Guidelines to promote accessibility for users with disabilities were included in the U. S. Rehabilitation Act Amendments of 1998. Its Section 508, with guidelines for web design, are published by the Access Board (http://www.access-board.gov/508.htm), an independent U. S. government agency devoted to accessibility for people with disabilities. In 1999, the World Wide Web Consortium (W3C) adapted these guidelines (http://www.w3.org/TR/WCAG10/) and organized them into three priority levels for which they provided automated checking tools. A few of the Priority 1 Accessibility Guidelines are:

- Provide a text equivalent for every nontext element (for example, via "alt", "longdesc", or in the element content), including images, graphical representations of text (including symbols), image map regions, animations (such as animated GIFs), applets and programmatic objects, ASCII art, frames, scripts, images used as list bullets, spacers, graphical buttons, sounds (played with or without user interaction), stand-alone audio files, audio tracks of video, and video.
- For any time-based multimedia presentation (for example, a movie or animation), synchronize equivalent alternatives, such as captions or auditory descriptions of the visual track, with the presentation.
- Ensure that all information conveyed with color is also available without color—for example, from context or markup.
- Title each frame to facilitate frame identification and navigation.

The goal of these guidelines is to have web-page designers use features that permit users with disabilities to employ screen readers or other special technologies to give them access to web-page content.

2.2.2   Organizing the display

Display design is a large topic with many special cases. Smith and Mosier (1986) offer five high-level goals as part of their guidelines for data display:

1. *Consistency of data display.* During the design process, the terminology, abbreviations, formats, colors, capitalization, and so on should all be standardized and controlled by use of a written (or computer-managed) dictionary of these items.

2. *Efficient information assimilation by the user.* The format should be familiar to the operator and should be related to the tasks required to be performed with the data. This objective is served by rules for neat columns of data, left justification for alphanumeric data, right justification of integers, lining up of decimal points, proper spacing, use of comprehensible labels, and appropriate measurement units and numbers of decimal digits.

3. *Minimal memory load on the user.* Users should not be required to remember information from one screen for use on another screen. Tasks should be arranged such that completion occurs with few actions, minimizing the chance of forgetting to perform a step. Labels and common formats should be provided for novice or intermittent users.

4. *Compatibility of data display with data entry.* The format of displayed information should be linked clearly to the format of the data entry. Where possible and appropriate, the output fields should also act as editable input fields.

5. *Flexibility for user control of data display.* Users should be able to get the information from the display in the form most convenient for the task on which they are working. For example, the order of columns and sorting of rows should be easily changeable by the users.

This compact set of high-level objectives is a useful starting point, but each project needs to expand these into application-specific and hardware-dependent standards and practices. For example, these generic guidelines, which emerged from a report on design of control rooms for electric-power utilities (Lockheed, 1981), remain valid:

- Be consistent in labeling and graphic conventions.
- Standardize abbreviations.
- Use consistent formatting in all displays (headers, footers, paging, menus, and so on).

- Present data only if they assist the operator.
- Present information graphically where appropriate by using widths of lines, positions of markers on scales, and other techniques that relieve the need to read and interpret alphanumeric data.
- Present digital values only when knowledge of numerical values is necessary and useful.
- Use high-resolution monitors and maintain them to provide maximum display quality.
- Design a display in monochromatic form using spacing and arrangement for organization and then judiciously add color where it will aid the operator.
- Involve users in the development of new displays and procedures.

Chapter 12 further discusses data-display issues.

2.2.3   Getting the user's attention

Since substantial information may be presented to users for the normal performance of their work, exceptional conditions or time-dependent information must be presented so as to attract attention (Wickens and Hollands, 2000). These guidelines detail several techniques for getting the user's attention:

- *Intensity.* Use two levels only, with limited use of high intensity to draw attention.
- *Marking.* Underline the item, enclose it in a box, point to it with an arrow, or use an indicator such as an asterisk, bullet, dash, plus sign, or X.
- *Size.* Use up to four sizes, with larger sizes attracting more attention.
- *Choice of fonts.* Use up to three fonts.
- *Inverse video.* Use inverse coloring.
- *Blinking.* Use blinking displays (2–4 Hz) or blinking color changes with great care and in limited areas.
- *Color.* Use up to four standard colors, with additional colors reserved for occasional use.
- *Audio.* Use soft tones for regular positive feedback and harsh sounds for rare emergency conditions.

A few words of caution are necessary. There is a danger in creating cluttered displays by overusing these techniques. Some web designers use blinking advertisements or animated icons to attract attention, but users almost universally disapprove. Animation is appreciated primarily when it provides meaningful information, such as for a progress indicator. Novices need simple, logically organized, and well-labeled displays that guide their actions. Expert users prefer limited labels on fields so data values are easier to extract; subtle highlighting of changed values or positional presentation is sufficient. Display formats must be tested with users for comprehensibility.

Similarly highlighted items will be perceived as being related. Color-coding is especially powerful in linking related items, but this use makes it more difficult to cluster items across color codes (see Section 12.6). User control over highlighting—for example, allowing the operator in an air-traffic–control environment to assign orange to images of aircraft above 18,000 feet—may provide a useful resolution to concerns about personal preferences.

Audio tones, like the clicks in keyboards or ringing sounds in telephones, can provide informative feedback about progress. Alarms for emergency conditions do alert users rapidly, but a mechanism to suppress alarms must be provided. If several types of alarms are used, testing is necessary to ensure that users can distinguish between the alarm levels. Prerecorded or synthesized voice messages are an intriguing alternative, but since they may interfere with communications between operators, they should be used cautiously (see Section 9.4).

2.2.4 Facilitating data entry

Data-entry tasks can occupy a substantial fraction of the users' time and can be the source of frustrating and potentially dangerous errors. Smith and Mosier (1986) offer five high-level objectives as part of their guidelines for data entry:

1. *Consistency of data-entry transactions.* Similar sequences of actions should be used under all conditions; similar delimiters, abbreviations, and so on should be used.

2. *Minimal input actions by user.* Fewer input actions mean greater operator productivity and—usually—fewer chances for error. Making a choice by a single keystroke, mouse selection, or finger press, rather than by typing in a lengthy string of characters, is potentially advantageous. Selecting from a list of choices eliminates the need for memorization, structures the decision-making task, and eliminates the possibility of typographic errors. However, if users must move their hands from a keyboard to a separate input device, the advantage is negated, because home-row position is lost. Expert users often prefer to type six to eight characters instead of moving to a mouse, joystick, or other selection device.

   A second aspect of this guideline is that redundant data entry should be avoided. It is annoying for users to enter the same information in two locations, since the double entry is perceived as a waste of effort and an opportunity for error. When the same information is required in two places, the system should copy the information for the user, who should still have the option of overriding by retyping.

3. *Minimal memory load on users.* When doing data entry, users should not be required to remember lengthy lists of codes and complex syntactic command strings.

4. *Compatibility of data entry with data display.* The format of data-entry information should be linked closely to the format of displayed information.

5. *Flexibility for user control of data entry.* Experienced data-entry operators may prefer to enter information in a sequence that they can control. For example, on some occasions in an air-traffic–control environment, the arrival time is the prime field in the controller's mind; on other occasions, the altitude is the prime field. However, flexibility should be used cautiously, since it goes against the consistency principle.

Guidelines documents are a wonderful starting point to give designers the benefit of experience, but they will always need management processes to facilitate education, enforcement, exemption, and enhancement (see Section 3.3.1).

2.3   Principles

While guidelines are narrowly focused, principles tend to be more fundamental, widely applicable, and enduring. However, they also tend to need more clarification. For example, the principle of recognizing user diversity makes sense to every designer, but it must be thoughtfully interpreted. A preschooler playing an animated computer game is a long way from a reference librarian doing bibliographic searches for anxious and hurried patrons. Similarly, a grandmother sending a text message is a long way from a highly trained and experienced air-traffic controller. These sketches highlight the differences in users' background knowledge, training in the use of the system, frequency of use, and goals, as well as in the impact of a user error. Since no single design could satisfy all these users and situations, successful designers must characterize their users and the situations in which their products will be used as precisely and completely as possible.

Section 1.5 offered an introduction to the variety of individual differences that a designer must address to work towards universal usability. This section focuses on a few fundamental principles, beginning with accommodating user skill levels and profiling tasks and user needs. We then discuss the five primary interaction styles (direct manipulation, menu selection, form fillin, command language, and natural language) and the "eight golden rules of interface design," followed by a section on error prevention. Finally, we cover the controversial strategies for integrating automation with human control.

2.3.1   Determine users' skill levels

"Know thy user" was the first principle in Hansen's (1971) classic list of user-engineering principles. It is a simple idea but a difficult and, unfortunately, often undervalued goal. No one would argue against this principle, but many designers assume that they understand the users and users' tasks. Successful designers are aware that other people learn, think, and solve problems in different ways. Some users really do prefer to deal with tables rather than with graphs, with words instead of numbers, or with a rigid structure rather than an open-ended form.

All design should begin with an understanding of the intended users, including population profiles that reflect age, gender, physical and cognitive abilities, education, cultural or ethnic background, training, motivation, goals, and personality. There are often several communities of users for an interface, especially for web applications and mobile devices, so the design effort is multiplied. Typical user communities—such as nurses, doctors, storekeepers, high-school students, or librarians—can be expected to have various combinations of knowledge and usage patterns. Users from different countries may each deserve special attention, and regional differences often exist within countries. Other variables that characterize users include location (for example, urban versus rural), economic profile, disabilities, and attitudes towards using technology. Users with poor reading skills, limited education, and low motivation require special attention.

In addition to these profiles, an understanding of users' skills with interfaces and with the application domain is important. Users might be tested for their familiarity with interface features such as traversing hierarchical menus or drawing tools. Other tests might cover domain-specific abilities such as knowledge of airport city codes, stockbrokerage terminology, insurance-claims concepts, or map icons.

The process of getting to know the users is never-ending because there is so much to know and because the users keep changing. Every step in understanding the users and in recognizing them as individuals with outlooks different from the designer's own is likely to be a step closer to a successful design.

For example, a generic separation into novice or first-time, knowledgeable intermittent, and expert frequent users might lead to these differing design goals:

- *Novice or first-time users.* True novice users—for example, grandparents sending their first e-mail to a grandchild—are assumed to know little of the task or interface concepts. By contrast, first-time users are professionals who know the task concepts but have shallow knowledge of the interface concepts (for example, a business traveler using a rental car's navigation system). Both groups of users may arrive with learning-inhibiting anxiety about using computers. Overcoming these limitations, via instructions, dialog boxes, and online help, is a serious challenge to the designer of the interface. Restricting vocabulary to a small number of familiar, consistently used concept terms is essential to begin developing the user's knowledge. The number of actions should also be small, so that novice and first-time users can carry out simple tasks successfully and thus reduce anxiety, build confidence, and gain positive reinforcement. Informative feedback about the accomplishment of each task is helpful, and constructive, specific error messages should be provided when users make mistakes. Carefully designed user manuals, video demonstrations, and task-oriented online tutorials may be effective.

- *Knowledgeable intermittent users.* Many people are knowledgeable but intermittent users of a variety of systems—for example, corporate managers using word processors to create templates for travel reimbursements. They have stable task concepts and broad knowledge of interface concepts, but they may have difficulty retaining the structure of menus or the location of features. The burden on their memories will be lightened by orderly structure in the menus, consistent terminology, and high interface apparency, which emphasizes recognition rather than recall. Consistent sequences of actions, meaningful messages, and guides to frequent patterns of usage will help knowledgeable intermittent users to rediscover how to perform their tasks properly. These features will also help novices and some experts, but the major beneficiaries are knowledgeable intermittent users. Protection from danger is necessary to support relaxed exploration of features or usage of partially forgotten action sequences. These users will benefit from context-dependent help to fill in missing pieces of task or interface knowledge. Well-organized reference manuals are also useful.

- *Expert frequent users.* Expert "power" users are thoroughly familiar with the task and interface concepts and seek to get their work done quickly. They demand rapid response times, brief and nondistracting feedback, and the shortcuts to carry out actions with just a few keystrokes or selections. When a sequence of three or four actions is performed regularly, frequent users are willing to create a *macro* or other abbreviated form to reduce the number of steps. Strings of commands, shortcuts through menus, abbreviations, and other accelerators are requirements.

The characteristics of these three classes of usage must be refined for each environment. Designing for one class is easy; designing for several is much more difficult.

When multiple usage classes must be accommodated in one system, the basic strategy is to permit a *multi-layer* (sometimes called *level-structured* or *spiral*) approach to learning. Novices can be taught a minimal subset of objects and actions with which to get started. They are most likely to make correct choices when they have only a few options and are protected from making mistakes— that is, when they are given a *training-wheels* interface. After gaining confidence from hands-on experience, these users can choose to progress to ever-greater levels of task concepts and the accompanying interface concepts. The learning plan should be governed by the users' progress through the task concepts, with new interface concepts being chosen when they are needed to support a more complex task. For users with strong knowledge of the task and interface concepts, rapid progress is possible.

For example, novice users of a cell phone can quickly learn to make/receive calls first, then to use the menus, and later to store numbers for frequent callees. Their progress is governed by the task domain, rather than by an alphabetical list of commands that are difficult to relate to the tasks. The multi-layer approach must be carried out in the design of not only the software, but also the user manuals, help screens, error messages, and tutorials (McGrenere, Baecker, and Booth, 2002; Shneiderman, 2003). Multi-layer designs seem to be the most promising approach to promoting universal usability.

Another component of accommodating different usage classes is to permit user control of the density of informative feedback that the system provides. Novices want more informative feedback to confirm their actions, whereas frequent users want less distracting feedback. Similarly, it seems that frequent users like displays to be more densely packed than do novices. Finally, the pace of interaction may be varied from slow for novices to fast for frequent users.

2.3.2 Identify the tasks

After carefully drawing the user profile, the developers must identify the tasks to be carried out. Every designer would agree that the set of tasks must be determined before design can proceed, but too often the task analysis is done informally or implicitly. Task analysis has a long, mixed history (Bailey, 1996; Hackos and Redish, 1998), but successful strategies usually involve long hours of observing and interviewing users. This helps designers to understand task frequencies and sequences and make the tough decisions about what tasks to support. Some implementers prefer to include all possible actions in the hope that some users will find them helpful, but this can cause unfortunate clutter. The Palm Pilot designers were dramatically successful because they ruthlessly limited functionality (calendar, contacts, to-do list, and notes) to guarantee simplicity.

High-level task actions can be decomposed into multiple middle-level task actions, which can be further refined into atomic actions that users execute with a single command, menu selection, and so on. Choosing the most appropriate set of atomic actions is a difficult task. If the atomic actions are too small, the users will become frustrated by the large number of actions necessary to accomplish a higher-level task. If the atomic actions are too large and elaborate, the users will need many such actions with special options, or they will not be able to get exactly what they want from the system.

The relative task frequencies are important in shaping, for example, a set of commands or a menu tree. Frequent tasks should be simple and quick to carry out, even at the expense of lengthening some infrequent tasks. Relative frequency of use is one of the bases for making architectural design decisions. For example, in a word processor:

- Frequent actions might be performed by special keys, such as the four cursor arrows, Insert, and Delete.
- Less frequent actions might be performed by a single letter plus the Ctrl key, or by a selection from a pull-down menu—examples include underscore, bold, or save.
- Infrequent actions or complex actions might require going through a sequence of menu selections or form fillins—for example, to change the printing format or to revise network-protocol parameters.

A matrix of users and tasks can help designers sort out these issues (Fig. 2.1). In each box, the designer can put a check mark to indicate that this user carries out this task. A more precise analysis would include frequencies instead of just simple check marks. Such user-needs assessment clarifies what tasks are essential for the design and which ones could be left out to preserve system simplicity and ease of learning.

			TASK		
Job title	Query by Patient	Update Data	Query across Patients	Add Relations	Evaluate System
Nurse	0.14	0.11			
Physician	0.06	0.04			
Supervisor	0.01	0.01	0.04		
Appointment personnel	0.26				
Medical-record maintainer	0.07	0.04	0.04	0.01	
Clinical researcher			0.08		
Database programmer			0.02	0.02	0.05

Figure 2.1

FREQUENCY OF TASK BY JOB TITLE
Hypothetical frequency-of-use data for a medical clinic information system. Answering queries from appointments personnel about individual patients is the highest-frequency task.

2.3.3   Choose an interaction style

When the task analysis is complete and the task objects and actions have been identified, the designer can choose from these primary interaction styles: direct amnipulation, menu selection, form fillin, command language, and natural language (Box 2.1 and Box 2.2). Chapters 6 through 8 explore these styles in detail; this summary gives a brief comparative overview.

Direct manipulation.   When a clever designer can create a visual representation of the world of action, the users' tasks can be greatly simplified, because direct manipulation of familiar objects is possible. Examples of such systems include the desktop metaphor, computer-assisted design tools, air-traffic–control systems, and games. By pointing at visual representations of objects and actions, users can carry out tasks rapidly and can observe the results immediately (for example, dragging and dropping an icon into a trash can). Keyboard entry of commands or menu choices is replaced by use of pointing devices to select from a visible set of objects and actions. Direct manipulation is appealing to novices, is easy to remember for intermittent users, and, with careful design, can be rapid for frequent users. Chapter 6 describes direct manipulation and its application.

Menu selection.   In menu-selection systems, users read a list of items, select the one most appropriate to their task, and observe the effect. If the terminology and meaning of the items are understandable and distinct, users can accomplish their tasks with little learning or memorization and just a few actions. The greatest benefit may be that there is a clear structure to decision making, since all possible choices are presented at one time. This interaction style is appropriate for novice and intermittent users and can be appealing to frequent users if the display and selection mechanisms are rapid. For designers, menu-selection systems require careful task analysis to ensure that all functions are supported conveniently and that terminology is chosen carefully and used consistently. Advanced user-interface building tools to support menu selection provide an enormous benefit by ensuring consistent screen design, validating completeness, and supporting maintenance. Menu selection is discussed in Chapter 7.

Form fillin.   When data entry is required, menu selection alone usually becomes cumbersome, and form fillin (also called *fill in the blanks*) is appropriate. Users see a display of related fields, move a cursor among the fields, and enter data where desired. With the form fillin interaction style, users must understand the field labels, know the permissible values and the data-entry method, and be capable of responding to error messages. Since knowledge of the keyboard, labels, and permissible fields is required, some training may be necessary. This interaction style is most appropriate for knowledgeable intermittent users or frequent users. Chapter 7 provides a thorough treatment of form fillin.

Box 2.1

Advantages and disadvantages of the five primary interaction styles.

Advantages	Disadvantages
Direct manipulation	
Visually presents task concepts	May be hard to program
Allows easy learning	May require graphics display and pointing devices
Allows easy retention	
Allows errors to be avoided	
Encourages exploration	
Affords high subjective satisfaction	
Menu selection	
Shortens learning	Presents danger of many menus
Reduces keystrokes	May slow frequent users
Structures decision making	Consumes screen space
Permits use of dialog-management tools	Requires rapid display rate
Allows easy support of error handling	
Form fillin	
Simplifies data entry	Consumes screen space
Requires modest training	
Gives convenient assistance	
Permits use of form-management tools	
Command language	
Is flexible	Has poor error handling
Appeals to "power" users	Requires substantial training and memorization
Supports user initiative	
Allows convenient creation of user-defined macros	
Natural language	
Relieves burden of learning syntax	Requires clarification dialog
	May not show context
	May require more keystrokes
	Is unpredictable

Box 2.2

Spectrum of directness.

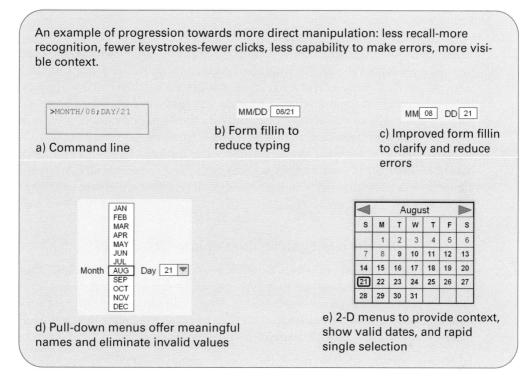

An example of progression towards more direct manipulation: less recall-more recognition, fewer keystrokes-fewer clicks, less capability to make errors, more visible context.

a) Command line

b) Form fillin to reduce typing

c) Improved form fillin to clarify and reduce errors

d) Pull-down menus offer meaningful names and eliminate invalid values

e) 2-D menus to provide context, show valid dates, and rapid single selection

Command language.   For frequent users, command languages (discussed in Chapter 8) provide a strong feeling of being in control. Users learn the syntax and can often express complex possibilities rapidly, without having to read distracting prompts. However, error rates are typically high, training is necessary, and retention may be poor. Error messages and online assistance are hard to provide because of the diversity of possibilities and the complexity of mapping from tasks to interface concepts and syntax. Command languages and lengthier query or programming languages are the domain of expert frequent users, who often derive great satisfaction from mastering a complex set of semantics and syntax. Powerful advantages include easy history keeping and simple macro creation.

Natural language.   The hope that computers will respond properly to arbitrary natural-language sentences or phrases engages many researchers and system developers, in spite of limited success thus far. Natural-language interaction usually provides little context for issuing the next command, frequently requires clarification dialog, and may be slower and more cumbersome than the alternatives. Still, where users are knowledgeable about a task domain whose scope is limited and where intermittent use inhibits command-language training, there exist opportunities for natural-language interfaces (discussed at the end of Chapter 8).

Blending several interaction styles may be appropriate when the required tasks and users are diverse. For example, commands can lead the user to a form fillin where data entry is required, or menus can be used to control a direct-manipulation environment when a suitable visualization of actions cannot be found. Also, keyboard commands can provide shortcuts for experts who seek more rapid performance than mouse selection. Chapters 6–8 expand on the constructive guidance for using the interaction styles outlined here, and Chapter 9 describes how input and output devices influence these interaction styles. Chapter 10 deals with the relationship between interaction styles and collaborative interfaces.

2.3.4   Use the eight golden rules of interface design

This section focuses attention on eight principles, called "golden rules," that are applicable in most interactive systems. These principles, derived from experience and refined over two decades, need validation and tuning for specific design domains. No list such as this can be complete, but it has been well received as a useful guide to students and designers.

1. *Strive for consistency.* This rule is the most frequently violated one, but following it can be tricky because there are many forms of consistency. Consistent sequences of actions should be required in similar situations; identical terminology should be used in prompts, menus, and help screens; and consistent color, layout, capitalization, fonts, and so on should be employed throughout. Exceptions, such as required confirmation of the delete command or no echoing of passwords, should be comprehensible and limited in number.

2. *Cater to universal usability.* Recognize the needs of diverse users and design for *plasticity*, facilitating transformation of content. Novice-expert differences, age ranges, disabilities, and technology diversity each enrich the spectrum of requirements that guides design. Adding features for novices, such as explanations, and features for experts, such as shortcuts and faster pacing, can enrich the interface design and improve perceived system quality.

3. *Offer informative feedback.* For every user action, there should be system feedback. For frequent and minor actions, the response can be modest, whereas for infrequent and major actions, the response should be more substantial. Visual presentation of the objects of interest provides a convenient environment for showing changes explicitly (see the discussion of direct manipulation in Chapter 6).

4. *Design dialogs to yield closure.* Sequences of actions should be organized into groups with a beginning, middle, and end. Informative feedback at the completion of a group of actions gives operators the satisfaction of accomplishment, a sense of relief, the signal to drop contingency plans from their minds, and a signal to prepare for the next group of actions. For example, e-commerce web sites move users from selecting products to the checkout, ending with a clear confirmation page that completes the transaction.

5. *Prevent errors.* As much as possible, design the system such that users cannot make serious errors; for example, gray out menu items that are not appropriate and do not allow alphabetic characters in numeric entry fields (see Section 2.3.5). If a user makes an error, the interface should detect the error and offer simple, constructive, and specific instructions for recovery. For example, users should not have to retype an entire name-address form if they enter an invalid zip code, but rather should be guided to repair only the faulty part. Erroneous actions should leave the system state unchanged, or the interface should give instructions about restoring the state.

6. *Permit easy reversal of actions.* As much as possible, actions should be reversible. This feature relieves anxiety, since the user knows that errors can be undone, thus encouraging exploration of unfamiliar options. The units of reversibility may be a single action, a data-entry task, or a complete group of actions, such as entry of a name and address block.

7. *Support internal locus of control.* Experienced operators strongly desire the sense that they are in charge of the interface and that the interface responds to their actions. Surprising interface actions, tedious sequences of data entries, inability to obtain or difficulty in obtaining necessary information, and inability to produce the action desired all build anxiety and dissatisfaction. Gaines (1981) captured part of this principle with his rule *avoid acausality* and his encouragement to make users the *initiators* of actions rather than the *responders* to actions.

8. *Reduce short-term memory load.* The limitation of human information processing in short-term memory (the rule of thumb is that humans can remember "seven plus or minus two chunks" of information) requires that displays be kept simple, multiple-page displays be consolidated, window-motion frequency be reduced, and sufficient training time be allotted for codes, mnemonics, and sequences of actions. Where appropriate, online access to command-syntax forms, abbreviations, codes, and other information should be provided.

These underlying principles must be interpreted, refined, and extended for each environment. They have their limitations, but they provide a good starting point for mobile, desktop, or web designers. The principles presented in the ensuing sections focus on increasing the productivity of users by providing simplified data-entry procedures, comprehensible displays, and rapid informative feedback to increase feelings of competence, mastery, and control over the system.

2.3.5 Prevent errors

> There is no medicine against death, and against error no rule has been found.
>
> *Sigmund Freud*
> *(Inscription he wrote on his portrait)*

The importance of error prevention (the fifth golden rule) is so strong that it deserves its own section. Users of cell phones, e-mail, spreadsheets, air-traffic–control systems, and other interactive systems make mistakes far more frequently than might be expected. Even experienced analysts make errors in almost half their spreadsheets (Brown and Gould, 1987; Galleta et al., 1993). Other studies reveal the magnitude of the problem of and the loss of productivity due to user errors (Panko and Halverson, 1996).

One way to reduce the loss in productivity due to errors is to improve the error messages provided by the interface. Better error messages can raise success rates in repairing the errors, lowering future error rates, and increasing subjective satisfaction (Shneiderman, 1982). Superior error messages are more specific, positive in tone, and constructive (telling the user what to do, rather than merely reporting the problem). Rather than using vague ("?" or "What?") or hostile ("Illegal Operation" or "Syntax Error") messages, designers are encouraged to use informative messages, such as "Printer is off, please turn it on" or "Months range from 1 to 12".

Improved error messages, however, are only helpful medicine. A more effective approach is to prevent the errors from occurring. This goal is more attainable than it may seem in many interfaces.

The first step is to understand the nature of errors. One perspective is that people make mistakes or "slips" (Norman, 1983) that designers can help them to avoid by organizing screens and menus functionally, designing commands or menu choices to be distinctive, and making it difficult for users to take irreversible actions. Norman offers other guidelines, such as providing feedback about the state of the interface (changing the cursor to show whether a map interface is in zoom-in or select mode) and designing for consistency of actions (ensuring that Yes/No buttons are always in the same order). Norman's analysis provides practical examples and a useful theory. Additional design techniques to reduce errors include correct actions and complete sequences.

Correct actions. Industrial designers recognize that successful products must be safe and must prevent users from making dangerously incorrect use of the products. Airplane engines cannot be put into reverse until the landing gear has touched down, and cars cannot be put into reverse while traveling forward at faster than five miles per hour. Similar principles can be applied to interactive systems—for example, graying out inappropriate menu items so they can't be inadvertently selected, or allowing web users to simply click on the date on a calendar instead of having to type a month and date for a desired airline flight departure. Likewise, instead of having to enter a 10-digit phone number, cell phone users can scroll through a list of frequently or recently dialed phone numbers and select one with a single button. Another option used by some systems, such as the Visual Basic programming environment, is to offer automatic command completion to reduce the likelihood of user errors: the user types the first few letters of a command and the computer completes it as soon as the input is sufficient to distinguish the command from others. Techniques such as these do some of the work for the user, thereby reducing opportunities for user errors.

Complete sequences.   Sometimes, an action requires several steps to reach completion. Since people may forget to complete every step of an action, designers attempt to offer a sequence of steps as a single action. In an automobile, the driver does not have to set two switches to signal a left turn. A single switch causes both (front and rear) turn-signal lights on the left side of the car to flash. When a pilot throws a switch to lower the landing gear, hundreds of steps and checks are invoked automatically. This same concept can be applied to interactive uses of computers. For example, the sequence of dialing up, setting communication parameters, logging on, and loading files is frequently executed by many users. Fortunately, most communications-software packages enable users to specify these processes once and then to execute them by simply selecting the appropriate process name.

As another example, users of a word processor can indicate that all section titles are to be centered, set in uppercase letters, and underlined, without having to issue a series of commands each time they enter a section title. Then, if users want to change the title style—for example, to eliminate underlining—a single command will guarantee that all section titles are revised consistently. As a final example, air-traffic controllers may formulate plans to change the altitude of a plane from 14,000 feet to 18,000 feet in two increments; after raising the plane to 16,000 feet, however, the controller may get distracted and may thus fail to complete the action. The controller should be able to record the plan and then have the computer prompt for completion. The notion of complete sequences of actions may be difficult to implement because users may need to issue atomic actions as well as complete sequences. In this case, users should be allowed to define sequences of their own; the macro or subroutine concept should be available at every level of usage. Designers can gather information about potential complete sequences by studying sequences of commands that people actually issue and the patterns of errors that people actually make.

Thinking about universal usability also contributes to reducing errors—for example, a design with too many small buttons may cause unacceptably high error rates among older users or others with limited motor control, but enlarging the buttons will benefit all users. Section 4.6.2 addresses the idea of logging user errors so designers can continuously improve designs.

⾞ . ⾞ . ⾞   Integrating automation while preserving human control

The guidelines and principles described in the previous sections are often devoted to simplifying the users' tasks. Users can then avoid routine, tedious, and error-prone tasks and can concentrate on making critical decisions, coping with unexpected situations, and planning future actions (Sanders and McCormick, 1993). (Box 2.3 provides a detailed comparison of human and machine capabilities.)

The degree of automation increases over time as procedures become more standardized and the pressure for productivity grows. With routine tasks, automation is desirable, since the potential for errors and the users' workload are reduced. However, even with increased automation, designers can still offer the predictable and controllable interfaces that users often prefer. The human supervisory role needs to be maintained because the real world is an *open system* (that is, there is a nondenumerable number of unpredictable events and system failures). By contrast, computers constitute a *closed system* (there is only a denumerable number of normal and failure situations that can be accommodated in hardware and software). Human judgment is necessary for the unpredictable events in which some action must be taken to preserve safety, to avoid expensive failures, or to increase product quality (Hancock and Scallen, 1996).

For example, in air-traffic control, common actions include changes to altitude, heading, or speed. These actions are well understood and can potentially be automatable by a scheduling and route-allocation algorithm, but the controllers must be present to deal with the highly variable and unpredictable emergency situations. An automated system might deal successfully with high volumes of traffic, but what would happen if the airport manager closes runways because of turbulent weather? The controllers would have to reroute planes quickly. Now suppose that one pilot requests clearance for an emergency landing because of a failed engine, while another pilot reports a passenger needing treatment for a potential heart attack. Human judgment is necessary to decide which plane should land first, and how much costly and risky diversion of normal traffic is appropriate. Air-traffic controllers cannot just jump into the emergency; they must be intensely involved in the situation as it develops if they are to make an informed and rapid decision. In short, many real-world situations are so complex that it is impossible to anticipate and program for every contingency; human judgment and values are necessary in the decision-making process.

Box 2.3

Relative capabilities of humans and machines. *Sources*: Compiled from Brown, 1988; Sanders and McCormick, 1993.

Humans Generally Better	Machines Generally Better
Sense low-level stimuli	Sense stimuli outside human's range
Detect stimuli in noisy background	Count or measure physical quantities
Recognize constant patterns in varying situations	Store quantities of coded information accurately
Sense unusual and unexpected events	Monitor prespecified events, especially infrequent ones
Remember principles and strategies	
Retrieve pertinent details without *a priori* connection	Make rapid and consistent responses to input signals
Draw on experience and adapt decisions to situation	Recall quantities of detailed information accurately
Select alternatives if original approach fails	Process quantitative data in prespecified ways
Reason inductively: generalize from observations	Reason deductively: infer from a general principle
Act in unanticipated emergencies and novel situations	Perform repetitive preprogrammed actions reliably
Apply principles to solve varied problems	Exert great, highly controlled physical force
Make subjective evaluations	Perform several activities simultaneously
Develop new solutions	
Concentrate on important tasks when overload occurs	Maintain operations under heavy information load
Adapt physical response to changes in situation	Maintain performance over extended periods of time

Another example of the complexity of life-critical situations in air-traffic control emerges from an incident on a plane that had a fire on board. The controller cleared other traffic from the flight path and began to guide the plane in for a landing. The smoke was so thick that the pilot had trouble reading his instruments. Then the onboard transponder burned out, so the air-traffic controller could no longer read the plane's altitude from the situation display. In spite of these multiple failures, the controller and the pilot managed to bring down the plane quickly enough to save the lives of many—but not all—of the passengers. A computer could not have been programmed to deal with this particular unexpected series of events.

A tragic outcome of excess automation occurred during a 1995 flight to Cali, Colombia. The pilots relied on the automatic pilot and failed to realize that the plane was making a wide turn to return to a location that they had already passed. When the ground-collision alarm sounded, the pilots were too disoriented to pull up in time; they crashed 200 feet below a mountain peak, killing all but four people on board.

The goal of system design in many applications is to give operators sufficient information about current status and activities so that, when intervention is necessary, they have the knowledge and the capacity to perform correctly, even under partial failures (Sheridan, 1997; Billings, 1997). The U. S. Federal Aviation Agency stresses that designs should place the user in control and automate only to "improve system performance, without reducing human involvement" (FAA, 2003). These standards also encourage managers to "train users when to question automation."

The entire system must be designed and tested, not only for normal situations, but also for as wide a range of anomalous situations as can be anticipated. An extensive set of test conditions might be included as part of the requirements document. Operators need to have enough information that they can take responsibility for their actions. Beyond supervision of decision making and handling of failures, the role of the human operator is to improve the design of the system.

Questions of integrating automation with human control also emerge in systems for home and office automation. Many designers are eager to create an autonomous agent that knows people's likes and dislikes, makes proper inferences, responds to novel situations, and performs competently with little guidance. They believe that human-human interaction is a good model for human-computer interaction, and they seek to create computer-based partners, assistants, or agents (Berners-Lee, Hendler, and Lassila, 2001).

The controversy is over whether to create tool-like interfaces or to pursue autonomous, adaptive, or anthropomorphic agents that carry out the users' intents and anticipate needs (Cassell et al., 2000; Gratch et al., 2002). The agent scenarios often show a responsive, butler-like human, such as the bow-tied, helpful young man in Apple Computer's 1987 video on the *Knowledge Navigator*. Microsoft's 1995 BOB program, which used cartoon characters to create onscreen partners, was unsuccessful; their much-criticized Clippie character was also withdrawn. Web-based characters (such as Ananova) to read the news have also faded. On the other hand, avatars representing users, not computers, in game-playing and three-dimensional social environments (see Section 6.6) have remained popular, possibly because they have a puppet-like theatrical quality.

To succeed in this path, promoters of anthropomorphic representations (see Section 12.3) of computers will have to understand and overcome the history of their unsuccessful application in the products mentioned above, as well as in bank terminals, computer-assisted instruction, talking cars, and postal-service stations. Hopeful scenarios include anthropomorphic pedagogical agents that instruct, respond to, or guide students using natural-language interaction (Rickel and Johnson, 1997; Graesser et al., 2001; Moreno et al., 2001; and see Section 8.6.5).

A variant of the agent scenario, which does not include an anthropomorphic realization, is that the computer employs a *user model* to guide an adaptive interface. The system keeps track of user performance and adapts the interface to suit the users' needs. For example, when users begin to make menu selections rapidly, indicating proficiency, advanced menu items or a command-line interface should appear. Automatic adaptations have been proposed for interface features such as content of menus, order of menu items (see Section 7.5.2 for evidence against the helpfulness of this strategy), type of feedback (graphic or tabular), and content of help screens. Advocates point to video games that increase the speed or number of dangers as users progress though stages of the game. However, games are notably different from most work situations, where users have goals and motivations to accomplish their tasks.

There are some opportunities for adaptive user models to tailor system designs (such as e-mail spam filters), but even occasional unexpected behavior has serious negative effects that discourage use. If adaptive systems make surprising changes, users must pause to see what has happened. Then users may become anxious, because they may not be able to predict the next change, interpret what has happened, or restore the system to the previous state. Suggestions that users could be consulted before a change is made are helpful, but such intrusions may still disrupt problem-solving processes and annoy users. Empirical evidence has begun to clarify that the more acceptable direction is content adaptation, such as allowing users to specify that more sports stories be shown in a newspaper web site (Kobsa, 2004).

An extension of user modeling is the notion of recommender systems or collaborative filtering in distributed World Wide Web applications. There is no agent or adaptation in the interface, but the system aggregates information from multiple sources in some (often proprietary) way. Such approaches have great entertainment and practical value in cases such as selecting movies, books, or music; users are often intrigued and amused to see what suggestions emerge from aggregated patterns of preferences or purchases (Riedl, Konstan, and Vrooman, 2002).

The philosophical alternative to agents and user modeling is comprehensible systems that provide consistent interfaces, user control, and predictable behavior. Designers who emphasize a direct-manipulation style believe that users have a strong desire to be in control and to gain mastery over the system, which allows them to accept responsibility for their actions and derive feelings of accomplishment (Lanier, 1995; Shneiderman, 1995). Historical evidence suggests that users seek comprehensible and predictable systems and shy away those that are complex or unpredictable; for example, pilots may disengage automatic piloting devices if they perceive that these systems are not performing as they expect.

Another resolution of the controversy is to accept user control at the interface, but consider agent-like or multi-agent programming to automate internal processes such as disk-space allocation or network routing based on current loads. However, these are adaptations based on system features, not user profiles.

Since agent advocates promote autonomy, it seems they must take on the issue of responsibility for failures. Who is responsible when an agent violates copyright, invades privacy, or destroys data? Agent designs might be better received if they supported performance monitoring while allowing users to examine and revise the current user model.

An alternative to agents with user models may be to expand the control-panel model. Computer control panels, like automobile cruise-control mechanisms and television remote controls, are designed to convey the sense of control that users seem to expect. Users employ control panels to set physical parameters, such as the cursor blinking speed or speaker volume, and to establish personal preferences such as time/date formats or color schemes (Figs 2.2 and 2.3). Some software packages allow users to set parameters such as the speed of play in games—users start at layer 1 and can then choose when to progress to higher levels; often they are content remaining experts at layer 1 of a complex interface rather than dealing with the uncertainties of higher layers. More elaborate control panels exist in style sheets of word processors, specification boxes of query facilities, and information-visualization tools. Similarly, scheduling software may have elaborate controls to allow users to execute planned procedures at regular intervals or when triggered by events.

2.4   Theories

One goal for the discipline of human-computer interaction is to go beyond the specifics of guidelines and build on the breadth of principles to develop tested, reliable, and broadly useful theories. Of course, for a topic as large as user-interface design, many theories are needed. Some theories are descriptive and explanatory; these theories are helpful in developing consistent terminology for objects and actions, thereby supporting collaboration and training. Some theories are predictive; these theories enable designers to compare proposed designs for execution time or error rates.

Another way to group theories is according to motor-task performance (pointing with a mouse), perceptual activities (finding an item on a display), or cognitive aspects (planning the conversion of a boldfaced character to an italic one). Motor-task performance predictions are well established and accurate for predicting keystroking or pointing times (see Fitts's Law, Section 9.3.5). Perceptual theories have been successful in predicting reading times for free text, lists, for-

Figure 2.2

Mac OS X system preferences for Universal Access features, which allow options to help vision-impaired users to see or hear what is on the screen. Zoom can magnify the contents of the screen, and the White on Black option gives the display higher contrast. The system can speak selected text and text underneath the mouse, and speech recognition allows users to launch applications as well as to execute application commands by simply speaking. Preferences can be set for many aspects of the user experience, from screen-saver settings, to the Dock (menu display), to keyboard and mouse settings. The bottom-left Finder screen allows users to see several levels of the directory hierarchies.

matted displays, and other visual or auditory tasks. Cognitive theories, involving short-term, working, and long-term memory, are central to problem solving and play a key role in understanding productivity as a function of response time (Chapter 11). However, predicting performance on complex cognitive tasks (combinations of subtasks) is especially difficult because of the many strategies that might be employed and the many opportunities for going astray. The ratio for times to perform complex tasks between novices and experts or between first-time and frequent users can be as high as 100 to 1. Actually, the contrast is even

Figure 2.3

Microsoft Windows XP Control Panel, showing how users can easily set regional and language options.

more dramatic, because novices and first-time users often are unable to complete the tasks.

Web designers have emphasized information-architecture models with navigation as the key to user success. Web users can be considered as *foraging* for information, and therefore the effectiveness of the *information scent* of links is the issue (Pirolli, 2003). A high-quality link, relative to a specifc task, gives users a good scent (or indication) of what is at the destination. For example, if users are trying to find an executable demonstration of a software package, then a link with the text "download demo" has a good scent. The challenge to designers is to understand user tasks well enough to design a large web site such that users will be able to find their way successfully from a home page to the right destination, even if it is three or four clicks away. Information-foraging theory attempts to predict user success rates given a set of tasks and a web site, so as to guide refinements.

Another tool for understanding is a *taxonomy*, which can be a part of a descriptive or explanatory theory. A taxonomy imposes order by classifying a complex set of phenomena into understandable categories; for example, a taxonomy might be created for different kinds of input devices (direct versus indirect, linear versus rotary, 1-, 2-, 3- or higher dimensional) (Card, Mackinlay, and Robertson, 1990). Other taxonomies might cover tasks (structured versus unstructured, novel versus regular) (Norman, 1991), personality styles (convergent versus divergent, field-dependent versus independent), technical aptitudes (spatial visualization, reasoning) (Egan, 1988), user experience levels (novice, knowledgeable, expert), or user-interface styles (menus, form fillin, commands). Taxonomies facilitate useful comparisons, organize topics for newcomers, guide designers, and often indicate opportunities for novel products—for example, a task-by-type taxonomy organizes the information visualizations in Chapter 14.

Any theory that might help designers to predict performance for even a limited range of users, tasks, or designs is a contribution (Card, 1989). At the moment, the field is filled with hundreds of theories competing for attention while being refined by their promoters, extended by critics, and applied by eager and hopeful—but skeptical—designers (Carroll, 2003). This development is healthy for the emerging discipline of human-computer interaction, but it means that practitioners must keep up with the rapid developments not only in software tools, design guidelines, but also in theories. Critics raise two challenges:

- *Theories should be more central to research and practice.* A good theory should guide researchers in understanding relationships between concepts and generalizing results. It should also guide practitioners when making design tradeoffs for products. The power of theories to shape design is most apparent in focused theories such as GOMS or Fitts's Law; it is more difficult to demonstrate for explanatory theories, whose main impact may be in educating the next generation of designers or guiding research.

- *Theories should lead rather than lag behind practice.* Critics remark that too often a theory is used to explain what has been produced by commercial product designers. A robust theory should predict or at least guide practitioners in designing new products. Effective theories should suggest novel products and help refine existing ones.

Another direction for theoreticians is to predict subjective satisfaction or emotional reactions of users. Researchers in media and advertising have recognized the difficulty in predicting emotional reactions, so they complement theoretical predictions with their intuitive judgments and extensive market testing.

Broader theories of small-group behavior, organizational dynamics, and sociology are proving to be useful in understanding usage of collaborative interfaces (Chapter 10). Similarly, the methods of anthropology or social psychology may be helpful in understanding technology adoption and overcoming barriers to new technology that build resistance to change.

There may be "nothing so practical as a good theory," but coming up with an effective theory is often difficult. By definition, a theory, taxonomy, or model is an abstraction of reality and therefore must be incomplete. However, a good theory should at least be understandable, produce similar conclusions for all who use it, and help to solve specific practical problems. This section reviews a range of descriptive and explanatory theories, in preparation for the discussion of the object-action interface model in the next section.

2.4.1   Levels of analysis theories

One approach to descriptive theory is to separate concepts according to levels. Such theories have been helpful in software engineering and network design. An appealing and easily comprehensible model for interfaces is the four-level conceptual, semantic, syntactic, and lexical model developed in the late 1970s (Foley et al., 1995):

1. The *conceptual level* is the user's "mental model" of the interactive system. Two mental models for image creation are paint programs that manipulate pixels and drawing programs that operate on objects. Users of paint programs think in terms of sequences of actions on pixels and groups of pixels, while users of drawing programs apply operators to alter and group objects. Decisions about mental models affect each of the lower levels.

2. The *semantic level* describes the meanings conveyed by the user's input and by the computer's output display. For example, deleting an object in a drawing program could be accomplished by undoing a recent action or by invoking a delete-object action. Either action should eliminate a single object and leave the rest untouched.

3. The *syntactic level* defines how the user actions that convey semantics are assembled into complete sentences that instruct the computer to perform certain tasks. For example, the delete-files action could be invoked by a multiple-object selection, followed by a keystroke, followed by a confirmation.

4. The *lexical level* deals with device dependencies and with the precise mechanisms by which users specify the syntax (for example, a function key or a mouse double-click within 200 milliseconds).

This approach is convenient for designers because its top-down nature is easy to explain, matches the software architecture, and allows for useful modularity during design. Designers are expected to move from conceptual to lexical and to record carefully the mappings between levels. This model was very effective in the early days of computing, when command-line input was common and implementers had to write low-level syntax and lexical-analysis programs. Since modern graphical user interface standards and toolkits have greatly reduced the need to design or implement syntactic and lexical levels, this model is less relevant today.

⪽.Ϥ.⪽   Stages-of-action models

Another approach to forming theories is to portray the stages of action that users go through in trying to use interactive products such as information appliances, office tools, and web interfaces. Norman (1988) offers seven stages of action, arranged in a cyclic pattern, as an explanatory model of human-computer interaction:

1. Forming the goal
2. Forming the intention
3. Specifying the action
4. Executing the action
5. Perceiving the system state
6. Interpreting the system state
7. Evaluating the outcome

Some of Norman's stages correspond roughly to Foley et al.'s separation of concerns; that is, the user forms a conceptual intention, reformulates it into the semantics of several commands, constructs the required syntax, and eventually produces the lexical token by the action of moving the mouse to select a point on the screen. Norman makes a contribution by placing his stages in the context of *cycles of action* and *evaluation*. This dynamic process of action distinguishes Norman's approach from the other models, which deal mainly with knowledge that must be in the user's mind. Furthermore, the seven-stages model leads naturally to identification of the *gulf of execution* (the mismatch between the user's intentions and the allowable actions) and the *gulf of evaluation* (the mismatch between the system's representation and the user's expectations).

This model leads Norman to suggest four principles of good design. First, the state and the action alternatives should be visible. Second, there should be a good conceptual model with a consistent system image. Third, the interface should include good mappings that reveal the relationships between stages. Fourth, users should receive continuous feedback. Norman places a heavy emphasis on studying errors, describing how errors often occur in moving from goals to intentions to actions and to executions.

A stages-of-action model helps us to describe user exploration of an interface (Polson and Lewis, 1990). As users try to accomplish their goals, there are four critical points where user failures can occur: (1) users can form an inadequate goal, (2) users might not find the correct interface object because of an incomprehensible label or icon, (3) users may not know how to specify or execute a desired action, and (4) users may receive inappropriate or misleading feedback. The latter three failures may be prevented by improved design or overcome by time-consuming experience with the interface (Franzke, 1995).

Refinements of the stages-of-action model have been developed for other domains. For example, information-seeking has been characterized by these stages: (1) recognize and accept an information problem, (2) define and understand the problem, (3) choose a search system, (4) formulate a query, (5) execute the search, (6) examine the results, (7) make relevance judgments, (8) extract information, and (9) reflect/iterate/stop (Marchionini, 1995).

2.4.3   GOMS and the keystroke-level model

An influential group of theorists at Carnegie-Mellon University carried forward the idea of levels of analysis by decomposing user actions into small measurable steps. They proposed two important models: the *goals, operators, methods, and selection rules* (GOMS) model and the *keystroke-level model* (Card, Moran, and Newell, 1980; 1983). The GOMS model postulated that users begin by formulating goals (edit document) and subgoals (insert word). Then users think in terms of operators, which are "elementary perceptual, motor, or cognitive acts, whose execution is necessary to change any aspect of the user's mental state or to affect the task environment" (Card, Moran, and Newell, 1983, p. 144) (press up-arrow key, move hand to mouse, recall file name, verify that the cursor is at end of file). Finally, users achieve their goals by using methods (move cursor to desired location by following a sequence of arrow keys). The selection rules are the control structures for choosing between the several methods available for accomplishing a goal (delete by repeated backspace versus delete by selecting a region and pressing the Delete button).

The keystroke-level model is a simplified version of GOMS that predicts times for error-free expert performance of tasks by summing up the times for keystroking, pointing, homing, drawing, thinking, and waiting for the system to respond. Card, Moran, and Newell describe an idealized model human processor whose activity displays the essential features of user behavior. However, critics complained that these models concentrate on expert users and error-free performance and place insufficient emphasis on learning, problem solving, error handling, subjective satisfaction, and retention.

GOMS works nicely for describing steps in decision making while carrying out interaction tasks, such as text editing in a manuscript. For example, a user can move a fragment of text by highlighting, cutting, and then pasting (Fig. 2.4). A selection rule determines how to highlight the text if it is a single word (by double clicking) or a phrase (by clicking, moving, and SHIFT-clicking).

Extending GOMS with *if-then* rules to describe the conditions and actions in an interactive text editor proved to be a powerful addition (Kieras and Polson, 1985). The number and complexity of production rules gave accurate predictions of learning and performance times for five text-editing operations: insert, delete, copy, move, and transpose. Other strategies for modeling interactive-system usage involve *transition diagrams* (Fig. 2.5). These diagrams are helpful during design, for instruction, and as a predictor of learning time, performance time, and errors.

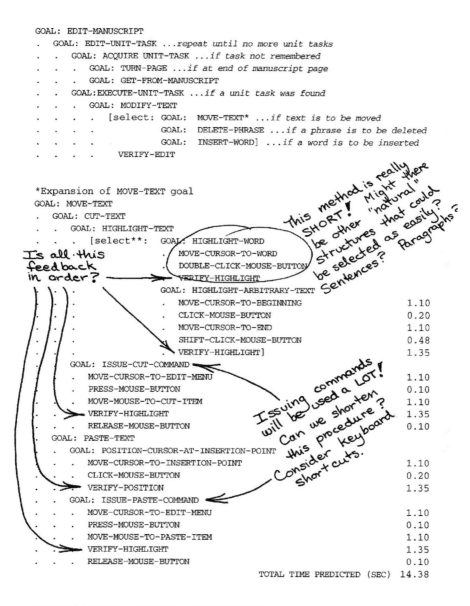

```
GOAL: EDIT-MANUSCRIPT
 .   GOAL: EDIT-UNIT-TASK ...repeat until no more unit tasks
 .   .   GOAL: ACQUIRE UNIT-TASK ...if task not remembered
 .   .   .   GOAL: TURN-PAGE ...if at end of manuscript page
 .   .   .   GOAL: GET-FROM-MANUSCRIPT
 .   .   GOAL:EXECUTE-UNIT-TASK ...if a unit task was found
 .   .   .   GOAL: MODIFY-TEXT
 .   .   .   .   [select: GOAL:  MOVE-TEXT* ...if text is to be moved
 .   .   .   .                   GOAL:  DELETE-PHRASE ...if a phrase is to be deleted
 .   .   .   .                   GOAL:  INSERT-WORD] ...if a word is to be inserted
 .   .   .   .            VERIFY-EDIT
```

```
*Expansion of MOVE-TEXT goal
GOAL: MOVE-TEXT
 .   GOAL: CUT-TEXT
 .   .   GOAL: HIGHLIGHT-TEXT
 .   .   .   [select**:   GOAL: HIGHLIGHT-WORD
 .   .                          MOVE-CURSOR-TO-WORD
 .   .                          DOUBLE-CLICK-MOUSE-BUTTON
 .   .                          VERIFY-HIGHLIGHT
 .   .   .   .   GOAL: HIGHLIGHT-ARBITRARY-TEXT
 .   .                          MOVE-CURSOR-TO-BEGINNING            1.10
 .   .                          CLICK-MOUSE-BUTTON                  0.20
 .   .                          MOVE-CURSOR-TO-END                  1.10
 .   .                          SHIFT-CLICK-MOUSE-BUTTON            0.48
 .   .                          VERIFY-HIGHLIGHT]                   1.35
 .   .   GOAL: ISSUE-CUT-COMMAND
 .   .                   MOVE-CURSOR-TO-EDIT-MENU                   1.10
 .   .                   PRESS-MOUSE-BUTTON                         0.10
 .   .                   MOVE-MOUSE-TO-CUT-ITEM                     1.10
 .   .                   VERIFY-HIGHLIGHT                           1.35
 .   .   .   RELEASE-MOUSE-BUTTON                                   0.10
 .   GOAL: PASTE-TEXT
 .   .   GOAL: POSITION-CURSOR-AT-INSERTION-POINT
 .   .                   MOVE-CURSOR-TO-INSERTION-POINT             1.10
 .   .                   CLICK-MOUSE-BUTTON                         0.20
 .   .                   VERIFY-POSITION                            1.35
 .   .   GOAL: ISSUE-PASTE-COMMAND
 .   .                   MOVE-CURSOR-TO-EDIT-MENU                   1.10
 .   .                   PRESS-MOUSE-BUTTON                         0.10
 .   .                   MOVE-MOUSE-TO-PASTE-ITEM                   1.10
 .   .                   VERIFY-HIGHLIGHT                           1.35
 .   .   .   RELEASE-MOUSE-BUTTON                                   0.10
                           TOTAL TIME PREDICTED (SEC)  14.38
```

```
**Selection Rule for GOAL: HIGHLIGHT-TEXT:
    If the text to be highlighted is a single word, use the
    HIGHLIGHT-WORD method. else use the HIGHLIGHT-ARBITRARY-TEXT method.
```

Handwritten annotations: This method is really SHORT! Might there be other "natural" structures that could be selected as easily? Sentences? Paragraphs? — Is all this feedback in order? — Issuing commands will be used a LOT! Can we shorten this procedure? Consider keyboard short cuts.

Figure 2.4

Example of CMN-GOMS text-editing methods with annotations showing the top-level unit-task method structure, an expansion of one method, and a selection rule, from "The GOMS family of user interface analysis techniques: Comparison and contrast" (John and Kieras, 1996b).

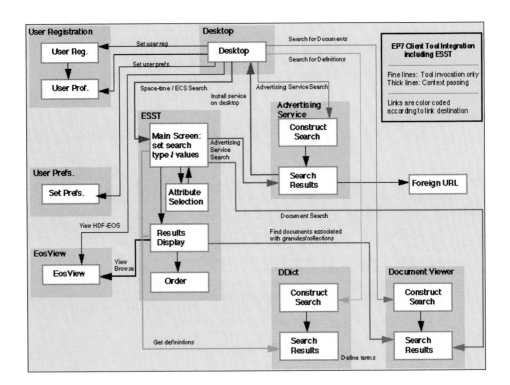

Figure 2.5

Transition diagram from NASA search system.

Kieras (1988), however, complains that the Card, Moran, and Newell presentation "does not explain in any detail how the notation works, and it seems somewhat clumsy to use. Furthermore, the notation has only a weak connection to the underlying cognitive theory." Kieras offers a refinement, with the *Natural GOMS Language* (NGOMSL), and an analysis method for writing down GOMS models. He tries to clarify the situations in which the GOMS task analyst must make a *judgment call*, must make assumptions about how users view the system, must bypass a complex and hard-to-analyze task (such as choosing the wording of a sentence or finding a bug in a program), or must check for consistency.

The development of GOMS modeling has continued, with progress in both techniques and tools. A version called CPM-GOMS (CPM stands for both "cognitive, perceptual, and motor" and "critical path method") can model the overlapping (multitasking) behavior displayed by extremely skilled users. It was used to predict the efficiency of a proposed workstation for telephone operators, saving the company $2,000,000 a year in operating costs. John and Kieras (1996a, b) compare four variants of GOMS techniques and describe nine cases of their use in practical applications. Baumeister, John, and Byrne (2000) review three GOMS tools designed to make modeling easier.

Another avenue for progress in GOMS modeling has been to implement GOMS models within more complex computational cognitive architectures, such as Soar and ACT-RPM (Anderson and Lebiere, 1998; Pew and Gluck, 2004). These architectures are embodied in software systems that model cognitive, motor, and perceptual processes, but these models inherit the limitations of GOMS models, predicting only skilled user execution time for familiar tasks. A current goal is to employ these architectures to predict a broader spectrum of human performance, including learning time, errors, performance under stress, and retention over time.

2.4.4 Consistency through grammars

An important goal for designers is a *consistent* user interface. However, the definition of consistency is elusive and has multiple levels that are sometimes in conflict; it is also sometimes advantageous to be inconsistent. The argument for consistency is that a command language or set of actions should be orderly, predictable, describable by a few rules, and therefore easy to learn and retain. These overlapping concepts are conveyed by an example that shows two kinds of inconsistency (A illustrates lack of any attempt at consistency, and B shows consistency except for a single violation):

Consistent	Inconsistent A	Inconsistent B
delete/insert table	delete/insert table	delete/insert table
delete/insert column	remove/add column	remove/insert column
delete/insert row	destroy/create row	delete/insert row
delete/insert border	erase/draw border	delete/insert border

Each of the actions in the consistent version is the same, whereas the actions vary for the inconsistent version A. The inconsistent action verbs are all acceptable, but their variety suggests that they will take longer to learn, will cause more errors, will slow down users, and will be harder for users to remember. Inconsistent version B is somehow more startling, because there is a single unpredictable inconsistency that stands out so dramatically that this language is likely to be remembered for its peculiar inconsistency.

To capture these notions, Reisner (1981) proposed an *action grammar* to describe two versions of a graphics-system interface. She demonstrated that the version that had a simpler grammar was easier to learn. Payne and Green (1986) expanded her work by addressing the multiple levels of consistency (lexical, syntactic, and semantic) through a notational structure they call *task-action grammars* (TAGs). They also address some aspects of completeness of a language by trying to characterize a complete set of tasks; for example, *up*, *down,* and *left* constitute an incomplete set of arrow-cursor movement tasks, because *right* is missing. Once the full set of task-action mappings is written down, the grammar of the command language can be tested against it to demonstrate completeness. Of course, a designer might leave out something from the task-action mapping, such that the grammar could not be checked accurately, but it still seems useful to have an approach to checking for completeness and consistency. For example, a TAG definition of cursor control would have a dictionary of tasks:

move-cursor-one-character-forward	[Direction = forward, Unit = char]
move-cursor-one-character-backward	[Direction = backward, Unit = char]
move-cursor-one-word-forward	[Direction = forward, Unit = word]
move-cursor-one-word-backward	[Direction = backward, Unit = word]

The high-level rule schemas that describe the syntax of the commands would be as follows:

1. task [Direction, Unit] → symbol [Direction] + letter [Unit]
2. symbol [Direction = forward] → "CTRL"
3. symbol [Direction = backward] → "ESC"
4. letter [Unit = word] → "W"
5. letter [Unit = char] → "C"

These schemas will generate a consistent grammar:

move cursor one character forward	CTRL-C
move cursor one character backward	ESC-C
move cursor one word forward	CTRL-W
move cursor one word backward	ESC-W

Payne and Green are careful to state that their notation and approach are flexible and extensible, and they provide appealing examples in which their approach sharpened the thinking of designers.

Reisner (1990) extends this work by defining consistency more formally, but Grudin (1989) points out flaws in some arguments for consistency. Certainly consistency is subtle and has multiple levels; however, there are conflicting forms of consistency, and sometimes inconsistency is a virtue (for example, to draw attention to a dangerous operation). Nonetheless, understanding consistency is an important goal for designers and researchers.

Consistency issues are critical in design of mobile devices. In successful products, users get accustomed to consistent patterns, such as initiating actions by a left-side button while terminating actions by a right-side button. Similarly, up and down scrolling actions should be done consistently by buttons that are vertically aligned. A frequent problem is the inconsistent placement of the Q and Z characters on phone buttons.

2.4.5   Widget-level theories

Hierarchical decomposition is often a useful tool for dealing with complexity, but many of the theories and predictive models follow an extreme reductionist approach, which may not always be valid. In some situations, it is hard to accept the low level of detail, the precise numbers that are sometimes attached to subtasks, and the validity of simple summations of time periods. Furthermore, models requiring numerous subjective judgments raise the question of whether several analysts would come up with the same results.

An alternative approach is to follow the simplifications made in the higher-level user-interface building tools (see Chapter 5). Instead of dealing with atomic-level features, why not create a model based on the widgets (interface components) supported in the tool? Once a scrolling-list widget was tested to determine user performance as a function of the number of items and the size of the window, the performance of future widget users could be predicted automatically. The prediction would have to be derived from some declaration of the task frequencies, but the description of the interface would emerge from the process of designing the interface. A measure of layout appropriateness (frequently used pairs of widgets should be adjacent, and the left-to-right sequence should be in harmony with the task-sequence description) would also be produced to guide the designer in a possible redesign. Estimates of the perceptual and cognitive complexity plus the motor load would be generated automatically (Sears, 1992).

As widgets become more sophisticated and more widely used, the investment in determining the complexity of each widget will be amortized over the many designers and projects.

Gradually, richer patterns of interface usage are appearing, resembling what Christopher Alexander has described for architecture (1977). Familiar patterns of building fireplaces, stairways, or roofs become modular components that acquire names and are combined to form still larger patterns. Patterns are akin to guidelines, with the distinguishing feature that patterns promise an orderly structure of problem, context, solution, examples, and cross-referencing. Patterns for human-computer interaction—such as "multiple ways to navigate," "process funnel," and "internationalized and localized content"—have been identified for desktop applications, web design (Van Duyne, Landay, and Hong, 2002), and mobile devices.

⌶.4.Ь   Context-of-use theories

While the scientific methods of experimental and cognitive psychology were a profound influence on early work in human-computer interaction, a growing awareness of the special needs of this new discipline led to the rise of alternative theories. The complaints against tightly controlled laboratory studies of isolated phenomena grew from researchers and practitioners. Investigators of workplace and home computing identified the critical role of users' complex interactions with other people, other electronic devices, and paper resources. For example, successful users of interfaces often have nearby colleagues to ask for help or require diverse documents to complete their tasks. Unexpected interruptions are a regular part of life, and sticky notes attached to the sides of computer monitors are often consulted for vital information. In short, the physical and social environments are inextricably intertwined with use of information and computing technologies. Design cannot be separated from patterns of use.

Suchman's (1987) analysis in her book *Plans and Situated Action* is often credited with launching this reconsideration of human-computer interaction. She argued that the cognitive model of orderly human plans that were executed when needed was insufficient to describe the richer and livelier world of work or personal usage. She proposed that users' actions were situated in time and place, making user behavior highly responsive to other people and to environmental contingencies. If users got stuck in using an interface, they might ask for help, depending on who was around, or consult a manual (if it were available). If they were pressed for time, they might risk some shortcuts, but if the work was life-critical they would be extra cautious. Rather than having fixed plans, users were constantly changing their plans in response to the circumstances.

The argument of distributed cognition is that knowledge is not only in the users' minds, but distributed in their environments—some knowledge is stored on paper documents, maintained by computers, or available from colleagues. Proponents of distributed cognition emphasize this distinction from the model human processor described by Card, Moran, and Newell as the basis for GOMS (Scaife and Rogers, 1996).

Physical space became an important notion for those who began to think more about ubiquitous, pervasive, and embedded devices. However, they sought to shift attention from place to space, implying that the social/psychological space had to be considered in addition to the physical place (Dourish, 2002). These notions are likely to become still more important as varied sensors become more common. Sensors to activate doors in supermarkets or faucets and hand-dryers in bathrooms are first steps, but newer sensors that detect and monitor human activity seem likely to proliferate. The goals are often positive, such as safety, security, or healthcare, but threats to privacy, dangers of errors, and the need to preserve human control will have to be considered carefully.

Other alternative models of technology use emphasize the social environment, motivations of users, or the role of experience. Innovators believe that turbulence of actual usage, as opposed to idealized task specifications, means that users have to be more than test subjects—they have to be participants in design processes (Greenbaum and Kyng, 1991). Breakdowns are often seen as a source of insight about design, and users are encouraged to become reflective practitioners who are continuously engaged in the process of design refinement. Understanding the transition from novice to expert and the differences in skill levels has become a focus of attention, further calling into question the utility of hour-long laboratory or half-day usability-testing studies as a guide to behavior of users after a month or more of experience. These movements encourage greater attention to detailed ethnographic observation, longitudinal case studies, and action research by participant observers (Nardi, 1997; Redmiles, 2002).

Context-of-use theories are especially relevant to mobile devices and ubiquitous computing innovations. Such devices are portable or installed in a physical space, and they are often designed specifically to provide place-specific information, such as a city guide on a portable computer or a museum guide that gives information on a nearby painting. A taxonomy of mobile device applications could guide innovators:

- *Monitor* blood pressure, stock prices, or air quality and give *alerts* when normal ranges are exceeded.
- *Gather* information from meeting attendees or rescue team members and *spread* the action list or current status to all.
- *Participate* in a large group activity by voting and *relate* to specific individuals by sending private messages.
- *Locate* the nearest restaurant or waterfall and *identify* the details of the current location.
- *Capture* information or photos left by others and *share* yours with future visitors.

These five pairs of actions could be tied to a variety of objects (such as photos, annotations, or documents), suggesting new mobile devices and services. They also suggest that one way of thinking about user interfaces is by way of the objects that users encounter and actions that they take.

2.5 Object-Action Interface Model

The cognitive model described in this book's first edition stressed the separation between task-domain concepts (for example, stock-market portfolios) and the computer-domain concepts that represent them (for example, folders, spread-sheets, or databases). The second edition amplified the important distinction between objects and actions, paralleling the familiar separation between nouns and verbs. In the third edition, the underlying theory of design was called the *object-action interface* (OAI—let's pronounce it Oo-Ah!) *model*. The OAI model is descriptive and explanatory, and it can also be prescriptive, in that it provides valuable guidance for designers of interfaces, online help, and training processes.

As GUIs have replaced command languages, intricate syntax has given way to relatively simple direct manipulations applied to visual representations of objects and actions. The emphasis is now on the visual display of user-task objects and actions. For example, a collection of stock-market portfolios might be represented by leather folders with icons of engraved share certificates; like-wise, actions might be represented by trash cans for deletion, or shelf icons to represent destinations for portfolio copying. Of course, there are syntactic aspects of direct manipulation, such as knowing whether to drag the file to the trash can or vice versa, but the amount of syntax is small and can be thought of as being at the lowest level of the interface actions. Even syntactic forms such as double-clicking, mouse-down-and-wait, or gestures seem simple compared to the pages of grammars for early command languages.

Doing object-action design starts with understanding the task. That task includes the universe of real-world objects with which users work to accomplish their intentions and the actions that they apply to those objects (Fig. 2.6). The high-level task objects might be stock-market listings, a photo library, or a per-sonal phone book. These objects can be decomposed into information on a single stock, for example, and finally into atomic units, such as a share price. Task actions start from high-level intentions that are decomposed into intermediate goals and individual steps.

To accommodate the arguments of situated action and distributed cognition, the objects may include real-world items (such as books, maps, or other devices) and the actions may include common activities (such as speaking to colleagues, handling interruptions, or answering telephones). These may be described as part of a model of user activity, but they form a separate category since design-ers may have little influence on them or how they are used.

Once there is agreement on the task objects and actions and their decomposi-tion, the designer can create the metaphoric representations of the interface objects and actions. Interface objects do not have weight or thickness; they are pixels that can be moved or copied in ways that represent real-world task objects with feedback to guide users. Finally, the designer must make the interface actions visible to users, so that users can decompose their plans into a series of intermediate actions, such as opening a dialog box, all the way down to a series of detailed keystrokes and clicks.

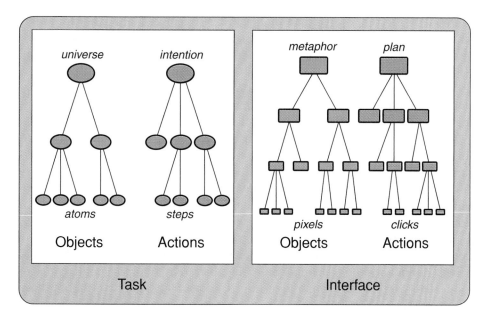

Figure 2.6

Task and interface concepts, separated into hierarchies of objects and actions.

In outline, the OAI model is a descriptive and explanatory model that focuses on task and interface objects and actions. Because the syntactic details are minimal, users who know the task-domain objects and actions can learn the interface relatively easily (see Chapter 13). The OAI model also reflects the higher level of design with which most designers deal when they use the widgets in user-interface building tools. The standard widgets have familiar and simple syntax (click, double-click, drag, or drop) and simple forms of feedback (highlighting, scrolling, or movement), leaving designers free to focus on how these widgets create a business-oriented solution. The OAI model is in harmony with the common software-engineering method of object-oriented design.

2.5.1   Task hierarchies of objects and actions

The primary way people deal with large and complex problems is to decompose them into several smaller problems, in a hierarchical manner, until each subproblem is manageable. For example, a human body is discussed in terms of neural, muscular, skeletal, reproductive, digestive, circulatory, and other subsystems, which in turn might be described by organs, tissues, and cells. Most real-world objects have similar decompositions: buildings, cities, computer programs, human genomes, and plays, for example. Some objects are more neatly decomposable than others, and some objects are easier to understand than others.

A symphony performance has movements, measures, and notes; a baseball game has innings, outs, and pitches. A building-construction plan can be reduced to a series of steps, such as surveying the property, laying the foundation, building the frame, raising the roof, and completing the interior. Similarly, intentions can be decomposed into smaller action steps.

People generally learn the task objects and actions independently of their implementation on a computer. Likewise, people learn about buildings or books through developmental experiences in their youth, but many tasks require specialized training, such as in how to manage stock-market portfolios, to design buildings, or to diagnose medical problems. It may take years to learn the terminology, to acquire the decision-making skills, and to become proficient.

Designers who develop user interfaces to support professionals may have to take training courses, read workbooks, and interview users. Then, the designers can sit down with the users and generate a hierarchy of objects and actions to model the users' tasks. This model forms a basis for designing the interface objects and actions as well as their representations in pixels on a screen, in physical devices, or by a voice or other audio cue.

Users who must learn to use interfaces to accomplish real-world tasks must first become proficient in the task domain. An expert interfaces user who has not studied architecture will not be able to effectively use a building-design package; nor will a computer-savvy amateur be able to make reliable medical diagnoses without extensive training.

In summary, tasks include hierarchies of objects and actions at high and low levels. Hierarchies are not perfect, but they are comprehensible and useful. Most users accept a separation of their tasks into high- and low-level objects and actions.

2 · 5 · 2   Interface hierarchies of objects and actions

Like tasks, interfaces include hierarchies of objects and actions at high and low levels. For example, a central set of *interface object* concepts deals with storage. Users come to understand the high-level concept that computers store information. The stored information can then be refined into objects, such as a directory and the files of information it contains. In turn, the directory object is refined into a set of directory entries, each of which has a name, length, date of creation, owner, access-control setting, and so on. Likewise, each file is an object that has a lower-level structure consisting of lines, fields, characters, fonts, pointers, and so on.

The *interface actions* also are decomposable into lower-level actions. The high-level plans, such as backing up a data file, may require selection, duplication, and save actions. The mid-level action of saving a file is refined into the actions of selecting a destination and moving the file onto a remote disk, providing a password, overwriting previous versions, assigning a name to the file, and so on. There are also many low-level details about permissible file types or sizes, error conditions such as shortage of storage space, or responses to hardware or software errors. Finally, users carry out each low-level action by selecting a button in a dialog box or clicking on a pull-down menu item.

Designers craft interface objects and actions based on familiar examples, then tune those objects and actions to fit the task. For example, in developing a system to manage stock-market portfolios, the designer might consider spreadsheets, databases, word processors, or a specialized graphical design that allows users to drag stock symbols to a buying or selling icon.

Users can learn about interface objects and actions by seeing a demonstration, hearing an explanation of features, or conducting trial-and-error sessions. The metaphoric representation—abstract, concrete, or analogical—conveys the interface objects and actions. For example, to explain saving a file, an instructor might draw a picture of a disk drive and a directory to show where the file goes and how the directory references the file. Alternatively, the instructor might describe how the card catalog acts as a directory for books saved in the library.

When interface objects and actions have a logical structure that can be anchored to familiar task objects and actions, we expect that structure to be relatively stable in human memory. If users remember the mid-level concept of saving a file, they will be able to conclude that the file must have a name, a size, and a storage location. The linkage to other objects and the visual presentation can enhance the memorability of this knowledge.

These interface objects and actions were once novel, known by only a small number of scientists, engineers, and data-processing professionals. Now, these concepts are taught at the elementary-school level, argued over during coffee breaks in the office, and exchanged in the aisles of corporate jets. When educators talk of computer literacy, part of their plans cover these interface concepts.

The OAI model helps us to understand the multiple complex processes that must occur for users to be successful in using an interface to accomplish a task. For example, in writing a business letter using computer software, users have to integrate smoothly their knowledge of the task objects and actions and of the interface objects and actions. They must have the high-level concept of writing (task action) a letter (task object), recognize that the letter will be stored as a document (interface object), and know the details of the save command (interface action). Users must be fluent with the middle-level concept of composing a sentence and must recognize the mechanisms for beginning, writing, and ending a sentence. Finally, users must know the proper low-level details of spelling each word (low-level task object) and must know where the keys are for each letter (low-level interface object). The goal of minimizing interface concepts (such as the syntax of a command language) while presenting a visual representation of the task objects and actions is at the heart of the direct-manipulation approach to design (see Chapter 6).

Integrating the multiple levels of task and interface concepts is a substantial challenge that requires great motivation and concentration. Educational materials that facilitate the acquisition of this knowledge are difficult to design, especially because of the diversity of background knowledge and motivation levels of typical learners. The OAI model of user knowledge can provide a guide to educational designers by highlighting the different kinds of knowledge that users need to acquire (see Chapter 13).

Designers of interactive systems can apply the OAI model to systematize their work. Where possible, the task objects should be made explicit, and the users' task actions should be laid out clearly. Then, the interface objects and actions can be identified, and appropriate representations can be created. These designs are likely to increase comprehensibility to users and independence from specific hardware. Criteria for design quality are emerging based on the fact that small numbers of objects and actions tend to be easier to learn. Designers would do well to determine how fine a granularity of objects to use and how many different actions are needed.

2.5.3   The disappearance of syntax

In the early days of computers, users had to maintain a profusion of device-dependent details in their human memories. These low-level syntactic details included the knowledge of which action erases a character (Delete, Backspace, Ctrl-H, Ctrl-G, Ctrl-D, rightmost mouse button, or Escape), which action inserts a new line after the third line of a text file (Ctrl-I, Insert key, I3, I 3, or 3I), which abbreviations are permissible, and which of the numbered function keys produces the previous screen.

The learning, use, and retention of this knowledge are hampered by two problems. First, these details vary across interfaces in an unpredictable manner. Second, acquiring syntactic knowledge is often a struggle because the arbitrariness of these minor design features greatly reduces the effectiveness of paired-associate learning. Rote memorization requires repeated rehearsals to reach competence, and retention over time is poor unless the knowledge is applied frequently.

A further problem with syntactic knowledge lies in the difficulty of providing a hierarchical structure or even a modular structure to cope with the complexity. For example, it may be hard for users to remember these details of using an electronic-mail system: press Return to terminate a paragraph, Ctrl-D to terminate a message, Q to quit the electronic-mail subsystem, and log out to terminate the session. The knowledgeable computer user understands these four forms of termination as commands in the context of the full system, but the novice may be confused by four seemingly similar situations that have radically inconsistent syntactic forms.

A final difficulty is that syntactic knowledge is system-dependent. Users who switch from one machine to another may face different keyboard layouts, commands, function-key usage, and sequences of actions. One system may use K to keep a file and Ctrl-S to save, while another uses K to kill the file and Ctrl-S to send.

Expert frequent users can overcome these difficulties, and they tend to be less troubled by syntactic knowledge problems. Novices and knowledgeable but intermittent users, however, are especially troubled by syntactic irregularities. Their burden can be lightened by use of menus (see Chapter 7), a reduction in the arbitrariness of the keypresses, use of consistent patterns of commands, meaningful command names and labels on keys, and fewer details that must be memorized (see Chapter 8).

Minimizing these burdens is the goal of most interface designers. Modern direct-manipulation styles (see Chapter 6) support the process of presenting users with screens filled with familiar objects and actions representing their task objects and actions. Modern user-interface building tools (see Chapter 5) facilitate the design process by making standard widgets easily available. Innovative designers may recognize opportunities for novel widgets that provide a closer match between the screen representation and the user's workplace.

Practitioner's Summary

Design principles and guidelines are emerging from practical experience and empirical studies. Organizations can benefit by reviewing available guidelines documents and then constructing local versions. A guidelines document records organizational policies, supports consistency, aids the application of tools for user-interface building, facilitates training of new designers, records results of practice and experimental testing, and stimulates discussion of user-interface issues. More established principles—such as recognizing user diversity, striving

WORLD WIDE WEB RESOURCES

Web sites include guidelines documents for desktop, web, and mobile device interfaces and recommendations for universal usability strategies to accommodate users with disabilities or other special needs. Theories are proliferating, so the Web is a good place to keep up with the latest ones. Debates over hot topics can be found in newsgroups, which are searchable from many standard services such as Yahoo! or Google.

http://www.aw.com/DTUI

for consistency, and preventing errors—have become widely accepted, but they require fresh interpretation as technology and applications evolve. Automation is increasingly present, but preserving human control is still a beneficial goal. A variety of reliable and broadly applicable theories are beginning to emerge for user interfaces.

In spite of the growing set of guidelines, principles, and theories, user-interface design is a complex and highly creative process. Successful designers begin with a thorough task analysis and a careful specification of the user communities. For expert users with established sequences of action, predictive models that reduce the time required to perform each step are effective. For novel applications and novice users, focusing on task objects and actions (for example, flight departure airports and upgrading reservations) can lead to construction of useful metaphors for interface objects and actions (such as form fillin and pull-down menu selections). Still, extensive testing and iterative refinement are necessary parts of every development project.

Researcher's Agenda

The central problem for human-computer–interaction researchers is to develop adequate theories and models. Traditional psychological theories must be extended and refined to accommodate the complex human learning, memory, and problem solving required in user interfaces. Useful goals include descriptive taxonomies, explanatory theories, and predictive models.

A first step might be to investigate a limited task for a single community and to develop a notation for describing task actions and objects. Then the mapping to interface actions and objects can be made. This process would lead to predictions of learning times, performance speeds, error rates, subjective satisfaction, or human retention over time, for competing designs.

Next, the range of tasks and user communities could be expanded to domains of interest, such as word processing, web searching, or cell-phone data entry. Applied research problems are suggested by each of the hundreds of design principles or guidelines that have been proposed. Each validation of these principles and clarification of the breadth of applicability is a small but useful contribution to the emerging mosaic of human performance with interactive systems.

References

Alexander, Christopher, Ishikawa, Sara, and Silverstein, Murray, *A Pattern Language: Towns, Buildings, Construction*, Oxford University Press, New York (1977).

Anderson, J. R. and Lebiere, C., *The Atomic Components of Thought*, Lawrence Erlbaum Associates, Mahwah, NJ (1998).

Bailey, Robert W., *Human Performance Engineering: Using Human Factors/Ergonomics to Achieve Computer Usability, Third Edition*, Prentice-Hall, Englewood Cliffs, NJ (1996).

Bauer, Malcolm I. and John, Bonnie E., Modeling time-constrained learning in a highly interactive task, *Proc. CHI '95 Conference: Human Factors in Computing Systems*, ACM, New York (1995), 19–26.

Baumeister , L., John, B. E., and Byrne, M., A comparison of tools for building GOMS models, *Proc. CHI 2000 Conference: Human Factors in Computing Systems*, ACM Press, New York (2000), 502–509.

Berners-Lee, Tim, Hendler, James, and Lassila, Ora, Semantic web, *Scientific American* (May 2001).

Billings, Charles E., *Animation Automation: The Search for a Human-Centered Approach*, Lawrence Erlbaum Associates, Hillsdale, NJ (1997).

Bridger, R. S., *Introduction to Ergonomics*, McGraw-Hill, New York (1995).

Brown, C. Marlin, *Human-Computer Interface Design Guidelines*, Ablex, Norwood, NJ (1988).

Brown, P. and Gould, J., How people create spreadsheets, *ACM Transactions on Office Information Systems*, 5 (1987), 258–272.

Card, Stuart K., Theory-driven design research, in McMillan, Grant R., Beevis, David, Salas, Eduardo, Strub, Michael H., Sutton, Robert, and Van Breda, Leo (Editors), *Applications of Human Performance Models to System Design*, Plenum Press, New York (1989), 501–509.

Card, Stuart K., Mackinlay, Jock D., and Robertson, George G., The design space of input devices, *Proc. CHI '90 Conference: Human Factors in Computing Systems*, ACM, New York (1990), 117–124.

Card, Stuart, Moran, Thomas P., and Newell, Allen, The keystroke-level model for user performance with interactive systems, *Communications of the ACM*, 23 (1980), 396–410.

Card, Stuart, Moran, Thomas P., and Newell, Allen, *The Psychology of Human-Computer Interaction*, Lawrence Erlbaum Associates, Hillsdale, NJ (1983).

Carroll, John M. (Editor), *HCI Models, Theories, and Frameworks: Toward a Multidisciplinary Science*, Morgan Kaufmann Publishers, San Francisco, CA (2003).

Cassell, Justine, Sullivan, Joseph, Prevost, Scott, and Churchill, Elizabeth, *Embodied Conversational Agents*, MIT Press, Cambridge, MA (2000).

Dourish, Paul, *Where the Action Is: The Foundations of Embodied Interaction*, MIT Press, Cambridge, MA (2001).

Eberts, Ray E., *User Interface Design*, Prentice-Hall, Englewood Cliffs, NJ (1993).

Egan, Dennis E., Individual differences in human–computer interaction, in Helander, Martin (Editor), *Handbook of Human-Computer Interaction*, Elsevier Science Publishers, Amsterdam, The Netherlands (1988), 543–568.

Federal Aviation Administration, *The Human Factors Design Standard*, Atlantic City, NJ (June 2003). Available at http://acb220.tc.faa.gov/hfds/.

Foley, James D., van Dam, Andries, Feiner, Steven K., and Hughes, John F., *Computer Graphics: Principles and Practice in C, Second Edition*, Addison-Wesley, Reading, MA (1995).

Franzke, Marita, Turning research into practice: Characteristics of display-based interaction, *Proc. CHI '95 Conference: Human Factors in Computing Systems*, ACM, New York (1995), 421–428.

Gaines, Brian R., The technology of interaction: Dialogue programming rules, *International Journal of Man-Machine Studies*, 14 (1981), 133–150.

Galitz, Wilbert O., *The Essential Guide to User Interface Design: An Introduction to GUI Design Principles and Techniques, Second Edition*, John Wiley & Sons, New York (2003).

Galletta, D.F., Abraham, D., El Louadi, M., Lekse, W., Pollalis, Y., and Sampler, J., An empirical study of spreadsheet error-finding performance, *Accounting, Management, and Information Technology*, 3, 2 (1993), 79–95.

Gilbert, Steven W., Information technology, intellectual property, and education, *EDUCOM Review*, 25 (1990), 14–20.

Graesser, Arthur C., VanLehn, Kurt, Rose, Carolyn P., Jordan, Pamela W., and Harter, Derek, Intelligent tutoring systems with conversational dialogue, *AI Magazine*, 22, 4 (Winter 2001), 39–52.

Gratch, J., Rickel, J., Andre, E., Badler, N., Cassell, J., and Petajan, E., Creating interactive virtual humans: Some assembly required, *IEEE Intelligent Systems*, 17, 4 (2002), 54–63.

Greenbaum, Joan and Kyng, Morten, *Design at Work: Cooperative Design of Computer Systems*, Lawrence Erlbaum Associates, Hillsdale, NJ (1991).

Grudin, Jonathan, The case against user interface consistency, *Communications of the ACM*, 32, 10 (1989), 1164–1173.

Hackos, JoAnn T. and Redish, Janice C., *User and Task Analysis for Interface Design*, John Wiley & Sons, New York (1998).

Hancock, P. A. and Scallen, S. F., The future of function allocation, *Ergonomics in Design*, 4, 4 (October 1996), 24–29.

Hansen, Wilfred J., User engineering principles for interactive systems, *Proc. Fall Joint Computer Conference*, 39, AFIPS Press, Montvale, NJ (1971), 523–532.

John, Bonnie and Kieras, David E., Using GOMS for user interface design and evaluation: Which technique?, *ACM Transactions on Computer-Human Interaction*, 3, 4 (December 1996a), 287–319.

John, Bonnie and Kieras, David E., The GOMS family of user interface analysis techniques: Comparison and contrast, *ACM Transactions on Computer-Human Interaction*, 3, 4 (December 1996b), 320–351.

Kieras, David, Towards a practical GOMS model methodology for user interface design. in Helander, Martin (Editor), *Handbook of Human-Computer Interaction*, Elsevier Science Publishers, Amsterdam, The Netherlands (1988), 135–157.

Kieras, David and Polson, Peter G., An approach to the formal analysis of user complexity, *International Journal of Man Machine Studies*, 22 (1985), 365–394.

Kobsa, Alfred, Adaptive interfaces, in Bainbridge, W. S. (Editor), *Encyclopedia of Human-Computer Interaction*, Berkshire Publishing, Great Barrington, MA (2004).

Koyani, Sanjay J., Bailey, Robert W., Nall, Janice R., and others, *Research-based Web Design & Usability Guidelines*, Dept of Health & Human Services, National Institutes of

Health Publication 03-5424, National Cancer Institute, Washington, DC (Sept 2003). Available at http://www.usability.gov/.

Lanier, Jaron, Agents of alienation, *ACM interactions*, 2, 3 (1995), 66–72.

Lockheed Missiles and Space Company, *Human Factors Review of Electric Power Dispatch Control Centers, Volume 2: Detailed Survey Results*, (Prepared for) Electric Power Research Institute, Palo Alto, CA (1981).

Lynch, Patrick J. and Horton, Sarah, *Web Style Guide: Basic Design Principles for Creating Web Sites*, Yale University Press, New Haven, CT (1999).

Marchionini, Gary, *Information Seeking in Electronic Environments*, Cambridge University Press, Cambridge, U.K. (1995).

McGrenere, Joanna, Baecker, Ronald M., and Booth, Kellogg S., An evaluation of a multiple interface design solution for bloated software, *Proc. ACM CHI 2002, ACM CHI Letters*, 4, 1 (2002), 164-170.

Moreno, R., Mayer, R. E., Spires, H., and Lester, J., The case for social agency in computer-based teaching: Do students learn more deeply when they interact with animated pedagogical agents? *Cognition and Instruction*, 19 (2001), 177–213.

Mullet, Kevin and Sano, Darrell, *Designing Visual Interfaces: Communication Oriented Techniques*, Sunsoft Press, Englewood Cliffs, NJ (1995).

Nardi, Bonnie A., *Context and Consciousness: Activity Theory and Human-Computer Interaction*, MIT Press, Cambridge, MA (1997).

National Research Council, *Intellectual Property Issues in Software*, National Academy Press, Washington, DC (1991).

Norman, Donald A., Design rules based on analyses of human error, *Communications of the ACM*, 26, 4 (1983), 254–258.

Norman, Donald A., *The Psychology of Everyday Things*, Basic Books, New York (1988).

Norman, Kent L., Models of the mind and machine: Information flow and control between humans and computers, *Advances in Computers*, 32 (1991), 119–172.

Panko, Raymond R. and Halverson, Jr., Richard P., Spreadsheets on trial: A survey of research on spreadsheet risks, *Proc. Twenty-Ninth Hawaii International Conference on System Sciences* (1996).

Payne, S. J. and Green, T. R. G., Task-action grammars: A model of the mental representation of task languages, *Human-Computer Interaction*, 2 (1986), 93–133.

Payne, S. J. and Green, T. R. G., The structure of command languages: An experiment on task-action grammar, *International Journal of Man-Machine Studies*, 30 (1989), 213–234.

Pew, R. W. and Gluck, K. A. (Editors), *Modeling Human Behavior with Integrated Cognitive Architectures: Comparison, Evaluation, and Validation*, Lawrence Erlbaum Associates, Mahwah, NJ (2004).

Pirolli, Peter, Exploring and finding information, in Carroll, John M. (Editor), *HCI Models, Theories, and Frameworks: Toward a Multidisciplinary Science*, Morgan Kaufmann Publishers, San Francisco, CA (2003).

Polson, Peter and Lewis, Clayton, Theory-based design for easily learned interfaces, *Human-Computer Interaction*, 5 (1990), 191–220.

Redmiles, David (Editor), Special Issue on Activity Theory and the Practice of Design, *Computer Supported Cooperative Work*, 11, 1–2 (2002).

Reeves, Byron and Nass, Clifford, *The Media Equation: How People Treat Computers, Television, and New Media Like Real People and Places*, Cambridge University Press, Cambridge, U.K. (1996).

Reisner, Phyllis, Formal grammar and design of an interactive system, *IEEE Transactions on Software Engineering*, SE–5 (1981), 229–240.

Reisner, Phyllis, What is consistency? in Diaper et al. (Editors), *INTERACT '90: Human-Computer Interaction*, North-Holland, Amsterdam, The Netherlands (1990), 175–181.

Rickel, J. and Johnson, W., Steve: An animated pedagogical agent for procedural training in virtual environments, *Proc. Animated Interface Agents: Making Them Intelligent* (1997), 71–76.

Riedl, John, Konstan, Joseph, and Vrooman, Eric, *Word of Mouse: The Marketing Power of Collaborative Filtering*, Warner Books, New York (2002).

Sanders, M. S. and McCormick, E. J., *Human Factors in Engineering and Design, Seventh Edition*, McGraw-Hill, New York (1993).

Scaife, Michael and Rogers, Yvonne, External cognition: how do graphical representations work?, *International Journal of Human-Computer Studies*, 45 (1996), 185-213.

Sears, Andrew, *Widget-Level Models of Human-Computer Interaction: Applying Simple Task Descriptions to Design and Evaluation*, Ph.D. Dissertation, Department of Computer Science, University of Maryland, College Park, MD (1992).

Sheridan, Thomas B., Supervisory control, in Salvendy, Gavriel (Editor), *Handbook of Human Factors, Second Edition*), John Wiley & Sons, New York (1997), 1295–1327.

Shneiderman, Ben, System message design: Guidelines and experimental results, in Badre, A. and Shneiderman, B. (Editors), *Directions in Human-Computer Interaction*, Ablex, Norwood, NJ (1982), 55–78.

Shneiderman, Ben, Direct manipulation: A step beyond programming languages, *IEEE Computer*, 16, 8 (1983), 57–69.

Shneiderman, Ben, Looking for the bright side of agents, *ACM interactions*, 2, 1 (January 1995), 13–15.

Shneiderman, Ben, Promoting universal usability with multi-layer interface design, *ACM Conference on Universal Usability*, ACM Press, New York (2003), 1–8.

Smith, Sid L. and Mosier, Jane N., *Guidelines for Designing User Interface Software*, Report ESD-TR-86–278, Electronic Systems Division, MITRE Corporation, Bedford, MA (1986). Available from National Technical Information Service, Springfield, VA.

Suchman, Lucy A., *Plans and Situated Actions: The Problem of Human-Machine Communication*, Cambridge University Press, Cambridge, U.K. (1987).

Van Duyne, Douglas K., Landay, James A., and Hong, Jason I., *The Design of Sites: Patterns, Principles, and Processes for Crafting a Customer-Centered Web Experience*, Addison-Wesley, Reading, MA (2002).

Wickens, Christopher D. and Hollands, Justin G., *Engineering Psychology and Human Performance*, Prentice-Hall, Englewood Cliffs, NJ (2000).

PART

II

Development Processes

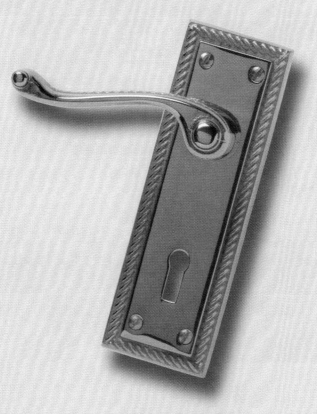

3 Managing Design Processes

Just as we can assert that no product has ever been created in a single moment of inspiration... nobody has ever produced a set of requirements for any product in a similarly miraculous manner. These requirements may well begin with an inspirational moment but, almost certainly, the emergent bright idea will be developed by iterative processes of evaluation until it is thought to be worth starting to put pencil to paper. Especially when the product is entirely new, the development of a set of requirements may well depend upon testing initial ideas in some depth.

W. H. MAYALL
Principles in Design, 1979

The Plan is the generator. Without a plan, you have lack of order and willfulness. The Plan holds in itself the essence of sensation.

LE CORBUSIER
Towards a New Architecture, 1931

3.1 Introduction

In the first decades of computer-software development, technically oriented programmers designed text editors, programming languages, and applications for themselves and their peers. The substantial experience and motivation of these users meant that complex interfaces were accepted and even appreciated. Now, the user population for mobile devices, instant messaging, e-business, and digital libraries is so vastly different from the original that programmers' intuitions may be inappropriate. Current users are not dedicated to the technology; their background is more tied to their work needs, while their use of computers for entertainment is discretionary. Designs should be based on careful observation of current users, refined by thoughtful analysis of task frequencies and sequences, and validated through early usability and thorough acceptance tests.

In the best organizations, the technocentric style of the past is yielding to a genuine desire to accommodate the users' skills, goals, and preferences. Designers seek direct interaction with users during the design phase, the development process, and throughout the system lifecycle. Iterative design methods that allow early testing of low-fidelity prototypes, revisions based on feedback from users, and incremental refinements suggested by usability-test administrators are catalysts for high-quality systems.

Around the world, *usability engineering* is becoming a recognized discipline with maturing practices and a growing set of standards. The Usability Professionals Association has become a respected community with active participation from large corporations and numerous small design, test, and build firms. Also, usability test reports are becoming standardized (for example, via the Common Industry Format), so that buyers of software can compare products across suppliers.

The variety of design situations precludes a comprehensive strategy. Managers will have to adapt the strategies offered in this chapter to suit their organizations, projects, schedules, and budgets. These strategies begin with the organizational design that gives appropriate emphasis to support usability. Next are the three pillars of successful user-interface development: guidelines documents and processes, user-interface software tools, and expert review and usability testing. The Logical User-Centered Interaction Design (LUCID) methodology is a framework for scheduling, on which strategies such as ethnographic observation, participatory design, scenario development, and possibly a Social Impact Statement review can be hung. Finally, legal concerns should be addressed during the design process.

3.2   Organizational Design to Support Usability

Corporate marketing and customer-assistance departments are becoming more aware of the importance of usability and are a source of constructive encouragement. When competitive products provide similar functionality, usability engineering is vital for product acceptance. Many organizations have created usability laboratories to provide expert reviews and to conduct usability tests of products during development. Outside experts can provide fresh insights, while usability-test subjects perform benchmark tasks in carefully supervised conditions (Nielsen, 1993; Dumas and Redish, 1999). These and other evaluation strategies are covered in Chapter 4.

Companies may not yet have chief usability officers (CUOs) or vice presidents for usability, but they often have user-interface architects and usability-engineering managers. High-level commitment helps to promote attention at every level. Organizational awareness can be stimulated by "Usability Day" presentations, internal seminars, newsletters, and awards. However, resistance to new techniques and a changing role for software engineers can cause problems in organizations.

Organizational change is difficult, but creative leaders blend inspiration and provocation. The high road is to appeal to the desire for quality that most professionals share. When they are shown data on shortened learning times, faster performance, or lower error rates on well-designed interfaces, they are likely to be more sympathetic to applying usability-engineering methods. Even more compelling for e-commerce managers is evidence of higher rates of conversion, enlarged market share, and increased customer retention. For managers of consumer products the goals include fewer returns/complaints, increased brand loyalty, and more referrals. The low road is to point out the frustration, confusion, and high error rates caused by the current complex designs, while citing the successes of competitors who apply usability-engineering methods.

Most large and many small organizations maintain a centralized human-factors group or a usability laboratory as a source of expertise in design and testing techniques (Mayhew, 1999; Nielsen, 1999). However, each project should have its own user-interface architect who develops the necessary skills, manages the work of other people, prepares budgets and schedules, and coordinates with internal and external human-factors professionals when further expertise, references to the literature, or usability tests are required. This dual strategy balances the needs for centralized expertise and decentralized application. It enables professional growth in the user-interface area and in the application domain (for example, in geographic information or web-based product catalogs).

As the field of user-interface design has matured, projects have grown in complexity, size, and importance. Role specialization is emerging, as it has in architecture, aerospace, and book design. Eventually, individuals will become highly skilled in specific problems, such as user-interface building tools, graphic-display strategies, voice and audio tone design, and online tutorial writing. Consultation with graphic artists, book designers, advertising copywriters, instructional-textbook authors, or film-animation creators is expected. Perceptive system developers recognize the need to employ psychologists for conducting experimental tests, sociologists for evaluating organizational impact, educational psychologists for refining training procedures, and social workers for guiding customer-service personnel.

As design moves to implementation, the choice of user-interface building tools is vital to success. These rapidly emerging tools enable designers to build novel systems quickly and support the iterative design/test/refine cycle.

Guidelines documents were originally seen as the answer to usability questions, but they are now appreciated as a broader social process in which the initial compilation is only the first step. The management strategies for the four Es—education, enforcement, exemption, and enhancement—are only beginning to emerge and to become institutionalized.

The business case for focusing on usability has been made powerfully and repeatedly (Karat, 1994; Bias and Mayhew, 1994). It apparently needs frequent repetition, because traditional managers and engineers are often resistant to changes that would bring increased attention to the users' needs. Karat's (1994) businesslike reports within IBM became influential documents when they were published externally. She reported up to $100 payoffs for each dollar spent on usability, with identifiable benefits in reduced program-development costs, reduced program-maintenance costs, increased revenue due to higher customer satisfaction, and improved user efficiency and productivity. Other economic analyses showed fundamental changes in organizational productivity (as much as 720% improvements) when people kept usability in mind from the beginning of development projects (Landauer, 1995). Even minimal application of usability testing followed by correction of 20 of the easiest-to-repair faults improved user success rates from 19% to as much as 80%.

Usability engineers and *user-interface architects* are gaining experience in managing organizational change. As attention shifts from software-engineering or management-information systems, battles for control and power manifest themselves in budget and personnel allocations. Well-prepared managers who have a concrete organizational plan, defensible cost/benefit analyses, and practical development methodologies are most likely to be winners.

Design is inherently creative and unpredictable. Interactive system designers must blend a thorough knowledge of technical feasibility with a mystical esthetic sense of what attracts users. Carroll and Rosson (1985) characterize design in this way:

- Design is a *process*; it is not a state and it cannot be adequately represented statically.

- The design process is *nonhierarchical*; it is neither strictly bottom-up nor strictly top-down.

- The process is *radically transformational*; it involves the development of partial and interim solutions that may ultimately play no role in the final design.

- Design intrinsically involves the *discovery of new goals*.

These characterizations of design convey the dynamic nature of the process. But in every creative domain, there can also be discipline, refined techniques, wrong and right methods, and measures of success. Once the early data collection and preliminary requirements are established, more detailed design and early development can begin. This chapter covers strategies for managing early stages of projects and offers design methodologies. Chapter 4 focuses on evaluation methods.

∃·∃   The Three Pillars of Design

If standardization can be humanized and made flexible in design and the economics brought to the home owner, the greatest service will be rendered to our modern way of life. It may be really born—this democracy, I mean.

Frank Lloyd Wright
The Natural House, 1954

The three pillars described in this section can help user-interface architects to turn good ideas into successful systems (Fig. 3.1). They are not guaranteed to work, but experience has shown that each pillar can produce an order-of-magnitude speedup in the process and can facilitate the creation of excellent systems.

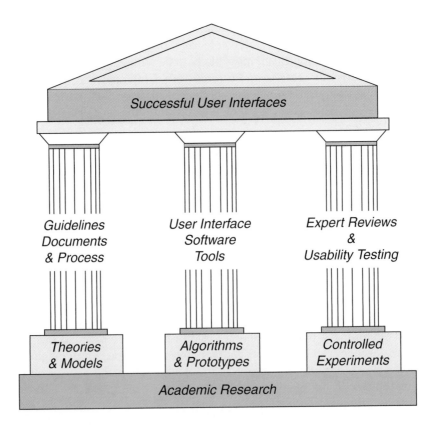

Figure 3.1

The three pillars of successful user-interface development.

3.3.1   Guidelines documents and processes

Early in the design process, the user-interface architect should generate, or require other people to generate, a set of working guidelines. Two people might work for one week to produce a 10-page document, or a dozen people might work for two years to produce a 300-page document. One component of Apple's success with the Macintosh was the machine's early and readable guidelines document, which provided a clear set of principles for the many application developers to follow and thus ensured harmony in design across products. Microsoft's Windows guidelines, which have been refined over the years, also provide a good starting point and an educational experience for many programmers. These and other guidelines documents are referenced and described briefly in the general reference section at the end of Chapter 1.

Each project has different needs, but guidelines should be considered for:

- Words, icons, and graphics
  - Terminology (objects and actions), abbreviations, and capitalization
  - Character set, fonts, font sizes, and styles (bold, italic, underline)
  - Icons, buttons, graphics, and line thickness
  - Use of color, backgrounds, highlighting, and blinking
- Screen-layout issues
  - Menu selection, form fillin, and dialog-box formats
  - Wording of prompts, feedback, and error messages
  - Justification, whitespace, and margins
  - Data entry and display formats for items and lists
  - Use and contents of headers and footers
  - Strategies for adapting to small and large displays
- Input and output devices
  - Keyboard, display, cursor control, and pointing devices
  - Audible sounds, voice feedback, touch input, and other special input modes or devices
  - Response times for a variety of tasks
  - Alternatives for users with disabilities
- Action sequences
  - Direct-manipulation clicking, dragging, dropping, and gestures
  - Command syntax, semantics, and sequences
  - Shortcuts and programmed function keys
  - Error handling and recovery procedures
- Training
  - Online help and tutorials
  - Training and reference materials

Guidelines creation should be a social process within an organization to gain visibility and build support. Controversial guidelines (for example, on when to use voice alerts) should be reviewed by colleagues or tested empirically. Procedures should be established to distribute the guidelines, to ensure enforcement, to allow exemptions, and to permit enhancements. Guidelines documents must be living texts that are adapted to changing needs and refined through experience. Acceptance may be increased by a three-level approach of rigid standards, accepted practices, and flexible guidelines. This approach clarifies which items are firmer and which items are susceptible to change.

The creation of a guidelines document (Box 3.1) at the beginning of an implementation project focuses attention on the interface design and provides an opportunity for discussion of controversial issues. When the guideline is adopted by the development team, the implementation proceeds quickly and with few design changes. For large organizations there may be two or more levels of guidelines, to provide organizational identity while allowing projects to have distinctive styles and local control of terminology.

The four Es provide a basis for creating a living document and a lively process:

- *Education*. Users need training and a chance to discuss the guidelines.
- *Enforcement*. A timely and clear process is necessary to verify that an interface adheres to the guidelines.

Box 3.1

Recommendations for guidelines documents.

- Provides a social process for developers
- Records decisions for all parties to see
- Promotes consistency and completeness
- Facilitates automation of design
- Allows multiple levels:
    Rigid standards
    Accepted practices
    Flexible guidelines
- Announces policies for:
    Education: how to get it?
    Enforcement: who reviews?
    Exemption: who decides?
    Enhancement: how often?

- *Exemption.* When creative ideas or new technologies are used, a rapid process for gaining exemption is needed.
- *Enhancement.* A predictable process for review, possibly annually, will help keep the guidelines up-to-date.

3.3.2   User-interface software tools

One difficulty in designing interactive systems is that customers and users may not have a clear idea of what the system will look like when it is done. Since interactive systems are novel in many situations, users may not realize the implications of design decisions. Unfortunately, it is difficult, costly, and time-consuming to make major changes to systems once those systems have been implemented.

Even though this problem has no complete solution, some of the more serious difficulties can be avoided if, at an early stage, the customers and users can be given a realistic impression of what the final system will look like (Gould and Lewis, 1985). A printed version of the proposed displays is helpful for pilot tests, but an onscreen display with an active keyboard and mouse is more realistic. The prototype of a menu system may have only one or two paths active, instead of the thousands of paths envisioned for the final system. For a form-fillin system, the prototype may simply show the fields but not actually process them. Prototypes have been developed with simple drawing or word-processing tools, but graphical design environments such as Macromedia's Director and Flash are widely used. Development environments such as Microsoft's Visual Basic/C++ are easy to get started with yet have a rich set of powerful features. More sophisticated tools such as Sun's Java provide cross-platform development and a variety of services. These tools are covered in Chapter 5.

3.3.3   Expert reviews and usability testing

Theatrical producers know that previews to critics and extensive rehearsals are necessary to ensure a successful opening night. Early rehearsals may require only one or two performers wearing street clothes, but as opening night approaches, dress rehearsals with the full cast, props, and lighting are expected. Aircraft designers carry out wind-tunnel tests, build plywood mockups of the cabin layout, construct complete simulations of the cockpit, and thoroughly flight-test the first prototype. Similarly, web-site designers now recognize that they must carry out many small and some large pilot tests of components before release to customers (Dumas and Redish, 1999). In addition to a variety of expert review methods, tests with the intended users, surveys, and automated analysis tools are proving to be valuable. Procedures vary greatly depending on the goals of the usability study, the number of expected users, the dangers of errors, and the level of investment. Chapter 4 covers expert reviews, usability testing, and other evaluation methods in depth.

3.4   Development Methodologies

Many software development projects fail to achieve their goals. Some estimates of the failure rate put it as high as 60%. Much of this problem can be traced to poor communication between developers and their business clients or between developers and their users.

Successful developers work carefully to understand the business' needs and refine their skills in eliciting accurate requirements from nontechnical business managers. In addition, since business managers may lack the technical knowledge to understand proposals made by the developers, dialog is necessary to reduce confusion about the organizational implications of design decisions.

Successful developers also know that careful attention to user-centered design issues at the early stages of software development dramatically reduces both development time and cost. User-centered design leads to systems that generate fewer problems during development and have lower maintenance costs over their lifetime. They are easier to learn, produce faster performance, reduce user errors substantially, and encourage users to explore features that go beyond the minimum required to get by. In addition, user-centered design practices help organizations align system functionality with their business needs and priorities.

Software developers have learned that consistently following established development methodologies can help them meet budgets and schedules (Sommerville, 2000; Pfleeger, 2001). While software-engineering methodologies are effective in facilitating the software development process, they have not always provided clear processes for studying the users, understanding their needs, and creating a usable interface. Small consulting firms that specialize in user-centered design have created innovative design methodologies such as Contextual Inquiry to guide developers (Beyer and Holtzblatt, 1998). Also, some large corporations have integrated user-centered design into their practices; for example, IBM's Ease of Use method fits with their existing corporate methods (Fig. 3.2).

These business-oriented approaches specify detailed deliverables for the various stages of design and incorporate cost/benefit and return-on-investment (ROI) analyses to facilitate decision making. They may also offer management strategies to keep projects on track and to facilitate effective collaboration among teams that include both business and technical participants. Since user-centered design is only a part of the overall development process, these method-

Role by phase: process navigator
Role by phase matrix

Role/phase matrix	All Phases	Business Opportunity	Understanding Users	Initial Design	Development	Deployment	Life Cycle
All Roles							
User Experience Leadership		User Engineering Plan - Initial	User Engineering Plan - Final	Execution of the User Engineering Plan	Satisfaction of established metrics	Project Assessment	Satisfaction Survey
Market Planning		Business and Market Requirements	Appropriate User Requirements	Draft Marketing Collateral	Detail Marketing Collateral	Final Marketing Collateral	
User Research			User Requirements	Appropriate Design			
User Experience Design			Design Direction	Conceptual Design, Low-Fidelity Prototypes	Detail Design, High-Fidelity Prototypes	Design Issue Resolution	
Visual & Industrial Design			Appearance Direction	Appearance Guidelines	Appearance Specification		
User Experience Evaluation			Competitive Evaluation	Conceptual Design Evalution	Detail Design Evaluations	User Feedback and Benchmark	Usage Issue Report

Figure 3.2

IBM's Ease of Use development methodology, which specifies activities by roles and phases.

ologies must also mesh with the various software-engineering methodologies that are used in industry today.

There are dozens of advertised development methods (such as GUIDE, STUDIO, and OVID), but we'll focus on Cognetics Corporation's well-tested and widely used method, The *Logical User-Centered Interactive Design Methodology* (LUCID) (Kreitzberg, 1996). It identifies six stages (see Table 3.1):

1. *Envision.* Align the agendas of all stakeholders with organizational strategy and the need for "extreme usability," and develop a clear, shared product vision, embodied in a concept sketch.
2. *Discovery.* Study users to determine high-level user requirements, terminology, and mental models.
3. *Design Foundation.* Develop a conceptual design and create a key screen prototype to convey the visual style. Usability test the design, revise, and repeat.
4. *Design Detail.* Flesh out the high-level design into complete specifications.
5. *Build.* Support the production process through review and late-stage change management.
6. *Release.* Develop a roll-out plan to support the users' transition to the new product; conduct a final usability test, and document the lessons learned.

Stage 1: Envision

Align the agendas of all stakeholders, balancing the needs to meet business objectives, manage technical constraints and support users' needs for a highly usable product.

Develop a clear, shared product vision among the stakeholders.

Identify and deal with potential problems that could impair the development team's ability to collaborate effectively.

Begin the design process at a concept sketch level.

Stage 2: Discovery

Develop a clear understanding of the characteristics of each distinct segment of the product's users.

Understand the tasks users perform, the information they need, the terminology they use, their priorities and their mental models.

Analyze the data gathered and create the product's user requirements.

Stage 3: Design Foundation

Develop and validate the basic conceptual design of the product.

Develop a visual look for the product.

Present the completed design as a key screen prototype.

Stage 4: Design Detail

Complete a style guide containing both the graphic design and UI policy decisions.

Flesh out the high-level design into a complete specification.

Conduct usability evaluations of specific screens or workflows.

Create detailed layouts for each screen and detailed specifications for each element of each screen.

Stage 5: Build

Answer questions and support developers during coding, redesigning screens if needed.

Conduct usability evaluation of critical screens, if necessary.

Support the build process through review and late-stage change management.

Stage 6: Release

Develop a rollout plan to support the new product.

Conduct usability evaluation of the "out of the box" or installation experience.

Measure user satisfaction.

Table 3.1

Logical User-Centered Interaction Design Methodology from Cognetics Corporation, Princeton Junction, NJ.

In the first stage, *envision*, a product concept is developed. Surprisingly, many software-development efforts are launched without a clear concept of the product or without agreement among stakeholders. At the center of the LUCID methodology is creation of a "high concept" for the product—that is, a brief statement that defines the goals, functionality, and benefits of the product. For example,

> The new home banking system will provide customers with unified access to their accounts. It will support balance inquiry, management of credit accounts and loans, transfer of funds between accounts, electronic bill payment, and investment in the bank's family of mutual funds. The system will provide the customer with year-end accounting for tax purposes.

As part of the envision stage, project leaders define business objectives, establish the design team, identify environmental, technical, or legal constraints, specify the user population, and prepare a project plan and budget. During this stage, the product concept is illustrated by simple screen sketches (which may be created on paper or onscreen). The goal of these sketches is to convey the system concept to nontechnical users.

With the project plan in place, the design team meets with users to learn about their needs and competencies, the business process to be supported, and the functional requirements of the system. LUCID uses participatory design sessions to solicit user input, construct workflow scenarios, and define the objects that are central to the design.

A distinctive aspect of LUCID is its focus on a key-screen prototype that incorporates the major navigational paths of the system. The key-screen prototype is used to show users the design of the proposed system and allow them to evaluate and refine it. The key-screen prototype is also used for usability testing and heuristic review. Key screens usually evoke strong reactions, generate early participation, and create momentum for the project.

Like most user-centered design methodologies, LUCID employs rapid prototyping and iterative usability testing (see Chapter 4). Because rapid prototyping is key to meeting schedule and budget requirements, LUCID relies on user-interface building tools (discussed Chapter 5). The prototypes are usually developed in conjunction with a programmer who is part of the software engineering team. One of this programmer's responsibilities is to identify interface issues that have implications for the technical architecture of the product. When completed and approved by users, the prototype serves as part of the programming specification for the software engineers.

Finally, LUCID describes a phased release stage built on theories of organizational change. Project leaders identify barriers to and construct incentives for adoption of the software. The goal is to ensure a positive reception by customers, users, and managers.

As a management strategy, LUCID makes the commitment to user-centered design explicit and highlights the role of usability engineering in software development by focusing on activities, deliverables, and reviews. At each of the LUCID stages there are specified deliverables and timely feedback through reviews, for components such as:

- *Product definition:* high concept for managers and marketers
- *Business case*: pricing, expected revenues, return on investment, competition
- *Resources*: duration, effort levels, team members, backup plans
- *Physical environment*: ergonomic design, physical installation, communication lines
- *Technical environment*: hardware and software for development and integration
- *Users*: multiple communities for interviews, user testing, and marketing
- *Functionality*: services provided to users
- *Prototype*: early paper prototypes, key screens, running prototypes
- *Usability*: set measurable goals, conduct tests, refine interface and goals
- *Design guidelines*: modify existing guidelines, implement review process
- *Content materials*: identify and acquire copyrighted text, audio, and video
- *Documentation, training and help*: specificy, develop, and test paper, video, and online versions

The thoroughness of the LUCID framework comes from its validation and refinement in multiple projects. The templates and techniques it provides help design teams structure their activities and deliverables. Because each project has special needs, a design methodology is only the starting point for project management. While LUCID is designed to promote an orderly process, with iterations within a stage and predictable progress between stages, the framework will need to be adapted to the realities of specific projects and organizations. And while the concept of flow from stage to stage is a useful structure for organizing user-centric design activities, some projects may require the design team to back up and redo earlier stages if elements of the product concept change dramatically.

3.5   Ethnographic Observation

The early stages of most methodologies include observation of users. Since interface users form a unique culture, ethnographic methods for observing them in the workplace are becoming increasingly important. Ethnographers join work or home environments to listen and observe carefully, sometimes stepping forward to ask questions and participate in activities (Fetterman, 1998; Harper, 2000; Millen, 2000) (Fig 3.3). As ethnographers, user-interface designers gain insight into individual behavior and the organizational context. User-interface designers differ from traditional ethnographers in that in addition to understanding their subjects, user-interface designers focus on interfaces for the purpose of changing and improving those interfaces. Also, whereas traditional ethnographers immerse themselves in cultures for weeks or months, user-interface designers usually need to limit this process to a period of days or even hours, and still to obtain the relevant data needed to influence a redesign (Hughes et al., 1997). Ethnographic methods have been applied to office work (Suchman, 1987), air-traffic control (Bentley et al., 1992), and other domains.

The goal of an observation is to obtain the necessary data to influence interface redesign. Unfortunately, it is easy to misinterpret observations, to disrupt normal practice, and to overlook important information. Following a validated ethnographic process reduces the likelihood of these problems. Guidelines for preparing for the evaluation, performing the field study, analyzing the data, and

Figure 3.3

Preteen researchers with the University of Baltimore's KidsTeam observe children's reading habits in the home (left). Researchers in Paris brainstorm ideas for new family technologies with families from France, Sweden, and the United States (right).

reporting the findings might include the following (Rose, Plaisant, and Shnei-derman, 1995):

- Preparation
  - Understand organization policies and work culture.
  - Familiarize yourself with the system and its history.
  - Set initial goals and prepare questions.
  - Gain access and permission to observe or interview.
- Field Study
  - Establish rapport with managers and users.
  - Observe or interview users in their workplace, and collect subjective and objective quantitative and qualitative data.
  - Follow any leads that emerge from the visits.
  - Record your visits.
- Analysis
  - Compile the collected data in numerical, textual, and multimedia databases.
  - Quantify data and compile statistics.
  - Reduce and interpret the data.
  - Refine the goals and the process used.
- Reporting
  - Consider multiple audiences and goals.
  - Prepare a report and present the findings.

These notions seem obvious when stated, but they require interpretation and attention in each situation. For example, understanding the differing percep-tions that managers and users have about the efficacy of the current interface will alert you to the varying frustrations that each group will have. Managers may complain about the unwillingness of staff to update information promptly, but staff may be resistant to using the interface because the login process takes six to eight minutes. In preparing for one observation, we appreciated that the manager called to warn us that graduate students should not wear jeans because the users were prohibited from doing so. Learning the technical lan-guage of the users is also vital for establishing rapport. It is useful to prepare a long list of questions that you can then filter down by focusing on the proposed goals. Awareness of the differences between user communities, such as those mentioned in Section 1.5, will help to make the observation and interview process more effective.

Data collection can include a wide range of subjective impressions that are qualitative or of subjective reactions that are quantitative, such as rating scales or rankings. Objective data can consist of qualitative anecdotes or critical incidents that capture user experiences, or can be quantitative reports about, for example, the number of errors that occur during a one-hour observation of six users. Deciding in advance what to capture is highly beneficial, but remaining alert to unexpected happenings is also valuable. Written report summaries have proved to be valuable, far beyond expectations; in most cases, raw transcripts of every conversation are too voluminous to be useful.

Making the process explicit and planning carefully may seem awkward to many people whose training stems from computing and information technology. However, a thoughtful applied ethnographic process has proved to have many benefits. It can increase trustworthiness and credibility, since designers learn about the complexities of an organization firsthand by visits to the workplace. Personal presence allows designers to develop working relationships with several end users to discuss ideas, and most importantly, the users may consent to be active participants in the design of their new interface.

3.6   Participatory Design

Many authors have urged participatory design strategies, but the concept is controversial. The arguments in favor suggest that more user involvement brings more accurate information about tasks and an opportunity for users to influence design decisions. However, the sense of participation that builds users' ego investment in successful implementation may be the biggest influence on increased user acceptance of the final system (Damodaran, 1996; Muller, 2002; Kujala, 2003).

On the other hand, extensive user involvement may be costly and may lengthen the implementation period. It may also generate antagonism from people who are not involved or whose suggestions are rejected and even force designers to compromise their designs to satisfy incompetent participants (Ives and Olson, 1984).

Participatory design experiences are usually positive, and advocates can point to many important contributions that would have been missed without user participation. People who are resistant might appreciate the somewhat formalized multiple-case-studies *plastic interface for collaborative technology initiatives through video exploration (PICTIVE)* approach (Muller, 1992). Users sketch interfaces, then use slips of paper, pieces of plastic, and tape to create low-fidelity early prototypes. A scenario walkthrough is then recorded on videotape for presentation to managers, users, or other designers. With the right leadership, PICTIVE can effectively elicit new ideas and be fun for all involved (Muller, Wildman, and White, 1993). Many variations of participatory design have been proposed that engage participants to create dramatic performances, photography exhibits, games, or merely sketches and written scenarios.

Careful selection of users helps to build a successful participatory design experience. A competitive selection increases participants' sense of importance and emphasizes the seriousness of the project. Participants may be asked to commit to repeated meetings and should be told what to expect about their roles and their influence. They may have to learn about the technology and business plans of the organization and be asked to act as a communication channel to the larger group of users that they represent.

The social and political environment surrounding the implementation of complex interfaces is not amenable to study by rigidly defined methods or controlled experimentation. Social and industrial psychologists are interested in these issues, but dependable research and implementation strategies may never emerge. The sensitive project leader must judge each case on its merits and must decide what is the right level of user involvement. The personalities of the participatory design team members are such critical determinants that experts in group dynamics and social psychology may be useful as consultants. Many questions remain to be studied, such as whether homogeneous or diverse groups are more successful, how to tailor processes for small and large groups, and how to balance decision-making control between typical users and professional designers.

The experienced user-interface architect knows that organizational politics and the preferences of individuals may be more important than technical issues in governing the success of an interactive system. For example, warehouse managers who see their positions threatened by an interactive system that provides senior managers with up-to-date information through desktop displays may ensure that the system fails by delaying data entry or by being less than diligent in guaranteeing data accuracy. The interface designer should take into account the system's effect on users and should solicit their participation to ensure that all concerns are made explicit early enough to avoid counterproductive efforts and resistance to change. Novelty is threatening to many people, so clear statements about what to expect can be helpful in reducing anxiety.

Ideas about participatory design are being refined with diverse users, ranging from children to older adults. Arranging for participation is difficult for some users, such as those with cognitive disabilities or those whose time is precious (for example, surgeons). The levels of participation are becoming clearer; one taxonomy describes the roles of children in developing interfaces for children, varying from testers to informants to partners (Druin, 2002) (Fig. 3.4). Testers are merely observed as they try out novel designs, while informants comment to designers through interviews and focus groups. Design partners are active members of a design team, which in the case of children's software will naturally involve participants of many ages—the intergenerational team.

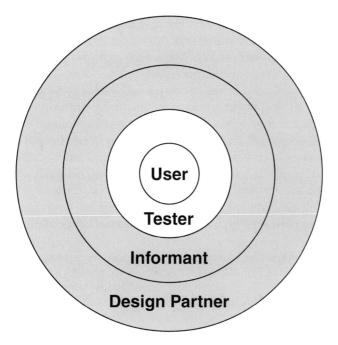

Figure 3.4

Druin's model of the four levels of user participation. The blue areas (informant and design partner) represent stages of participatory design.

∃.7 Scenario Development

When a current interface is being redesigned or a well-polished manual system is being automated, reliable data about the distribution of task frequencies and sequences is an enormous asset. If current data do not exist, then usage logs can quickly provide insight.

A table with user communities listed across the top and tasks listed down the side is helpful. Each box can then be filled in with the relative frequency with which each user performs each task. Another representation tool is a table of task sequences, indicating which tasks follow other tasks. Often, a flowchart or transition diagram helps designers to record and convey the sequences of possible actions; the thickness of the connecting lines indicates the frequency of the transitions.

In less well-defined projects, many designers have found day-in-the-life scenarios helpful to characterize what happens when users perform typical tasks.

During the early design stages, data about current performance should be collected to provide a baseline. Information about similar systems helps, and interviews can be conducted with stakeholders, such as users and managers (Bodker, 2000; Carroll, 2000; Rosson and Carroll, 2001).

An early and easy way to describe a novel system is to write scenarios of usage and then, if possible, to act them out as a form of theater. This technique can be especially effective when multiple users must cooperate (for example, in control rooms, cockpits, or financial trading rooms) or multiple physical devices are used (for example, at customer-service desks, medical laboratories, or hotel check-in areas). Scenarios can represent common or emergency situations with both novice and expert users.

In developing the National Digital Library, the design team began by writing 81 scenarios that portrayed typical needs of potential users. Here is an example:

> *K–16 Users:* A seventh-grade social-studies teacher is teaching a unit on the Industrial Revolution. He wants to make use of primary source material that would illustrate the factors that facilitated industrialization, the manner in which it occurred, and the impact that it had on society and on the built environment. Given his teaching load, he only has about four hours total to locate and package the supplementary material for classroom use.

Other scenarios might describe how users explore a system, such as this optimistic vision, written for the U.S. Holocaust Museum and Education Center:

> A grandmother and her 10- and 12-year old grandsons have visited the museum before. They have returned this time to the Learning Center to explore what life was like in her shtetl in Poland in the 1930s. One grandson eagerly touches the buttons on the welcome screen, and they watch the 45-second video introduction by the museum director. They then select the button on "History before the Holocaust" and choose to view a list of towns. Her small town is not on the list, but she identifies the larger nearby city, and they get a brief textual description, a map of the region, and a photograph of the marketplace. They read about the history of the town and view 15-second videos of the marketplace activity and a Yiddish theater production. They bypass descriptions of key buildings and institutions, choosing instead to read biographies of a famous community leader and a poet. Finally, they select "GuestBook" and add their names to the list of people who have indicated an affiliation with this town. Further up on the list, the grandmother notices the name of a childhood friend from whom she has not heard in 60 years—fortunately, the earlier visitor has left an address.

This scenario was written to give nontechnical museum planners and the Board of Directors an idea of what could be built if funding were provided. Such scenarios are easy for most people to grasp, and they convey design issues such as physical installation (room and seats for three or more patrons with sound isolation) and development requirements (video production for the director's introduction and conversion of archival films to video).

An elaborate scenario development process was conducted to help U.S. statistical agencies formulate a vision for a Statistical Knowledge Network. Patterns of citizen requests were combined with agency proposals to develop 15 brief scenarios, using first-person format, such as these two that were the basis of empirical tests of proposed interfaces:

> I'm a social activist in the Raleigh-Durham, North Carolina area and have become increasingly concerned about urban sprawl and the loss of rural areas for both farming and recreation. I need statistics to support my claim that significant differences occur when urban development occurs in rural and/or farming areas.

> I would like to open a grocery store specializing in organic products in the greater Seattle metropolitan area. What are the trends in production and consumption of organic food products? Would the Seattle area be a good place to locate?

Some scenario writers take a further step and produce a videotape to convey their intentions. There are famous future scenarios, such as Apple's *Knowledge Navigator*, made in 1988, which produced numerous controversies. It portrayed a professor using voice commands to talk with a bow-tied preppie character on the screen and touch commands to develop ecological simulations. Many viewers enjoyed the tape, but thought that it stepped over the bounds of reality by having the preppie agent recognize the professor's facial expressions, verbal hesitations, and emotional reactions. In 1994, Bruce Tognazzini's *Starfire* scenario for Sun Microsystems gave his elaborate but realistic impression of a large-screen work environment that supported rich collaborations with remote colleagues. By 2003, cell-phone developers were producing scenarios on how personal, family, and commercial relationships would change due to mobile video communications— an appealing example is the Japanese NTT DoCoMo's *Vision 2010: Beyond the Mobile Frontier*, which shows how a family can realize its goal of remaining in close contact while children go to study far away from home.

3.8 Social Impact Statement for Early Design Review

Interactive systems often have a dramatic impact on large numbers of users. To minimize risks, a thoughtful statement of anticipated impacts circulated among stakeholders can be a useful process for eliciting productive suggestions early in the development, when changes are easiest.

Information systems are increasingly required to provide services by governments, utilities, and publicly regulated industries. However, some critics have strong negative attitudes about modern technologies and see only a hopeless technological determinism: "Technopoly eliminates alternatives to itself. It consists in the deification of technology, which means that the culture seeks its authorization in technology, finds its satisfactions in technology, and takes its orders from technology" (Postman, 1993).

Postman's endless fears do not help us to shape more effective technology or to prevent damage from technology failures. However, constructive criticism and guidelines for design could be helpful in reversing the long history of incorrect credit histories, dislocation through de-skilling or layoffs, and deaths from flawed medical instruments. Current concerns focus on privacy invasion from surveillance systems, government attempts to restrict access to information, and voting fraud because of poor security. While guarantees of perfection are not possible, policies and processes can be developed that will more often than not lead to satisfying outcomes.

A *social impact statement,* similar to an environmental impact statement, might help to promote high-quality systems in government-related applications (reviews for private-sector corporate projects would be optional and self-administered). Early and widespread discussion can uncover concerns and enable stakeholders to state their positions openly. Of course, there is the danger that these discussions will elevate fears or force designers to make unreasonable compromises, but these risks seem reasonable in a well-managed project. An outline for a social impact statement might include these sections (Shneiderman and Rose, 1996):

- Describe the new system and its benefits
  - Convey the high-level goals of the new system.
  - Identify the stakeholders.
  - Identify specific benefits.
- Address concerns and potential barriers
  - Anticipate changes in job functions and potential layoffs.
  - Address security and privacy issues.
  - Discuss accountability and responsibility for system misuse and failure.
  - Avoid potential biases.
  - Weigh individual rights versus societal benefits.
  - Assess tradeoffs between centralization and decentralization.
  - Preserve democratic principles.
  - Ensure diverse access.
  - Promote simplicity and preserve what works.
- Outline the development process
  - Present an estimated project schedule.

- Propose a process for making decisions.
- Discuss expectations of how stakeholders will be involved.
- Recognize needs for more staff, training, and hardware.
- Propose a plan for backups of data and equipment.
- Outline a plan for migrating to the new system.
- Describe a plan for measuring the success of the new system.

A social impact statement should be produced early enough in the development process to influence the project schedule, system requirements, and budget. It can be developed by the system design team, which might include end users, managers, internal or external software developers, and possibly clients. Even for large systems, the social impact statement should be of a size and complexity that make it accessible to users with relevant backgrounds.

After the social impact statement is written, it should be evaluated by the appropriate review panel as well as by managers, other designers, end users, and anyone else who will be affected by the proposed system. Potential review panels include federal government units (for example, the General Accounting Organization or Office Personnel Management), state legislatures, regulatory agencies (for example, the Securities and Exchange Commission or Federal Aviation Administration), professional societies, and labor unions. The review panel will receive the written report, hold public hearings, and request modifications. Citizen groups also should be given the opportunity to present their concerns and to suggest alternatives.

Once the social impact statement is adopted, it must be enforced. A social impact statement documents the intentions for the new system, and the stakeholders need to see that those intentions are backed up by actions. Typically, the review panel is the proper authority for enforcement.

The effort, cost, and time should be appropriate to the project, while facilitating a thoughtful review. The process can offer large improvements by preventing problems that could be expensive to repair, improving privacy protection, minimizing legal challenges, and creating more satisfying work environments. Information-system designers take no Hippocratic Oath, but pledging themselves to strive for the noble goal of excellence in design can win respect and inspire others.

3.9   Legal Issues

As user interfaces have become prominent, serious legal issues have emerged. Every developer of software and information should review legal issues that may affect design, implementation, or marketing.

Privacy is always a concern whenever computers are used to store data or to monitor activity. Medical, legal, financial, and other data often have to be protected to prevent unapproved access, illegal tampering, inadvertent loss, or malicious mischief. Physical security to prohibit access is fundamental; in addition, privacy protection can involve user-interface mechanisms for controlling password access, identity checking, and data verification. Effective protection provides a high degree of privacy with a minimum of confusion and intrusion into work. Web-site developers should provide easily accessible and understandable privacy policies.

A second concern encompasses safety and reliability. User interfaces for aircraft, automobiles, medical equipment, military systems, or utility control rooms can affect life-or-death decisions. If air-traffic controllers are confused by the situation display, they can make fatal errors. If the user interface for such a system is demonstrated to be difficult to understand, it could leave the designer, developer, and operator open to a lawsuit alleging improper design. Designers should strive to make high-quality and well-tested interfaces that adhere to state-of-the-art design guidelines. Documentation of testing and usage to provide accurate records will protect designers in case problems arise.

A third issue is copyright or patent protection for software (Lessig, 1999; Samuelson, 2001). Software developers who have spent time and money to develop a package are frustrated in their attempts to recover their costs and to make a profit if potential users make illegal copies of the package, rather than buying it. Technical schemes have been tried to prevent copying, but clever hackers can usually circumvent the barriers. It is unusual for a company to sue an individual for copying a program, but cases have been brought against corporations and universities. A vocal community of developers, led by the League for Programming Freedom, opposes software copyright and patents, believing that broad dissemination is the best policy. An innovative legal approach, Creative Commons, enables authors to specify more liberal terms for others to use their works. The open-source software movement has enlivened these controversies. The Open Source Initiative describes their movement as follows: "When programmers can read, redistribute, and modify the source code for a piece of software, the software evolves. People improve it, people adapt it, people fix bugs. And this can happen at a speed that, if one is used to the slow pace of conventional software development, seems astonishing." Some open-source products, such as the Linux operating system and Apache web server, have become successful enough to take a substantial fraction of the market share.

A fourth concern is with copyright protection for online information, images, or music. If customers access an online resource, do they have the right to store the information electronically for later use? Can the customer send an electronic copy to a colleague or friend? Do individuals, their employers, or network operators own the information contained in e-mail messages? The expansion of the World Wide Web, with its vast digital libraries, has raised the temperature and pace of copyright discussions. Publishers seek to protect their intellectual assets, while librarians are torn between their desire to serve patrons and their obligations to publishers. If copyrighted works are disseminated freely, then what incentives will there be for publishers and authors? If it is illegal to transmit any copyrighted work without permission or payment, then science, education, and other fields will suffer. The fair-use doctrine of limited copying for personal and educational purposes helped cope with the questions raised by photocopying technologies. However, the perfect rapid copying and broad dissemination permitted by the Internet demand a thoughtful update (Lessig, 2001; Samuelson, 2003).

A fifth issue is freedom of speech in electronic environments. Do users have a right to make controversial or potentially offensive statements through e-mail or listservs? Are such statements protected by the First Amendment? Are networks like street corners, where freedom of speech is guaranteed, or are networks like television broadcasting, where community standards must be protected? Should network operators be responsible for or prohibited from eliminating offensive or obscene jokes, stories, or images? Controversy has raged over whether Internet service providers have a right to prohibit e-mail messages that are used to organize consumer rebellions against themselves. Another controversy emerged over whether a network operator has a duty to suppress racist e-mail remarks or postings to a bulletin board. If libelous statements are transmitted, can a person sue the network operator as well as the source?

Other legal concerns include adherence to laws requiring equal access for disabled users and attention to changing laws in countries around the world. Do Yahoo! and eBay have to enforce the laws of every country in which they have customers? These and other issues mean that developers of online services must be sure to consider all the legal implications of their design decisions.

Practitioner's Summary

Usability engineering is maturing rapidly, and once-novel ideas have become standard practices. Usability has increasingly taken center stage in organizational and product planning. Development methodologies such as LUCID or contextual design help by offering validated processes with predictable schedules and meaningful deliverables. Ethnographic observation can provide information to guide task analysis and to complement carefully supervised participatory design processes. Logs of usage provide valuable data about the task frequencies and sequences. Scenario writing helps to bring common understanding of design goals, is useful for managerial and customer presentations, and helps to plan usability tests. For interfaces developed by governments, public utilities, and regulated industries, an early social impact statement can elicit public discussion that is likely to identify problems and produce interfaces that have high overall societal benefits. Designers and managers should obtain legal advice to ensure adherence to laws and protection of intellectual property.

Researcher's Agenda

Human-interface guidelines are often based on best-guess judgments rather than on empirical data. More research could lead to refined standards that are more complete and dependable, and to more precise knowledge of how much improvement can be expected from a design change. Because of changing technology, we will never have a stable and complete set of guidelines, but the benefits of scientific studies will be enormous in terms of the reliability and quality of decision making about user interfaces. The design processes, ethnographic methods, participatory design activities, scenario writing, and social impact statements are evolving. Variations are needed to address international diversity, special populations such as children or older adults, and long-term studies of actual usage. Thoughtful case studies of design processes would lead to their refinement and promote more widespread application. Creative processes are notoriously difficult to study, but well-documented examples of success stories will inform and inspire.

WORLD WIDE WEB RESOURCES

Design processes promoted by companies and professional standards organizations, with information on how to develop style guidelines. References to guidelines documents are included in Chapter 1.

http://www.aw.com/DTUI

References

Bentley, R., Hughes, J., Randall, D., Rodden, T., Sawyer, P., Shapiro, D., and Sommerville, I., Ethnographically-informed systems design for air traffic control, *Proc. CSCW '92 Conference: Sharing Perspectives*, ACM Press, New York (1992), 123–129.

Beyer, Hugh and Holtzblatt, Karen, *Contextual Design: Defining Customer-Centered Systems*, Morgan Kaufmann Publishers, San Francisco, CA (1998).

Bias, Randolph, and Mayhew, Deborah (Editors), *Cost-Justifying Usability*, Academic Press, New York (1994).

Bodker, Susan, Scenarios in user-centered design—setting the stage for reflection and action, *Interacting with Computers*, 13, 1 (2000), 61–76.

Carroll, John M. (Editor), *Making Use: Scenario-Based Design of Human-Computer Interactions*, MIT Press, Cambridge, MA (2000).

Carroll, John M. and Rosson, Mary Beth, Usability specifications as a tool in iterative development. in Hartson, H. Rex (Editor), *Advances in Human-Computer Interaction 1*, Ablex, Norwood, NJ (1985), 1–28.

Constantine, Larry L. and Lockwood, Lucy A. D., *Software for Use: A Practical Guide to the Models and Methods of Usage-Centered Design*, Addison-Wesley, Reading, MA (1999).

Damodaran, Leela, User involvement in the systems design process—a practical guide for users, *Behaviour & Information Technology*, 15, 6 (1996), 363–377.

Druin, Allison, The role of children in the design of new technology, *Behaviour & Information Technology*, 21, 1 (2002), 1–25.

Dumas, Joseph and Redish, Janice, *A Practical Guide to Usability Testing: Revised Edition*, Intellect Books, Bristol, U.K. (1999).

Fetterman, D. M., *Ethnography: Step by Step, Second Edition*, Sage, Thousand Oaks, CA (1998).

Gould, John D. and Lewis, Clayton, Designing for usability: Key principles and what designers think, *Communications of the ACM*, 28, 3 (March 1985), 300–311.

Harper, R., The organization of ethnography, *Proc. CSCW 2000*, ACM, New York (2000), 239–264.

Hix, Deborah and Hartson, H. Rex, *Developing User Interfaces: Ensuring Usability Through Product and Process*, John Wiley & Sons, New York (1993).

Hughes, J., O'Brien, J., Rodden, T., and Rouncefield, M., Design with ethnography: A presentation framework for design, *Proc. of Design of Interaction Systems '97*, ACM, New York (1997), 147–159.

Ives, Blake and Olson, Margrethe H., User involvement and MIS success: A review of research, *Management Science*, 30, 5 (May 1984), 586–603.

Karat, Claire-Marie, A business case approach to usability, in Bias, Randolph and Mayhew, Deborah (Editors), *Cost-Justifying Usability*, Academic Press, New York (1994), 45–70.

Kreitzberg, Charles, Managing for usability, in Alber, Antone F. (Editor), *Multimedia: A Management Perspective*, Wadsworth, Belmont, CA (1996), 65–88.

Kujala, Sari, User involvement: A review of the benefits and challenges, *Behaviour & Information Technology*, 22, 1 (2003), 1–16.

Landauer, Thomas K., *The Trouble with Computers: Usefulness, Usability, and Productivity*, MIT Press, Cambridge, MA (1995).

Lessig, Lawrence, *Code and Other Laws of Cyberspace*, Basic Books, New York (1999).

Lessig, Lawrence, *The Future of Ideas: The Fate of the Commons in a Connected World*, Random House, New York (2001).

Mayhew, Deborah J., *The Usability Engineering Lifecycle: A Practitioner's Guide to User Interface Design*, Morgan Kaufmann Publishers, San Francisco, CA (1999).

Millen, David, Rapid ethnography: Time deepening strategies for HCI field, *Proc. ACM Symposium on Designing Interactive Systems*, ACM, New York (2000), 280–286.

Muller, Michael J., Retrospective on a year of participatory design using the PICTIVE technique, *Proc. CHI '92: Human Factors in Computing Systems*, ACM, New York (1992), 455–462.

Muller, M., Wildman, D., and White, E., Taxonomy of PD practices: A brief practitioner's guide, *Communications of the ACM*, 36, 4 (1993), 26–27.

Muller, Michael, Participatory design, in Jacko, Julie and Sears, Andrew (Editors), *Handbook of Human-Computer Interaction*, Lawrence Erlbaum Associates, Hillsdale, NJ (2002), 1051–1068.

Nielsen, Jakob, *Designing Web Usability: The Practice of Simplicity*, New Riders Publishing, Indianapolis, IN (1999).

Nielsen, Jakob, *Usability Engineering*, Academic Press, New York (1993).

Pfleeger, Shari Lawrence, *Software Engineering: Theory and Practice, Second Edition*, Prentice-Hall, Englewood Cliffs, NJ (2001).

Postman, Neil, *Technopoly: The Surrender of Culture to Technology*, Vintage Books, New York (1993).

Rose, Anne, Plaisant, Catherine, and Shneiderman, Ben, Using ethnographic methods in user interface re-engineering, *Proc. DIS '95: Symposium on Designing Interactive Systems*, ACM Press, New York (August 1995), 115–122.

Rosson, Mary Beth and Carroll, John M., *Usability Engineering: Scenario-Based Development of Human Computer Interaction*, Morgan Kaufmann Publishers, San Francisco, CA (2001).

Samuelson, Pamela, Digital Rights Management {and, or, vs.} the Law, *Communications of the ACM*, 46, 4 (April 2003), 41–45.

Samuelson, Pamela, Intellectual property for an information age: How to balance the public interest, traditional legal principles, and the emerging digital reality, *Communications of the ACM*, 44, 2 (February 2001), 67–68.

Shneiderman, Ben and Rose, Anne, Social impact statements: Engaging public participation in information technology design, *Proc. CQL '96: ACM SIGCAS Symposium on Computers and the Quality of Life* (February 1996), 90–96.

Sommerville, Ian, *Software Engineering, Sixth Edition*, Addison-Wesley, Boston, MA (2000).

Suchman, Lucy A., *Plans and Situated Actions: The Problem of Human-Machine Communication*, Cambridge University Press, Cambridge, U.K. (1987).

chapter

4

Evaluating Interface Designs

The test of what is real is that it is hard and rough.
. . . What is pleasant belongs in dreams.

SIMONE WEIL
Gravity and Grace, 1947

4.1 Introduction

Designers can become so entranced with their creations that they may fail to evaluate them adequately. Experienced designers have attained the wisdom and humility to know that extensive testing is a necessity. If feedback is the "breakfast of champions," then testing is the "dinner of the gods." However, careful choices must be made from the large menu of evaluation possibilities to create a balanced meal.

The determinants of the evaluation plan (Nielsen, 1993; Dumas and Redish, 1999; Preece, Rogers, and Sharp, 2002) include at least:

- Stage of design (early, middle, late)
- Novelty of project (well defined versus exploratory)
- Number of expected users
- Criticality of the interface (for example, life-critical medical system versus museum-exhibit support)
- Costs of product and finances allocated for testing
- Time available
- Experience of the design and evaluation team

The range of evaluation plans might be from an ambitious two-year test with multiple phases for a new national air-traffic–control system to a three-day test with six users for a small internal web site. The range of costs might be from 20% of a project down to 5%.

A few years ago, it was just a good idea to get ahead of the competition by focusing on usability and doing testing, but now the rapid growth of interest in usability means that failure to test is risky indeed. The dangers are not only that the competition has strengthened, but also that customary engineering practice now requires adequate testing. Failure to perform and document testing could lead to failed contract proposals or malpractice lawsuits from users when errors arise. At this point, it is irresponsible to bypass some form of usability testing.

One troubling aspect of testing is the uncertainty that remains even after exhaustive testing by multiple methods. Perfection is not possible in complex human endeavors, so planning must include continuing methods to assess and repair problems during the lifecycle of an interface. Second, even though problems may continue to be found, at some point a decision has to be made about completing prototype testing and delivering the product. Third, most testing methods will account appropriately for normal usage, but performance in unpredictable situations with high levels of input, such as in nuclear-reactor–control or air-traffic–control emergencies, is extremely difficult to test. Development of testing methods to deal with stressful situations and even with partial equipment failures will have to be undertaken as user interfaces are developed for an increasing number of life-critical applications.

4.2   Expert Reviews

A natural starting point for evaluating new or revised interfaces is to ask colleagues or customers for their feedback. Such informal demos with test subjects can provide some useful feedback, but more formal expert reviews have proven to be far more effective (Nielsen and Mack, 1994). These methods depend on having experts (whose expertise may be in the application or user-interface domains) available on staff or as consultants. Expert reviews can then be conducted on short notice and rapidly.

Expert reviews can occur early or late in the design phase. The outcome can be a formal report with problems identified or recommendations for changes. Alternatively, the expert review may result in a discussion with or presentation to designers or managers. Expert reviewers should be sensitive to the design team's ego involvement and professional skill, so suggestions should be made cautiously: It is difficult for someone just freshly inspecting an interface to understand fully the design rationale and development history. The reviewers note possible problems for discussion with the designers, but solutions generally should be left for the designers to produce. Expert reviews usually take from half a day to one week, although a lengthy training period may be required to explain the task domain or operational procedures. It may be useful to have the same as well as fresh expert reviewers as the project progresses. There are a variety of expert-review methods from which to choose:

- *Heuristic evaluation.* The expert reviewers critique an interface to determine conformance with a short list of design heuristics, such as the eight golden rules (see section 2.3.4). It makes an enormous difference if the experts are familiar with the rules and are able to interpret and apply them.

- *Guidelines review.* The interface is checked for conformance with the organizational or other guidelines document. Because guidelines documents may contain a thousand items, it may take the expert reviewers some time to master the guidelines and days or weeks to review a large interface.

- *Consistency inspection.* The experts verify consistency across a family of interfaces, checking for consistency of terminology, fonts, color schemes, layout, input and output formats, and so on within the interface as well as in the training materials and online help. Software tools can help automate the process, as well as produce concordances of words and abbreviations.

- *Cognitive walkthrough.* The experts simulate users walking through the interface to carry out typical tasks. High-frequency tasks are a starting point, but rare critical tasks, such as error recovery, also should be walked through. Some form of simulating the day in the life of the user should be part of the expert-review process. Cognitive walkthroughs were developed for interfaces that can be learned by exploratory browsing (Wharton et al., 1994), but they are useful even for interfaces that require substantial training. An expert might try the walkthrough privately and explore the system, but there also should be a group meeting with designers, users, or managers to conduct the walkthrough and provoke discussion. Extensions to cover web-site navigation incorporate richer descriptions of users and their goals plus linguistic-analysis programs to estimate the similarity of link labels and destinations (Blackmon et al., 2002).

- *Formal usability inspection.* The experts hold a courtroom-style meeting, with a moderator or judge, to present the interface and to discuss its merits and weaknesses. Design-team members may rebut the evidence about problems in an adversarial format. Formal usability inspections can be educational experiences for novice designers and managers, but they may take longer to prepare and more personnel to carry out than do other types of review.

Expert reviews can be scheduled at several points in the development process, when experts are available and when the design team is ready for feedback. The number of expert reviews will depend on the magnitude of the project and on the amount of resources allocated.

An expert-review report should aspire to comprehensiveness, rather than making opportunistic comments about specific features or presenting a random collection of suggested improvements. It might use a guidelines document to structure the report, then comment on novice, intermittent, and expert features and review consistency across all displays. Another strategy would be to use a theory or model, such as the object-action interface model (see Section 2.5), to organize a report. An evaluation of the task objects and actions (nouns and verbs) is a good starting point, followed by comments on the corresponding interface objects and actions.

If the report ranks recommendations by importance and expected effort level, managers are more likely to implement them (or at least the high-payoff, low-cost ones). In one expert review, the highest priority was to shorten a three-to-five minute log-in procedure that required eight dialog boxes and passwords on two networks. The obvious benefit to already over-busy users was apparent, and they were delighted with the improvement. Common middle-level recommendations include reordering the sequence of displays, providing improved instructions or feedback, and removing nonessential actions. Expert reviews should also include required small fixes such as spelling mistakes, poorly aligned data-entry fields, or inconsistent button placement. A final category includes less vital fixes and novel features that can be addressed in the next version of the interface.

Comparative evaluation of expert-review methods and usability-testing methods is difficult because of the many uncontrollable variables. However, the studies that have been conducted provide evidence for the benefits of expert reviews (Jeffries et al., 1991; Karat, Campbell, and Fiegel, 1992). Different experts tend to find different problems in an interface, so three to five expert reviewers can be highly productive, as can complementary usability testing.

Expert reviewers should be placed in the situation most similar to the one that intended users will experience. The expert reviewers should take training courses, read manuals, take tutorials, and try the interface in as close as possible to a realistic work environment, complete with noise and distractions. However, expert reviewers may also retreat to a quieter environment for detailed review of each screen.

Another approach, getting a *bird's-eye view* of an interface by studying a full set of printed screens laid out on the floor or pinned to walls, has proved to be enormously fruitful in detecting inconsistencies and spotting unusual patterns. The bird's-eye view enables reviewers to quickly see if the fonts, colors, and terminology are consistent, and to appreciate whether the multiple developers have adhered to a common style.

Expert reviewers may also use software tools to speed their analyses, especially with large interfaces. Sometimes string searches on design documents, help text, or program code can be valuable, but more specific interface-design analyses—such as web-accessibility validation, privacy-policy checks, and download-time reduction—are growing more effective. These tools usually provide specific instructions for improvements.

The danger with expert reviews is that the experts may not have an adequate understanding of the task domain or user communities. Experts come in many flavors, and conflicting advice can further confuse the situation (cynics say, "For every Ph.D., there is an equal and opposite Ph.D."). To strengthen the possibility of successful expert review, it helps to choose knowledgeable experts who are familiar with the project and who have a long-term relationship with the organization. These people can be called back to see the results of their intervention, and they can be held accountable. However, even experienced expert reviewers have difficulty knowing how typical users, especially first-time users, will behave.

4.3   Usability Testing and Laboratories

The emergence of usability testing and laboratories since the early 1980s is an indicator of the profound shift in attention to user needs. Traditional managers and developers resisted at first, saying that usability testing seemed like a nice idea, but that time pressures or limited resources prevented them from trying it. As experience grew and successful projects gave credit to the testing process, demand swelled and design teams began to compete for the scarce resource of the usability-laboratory staff. Managers came to realize that having a usability test on the schedule was a powerful incentive to complete a design phase. The usability-test report provided supportive confirmation of progress and specific recommendations for changes. Designers sought the bright light of evaluative feedback to guide their work, and managers saw fewer disasters as projects approached delivery dates. The remarkable surprise was that usability testing not only sped up many projects, but also produced dramatic cost savings (Karat, 1994; Rubin, 1994; Dumas and Redish, 1999).

Usability-laboratory advocates split from their academic roots as these practitioners developed innovative approaches that were influenced by advertising and market research. While academics were developing controlled experiments to test hypotheses and support theories, practitioners developed usability-testing methods to refine user interfaces rapidly. Controlled experiments have at least two treatments and seek to show statistically significant differences; usability tests are designed to find flaws in user interfaces. Both strategies use a carefully prepared set of tasks, but usability tests have fewer participants (maybe as few as three), and their outcome is a report with recommended changes, as opposed to validation or rejection of a hypothesis. Of course, there is a useful spectrum of possibilities between rigid controls and informal testing, and sometimes a combination of approaches is appropriate.

The movement towards usability testing stimulated the construction of usability laboratories (Nielsen, 1993; Dumas and Redish, 1999). Having a physical laboratory makes an organization's commitment to usability clear to employees, customers, and users (Fig. 4.1). A typical modest usability laboratory would have two 10- by 10-foot areas, divided by a half-silvered mirror: one for the participants to do their work and another for the testers and observers (designers, managers, and customers) (Fig. 4.2). IBM was an early leader in developing usability laboratories. Microsoft started later but embraced the idea with more than 25 usability-test labs. Hundreds of software-development companies have followed suit, and a consulting community that will do usability testing for hire also has emerged.

Usability laboratories are typically staffed by one or more people with expertise in testing and user-interface design, who may serve 10 to 15 projects per year throughout an organization. The laboratory staff meet with the user-interface architect or manager at the start of the project to make a test plan with scheduled dates and budget allocations. Usability-laboratory staff members participate in early task analysis or design reviews, provide information on software tools or literature references, and help to develop the set of tasks for the usability test.

Figure 4.1

Usability lab test, with participant and observer seated at a workstation. Video recorders capture the user's actions and the contents of the screens, while microphones capture thinking-aloud comments. (Indiana University School of Library and Information Science)

Figure 4.2

Usability lab control room, with test controllers and observers watching the subject through a half-silvered window. Video controls allow zooming and panning to focus on user actions. (Indiana University School of Library and Information Science)

Two to six weeks before the usability test, the detailed test plan is developed; it contains the list of tasks plus subjective satisfaction and debriefing questions. The number, types, and sources of participants are also identified—sources might be customer sites, temporary personnel agencies, or advertisements placed in newspapers. A pilot test of the procedures, tasks, and questionnaires with one to three participants is conducted one week ahead of time, while there is still time for changes. This typical preparation process can be modified in many ways to suit each project's unique needs.

After changes are approved, participants are chosen to represent the intended user communities, with attention to background in computing, experience with the task, motivation, education, and ability with the natural language used in the interface. Usability-laboratory staff also must control for physical concerns (such as eyesight, left- versus right-handedness, age, gender, education, and computer experience) and for other experimental conditions (such as time of day, day of week, physical surroundings, noise, room temperature, and level of distractions).

Participants should always be treated with respect and should be informed that it is not *they* who are being tested; rather, it is the software and user interface that are under study. They should be told about what they will be doing (for example, finding products on a web site, creating a diagram using a mouse, or studying a restaurant guide on a touchscreen kiosk) and how long they will be expected to stay. Participation should always be voluntary, and *informed consent* should be obtained. Professional practice is to ask all participants to read and sign a statement like this one:

- I have freely volunteered to participate in this experiment.
- I have been informed in advance what my task(s) will be and what procedures will be followed.
- I have been given the opportunity to ask questions and have had my questions answered to my satisfaction.
- I am aware that I have the right to withdraw consent and to discontinue participation at any time, without prejudice to my future treatment.
- My signature below may be taken as affirmation of all the above statements; it was given prior to my participation in this study.

An effective technique during usability testing is to invite users to *think aloud* about what they are doing. The designer or tester should be supportive of the participants, not taking or giving instructions, but prompting and listening for clues about how they are dealing with the interface. Thinking-aloud protocols yield interesting clues for the observant usability tester; for example, "This web page text is too small… so I'm looking for something on the menus to make the text bigger… maybe it is on the top in the icons… I can't find it… so I'll just carry on."

After a suitable time period for accomplishing the task list—usually one to three hours—the participants can be invited to make general comments or suggestions, or to respond to specific questions. The informal atmosphere of a thinking-aloud session is pleasant and often leads to many spontaneous suggestions for improvements. In their efforts to encourage thinking aloud, some usability laboratories have found that having two participants working together produces more talking, as one participant explains procedures and decisions to the other.

Videotaping participants performing tasks is often valuable for later review and for showing designers or managers the problems that users encounter. Reviewing videotapes is a tedious job, so careful logging and annotation during the test is vital to reduce the time spent finding critical incidents. Most usability laboratories have acquired or developed software to facilitate logging of user activities (typing, mousing, reading screens, reading manuals, and so on) by observers with automatic time stamping. Participants may be anxious about the video cameras at the start of the test, but within minutes they usually focus on the tasks and ignore the videotaping. The reactions of designers to seeing videotapes of users failing with their interfaces is sometimes powerful and may be highly motivating. When designers see participants repeatedly picking the wrong menu item, they realize that the label or placement needs to be changed.

At each design stage, the interface can be refined iteratively and the improved version can be tested. It is important to fix quickly even small flaws, such as spelling errors or inconsistent layout, since they influence user expectations. Many variant forms of usability testing have been tried:

- *Paper mockups.* Early usability studies can be conducted using paper mockups of screen displays to assess user reactions to wording, layout, and sequencing. A test administrator plays the role of the computer by flipping the pages while asking a participant user to carry out typical tasks. This informal testing is inexpensive, rapid, and usually productive.

- *Discount usability testing.* This quick-and-dirty approach to task analysis, prototype development, and testing has been widely influential because it lowered the barriers to newcomers (Nielsen, 1993). A controversial aspect is the recommendation to use only three to six test participants. Advocates point out that most serious problems are found with a few participants, enabling prompt revision and repeated testing, while critics hold that a broader subject pool is required to thoroughly test more complex systems. One resolution to the controversy is that discount usability testing be used as a formative evaluation (while designs are changing substantially) and more extensive usability testing be used as a summative evaluation (near the end of the design process). The formative evaluation identifies problems that guide redesign, while the summative evaluation provides evidence for product announcements ("94% of our 120 testers completed their shopping tasks without assistance") and clarifies training needs ("with 4 minutes of instruction, every participant successfully programmed the videorecorder").

- *Competitive usability testing.* Competitive testing compares a new interface to previous versions or to similar products from competitors. This approach is close to a controlled experimental study, and staff must be careful to construct parallel sets of tasks and to counterbalance the order of presentation of the interfaces. Within-subjects designs seem the most powerful, because participants can make comparisons between the competing interfaces—fewer participants are needed, although each is needed for a longer time period.

- *Universal usability testing.* This approach tests interfaces with highly diverse users, hardware, software platforms, and networks. When a wide range of international users is anticipated, such as for consumer electronics products, web-based information services, or e-government services, ambitious testing is necessary to clean up problems and thereby help ensure success. Trials with small and large displays, slow and fast networks, and a range of operating systems or Internet browsers will do much to raise the rate of customer success.

- *Field tests and portable labs.* This testing method puts new interfaces to work in realistic environments for a fixed trial period. Field tests can be made more fruitful if logging software is used to capture error, command, and help frequencies, as well as productivity measures. Portable usability laboratories with videotaping and logging facilities have been developed to support more thorough field testing (Fig. 4.3). A different kind of field testing is to supply users with test versions of new software or consumer products; tens or even thousands of users might receive beta versions and be asked to comment.

- *Remote usability testing.* Since web-based applications are available internationally, it is tempting to conduct usability tests online, without incurring the complexity and cost of bringing participants to a lab. This makes it possible to have larger numbers of participants with more diverse backgrounds, and may add to the realism since participants do their tests in their own environments, using their own equipment. Participants can be recruited by e-mail from customer lists or through online communities. The downside is that there is less control over user behavior and less chance to observe their reactions, although usage logs and phone interviews are useful supplements.

Figure 4.3

UserWorks, Inc.'s "Lab-in-a-Box," a high-end portable audio/video data collection and analysis lab with all the functionality that most investigators would need in even the most demanding field situations.

- *Can-you-break-this tests*. Game designers pioneered the *can-you-break-this* approach to usability testing by providing energetic teenagers with the challenge of trying to beat new games. This destructive testing approach, in which the users try to find fatal flaws in the system or otherwise destroy it, has been used in other projects and should be considered seriously. Software purchasers have little patience with flawed products, and the cost of sending out thousands of replacement disks is high. Furthermore, the loss of goodwill when customers have to download and install revised versions is one that few companies can bear.

For all its success, usability testing does have at least two serious limitations: it emphasizes first-time usage and has limited coverage of the interface features. Since usability tests are usually only one to three hours long, it is difficult to ascertain how performance will be after a week or a month of regular usage. Within the short time of a usability test, the participants may get to use only a small fraction of the system's features, menus, dialog boxes, or help screens. These and other concerns have led design teams to supplement usability testing with the varied forms of expert reviews.

Further criticisms of usability lab testing come from proponents of activity theory and those who believe that realistic test environments are necessary to evaluate information appliances, ambient technologies, and consumer-oriented mobile devices. They argue that longer-term testing, such as a six-month trial for a home TV interface, is necessary to understand adoption and learning processes (Petersen, Madsen, and Kjaer, 2002).

A major step in standardizing usability-test reports was taken by the U.S. National Institute for Standards and Technology in 1997. They convened a group of software manufacturers and large purchasers to work for several years to produce the Common Industry Format for summative usability testing results. The format describes the testing environment, tasks, participants, and results in a standard way, so as to enable consumers to make comparisons.

4.4   Survey Instruments

Written user surveys are a familiar, inexpensive, and generally acceptable companion for usability tests and expert reviews. Managers and users can easily grasp the notion of surveys, and the typically large numbers of respondents (hundreds to thousands of users) offer a sense of authority compared to the potentially biased and highly variable results from small numbers of usability-test participants or expert reviewers. The keys to successful surveys are clear goals in advance and development of focused items that help to attain those goals. Experienced surveyors know that care is also needed during administration and data analysis (Oppenheim, 1992).

A survey form should be prepared, reviewed by colleagues, and tested with a small sample of users before a large-scale survey is conducted. Methods of statistical analysis (beyond means and standard deviations) and presentation (histograms, scatterplots, and so on) should also be developed before the final survey is distributed. In short, directed activities are more successful than unplanned statistics-gathering expeditions. Our experience is that directed activities also seem to provide the most fertile frameworks for unanticipated discoveries. Since biased samples of respondents can produce erroneous results, survey planners need to build in methods to verify that respondents represent the population in terms of age, gender, experience, and so on.

Survey goals can be tied to the components of the OAI model of interface design (see Section 2.5). That is, users can be asked for their subjective impressions about specific aspects of the interface, such as the representation of

- Task domain objects and actions
- Interface domain metaphors and action handles
- Syntax of inputs and design of displays

Other goals would be to ascertain the user's

- Background (age, gender, origins, education, income)
- Experience with computers (specific applications or software packages, length of time, depth of knowledge)
- Job responsibilities (decision-making influence, managerial roles, motivation)
- Personality style (introvert versus extrovert, risk taking versus risk averse, early versus late adopter, systematic versus opportunistic)
- Reasons for not using an interface (inadequate services, too complex, too slow)
- Familiarity with features (printing, macros, shortcuts, tutorials)
- Feelings after using an interface (confused versus clear, frustrated versus in control, bored versus excited)

Online and web-based surveys avoid the cost and effort of printing, distributing, and collecting paper forms. Many people prefer to answer a brief survey displayed on a screen instead of filling in and returning a printed form, although there is a potential bias in the self-selected sample. Some surveys of World Wide Web utilization include more than 50,000 respondents. Survey companies such as Nielsen NetRatings and Knowledge Networks produce high-quality results by collecting demographic data and automated logging of web use sessions.

In one survey (Gefen and Straub, 2000), e-commerce users were asked to respond to five statements according to the following commonly used scale:

Strongly agree   Agree   Neutral   Disagree   Strongly disagree

The items in the survey were these:

- Improves my performance in book searching and buying
- Enables me to search and buy books faster
- Enhances my effectiveness in book searching and buying
- Makes it easier to search for and purchase books
- Increases my productivity in searching and purchasing books

Such a list of questions can help designers to identify problems users are having and to demonstrate improvement to the interface as changes are made in training, online assistance, command structures, and so on; progress is demonstrated by improved scores on subsequent surveys.

Coleman and Williges (1985) developed a set of bipolar semantically anchored items (pleasing versus irritating, simple versus complicated, concise versus redundant) that asked users to describe their reactions to using a word processor. In one of our pilot studies of error messages in text-editor usage, users had to rate the messages on 1-to-7 scales:

Hostile	1 2 3 4 5 6 7	Friendly
Vague	1 2 3 4 5 6 7	Specific
Misleading	1 2 3 4 5 6 7	Beneficial
Discouraging	1 2 3 4 5 6 7	Encouraging

Another approach is to ask users to evaluate aspects of the interface design, such as the readability of characters, the meaningfulness of command names, or the helpfulness of error messages. If users rate as poor one aspect of the interactive system, the designers have a clear indication of what needs to be redone. If precise—as opposed to general—questions are used in surveys, there is a greater chance that the results will provide useful guidance for taking action.

The *Questionnaire for User Interaction Satisfaction* (QUIS) was developed by Shneiderman and refined by Chin, Diehl, and Norman (1988) (http://www.lap.umd.edu/quis). It was based on the early versions of the OAI model and therefore covered interface details, such as readability of characters and layout of displays; interface objects, such as meaningfulness of icons; interface actions, such as shortcuts for frequent users; and task issues, such as appropriate terminology and screen sequencing. It has proved useful in demonstrating the benefits of improvements to a videodisc-retrieval program, in comparing two programming environments, in assessing word processors, and in setting requirements for redesign of an online public-access library catalog. We have since applied QUIS in many projects with thousands of users and have created new versions that include items relating to web-site design and videoconferencing. The University of Maryland Office of Technology Commercialization licenses QUIS in electronic and paper forms to hundreds of organizations internationally, with special licensing terms for student researchers. The licensees sometimes use only parts of QUIS or extend its domain-specific items.

Table 4.1 contains the long form, which was designed to have two levels of questions: general and detailed. If participants are willing to respond to every item, then the long-form questionnaire can be used. If participants are not likely to be patient, then only the general questions in the short form need to be asked.

Identification number: _____ System: _____ Age: _____ Gender: __ male __ female

PART 1: System Experience

1.1 How long have you worked on this system?

____ less than 1 hour   ____ 6 months to less than 1 year

____ 1 hour to less than 1 day   ____ 1 year to less than 2 years

____ 1 day to less than 1 week   ____ 2 years to less than 3 years

____ 1 week to less than 1 month   ____ 3 years or more

____ 1 month to less than 6 months

1.2 On the average, how much time do you spend per week on this system?

____ less than one hour   ____ 4 to less than 10 hours

____ one to less than 4 hours   ____ over 10 hours

PART 2: Past Experience

2.1 How many operating systems have you worked with?

____ none   ____ 3–4

____ 1   ____ 5–6

____ 2   ____ more than 6

2.2 Of the following devices, software, and systems, check those that you have personally used and are familiar with:

____ computer terminal	____ personal computer	____ lap top computer
____ color monitor	____ touch screen	____ floppy drive
____ CD-ROM drive	____ keyboard	____ mouse
____ track ball	____ joy stick	____ pen based computing
____ graphics tablet	____ head mounted display	____ modems
____ scanners	____ word processor	____ graphics software
____ spreadsheet software	____ database software	____ computer games
____ voice recognition	____ video editing systems	____ internet
____ CAD computer aided design	____ rapid prototyping systems	____ e-mail

Table 4.1

Questionnaire for User Interaction Satisfaction (© University of Maryland, 1997)

PART 3: Overall User Reactions

Please circle the numbers which most appropriately reflect your impressions about using this computer system. Not Applicable = NA.

3.1   Overall reactions to the system: terrible   wonderful
                                                 1 2 3 4 5 6 7 8 9   NA

3.2   frustrating   satisfying
                                                 1 2 3 4 5 6 7 8 9   NA

3.3   dull   stimulating
                                                 1 2 3 4 5 6 7 8 9   NA

3.4   difficult   easy
                                                 1 2 3 4 5 6 7 8 9   NA

3.5   inadequate power   adequate power
                                                 1 2 3 4 5 6 7 8 9   NA

3.6   rigid   flexible
                                                 1 2 3 4 5 6 7 8 9   NA

PART 4: Screen

4.1   Characters on the computer screen   hard to read   easy to read
                                                 1 2 3 4 5 6 7 8 9   NA

    4.1.1 Image of characters   fuzzy   sharp
                                                 1 2 3 4 5 6 7 8 9   NA

    4.1.2 Character shapes (fonts)   barely legible   very legible
                                                 1 2 3 4 5 6 7 8 9   NA

4.2   Highlighting on the screen   unhelpful   helpful
                                                 1 2 3 4 5 6 7 8 9   NA

    4.2.1 Use of reverse video   unhelpful   helpful
                                                 1 2 3 4 5 6 7 8 9   NA

    4.2.2 Use of blinking   unhelpful   helpful
                                                 1 2 3 4 5 6 7 8 9   NA

    4.2.3 Use of bolding   unhelpful   helpful
                                                 1 2 3 4 5 6 7 8 9   NA

4.3   Screen layouts were helpful   never   always
                                                 1 2 3 4 5 6 7 8 9   NA

    4.3.1 Amount of information that   inadequate   adequate
       can be displayed on screen   1 2 3 4 5 6 7 8 9   NA

    4.3.2 Arrangement of information   illogical   logical
       can be displayed on screen   1 2 3 4 5 6 7 8 9   NA

Table 4.1

(continued)

4.4	Sequence of screens	confusing	clear	
		1 2 3 4 5 6 7 8 9		NA
	4.4.1 Next screen in a sequence	unpredictable	predictable	
		1 2 3 4 5 6 7 8 9		NA
	4.4.2 Going back to the previous screen	impossible	easy	
		1 2 3 4 5 6 7 8 9		NA
	4.4.3 Progression of work related tasks	confusing	clearly marked	
		1 2 3 4 5 6 7 8 9		NA

Please write your comments about the screens here:

PART 5: Terminology and System Information

5.1	Use of terminology throughout system	inconsistent	consistent	
		1 2 3 4 5 6 7 8 9		NA
	5.1.2 Work related terminology	inconsistent	consistent	
		1 2 3 4 5 6 7 8 9		NA
	5.2.3 Computer terminology	inconsistent	consistent	
		1 2 3 4 5 6 7 8 9		NA
5.2	Terminology relates well to the work you are doing?	never	always	
		1 2 3 4 5 6 7 8 9		NA
	5.2.1 Computer terminology is used	too frequently	appropriately	
		1 2 3 4 5 6 7 8 9		NA
	5.2.2 Terminology on the screen	ambiguous	precise	
		1 2 3 4 5 6 7 8 9		NA
5.3	Messages which appear on screen	inconsistent	consistent	
		1 2 3 4 5 6 7 8 9		NA
	5.3.1 Position of instructions on the screen	inconsistent	consistent	
		1 2 3 4 5 6 7 8 9		NA
5.4	Messages which appear on screen	confusing	clear	
		1 2 3 4 5 6 7 8 9		NA
	5.4.1 Instructions for commands or functions	confusing	clear	
		1 2 3 4 5 6 7 8 9		NA
	5.4.2 Instructions for correcting errors	confusing	clear	
		1 2 3 4 5 6 7 8 9		NA
5.5	Computer keeps you informed about what it is doing	never	always	
		1 2 3 4 5 6 7 8 9		NA
	5.5.1 Animated cursors keep you informed	never	always	
		1 2 3 4 5 6 7 8 9		NA

Table 4.1

(continued)

5.5.2 Performing an operation leads to a predictable result	never 1 2 3 4 5 6 7 8 9	always	NA
5.5.3 Controlling amount of feedback	impossible 1 2 3 4 5 6 7 8 9	easy	NA
5.5.4 Length of delay between operations	unacceptable 1 2 3 4 5 6 7 8 9	acceptable	NA
5.6 Error messages	unhelpful 1 2 3 4 5 6 7 8 9	helpful	NA
5.6.1 Error messages clarify the problem	never 1 2 3 4 5 6 7 8 9	always	NA
5.6.2 Phrasing of error messages	unpleasant 1 2 3 4 5 6 7 8 9	pleasant	NA

Please write your comments about terminology and system information here:

PART 6: Learning

6.1 Learning to operate the system	difficult 1 2 3 4 5 6 7 8 9	easy	NA
6.1.1 Getting started	difficult 1 2 3 4 5 6 7 8 9	easy	NA
6.1.2 Learning advanced features	difficult 1 2 3 4 5 6 7 8 9	easy	NA
6.1.3 Time to learn to use the system	difficult 1 2 3 4 5 6 7 8 9	easy	NA
6.2 Exploration of features by trial and error	discouraging 1 2 3 4 5 6 7 8 9	encouraging	NA
6.2.1 Exploration of features	risky 1 2 3 4 5 6 7 8 9	safe	NA
6.2.2 Discovering new features	difficult 1 2 3 4 5 6 7 8 9	easy	NA
6.3 Remembering names and use of commands	difficult 1 2 3 4 5 6 7 8 9	easy	NA
6.3.1 Remembering specific rules about entering commands	difficult 1 2 3 4 5 6 7 8 9	easy	NA
6.4 Tasks can be performed in a straight-forward manner	never 1 2 3 4 5 6 7 8 9	always	NA
6.4.1 Number of steps per task	too many 1 2 3 4 5 6 7 8 9	just right	NA

Table 4.1

(continued)

6.4.2 Steps to complete a task follow
a logical sequence

never   always
1 2 3 4 5 6 7 8 9   NA

6.4.3 Feedback on the completion of
sequence of steps

unclear   clear
1 2 3 4 5 6 7 8 9   NA

Please write your comments about learning here:

PART 7: System Capabilities

7.1   System speed

too slow   fast enough
1 2 3 4 5 6 7 8 9   NA

7.1.1 Response time for most operations

too slow   fast enough
1 2 3 4 5 6 7 8 9   NA

7.1.2 Rate information is displayed

too slow   fast enough
1 2 3 4 5 6 7 8 9   NA

7.2   The system is reliable

never   always
1 2 3 4 5 6 7 8 9   NA

7.2.1 Operations

undependable   dependable
1 2 3 4 5 6 7 8 9   NA

7.2.2 System failures occur

frequently   seldom
1 2 3 4 5 6 7 8 9   NA

7.2.3 System warns you about
potential problems

never   always
1 2 3 4 5 6 7 8 9   NA

7.3   System tends to be

noisy   quiet
1 2 3 4 5 6 7 8 9   NA

7.3.1 Mechanical devices such as
fans, disks, and printers

noisy   quiet
1 2 3 4 5 6 7 8 9   NA

7.3.2 Computer generated sounds

annoying   pleasant
1 2 3 4 5 6 7 8 9   NA

7.4   Correcting your mistakes

difficult   easy
1 2 3 4 5 6 7 8 9   NA

7.4.1 Correcting typos

complex   simple
1 2 3 4 5 6 7 8 9   NA

7.4.2 Ability to undo operations

inadequate   adequate
1 2 3 4 5 6 7 8 9   NA

7.5   Ease of operation depends on your
level of experience

never   always
1 2 3 4 5 6 7 8 9   NA

Table 4.1

(continued)

7.5.1 You can accomplish tasks knowing only a few commands	with difficulty	easily	
	1 2 3 4 5 6 7 8 9		NA
7.5.2 You can use features/shortcuts	with difficulty	easily	
	1 2 3 4 5 6 7 8 9		NA

Please write your comments about system capabilities here:

PART 8: User Manuals and On-line help

8.1 Technical manuals are	confusing	clear	
	1 2 3 4 5 6 7 8 9		NA
8.1.1 The terminology used in the	confusing	clear	
	1 2 3 4 5 6 7 8 9		NA
8.2 Information from the manual is easily understood	never	always	
	1 2 3 4 5 6 7 8 9		NA
8.2.1 Finding a solution to a problem using the manual	impossible	easy	
	1 2 3 4 5 6 7 8 9		NA
8.3 Amount of help given	inadequate	adequate	
	1 2 3 4 5 6 7 8 9		NA
8.3.1 Placement of help messages on the screen	confusing	clear	
	1 2 3 4 5 6 7 8 9		NA
8.3.2 Accessing help messages	difficult	easy	
	1 2 3 4 5 6 7 8 9		NA
8.3.3 Content of on-line help messages	confusing	clear	
	1 2 3 4 5 6 7 8 9		NA
8.3.4 Amount of help given	inadequate	adequate	
	1 2 3 4 5 6 7 8 9		NA
8.3.5 Help defines specific aspects of the system	inadequately	adequately	
	1 2 3 4 5 6 7 8 9		NA
8.3.6 Finding specific information using the on-line help	difficult	easy	
	1 2 3 4 5 6 7 8 9		NA
8.3.7 On-line help	useless	helpful	
	1 2 3 4 5 6 7 8 9		NA

Please write your comments about technical manuals and on-line help here:

Table 4.1

(continued)

PART 9: On-line Tutorials

9.1 Tutorial was	useless helpful	
	1 2 3 4 5 6 7 8 9	NA
9.1.1 Accessing on-line tutorial	difficult easy	
	1 2 3 4 5 6 7 8 9	NA
9.2 Maneuvering through the tutorial was	difficult easy	
	1 2 3 4 5 6 7 8 9	NA
9.2.1 Tutorial is meaningfully structured	never always	
	1 2 3 4 5 6 7 8 9	NA
9.2.2 The speed of presentation was	unacceptable acceptable	
	1 2 3 4 5 6 7 8 9	NA
9.3 Tutorial content was	useless helpful	
	1 2 3 4 5 6 7 8 9	NA
9.3.1 Information for specific aspects of the system were complete and informative	never always	
	1 2 3 4 5 6 7 8 9	NA
9.3.2 Information was concise and to the point	never always	
	1 2 3 4 5 6 7 8 9	NA
9.4 Tasks can be completed	with difficulty easily	
	1 2 3 4 5 6 7 8 9	NA
9.4.1 Instructions given for completing tasks	confusing clear	
	1 2 3 4 5 6 7 8 9	NA
9.4.2 Time given to perform tasks	inadequate adequate	
	1 2 3 4 5 6 7 8 9	NA
9.5 Learning to operate the system using the tutorial was	difficult easy	
	1 2 3 4 5 6 7 8 9	NA
9.5.1 Completing system tasks after using only the tutorial	difficult easy	
	1 2 3 4 5 6 7 8 9	NA

Please write your comments about on-line tutorials here:

PART 10: Multimedia

10.1 Quality of still pictures/photographs	bad good	
	1 2 3 4 5 6 7 8 9	NA
10.1.1 Pictures/Photos	fuzzy clear	
	1 2 3 4 5 6 7 8 9	NA
10.1.2 Picture/Photo brightness	dim bright	
	1 2 3 4 5 6 7 8 9	NA

Table 4.1

(continued)

10.2 Quality of movies	bad	good	
	1 2 3 4 5 6 7 8 9		NA
10.2.1 Focus of movie images	fuzzy	clear	
	1 2 3 4 5 6 7 8 9		NA
10.2.2 Brightness of movie images	dim	bright	
	1 2 3 4 5 6 7 8 9		NA
10.2.3 Movie window size is adequate	never	always	
	1 2 3 4 5 6 7 8 9		NA
10.3 Sound output	inaudible	audible	
	1 2 3 4 5 6 7 8 9		NA
10.3.1 Sound output	choppy	smooth	
	1 2 3 4 5 6 7 8 9		NA
10.3.2 Sound output	garbled	clear	
	1 2 3 4 5 6 7 8 9		NA
10.4 Colors used are	unnatural	natural	
	1 2 3 4 5 6 7 8 9		NA
10.4.1 Amount of colors available	inadequate	adequate	
	1 2 3 4 5 6 7 8 9		NA

Please write your comments about multimedia here:

PART 11: Teleconferencing

11.1 Setting up for conference	difficult	easy	
	1 2 3 4 5 6 7 8 9		NA
11.1.1 Time for establishing the connections to others	too long	just right	
	1 2 3 4 5 6 7 8 9		NA
11.1.2 Number of connections possible	too few	enough	
	1 2 3 4 5 6 7 8 9		NA
11.2 Arrangement of windows showing connecting groups	confusing	clear	
	1 2 3 4 5 6 7 8 9		NA
11.2.1 Window with view of your own group is of appropriate size	never	always	
	1 2 3 4 5 6 7 8 9		NA
11.2.2 Window(s) with view of connecting group(s) is of appropriate size	never	always	
	1 2 3 4 5 6 7 8 9		NA
11.3 Determining the focus of attention during conference was	confusing	clear	
	1 2 3 4 5 6 7 8 9		NA

Table 4.1

(continued)

11.3.1 Telling who is speaking	difficult	easy	
	1 2 3 4 5 6 7 8 9		NA
11.4 Video image flow	choppy	smooth	
	1 2 3 4 5 6 7 8 9		NA
11.4.1 Focus of video image	fuzzy	clear	
	1 2 3 4 5 6 7 8 9		NA
11.5 Audio output	inaudible	audible	
	1 2 3 4 5 6 7 8 9		NA
11.5.1 Audio is in sync with video images	never	always	
	1 2 3 4 5 6 7 8 9		NA
11.6 Exchanging data	difficult	easy	
	1 2 3 4 5 6 7 8 9		NA
11.6.1 Transmitting files	difficult	easy	
	1 2 3 4 5 6 7 8 9		NA
11.6.2 Retrieving files	difficult	easy	
	1 2 3 4 5 6 7 8 9		NA
11.6.3 Using on-line chat	difficult	easy	
	1 2 3 4 5 6 7 8 9		NA
11.6.4 Using shared workspace	difficult	easy	
	1 2 3 4 5 6 7 8 9		NA

Please write your comments about teleconferencing here:

PART 12: Software Installation

12.1 Speed of installation	slow	fast	
	1 2 3 4 5 6 7 8 9		NA
12.2 Customization	difficult	easy	
	1 2 3 4 5 6 7 8 9		NA
12.2.1 Installing only the software	confusing	clear	
	1 2 3 4 5 6 7 8 9		NA
12.3 Informs you of its progress	never	always	
	1 2 3 4 5 6 7 8 9		NA
12.4 Gives a meaningful explanation when failures occur	never	always	
	1 2 3 4 5 6 7 8 9		NA

Please write your comments about software installation here:

Table 4.1

(continued)

Other scales include the Post-Study System Usability Questionnaire, developed by IBM, which has 48 items that focus on system usefulness, information quality, and interface quality (Lewis, 1995); the Software Usability Measurement Inventory, which contains 50 items designed to measure users' perceptions of their effect, efficiency, and control (Kirakowski and Corbett, 1993); and the WAMMI Web Usability Questionnaire, which does web-based evaluations and is available in more than a dozen languages.

4 . 5   Acceptance Tests

For large implementation projects, the customer or manager usually sets objective and measurable goals for hardware and software performance. Many authors of requirements documents are even so bold as to specify mean time between failures, as well as the mean time to repair for hardware and, in some cases, software failures. More typically, a set of test cases is specified for the software, with possible response-time requirements for the hardware/software combination. If the completed product fails to meet these acceptance criteria, the system must be reworked until success is demonstrated.

These notions can be neatly extended to the human interface. Explicit acceptance criteria should be established when the requirements document is written or when a contract is offered. Rather than using the vague and misleading criterion of "user friendly," measurable criteria for the user interface can be established for the following:

- Time for users to learn specific functions
- Speed of task performance
- Rate of errors by users
- User retention of commands over time
- Subjective user satisfaction

An acceptance test for a food-shopping web site might specify the following:

> The participants will be 35 adults (25–45 years old), native speakers with no disabilities, hired from an employment agency. They have moderate web-use experience: 1–5 hours/week for at least a year. They will be given a 5-minute demonstration on the basic features. At least 30 of the 35 adults should be able to complete the benchmark tasks, within 30 minutes.

Another testable requirement for the same interface might be this:

> Special participants in three categories will also be tested: (a) 10 older adults aged 55–65; (b) 10 adult users with varying motor, visual, and auditory dis-

abilities; and (c) 10 adult users who are recent immigrants and use English as a second language.

Since the choice of the benchmark tasks is critical, the materials and procedures must be refined by pilot testing. A third item in the acceptance test plan might focus on retention:

> Ten participants will be recalled after one week, and asked to carry out a new set of benchmark tasks. In 20 minutes, at least 8 of the participants should be able to complete the tasks correctly.

In a large interface, there may be 8 or 10 such tests to carry out on different components of the interface and with different user communities. Other criteria, such as subjective satisfaction, output comprehensibility, system response time, installation procedures, printed documentation, or graphics appeal, may also be considered in acceptance tests of complete commercial products.

If precise acceptance criteria are established, both the customer and the interface developer can benefit. Arguments about user friendliness are avoided, and contractual fulfillment can be demonstrated objectively. Acceptance tests differ from usability tests in that the atmosphere may be adversarial, so outside testing organizations are often appropriate to ensure neutrality. The central goal of acceptance testing is not to detect flaws, but rather to verify adherence to requirements.

After successful acceptance testing, there may be a period of field testing before national or international distribution. In addition to further refining the user interface, field tests can improve training methods, tutorial materials, telephone-help procedures, marketing methods, and publicity strategies.

The goal of early expert reviews, usability testing, surveys, acceptance testing, and field testing is to force as much as possible of the evolutionary development into the prerelease phase, when change is relatively easy and inexpensive to accomplish.

4.6   Evaluation During Active Use

A carefully designed and thoroughly tested interface is a wonderful asset, but successful active use requires constant attention from dedicated managers, user-service personnel, and maintenance staff. Everyone involved in supporting the user community can contribute to interface refinements that provide ever higher levels of service. You cannot please all of the users all of the time, but earnest effort will be rewarded by the appreciation of a grateful user community. Perfection is not attainable, but percentage improvements are possible and are worth pursuing.

Gradual interface dissemination is useful so that problems can be repaired with minimal disruption. As more and more people use the interface, major changes should be limited to an announced annual or semiannual interface revision. If interface users can anticipate the change, then resistance will be reduced, especially if they have positive expectations of improvement. More frequent changes are expected in the rapidly developing World Wide Web environment, but stable access to key resources even as novel services are added may be the winning policy.

4.6.1   Interviews and focus-group discussions

Interviews with individual users can be productive because the interviewer can pursue specific issues of concern. After a series of individual discussions, focus-group discussions are valuable to ascertain the universality of comments (Kuhn, 2000). Interviewing can be costly and time-consuming, so usually only a small fraction of the user community is involved. On the other hand, direct contact with users often leads to specific, constructive suggestions. Professionally led focus groups can elicit surprising patterns of usage or hidden problems, which can be quickly explored and confirmed by participants. On the other hand, outspoken individuals can sway the group or dismiss comments from weaker participants.

A large corporation conducted 45-minute interviews with 66 of the 4,300 users of an internal message system. The interviews revealed that the users were happy with some aspects of the functionality, such as the capacity to pick up messages at any site, the legibility of printed messages, and the convenience of after-hours access. However, the interviews also revealed that 23.6% of the users had concerns about reliability, 20.2% thought that using the system was confusing, and 18.2% said convenience and accessibility could be improved, whereas only 16.0% expressed no concerns. Later questions in the interview explored specific features. As a result of this interview project, a set of 42 enhancements to the interface was proposed and implemented. The designers of the interface had earlier proposed an alternate set of enhancements, but the results of the interviews led to a changed set of priorities that more closely reflected the users' needs.

4.6.2   Continuous user-performance data logging

The software architecture should make it easy for system managers to collect data about the patterns of interface usage, speed of user performance, rate of errors, or frequency of requests for online assistance. Logging data provide guidance in the acquisition of new hardware, changes in operating procedures, improvements to training, plans for system expansion, and so on.

For example, if the frequency of each error message is recorded, the highest-frequency error is a candidate for attention. The message could be rewritten, training materials could be revised, the software could be changed to provide more specific information, or the command syntax could be simplified. Without specific logging data, however, the system-maintenance staff has no way of knowing which of the many hundreds of error-message situations is the biggest problem for users. Similarly, staff should examine messages that never appear, to see whether there is an error in the code or whether users are avoiding use of some facility.

If logging data are available for each command, each help screen, and each database record, changes to the human-computer interface can be made to simplify access to frequently used features. For example, logging of the THOMAS system for access to U.S. Congress legislation revealed high-frequency terms, such as *abortion, gun control,* and *balanced budget,* that could be used in a browse list of hot topics (Croft, Cook, and Wilder 1995). Managers also should examine unused or rarely used facilities to understand why users are avoiding those features.

A major benefit of usage-frequency data is the guidance that they provide to system maintainers in optimizing performance and in reducing costs for all participants. This latter argument may yield the clearest advantage to cost-conscious managers, whereas the increased quality of the interface is an attraction to service-oriented managers.

Logging may be well intentioned, but users' rights to privacy deserve to be protected. Links to specific user names should not be collected unless necessary. When logging aggregate performance crosses over to monitoring individual activity, managers must inform users of what is being monitored and how the information will be used. Although organizations may have a right to ascertain workers' performance levels, workers should be able to view the results and to discuss the implications. If monitoring is surreptitious and is later discovered, resulting worker mistrust of management could be more damaging than the benefits of the collected data. Manager and worker cooperation to improve productivity, and worker participation in the process and benefits, are advised.

Commercial services such as Nielsen NetRatings and Knowledge Networks are making a success of providing clients with log data and analyses of web visits from their panels of users. These users have provided their demographic information and are paid to answer surveys or allow their web visitation patterns to be logged. The purchasers of data are interested to know what kinds of people buy books, visit news sites, or seek healthcare information, so as to guide their marketing, product development, and web-site design.

4.6.3   Online or telephone consultants

Online or telephone consultants can provide extremely effective and personal assistance to users who are experiencing difficulties. Many users feel reassured if they know that there is a human being to whom they can turn when problems arise. These consultants are an excellent source of information about problems users are having and can suggest improvements and potential extensions.

Many organizations offer toll-free numbers via which the users can reach a knowledgeable consultant; others charge for consultation by the minute. On some network systems, the consultants can monitor the user's computer and see the same displays that the user sees while maintaining telephone voice contact. This service can be extremely reassuring: Users know that someone can walk them through the correct sequence of displays to complete their tasks.

America Online provides live (real-time) chat rooms for discussion of user problems. Users can type their questions and get responses promptly. Many groups maintain a standard electronic-mail address of staff@<organization> that allows users to get help from whomever is on duty. Such services help users, build customer loyalty, and provide insights that can lead to design refinements as well as novel product extensions.

4.6.4   Online suggestion box or e-mail trouble reporting

Electronic mail can be employed to allow users to send messages to the maintainers or designers. Such an *online suggestion box* encourages some users to make productive comments, since writing a letter may be seen as requiring too much effort.

A Library of Congress web site that invites comments gets 10 to 20 per day, including thoughtful ones such as this:

> I find as I get searching through the various Web pages… that I am left with an unsatisfied feeling. I have been sitting in front of the PC for close to an hour… and have been stopped and/or slowed due to items that can be directly related to web server design.
>
> First off, the entry pages are too big and disorganized. Those links that do exist do not have adequate enough descriptions to direct a user to the information they desire. In addition, the use of a search engine would greatly facilitate sifting through the abundance of information that is thrown at the user with any one of these links. Links should be short, sweet, and specific. Large amounts of material should not be included in one document on a busy server. . . .
>
> Breaking up these larger documents into smaller, well organized documents may seem to create an additional burden on programming. However, if intelligence is used in the creation of such systems, it would not take much….

In fact, the search engine that this user wanted was available, but he could not find it, and larger documents were broken into smaller segments. A reply helped to get this user what he was seeking, and his message also led to design changes that made the interface features more visible.

Web-based error reporting schemes are growing in popularity. Netscape's Quality Feedback System, Microsoft's Dr. Watson, and Bugtoaster are programs that automatically file reports after a crash. Bugtoaster's public summary of the results covers more than half a million incidents, organized by operating system and application. Their staff approaches the software developers to request or pressure for bug fixes and guides corporate administrators in how to reduce problems.

Suggestion boxes and complaint facilities are becoming common in web sites for organizations that are eager to provide high levels of customer support. Microsoft's Feedback page requests suggestions in these categories: installation or deployment, ease of use, customization or preferences, interoperability or integration, security, performance, networking or connectivity, help and documentation, accessibility, and localization. User bug reports have also gained popularity in the open-source community with web-based tools such as Bugzilla.

4.6.5   Discussion groups and newsgroups

Some users may have questions about the suitability of a software package for their application, or may be seeking someone who has had experience using an interface feature. They do not have any individual in mind, so e-mail does not serve their needs. Many interface designers and web-site managers offer users discussion groups or newsgroups (see Section 10.3) to permit posting of open messages and questions. More independent (and controversial) discussion groups are hosted by services such as America Online, Yahoo! Groups, and Microsoft Network.

Discussion groups usually offer lists of item headlines, allowing users to scan items for relevant topics. New items can be added by anyone, but usually someone moderates the discussion to ensure that offensive, useless, or repetitious items are removed. When there are a substantial number of users who are geographically dispersed, moderators may have to work hard to create a sense of community.

Personal relationships established by face-to-face meetings also increase the sense of community among users. Ultimately, it is the people who matter, and human needs for social interaction should be satisfied. Every technical system is also a social system that needs to be encouraged and nurtured.

By soliciting user feedback in any of these ways, managers can gauge user attitudes and elicit useful suggestions. Furthermore, users may have more positive attitudes towards interfaces or web services if they see that the managers genuinely desire comments and suggestions.

4.7   Controlled Psychologically Oriented Experiments

Scientific and engineering progress is often stimulated by improved techniques for precise measurement. Rapid progress in the designs of interfaces will be stimulated as researchers and practitioners evolve suitable human-performance measures and techniques. We have come to expect that automobiles will have miles-per-gallon reports pasted to their windows, appliances will have energy-efficiency ratings, and textbooks will be given grade-level designations; soon, we will expect software packages to show learning-time estimates and user-satisfaction indices from appropriate evaluation sources.

Academic and industrial researchers are discovering that the power of the traditional scientific method can be fruitfully employed in the study of interfaces. They are conducting numerous experiments that are uncovering basic design principles. The outline of the scientific method as applied to human-computer interaction might include these tasks:

- Deal with a practical problem and consider the theoretical framework.
- State a lucid and testable hypothesis.
- Identify a small number of independent variables that are to be manipulated.
- Carefully choose the dependent variables that will be measured.
- Judiciously select participants, and carefully or randomly assign participants to groups.
- Control for biasing factors (nonrepresentative sample of participants or selection of tasks, inconsistent testing procedures).
- Apply statistical methods to data analysis.
- Resolve the practical problem, refine the theory, and give advice to future researchers.

The classic experimental methods of psychology are being enhanced to deal with the complex cognitive tasks of human performance with information and computer systems. The transformation from Aristotelian introspection to Galilean experimentation that took two millennia in physics is being accomplished in two decades in the study of human-computer interaction.

The reductionist approach required for controlled experimentation yields narrow but reliable results. Through multiple replications with similar tasks, participants, and experimental conditions, reliability and validity can be enhanced. Each small experimental result acts like a tile in the mosaic of human performance with computer-based information systems.

Managers of actively used systems are also coming to recognize the power of controlled experiments in fine-tuning the human-computer interface. As proposals are made for new menu structures, novel cursor-control devices, and reorganized display formats, a carefully controlled experiment can provide data to support a management decision. Fractions of the user population can be given proposed improvements for a limited time, and then performance can be compared with the control group. Dependent measures may include performance times, user-subjective satisfaction, error rates, and user retention over time.

For example, the competition over mobile device input methods has led to numerous experimental studies of keyboard arrangements, with similar training methods, standard benchmark tasks, common dependent measures that account for error rates, and strategies for testing frequent users. Such careful controls are necessary because a 10-minute reduction in learning time, a 10% speed increase, or 10 fewer errors could be a vital advantage in a competitive consumer market.

Experimental design and statistical analysis are complex topics (Runyon et al., 1996; Cozby, 2000; Elmes, Kantowitz, and Roediger, 2002). Novice experimenters would be well advised to collaborate with experienced social scientists and statisticians.

Practitioner's Summary

Interface developers evaluate their designs by conducting expert reviews, usability tests, surveys, and rigorous acceptance tests. Once interfaces are released, developers perform continuous performance evaluations by interviews or surveys, or by logging users' performance in a way that respects their privacy. If you are not measuring user performance, you are not focusing on usability!

Successful interface project managers understand that they must work hard to establish a relationship of trust with the user community. As markets are opened, (for example, in another country or vertical market segment), managers have to start fresh in gaining recognition and customer loyalty. Special attention may need to be devoted to novice users and users with disabilities. In addition to providing a properly functioning system, successful managers recognize the need to create social mechanisms for feedback, such as online surveys, interviews, discussion groups, consultants, suggestion boxes, newsletters, and conferences.

Researcher's Agenda

Researchers can contribute their experience with experimentation to develop improved techniques for interface evaluation. Guidance in conducting pilot studies, acceptance tests, surveys, interviews, and discussions would benefit commercial development groups. Strategies are needed to cope with evaluation for the numerous specific populations of users and the diverse forms of disabilities that users may have. Experts in constructing psychological tests can help in preparing validated and reliable test instruments for subjective evaluation of web-based, desktop, and mobile interfaces. Such standardized tests would allow independent groups to compare the acceptability of interfaces. Would benchmark data sets and task libraries help standardize evaluation? How useful can researchers make automated testing against requirements documents? How can life-critical applications for experienced professionals be tested reliably?

Psychotherapists and social workers could contribute to training online or telephone consultants—after all, helping troubled users is a human-relationships issue. Finally, more input from experimental, cognitive, and clinical psychologists would help computer specialists to recognize the importance of the human aspects of computer use. Can psychological principles be applied to reduce novice users' anxiety or expert users' frustration? Could profiles of users' skill levels with interfaces be helpful in job-placement and training programs?

WORLD WIDE WEB RESOURCES

Prototyping and usability-testing methods are covered, with some information on evaluation methods such as surveys.

http://www.aw.com/DTUI

References

Blackmon, M.H., Polson, P.G., Kitajima, M., and Lewis, C., Design methods: Cognitive walkthrough for the Web, *Proc. CHI 2002: Human Factors in Computing Systems*, ACM, New York (2002), 463–470.

Chin, John P., Diehl, Virginia A., and Norman, Kent L., Development of an instrument measuring user satisfaction of the human-computer interface, *Proc. CHI '88: Human Factors in Computing Systems*, ACM, New York (1988), 213–218.

Coleman, William D. and Williges, Robert C., Collecting detailed user evaluations of software interfaces, *Proc. Human Factors Society: Twenty-Ninth Annual Meeting*, Santa Monica, CA (1985), 204–244.

Cozby, Paul C., *Methods in Behavioral Research, Seventh Edition*, McGraw-Hill, New York (2000).

Croft, W. Bruce, Cook, Robert, and Wilder, Dean, Providing government information on the Internet: Experiences with THOMAS, *Proc. Digital Libraries '95 Conference*, ACM, New York (1995). Also available at http://www.csdl.tamu.edu/DL95/papers/croft/croft.html.

Dumas, Joseph and Redish, Janice, *A Practical Guide to Usability Testing, Revised Edition*, Intellect Books, Bristol, U.K. (1999).

Elmes, David G., Kantowitz, Barry H., and Roediger, Henry L., *Research Methods in Psychology, Seventh Edition*, Wadsworth Publishing, Belmont, CA (2002).

Gefen, David and Straub, Detmar, The relative importance of perceived ease of use in IS adoption: A study of e-commerce adoption, *Journal of the Association for Information Systems*, 1, 8 (October 2000), Available at http://jais.isworld.org/articles/default.asp?vol=1&art=8.

Jeffries, R., Miller, J. R., Wharton, C., and Uyeda, K. M., User interface evaluation in the real world: A comparison of four techniques, *Proc. ACM CHI '91 Conf.*, ACM, New York (1991), 119–124.

Karat, Claire-Marie, A business case approach to usability, in Bias, Randolph and Mayhew, Deborah (Editors), *Cost-Justifying Usability*, Academic Press, New York (1994), 45–70.

Karat, Claire-Marie, Campbell, Robert, and Fiegel, T., Comparison of empirical testing and walkthrough methods in user interface evaluation, *Proc. CHI '92: Human Factors in Computing Systems*, ACM, New York (1992), 397–404.

Kirakowski, J. and Corbett, M., SUMI: The Software Usability Measurement Inventory, *British Journal of Educational Technology*, 24, 3 (1993), 210–212.

Kuhn, Klaus, Problems and benefits of requirements gathering with focus groups: A case study, *International Journal of Human-Computer Interaction* 12, 3/4 (2000), 309–325.

Landauer, Thomas K., *The Trouble with Computers: Usefulness, Usability, and Productivity*, MIT Press, Cambridge, MA (1995).

Lewis, James R., IBM computer usability satisfaction questionnaires: Psychometric evaluation and instructions for use, *International Journal of Human-Computer Interaction*, 7, 1 (1995), 57–78.

Nielsen, Jakob (Editor), Special Issue on Usability Laboratories, *Behaviour & Information Technology*, 13, 1 & 2 (January–April 1994).

Nielsen, Jakob, *Usability Engineering*, Academic Press, New York (1993).

Nielsen, Jakob and Mack, Robert (Editors), *Usability Inspection Methods*, John Wiley & Sons, New York (1994).

Oppenheim, Abraham N., *Questionnaire Design, Interviewing, and Attitude Measurement*, Pinter Publishers, New York (1992).

Petersen, Marianne Graves, Madsen, Kim Halskov, and Kjaer, Arne, The usability of everyday technology—Emerging and fading opportunities, *ACM Trans. on Computer Human Interaction*, 9, 2 (June 2002), 74–105.

Preece, Jenny, Rogers, Yvonne, and Sharp, Helen, *Interaction Design: Beyond Human-Computer Interaction*, John Wiley & Sons, New York (2002).

Rubin, Jeffrey, *Handbook of Usability Testing: How to Plan, Design, and Conduct Effective Tests*, John Wiley & Sons, New York (1994).

Runyon, Richard P., Haber, Audrey, Pittenger, David J., and Coleman, Kay A., *Fundamentals of Behavioral Statistics, Eighth Edition*, McGraw-Hill, New York (1996).

Wharton, Cathleen, Rieman, John, Lewis, Clayton, and Polson, Peter, The cognitive walkthrough method: A practitioner's guide, in Nielsen, Jakob and Mack, Robert (Editors), *Usability Inspection Methods*, John Wiley & Sons, New York (1994).

5 Software Tools

There is great satisfaction in building good tools for other people to use.

FREEMAN DYSON
Disturbing the Universe, 1979

written in collaboration with Jean-Daniel Fekete

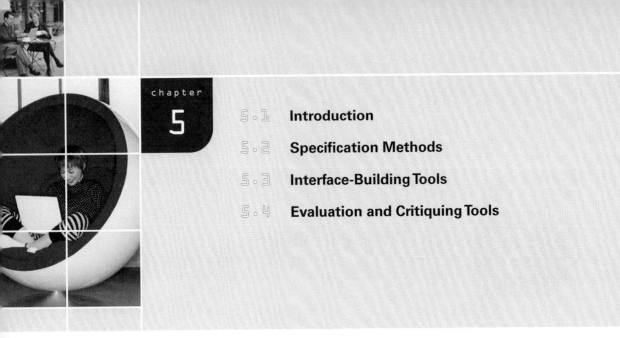

5.1 Introduction

Log cabins were often built by settlers for personal housing on the American frontier, just as early user interfaces were built by programmers for their own use. As housing needs changed, windows and rooms were added in a process of iterative refinement, and dirt floors gave way to finished wood. Log cabins are still being built according to personal taste by rugged individualists, but the building of more complex modern private homes, apartment buildings, schools, hospitals, and offices requires specialist training, careful planning, and special equipment.

The emergence of user-interface architects, design and specification methods, standard components, and automated tools for construction are indicators of the maturation of our field. There will always be room for the innovator and the eccentric, but the demands of modern life require user-interface architects to build reliable, standard, safe, inexpensive, effective, and widely acceptable user interfaces on a predictable schedule (Carey, 1988).

Building and user-interface architects must have simple and quick methods of sketching to give their clients a way to identify needs and preferences. They also need precise methods for working out the details with the clients (detailed floorplans or transition diagrams, screen layouts, and menu trees), for coordinating with specialized colleagues (plumbers and electricians or graphic designers and technical writers), and for telling the craftspeople (builders or software engineers) what to do.

Like building architects, successful user-interface architects know that it makes good sense to complete the design before they start building, even though they know that, in the process of construction, some changes will have to be made. With large projects, multiple designers (structural engineers for the steel framework, interior designers for space planning, and decorators for the esthetics) will be necessary. The size and importance of each project will determine the level of design effort and the number of participants. Just as there are building specialists for airports, hospitals, and schools, there are user-interface specialists for e-commerce, medical, and educational applications.

This chapter begins with user-interface specification methods (Section 5.2), moves to software tools to support design and software engineering (Section 5.3), and then closes with evaluation and critiquing tools (Section 5.4). These tools are increasingly graphical in their user interfaces, enabling designers and programmers to build interfaces rapidly by dragging components and linking functions together. User-interface building tools have matured rapidly in the past few years and have radically changed the nature of software development (Myers, Hudson, and Pausch, 2000). Productivity gains of 50 to 500% above previous methods have been documented for many standard graphical user interfaces (GUIs). But, even as the power tools for established styles improve and gain acceptance, the need remains for programmers to handcraft novel interface styles.

A major development in the field of user-interface design is that the desktop computer is losing its predominance as the primary platform for interactive applications. In addition to the huge and diverse web environment, there are a growing number of interaction-capable machines such as mobile devices, cell phones, pocket PCs, game consoles, auditory interfaces, and appliances with displays. This means that new software tools must support greater plasticity in the interface; users should be able to switch from large to small displays or even to telephone access to web services. Users should also be able to control the window size, fonts, colors, and background, and possibly convert the text to foreign languages. The requirements of universal usability mean that content transformations need to be specified and that device-independent programming is of greater importance. Hopefully, even if the details change in the software tools, the principles will remain stable and valid across all the platforms.

5.2 Specification Methods

The first asset in making designs is a good notation to record and discuss alternate possibilities. The default language for specifications in any field is the designer's natural language, such as English, and the initial specifications are generally drawn up on a sketchpad or blackboard. But *natural-language specifications* tend to be lengthy, vague, and ambiguous, and therefore often are difficult to prove correct, consistent, or complete. *Formal* and *semiformal languages* have proved their value in many areas, including mathematics, physics, circuit design, music, and even knitting. Formal languages have a specified grammar, and effective procedures exist to determine whether a string adheres to the language's grammar. Grammars for command languages are effective, but for graphical user interfaces the amount of syntax for specifying commands is small. In graphical user interfaces, a grammar might be used to describe sequences of actions, but these grammars tend to be short, making transition diagrams and graphical specifications more appealing. Grammars are discussed in detail in Section 5.2.1.

Several other specification methods are also available. *Menu-tree structures* are popular, and therefore specifying menu trees by simply drawing the tree and showing the menu layout deserves attention (Section 5.2.2). The more general method of *transition diagrams* also has wide applicability in user-interface design (Section 5.2.3), while improvements such as *statecharts* (Section 5.2.4) have features that are attuned to the needs of interactive systems, for widget specification and more generally for software behavior modeling

5.2.1   Grammars

Grammars are useful to specify textual commands or expressions that a program should understand. They were necessary with older terminal-based interfaces and are still used on interactive systems that need powerful and extensible symbolic expressions, such as spreadsheet calculators where the values of some cells are computed from others using a combination of mathematical functions. Grammars are also useful to verify the validity of stereotypical computer forms filled in by users, such as telephone-book entries.

In computer programming, *Backus-Naur form* (BNF), also called *Backus normal form*, is often used to describe programming languages. High-level components are described by nonterminals, and specific strings are terminals. Let us use the example of the telephone-book entry. The nonterminals describe a person's name and a telephone number. Names consist of strings of characters: a last name followed by a comma and a first name. The telephone number has three components: a three-digit area code, a three-digit exchange, and a four-digit local number.

```
<Telephone book entry> ::= <Name> <Telephone number>
<Name> ::= <Last name>, <First name>
<Last name> ::= <string>
<First name> ::= <string>
<string> ::= <character>|<character><string>
<character> ::=
   A|B|C|D|E|F|G|H|I|J|K|L|M|N|O|P|Q|R|S|T|U|V|W|X|Y|Z
<Telephone number> ::= (<area code>) <exchange>-<local number>
<area code> ::= <digit><digit><digit>
<exchange> ::= <digit><digit><digit>
<local number> ::= <digit><digit><digit><digit>
<digit> ::= 0|1|2|3|4|5|6|7|8|9
```

The left-hand side of each specification line is a nonterminal (within angle brackets) that is defined by the right-hand side. Vertical bars indicate alternatives for nonterminals and terminals. Acceptable telephone-book entries include the following:

```
WASHINGTON, GEORGE (301) 555-1234
BEEF, STU (726) 768-7878
A, Z (999) 111-1111
```

BNF notation is used widely, even though it is incomplete and must be supplemented by ad-hoc techniques for specifying the semantics, such as permissible names or area codes. The benefits of this technique are that some aspects can be written down precisely and that software tools can be employed to verify some aspects of completeness and correctness of the grammar and of strings in the language. On the other hand, grammars are difficult to follow as they grow and are confusing for many users.

Command languages are nicely specified by BNF-like grammars, such as the task-action grammar (Section 2.4.4). Over the years attempts have been made to extend BNF with strategies for specifying sequences of actions, describing time delays, and accommodating interface actions such as double-clicking and dragging. Other notations have addressed the specification of visual feedback, such as highlighting an icon or opening a folder, but these temporal and visual additions have not caught on in widely used tools.

To accommodate the richness of interactive software, *multiparty grammars* (Shneiderman, 1982) have nonterminals that are labeled by the party that produces the string (typically the user, U, or the computer, C). Nonterminals acquire values during parsing for use by other parties, and therefore error-handling rules can be included easily. This grammar describes the opening steps in a login process:

```
<Session> ::= <U: Opening> <C: Responding>
<U: Opening> ::= LOGIN <U: Name>
<U: Name> ::= <U: string>
<C: Responding> ::= HELLO [<U: Name>]
```

Here, square brackets indicate that the value of the user's name should be produced by the computer in responding to the login command.

Multiparty grammars are effective for text-oriented command sequences that have repeated exchanges, such as at a bank terminal. They are also widely used to specify the grammars recognized by voice-recognition systems (Hunt, 2000). A simple travel command such as "go from Paris to Bangkok and Singapore" can be specified using the following JSpeech grammar, where the list of city names is stored in an external grammar file that defines the "city" nonterminal:

```
import <com.acme.cities.*>;
public <travel> = go from <city> ( to <city> )+;
```

Unfortunately, two-dimensional styles, such as form fillin or direct manipulation and graphical layouts, are more difficult to describe with multiparty grammars. Menu selection can be described by multiparty grammars, but the central aspect of tree structure and traversal is not shown conveniently in a grammar-based approach.

5.2.2   Menu-selection and dialog-box trees

A *menu-selection tree* has a simple structure that guides designers and users alike, making it an excellent selection style for many applications. Guidelines for the contents of menu trees are covered in Chapter 7. Specification methods include online tools to help in the construction of menu trees and simple drawing tools that enable designers and users to see the entire tree at one time.

Menu trees are powerful as a specification tool because they show users, managers, implementers, and other interested parties complete and detailed coverage of the system. Like any map, a menu tree shows high-level relationships and low-level details. With large systems, the menu tree may have to be laid out on a large wall or floor, but it is important to be able to see the entire structure at once to check for consistency, completeness, and lack of ambiguity or redundancy.

Similar comments apply for dialog-box trees. Printing out the dialog boxes and showing their relationships by mounting them on a wall is enormously helpful in gaining an overview of the entire system to check for consistency and completeness.

5.2.3   Transition diagrams

Menu trees are incomplete because they do not show the entire structure of possible user actions, such as returns to the previous menu, jumps to the starting menu, or detours to error handling or help screens. This is intentional, as adding all these transitions would clutter the clean structure of a menu tree. However, for some aspects of the design process, more precise specification of every possible transition is required. Also, for many nonmenu interaction styles, there is a set of possible states and permissible transitions among the states that may not form a tree structure. For these and other circumstances, a more general design notation, known as *transition diagrams*, has been used widely.

Typically, a transition diagram has a set of *nodes* that represent system states and a set of *links* between the nodes that represent possible transitions. Each link is labeled with the user action that selects that link and possible computer responses. The simple transition diagram in Figure 5.1 (Wasserman and Shewmake, 1985) represents a numbered menu-selection system for restaurant reviews that shows what happens when the user selects numbered choices: 1 (add a restaurant to the list), 2 (provide a review of a restaurant), 3 (read a

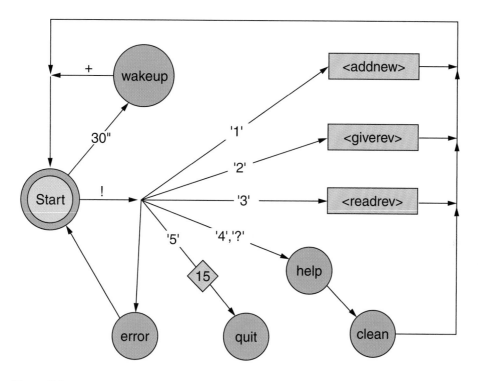

Figure 5.1

Transition diagram for a simple menu system. (Wasserman and Shewmake, 1985.)

review), 4 (get help, also accessed by a ?), 5 (quit), or any other character (error message). Figure 5.2 shows its text form. Figure 5.3 shows another form of transition diagram that displays frequencies along the links.

Many forms of transition diagrams have been created with special notations to fit the needs of specific application areas, such as e-commerce or word processing. Tools for creating and maintaining transition diagrams, dataflow diagrams, and other graphical displays are part of most software design tools, such as the IBM Rational Suite of products. In most systems, the diagrams are created by direct-manipulation actions, but designers can get textual outputs of the transition diagrams as well.

Unfortunately, transition diagrams get unwieldy as system complexity grows, and too many transitions can lead to complex spaghetti-like displays. One improvement is to replace a state transition node with a screen print, to give readers a better sense of movement through the displays and dialog boxes. Such overviews are helpful in design and in training.

Designs for interfaces with hundreds of dialog boxes, or for web sites with hundreds of screens, are easier to study when hung on the wall. In one memorable

```
node start
       cs, r2, rv, c_' Interactive Restaurant Guide', sv,
       r6, c5,  'Please make a choice:  ',
       r+2, c10,  '1:  Add new restaurant to database',
       r+2, c10,  '2:  Give review of a restaurant  ',
       r+2, c10,  '3:  Read reviews for a given restaurant',
       r+2, c10,  '4:  Help', r+2, c10,  '5:  Quit',  r+3,c5,  'Your choice:  ',  mark_A

node help
       cs, r5, c0,  'This program stores and retrieves information on',
       r+1,  c0, 'restaurants,  with emphasis on San Francisco.',
       r+1,  c0,  'You can add or update information about restaurants',
       r+1,  c0,  'already in the database,  or obtain information about',
       r+1,  c0,  'restaurants,  including the reviews of others.',
       r+2,  c0,  'To continue, type RETURN.'

node error
       r$-1, rv, 'Illegal command.',  sv,  'Please type a number from 1 to 5.',
       r$,  'Press RETURN to continue.'
node clean
       r$-1, cl,r$,cl
node wakeup
       r$,cl,rv,'Please make a choice',sv,  tomark_A
node quit
       cs,  'Thank you very much.  Please try this program again',
       nl,'and continue to add information on restaurants.'
arc start single_key
       on  '1'  to  <addnew>
       on  '2'  to  <giverev>
       on  '3'  to  <readrev>
       on  '4',  '?'  to help
       on  '5'  to quit
       alarm 30 to wakeup
       else to error
arc error
       else to start
arc help
       skip to clean
arc clean
       else to start
arc <addnew>
       skip to start
arc <readrev>
       skip to start
arc <giverev>
       skip to start
```

Figure 5.2

Text form of Fig. 5.1. Additional information is provided by the comment lines.

encounter, 350 screens of a satellite-control system were pasted on three walls of a conference room, quickly revealing the disparate styles of the design teams of the six modules. Compressed overview diagrams may be squeezed onto a single sheet of paper for user manuals, or printed as a poster to hang on users' walls.

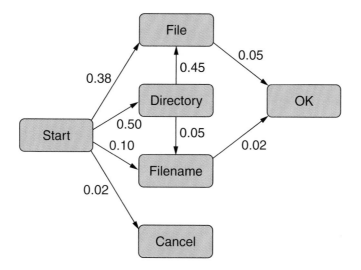

Figure 5.3

Sample transition diagram for file-manipulation actions. Link labels indicate how frequently each transition is made.

Transition diagrams translate directly into finite-state automata, which are well studied in computer science. Several properties can be verified automatically, such as reachability (is there a possible path to reach all states?) or liveliness (is there a way out from all states?). However, user-centered properties such as the visibility of system status are notoriously hard to express and verify in terms of automata (Dix et al., 1998).

5.2.4   Statecharts

Although transition diagrams are effective for following flow or action and for keeping track of the current state and current options, they can rapidly become large and confusing. Modularity is possible if nodes are included with subgraphs, but this strategy works well only with orderly, one-in, one-out graphs. Transition diagrams also become confusing when each node must show links to a help state, jumps back to the previous or start state, and a quit state. Concurrency and synchronization are poorly represented by transition diagrams, although some variations, such as petri-nets, can help. An appealing alternative is *statecharts* (Harel, 1988), which have several virtues in specifying interfaces. Because a grouping feature is offered through nested roundtangles (Fig. 5.4), repeated transitions can be factored out to the surrounding roundtangle. Extensions to statecharts—such as concurrency, external interrupt events, and user actions—are represented in Ilogix's Statemate, which is a user-interface tool based on statecharts. The Unified Modeling Language (UML), an emerging industry standard for visualizing and documenting software systems (Booch et al., 1998) also uses statecharts to specify the behavior of general programs; thus they should be familiar to software engineers.

Statecharts can also be extended with dataflow and constraint specification, plus embedded screen prints to show the visual states of graphical widgets (Carr, 1994). For example, in the simple case of a secure toggle switch there are five states, so showing the visual feedback on the statechart with triggering events on the arcs helps readers to understand what is happening (Fig. 5.5).

Specifications are useful to ensure consistency between the design of the user interface and its implementation, but they would become more widely used if they were linked to interface-building tools. Linking specifications to building tools and evaluation tools has been the goal of user-interface management systems (Myers, 1995) and model-based systems (Szekely, 1996). However, this goal has not yet been achieved, and most model-based systems remain academic prototypes. Novel approaches are still appearing, such as "scenario-based programming," which is based on specifying scenarios of behavior from widget-level formal specification of interface actions and feedback (Harel and Marelly, 2003). This system allows designers to create dialog boxes with graphic elements and then specify how user actions generate system changes. They can also specify what scenarios are allowed or forbidden, allowing these specifications to be tested against the final implementation.

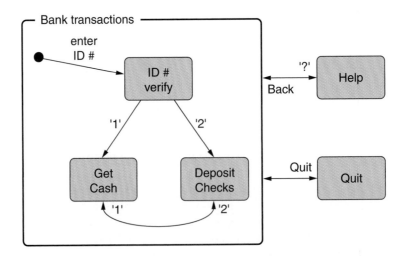

Figure 5.4

Statechart of a simplified bank transaction system showing grouping of states.

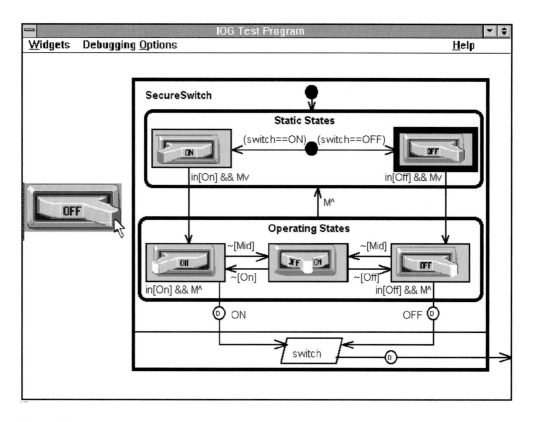

Figure 5.5

Interaction-object graphs extend statecharts with dataflow features. This example shows a secure switch with bitmaps of the states at each node (Carr, 1994). The switch is secure, as its status can only be changed by a sweep through three states, as opposed to by a simple click.

Given the growing interest in software quality in industry and the rise of UML, tools linking specification, interface building, verification, and evaluation may soon be available.

5.3   Interface-Building Tools

Specification methods are important for the design of components of a system, such as command languages, data-entry sequences, and widgets. Screen-transition diagrams drawn or printed on paper are an excellent means of providing an overview of the system. They allow user-interface architects, designers, managers, users, and software engineers to sit around a table, discuss the design, and prepare for the big job that lies ahead. Paper-based designs are a great way to start, but the detailed specification of complete user interfaces requires software tools.

The good news is that there has been a rapid and remarkable proliferation of software tools to accommodate most designers and software engineers in accomplishing many design goals. These tools come in colorful shrink-wrapped boxes that emphasize convenient and rapid building of onscreen prototypes. They generally allow visual editing, so designers can immediately assess the "look" of the system and can easily change colors, fonts, and layout. These direct-manipulation design tools have enabled large numbers of task-domain experts who have only modest technical training to become user-interface designers.

Thanks to the stabilization of desktop platforms, these tools are now mature and very similar across the three standard platforms: Windows, Macintosh, and the UNIX family, including Linux. An important consideration in choosing tools is whether they support cross-platform development, a strategy in which the interface can run on multiple platforms. There is a great benefit if only one program needs to be written and maintained, but the product is available on multiple platforms.

Another important consideration is whether the application allows the user interface to run under a web browser such as Netscape Navigator or Microsoft Internet Explorer. Since these browsers are written for multiple platforms, if the application runs on them the cross-platform goal is automatically met. Web browsers can now host full interactive applications, thanks to the standardization of formats and languages on the World Wide Web.

The bad news—at least from the designer's point of view—is that there has been a rapid and remarkable proliferation of non-desktop platforms in recent years. These include mobile devices, cell phones, Tablet PCs, programmable appliances, and set-top boxes for televisions offering cable TV and Internet access. Since these new platforms come with extensive design environments, interfaces must be built using low-level tools. Still, the principles underlying the construction of these interfaces are very much the same as for desktop applications, and the structure of programming is similar for all the platforms. Improved tools are being created for these platforms, but there is often a delay between the availability of the platform and the availability of interactive design environments, forcing innovative designers to use low-level tools.

Where possible, the use of high-level software tools brings great benefits (Box 5.1). The tools improve rapidly with successive versions, and their use is spreading widely. Their central advantage stems from the notion of *user-interface independence*: the decoupling of the user-interface design from the complexities of programming. This decoupling allows the designers to lay out sequences of displays in just a few hours, to make revisions in minutes, and to support the

Box 5.1

Features of user-interface building tools.

User-interface independence
- Separate interface design from internals
- Enable multiple user-interface strategies
- Enable multiple-platform support
- Establish role of user-interface architect
- Enforce standards

Methodology and notation
- Develop design procedures
- Find ways to talk about design
- Create project management

Rapid prototyping
- Try out ideas very early
- Test, revise, test, revise, . . .
- Engage end users, managers, and customers

Software support
- Increase productivity
- Offer constraint and consistency checks
- Facilitate team approaches
- Ease maintenance

expert-review and usability-testing processes. The programming needed to complete the underlying system can be applied once the user-interface design has been stabilized. The user-interface prototypes can serve as specifications from which writers create user manuals and from which software engineers build the system using other tools. The latter are required to produce a system that works just like the prototype. In fact, prototypes can be the specifications in government or commercial contracts for novel software.

Some early tools were limited to doing prototyping only, but most modern tools allow for quick prototyping and then system development. The design tools enable construction of complete systems, but they may run slowly, limit the database size, or restrict users in many ways. The software-engineering tools allow construction of more robust systems, but the complexity, cost, and development time are usually greater.

5.3.1   Interface mockup tools

User-interface architects recognize that creating quick sketches is important during the early stages of design to explore multiple alternatives, to allow communication within the design team, and to convey to clients what the product will look like. User-interface mockups can be created with paper and pencil, word processors, or slide-show presentation software (such as Microsoft PowerPoint or Apple Keynote). Resourceful designers have also built user-interface prototypes with multimedia construction tools, such as Macromedia Director, Flash MX (Fig. 5.6), or Dreamweaver. These programs can quickly generate animated or even interactive programs and be distributed via the Web.

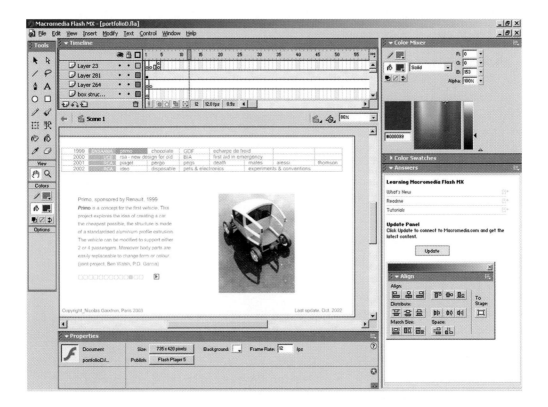

Figure 5.6

This Flash MX design shows a multimedia presentation with a time line on top, a color palette on the top right, alignment options on the bottom right, and standard graphic tools on the left. Once created, a Flash file is saved that can be made available through the Internet and run on most web browsers using a free plug-in. (This example was created by Nicolas Gaudron.)

In the simplest case, designers create a slide show of still images, which are switched at a user-controlled pace. Most tools support more complete prototyping that allows users to select from menus, click on buttons, use scrolling lists, and even drag icons. Users can navigate through screens and go back to previous screens. Graphics tools such as Microsoft Visio can be configured for designing interfaces. The prototype may not have a full database, help, or other facilities, but it offers a carefully chosen path that gives a realistic presentation of what the interface will do. Visual editing tools usually permit designers to lay out displays with cursor movements or mouse clicks and to mark regions for selection, highlighting, or data entry. Then, designers can specify which button selection is linked to a related display or dialog box. Prototypes are excellent aids to design discussions and are effective in winning contracts, because they give clients a rough idea of what the finished system will be like.

Visual development tools such as Microsoft Visual Studio.NET (Fig. 5.7) and Borland JBuilder (Fig. 5.8) have easy-to-use design tools for dragging buttons, labels, data-entry fields, combo boxes, and more onto a workspace to assemble the visual interface. Then, programmers or designers write code in languages like Visual Basic or Java to implement the actions. The visual editors in these products dramatically reduce design time for user interfaces if the designers are content to use the supplied widgets, such as labels, data-entry boxes, scroll bars, scrolling lists, and text-entry areas. Adding new widgets takes programming skill, but there are large libraries of widgets for sale. JBuilder Java code runs faster than the interpreted Basic, and JBuilder also provides good support for database access, but newer versions of each product are likely to challenge each other.

5.3.2 Software-engineering tools

Experienced programmers sometimes build user interfaces with general-purpose programming languages such as Java, C#, or C++, but this approach is giving way to using facilities that are specially tuned to user-interface development and web access (Olsen, 1991; Myers, 1995; Myers, Hudson, and Pausch, 2000). Choosing among them is sometimes a complex and confusing task, due to the lack of uniform terminology used to describe the tools and their features.

There are a large number of tools available for building user interfaces. Table 5.1 lists the four software layers that can be used to build a user interface and their associated interactive tools.

The higher-level tools (layer 4) are interface generators, sometimes called user-interface management systems or model-based building tools. Most if not all of an application can be built quickly using these visual tools. However, these tools are currently available only for a small class of applications, such as database front-ends (Microsoft Access, Sybase PowerDesigner); or remain research prototypes (Szekely, 1996).

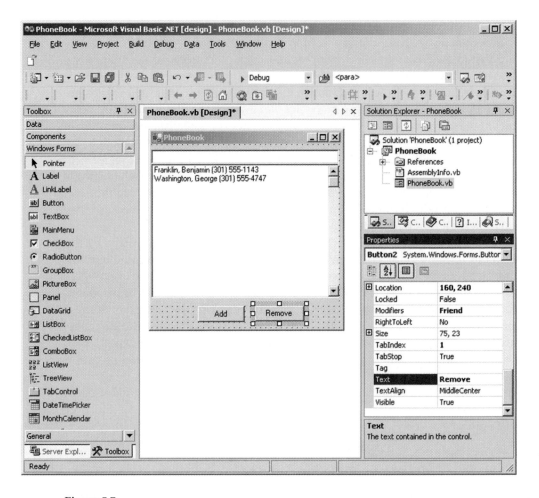

Figure 5.7

This Microsoft Visual Basic.NET design shows a mock-up of a PhoneBook interface with a text box for the phone number and two action buttons. The palette of tools on the left includes tools for adding a Label, TextBox, CheckBox, RadioButton, ComboBox, ListBox, and Scrollbar; the Properties window at the right allows users to set object properties.

Layer-3 tools include specialized languages or application frameworks. These are software architectures specially designed for building graphical user interfaces (GUIs). Compared to layer-4 tools, they provide almost no support for the nongraphical part of the application. At this layer, a key distinction is how extensively the software-engineering tool uses convenient visual programming, a relatively simple scripting language (event or object oriented), or a more powerful general-purpose programming language.

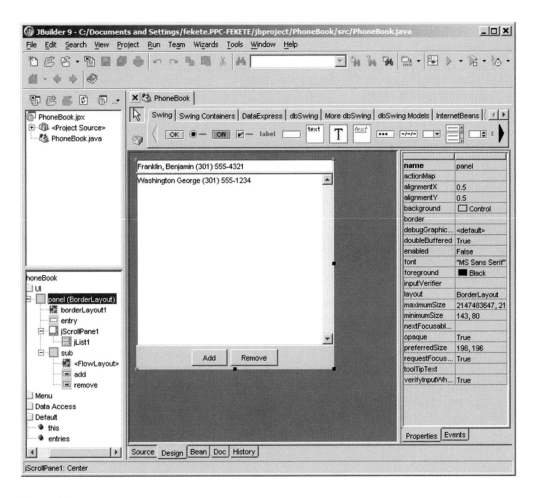

Figure 5.8

This Borland JBuilder design shows the same mock-up of a PhoneBook as Fig. 5.7.
The palette of tools, which is located across the top under the main menu bar,
includes Swing components, Swing Containers, and other groups of components.
The selected group shows Swing components such as Button, RadioButton, Toggle-
Button, CheckBox, Label, TextField, TextArea, TextPane, EditorPane, PasswordField,
FormattedTextField, ComboBox, and List. More can be accessed by scrolling to the
right. The Object Inspector window, which allows setting of properties, is at the right,
and the code window is accessible from the Source tab under the Design pane.

The terminology for GUI toolkits (layer 2) varies depending on the vendor.
Popular terms for these toolkits include Rapid Prototyper, Rapid Application
Developer, User Interface Builder, and User Interface Development Environment.
This layer provides software libraries and widgets as building blocks but requires

Software Layers	Visual Tools	Examples
4 Application	Model-Based Building Tools	Microsoft Access, Sybase PowerDesigner
3 Application Framework/ Specialized Language	Conceptual Building Tools	Macromedia Director, Tcl/Tk, Microsoft MFC
2 GUI Toolkit	Interface Builder	Eclipse, Borland JBuilder Microsoft Visual Studio
1 Windowing System	Resources Editor	Microsoft Win32/GDI+ Apple Quartz X11 Windowing System

Table 5.1

The four software layers available to build a user interface, their related visual tools, and examples of popular tools at each level.

extensive programming to connect these components to each other and to the non-GUI part of the application.

The layer 1 windowing system tools require extensive programming by experienced software engineers and offer little support from interactive tools.

Given this list of layers, the obvious recommendation is to use the highest available. However, with increased support also comes more constraints: full application generators will quickly build stereotyped applications that, like prefab houses, are cheap and easy to build but offer very little variety or adaptability. Finding the right tool is a tradeoff between six main criteria:

1. *Part of the application built using the tool.* Some tools only support building the presentation part of the application; others also help with low-level interaction, and some support general programming mechanisms usable in other parts of the application as well.

2. *Learning time.* The time required to learn the tool varies.

3. *Building time.* The time required to build a user interface using the tool varies.

4. *Methodology imposed or advised.* Some tools strongly impose a methodology for building the application, such as building the visual part first and connecting it to the remainder of the application afterwards, whereas other tools are more flexible.

5. *Communication with other subsystems.* Applications frequently use databases, files located on the Web, or other resources that, when supported by the building tool, simplify the development.

6. *Extensibility and modularity.* Applications evolve, and new applications may want to reuse parts of existing applications. Supporting the evolution and reuse of software remains a challenge. Level-4 tools and application frame-

works inherently promote good software organization, but the others usually lead to poor extensibility and modularity.

Tool price is rarely an important criteria, because it is usually negligible compared to the cost of good designers and engineers. Furthermore, there is a growing trend to distribute free tools suitable for building standard GUIs. Table 5.2 summarizes the six criteria applied to the software layers.

Regardless of the tools used to design the user interface, designing for good usability has important implications for the quality and complexity of software development. For the past twenty years, usability has been treated by many software architects as a problem in modifiability. They have designed software architectures that separate the user interface of an application (the visual presentation with graphical user interfaces) from the internal functions of that application. This separation makes it easier to make modifications to the user interface without changing the internals and to maintain multiple views of application data. It is also consistent with standard iterative design methods that determine necessary changes to the user interface from user testing and then modify the system to implement these changes. Separating the user interface from the remainder of the application has been quite successful and is now standard practice in interactive system development. This separation also facilitates cross-platform development,

Layer	Part of the application built	Learning time	Building time	Methodology imposed or advised	Communication with other subsystems	Extensibility and modularity
4	All for a specific domain	Long	Short	Specification first, then visual, then programming (if required)	Very good for the specific domain of the tool	Very good
3	Presentation, interaction	Short (days)	Short	Visual first	Depends on the tool	Languages: Bad Frameworks: Good
2	Presentation	Long (weeks)	Long	Visual first with tools, none otherwise	Good	Medium/good
1	All	Very long (months)	Very long	None	Very good	Very bad

Table 5.2

Comparison between six features of design tools (horizontal) depending on the software layer (vertical)

which makes it easier to generate interfaces for standard platform families (Windows, Macintosh, UNIX).

Treating usability as a problem in modifiability, however, has the effect of postponing attending to many usability requirements to the end of the development cycle, where they are overtaken by time and budget pressures. Consequently, some systems are being fielded that are less usable than they could be.

Some usability problems cannot easily be solved late in the life cycle because they come from fundamental design flaws in the software architecture (Bass and John, 2003). For example, providing users with the ability to cancel commands can be very difficult to program if not planned for early in the development process. Likewise, the ability to ascertain the system state and present appropriate feedback to users—such as via a progress bar—can be surprisingly hard to add late in the process. The general "undo" facility often associated with direct manipulation is another example of a capability that needs to be planned early in the software design.

The three following sections describe software layers 1, 2, and 3 and their associated tools. An example of a visual layer-4 tool, LabVIEW, is discussed at the end of Section 5.3.5.

5.3.3   The windowing-system layer

Some platforms are too new to offer high-level building tools, forcing the software engineer to work at a low level. Only some graphics resources—such as icons, images, cursors, or fonts—can be edited interactively at this level. Although better tools are being created every day, new platforms are being created too. Interfaces for some mobile devices or cell phones should currently be done at the windowing-system level. All the programs have the following form:

```
main() {
    InitializeSystem();
    SetInitialState();
    DisplayInitialGraphics();
    while(true) {
        Event event = readNextEvent();
        switch(event.type) {
            case EVENT_REDISPLAY: redisplay(); break;
            case EVENT_PEN_DOWN: doPenDown(event.x, event.y); break;
            case EVENT_CHAR: doInputChar(event.detail); break;
            ...
            default: doSystemDefault(event); break;
        }
    }
}
```

In this small stereotypical program, the "while(true)…" loop is referred to as the "main loop"; it exists in each and every interactive application, even if higher-level tools hide it. This loop manages the state transitions, triggered by events arriving from the windowing system or the operating system. Procedures called "doPenDown," "doInputChar," and so on perform the actions required to change the display or the internal state of the program. Events not explicitly managed by the user program are passed to a special procedure ("doSystemDefault" here) provided by the windowing system.

Programming at this level, while challenging, is sometimes appropriate when no higher-level tool exists or when memory or performance is critical. Higher-level tools all rely on this level but provide programming abstractions and interactive tools to simplify the programming. As a comparison, displaying a window with just one text label requires 237 lines of code using the low-level Xlib and only 2 using the specialized Tcl/Tk language (Ousterhout, 1994). The ratio decreases a little bit when the application becomes larger, but the scale factor remains dramatic. Since no visual tool exists at this level, designers can only use drawing programs to express their graphical intents to software engineers.

5.3.4 The GUI toolkit layer

Most products provide user-interface program libraries called *GUI toolkits* that offer common widgets, such as windows, scroll bars, pull-down or pop-up menus, data-entry fields, buttons, and dialog boxes. Programming languages with accompanying libraries are familiar to experienced programmers and afford great flexibility. However, toolkits without interactive support can become complex, and the programming environments for those, such as the Microsoft Windows Forms, Apple Macintosh Toolkit, and Unix X Toolkit (Xtk), require months of learning for programmers to gain proficiency. Even then, the burden in creating applications is great, and maintenance is difficult. The advantage is that programmers have extensive control and great flexibility in creating the interfaces. Toolkits have become popular with programmers, but they provide only partial support for consistency, and designers and managers must still depend heavily on experienced programmers. The Motif example in Fig. 5.9 conveys the challenge of programming user interfaces in X, which lacks a standard visual GUI editor.

Cross-platform toolkits such as ILOG Views (Fig. 5.10), Gtk, and Qt are becoming common and are sometimes even free (the last two are free software.) They offer cross-platform capability by emulating GUIs on Macintosh, Windows, and other platforms. They come with visual editors rich in functionality that allows users to specify layouts to preserve the designer's intent even when

```
X/* Written by Dan Heller. Copyright 1991, O'Reilly & Associates.
X * This program is freely distributable without licensing fees and
X * is provided without guarantee or warrantee expressed or implied.
X * This program is -not- in the public domain.
X========================================================================
X       /* main window contains a MenuBar and a Label displaying a pixmap */
X       main_w = XtVaCreateManagedWidget("main_window",
X           xMainWindowWidgetClass,    toplevel,
X           XmNscrollBarDisplayPolicy, XmAS_NEEDED,
X           XmNscrollingPolicy,        XmAUTOMATIC,
X           NULL);
X
X       /* Create a simple MenuBar that contains three menus */
X       file = XmStringCreateSimple("File");
X       edit = XmStringCreateSimple("Edit");
X       help = XmStringCreateSimple("Help");
X       menubar = XmVaCreateSimpleMenuBar(main_w, "menubar",
X           XmVaCASCADEBUTTON, file, 'F',
X           XmVaCASCADEBUTTON, edit, 'E'
X           XmVaCASCADEBUTTON, help, 'H',
X           NULL);
X    XmStringFree(file);
X    XmStringFree(edit);
X    /* don't free "help" compound string yet — reuse it for later */
X
X    /* Tell the menubar which button is the help menu */
X    if (widget - XtNameToWidget(menubar, "button_2"))
X        XtVaSetValues(menubar, XmNmenuHelpWidget, widget, NULL);
```

Figure 5.9

Programming of user interfaces in Motif.

display sizes or widget sizes are changed (Hudson and Mohamed, 1990). They also provide rich object-oriented libraries that can be invoked from C or C++ programs, plus tools for managing network services and file directories. These toolkits require software-engineering skills to use, but the visual editors enable prompt construction of prototypes.

Sun Microsystems has created the largest tremors in the realm of cross-platform toolkits and the Web with its offering of Java. Java is a complete system and programming language that is specially designed for platform independence and the World Wide Web. Java is based on a portable virtual machine and low-level libraries (all together called the Java Runtime Environment, or JRE), available for free for all the popular platforms. This virtual machine can run any compiled Java program as if it were on a special Java machine, justifying Sun's motto "Write once, run everywhere." All the low-level layers are included in the Java Runtime System, guaranteeing full portability of Java applications across platforms and even on web browsers. Java can be used to create complete applications that are distributed like any other programs, but one of its charms is its capacity to create "applets." These small

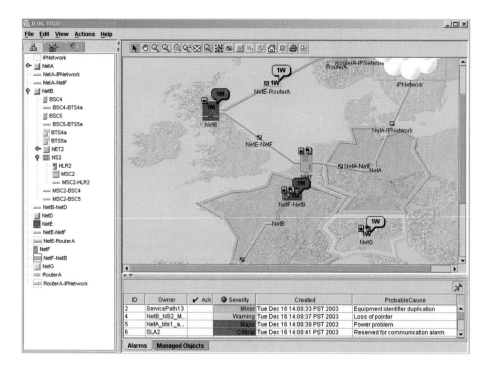

Figure 5.10

ILOG JViews allows designers to define application-specific displays and icons using high-level components such as maps or graphs. Programmers then connect the design to the underlying software using a scripting language. Once the design has been tested and stabilized, the connection between the program and the displays can be rewritten in Java for higher performance.

program fragments can be stored on a web server, downloaded from a web page, and executed on the user's machine, regardless of what platform the user is running. This enables programmers to easily make dynamic web pages and provide animations or error checking on data-entry forms. This extreme form of modularity allows software packages to be updated by way of the World Wide Web and permits users to acquire only the components that they use, rather than the entire package.

Java is object oriented but eliminates some of the complexity of C++, such as operator overloading, multiple inheritance, pointers, and extensive automatic coercions. Automatic garbage collection and the absence of pointers eliminate common sources of bugs. Security and robustness goals were achieved by techniques such as strong typing, which requires explicit data declarations, and static binding, which means that references must be made during compilation.

Software engineers have celebrated Java because of its features and its familiar programming-language style, as indicated in this brief example:

```
class PhoneBook {
  public static void main(String[] args) {
    Frame frame = new Frame("PhoneBook");    // create the main window
    final TextField entry = new TextField(); // create a text field
    frame.add(entry, BorderLayout.NORTH);    // add the text field on the upper
                                             // side of the window
    Panel panel = new Panel();               // create a composite panel to store
                                             // the two "Add" and "Remove" buttons
    panel.setLayout(new FlowLayout());       // specify how the widgets will be
                                             // laid out in the panel
    Button add = new Button("Add");          // create the "Add" button
    panel.add(add);                          // add it to the panel
    Button remove = new Button("Remove");    // create the "Remove" button
    panel.add(remove);                       // add it to the panel
    frame.add(panel, BorderLayout.SOUTH);    // add the panel on the lower side
    final List list = new List();            // create a new item list widget
    frame.add(list, BorderLayout.CENTER);    // add it to the  window's center
    list.add("Washington George
      (301) 555-1234");                      // add one item to the list
    frame.pack();                            // compute the final widgets' sizes
                                             // and positions
    frame.setVisible(true);                  // show the window
    add.addActionListener(new
      ActionListener() {                     // add action to the "Add" button
public void actionPerformed(ActionEvent e)
{ list.add(entry.getText()); }              // add the text field's text
      });                                    // to the list
    remove.addActionListener
    (new ActionListener() {                  // add action to the "Remove" button
    public void actionPerformed
    (ActionEvent e)
{ try { list.remove(entry.getText()); } catch(Exception ex) {}}
      });
  }
}
```

Several Java programming environments, such as Borland JBuilder (Fig. 5.8) and Sun NetBeans for Java, support visual editing of widgets, simplifying the design of user interfaces and increasing the productivity of programmers. Despite these great advantages, Java also suffers from its portability. The first versions of Java provided the Abstract Widget Toolkit (AWT), which was portable and consistent across all platforms but not consistent with the style guides of any platform. To solve that problem, Java now includes the Swing Toolkit, which is much more sophisticated than AWT, is entirely written in Java, and is able to mimic the look of all the popular platforms. Using Swing, an application can take the look of a Windows application, an X/Motif application, or a Macintosh application wherever it runs by just changing one parameter in the program; the Java demos even offer a menu to do that. Still, emulating platform looks is sometimes not enough—in particular, when applications need to communicate. This is certainly the limit of portability, because not all the system services can be emulated in a similar way across platforms. To add more choice and confusion for the sake of integration and performance, IBM has introduced the Standard Widget Toolkit (SWT) a bridge and an abstraction layer between Java and standard GUI toolkits supplied by the operating system. SWT has a smaller memory footprint and is faster than Swing, and it is much richer than AWT. The popularity of SWT mainly comes from its use in the popular Eclipse Interactive Development Environment for programming in Java.

Java's popularity is still growing, partly due to its availability for free and to its comprehensive library of classes (for example Java2 Enterprise Edition or J2EE), which streamline the access to popular development technologies such as SQL for databases and CORBA for network services.

The integration of large programming libraries with network-aware languages and a standard GUI toolkit is becoming so important for industrial development that Microsoft has designed its own platform called .NET (pronounced "Dotnet"), made of a virtual machine compiler and a large library. .NET includes compilers for several languages, including C#, C++, and Visual Basic. Compared to Java/J2EE, C#/.NET has several similarities, several advantages, and some pitfalls. The C# language is similar to the Java language, with small syntactic enhancements. The main advantages of .NET come from the simplicity of using different programming languages and sharing the same programming libraries, thanks to its more versatile virtual machine. The .NET GUI toolkit is very similar to Java Swing but can be used with C++, Visual Basic, C#, and a large number of other languages, cutting the training costs of professional programmers and simplifying the porting of existing programs. Despite being language-neutral, though, .NET is deeply tied to the Windows platform, making it less attractive for cross-platform development (where Java has no serious competitors).

A third potential alternative is appearing in the open source and free software community with the Gtk and Qt toolkits and the Gnu compiler suite, providing compilers for the most popular languages, including C, C++, Java, Fortran, and

Ada. These compilers are portable across a wide range of platforms, including embedded systems, and provide libraries similar to .NET or J2EE, although not yet as complete and unified.

Standardizing the user interface has been very important for computer novices, but new interaction and visualization paradigms can improve the productivity and satisfaction of knowledgeable computer users, who are becoming a majority in the younger populations of industrialized countries. An important new trend in interaction research involves going beyond the standard set of widgets and inter-action techniques provided by the desktop toolkits (usually called "WIMP toolk-its," because they manage windows, icons, menus and a pointer). Post-WIMP toolkits are very diverse, since each explores a new visual or interaction paradigm. Popular post-WIMP toolkits include Jazz (Bederson, Meyer, and Good, 2000) with its successor Piccolo, for building zoomable user interfaces, and SATIN (Hong and Landay, 2000), for building informal ink-based applications.

The proliferation of GUI toolkits shows the liveliness of the domain but unfortunately also dilutes efforts that could otherwise be spent on better usabil-ity, formalization, or true innovation.

5.3.5   The Application Framework and Specialized Language layer

Even with a sophisticated toolkit in a supporting environment with visual edi-tors, programming remains a difficult and long process. Two paths have been tried to simplify the programming of user interfaces: application frameworks and specialized languages.

Application frameworks (Lewis et al., 1995) are based on object-oriented pro-gramming; they started with MacApp (Schmucker, 1986), an extended toolkit written in Object Pascal. The idea behind frameworks is that all the user-interface programs have a similar structure. Capturing this structure and trans-lating it into classes, objects, and methods means that an application can be built by just completing the framework instead of recreating everything from scratch. Popular frameworks include NextStep, its successor Cocoa, and the Microsoft Foundation Classes (MFC). Application frameworks are very effective at quickly building sophisticated user interfaces but require intensive learning because they are very abstract, forcing the programmer to understand a large number of concepts and how classes and methods interrelate. Powerful visual tools exist to help organize the user interface and the application structure; the latter are aimed at engineers rather than designers.

Instead of extending libraries of existing languages, another approach is to craft a programming language specially to build user interfaces and to lighten the burden of programming. Ousterhout (1994) successfully attempted this by developing a simple scripting language called Tcl and an accompanying toolkit called Tk (a scripting language is a programming language designed to be embedded into applications to add new functionalities or to glue applications together). Their great success was due to the relative ease of use of Tcl and the useful widgets in Tk, such as the text and canvas widgets. Tcl is interpreted, so development is rapid, and its cross-platform capabilities are further attractions. The absence of a simple visual editor discourages some users, but Tcl's convenience in gluing together components has overcome the objections of most critics. Here is a simple phone-book interface in Tcl/Tk:

```
entry .entry -width 30;              # create a text entry for typing new name/telephone lines
pack .entry -side top;               # place it on the top of the window
frame .buttons;                      # create a frame for two buttons
pack .buttons -side top;             # place it on top, under the text entry
button .buttons.add -text "Add" -command { add [.entry get]};          # create the "Add" button
button .buttons.remove -text "Remove" -command { remove [.entry get]}; # and the "Remove" button
pack .buttons.add .buttons.remove -side left -fill x;   # place the buttons side by side
listbox .phoneEntryList -width 30 -listvariable entries;  # create the list box
pack .phoneEntryList -side bottom -fill both;           # place it at the bottom of the window
proc add {e} {                       # procedure called to add an entry
    global entries
    .entry delete 0 end
    lappend entries $e
    set entries [lsort -uniq -dictionary $entries ]
}
proc remove {e} {                    # procedure called to remove an entry
    global entries
    set i [lsearch -sorted -dictionary $entries $e]
    if {$i >= 0} {
        set entries [lreplace $entries $i $i]
        .entry delete 0 end
    }
}
add "Washington George (301) 555-1234";   # Add an initial entry
```

The popularity of Tcl/Tk showed that scripting languages were good at proto-typing user interfaces. Several scripting languages are now connected to powerful toolkits to fit the needs and tastes of programmers. Popular scripting languages include Perl/Tk, Python/Tk, and Visual Basic (embedded in several Microsoft applications to extend them). Scripting languages are also used extensively to add interaction to web pages initially intended to display static contents.

JavaScript, officially known as ECMAScript, is a simple scripting language that is embedded in all major web browsers and can be combined with the Hypertext Markup Language (HTML) to interactively modify web pages. It achieves the goals of network distribution and cross-platform capability, since it is distributed within the HTML for a web page and is interpreted by the client's browser on the local machine—Macintosh, Windows, or Unix. JavaScript is relatively easy to learn, especially for someone who has learned HTML, and it supplies common features. This example shows a script to manage a phone book in an HTML form:

```
<html><head><script><!– /* Definition of JavaScript functions inside an HTML document */
function add() /* function to add a new entry to the HTML option list */
{
    var list = document.forms[0].phoneBookList;
    list.options[list.length] = new Option(document.forms[0].entry);
}
 function remove() /* function to remove a selected entry */
{
    var list = document.forms[0].phoneBookList;
    for (var i = 0; i < list.length; i++) {
      if (list.options[i].text== document.forms[0].entry.value) {
          list.options[i]=null;
          return;
      }
    }
}
–>
</script> </head><body>  <form>
<input type="text" name="entry"><br>
<input TYPE="button" VALUE="Add" onclick="add()">
    <!–associate the function with the "Add" button –>
<input TYPE="button" VALUE="Remove" onclick="remove()">
    <!–associate the function with the "Remove" button –>
<br><select name="phoneBookList">
    <option>Washington George (301) 555-1234</option>
</select></form></body></html>
```

Although JavaScript did not contain visual editors at its beginning, development environments are now supplying those tools. Security problems have arisen, but new browsers are starting to provide adequate configuration options to avoid JavaScript abuses such as annoying pop-up windows or more malicious programs.

Coupling of visual editors and scripting languages was made popular by Apple's HyperCard, whose early success stimulated many competitors. These systems combine visual editing—by allowing designers to include buttons and other fields—with simple interface actions provided automatically (for example, clicking on a back-arrow takes users to the previous card). For more complex actions, the innovative HyperTalk scripting language enables users to create useful interfaces with only moderate training. Designers can write programs with easy-to-understand terms:

```
on mouseUp
    play "boing"
    wait for 3 seconds
    visual effect wipe left very fast to black
    click at 150,100
    type "goodbye"
end mouseUp
```

Of course, programming in such languages can become complex as the number of short code segments grows and their interrelationships become difficult to fathom.

Macromedia Director has followed HyperCard's path. Its development environment has been visual and interactive since the beginning and has been augmented by a scripting language called Lingo, allowing designers to build the graphical parts of applications and leave the programming to engineers. Although not designed for developing large applications, Director achieves a seducing compromise that meets the needs of several smaller graphically oriented designers. Director's interactive animations can be exported using the popular Flash format, which can be played on most platforms through free web-browser plug-ins. The Flash file format has become a recognized infrastructure for creating small and fast multimedia applications and interface mockups. Several interactive tools, such as Flash MX (Fig. 5.6), have been created to allow designers to easily create Flash documents.

Ultimately, the scripting language can itself be visual: *Visual programming tools* can build interactive applications interactively. The domain of laboratory instruments was the motivating influence for National Instruments Corporation's LabVIEW (Fig. 5.11), which has a flat structure of function boxes (arithmetic, Boolean, and more) linked with wires (Green and Petre, 1996). LabVIEW is popular in the domain of electronics and electrical engineering, but general-purpose visual programming tools have yet to prove their effectiveness for building large-scale applications.

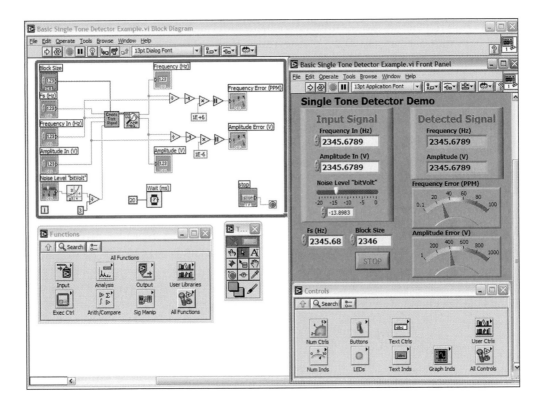

Figure 5.11

LabVIEW enables users to develop virtual instruments in a visual programming environment. In this simple demo, the program on the left controls the virtual instrument on the right. An animation of the program execution can be shown in the visual program, which is constructed by connecting sensors, gauges, counters, or logic components.

The rapid pace of change on the Internet is stimulated by the easy sharing of code and the capacity to build quickly on top of the work of other programmers. The frenzy is sometimes alarming but usually irresistible. The importance of the World Wide Web has led developers of many tools—including Tcl/Tk, Java, Flash, and Visual Basic—to enable their programs to run on the Web, and this capability provides a strong competitive advantage.

5.4   Evaluation and Critiquing Tools

Software tools are natural environments in which to add procedures to evaluate or critique user interfaces. Even straightforward tools to check spelling or concordance of terms benefit interface designers. Simple metrics that report numbers of displays, widgets, or links between displays capture the size of a user-interface project, but the inclusion of more sophisticated evaluation procedures can allow interface designers to assess whether a menu tree is too deep or contains redundancies, whether widget labels have been used consistently, whether all buttons have proper transitions associated with them, and so on (Olsen and Halversen, 1988).

A second set of tools is *run-time logging software,* which captures the users' patterns of activity. Simple reports—such as on the frequency of each error message, menu-item selection, dialog-box appearance, help invocation, form-field usage, or web-page access—are of great benefit to maintenance personnel and to revisers of the initial design. Experimental researchers can also capture performance data for alternative designs to guide their decision making. Software to analyze and summarize the performance data is improving steadily.

An early example is Tullis's Display Analysis Program, which takes alphanumeric screen designs (no color, highlighting, separator lines, or graphics) and produces Tullis's display-complexity metrics plus some advice, such as this (Tullis, 1988):

```
Upper-case letters: 77% The percentage of upper-case letters is high.
    Consider using more lower-case letters, since text printed
    in normal upper- and lower-case letters is read about 13%
    faster than text in all upper case. Reserve all upper-case
    for items that need to attract attention.
Maximum local density = 89.9% at row 9, column 8.
Average local density = 67.0%
    The area with the highest local density is identified
    ...you can reduce local density by distributing the
    characters as evenly as feasible over the entire screen.
Total layout complexity = 8.02 bits
Layout complexity is high.
This means that the display items (labels and data) are not
well aligned with each other...Horizontal complexity can be
reduced by starting items in fewer different columns on the
screen (that is, by aligning them vertically).
```

The movement towards graphical user interfaces with richer fonts and layout possibilities has reduced interest in Tullis's metrics, but better analyses of layouts seem possible (see Section 12.4.3). One approach is to base evaluations on formal user-task descriptions using NGOMSL (Byrne et al., 1994) or simpler task sequences and frequencies (Sears, 1993; 1995). Task-dependent metrics are likely to be more accurate, but the effort and uncertainty in collecting sequences and frequencies of tasks discourages some potential users.

Task-independent measurement and evaluation tools can be easily applied at low cost early in the development process (Mahajan and Shneiderman, 1997). Simple measures such as the number of widgets per dialog box, widget density, nonwidget areas, aspect ratio, and balance of top to bottom or left to right are useful to gain some idea of the designer's style, but they have limited value in detecting anomalies. However, reports on the top, bottom, left, and right margins and the list of distinct colors and typefaces used detected unreasonable variations in four systems developed using Visual Basic. Separate tools to perform spell checking and to produce interface concordances were helpful in revealing errors and inconsistencies. Software tools to check button size, position, color, and wording also revealed inconsistencies that were produced because multiple members of design teams failed to coordinate on a common style. An empirical study demonstrated that increased variations in terminology—for example, switching from *search* to *browse* to *query*—slowed performance times by 10 to 25%.

Web-page and web-site analyzers offer designers a wide range of guidance and automated tools. Bobby from Watchfine Corp. and HTML Tidy are useful free tools for HTML checking and cleaning and analysis of accessibility guidelines. Tidy produces advice like:

```
line 6 column 5 - Warning: <table> lacks "summary" attribute
line 10 column 22 - Warning: <img> lacks "alt" attribute
line 15 column 22 - Warning: <img> lacks "alt" attribute
line 86 column 17 - Warning: <table> lacks "summary" attribute
line 151 column 55 - Warning: unescaped & or unknown entity "&r"
5 warnings, 0 errors were found!

The table summary attribute should be used to describe the table
structure. It is very helpful for people using non-visual
browsers. The scope and headers attributes for table cells are
useful for specifying which headers apply to each table cell,
enabling non-visual browsers to provide a meaningful context for
each cell.
The alt attribute should be used to give a short description of
an image; longer descriptions should be given with the longdesc
attribute which takes a URL linked to the description.
```

The U.S. National Institute of Standards and Technology (NIST) Web Metrics page provides extensive testing tools, such as a static analyzer (WebSAT) for pages or sites, a categorical analyzer (WebCAT) to check whether categories extracted from web pages fit the designers' intents, an "instrumenter" (WebVIP) to quickly instrument existing web pages for collecting measures of interactive uses of web pages, and other tools to guide web designers.

To guide designers seeking to make appealing web pages, researchers correlated site ratings with 141 layout metrics (Ivory and Hearst, 2002). The ratings were assigned by Internet professionals, acting as judges for the Webby Awards. The researchers analyzed the informational, navigational, and graphical aspects of 5,300 web pages to build statistical models that can predict, with over 90% accuracy in most cases, the scores assigned to the web sites. The resulting predictive models, collectively labeled WebTango, were then examined to determine which design features they recommend. The results were complex—for instance, showing interactions between the functional types and sizes of web pages. Some of the easily applicable results for page design were that high ratings were assigned when large pages had columnar organization, headings were used in proportion to the amount of text, and animated graphical ads were limited. Other recommendations for text design included keeping average link text to two to three words, using sans-serif fonts for body text, and applying colors to highlight headings. One intriguing finding was that preferred web sites did not always have the fastest user performance, suggesting that in e-commerce and entertainment applications attractiveness may be more important than rapid task execution. Further analysis of the results could lead to conjectures about the design goals that bring about high preference: for example, designs that are comprehensible, predictable and visually appealing and that incorporate relevant content.

The standardization of web formats and languages has led to major improvements in automated evaluation and critiquing tools. Given the potential audience of documents published on the Web, improving their quality and accessibility is crucial. The proliferation of development environments, GUI toolkits, and languages explains the relative lack of automated tools for traditional GUI applications, despite the rich literature on metrics and rules for assessing GUI quality. Several initiatives to describe interfaces using Extensible Markup Language (XML) formats, such as User Interface Markup Language (UIML) or XML User Interface Language (XUL), may solve the proliferation problem and open the way to more generic tools.

Practitioner's Summary

There will always be a need to write some user interfaces with traditional programming tools, but the advantages of specialized user-interface software tools for designers and software engineers are large. They include an order-of-magnitude increase in productivity, shorter development schedules, support for expert reviews and usability testing, ease in making changes and ensuring consistency, better management control, and reduced training necessary for designers.

The profusion of current tools and the promises of improved tools require that managers, designers, and programmers stay informed and make fresh choices for each project. This educational process can be enlightening, since the benefits of improved and appropriate tools are enormous if the right tools are selected (Hix and Schulman, 1991). Box 5.2 details some of the considerations in evaluating user-interface building tools.

From the toolmaker's viewpoint, there are still great opportunities to create effective tools that handle more user-interface widgets, produce output for multiple software and hardware platforms (Thévenin and Coutaz, 1999), are easier to learn, and provide more useful and accurate evaluation.

There is a clear trend towards enhancing software quality using methods such as the Unified Modeling Language (UML) and several associated tools. Integrating these tools in a coherent development tool seems like the next logical step. It remains to be seen whether the current fragmentation of GUI toolkits will slow down this trend or if convergence towards a unified set of tools for specifying the user interface will emerge.

Researcher's Agenda

The narrow focus of formal models of user interfaces and specification languages means that these models are beneficial for only small components. Scalable formal methods and automatic checking of user-interface features would be a major contribution. Innovative methods of specification involving graphical constraints or visual programming seem to be a natural match for creating graphical user interfaces. Improved software architectures are needed to ease the burden during revision and maintenance of user interfaces. Collaborative computing tools may provide powerful authoring tools that enable multiple designers to work together effectively on large projects.

Other opportunities exist to create tools for designers of interfaces in novel environments using sound, animation, video, and virtual reality, and in operating mobile or embedded devices. Other challenges are to specify dynamic processes (gestural input), to handle continuous input (datastreams from sensors), and to synchronize activities (to pop up a reminder box for 10 seconds if a file has not been saved after 30 minutes of editing). As new interface styles emerge, there will always be a need to develop new tools to facilitate their construction. Metrics and evaluation tools are still open topics for user-interface and web-site developers. Specification by demonstration is an appealing notion (Lieberman, 2001), but practical application remains elusive (see Section 6.3.4).

Box 5.2

User experience features that can be created by common user-interface building tools.

Widgets supported
- Windows and dialog boxes
- Pull-down or pop-up menus
- Buttons (rectangles, roundtangles, etc.)
- Radio buttons and switches
- Scroll bars (horizontal and vertical)
- Data-entry fields
- Field labels
- Compound objects for lists, tables, trees, calendars
- Boxes and separator lines
- Sliders, gauges, meters
- User-created widgets

Interface features
- Color, graphics, images
- Animation, zooming, video
- Varying display size (low to high resolution)
- User-controlled window resizing
- Toolbars
- Sounds, music, voice input-output
- Mouse, arrow keys, touchscreen, stylus, novel input devices
- Alternate input methods
- International languages
- Universal usability

Run-time support
- Online help
- Easy interface with database, graphics, spreadsheets, and so on.
- Web-services and networking
- Logging during use
- Customization and user tailoring
- Debugging and reporting services

WORLD WIDE WEB RESOURCES

User-interface tools are widely promoted on the Web by companies and others. The World Wide Web is a great resource here, because the technology changes so rapidly that books are immediately out of date. Online white papers, manuals, and tutorials are often effective and enable contact with developers. An imaginative idea is to have web sites that will critique your web site. Such online services are likely to expand in the coming years.

http://www.aw.com/DTUI

References

Bass, Len and John, Bonnie. E., Linking usability to software architecture patterns through general scenarios, *Journal of Systems and Software*, 66, 3 (2003), 187–197.

Bederson, Ben B., Meyer, Jon, and Good, Lance, Jazz: An extensible zoomable user interface graphics toolkit in Java, *ACM Symposium on User Interface Software and Technology: UIST 2000, CHI Letters*, 2, 2 (2000), 171–180.

Booch, Grady, Rumbaugh, James, and Jacobson, Ivar, *The Unified Modeling Language User Guide*, Addison-Wesley, Reading, MA (1998).

Byrne, Michael D., Wood, Scott D., Sukaviriya, Piyawadee, Foley, James D., and Kieras, David E., Automating interface evaluation, *Proc. CHI '94 Conference: Human Factors in Computing Systems*, ACM, New York (1994), 232–237.

Carey, Tom, The gift of good design tools, in Hartson, H. R. and Hix, D. (Editors), *Advances in Human-Computer Interaction, Volume II*, Ablex, Norwood, NJ (1988), 175–213.

Carr, David, Specification of interface interaction objects, *Proc. CHI '94 Conference: Human Factors in Computing Systems*, ACM, New York (1994), 372–378.

Dix, Alan, Finlay, Janet, Abowd, Gregory, Beale, Russell, Finley, Janet, *Human-Computer Interaction*, Prentice-Hall, Englewood Cliffs, NJ (1998).

Green, Thomas R. G. and Petre, Marian, Usability analysis of visual programming environments: A "cognitive dimensions" framework, *Journal of Visual Languages and Computing*, 7 (1996), 131–174.

Harel, David, On visual formalisms, *Communications of the ACM*, 31, 5 (May 1988), 514–530.

Harel, David and Marelly, Rami, *Come Let's Play: Scenario-based Programming Using LSCs and the Play-Engine*, Springer-Verlag, Berlin, Germany (2003).

Hix, Deborah and Schulman, Robert S., Human-computer interface development tools: A methodology for their evaluation, *Communications of the ACM*, 34, 3 (March 1991), 74–87.

Hong, Jason I. and Landay, James A., SATIN: A toolkit for informal ink-based applications, *ACM Symposium on User Interface Software and Technology: UIST 2000, CHI Letters*, 2, 2 (2000), 63–72.

Hudson, Scott E. and Mohamed, Shamim P., Interactive specification of flexible user interface displays, *ACM Transactions on Information Systems*, 8, 3 (July 1990), 269–288.

Hunt, Andrew, JSpeech Grammar Format, W3C Note (05 June 2000). Available at http://www.w3.org/TR/jsgf.

Ivory, Melody Y and Hearst, Marti A., Statistical profiles of highly-rated web site interfaces, *Proc. CHI 2002 Conference: Human Factors in Computing Systems*, ACM, New York (2002), 367–374.

Lewis, Ted, Rosenstein, Larry, Pree, Wolfgang, Weinand, Andre, Gamma, Erich, Calder, Paul Andert, Glenn, Vlissides, John, and Schmucker, Kurt, *Object-Oriented Application Frameworks*, Prentice-Hall, Englewood Cliffs, NJ (1995).

Lieberman, Henry (Editor), *Your Wish Is My Command: Programming by Example,* Morgan Kaufmann Publishers, San Francisco, CA (2001).

Mahajan, Rohit and Shneiderman, Ben, Visual and textual consistency checking tools for graphical user interfaces, *IEEE Transaction on Software Engineering*, 23, 11 (November 1997), 722–735.

Myers, Brad A., User interface software tools, *ACM Transactions on Computer-Human Interaction*, 2, 1 (March 1995), 64–103.

Myers, Brad A., Hudson, Scott E., and Pausch, Randy, Past, present and future of user interface software tools, *ACM Transactions on Computer-Human Interaction*, 7, 1 (2000), 3–28.

Olsen, Jr., Dan R., *User Interface Management Systems: Models and Algorithms,* Morgan Kaufmann Publishers, San Mateo, CA (1991).

Olsen, Jr., Dan R. and Halversen, Bradley W., Interface usage measurement in a user interface management system, *Proc. ACM SIGGRAPH Symposium on User Interface Software and Technology*, ACM, New York (1988), 102–108.

Ousterhout, John K., *Tcl and the Tk Toolkit*, Addison-Wesley, Reading, MA (1994).

Schmucker, Kurt J., MacApp: An application framework, *Byte*, 11, 8 (August 1986), 189–193.

Sears, Andrew, Layout appropriateness: Guiding user interface design with simple task descriptions, *IEEE Transactions on Software Engineering*, 19, 7 (1993), 707–719.

Sears, Andrew, AIDE: A step towards metrics-based interface development tools, *Proc. UIST '95 User Interface Software and Technology*, ACM, New York (1995), 101–110.

Shneiderman, Ben, Multi-party grammars and related features for defining interactive systems, *IEEE Systems, Man, and Cybernetics*, SMC-12, 2 (March–April 1982), 148–154.

Szekely, Pedro, Retrospective and challenges for model-based interface development, in Vanderdonckt, J. (Editor), *Proc. Second International Workshop on Computer-Aided Design of User Interfaces*, Namur University, Belgium (1996), 1–27.

Thévenin, David and Coutaz, Joëlle, Plasticity of user interfaces: Framework and research agenda, in *Proc. Interact '99*, 1, IFIP, IOS Press, Edinburgh, Scotland (1999), 110–117.

Tullis, Thomas S., A system for evaluating screen formats: Research and application, in Hartson, H. Rex and Hix, D. (Editors), *Advances in Human-Computer Interaction, Volume II*, Ablex, Norwood, NJ (1988), 214–286.

Wasserman, Anthony I. and Shewmake, David T., The role of prototypes in the User Software Engineering (USE) methodology, in Hartson, H. Rex (Editor), *Advances in Human-Computer Interaction, Volume I*, Ablex, Norwood, NJ (1985), 191–210.

PART

III

Interaction
Styles

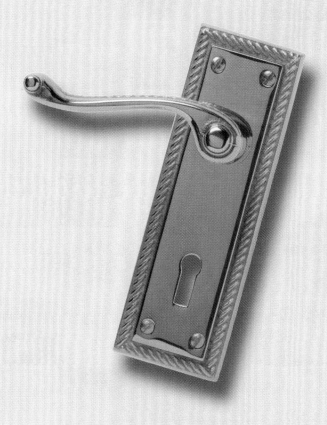

Direct Manipulation
and Virtual Environments

Leibniz sought to make the form of a symbol reflect its content. "In signs," he wrote, "one sees an advantage for discovery that is greatest when they express the exact nature of a thing briefly and, as it were, picture it; then, indeed, the labor of thought is wonderfully diminished."

FREDERICK KREILING, "LEIBNIZ,"
Scientific American, May 1968

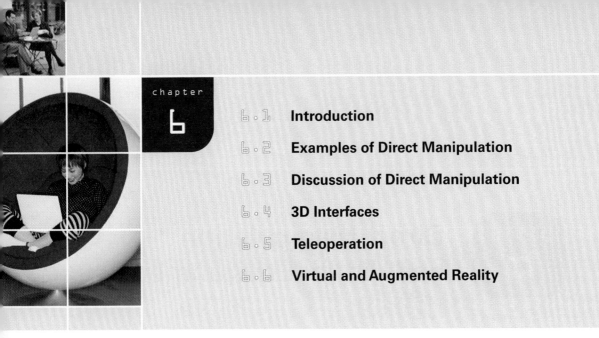

6.1   Introduction

Certain interactive systems generate a glowing enthusiasm among users that is in marked contrast with the more common reaction of reluctant acceptance or troubled confusion. The enthusiastic users report the following positive feelings:

- Mastery of the interface
- Competence in performing tasks
- Ease in learning originally and in assimilating advanced features
- Confidence in the capacity to retain mastery over time
- Enjoyment in using the interface
- Eagerness to show off the interface to novices
- Desire to explore more powerful aspects

These feelings convey an image of the truly pleased user. The central ideas in such satisfying interfaces, now widely referred to as *direct-manipulation interfaces* (Shneiderman, 1983), are visibility of the objects and actions of interest; rapid, reversible, incremental actions; and replacement of typed commands by a pointing action on the object of interest (see Chapter 8). Dragging a file to a trash can is a familiar example of direct manipulation, but direct-manipulation ideas are also at the heart of many contemporary and advanced non-desktop interfaces. Game designers led the way in creating visually compelling three-dimensional (3D) scenes with characters controlled by novel pointing devices. At the same time, interest in teleoperated devices blossomed, enabling operators to look through distant microscopes or fly reconnaissance drones. As the technology platforms mature, direct manipulation increasingly influences designers of mobile devices and web pages. It also inspires designers of information-visualization systems that present thousands of objects on the screen with dynamic user controls (see Chapter 14).

Newer concepts that extend direct manipulation include virtual reality, augmented reality, and tangible user interfaces. Virtual reality puts users in an immersive environment in which the normal surroundings are blocked out by a head-mounted display that presents artificial worlds. Hand gestures in a data glove allow users to point, select, grasp, and navigate. Augmented reality keeps users in the normal surroundings but adds a transparent overlay with information such as the names of buildings or the location of hidden plumbing. Tangible user interfaces give users physical objects to manipulate so as to operate the interface: for example, putting several plastic blocks near to each other to create an office floorplan.

This chapter develops the principles of direct manipulation by reviewing some historically important examples (Section 6.2) and providing psychological justification while raising some concerns (Section 6.3). The object-action interface (OAI) model provides a foundation for understanding direct manipulation, since it steers designers to represent the task-domain objects and actions while minimizing the interface concepts and the syntax-memorization load. Further applications of direct manipulation are covered in sections on 3D interfaces (6.4), teleoperation (6.5), and virtual and augmented reality (6.6).

6.2   Examples of Direct Manipulation

No single interface has every admirable attribute or design feature—such an interface might not be possible. Each of the following examples, however, has sufficient numbers of them to win the enthusiastic support of many users.

A favorite example of using direct manipulation is driving an automobile. The scene is directly visible through the front window, and performance of actions such as braking or steering has become common knowledge in our culture. To turn left, the driver simply rotates the steering wheel to the left. The response is immediate and the scene changes, providing feedback to refine the turn. You probably can't imagine trying to accurately turn a car by typing a command or selecting "turn left 30 degrees" from a menu, but that is the level of operation of many of today's productivity tools!

6.2.1   Command-line versus display editors versus word processors

It may be hard for users of word processors to believe, but in the early 1980s, text editing was done with line-oriented command languages. Users might see only one line at a time! Typed commands were needed to move the one-line window up or down, or to make any changes. The enthusiastic users of novel *full-page display editors* were great advocates of their two-dimensional interfaces with cursor controls. A typical comment was, "Once you've used a display editor, you will never go back to a line editor—you'll be spoiled." Similar comments came from users of early personal-computer word processors, such as WORDSTAR, or display editors such as emacs on the Unix system. A beaming advocate called emacs "the one true editor." In these interfaces, users viewed a full screen of text and could edit by using the backspace key or insert directly by typing.

Researchers found that performance was improved and training times were reduced with display editors, so there was evidence to support the enthusiasm of display-editor devotees. Furthermore, office-automation evaluations consistently favored full-page display editors, and the clarity of seeing italic, bold, underscore, or centered text onscreen enabled users to concentrate on the contents.

There are some advantages to command-language approaches: history keeping is easier, more flexible markup languages are available (for example, SGML), macros tend to be more powerful, and some tasks are simpler to express (for example, change all italics to bold). Strategies for accommodating these needs are finding their way into modern direct-manipulation word processors.

By the early 1990s, the display editors, described as *what you see is what you get* (WYSIWYG), had become standard for word processors. Microsoft Word (Fig. 6.1) is now dominant on the Macintosh and IBM PC compatibles, with Lotus Word Pro and Corel's WordPerfect taking second place. The advantages of WYSIWYG word processors include the following:

- *Users see a full page of text.* Showing 20 to 60 lines of text simultaneously gives the reader a clearer sense of context for each sentence, while permitting easier reading and scanning of the document. By contrast, working with the one-line view offered by line editors is like seeing the world through a narrow cardboard tube. Modern displays can support two or more full pages of text, set side by side.

- *The document is seen as it will appear when printed.* Eliminating the clutter of formatting commands also simplifies reading and scanning of the document. Tables, lists, page breaks, skipped lines, section headings, centered text, and figures can be viewed in their final form. The annoyance and delay of debugging the format commands are almost eliminated because the errors are usually immediately apparent.

- *Cursor action is visible.* Seeing an arrow, underscore, or blinking box on the screen gives the operator a clear sense of where to focus attention and to apply action.

- *Cursor motion is natural.* Arrow keys or cursor-motion devices—such as a mouse, trackpad, or tablet—provide natural physical mechanisms for moving the cursor. This setup is in marked contrast to commands, such as UP 6, that require an operator to convert the physical action into a correct syntactic

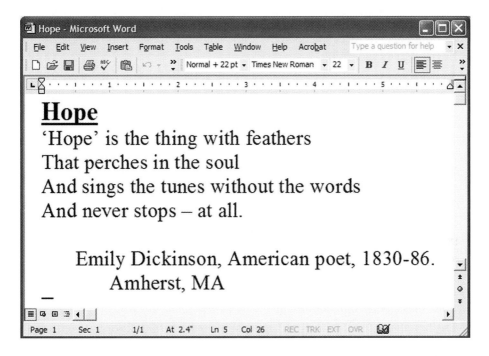

Figure 6.1

An example of a WYSIWYG (what you see is what you get) editor: Microsoft Word for Office XP.

form that may be difficult to learn and hard to recall, and thus may be a source of frustrating errors.

- *Labeled icons make frequent actions rapid.* Most word processors have labeled icons in a toolbar for frequent actions. These buttons act as a permanent menu-selection display to remind users of the features and to enable rapid selection.

- *Immediate display of the results of an action.* When users press a button to move the cursor or center text, the results are shown immediately on the screen. Deletions are apparent immediately: the character, word, or line is erased, and the remaining text is rearranged. Similarly, insertions or text movements are shown after each keystroke or function-key press. In contrast, with line editors, users must issue print or display commands to see the results of changes.

- *Rapid response and display.* Most display editors operate at high speed; a full page of text appears in a fraction of a second. This high display rate, coupled with short response time, produces a satisfying sense of power and speed. Cursors can be moved quickly, large amounts of text can be scanned rapidly, and the results of actions can be shown almost instantaneously. Rapid response also reduces the need for additional commands and thereby simplifies design and learning.

- *Easily reversible actions.* When users enter text, they can repair an incorrect keystroke by merely backspacing and retyping. They can make simple changes by moving the cursor to the problem area and inserting or deleting characters, words, or lines. A useful design strategy is to include natural inverse actions for each action (for example, to increase or decrease type sizes). An alternative offered by many display editors is a simple undo action to return the text to the state that it was in before the previous action. Easy reversibility reduces user anxiety about making a mistake or destroying the file.

So many of these issues have been studied empirically that someone once joked that the word processor was the white rat for researchers in human-computer interaction. Switching metaphors, for commercial developers, we might say the word processor is the root for many technological sprouts:

- *Integration* of graphics, spreadsheets, animations, photographs, and so on is done in the body of a document.

- *Desktop-publishing software* produces sophisticated printed formats with multiple columns and allows output to high-resolution printers. Multiple fonts, grayscales, and color permit preparation of high-quality documents, newsletters, reports, newspapers, or books. Examples include Adobe PageMaker and QuarkXPress.

- *Presentation software* produces color text and graphic layouts for use directly from the computer with a large-screen projector to allow animations. Examples include Microsoft PowerPoint, Adobe Persuasion, and Apple Keynote.

- *Hypermedia environments and the World Wide Web* allow users to jump from one page or article to another with selectable buttons or embedded hot links. Readers can add bookmarks, annotations, and tours.

- *Improved macro facilities* enable users to construct, save, and edit sequences of frequently used actions. A related feature is a style sheet that allows users to specify and save a set of options for spacing, fonts, margins, and so on. Likewise, the saving of templates allows users to take the formatting work of colleagues as a starting point for their own documents. Most word processors come with dozens of standard templates for business letters, newsletters, or brochures.

- *Spell checkers and thesauri* are standard on most full-featured word processors. Spell checking can also be set to function while users are typing, and to make automatic changes for common mistakes, such as changing "teh" to "the".

- *Grammar checkers* offer users comments about potential problems in writing style, such as use of passive voice, excessive use of certain words, or lack of parallel construction. Some writers—both novices and professionals—appreciate the comments and know that they can decide whether to apply the suggestions. Critics point out, however, that the advice is often inappropriate and therefore wastes time.

- *Document assemblers* allow users to compose complex documents, such as contracts or wills, from standard paragraphs using appropriate language for males or females; citizens or foreigners; high-, medium-, or low-income earners; renters or home owners, and so on.

6.2.2 The VisiCalc spreadsheet and its descendants

The first electronic spreadsheet, VisiCalc, was the 1979 product of a Harvard Business School student, Dan Bricklin, who became frustrated when trying to carry out repetitious calculations for a graduate course in business. He and a friend, Bob Frankston, built an "instantly calculating electronic worksheet" (as the user manual described it) that permitted computation and immediate display of results across 254 rows and 63 columns.

The spreadsheet can be programmed so that column 4 displays the sum of columns 1 through 3; then, every time a value in the first three columns changes, the fourth column changes as well. Complex dependencies between, for example, manufacturing costs, distribution costs, sales revenue, commissions, and profits can be stored for several sales districts and for various months. Spreadsheet users can try out alternate plans and immediately see the effects of changes on profits. This simulation of an accountant's spreadsheet makes it easy for business analysts to comprehend the objects and permissible actions. The distributor of VisiCalc explained the system's appeal as "it jumps," referring to the user's delight in watching the propagation of changes across the screen.

Competitors to VisiCalc emerged quickly; they made attractive improvements to the user interface and expanded the tasks that were supported. Lotus 1-2-3 dominated the market in the 1980s (Fig. 6.2), but the current leader is Microsoft's Excel (Fig. 6.3), which has numerous features and specialized additions. Excel and other modern spreadsheet programs offer numerous graphics displays, multiple windows, statistical routines, and database access. The huge numbers of features are invoked with menus or toolbars, and extensibility is provided by powerful macro facilities.

6.2.3 Spatial data management

In geographic applications, it seems natural to give a spatial representation in the form of a map that provides a familiar model of reality. The developers of the prototype Spatial Data Management System (Herot, 1980; 1984) attribute the

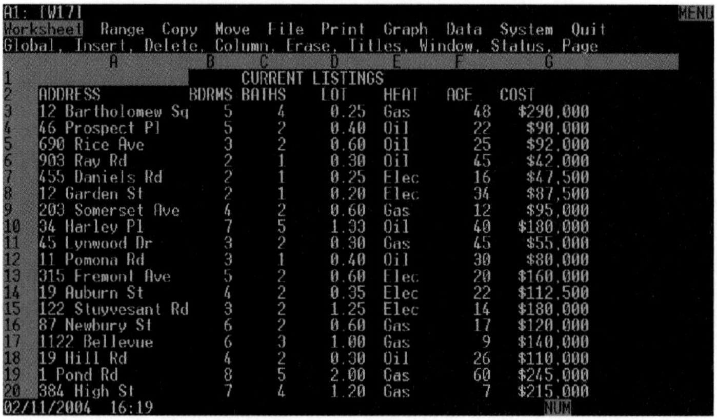

Figure 6.2

Early version of Lotus 1-2-3, the spreadsheet program that was dominant through the 1980s.

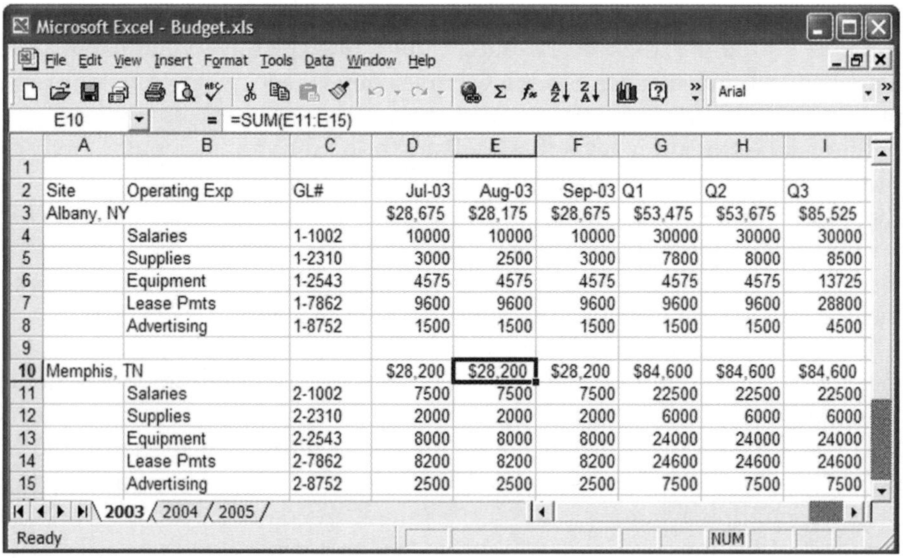

Figure 6.3

Microsoft Excel spreadsheet for Office XP.

basic idea to Nicholas Negroponte of MIT. In one early scenario, users were seated before a color-graphics display of the world and could zoom in on the Pacific Ocean to see markers for convoys of military ships. By moving a joystick, users caused the screen to be filled with silhouettes of individual ships; zooming displayed detailed data, such as, ultimately, a full-color picture of the captain.

Later attempts at spatial data management included the Xerox PARC Information Visualizer, which was an ensemble of tools for three-dimensional animated explorations of buildings, cone-shaped file directories, organization charts, a perspective wall that puts featured items up front and centered, and several two- and three-dimensional information layouts (Robertson, Card, and Mackinlay, 1993).

ArcView (by ESRI, Inc.) is a widely used geographic-information system that offers rich, layered databases of map-related information (Fig. 6.4). Users can zoom in on areas of interest, select the kinds of information they wish to view (roads, population density, topography, rainfall, political boundaries, and much

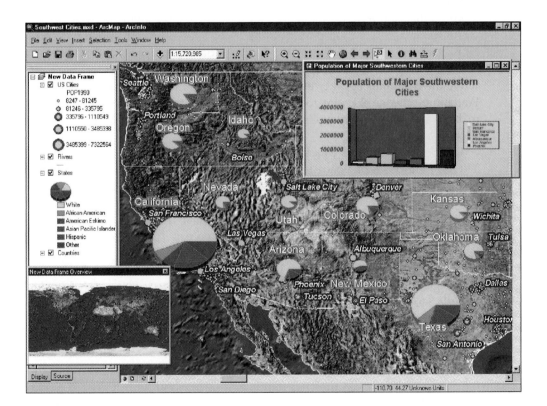

Figure 6.4

ArcView geographic information system (GIS) provides comprehensive mapping functions and management of related data. Users can see the population of major cities. An overview map provides the context for the detail map.

more), and do limited searches. Much simpler but widely popular highway, weather, and economic maps covering whole continents are available on the Web, on CD-ROMs, and on mobile devices.

The success of a spatial data-management system depends on the skill of the designers in choosing icons, graphical representations, and data layouts that are natural and comprehensible to users. The joy of zooming in and out or of gliding over data entices even anxious users, who quickly demand additional power and data.

6.2.4   Video games

For many people, the most exciting, well-engineered, and commercially success-ful application of the direct-manipulation concepts lies in the world of video games (Provenzo, 1991). The early but simple and popular game PONG required the user to rotate a knob that moved a white rectangle on the screen. A white spot acted as a ping-pong ball that ricocheted off the wall and had to be hit back by the movable white rectangle. Users developed speed and accuracy in placing the "paddle" to keep the increasingly speedy ball from getting past, while the computer speaker emitted a ponging sound when the ball bounced. Watching someone else play for 30 seconds is all the training that a person needs to become a competent novice, but many hours of practice are required to become a skilled expert.

Later games, such as Missile Command, Donkey Kong, Pacman, Tempest, TRON, Centipede, or Space Invaders, were much more sophisticated in their rules, color graphics, and sound effects. Recent games include multiperson com-petitions (for example, in tennis or karate), three-dimensional graphics, still higher resolution, and stereo sound. The designers of these games provide stim-ulating entertainment, a challenge for novices and experts, and many intriguing lessons in the human factors of interface design—somehow, they have found a way to get people to put quarters in the sides of computers. Forty million Nin-tendo game players reside across 70% of those American households that include 8 to 12 year olds. Brisk sales of games like the Mario series testify to the games' strong attraction, in marked contrast to the anxiety about and resistance to office-automation equipment that many users have shown.

The Nintendo GameCube (Fig 6.5), Sony PlayStation 2, and Microsoft Xbox have brought powerful three-dimensional graphics hardware to the home and have created a remarkable international market. Wildly successful games include violent first-person shooters, fast-paced racing games, and more sedate golfing games. Small handheld game devices, such as the Game Boy, provide portable fun for kids on the street as well as executives in their well-appointed offices. These game boxes also support two-person games based on competition, such as car racing, tennis, or more violent boxing or shooting games. Multi-player games on the Internet have also caught on with many users because of

Figure 6.5

Home video games are a huge success and employ advanced graphics hardware for rapid movement in rich three-dimensional worlds. Here, two teenagers are using the Nintendo GameCube to play the Tony Hawk Underground skateboarding game, from Activision, Inc.

the additional opportunity for social encounters and competitions. Gaming magazines and conferences attest to the widespread interest.

Typical games provide a field of action that is visual and compelling. The physical actions—such as button presses, joystick motions, or knob rotations—produce rapid responses on the screen. There is no syntax to remember, and therefore there are no syntax-error messages. If users move their spaceships too far to the left, they merely use the natural inverse action of moving back to the right. Error messages are rare, because the results of actions are obvious and can be reversed easily. These principles can be applied to office automation, personal computing, or other interactive environments.

Most games continuously display a numeric score so that users can measure their progress and compete with their previous performance, with friends, or with the highest scorers. Typically, the 10 highest scorers get to store their initials in the game for public display. This strategy provides one form of positive reinforcement that encourages mastery. Malone's (1981), Provenzo's (1991), and our studies with elementary-school children have shown that continuous display of scores is extremely valuable. Machine-generated feedback—such as "Very good" or "You're doing great!"—is not as effective, since the same score carries different meanings for different people. Most users prefer to make their own subjective judgments and perceive the machine-generated messages as an annoyance and a deception.

Many educational games use direct manipulation effectively. For example, elementary- or high-school students can learn about urban planning by using SimCity and its variants, which show urban environments visually and let students build roads, airports, housing, and so on by direct-manipulation actions. The social simulation game, The Sims, and its online version broke new ground because of their stronger attraction to women than men.

The esthetically appealing Myst, with its successors Riven and Exile, have drawn widespread approval even in some literary circles, while the more violent but successful DOOM and Quake series have provoked controversy over their psychological effects on teens. Studying game design is fun, but there are limits to the applicability of the lessons. Game players are engaged in competition with the system or with other players, whereas applications-systems users prefer a strong internal locus of control, which gives them the sense of being in charge. Likewise, whereas game players seek entertainment and focus on the challenge, applications users focus on their tasks and may resent too many playful distractions. The random events that occur in most games are meant to challenge the users; in nongame designs, however, predictable system behavior is preferred.

6.2.5   Computer-aided design

Most computer-aided design (CAD) systems for automobiles, electronic circuitry, aircraft, or mechanical engineering use principles of direct manipulation. Building and home architects now have powerful tools such as AutoCAD (see Fig 1.14) with components to handle structural engineering, floorplans, interiors, landscaping, plumbing, electrical installation, and much more. With programs like this, the operator may see a circuit schematic on the screen and, with mouse clicks, be able to move components into or out of the proposed circuit.

When the design is complete, the computer can provide information about current, voltage drops, and fabrication costs, and warnings about inconsistencies or manufacturing problems. Similarly, newspaper-layout artists or automobile-body designers can easily try multiple designs in minutes and can record promising approaches until they find even better ones. The pleasures in using these systems stem from the capacity to manipulate the object of interest directly and to generate multiple alternatives rapidly.

Related applications are for computer-aided manufacturing (CAM) and process control. Honeywell's Experion Process Knowledge System provides the manager of an oil refinery, paper mill, or power-utility plant with a colored schematic view of the plant. The schematic may be displayed on multiple displays or on a large wall-sized map, with red lines indicating a sensor value that is out of normal range. With a single click, the operator can get a more detailed view of the troubling component; with a second click, the operator can examine individual sensors or can reset valves and circuits.

A basic strategy for this design is to eliminate the need for complex commands that the operator might only need to recall during a once-a-year emergency. The visual overview provided by the schematic facilitates problem solving by analogy, since the linkage between the screen representations and the plant's temperatures or pressures is so close.

6.2.6   Office automation

Designers of early office-automation systems used direct-manipulation principles. The pioneering Xerox Star (Smith et al., 1982) offered sophisticated text-formatting options, graphics, multiple fonts, and a high-resolution, cursor-based user interface (Fig. 6.6). Users could move (but not drag) a document icon to a printer icon to generate a hardcopy printout. The Apple Lisa system also elegantly applied many of the principles of direct manipulation; although it was not a commercial success, it laid the groundwork for the successful Macintosh. The Macintosh designers drew from the Star and Lisa experiences, but made many simplifying decisions while preserving adequate power for users (Fig. 6.7). The hardware and software designs supported rapid and continuous graphical interaction for pull-down menus, window manipulation, editing of graphics and text, and dragging of icons. Variations on the Macintosh appeared soon afterward for other popular personal computers, and Microsoft now dominates the office-automation market (Fig. 6.8). The Microsoft Windows design is still a close relative of the Macintosh design, and both are candidates for substantial improvements in window management, with simplifications for novices and increased power for sophisticated users.

Early studies of direct-manipulation interfaces confirmed the advantages for at least some users and tasks. In a study of novices, MS-DOS commands for

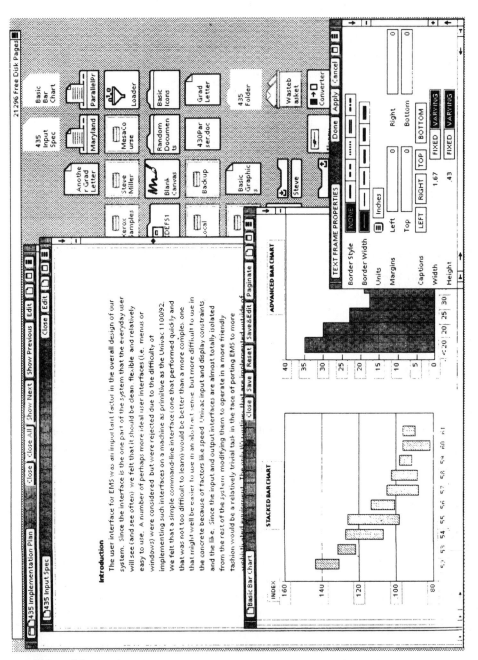

Figure 6.6

The Xerox Star 8010 with the ViewPoint system enables users to create documents with multiple fonts and graphics. This session shows the Text Frame Properties sheet over sample bar charts, with a document in the background and many desktop icons available for selection.

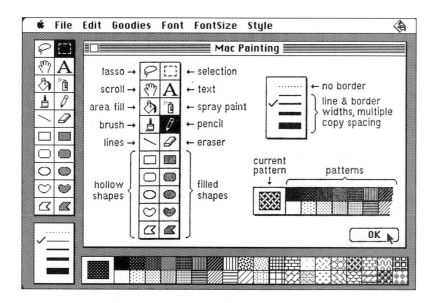

Figure 6.7

The original Apple Macintosh MacPaint. This program offers a command menu on the top, a menu of action icons on the left, a choice of line thicknesses on the lower left, and a palette of textures on the bottom. All actions can be accomplished with only the mouse.

creating, copying, renaming, and erasing files were contrasted with the Macintosh's direct-manipulation actions. After user training and practice, average task times were 5.8 minutes (MS-DOS) versus 4.8 minutes (Macintosh), and average errors were 2.0 versus 0.8 (Margono and Shneiderman, 1987). Subjective preference also favored the direct-manipulation interface. In a study of a command-line versus a direct-manipulation database interface, "computer naive but keyboard literate" users made more than twice as many errors with the command-line format. No significant differences in time were found (Morgan, Morris, and Gibbs, 1991). These users preferred the direct-manipulation interface overall, and they rated it as more stimulating, easier, and more powerful.

Both of the above reports caution about generalizing their results to more experienced users. However, a study with novices and experienced users was cosponsored by Microsoft and Zenith Data Systems (Temple, Barker, and Sloane, Inc., 1990). Although details about subjects, interfaces, and tasks were not reported, the results showed improved productivity and reduced fatigue for experienced users with a GUI as compared with a character-based user interface. The benefits of direct manipulation were confirmed in other studies (Benbasat and Todd, 1993); one such study also demonstrated that the advantage was greater for experienced than for novice users (Ulich et al., 1991).

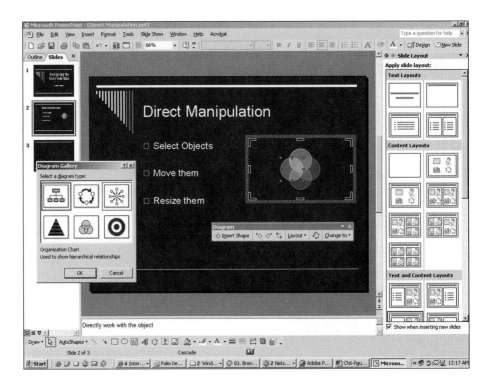

Figure 6.8

Presentation graphics or slide programs, such as Microsoft's PowerPoint for Office XP, have multiple toolbars and palettes that support a direct-manipulation style of selecting objects, moving them, and resizing them.

6.2.7   The continuing evolution of direct manipulation

The insight needed to create a successful direct-manipulation interface is an appropriate representation or model of reality. With some applications the jump to visual language may be difficult, but after using visual direct-manipulation interfaces most users and designers can hardly imagine why anyone would want to use a complex syntactic notation to describe an essentially visual process. It is hard to conceive of learning the commands for the vast number of features in modern word processors, drawing programs, or spreadsheets, but the visual cues, icons, menus, and dialog boxes make it possible for even intermittent users to succeed.

Several designers have applied direct manipulation using the metaphor of a stack of cards to portray a set of addresses, telephone numbers, events, and so on. Clicking on a card brings it to the front, and the stack of cards moves to preserve alphabetic ordering. This simple card-deck metaphor, combined with other notions (Heckel, 1991), led to Bill Atkinson's innovative development of HyperCard stacks in 1987. Promoted as a way to "create your own applications for gathering, organizing, presenting, searching, and customizing information," HyperCard quickly spawned variants, such as SuperCard and ToolBook. Each had a scripting language to enable users to create appealing graphics applications. However, these products faded as the World Wide Web and development tools such as Microsoft Frontpage and Macromedia Dreamweaver became widely used.

Direct-manipulation interfaces are now being used for a wide range of purposes, including personal finance and travel arrangements. Direct-manipulation checkbook-maintenance and checkbook-searching interfaces, such as Quicken (by Intuit, Inc.), display a checkbook register with labeled columns for check number, date, payee, and amount. Changes can be made in place, new entries can be made at the first blank line, and a check mark can be made to indicate verification against a monthly report or bank statement; users can search for a particular payee by filling in a blank payee field and then typing a "?". Some web-based airline-reservations systems show users a map and prompt for clicks on the departing and arriving cities. Then users can select the date from a calendar and the time from a clock and make their seat selections by clicking on the plane's seating plan.

Another emerging use of direct manipulation involves home automation. Since so much of home control involves floorplans, direct-manipulation actions naturally take place on a display of the floorplan (Fig. 6.9), with selectable icons for each status indicator (such as a burglar alarm, heat sensor, or smoke detector) and for each activator (such as contols for opening and closing curtains or shades, for air conditioning and heating, or for audio and video speakers or screens) (Norman, 2002). For example, users can route sound from a CD player located in the living room to the bedroom and kitchen by merely dragging the CD icon into those rooms, and they can adjust the volume by moving a marker on a linear scale.

"Direct manipulation" is also an accurate description of the programming of certain industrial robotics tools. In one such scenario, often used on automobiles, the operator holds the robot's "hand" and guides it through a spray-painting or welding task while the controlling computer records every action. The computer can then operate the robot automatically, repeating the precise action as many times as is necessary.

By the 1990s, direct-manipulation variations had become influential in beyond-the-desktop designs such as virtual reality, ubiquitous computing, augmented reality, and tangible user interfaces. Virtual reality places users in an immersive environment that blocks out the world. They see an artificial world inside their stereoscopic goggles, which is updated as they turn their heads. Users typically control activity by hand gestures inside a data glove, which allows them to point, select, grasp, and navigate. Handheld controllers allow

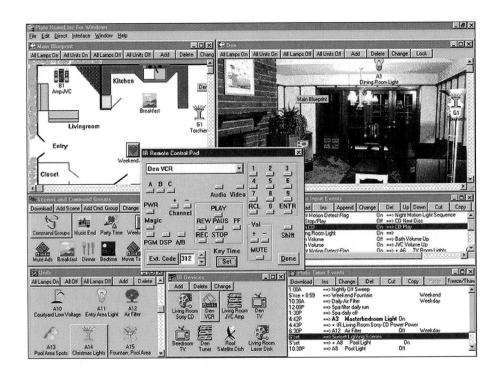

Figure 6.9

Floorplan and general control system for a private home. Direct-manipulation designs emphasize task-domain graphics. (http://smarthome.com)

users to have a six-degree-of-freedom pointer (three dimensions of position and three dimensions of orientation), to simulate mouse clicks, or to fly in the direction that they point. Virtual worlds allow users to travel through the human body, swim through oceans, ride an electron cloud as it spins around a nucleus, or participate in fantasy worlds with distant Inernet-connected collaborators.

Weiser's (1991) influential vision of ubiquitous computing described a world where computational devices were everywhere—in your hands, on your body, in your car, built into your home, and pervasively distributed in your environment. The 1993 special issue of *Communications of the ACM* (Wellner, Mackay, and Gold, 1993) showed provocative prototypes that refined Weiser's vision. It offered multiple visions of beyond-the-desktop designs that used freehand gestures and small mobile devices whose displays changed depending on where users stood and how they pointed the device. Another prototype showed how users of paper documents on a digital desk could control a desktop display interface (Wellner, 1993).

Another innovation was augmented reality, in which users see the real world with an overlay of additional information, such as instructions on how to repair a laser printer or information about the location of plumbing behind a wall (Feiner, MacIntyre, and Seligmann, 1993). At the same time, the notion of tangible user interfaces—in which users grasp physical objects such as bricks, plastic tiles, or marbles to manipulate a graphical display that represents, for example, an urban plan, an optical workbench, or an e-mail interface—was being developed (Ishii and Ullmer, 1997). Virtual, artificial, and augmented reality are discussed further in Section 6.6.

There will certainly be many future variations of and extensions to direct manipulation, but the basic goals will remain similar: comprehensible interfaces that enable rapid learning, predictable and controllable actions, and appropriate feedback to confirm progress. Direct manipulation has the power to attract users because it is rapid, and even enjoyable. If actions are simple, reversibility is ensured, and retention is easy, then anxiety recedes, users feel in control, and satisfaction flows in.

6.3 Discussion of Direct Manipulation

Several authors have attempted to describe the component principles of direct manipulation. An imaginative and early interactive system designer, Ted Nelson (1980), perceived user excitement when the interface was constructed by what he calls the *principle of virtuality*—a representation of reality that can be manipulated. Rutkowski (1982) conveyed a similar concept in his *principle of transparency*: "The user is able to apply intellect directly to the task; the tool itself seems to disappear." Heckel (1991) laments that "Our instincts and training as engineers encourage us to think logically instead of visually, and this is counterproductive to friendly design." His description is in harmony with the popular notions of the logical, symbolic, sequential left-brain and the visual, artistic, all-at-once right-brain problem-solving styles.

Hutchins, Hollan, and Norman (1986) review the concepts of direct manipulation and offer a thoughtful decomposition of concerns. They describe the "feeling of involvement directly with a world of objects rather than of communicating with an intermediary," and clarify how direct manipulation breaches the *gulf of execution* and the *gulf of evaluation*.

These writers and others (Ziegler and Fähnrich, 1988; Thimbleby, 1990; Phillips and Apperley, 1991; Frohlich, 1993) validate the significance of direct manipulation and improve our understanding of how to apply its principles. Much credit also goes to the individual designers who created systems that exemplify aspects of direct manipulation.

Another perspective on direct manipulation comes from the psychology literature on *problem-solving* and *learning research*. Suitable representations of problems have been clearly shown to be critical to solution finding and to learning.

This approach is in harmony with Maria Montessori's (1964) teaching methods for children. She proposed use of physical objects, such as beads or wooden sticks, to convey such mathematical principles as addition, multiplication, or size comparison. The durable abacus is appealing because it gives a direct-manipulation representation of numbers.

Similarly, feedback in direct-manipulation designs reduced users' errors in a task requiring statistical analysis of student grades (Te'eni, 1990). The advantage appears to stem from having the data entry and display combined in a single location on the screen. Physical, spatial, and visual representations also appear to be easier to retain and manipulate than textual or numeric representations (Arnheim, 1972; McKim, 1980).

Papert's (1980) LOGO language created a mathematical microworld in which the principles of geometry are visible. Based on the Swiss psychologist Jean Piaget's theory of child development, LOGO offers students the opportunity to easily create line drawings with an electronic turtle displayed on the screen. In this environment, users derive rapid feedback about their programs, can easily determine what has happened, can spot and repair errors quickly, and can gain satisfaction from creative production of drawings. These features are all characteristic of a direct-manipulation environment.

6.3.1   Problems with direct manipulation

Spatial or visual representations are not necessarily an improvement over text, especially for blind or vision-impaired users who will need special software. Graphical user interfaces were a setback for vision-impaired users, who appreciated the simplicity of linear command languages. However, screen readers for desktop interfaces, page readers for Internet browsers, and audio designs for mobile devices enable vision-impaired users to understand some of the spatial relationships necessary to achieve their goals.

A second problem is that direct-manipulation designs may consume valuable screen space and thus force valuable information offscreen, requiring scrolling or multiple actions. Studies of graphical plots versus tabular business data and of flowcharts versus program text demonstrate advantages for compact graphical approaches when pattern-recognition tasks are relevant, but disadvantages when the graphic gets too large and the tasks require detailed information. For experienced users, a tabular textual display of 50 document names may be more appropriate than only 10 graphic document icons with the names abbreviated to fit the icon size.

A third problem is that users must learn the meanings of visual representations. A graphic icon may be meaningful to the designer, but for users may require as much learning time as a word, or more. Some airports that serve multilingual communities use graphic icons extensively, but the meanings of these icons may not be obvious. Similarly, some computer terminals designed for international use have icons in place of names, but their meanings are not always clear. Titles that appear on icons when the cursor is over them offer only a partial solution.

A fourth problem is that the visual representation may be misleading. Users may grasp the analogical representation rapidly, but then may draw incorrect conclusions about permissible actions. Users may overestimate or underestimate the functions of the computer-based analogy. Ample testing must be carried out to refine the displayed objects and actions and to minimize negative side effects.

A fifth problem is that, for experienced typists, taking a hand off the keyboard to move a mouse or point with a finger may take more time than typing the relevant command. This problem is especially likely to occur if users are familiar with a compact notation, such as for arithmetic expressions, that is easy to enter from a keyboard but that may be more difficult to select with a mouse. While direct manipulation is often defined as replacing typed commands by pointing devices, sometimes the keyboard is the most effective direct-manipulation device. Rapid keyboard interaction can be extremely attractive for expert users, but the visual feedback must be equally rapid and comprehensible. The non-graphical emacs text editor is an excellent example of a powerful tool that was designed for rapid keyboard entry. It offers rich cursor-movement control that allows quick jumps to destinations, scrolling, and paging, as well as reversibility for actions and potent macro facilities.

In addition to these problems, choosing the right objects and actions for a direct-manipulation interface may be difficult. Simple metaphors or analogies with a minimal set of concepts—for example, pencils and paintbrushes in a drawing tool—are a good starting point. Mixing metaphors from two sources may add complexity that contributes to confusion. Also, the emotional tone of the metaphor should be inviting rather than distasteful or inappropriate (Carroll and Thomas, 1982)—sewage-disposal systems are an inappropriate metaphor for electronic-message systems. Since the users may not share understanding of the metaphor, analogy, or conceptual model with the designer, ample testing is required.

Some direct-manipulation principles can be surprisingly difficult to realize in software. Rapid and incremental actions have two strong implications: a fast perception/action loop (less than 100 ms) and reversibility (the undo action). A standard database query may take a few seconds to perform, so implementing a direct-manipulation interface on top of a database may require special programming techniques. The undo action may be even harder to implement, as it requires that each user action be recorded and that reverse actions be defined. It changes the style of programming, because a nonreversible action is implemented by a simple function call, whereas a reversible action requires recording the inverse action.

Web-based implementers of direct manipulation face further challenges, because the standard markup language (HTML) limits dynamic user interaction even with the addition of JavaScript. The newer Dynamic HTML offers greater flexibility (Golub and Shneiderman, 2003), but web-based direct manipulation is more easily accomplished in Java or Flash. As these tools become more widely accepted, web-based direct manipulation will spread, enabling users to move sliders, make selections, and perform drag-and-drop operations.

6.3.2   The OAI model explanation of direct manipulation

The attraction of direct manipulation is apparent in the enthusiasm of the users. The designers of the examples in Section 6.2 had an innovative inspiration and an intuitive grasp of what users would want. Each example has problematic features, but they demonstrate the potent advantages of direct manipulation, which can be summarized by three principles:

1. Continuous representations of the objects and actions of interest with meaningful visual metaphors.
2. Physical actions or presses of labeled buttons, instead of complex syntax.
3. Rapid, incremental, reversible actions whose effects on the objects of interest are visible immediately.

Using these three principles, it is possible to design systems that have these beneficial attributes:

- Novices can learn basic functionality quickly, usually through a demonstration by a more experienced user.
- Experts can work rapidly to carry out a wide range of tasks, even defining new functions and features.
- Knowledgeable intermittent users can retain operational concepts.
- Error messages are rarely needed.
- Users can immediately see whether their actions are furthering their goals, and, if the actions are counterproductive, they can simply change the direction of their activity.
- Users experience less anxiety because the interface is comprehensible and because actions can be reversed easily.
- Users gain confidence and mastery because they are the initiators of action, they feel in control, and they can predict the interface's responses.

The success of direct manipulation is understandable in the context of the OAI model. The object of interest is displayed so that interface actions are close to the high-level task domain. There is little need for the mental decomposition of tasks into multiple interface commands with complex syntactic forms. On the contrary, each action produces a comprehensible result in the task domain that is visible in the interface immediately. The closeness of the task domain to the interface domain reduces operator problem-solving load and stress. This basic principle is related to stimulus-response compatibility, as discussed in the human-factors literature. The task objects and actions dominate the users' concerns, and the distraction of dealing with a tedious interface is reduced (Fig. 6.10).

In contrast to textual descriptors, dealing with visual representations of objects may be more "natural" and closer to innate human capabilities: Action and visual skills emerged well before language in human evolution. Psychologists have long known that people grasp spatial relationships and actions more quickly when those people are given visual rather than linguistic representations. Furthermore, intuition and discovery are often promoted by suitable visual representations of formal mathematical systems.

The Swiss psychologist Jean Piaget described four *stages of development: sensorimotor* (from birth to approximately 2 years), *preoperational* (2 to 7 years), *concrete operational* (7 to 11 years), and *formal operations* (begins at approximately 11 years) (Copeland, 1979). According to this theory, physical actions on an object are comprehensible during the concrete operational stage, when children

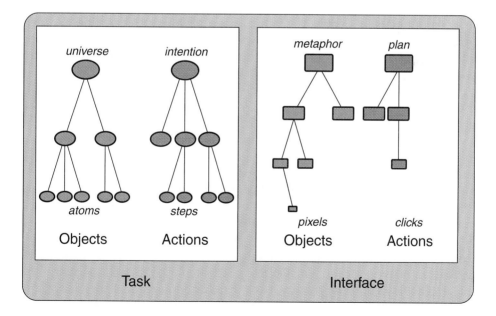

Figure 6.10

Direct-manipulation systems may require users to learn substantial task knowledge. However, users must acquire only a modest amount of interface knowledge and syntactic details.

acquire the concept of *conservation* or *invariance.* At about age 11, children enter the formal-operations stage, in which they use *symbol manipulation* to represent actions on objects. Since mathematics and programming require abstract thinking, they are difficult for children, and designers must link symbolic representations to actual objects. Direct manipulation brings activity to the concrete-operational stage, thus making certain tasks easier for children and adults.

6.3.3   Visual thinking and icons

The concepts of a *visual language* and of *visual thinking* were promoted by Arnheim (1972) and were embraced by commercial graphic designers (Verplank, 1988; Mullet and Sano, 1995), semiotically oriented academics (*semiotics* is the study of signs and symbols), and data-visualization gurus. The computer provides a remarkable visual environment for revealing structure, showing relationships, and enabling interactivity that attracts users who have artistic, right-brained, holistic, intuitive personalities. The increasingly visual nature of computer interfaces can sometimes challenge or even threaten the logical, linear, text-oriented, left-brained, compulsive, rational programmers who were the heart of the first generation of hackers. Although these stereotypes—or caricatures—will not stand up to scientific analysis, they do convey the dual paths that computing is following. The new visual directions are sometimes scorned by the traditionalists as *WIMP* (windows, icons, mouse, and pull-down menu) interfaces, whereas the command-line devotees are seen by visual system proponents as stubborn and inflexible.

There is evidence that different people have different cognitive styles, and it is quite understandable that individual preferences may vary. Just as there are multiple ice-cream flavors or car models, so too there will be multiple interface styles. It may be that preferences will vary by user and by tasks, so respect is due to each community, and the designer's goal is to provide the best of each style and the means to cross over when desired.

The conflict between text and graphics becomes most heated when the issue of *icons* is raised. Dictionary definitions of *icon* usually refer to religious images, but the central notion in computing is that an icon is an image, picture, or symbol representing a concept (Rogers, 1989; Marcus, 1992). In the computer world, icons are usually small (less than 1-inch-square or 64- by 64-pixel) representations of an object or action. Smaller icons are often used to save space or to be integrated within other objects, such as a window border or toolbar. It is not surprising that icons are often used in painting programs to represent tools or actions (for example, lasso or scissors to cut out an image, brush for painting, pencil for drawing, eraser to wipe clean), whereas word processors usually have textual menus for their actions. This difference appears to reflect the differing cognitive styles of visually and textually oriented users, or at least differences in the tasks. Maybe while users are working on visually oriented tasks, it is helpful to "stay visual" by using icons, whereas while working on a text document, it is helpful to "stay textual" by using textual menus.

For situations where both a visual icon or a textual item are possible—for example, in a directory listing—designers face two interwoven issues: how to decide between icons and text, and how to design icons. The well-established highway signs are a useful source of experience. Icons are unbeatable for showing ideas such as a road curve, but sometimes a phrase such as ONE WAY!—DO NOT ENTER is more comprehensible than an icon. Of course, the smorgasbord approach is to have a little of each (as with, for example, the octagonal STOP sign), and there is evidence that icons plus words are effective in computing situations (Norman, 1991). So the answer to the first question (deciding between icons and text) depends not only on the users and the tasks, but also on the quality of the icons or the words that are proposed. Textual menu choices are covered in Chapter 7; many of the principles carry over to icon use. In addition, these icon-specific guidelines should be considered:

- Represent the object or action in a familiar and recognizable manner.
- Limit the number of different icons.
- Make the icon stand out from its background.
- Carefully consider three-dimensional icons; they are eye-catching but also can be distracting.
- Ensure that a single selected icon is clearly visible when surrounded by unselected icons.
- Make each icon distinctive from every other icon.
- Ensure the harmoniousness of each icon as a member of a family of icons.
- Design the movement animation: when dragging an icon, the user might move the whole icon, just a frame, possibly a grayed-out or transparent version, or a black box.
- Add detailed information, such as shading to show the size of a file (larger shadow indicates larger file), thickness to show the breadth of a directory folder (thicker means more files inside), color to show the age of a document (older might be yellower or grayer), or animation to show how much of a document has been printed (document folder absorbed progressively into the printer icon).
- Explore the use of combinations of icons to create new objects or actions—for example, dragging a document icon to a folder, trash can, outbox, or printer icon has great utility. Can a document be appended or prepended to another document by pasting of adjacent icons? Can a user set security levels by dragging a document or folder to a guard dog, police car, or vault icon? Can two database icons be intersected by overlapping of the icons?

Marcus (1992) applies semiotics as a guide to four levels of icon design:

1. *Lexical qualities.* Machine-generated marks—pixel shape, color, brightness, blinking

2. *Syntactics.* Appearance and movement—lines, patterns, modular parts, size, shape

3. *Semantics.* Objects represented—concrete versus abstract, part versus whole

4. *Pragmatics.* Overall legibility, utility, identifiability, memorability, pleasingness

He recommends starting by creating quick sketches, pushing for consistent style, designing a layout grid, simplifying appearance, and evaluating the designs by testing with users. We might also consider a fifth level of icon design:

5. *Dynamics.* Receptivity to clicks—highlighting, dragging, combining

The dynamics of icons might include a rich set of gestures with a mouse, touch-screen, or pen. The gestures might indicate copy (up and down arrows), delete (a cross), edit (a circle), and so on. Icons might also have associated sounds. For example, if each document icon had a tone associated with it (the lower the tone, the bigger the document), when a directory was opened, each tone might be played simultaneously or sequentially. Users might get used to the symphony played by each directory and be able to detect certain features or anomalies, just as we often know telephone numbers by tune and can detect misdialings as discordant tones.

Icon design becomes more interesting as computer hardware improves and as designers become more creative. Animated icons that demonstrate their functions improve online help capabilities (see Section 13.4.2). Beyond simple icons, we are now seeing increasing numbers of visual programming languages (see Section 5.3) and specialized languages for mechanical engineering, circuit design, and database query.

6.3.4 Direct-manipulation programming

Performing tasks by direct manipulation is not the only goal. It should be possible to do programming by direct manipulation as well, at least for certain problems. As mentioned earlier, people often program car-painting robots by moving the robot arm through a sequence of steps that are later replayed, possibly at higher speed. This example seems to be a good candidate for generalization. How about moving a drill press or a surgical tool through a complex series of motions that are then repeated exactly? In fact, these direct-manipulation programming ideas are already being implemented in modest ways with automobile radios that users preset by tuning to their desired station and then pressing and holding a button. Later, when the button is pressed, the radio tunes to the preset frequency. Likewise, some professional television-camera supports allow the operator to program a sequence of pans or zooms and then to replay it smoothly when required.

Programming of physical devices by direct manipulation seems quite natural, and an adequate visual representation of information may make direct-manipulation programming possible in other domains. Several word processors allow users to create macros by simply performing a sequence of commands and storing it for later use—for example, emacs allows its rich set of functions, including regular-expression searching, to be recorded into macros. Spreadsheet packages, such as Lotus 1-2-3 and Excel, have rich programming languages and allow users to create portions of programs by carrying out standard spreadsheet actions. The result of the actions is stored in another part of the spreadsheet and can be edited, printed, and stored in a textual form. Similarly, Adobe PhotoShop records a history of user actions and then allows users to create programs with action sequences and repetition using direct manipulation.

It would be helpful if the computer could recognize repeated patterns reliably and create useful macros automatically, while the user was engaged in performing a repetitive interface task. Then, with the user's confirmation, the computer could take over and carry out the remainder of the task automatically (Lieberman, 2001). This hope for automatic programming is appealing, but a more effective approach may be to give users the visual tools to specify and record their intentions. Rule-based programming with graphical conditions and actions offers a fresh alternative that may be appealing to children and adults (Smith, Cypher, and Spohrer, 1994). The screen is portrayed as a set of tiles, and users specify graphical rewrite rules by showing before-and-after tile examples (Fig. 6.11). Another innovative environment initially conceived of for children is ToonTalk (Kahn, 1999), which offers animated cartoon characters who carry out actions in buildings using a variety of fanciful tools.

To create a reliable tool that works in many situations without unpredictable automatic programming, designers must meet the five challenges of *programming in the user interface* (PITUI) (Potter, 1993):

1. Sufficient computational generality (conditionals, iteration)

2. Access to the appropriate data structures (file structures for directories, structural representations of graphical objects) and operators (selectors, booleans, specialized operators of applications)

3. Ease in programming (by specification, by example, or by demonstration, with modularity, argument passing, and so on) and in editing programs

4. Simplicity in invocation and assignment of arguments (direct manipulation, simple library strategies with meaningful names or icons, in-context execution, and availability of results)

5. Low risk (high probability of bug-free programs, halt and resume facilities to permit partial executions, undo actions to enable repair of unanticipated damage)

The goal of PITUI is to allow users easily and reliably to repeat automatically the actions that they can perform manually in the user interface. Rather than

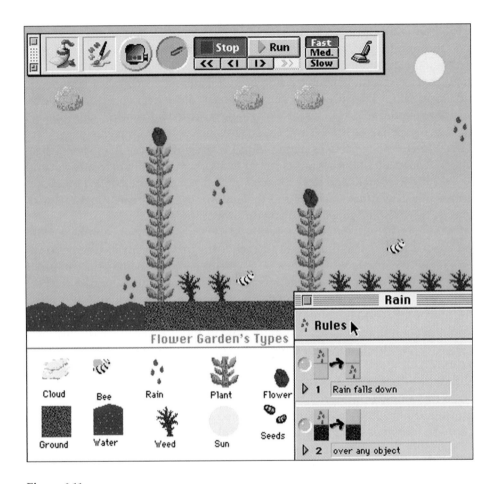

Figure 6.11

1994 Cocoa program display showing the Flower Garden world, with the control panel, the garden data types, and the graphical rules for the rain falling down and getting absorbed by any object.

depending on unpredictable inferencing, users will be able to indicate their intentions explicitly by manipulating objects and actions. The design of direct-manipulation systems will undoubtedly be influenced by the need to support PITUI. This influence will be a positive step that will also facilitate history keeping, undo functions, and online help.

The *cognitive-dimensions framework* may help us to analyze design issues of visual-programming environments, such as those needed for PITUI (Green and Petre, 1996). The framework provides a vocabulary to facilitate discussion of high-level design issues; for example, *viscosity* is used to describe the difficulty of making changes in a program, and *progressive evaluation* describes the capacity for execution of partial programs. Other dimensions are consistency, diffuseness, hidden dependencies, premature commitment, and visibility.

Direct-manipulation programming offers an alternative to the agent scenarios (see Section 2.3.6). Agent promoters believe that the computer can ascertain the users' intentions automatically, or can take action based on vague statements of goals. User intentions are unlikely to be so easily determined, though, and vague statements are not usually too effective. However, if users can specify what they want with comprehensible actions selected from a visual display, then they can often rapidly accomplish their goals while preserving their sense of control and accomplishment.

6.4   3D Interfaces

Some designers dream about building interfaces that approach the richness of three-dimensional (3D) reality. They believe that the closer the interfaces are to the real world, the easier usage will be. This extreme interpretation of direct manipulation is a dubious proposition, since user studies show that disorienting navigation, complex user actions, and annoying occlusions can slow performance in the real world as well as in 3D interfaces (Sutcliffe and Patel, 1996; Risden et al., 2000; Cockburn and McKenzie, 2002). Many interfaces are designed to be simpler than the real world (sometimes called 2D) by constraining movement, limiting interface actions, and ensuring visibility of interface objects. However, the strong utility of "pure" 3D interfaces for medical, architectural, product design, and scientific visualization purposes means that they remain an important challenge for interface designers.

An intriguing possibility is that "enhanced" interfaces may be better than 3D reality. Enhanced features might enable superhuman capabilities such as faster-than-light teleportation, flying through objects, multiple simultaneous views of objects, and x-ray vision. Playful game designers and creative applications developers have already pushed the technology further than those who seek merely to mimic reality.

For some computer-based tasks—such as medical imagery, architectural drawing, computer-assisted design, chemical-structure modeling, and scientific simulations—pure 3D representations are clearly helpful and have become major industries. However, even in these cases, the successes are often due to design features that make the interface better than reality. Users can magically change colors or shapes, duplicate objects, shrink/expand objects, group/ungroup components, send them by e-mail, and attach floating labels. In these representations users can also carry out other useful supernatural actions, such as going back in time by undoing recent actions.

Among the many innovations, there have been questionable 3D prototypes, such as for air-traffic control (showing altitude by perspective drawing only adds clutter when compared to an overview from directly above), digital libraries (showing books on shelves may be nice for browsing, but it inhibits search and linking), and file directories (showing tree structures in three dimensions sometimes leads to designs that increase occlusion and navigation problems). Other questionable applications include ill-considered 3D features for situations in which simple 2D representations would do the job. For example, adding a third dimension to bar charts may slow users and mislead them (Levy et al., 1996; Hicks et al., 2003), but they are such an attraction for some users that they are included in most business graphics packages (Cognos, SAS/GRAPH, SPSS/SigmaPlot).

Intriguing, successful applications of 3D representations are game environments. These include first-person action games in which users patrol city streets or race down castle corridors while shooting at opponents, as well as role-playing fantasy games with beautifully illustrated island havens or mountain strongholds (for example, Myst, RealMyst, or Riven). Many games are socially enriched by allowing users to choose 3D avatars to represent themselves. Users can choose avatars that resemble themselves, but often they choose bizarre characters or fantasy images with desirable characteristics such as unusual strength or beauty (Damer, 1997).

Some web-based game environments, such as ActiveWorlds (Fig. 6.12), may involve millions of users and thousands of user-constructed "worlds," such as

Figure 6.12

ActiveWorlds, a multi-user environment where users interact and create user-constructed "worlds" such as shopping malls (upper left), Yellowstone Park (bottom), and a user-created garden with a chat window open on the bottom (upper right).

Yellowstone Park, shopping malls, or urban neighborhoods. Game devotees may spend dozens of hours per week immersed in their virtual worlds, chatting with collaborators or negotiating with opponents. Sony's EverQuest (Fig. 6.13) attracts users with this ambitious description: "Welcome to the world of EverQuest, a real 3D massively multiplayer fantasy role-playing game. Prepare to enter an enormous virtual environment—an entire world with its own diverse species, economic systems, alliances, and politics." Another popular role-playing game, The Sims Online, has 3D characters who live in home environments with rich social behaviors that users control.

These environments may prove to be successful because of the increasingly rich social contexts based on spatial cognition—that is, users may come to appreciate the importance of the setting and value participants who choose to stand close to them. Such environments may come to support effective business meetings (as promoters of Adobe's Atmosphere, There.com, and Blaxxun envision), community discussion groups, and even contentious political forums. Promoters of Atmosphere invite users to "Imagine walking down the aisles of a

Figure 6.13

Sony's EverQuest virtual world. The upper-left picture is EverQuest, showing a chat box and character controls. The lower-right picture is EverQuest II, demonstrating real-time multi-player interaction.

virtual store and inspecting merchandise before you purchase it. Or imagine taking a virtual tour of the Great Pyramid of Giza, where you explore its internal corridors and view details down to the chisel marks on the stone."

Three-dimensional art and entertainment experiences, often delivered by web applications, provide another opportunity for innovative applications. Early web standards like VRML, which did not generate huge commercial successes, have given way to richer ones such as X3D. This standard has major corporate supporters who believe it will lead to viable commercial applications.

Many attempts have been made to provide 3D desktops and workspaces, sometimes based on office and room metaphors. These did not help early commercial products such as General Magic's office desktop or Microsoft's BOB home setting. Prototypes such as Microsoft's Task Gallery (Fig. 6.14), Intel's Grand Canyon, and Xerox PARC's Information Visualizer (see Chapter 14) have not yet spawned successful products (Card, Mackinlay, and Shneiderman, 1999).

Start-up companies continue to produce 3D designs, such as Clockwise3D's Win3D and its newer competitor 3DNA, that mix pure, constrained, and

Figure 6.14

A 3D window manager developed by Microsoft Research called the Task Gallery.

enhanced 3D features. These 3D front-ends for Windows, which offer rooms for shopping, games, the Internet, and office applications, are likely to remain attractive largely for games, entertainment, and sports enthusiasts. Another product, Browse3D, provides a limited 3D web-browsing experience based on perspective. Its main benefit is appropriate screen management for at least 16 web pages, but a skeptic might wonder if a 2D version would produce faster performance and better use of screen space.

A modest use of 3D techniques is to add highlights to 2D interfaces, such as buttons that appear to be raised or depressed, windows that overlap and leave shadows, or icons that resemble real-world objects. These may be enjoyable, recognizable, and memorable because of improved use of spatial memory (Ark et al., 1998), but they can also be visually distracting and confusing because of additional visual complexity. Attempts to build realistic devices, such as telephones, books, or CD-players, produce pleasant smiles from first-time users, but these ideas have not caught on, probably because the design compromises to produce 3D effects undermine usability.

This enumeration of features for effective 3D interfaces might serve as a checklist for designers, researchers, and educators:

- Use occlusion, shadows, perspective, and other 3D techniques carefully.
- Minimize the number of navigation steps for users to accomplish their tasks.
- Keep text readable (better rendering, good contrast with background, and no more than 30-degree tilt).
- Avoid unnecessary visual clutter, distraction, contrast shifts, and reflections.
- Simplify user movement (keep movements planar, avoid surprises like going through walls).
- Prevent errors (that is, surgical tools that cut only where needed and chemistry kits that produce only realistic molecules and safe compounds).
- Simplify object movement (facilitate docking, follow predictable paths, limit rotation).
- Organize groups of items in aligned structures to allow rapid visual search.
- Enable users to construct visual groups to support spatial recall (placing items in corners or tinted areas).

Breakthroughs based on clever ideas seem possible. Enriching interfaces with stereo displays (Ware and Franck, 1996), haptic feedback, and 3D sound may yet prove beneficial in more than specialized applications. Bigger payoffs are more likely to come sooner by following guidelines for inclusion of enhanced 3D features:

- Provide overviews so users can see the big picture (plan view display, aggregated views) (Wiss, Carr, and Jonsson, 1998).
- Allow teleportation (rapid context shifts by selecting destination in an overview).

- Offer x-ray vision so users can see into or beyond objects.
- Provide history keeping (recording, undoing, replaying, editing).
- Permit rich user actions on objects (save, copy, annotate, share, send).
- Enable remote collaboration (synchronous, asynchronous).
- Give users control over explanatory text (pop-up, floating, or ex-centric labels and screen tips) and let users select for details on demand.
- Offer tools to select, mark, and measure.
- Implement dynamic queries to rapidly filter out unneeded items.
- Support semantic zooming and movement (simple action brings object front and center and reveals more details).
- Enable landmarks to show themselves even at a distance (Darken and Sibert, 1996).
- Allow multiple coordinated views (users can be in more than one place at a time, users can see data in more than one arrangement at a time).
- Develop novel 3D icons to represent concepts that are more recognizable and memorable (Irani and Ware, 2003).

Three-dimensional environments are greatly appreciated by some users and are helpful for some tasks. They have the potential for novel social, scientific, and commercial applications, if designers go beyond the goal of mimicking 3D reality. Enhanced 3D interfaces could be the key to making some kinds of 3D teleconferencing, collaboration, and teleoperation popular. Of course, it will take good design of 3D interfaces (pure, constrained, or enhanced) and more research on finding the payoffs beyond the entertaining features that appeal to first-time users. Success will come to designers who provide compelling content, relevant features, appropriate entertainment, and novel social structure support. Then, by studying user performance and measuring satisfaction, they can polish their designs and refine guidelines for others to follow.

6.5   Teleoperation

Teleoperation has two parents: direct manipulation in personal computers, and process control, where human operators control physical processes in complex environments. Typical tasks are operating power or chemical plants, controlling manufacturing, flying airplanes, or steering vehicles. If the physical processes take place in a remote location, we talk about *teleoperation* or *remote control*. To perform the control task remotely, the human operator may interact with a computer, which may carry out some of the control tasks without any interference by the human operator. This idea is captured by the notion of *supervisory control* (Sheridan, 1992). Although supervisory control and direct manipulation stem from different problem domains and are usually applied to different system architectures, they carry a strong resemblance.

There are great opportunities for the remote control or teleoperation of devices if acceptable user interfaces can be constructed. When designers can provide adequate feedback in sufficient time to permit effective decision making, attractive applications in manufacturing, medicine, military operations, and computer-supported collaborative work are viable. Home-automation applications extend remote operation of telephone-answering machines to security and access systems, energy control, and operation of appliances. Scientific applications in space, underwater, or in hostile environments enable new research projects to be conducted economically and safely (Sheridan, 1992; Stanney, Mourant, and Kennedy, 1998).

In traditional direct-manipulation interfaces, the objects and actions of interest are shown continuously; users generally point, click, or drag rather than type, and feedback indicating change is immediate. However, when the devices being operated are remote, these goals may not be realizable, and designers must expend additional effort to help users to cope with slower responses, incomplete feedback, increased likelihood of breakdowns, and more complex error-recovery procedures. The problems are strongly connected to the hardware, physical environment, network design, and task domain.

A typical remote application is *telemedicine*: medical care delivered over communication links (Satava and Jones, 1996). This allows physicians to examine patients remotely and surgeons to carry out operations across continents. A growing application is telepathology, in which a pathologist examines tissue samples or body fluids under a remotely located microscope (Figs. 6.15). The transmitting workstation has a high-resolution camera mounted on a motorized light microscope. The pathologist at the receiving workstation can manipulate the microscope using a mouse or keypad and can see a high-resolution image of the magnified sample. The two caregivers talk by telephone to coordinate control and to request slides that are placed manually under the microscope. Controls include:

- Magnification (three or six objectives)
- Focus (coarse and fine bidirectional control)
- Illumination (bidirectional adjustment continuous or by step)
- Position (two-dimensional placement of the slide under the microscope objective)

The architecture of remote environments introduces several complicating factors:

- *Time delays.* The network hardware and software cause delays in sending user actions and receiving feedback: a *transmission delay*, or the time it takes for the command to reach the microscope (in our example, transmitting the

Figure 6.15

Telepathology suite at VA Milwaukee. From left, equipment consists of microscope with static/dynamic camera, computer screens (2), flat-bed scanner (behind pathologist), document reader, and printer. This setup enables a pathologist to use remote control to examine the slides.

command through the modem), and an *operation delay,* or the time until the microscope responds. These delays in the system prevent the operator from knowing the current status of the system. For example, if a positioning command has been issued, it may take several seconds for the slide to start moving.

- *Incomplete feedback.* Devices originally designed for direct control may not have adequate sensors or status indicators. For instance, the microscope can transmit its current position, but it operates so slowly that it does not indicate the *exact* current position.

- *Unanticipated interferences.* Since the devices operated are remote, unanticipated interferences are more likely to occur than in desktop direct-manipulation environments. For instance, if the slide under the microscope is moved accidentally by a local operator, the positions indicated might not be correct. A breakdown might also occur during the execution of a remote operation without a good indication of this event being sent to the remote site.

One solution to these problems is to make explicit the network delays and breakdowns as part of the system. The user sees a model of the starting state of the system, the action that has been initiated, and the current state of the system as it carries out the action. It may be preferable for users to specify a destination (rather than a motion) and wait until the action is completed before readjusting the destination if necessary.

Another common use of teleoperation is by the military and civilian space projects. Military applications for unmanned aircraft gained visibility during the wars in Afghanistan and Iraq. Reconnaisance drones were widely used, and teleoperated missile-firing aircraft were also tested. Military missions and harsh environments, such as undersea and space exploration, are strong drivers for improved designs.

6.6   Virtual and Augmented Reality

Flight-simulator designers work hard to create the most realistic experience for fighter or airline pilots. The cockpit displays and controls are taken from the same production line that create the real ones. Then, the windows are replaced by high-resolution computer displays, and sounds are choreographed to give the impression of engine start or reverse thrust. Finally, the vibration and tilting during climbing or turning are created by hydraulic jacks and intricate suspension systems. This elaborate technology may cost $100 million, but even then it is a lot cheaper, safer, and more useful for training than the $400-million jet that it simulates (and for training actual pilots, the $30 flight simulators that millions of home computer game players have purchased won't quite do the trick!). Flying a plane is a complicated and specialized skill, but simulators are available for more common—and for some surprising—tasks under the alluring name of *virtual reality* or the more descriptive *virtual environments.*

High above the office desktop, much beyond multimedia, the gurus of virtuality are promoting immersive experiences (Fig. 6.16). Whether soaring over Seattle, bending around bronchial tubes to find lung cancers, or grasping complex molecules, the cyberspace explorers are moving past their initial fantasies to create useful technologies. The imagery and personalities involved in virtual reality are often colorful (Rheingold, 1991), but many researchers have tried to present a balanced view by conveying enthusiasm while reporting on problems (Bryson, 1996; Stanney, 2002).

Architects have been using computers to draw three-dimensional representations of buildings for two decades. Their design tools show buildings on a standard display, but using a projector to create a wall-sized image gives prospective clients a more realistic impression. Now add animation that allows clients to see what happens if they move left or right, or approach the image. Then enable

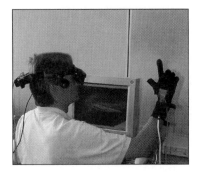

Figure 6.16

In the goggles-and-gloves approach to virtual reality, the system tracks the user's hand and head motions, plus finger gestures, to control the scene's movement and manipulation. To enter this virtual environment you need special gear. Any of several types of stereoscopic devices transform otherwise two-dimensional image data into three dimensional images. Some three-dimensional viewers, called head-mounted displays, resemble helmets with movie screens where the visor would be. In this example, the user experiences a flow field as if they were within the field. (www.5DT.com)

clients to control the animation by walking on a treadmill (faster walking brings the building closer more quickly), and allow them to walk through the doors or up the stairs. Finally, replace the projector with a head-mounted display, and monitor head movement with a head tracker (for example, Polhemus, Logitech, or Intertrax2). Each change takes users a bit farther along the range from "looking at" to "being in." Bumping into walls, falling (gently) down stairs, meeting other people, or having to wait for an elevator could be the next variations.

The architectural application is a persuasive argument for "being in," because we are used to "being in" buildings and moving around them. On the other hand, for many applications, "looking at" is often more effective, which is why air-traffic–control workstations place the viewer above the situation display. Similarly, seeing movies on the large wraparound screens that put viewers "in" race cars or airplanes are special events compared to the more common "looking at" television experience. The Living Theater of the 1960s created an immersive theatrical experience and "be-ins" were popular, but most theatergoers prefer to take their "suspension of disbelief" experiences from the "looking at" perspective, while seated safely in the audience (Laurel, 1991).

It remains to be seen whether doctors and surgeons, accustomed to "looking at" a patient, really want to crawl through the patient's colon or "be in" the patient's brain. Surgeons can benefit by "looking at" video images from inside a patient's heart taken through fiber-optic cameras and from use of remote direct-manipulation devices that minimize the invasive surgery, but they don't seem to want the immersive experience of being inside the patient with a head-mounted display. Surgery planning and teleoperation can also be done with three-dimensional "looking at" visualizations shown on desktop displays and guided by handheld props (Hinckley et al., 1994). There are more mundane applications for such video and fiber-optic magic, too—imagine the benefits to household plumbers of being able to see lost wedding rings around the bends of a sink drain or to see and grasp the child's toy that has fallen down the pipes of a clogged toilet.

Other concepts that were sources for the current excitement include *artificial reality*, pioneered by Myron Krueger (1991). His VideoPlace and VideoDesk installations with large-screen projectors and video sensors combined full-body movement with projected images of light creatures that walked along a performer's arm or of multicolored patterns and sounds generated by the performer's movement. Similarly, Vincent Vincent's demonstrations of the Mandala system carried performance art to a new level of sophistication and fantasy. The CAVE, a room with several walls of high-resolution rear-projected displays with three-dimensional audio, can offer satisfying experiences for several people at a time (Cruz-Neira, Sandin, and DeFanti 1993) (Fig. 6.17). The theatrical possibilities have attracted researchers and media pioneers who are merging reality with virtuality (Benford et al., 2001).

The telepresence aspect of virtual reality breaks the physical limitations of space and allows users to act as though they are somewhere else. Practical thinkers immediately grasp the connection to remote direct manipulation, remote control, and remote vision, but the fantasists see the potential to escape current reality and to visit science-fiction worlds, cartoonlands, previous times in history, galaxies with different laws of physics, or unexplored emotional territories (Whitton, 2003).

Medical successes for virtual environments include phobia treatment and pain control. Virtual worlds can be used to treat patients with fear of heights by giving them an immersive experience with control over their viewpoint and

Figure 6.17

The CAVE™, a multiperson, room-sized, high-resolution, 3D video and audio environment at the University of Illinois at Chicago. The CAVE is a 10 by 10 by 9-foot theater, made up of three rear-projection screens for walls and a down-projection screen for the floor. Projectors throw full-color workstation fields (1024 by 768 stereo) onto the screens at 96 Hz.

movement (Fig. 6.18) (Hodges et al., 1995). The safe immersive environment enables phobia sufferers to accommodate themselves to frightening stimuli in preparation for similar experiences in the real world. Another dramatic result is that immersive environments provide distractions for patients so that some forms of pain are controlled (Hoffman et al., 2001).

The direct-manipulation principles and the OAI model may be helpful to people who are designing and refining virtual environments. When users can select actions rapidly by pointing or gesturing, and display feedback occurs immediately, users have a strong sense of causality. Interface objects and actions should be simple, so that users view and manipulate task-domain objects. The surgeon's instruments should be readily available or easily called up. Similarly, an interior designer walking through a house with a client should be able to pick up a window-stretching tool or pull on a handle to try out a larger window, or to use a room-painting tool to change the wall colors while leaving the windows and furniture untouched. Navigation in large virtual spaces presents further

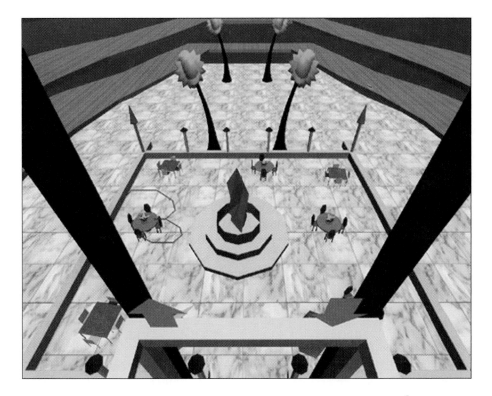

Figure 6.18

Virtual-reality therapy for users who have acrophobia. These users can accommodate to heights by going up in this virtual elevator with a guard rail located at waist level. The controls for the elevator are located on the guard rail: a green up arrow, a green down arrow, and a red stop square. © 1995 IEEE (Hodges et al., 1995.)

challenges, but overview maps have been demonstrated to provide useful orientation information (Darken and Sibert, 1996).

An important variant, called *augmented reality*, enables users to see the real world with an overlay of additional information; for example, while users are looking at the walls of a building, their semitransparent eyeglasses show where the electrical wires or plumbing are located. Medical applications, such as allowing surgeons to look at a patient while they see an overlay of an x-ray or sonogram to help locate a cancer tumor, also seem compelling. Augmented reality could show users how to repair electrical equipment or guide visitors through tourist attractions (Feiner, MacIntyre, and Seligman, 1993). Tourist-guide eyeglasses could allow visitors to view labels about architectural features in an historic town or to find dining halls at a large college campus. Augmented-reality strategies also enable users to manipulate real-world artifacts to see results on graphical models (Ishii and Ullmer, 1997; Poupyrev et al., 2002), with applications such as manipulating protein molecules to understand attractive/repulsive force fields between them (Fig. 6.19).

Alternatives to the immersive environment are appealing because they avoid the problems of simulator sickness, nausea, and discomfort from wearing head-mounted gear. *Desktop* or *fishtank* virtual environments (both references are to standard "looking-at" displays) are becoming more common, because they avoid the physically distressing symptoms and require only standard equipment. Three-dimensional graphics has led to user interfaces that support user-controlled exploration of real places, scientific visualizations, or fantasy worlds. Many applications run on high-performance workstations capable of rapid rendering, but some are appealing even over the Web, using the Virtual Reality Modeling Language (VRML) and its successors, such as X3D. Graphics researchers have been perfecting image display to simulate lighting effects, textured surfaces, reflections, and shadows. Data structures and algorithms for zooming in or panning across an object rapidly and smoothly are now practical on common computers.

Successful virtual environments will depend on smooth integration of multiple technologies:

- *Visual display.* The normal-size (12 to 17 inches diagonally) computer display at a normal viewing distance (70 centimeters) subtends an angle of about 5 degrees; large-screen (17- to 30-inch) displays can cover a 20- to 30-degree field, and the head-mounted displays cover 100 degrees horizontally and 60 degrees vertically. The head-mounted displays block other images, so the effect is more dramatic, and head motion produces new images, so the users can get the impression of 360-degree coverage. Flight simulators also block extraneous images, but they do so without forcing the users to wear sometimes-cumbersome head-mounted displays. Another approach is a boom-mounted display that senses the users' positions without requiring that they wear heavy goggles (Fig. 6.20).

  As hardware technology improves, it will be possible to provide more rapid and higher-resolution images. Most researchers agree that the displays must approach real time (probably under a 100-millisecond delay) in presenting the images to the users. Low-resolution displays are acceptable while users or the objects are moving, but when users stop to stare, higher resolution is necessary to preserve the sense of "being in." Improved hardware and algorithms are needed to display rough shapes rapidly and then to fill in the details when the motion stops. A further requirement is that motion be smooth; both incremental changes and continuous display of the objects of interest are required (Hendrix and Barfield, 1996; Allison et al., 2001).

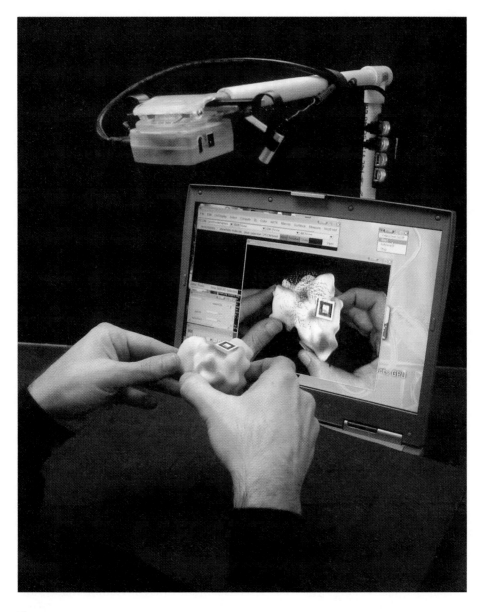

Figure 6.19

A tangible user interface for molecular biology, developed in Art Olson's Laboratory at The Scripps Research Institute, utilizes autofabricated molecular models tracked with the Augmented Reality Toolkit from the University of Washington Human Interface Technology Lab. The video camera on the laptop captures the molecule's position and orientation, enabling the molecular modeling software to display information such as the attractive/repulsive forces surrounding the molecule.

Figure 6.20

A head-couple stereoscopic display. The Boom Chameleon provides high-quality visual displays and tracking integrated with a counterbalanced articulated arm for full six-degree of freedom motion. (Tsang et al., 2002)

- *Head-position sensing.* Head-mounted displays can provide differing views depending on head position. Look to the right, and you see a forest; look to the left, and the forest gives way to a city. Some head trackers can be cumbersome to wear, but smaller versions embedded in a hat or eyeglasses facilitate mobility. Video recognition of head position is possible. Sensor precision should be high (within 1 degree and within 1 centimeter) and rapid (within 100 milliseconds). Eye tracking to recognize the focus of attention might be useful, but it is difficult to accomplish while the user is moving and is wearing a head-mounted display.

- *Hand-position sensing.* The DataGlove is an innovative invention that continues to be refined and improved beyond its current low resolution. Bryson (1996) complains that "the problems with glove devices include inaccuracies in measurement and lack of standard gestural vocabulary." It may turn out that accurate measurement of finger position is required only for one or two fingers or even one or two joints. Hand orientation is provided by a 6-degrees-of-freedom tracker mounted on the glove or wrist. Sensors for other body parts, such as knees, arms, or legs, are finding uses in sports training and movement capture. The potential for sensors and tactile feedback on more erotic body parts has been referred to by more than one journalist.

- *Handheld manipulatives.* Imaginative approaches have included electronically active surgical tools and small dolls (Pierce and Pausch, 2002). Users can manipulate these objects to produce input, operate devices, create drawings, or make sculptures. A variant, often called "worlds in miniature," is to have a small model of a house or of scientific equipment, which users can manipulate to create operations on the larger real-world object, often at a distant location.

- *Force feedback and haptics.* Hand-operated remote-control devices for performing experiments in chemistry laboratories or for handling nuclear materials provide force feedback that gives users a good sense of when they grasp an object or bump into one. Force feedback to car drivers and pilots is carefully configured to provide realistic and useful tactile information. Simulated feedback from software was successful in speeding docking tasks with complex molecules (Brooks, 1988). It might be helpful for surgeons to receive force feedback as they practice difficult operations. A palmtop display mounted on a boom was shown to produce faster and more accurate performance on a remote manipulation task when haptic (touch and force feedback) feedback was added (Noma, Miyasato, and Kishino 1996). Remote handshaking as part of a videoconference has been suggested, but it is not clear that the experience could be as satisfying as the real thing.

- *Sound input and output.* Sound output adds realism to bouncing balls, beating hearts, or dropping vases, as videogame designers found out long ago. Making convincing sounds at the correct moment with full three-dimensional effect is possible, but it too is hard work. The digital sound hardware is adequate, but the software tools are still inadequate. Music output from virtual instruments is promising; early work simulates existing instruments (such as a violin), but novel instruments have emerged. Speech recognition for initiating actions and making menu selections may be useful, because keyboard and mouse use is restricted.

- *Other sensations.* The tilting and vibration of flight simulators might provide an inspiration for some designers. Tilting and vibrating virtual roller coasters already exist and could become even more popular if users could travel at 60, 600, or 6,000 miles per hour and crash through mountains or go into orbit. Why not include real gusts of air with raindrops, made hot or cold to convey the virtual weather? Finally, the power of smells to evoke strong reactions has been understood by writers from Proust to Gibson. Olfactory computing has been tried, but appropriate and practical applications have yet to be found.

- *Collaborative and competitive virtual environments.* Collaboration (see Chapter 10) is a lively research area, as are collaborative virtual environments or, as one developer called it, "virtuality built for two." Two people at remote sites work together, possibly designing an object, while seeing each other's actions and the object of interest (Benford et al., 2001). Competitive games such as virtual racquetball have been built for two players. Software for training Army tank crews took on a much more compelling atmosphere when the designs shifted from playing against the computer to shooting at other tank crews and worrying about their attacks. The realistic sounds created such a sense of engagement that crews experienced elevated heart rates, more rapid breathing, and increased perspiration. By contrast, some virtual environments are designed to bring relaxation and pleasant encounters with other people.

The opportunities for artistic expression and public-space installations are being explored by performance artists, museum designers, and building architects. Creative installations include projected images, 3D sound, and sculptural components, sometimes combined with video cameras and user control by mobile devices.

Practitioner's Summary

Among interactive systems that provide equivalent functionality and reliability, some systems emerge to dominate the competition. Often, the most appealing systems have an enjoyable user interface that offers a natural representation of the task objects and actions—hence the term *direct manipulation* (Box 6.1). These interfaces are easy to learn, to use, and to retain over time. Novices can acquire a simple subset of the actions and then progress to more elaborate ones. Actions are rapid, incremental, and reversible, and they can be performed with physical movements instead of complex syntactic forms. The results of actions are visible immediately, and error messages are needed less often.

Using direct-manipulation principles in an interface does not ensure its success. A poor design, slow implementation, or inadequate functionality can undermine acceptance. For some applications, menu selection, form fillin, or command languages may be more appropriate. However, the potential for direct-manipulation programming, 3D interfaces, and teleoperation is great. Compelling demonstrations of virtual and augmented reality are being applied in a growing set of applications. Iterative design (see Chapter 3) is especially important in testing advanced direct-manipulation systems, because the novelty of these approaches may lead to unexpected problems for designers and users.

Researcher's Agenda

We need research to refine our understanding of the contributions of each feature of direct manipulation: analogical representation, incremental action, reversibility, physical action instead of syntax, immediate visibility of results,

Box 6.1

Definition, benefits, and drawbacks of direct manipulation.

Definition
- Visual representation (metaphor) of the "world of action"
  Objects and actions are shown
  Analogical reasoning is tapped
- Rapid, incremental, and reversible actions
- Replacement of typing with pointing and selecting
- Immediate visibility of results of actions

Benefits over commands
- Control/display compatibility
- Less syntax reduces error rates
- Errors are more preventable
- Faster learning and higher retention
- Encourages exploration

Concerns
- Increased system resources, possibly
- Some actions may be cumbersome
- Macro techniques are often weak
- History and other tracing may be difficult
- Visually impaired users may have more difficulty

and graphic display. Reversibility is easily accomplished by a generic undo action, but designing natural inverses for each action may be more attractive. Complex actions are well represented with direct manipulation, but multi-layer design strategies for graceful evolution from novice to expert usage could be a major contribution. For expert users, direct-manipulation programming is still an opportunity, but good methods of history keeping and editing of action sequences are needed. The allure of 3D interaction is great, but researchers need to provide a better understanding of how and when (and when not) to use features such as occlusion, reduced navigation, and enhanced 3D actions such as teleportation or x-ray vision.

Beyond the desktops and laptops, there is the allure of telepresence, virtual environments, augmented realities, and context-aware devices. The playful aspects will certainly be pursued, but the real challenge is to find the practical designs for being in and looking at three-dimensional worlds. Novel devices for walking through museums or supermarkets and teleoperation for repair seem good candidates for entrepreneurs.

WORLD WIDE WEB RESOURCES

Some creative direct-manipulation services and tools are linked to, but the majority of links cover direct-manipulation programming, teleoperation, and virtual environments. The Web3D standard enables creation of visually appealing web-based three-dimensional environments.

http://www.aw.com/DTUI

References

Allison, R. S., Harris, L. R., Jenkin, M., Jasiobedzka, J., and Zacher, J. E., Tolerance of temporal delay in virtual environments, *Proc. IEEE Virtual Reality 2001* (2001).

Ark, Wendy, Dryer, D. Christopher, Selker, Ted, and Zhai, Shumin, Representation matters: The effect of 3D objects and a spatial metaphor in a graphical user interface, *Proc. HCI '98 Conference on People and Computers XIII*, Springer-Verlag, London, U.K. (1998), 209–219.

Arnheim, Rudolf, *Visual Thinking*, University of California Press, Berkeley, CA (1972).

Barfield, W. and Robless, R., The effects of two- and three-dimensional graphics on the problem-solving performance of experienced and novice decision-makers, *Behaviour & Information Technology*, 8 (1989), 369–385.

Benbasat, I. and Todd, P., An experimental investigation of interface design alternatives: Icon versus text and direct manipulation versus menus, *International Journal of Man-Machine Studies*, 38, 3 (1993), 369–402.

Benford, Steve, Greenhalgh, Chris, Rodden, Tom, Pycock, James, Collaborative virtual environments, *Communications of the ACM*, 44, 7 (July 2001), 79–85.

Brooks, Frederick, Grasping reality through illusion: Interactive graphics serving science, *Proc. CHI '88 Conference: Human Factors in Computing Systems*, ACM, New York (1988), 1–11.

Bryson, Steve, Virtual reality in scientific visualization, *Communications of the ACM*, 39, 5 (May 1996), 62–71.

Card, Stuart, Mackinlay, Jock, and Shneiderman, Ben, *Readings in Information Visualization: Using Vision to Think*, Morgan Kaufmann Publishers, San Francisco, CA (1999).

Carroll, John M. and Thomas, John C., Metaphor and the cognitive representation of computing systems, *IEEE Transactions on Systems, Man, and Cybernetics*, SMC-12, 2 (March–April 1982), 107–116.

Cockburn, Andy and McKenzie, Bruce, Evaluating the effectiveness of spatial memory in 2D and 3D physical and virtual environments, *Proc. CHI 2001 Conference: Human Factors in Computing Systems,* ACM, New York (2002), 203–210.

Copeland, Richard W., *How Children Learn Mathematics, Third Edition,* MacMillan, New York (1979).

Cruz-Neira, C., Sandin, D. J., and DeFanti, T., Surround-screen projection-based virtual reality: The design and implementation of the CAVE, *Proc. SIGGRAPH '93 Conference,* ACM, New York (1993), 135–142.

Damer, Bruce, *Avatars: Exploring and Building Virtual Worlds on the Internet,* Peachpit Press, Berkeley, CA (1997).

Darken, Rudolph, P. and Sibert, John L., Navigating large virtual spaces, *International Journal of Human-Computer Interaction,* 8, 1 (1996), 49–71.

Feiner, Steven, MacIntyre, Blair, and Seligmann, Doree, Knowledge-based augmented reality, *Communications of the ACM,* 36, 7 (1993), 52–62.

Frohlich, David M., The history and future of direct manipulation, *Behaviour & Information Technology,* 12, 6 (1993), 315–329.

Golub, Evan and Shneiderman, Ben, Dynamic query visualizations on World Wide Web clients: A DHTML solution for maps and scattergrams, *International Journal of Web Engineering and Technology,* 1, 1 (2003), 63–78.

Green, T. R. G. and Petre, M., Usability analysis of visual programming environments: A "cognitive dimensions" framework, *Journal of Visual Languages and Computing,* 7 (1996), 131–174.

Heckel, Paul, *The Elements of Friendly Software Design: The New Edition,* SYBEX, San Francisco, CA (1991).

Hendrix, C., and Barfield, W., Presence within virtual environments as a function of visual display parameters, *Presence: Teleoperators and Virtual Environments,* 5, 3 (1996), 274–289.

Herot, Christopher F., Spatial management of data, *ACM Transactions on Database Systems,* 5, 4, (December 1980), 493–513.

Herot, Christopher, Graphical user interfaces, in Vassiliou, Yannis (Editor), *Human Factors and Interactive Computer Systems,* Ablex, Norwood, NJ (1984), 83–104.

Hicks, Martin, O'Malley, Claire, Nichols, Sarah, and Anderson, Ben, Comparison of 2D and 3D representations for visualising telecommunication usage, *Behaviour & Information Technology,* 22, 3 (2003), 185–201.

Hinckley, Ken, Pausch, Randy, Goble, John C., and Kassell, Neal F., Passive real-world props for neurosurgical visualization, *Proc. CHI '94 Conference: Human Factors in Computing Systems,* ACM, New York (1994), 452–458.

Hodges, L.F., Rothbaum, B.O., Kooper, R., Opdyke, D., Meyer, T., North, M., de Graff, J.J., and Williford, J., Virtual environments for treating the fear of heights, *IEEE Computer,* 28, 7 (1995), 27–34.

Hoffman, H.G., Patterson, D.R., Carrougher, G.J., Nakamura, D., Moore, M., Garcia-Palacios, A., and Furness, T.A. III, The effectiveness of virtual reality pain control with multiple treatments of longer durations: A case study, *International Journal of Human-Computer Interaction,* 13 (2001), 1–12.

Hutchins, Edwin L., Hollan, James D., and Norman, Don A., Direct manipulation interfaces, in Norman, Don A. and Draper, Stephen W. (Editors), *User Centered System
Design: New Perspectives on Human-Computer Interaction,* Lawrence Erlbaum Associates, Hillsdale, NJ (1986), 87–124.

Irani, Pourang and Ware, Colin, Diagramming information structures using 3D perceptual primitives, *ACM Transactions on Computer-Human Interaction,* 10, 1, ACM, New
York (March 2003), 1–19.

Ishii, Hiroshi and Ullmer, Brygg, Tangible bits towards seamless interfaces between people, bits, and atoms, *Proc. CHI '97 Conference: Human Factors in Computing Systems,*
ACM, New York (1997), 234–241.

Kahn, Ken, Helping children to learn hard things: Computer programming with familiar objects and actions, in Druin, Allison (Editor), *The Design of Children's Technology:
How We Design and Why,* Morgan Kaufmann, San Francisco, CA (1999).

Krueger, Myron, *Artificial Reality II,* Addison-Wesley, Reading, MA (1991).

Laurel, Brenda, *Computers as Theatre,* Addison-Wesley, Reading, MA (1991).

Levy, Ellen, Zacks, Jeff, Tversky, Barbara, and Schiano, Diane, Gratuitous graphics?
Putting preferences in perspective: Empirical studies of graphics and visual design,
Proc. CHI '96 Conference: Human Factors in Computing Systems, ACM, New York (1996),
42–49.

Lieberman, Henry, *Your Wish Is My Command: Programming by Example,* Morgan Kaufmann Publishers, San Francisco, CA (2001).

Malone, Thomas W., What makes computer games fun? *Byte,* 6, 12 (December 1981),
258–277.

Marcus, Aaron, *Graphic Design for Electronic Documents and User Interfaces,* ACM, New
York (1992).

Margono, Sepeedeh and Shneiderman, Ben, A study of file manipulation by novices
using commands versus direct manipulation, *Twenty-sixth Annual Technical Symposium,* ACM, Washington, D.C. (June 1987), 154–159.

McKim, Robert H., *Experiences in Visual Thinking, Second Edition,* Brooks/Cole, Monterey,
CA (1980).

Montessori, Maria, *The Montessori Method,* Schocken, New York (1964).

Morgan, K., Morris, R. L., and Gibbs, S., When does a mouse become a rat? or . . . Comparing performance and preferences in direct manipulation and command line environment, *The Computer Journal,* 34, 3 (1991), 265–271.

Mullet, Kevin and Sano, Darrell, *Designing Visual Interfaces: Communication Oriented Techniques,* Sunsoft Press, Englewood Cliffs, NJ (1995).

Nelson, Ted, Interactive systems and the design of virtuality, *Creative Computing,* 6, 11,
(November 1980), 56 ff., and 6, 12 (December 1980), 94 ff.

Noma, Haruo, Miyasato, Tsutomu, and Kishino, Fumio, A palmtop display for dexter-
ous manipulation with haptic sensation, *Proc. CHI '96 Conference: Human Factors in
Computing Systems,* ACM, New York (1996), 126–133.

Norman, Donald A., *The Design of Everyday Things,* Basic Books, New York (2002).

Norman, Kent, *The Psychology of Menu Selection: Designing Cognitive Control at the
Human/Computer Interface,* Ablex, Norwood, NJ (1991).

Papert, Seymour, *Mindstorms: Children, Computers, and Powerful Ideas,* Basic Books, New York (1980).

Phillips, C. H. E. and Apperley, M. D., Direct manipulation interaction tasks: A Macintosh-based analysis, *Interacting with Computers,* 3, 1 (1991), 9–26.

Pierce, Jeffrey S. and Pausch, Randy, Comparing voodoo dolls and HOMER: Exploring the importance of feedback in virtual environments, *Proc. CHI 2002 Conference: Human Factors in Computing Systems,* ACM, New York (2002), 105–112.

Potter, Richard, Just in time programming, in Cypher, Allen (Editor), *Watch What I Do: Programming by Demonstration,* MIT Press, Cambridge, MA (1993), 513–526.

Poupyrev, Ivan, Tan, Desney S., Billinghurst, Mark, Kato, Hirokazu, Regenbrecht, Holger, and Tetsutani, Nobuji, Developing a generic augmented-reality interface, *IEEE Computer,* 35, 3 (March 2002), 44–50.

Provenzo, Jr., Eugene R., *Video Kids: Making Sense of Nintendo,* Harvard University Press, Cambridge, MA (1991).

Rheingold, Howard, *Virtual Reality,* Simon and Schuster, New York (1991).

Risden, Kirsten, Czerwinski, Mary P., Munzner, Tamara, and Cook, Daniel, An initial examination of ease of use for 2D and 3D information visualizations of web content, *International Journal of Human-Computer Studies,* 53, 5 (November 2000), 695–714.

Robertson, George G., Card, Stuart K., and Mackinlay, Jock D., Information visualization using 3-D interactive animation, *Communications of the ACM,* 36, 4 (April 1993), 56–71.

Rogers, Yvonne, Icons at the interface: Their usefulness, *Interacting with Computers,* 1, 1 (1989), 105–117.

Rutkowski, Chris, An introduction to the Human Applications Standard Computer Interface, Part 1: Theory and principles, *Byte,* 7, 11 (October 1982), 291–310.

Satava, R. M. and Jones, S. B., Virtual reality and telemedicine: Exploring advanced concepts, *Telemedicine Journal,* 2, 3 (1996), 195–200.

Sheridan, T. B., *Telerobotics, Automation, and Human Supervisory Control,* MIT Press, Cambridge, MA (1992).

Shneiderman, Ben, Direct manipulation: A step beyond programming languages, *IEEE Computer,* 16, 8 (August 1983), 57–69.

Smith, D. Canfield, Irby, Charles, Kimball, Ralph, Verplank, Bill, and Harslem, Eric, Designing the Star user interface, *Byte,* 7, 4 (April 1982), 242–282.

Smith, David Canfield, Cypher, Allen, and Spohrer, Jim, KIDSIM: Programming agents without a programming language, *Communications of the ACM,* 37, 7 (July 1994), 55–67.

Stanney, Kay (Editor), *Handbook of Virtual Environments Technology: Design, Implementation, and Applications,* Lawrence Erlbaum Associates, Mahwah, NJ (2002).

Stanney, K.M., Mourant, R., and Kennedy, R.S., Human factors issues in virtual environments: A review of the literature, *Presence: Teleoperators and Virtual Environments,* 7, 4 (1998), 327–351.

Sutcliffe, A. and Patel, U., 3D or not 3D: Is it nobler in the mind?, *People and Computers: Proc. 1996 British HCI Conference,* Cambridge University Press, Cambridge, U.K. (1996).

Tang, M., Fitzmaurice, G., Khan, A., and Buxton, B., Boom chameleon: simultaneous capture of 3D viewpoint, voice and gesture annotations on a spatially-aware display, *Proceedings of the UIST2002 ACM Symposium on User Interface Software and Technology* (2002), 111–120.

Te'eni, Dov, Direct manipulation as a source of cognitive feedback: A human-computer experiment with a judgment task, *International Journal of Man-Machine Studies*, 33, 4 (1990), 453–466.

Temple, Barker, and Sloane, Inc., The benefits of the graphical user interface, *Multimedia Review* (Winter 1990), 10–17.

Thimbleby, Harold, *User Interface Design*, ACM, New York (1990).

Ulich, E., Rauterberg, M., Moll, T., Greutmann, T., and Strohm, O., Task orientation and user-orientated dialogue design, *International Journal of Human-Computer Interaction*, 3, 2 (1991), 117–144.

Verplank, William L., Graphic challenges in designing object-oriented user interfaces, in Helander, M. (Editor), *Handbook of Human-Computer Interaction*, Elsevier Science Publishers, Amsterdam, The Netherlands (1988), 365–376.

Ware, Colin and Franck, Glenn, Evaluating stereo and motion cues for visualizing information nets in three dimensions, *ACM Transactions on Graphics*, 15, 2 (1996), 121–139.

Weiser, M., The computer for the 21st century, *Scientific American*, 265, 3 (1991), 94–104.

Wellner, P., Interacting with paper on the digital desk, *Communications of the ACM*, 36, 7 (July 1993), 86–96.

Wellner, P., Mackay, W., and Gold, R., Computer augmented environments: Back to the real world, *Communications of the ACM*, 36, 7 (July 1993), 24–27.

Whitton, Mary C., Making virtual environments compelling, *Communications of the ACM*, 46, 7 (July 2003), 40–46.

Wiss, Ulrika, Carr, David, and Jonsson, Hakan, Evaluating three-dimensional information visualization designs: A case study of three designs, *Proc. 1998 International Conference on Information Visualization, IV '98.* Available from IEEE Press (July 1998), 137–144.

Ziegler, J. E. and Fähnrich, K.-P., Direct manipulation, in Helander, M. (Editor), *Handbook of Human-Computer Interaction*, Elsevier Science Publishers, Amsterdam, The Netherlands (1988), 123–133.

chapter

7

Menu Selection, Form Fillin, and Dialog Boxes

A man is responsible for his choice and must accept the consequences, whatever they may be.

W. H. AUDEN
A Certain World, 1970

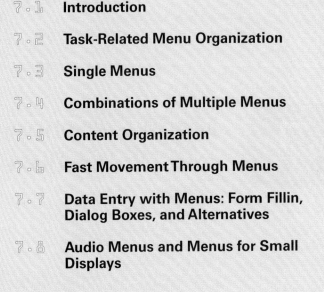

7.1   Introduction

When designers cannot create appropriate direct-manipulation strategies, menu selection and form fillin are attractive alternatives. Whereas early systems used full-screen menus with numbered items, modern menus are usually pull-downs, check boxes or radio buttons in dialog boxes, or embedded links on World Wide Web pages, all selectable by mouse clicks or a tap of the pen. When the menu items are written with familiar terminology and are organized in a convenient structure and sequence, users can select an item easily.

Menus are effective because they offer the cues to elicit recognition, rather than forcing users to recall the syntax of a command from memory. Users indicate their choices with a pointing device or keystroke and get feedback indicating what they have done. Simple menu selection is especially effective when users have little training, use the interface intermittently, are unfamiliar with the terminology, or need help in structuring their decision-making processes. With careful design of complex menus and high-speed interaction, menu selection can be made appealing even to expert frequent users.

However, just because a designer uses menu selection, form fillin, and dialog boxes, there is no guarantee that the interface will be appealing and easy to use. Effective interfaces emerge only after careful consideration of and testing for numerous design issues, such as task-related organization, phrasing of items, sequence of items, graphic layout and design, shortcuts for knowledgeable frequent users, online help, error correction, and selection mechanisms (keyboard, pointing device, touchscreen, voice, and so on) (Norman, 1991).

After introducing the importance of meaningful organization of menus (Section 7.2), this chapter reviews available menu techniques, from single menus (Section 7.3) to combinations of multiple menus (Section 7.4). Section 7.5 discusses issues related to the content of the menu, and Section 7.6 explores fast movement through menus for expert users. Form fillin, dialog boxes, and other methods of data entry using menus are covered in Section 7.7. Finally, the special cases of audio menus and menus for small devices are discussed in Section 7.8.

7.2 Task-Related Menu Organization

The primary goal for menu, form-fillin, and dialog-box designers is to create a sensible, comprehensible, memorable, and convenient organization relevant to the user's tasks. We can learn a few lessons by following the decomposition of a book into chapters, a program into modules, or the animal kingdom into species. Hierarchical decompositions—natural and comprehensible to most people—are appealing because every item belongs to a single category. Unfortunately, in some applications, an item may be difficult to classify as belonging to only one category, and designers are tempted to create duplicate pointers, thus forming a network.

Restaurant menus separate appetizers, soups, salads, main dishes, desserts, and beverages to help customers organize their selections. Menu items should fit logically into categories and have readily understood meanings. Restaurateurs who list dishes with idiosyncratic names such as "veal Monique," generic terms such as "house dressing," or unfamiliar labels such as "wor shu op" should expect that waiters will spend ample time explaining the alternatives, or should anticipate that customers will become anxious because of the unpredictability of their meals.

Similarly, for computer menus, the categories should be comprehensible and distinctive so that users are confident in making their selections. Users should have a clear idea of what will happen when they make a selection. Computer menus are more difficult to design than restaurant menus, because computer displays typically have less space than printed menus. In addition, the number of choices and the complexity is greater in many computer applications, and computer users do not have helpful waiters to turn to for explanations (Norman and Chin, 1989).

The importance of meaningful organization of menu items was demonstrated in an early study by Liebelt et al. (1982). Simple menu trees with 3 levels and 16 target items were constructed in both meaningfully organized and disorganized forms. Error rates were nearly halved and user think time (time from menu presentation to user's selection of an item) was reduced for the meaningfully organized form. In a later study, use of meaningful categories—such as food, animals, minerals, and cities—led to shorter response times than did random or alphabetic organizations (McDonald, Stone, and Liebelt, 1983). The authors concluded that "these results demonstrate the superiority of a categorical menu organization over a pure alphabetical organization, particularly when there is some uncertainty about the terms." With larger menu structures, the effect is even more dramatic.

These results and the OAI model suggest that the key to menu-structure design is first to consider the task-related objects and actions. For a music-concert ticketing system, the menus might separate out types of music (classical, folk, rock, jazz, and so on), concert locations, or dates, and might offer actions such as browsing lists, searching by performer name, or locating inexpensive performances. The interface objects might be dialog boxes with check boxes for types of music and scrolling menus of concert locations. Performer names might be in a scrolling list or typed in via form fillin. In mobile applications, where simplicity and ease of learning are important, frequency of use is a useful way of organizing menus. For a telephone interface, adding a phone number is a far more common task than removing a number, so the "add" command should be easily accessible, while "remove" can be pushed to a lower level of the menu.

Menu-selection applications range from trivial choices between two items to complex information systems that can lead through thousands of displays (Fig. 7.1). The simplest applications consist of a single menu, but even in these there are many possible variations. The second group of applications uses a linear sequence of menu selections; the progression of menus is independent of the user's choice. Strict tree structures make up the third and most common group. Acyclic (menus that are reachable by more than one path) and cyclic (structures with meaningful paths that allow users to repeat menus) networks constitute the fourth group. The World Wide Web structure is part of this last group. In addition, special traversal commands may enable users to jump around the branches of a tree, to go back to the previous menu, or to go to the beginning of a linear sequence or the top of the tree.

7.3   Single Menus

In some situations, a single menu is sufficient to accomplish a task. Single menus may require users to choose between two or more items, or may allow multiple selections. Single menus may pop up on the current work area or may remain permanently available (on a frame, in a separate window, or on a data table) while the main display is changed. The simplest case is a *binary menu* with, for example, true-false, male-female, or yes-no choices (Fig. 7.2).

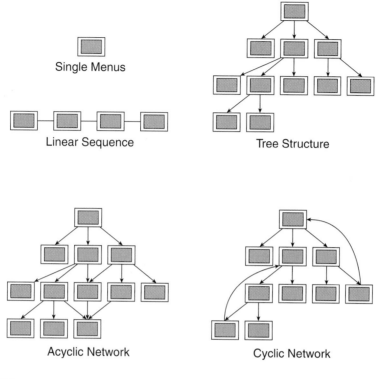

Figure 7.1

Menu systems can use a simple single menu or a linear sequence of menus. Tree-structured menus are the most common. Traversing deep trees or more elaborate acyclic or cyclic menu structures can be difficult for some users.

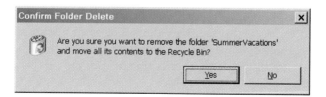

Figure 7.2

A binary menu allows users to choose between two options, here Yes or No. The thickened border on Yes indicates that this selection is the default and that pressing Return will select it. Keyboard shortcuts are available as indicated by the underlined letters. Typing the letter N will select No.

Single menus often have more than two items. One example is a quiz displayed on a touchscreen. Users simply touch a name to answer the question:

Who invented the telephone?

Thomas Edison
Alexander Graham Bell
Lee De Forest
George Westinghouse

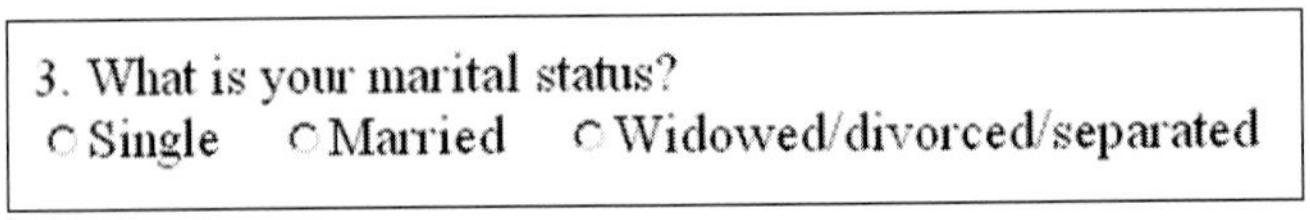

3. What is your marital status?
○ Single   ○ Married   ○ Widowed/divorced/separated

Figure 7.3

An online survey question uses radio buttons for users to select a single item in a three-item menu.

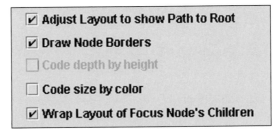

Figure 7.4

Users set their preferences by clicking on one or more check boxes in a menu. Feedback is provided by a check mark.

Radio buttons also support single-item selection from a multiple-item menu (Fig. 7.3), while check boxes can allow the selection of one or more items in a menu. A multiple-selection menu is a convenient selection method for handling multiple binary choices, since the user is able to scan the full list of items while deciding (Fig. 7.4).

7.3.1   Pull-down, pop-up, and toolbar menus

The two-dimensional layout in graphical user interfaces offered new opportunities for menu designers. The positioning of menus became more open, as did their invocation, selection, and visual presentation.

Pull-down menus are menus that are always available to the user by making selections on a top menu bar (Fig. 7.5). Introduced by the early Xerox Star, Apple Lisa, and Apple Macintosh interfaces, these menus are now used by a majority of desktop applications for Windows, Macintosh, and Unix. Common items in the menu bar are File, Edit, Format, View, and Help. Clicking on a menu item brings more items, shown in a vertical list menu; users can then make a selection by moving the pointing device over the menu items, which respond by highlighting, and clicking on the desired item. Since positional constancy is such a strong principle, when an item is not available for selection it is preferable to gray it out rather than to remove it from the list. *Keyboard shortcuts* such as Ctrl-C for copy are important for expert users, who can memorize the keystrokes for the menu items they use often and thus speed up the interaction considerably. The first letter of the command is often used for the shortcut to favor memorability, but caution is required to avoid collisions. If at all

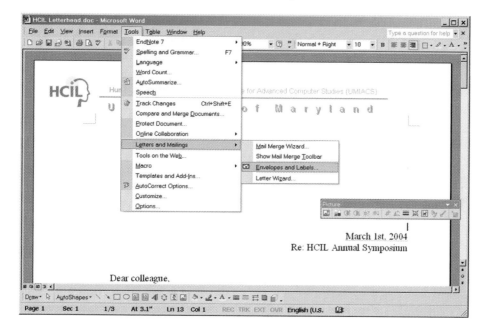

Figure 7.5

The cascading pull-down menus of Microsoft Word allow users to explore all the functions of the application. To facilitate the discovery and learning of icons and keyboard shortcuts, they are indicated on the left and right of the menu items, respectively (for example, the function key F7 is the keyboard shortcut for Spelling and Grammar, which the user can also select by clicking on the ABC/check mark icon). The small black triangles indicate that selection of the menu item will lead to an additional menu. Three dots (...) indicate that the selection will lead to a dialog box. Toolbars show groups of menu icons at the periphery of the window. A tool palette (such as the Picture palette shown here) can also be pulled away in a small separate window next to or on top of the document.

possible, shortcuts should be used consistently across applications; for example, Ctrl-S is usually used for Save and Ctrl-P for Print. Keyboard shortcuts should be indicated next to their corresponding menu items.

Toolbars, iconic menus, and palettes can offer many actions that users can select with a click and apply to a displayed object. These menus were first used in drawing and computer-assisted design applications but are now widely popular (Fig. 7.5.) Users should be able to customize the toolbars with their choices of items and to control the number and placement of those toolbars. Users who wish to conserve screen space for their workspace can eliminate the toolbars.

Pop-up menus appear on the display in response to a click or tap with a pointing device. The contents of the pop-up menu usually depend on where the cursor is when the pointing device is clicked. Since the pop-up menu covers a portion of the display, there is strong motivation to keep the menu text small so that it does not cover the context of the menu. Pop-up menus can also be organized in a circle to form *pie menus* (Fig. 7.6). Pie menus are convenient because selection is more rapid and, with practice, can be done without visual attention (Callahan et al., 1988). Improvements to appearance and behavior have been made in a pie-menu variant called *marking menus* (Tapia and Kurtenbach, 1995). Because pop-up menus can be initiated anywhere on the display, they are particularly adapted to large wall displays: they are unlikely to obscure too much of the screen, and users do not need to travel back to a fixed toolbar to access menus. Innovative designs such as the *FlowMenu* expand the capabilities of pop-up menus by integrating data entry with menu selection (see Section 7.7.4).

7.3.2   Menus for long lists

Sometimes the list of menu items may be longer than the 30 to 40 lines that can reasonably fit on a display. One solution is to create a tree-structured menu (Section 7.4.2), but sometimes the desire to limit the interface to one conceptual menu is strong—for example, when users must select a state from the 50 states in the United States or a country from an extensive list of possibilities. Typical lists are alphabetically ordered to support user typing of leading characters, but categorical lists may be useful. The principles of menu-list sequencing apply (Section 7.5.2).

Scrolling menus, combo boxes, and fisheye menus.   *Scrolling menus* display the first portion of the menu and an additional menu item, typically an arrow that leads to the next set of items in the menu sequence. The scrolling (or paging) menu might continue with dozens or thousands of items, using the list-box capabilities found in most graphical user interfaces. Keyboard shortcuts might allow users to type the letter "M" to scroll directly to the first word starting with the letter "M," but this feature is seldom discovered and remembered by novice users. *Combo boxes* make this option more evident by combining a scrolling menu with a text-entry field. Users can type in leading characters to scroll through the list. Another alternative is the *fisheye menu*, which displays all

Figure 7.6

The game The Sims allows players to buy and furnish houses, then create characters and make them interact with their environment. For example, clicking on the refrigerator pops up a pie menu of possible actions the character can take when looking into the refrigerator.

of the menu items on the screen at once but shows only items near the cursor at full size; items further away are displayed at a smaller size (Fig. 7.7). Fisheye menus have the potential to improve speed, but wide differences in users' preferences exist, making fisheye menus a useful option but not a recommended choice as a default menu style (Bederson, 2000).

Sliders and alphasliders. When items consist of ranges of numerical values, a *slider* is a natural choice to allow the selection of a value. Ranges of values can also be selected with double-sided (range) sliders. Users select values by using a pointing device to drag the slider thumb (scroll box) along the scale. When greater precision is needed, the slider thumb can be adjusted incrementally by clicking on arrows located at each end of the slider. A similar tool that can be useful for presenting menus with a vast number of selection options is an *alphaslider*. The alphaslider uses multiple levels of granularity in moving the slider thumb and therefore can support tens or hundreds of thousands of items (Ahlberg and Shneiderman, 1994). The following alphaslider covers the 10,000 actors in a film database. The dark upper part of the thumb jumps over 40 actors

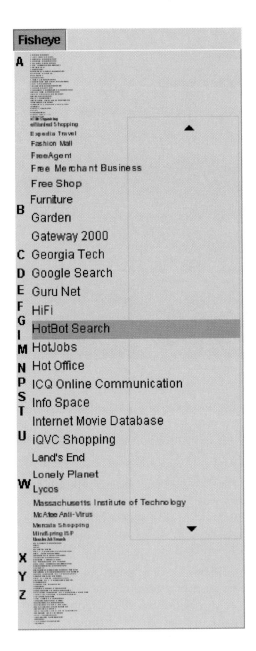

Figure 7.7

Fisheye menus allow rapid selection in very large menus. Users can rapidly move the cursor to the first letter of the word using the alphabet letters given on the left. Menu items around the cursor are shown full size, while further-away items are barely visible. Fine adjustments can be done by moving the cursor to the right side of the menu.

for each move of the mouse, and the lighter smaller lower part allows movement through each actor's name. The index at the bottom of the alphaslider gives users an idea of where to jump to start a new search.

Because of their compactness, sliders, range sliders, and alphasliders are often used in the control panels of interactive visualization systems (see Chapter 14 and Figs. 13.3 and 14.5).

Two-dimensional menus.   Alternatively, a multiple-column menu might be used. These "fast and vast" two-dimensional menus give users a good overview of the choices, reduce the number of required actions, and allow rapid selection. Multiple-column menus are especially useful in web-page design, to minimize the scrolling needed to see a long list and to give users a single-screen overview of the full set of choices (Figs. 7.8 and 7.9).

Figure 7.8

This online grocery-shopping web page includes multiple menus using icons and textual labels. Twenty-five labeled icons describe the General Grocery aisles. The icons are attractive and representative of the items. Their locations remain fixed, so users can remember that cereals, for example, are on the top-right corner of the menu. This page also demonstrates an effective tab design to provide access to other services. The order list and the total price tag remain visible at all times. (www.peapod.com)

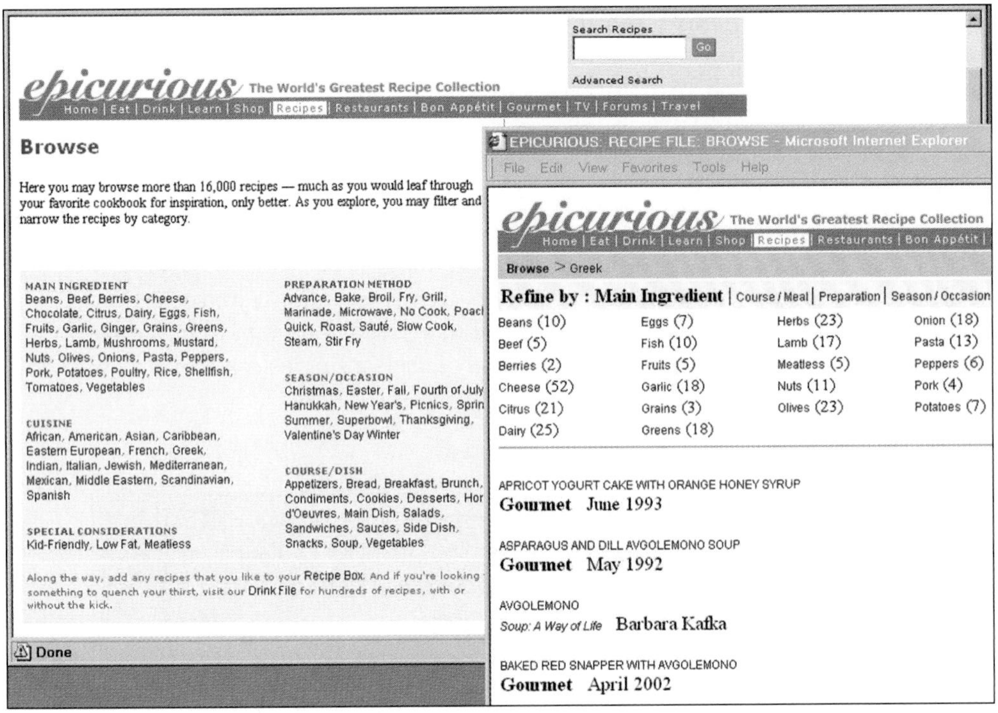

Figure 7.9

Epicurious proposes a menu of a hundred categories of recipes. Once the users have selected a category (here, Greek recipes), they can review the list or narrow it down by selecting from a list of 22 main ingredients. The number of recipes is listed next to each category (for example, there are 10 bean recipes). Other refinement options are course/meal, preparation time, and season/occasion. (www.epicurious.com)

7.3.3 Embedded menus and hotlinks

All the menus discussed thus far might be characterized as *explicit menus*, in that there is an orderly enumeration of the menu items with little extraneous information. In many situations, however, the menu items might be *embedded* in text or graphics and still be selectable. For example, it is natural to allow users reading about people, events, and places to retrieve detailed information by selecting names in context (Koved and Shneiderman, 1986). The highlighted names, places, or phrases are menu items embedded in meaningful text that informs users and helps to clarify the meaning of the menu items. Embedded links were popularized in the Hyperties system, which was used for two early commercial hypertext projects (Shneiderman, 1988; Shneiderman and Kearsley, 1989) and became the inspiration for the *hotlinks* of the World Wide Web (see Figs. 1.4 and 1.5).

Embedded links permit items to be viewed in context and eliminate the need for a distracting and screen-wasting enumeration of items. Contextual display helps to keep the users focused on their tasks and on the objects of interest. Graphical menus are a particularly attractive way to present many selection options while providing context to help users make their choices. For example, maps orient users about the geography of the area before they select a menu item (Fig. 7.10), and calendars can inform users of availability and constraints (Fig. 7.11). Information-abundant compact visualizations can enable the presentation of vast menus (see Chapter 14 and Figure 14.14).

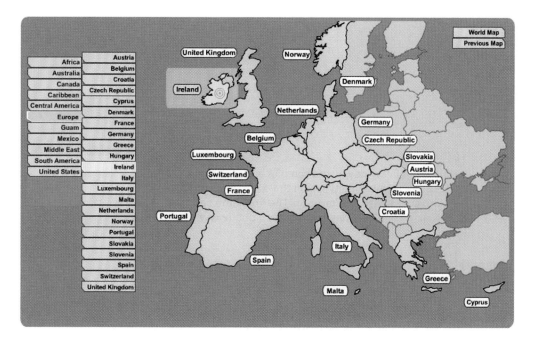

Figure 7.10

To search for rental-car office locations, users can select a country by using a cascading menu of regions of the world and countries, or by clicking directly on the area of interest. As users select the region of the world (here, Europe), the map is updated. Possible choices are shown in yellow, highlighting that the company has no offices in Sweden. The country under the cursor (here, Ireland) is highlighted on both the map and the menu. (www.alamo.com)

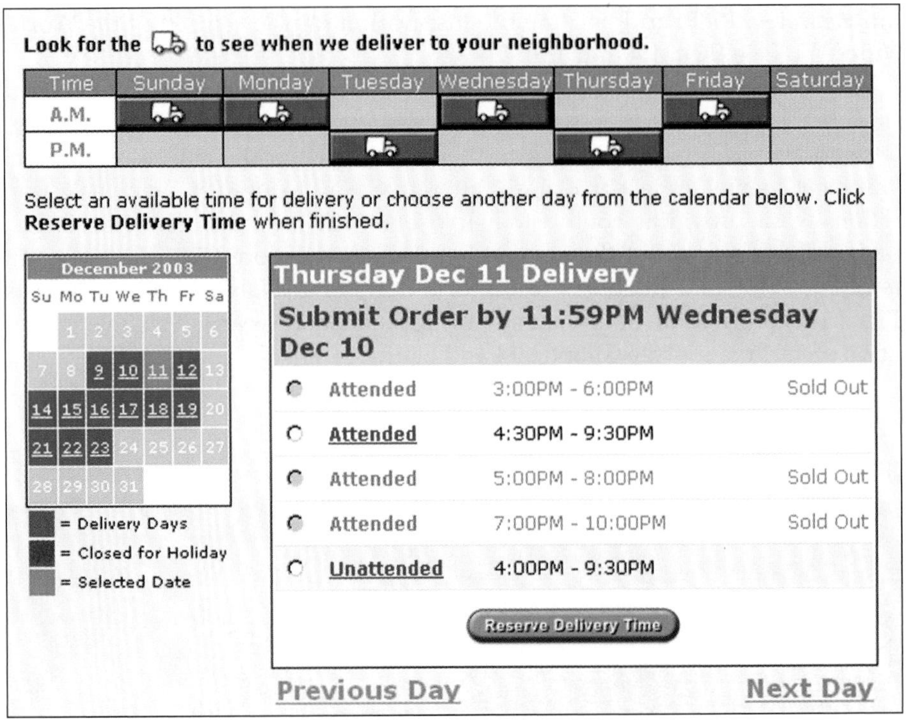

Look for the � to see when we deliver to your neighborhood.

Time	Sunday	Monday	Tuesday	Wednesday	Thursday	Friday	Saturday
A.M.	�	�		�		�	
P.M.			�		�		

Select an available time for delivery or choose another day from the calendar below. Click **Reserve Delivery Time** when finished.

December 2003

Su Mo Tu We Th Fr Sa

Su	Mo	Tu	We	Th	Fr	Sa
	1	2	3	4	5	6
7	8	9	10	11	12	13
14	15	16	17	18	19	20
21	22	23	24	25	26	27
28	29	30	31			

■ = Delivery Days
■ = Closed for Holiday
■ = Selected Date

Thursday Dec 11 Delivery

Submit Order by 11:59PM Wednesday Dec 10

○	Attended	3:00PM - 6:00PM	Sold Out
○	**Attended**	4:30PM - 9:30PM	
○	Attended	5:00PM - 8:00PM	Sold Out
○	Attended	7:00PM - 10:00PM	Sold Out
○	**Unattended**	4:00PM - 9:30PM	

(Reserve Delivery Time)

Previous Day   Next Day

Figure 7.11

To select a delivery day, users can pick a day on the current month calendar view (color-coded by availability) or on the week view, which indicates if deliveries are done in the morning or afternoon. The final time selection is made by clicking on the list, where unavailable times are grayed out. (www.peapod.com)

7.4   Combinations of Multiple Menus

Menus can be combined in linear series or presented simultaneously. A common strategy is to use a tree structure to organize large menus, but acyclic and cyclic networks are also possible.

7.4.1   Linear menu sequences and simultaneous menus

Often, a series of interdependent menus can be used to guide users through a series of choices in which they see a sequence of menus. For example, a pizza-ordering interface might include a linear sequence of menus to choose size (small, medium, or large), thickness (thick, normal, or thin), and finally ingredients. Other familiar examples are online examinations that have sequences of multiple-choice test items, each made up as a menu, or wizards (a Microsoft term) that guide users through complex decisions with a sequence of cue cards and menu options. Linear sequences guide the user by presenting one decision at a time and are effective for novice users performing simple tasks.

Simultaneous menus present multiple active menus on a screen at the same time and allow users to enter choices in any order (Fig. 7.12). They require more

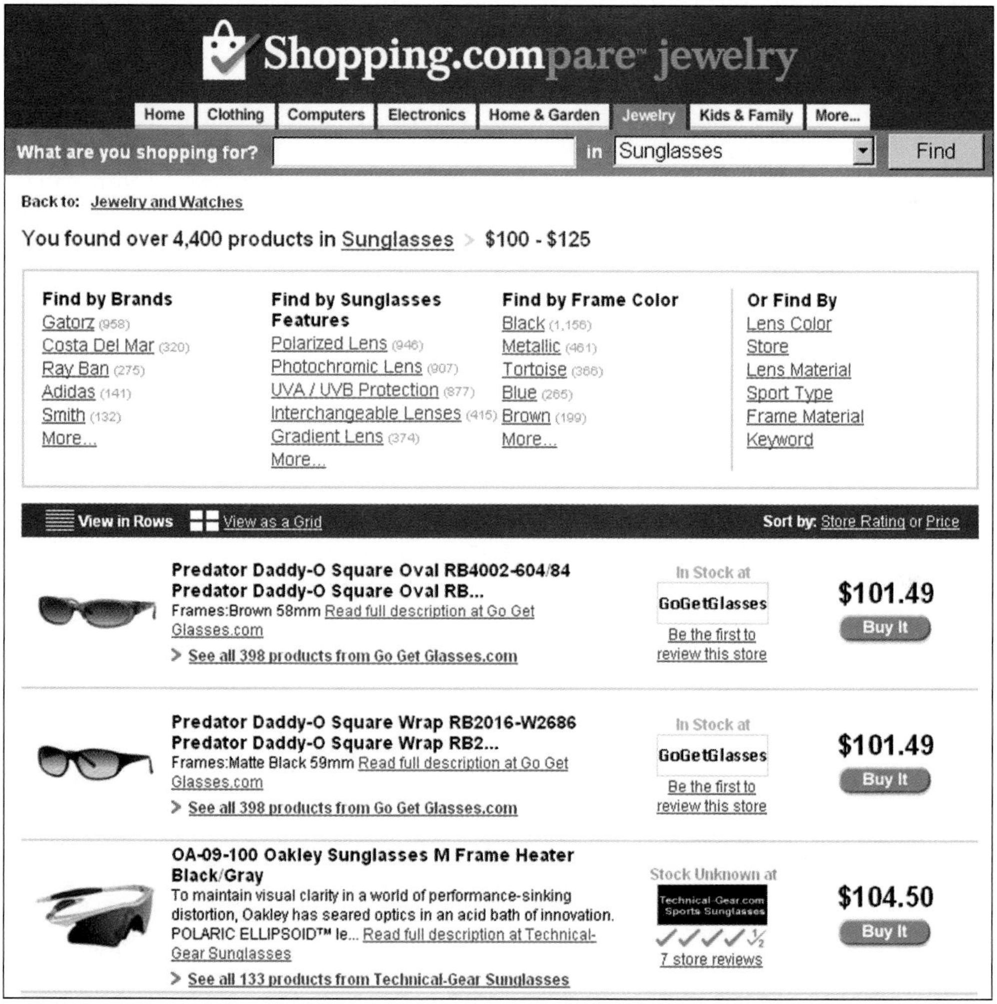

Figure 7.12

Shoppers looking for sunglasses can narrow the list of results by selecting any item in three simultaneous menus of brands, features, and frame color, without any particular order. Results can be laid out in a row or a grid, and sorting can be done by price or store rating. (www.shopping.com)

display space, which may render them inappropriate for certain display environments and menu structures; however, a study has shown that experienced users performing complex tasks benefit from simultaneous menus (Hochheiser and Shneiderman, 1999). The faceted metadata search interface of Flamenco (see Section 14.4 and Fig. 14.9) is a powerful application of simultaneous menus to browse large image databases.

7.4.2   Tree-structured menus

When a collection of items grows and becomes difficult to maintain under intellectual control, designers can form categories of similar items, creating a *tree structure*. Some collections can be partitioned easily into mutually exclusive groups with distinctive identifiers. For example, an online grocery store can be organized by categories such as produce, meat, dairy, cleaning products, and more. Produce can then be organized into vegetables, fruits, and nuts, while dairy is organized into milk, cheese, yogurt, and so on.

Even these groupings may occasionally lead to confusion or disagreement. Classification and indexing are complex tasks, and in many situations there is no single solution that is acceptable to everyone. The initial design can be improved as a function of feedback from users, though, and over time, as the structure is improved and as users gain familiarity with it, success rates will improve.

In spite of the associated problems, tree-structured menu systems have the power to make large collections of data available to novice or intermittent users. If each menu has 30 items, then a menu tree with 4 levels has the capacity to lead an untrained user through a collection of 810,000 destinations. That number would be excessively large for a set of commands in a word processor but would be realistic in a World Wide Web application such as a newspaper (Fig. 1.4), a library (Fig 1.7), or a web portal such as Yahoo! (Fig. 1.11).

If the groupings at each level are natural and comprehensible to users and if users know the target, menu traversal can be accomplished in a few seconds—it is faster than flipping through a book. On the other hand, if the groupings are unfamiliar and users have only vague notions of the items that they seek, they may get lost for hours in the tree menus (Norman and Chin, 1988). Terminology from the user's task domain can help orient the user. Instead of using a title that is vague and emphasizes the computer domain, such as "Main Menu Options," use terms such as "Friendlibank Services" or simply "Games."

Menus using large indexes such as library subject headings or comprehensive business classifications are challenging to navigate. With *expanding menus,* the full context of the choices is preserved while the user browses through the tree structure (as in Windows Explorer). At any point, users have access to the whole set of major and same-level categories. Sequential menus, on the other hand, do not display the full hierarchical context as they drop down to deeper levels in the hierarchy. Only elements in the selected category are displayed as options for browsing. A recent study showed that expandable menus were acceptable only for shallow menu hierarchies of depth 2 or 3, and should be avoided for deeper hierarchies. The study also showed that expandable menus should avoid hard-to-follow indentation schemes and long lists that require excessive scrolling in a browser window (Zaphiris, Shneiderman, and Norman, 2002).

The *depth,* or number of levels, of a menu tree depends in part on the *breadth,* or number of items per level. If more items are put into the main menu, then the tree spreads out and has fewer levels. This shape may be advantageous, but only if clarity is preserved. Several authors urge using four to eight items per menu, but at the same time, they urge using no more than three to four levels. With large menu applications, one or both of these guidelines must be compromised.

Several empirical studies have dealt with the depth/breadth tradeoff, and the evidence is strong that breadth should be preferred over depth (Kiger, 1984; Norman and Chin, 1988). In fact, there is reason to encourage designers to limit menu trees to three levels: when the depth goes to four or five, there is a good chance of users becoming lost or disoriented. Jacko and Salvendy (1996) examined the relationship between task complexity and performance for menus of various breadths and depths. They found that response time and number of errors increased as menu depth increased. Furthermore, users found deeper menus to be more complex. In an interesting variation, Wallace, Anderson, and Shneiderman, (1987) also confirmed that broader, shallower trees (64 items in 3 levels or 6 levels) produced superior performance, and showed that when users were stressed they made 96% more errors and took 16% longer to complete their tasks. The stressor was simply an instruction to work quickly ("It is imperative that you finish the task just as quickly as possible"); the control group received gentler verbal instruction to avoid rushing ("Take your time; there is no rush").

Recent empirical work has demonstrated that hierarchical-menu design experiments can be replicated when applied to hierarchies of web links (Larson and Czerwinski, 1998). The navigation problem (getting lost or using an inefficient path) becomes more and more treacherous as the depth of the hierarchy increases.

A critical variable that may determine the attractiveness of menu organization is the speed at which users can move through the menus. For most modern computers, response time (the time it takes to display a new screen after users make a selection) is so rapid that this issue is less of a concern, but delays on the World Wide Web have revived this topic. Deep menu trees or complex traversals become annoying to the user if system response time is slow, resulting in long and multiple delays.

Landauer and Nachbar (1985) developed predictive equations for traversal times. They varied the number of items per level from 2 to 4 to 8 to 16, to reach 4,096 target items of numbers or words. The times for the task with words ranged from 23.4 seconds down to 12.5 seconds as the breadth increased and the number of levels decreased. Over the range studied, the authors suggest that a simple function of the number of items on the screen will predict the time, T, for a selection:

$$T = k + c*\log b,$$

where k and c are empirically determined constants for scanning the screen to make a choice, and b is the breadth at each level. Then, the total time to traverse the menu tree depends on only the depth, D, which is

$$D = \log bN,$$

where N is the total number of items in the tree. With $N = 4,096$ target items and a branching factor of $b = 16$, the depth $D = 3$, and the total time is $3*(k + c*\log 16)$. Correction factors can be defined for special populations, such as older adult users (Zaphiris and Ellis, 2000).

Even though the semantic structure of the items cannot be ignored, these studies suggest that the fewer levels there are, the greater the ease of decision making is. Of course, screen clutter must be considered, in addition to the semantic organization.

7.4.3   Menu maps

As the depth of a menu tree grows, users find it increasingly difficult to maintain a sense of position in the tree; their sense of disorientation, or of "getting lost," grows. Viewing one menu at a time makes it hard to grasp the overall pattern and to see relationships among categories. Evidence from several early studies demonstrated the advantage of offering a spatial map to help users stay oriented. Sometimes menu maps are shown on web pages as site maps (Fig. 7.13); sometimes they are printed as large posters to give users a visual overview of hundreds of items at several levels. Another approach is to have the overview in the user manual as a fold-out, or spread over several pages as a tree diagram or indented-text display to show levels.

7.4.4   Acyclic and cyclic menu networks

Although tree structures are appealing, sometimes network structures are more appropriate. For example, in a commercial online service, it might make sense to provide access to banking information from both the financial and consumer parts of a tree structure. A second motivation for using *menu networks* is that it may be desirable to permit paths between disparate sections of a tree, rather than requiring users to begin a new search from the main menu. Network struc-

Tools	Lycos Topics	Search	Shopping
• Chat	**Autos**	• Add Your Site to	• Autos
• Classifieds	Buy, Sell, Research, Website Directory ...	Lycos	• Babies & Kids
• Clubs	**Back To School**	• Advanced Search	• Back to School
• Domain Name	Electronics, School Supplies, College Life,	• Audio	• Books
Registration	Win a Computer ...	• E-mail Addresses	• Clothing &
• eBay Auctions	**College**	• HotBot Search	Accessories
• E-mail	Dating, Entertainment, Jobs, Library ...	• The Lycos 50	• Computers
• E-mail Address	**Entertainment**	• MP3s	• Electronics
Search	Celebrities, Pictures, TV,	• Parental Controls	• Health & Beauty
• Greeting Cards	Website Directory ...	• Pictures	• Music
• Help	**Finance**	• Stocks	• Software
• Horoscopes	Insurance, Live Charts, Trading,	• Video	• More Shopping
• Lycos Messenger	Website Directory ...	• Websites	
• Internet Access	**Games**	Directory	**Shopping Services**
• Maps	Prize Games, Classic Games, Lottery,	• White Pages	• Classifieds
• Message Boards	Website Directory ...	• Yellow Pages	• eBay Auctions
• Mobile/Wireless	**Health**		
• MP3s	Conditions A-Z, Medical Library, News,	**Personalize Lycos**	**About Lycos**
• Multimedia Search	Website Directory ...	• E-mail	• Add Your Site to
• Parental Controls	**Kids**	• My Investing	Lycos
• Personalize Lycos	Games, Home and Family, Homework,	• My Lycos	• Advertise on
• Personals & Dating	Recipes and Entertainment,	• Web Site Building	Lycos
• Stocks	Website Directory ...		• Corporate
• Translate	**Movies**	**Lycos Network**	Information
• TV Listings	Coming Soon, Trailers,	• Angelfire	• Jobs at Lycos
• WAP/SMS	Website Directory ...	• Gamesville	• Press Releases
• Weather	**Music**	• htmlGEAR	• Send Us Feedback
• Web Site Building	Downloads, Website Directory ...	• HotBot	
• White Pages	**News**	• HotWired	
• Yellow Pages	Breaking News, Photos, Cartoons,	• Matchmaker	
	Website Directory ...	• Sonique	
	Reference	• Tripod	
	Education, Maps, Website Directory ...	• Wired News	
	Relationships	• Webmonkey	
	Dating, Personals, Romance	• WhoWhere	
	Shopping		
	Departments ...		
	Small Business		
	Business-to-business, News, Tools,		
	Website Directory ...		

Figure 7.13

The Lycos site-map page presents the entire menu structure of the web site. (www.lycos.com)

tures in the form of *acyclic* or *cyclic graphs* arise naturally in social relationships, transportation routing, and of course the World Wide Web. As users move from trees to acyclic networks to cyclic networks, the potential for getting lost increases. Confusion and disorientation are often reported by World Wide Web users who have difficulty navigating that large cyclic network.

With a tree structure, the user can form a mental model of the structure and of the relationships between the menus. Developing this mental model may be more difficult with a network. With a tree structure, there is a single parent menu, so backward traversals towards the main menu are straightforward. In networks, a stack of visited menus must be kept to allow backward traversals. It may be helpful to preserve a notion of "level," as users may feel more comfortable if they have a sense of how far they are from the main menu.

Many other specialized or hybrid menu structures can also be designed. For example, computerized surveys typically use linear sequences of menus, but conditional branching might alter the sequence of menus and item values might vary according to answers to previous questions. Pursuing new structures and refining existing ones should lead to improved user performance and satisfaction.

7 · 5   Content Organization

Meaningful grouping and sequencing of menu items, along with careful editing of titles and labels and appropriate layout design, can lead to easier-to-learn menus and increased selection speed. In this section, we review the content-organization issues and provide guidelines for design.

7 · 5 · 1   Task-related grouping in tree structures

Grouping menu items in a tree such that they are comprehensible to users and match the task structure is sometimes difficult. The problems are akin to putting kitchen utensils in order; steak knives go together and serving spoons go together, but where do you put butter knives or carving sets? Computer-menu problems include overlapping categories, extraneous items, conflicting classifications in the same menu, unfamiliar jargon, and generic terms. Based on this set of problems, here are several suggested rules for forming menu trees:

- *Create groups of logically similar items.* For example, a comprehensible menu would list countries at level 1, states or provinces at level 2, and cities at level 3.

- *Form groups that cover all possibilities.* For example, a menu with age ranges 0–9, 10–19, 20–29, and > 30 makes it easy for the user to select an item.

- *Make sure that items are nonoverlapping.* Lower-level items should be naturally associated with a single higher-level item. Overlapping categories such as "Entertainment" and "Events" are poor choices compared to "Concerts" and "Sports."

- *Use familiar terminology, but ensure that items are distinct from one another.* Generic terms such as "Day" and "Night" may be too vague; more specific options such as "6 A.M. to 6 P.M." and "6 P.M. to 6 A.M." may be more useful and precise.

There is no perfect menu structure that matches every person's knowledge of the application domain. Designers must use good judgment for the initial implementation, but then must be receptive to suggested improvements and empirical data. Users will gradually gain familiarity, even with extremely complex tree structures, and will be increasingly successful in locating required items.

7.5.2 Item presentation sequence

Once the items in a menu have been chosen, the designer is still confronted with the choice of *presentation sequence*. If the items have a natural sequence—such as days of the week, chapters in a book, or sizes of eggs—then the decision is trivial. Typical bases for sequencing items include these:

- *Time* (chronological ordering)
- *Numeric ordering* (ascending or descending ordering)
- *Physical properties* (increasing or decreasing length, area, volume, temperature, weight, velocity, and so on)

Many cases have no task-related ordering, though, and the designer must choose from such possibilities as these:

- *Alphabetic sequence of terms*
- *Grouping of related items* (with blank lines or other demarcation between groups)
- *Most frequently used items first*
- *Most important items first* (importance may be difficult to determine and may vary among users)

Card (1982) experimented with a single 18-item vertical permanent menu of text-editing commands such as INSERT, ITALIC, and CENTER. He presented subjects with a command, and they had to locate the command in the list, move a mouse-controlled cursor, and select the command by pressing a button on the mouse. The menu items were sequenced in one of three ways: alphabetically, in categorical groups (Card called them "functional"), and randomly. The mean times were as follows:

Strategy	Time per trial (seconds)
alphabetic	0.81
categorical	1.28
random	3.23

Since subjects were given the target item, they did best when merely scanning to match the menu items in an alphabetic sequence. The performance with the categorical groupings was remarkably good, indicating that subjects began to remember the groupings and could go directly to the appropriate group. In menu applications where the users must make a decision about the most suitable menu item, the categorical arrangement might be more appealing. Users' memory for the categorically grouped items is likely to surpass their memory for the alphabetic or random sequences. The poor performance that Card observed with the random sequence confirms the importance of considering alternative presentation sequences for the items.

With a 64-item menu, the time for locating a target word was found to increase from just over 2 seconds for an alphabetic menu to more than 6 seconds for a random menu (McDonald, Stone, and Liebelt, 1983). When the target word was replaced with a single-line definition, the subjects could no longer scan for a simple match and had to consider each menu item carefully. The advantage of alphabetic ordering nearly vanished. User reaction time went up to about 7 seconds for the alphabetic and about 8 seconds for the random organization. Somberg and Picardi (1983) studied user reaction times in a five-item menu. Their three experiments revealed a significant and nearly linear relationship between the user's reaction time and the serial position in the menu. Furthermore, there was a significant increase in reaction time if the target word was unfamiliar, rather than familiar.

Finally a recent study compared the use of an alphabetical list (645 terms) versus a categorical organization (16 categories) of the same terms in FedStats, a World Wide Web government statistics portal (Ceaparu and Shneiderman, 2004). Users who answered complex questions showed a significant performance improvement when a categorical organization was used. A further improvement was seen when the categorically organized terms provided links to 215 agency or project home pages, instead of to low-level pages where users may feel lost if they do not find the information they need.

If frequency of use is a potential guide to sequencing menu items, it might make sense to vary the sequence adaptively to reflect the current pattern of use. Unfortunately, adaptations can be disruptive, increasing confusion and undermining the users' learning of menu structures. In addition, users might become anxious that other changes might occur at any moment. Evidence against the utility of such changes was found in a study in which a pull-down list of food items was resequenced to ensure that the most frequently selected items migrated towards the top (Mitchell and Shneiderman, 1989). Users were clearly unsettled by the changing menus, and their performance was better with static menus. In contrast, evidence in favor of adaptation was found in a study of a telephone-book menu tree that had been restructured to make frequently used telephone numbers more easily accessible (Greenberg and Witten, 1985). However, this study did not deal with the issue of potentially disorienting changes to the menu during usage. To avoid disruption and unpredictable behavior, it is probably a wise policy to allow users to specify when they want the menu restructured.

When some menu items are much more frequently selected than others, there is a temptation to organize the menu in descending frequency. This organization does speed up selection of the topmost items, but the loss of a meaningful ordering for low-frequency items is disruptive. A sensible compromise is to extract three or four of the most frequently selected items and to put them on the top, while preserving the order of the remaining items. In controlled experiments and field studies with a lengthy font menu, the three most popular fonts (Courier, Helvetica, and Times) were put on top, and the remaining list was left in alphabetical order. This split-menu strategy proved appealing and statistically significantly improved performance (Sears and Shneiderman, 1994). An improved theory of menu-selection performance emerged that showed that familiar items were selected in logarithmic time, whereas unfamiliar items were found in linear time, with respect to their position in the menu. The software collected usage frequency, but the split-menu ordering remained stable until the system administrator decided to make a change.

Microsoft introduced adaptive menus in Office 2000. As users work with the programs, the menu items that have not been selected disappear from the menu, making it shorter. To see the missing items again, users have to click on the arrow at the bottom of the menu or hover over it for a few seconds, causing the menu to show all items. Items that have recently been selected remain on the short version of the menu, while items that have not been used for a while disappear (Fig. 7.14). This complex approach is appreciated by some users who have regular patterns of use, but highly disliked by many users who are confused by the constantly changing menus.

Adaptable (user-controlled) menus are an attractive alternative to adaptive menus. One study compared the Microsoft Word version using adaptive menus with a variant providing users with the ability to switch between two modes of operation: the normal full-feature mode, and a personal mode that users could customize by selecting which items were included in the menus (McGrenere, Baecker, and Booth, 2002). Results showed that participants were better able to learn and navigate through the menus with the personally adaptable version. Preferences varied greatly among users, and the study revealed some users' overall dissatisfaction with adaptive menus but also the reluctance of others to spend significant time customizing the interface.

7.5.3   Menu layout

Little experimental research has been done on menu layout. This section contains many subjective judgments, which are in need of empirical validation (Box 7.1).

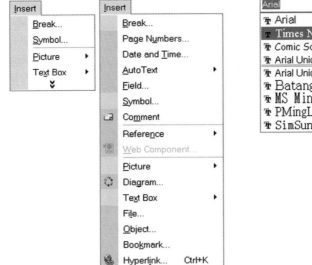

Figure 7.14

Adaptive menus found in Microsoft Office. At first the Insert menu only shows items used recently, but it can be expanded to show all items (center). On the right, a font-selection menu lists the recently selected fonts at the top of the menu (as well as in the full list), making it easier to quickly select the popular fonts.

Box 7.1

Menu-selection guidelines.

- Use task semantics to organize menus (single, linear sequence, tree structure, acyclic and cyclic networks)
- Prefer broad–shallow to narrow–deep
- Show position by graphics, numbers, or titles
- Use items as titles for subtrees
- Group items meaningfully
- Sequence items meaningfully
- Use brief items, begin with the keyword
- Use consistent grammar, layout, terminology
- Allow type ahead, jump ahead, or other shortcuts
- Enable jumps to previous and main menu
- Consider online help; novel selection mechanisms; and optimal response time, display rate, screen size

Titles.   Choosing the title for a book is a delicate matter for an author, editor, or publisher. A particularly descriptive or memorable title can make a big difference in reader responses. Similarly, choosing titles for menus is a complex matter that deserves serious thought.

For single menus, a simple descriptive title that identifies the situation is all that is necessary. With a linear sequence of menus, the titles should accurately represent the stages in the linear sequence. Consistent grammatical style can reduce confusion, and brief but unambiguous noun phrases are often sufficient.

For tree-structured menus, choosing titles is more difficult. Titles such as "Main menu" or topic descriptions such as "Bank transactions" for the root of the tree clearly indicate that the user is at the beginning of a session. One potentially helpful rule is to use the high-level menu items as the titles for the next lower-level menus. It is reassuring to users to find that when they select an item such as "Business and financial services" they are shown a screen that is titled "Business and financial services." It might be unsettling to get a screen titled "Managing your money," even though the intent is similar. Imagine looking in the table of contents of a book and seeing a chapter titled "The American Revolution," but, when you turn to the indicated page, finding instead "Our Early History"—you might wonder if you've made a mistake, and your confidence might be undermined. Similarly, when designing World Wide Web pages, you should ensure that the embedded menu item matches the title on the destination page. Using menu items as titles may encourage the menu author to choose items more carefully, so that they are descriptive in the context of the other menu items and as the title of the next menu.

A further concern is consistency in placement of titles and other features in a menu screen. Teitelbaum and Granda (1983) demonstrated that user think time nearly doubled when the position of information such as titles or prompts was varied on menu screens, so efforts should be made to keep the placement constant.

Phrasing of menu items.   Just because an interface has English words, phrases, or sentences as menu choices, that is no guarantee that it is comprehensible. Individual words may not be familiar to some users (for example, "repaginate"), and often two menu items may appear to satisfy the user's needs, whereas only one actually does (for example, "put away" or "eject"). This enduring problem has no perfect solution, but designers can gather useful feedback from colleagues, users, pilot studies, acceptance tests, and user-performance monitoring. The following guidelines may seem obvious, but we state them because they are so often violated:

- *Use familiar and consistent terminology.* Carefully select terminology that is familiar to the designated user community and keep a list of these terms to facilitate consistent use.

- *Ensure that items are distinct from one another.* Each item should be distinguished clearly from other items. For example, "Slow tours of the countryside,"

"Journeys with visits to parks," and "Leisurely voyages" are less distinctive than are "Bike tours," "Train tours to national parks," and "Cruise-ship tours."

- *Use consistent and concise phrasing.* Review the collection of items to ensure consistency and conciseness. Users are likely to feel more comfortable and to be more successful with "Animal," "Vegetable," and "Mineral" than with "Information about animals," "Vegetable choices you can make," and "Viewing mineral categories."

- *Bring the keyword to the fore.* Try to write menu items such that the first word aids the user in recognizing and discriminating between items—use "Size of type" instead of "Set the type size." Then, if the first word indicates that this item is not relevant, users can begin scanning the next item.

Graphic layout and design. The constraints of screen width and length, display rate, character set, and highlighting techniques strongly influence the graphic layout of menus. Presenting 50 states as menu items is easy enough on a large screen with a rapid display rate. On the other hand, systems with small text-only displays or slow modems must add levels of subcategories to present the same information.

Consistent formats help users to locate necessary information, focus users' attention on relevant material, and reduce users' anxiety by offering predictability. Menu designers should establish guidelines for consistency of at least these menu components:

- *Titles.* Some people prefer centered titles, but left justification is an acceptable approach, especially with slow display rates.

- *Item placement.* Typically, items are left justified, with the item number or letter preceding the item description. Blank lines may be used to separate meaningful groups of items. If multiple columns are used, a consistent pattern of numbering or lettering should be used (for example, down the columns is easier to scan than across the rows).

- *Instructions.* The instructions should be identical in each menu and should be placed in the same position. This rule includes instructions about traversals, help, or function-key usage.

- *Error messages.* If the users make unacceptable choices, the error messages should appear in a consistent position and should use consistent terminology and syntax.

- *Status reports.* Some systems indicate which portion of the menu structure is currently being searched, which page of the structure is currently being viewed, or which choices must be made to complete a task. This information should appear in a consistent position and should have a consistent structure.

In addition, since disorientation is a potential problem, techniques to indicate position in the menu structure can be useful. In books, different fonts and typefaces may indicate chapter, section, and subsection organization. Similarly, in menu trees, as the user goes down the tree structure, the titles can be designed to indicate the level or distance from the main menu. Graphics, fonts, typefaces, or highlighting techniques can be used beneficially.

Main Menu

HOME SERVICES

NEWSPAPERS

The New York Times

This display gives a clear indication of progress down the tree. When users want to do a traversal back up the tree or to an adjoining menu at the same level, they will feel confident about what action to take.

With linear sequences of menus, the users can be given a simple visual presentation of position in the sequence: a *position marker*. In a computer-assisted instruction sequence with 12 menu frames, a position marker (+) just below the menu items might show progress. In the first frame, the position marker is

```
+ — — — — — —
```

in the second frame, it is

```
— + — — — — —
```

and in the final frame, it is

```
— — — — — — +
```

The users can use this marker to gauge their progress and see how much remains to be done. Figure 7.19 shows a similar example in a mobile phone.

With GUIs, many possibilities exist for showing progress through successive levels of a tree-structured menu or through linear sequences. A common approach is to show a cascade of successive menu boxes set slightly lower than and slightly to the right of the previous items. For pull-down menus, *cascading* or *walking menus* (in which users walk through several levels at a time) are perceptually meaningful, but they can present a motor challenge to users who must move the cursor in the appropriate direction. Another graphic innovation is to use transparent or see-through menus or tool palettes, called *magic lenses*, that can be dragged near to the object of interest while only partially obscuring it (Bier et al., 1994). Harrison and Vicente (1996) showed that user performance remains unchanged as the menu becomes up to 50% transparent, but the users make significantly more errors and their performance slows as the transparency reaches 75%.

With rapid high-resolution displays, more elegant visual representations are possible. Given sufficient screen space, it is possible to show a large portion of the menu map and to allow users to point to menu items anywhere in the tree. Graphic designers and layout artists are useful partners in such design projects.

7.6   Fast Movement Through Menus

After optimizing the grouping and sequencing of menu items and considering adaptable menu strategies, there are still techniques available to accelerate the movement through menus, particularly for expert users.

A standard way to permit frequent menu users to speed through the options is to provide *keyboard shortcuts*. For example, an expert user might memorize that in Microsoft Word the shortcut Alt-V for View followed by Alt-O for Outline will change a document's presentation to outline view. Even if the display of the menu items is very fast, the user will still avoid reaching for the mouse, locating the correct option, and reaching two targets with the mouse. This approach is attractive because it is rapid and allows graceful evolution from novice to expert. Using the mnemonic-letters approach to type ahead requires caution in avoiding collisions and increases the effort of translation to foreign languages, but its clarity and memorability are an advantage in many applications. Shortcuts should be indicated next to the menu item label so that users can progressively learn new shortcuts as needed (Fig. 7.5).

Pie menus, marking menus, and other variations of circular menus can insert a short delay before menu items are displayed, allowing users to *mouse ahead* by relying on their muscle memory to reproduce the series of angular displacements necessary for a command selection (for example, in a drawing program a "click-up-left-up" can start dragging an object before the menu appears). When unsure, users can wait until the menu appears.

In web browsers, *bookmarks* provide a way for users to take shortcuts to destinations that they have visited previously. For many users, this menu of destinations can grow quickly and require hierarchical management strategies, becoming a challenge in itself.

Another approach to serving frequent menu users is to allow regularly used paths to be recorded by users as *menu macros* or to be placed in the toolbar as a user-selected icon. Users can invoke the macro or customization facility, traverse the menu structure, and then assign a name or icon. When the name or icon is invoked, the traversal is executed automatically. This mechanism allows tailoring of the interface and can provide a simplified access mechanism for repetitive tasks. Many word processors allow users to define their preferred character styles through multiple menu selections and then to name each of the styles and place them on a toolbar. For example, the style for chapter titles might be set to boldface, 24-point, italic, Times font, and centered text. Then, this chapter-title style can be saved and later invoked when needed as a form of macro.

Finally, when items of a lower-level menu need to be used multiple times in a row, *tear-off menus* can be useful to keep the list of options visible on the screen.

7·7   Data Entry with Menus: Form Fillin, Dialog Boxes, and Alternatives

Menu selection is effective for choosing an item from a list, but some tasks are cumbersome (or even impossible) with menus. If data entry of personal names or numeric values is required, then keyboard typing becomes more attractive. When many fields of data are necessary, the appropriate interaction style is *form fillin*—for example, the user might be presented with a name and address form. Form fillin was an important strategy in the early days of 80 × 24 textual displays, and it has flourished in the world of graphical dialog boxes. It has also became the standard interface for specifying complex searches (Figs. 7.15, 13.10, and 14.1) and doing data entry on the World Wide Web.

The form-fillin approach is attractive because the full complement of information is visible, giving users a feeling of being in control of the dialog. Few instructions are necessary, since the display resembles familiar paper forms. A combination of form fillins, pop-up or scrolling menus, and custom widgets such as calendars or maps can support rapid selection, even for a multistep task such as airline-ticket booking, seat selection, and purchasing.

7·7·1   Form fillin

There is a paucity of empirical work on form fillin, but several design guidelines have emerged from practitioners (Galitz, 2002; Brown, 1988). Software tools simplify design, help to ensure consistency, ease maintenance, and speed implementation. But even with excellent tools, the designer must still make many complex decisions (Box 7.2).

The elements of form-fillin design include the following:

- *Meaningful title.* Identify the topic and avoid computer terminology.

- *Comprehensible instructions.* Describe the user's tasks in familiar terminology. Be brief; if more information is needed, make a set of help screens available to the novice user. In support of brevity, just describe the necessary action ("Type the address" or simply "Address:") and avoid pronouns ("You should type the address") or references to "the user" ("The user of the form should type the address"). Another useful rule is to use the word "type" for entering information and "press" for special keys such as the Tab, Enter, or cursor-movement keys. Since "Enter" often refers to the special key, avoid using it in the instructions (for example, do not use "Enter the address"; instead, stick to "Type the address"). Once a grammatical style for instructions is developed, be careful to apply that style consistently.

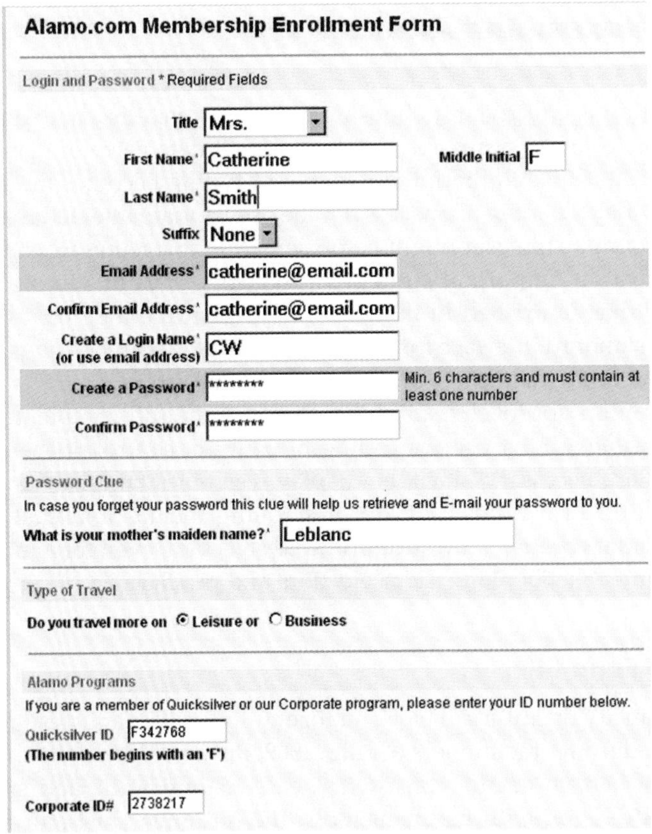

Figure 7.15

Form fillin allows users to enter their personal information when registering on this car-rental web site. Required fields are indicated with a red star. Fields are grouped meaningfully, and field-specific rules such as password requirements are provided next to the fields.

Box 7.2

Form-fillin design guidelines.

- Meaningful title
- Comprehensible instructions
- Logical grouping and sequencing of fields
- Visually appealing layout of the form
- Familiar field labels
- Consistent terminology and abbreviations
- Visible space and boundaries for data-entry fields
- Convenient cursor movement
- Error correction for individual characters and entire fields
- Error prevention where possible
- Error messages for unacceptable values
- Marking of optional fields
- Explanatory messages for fields
- Completion signal to support user control

- *Logical grouping and sequencing of fields.* Related fields should be adjacent and should be aligned with blank spaces for separation between groups. The sequencing should reflect common patterns—for example, city followed by state followed by zip code.

- *Visually appealing layout of the form.* Alignment creates a feeling of order and comprehensibility. For example, the field labels "Name," "Address," and "City" can be right justified so that the data-entry fields are vertically aligned. This layout allows the frequent user to concentrate on the entry fields and to ignore the labels.

- *Familiar field labels.* Common terms should be used. If "Home Address" were replaced by "Domicile," many users would be uncertain or anxious about what to enter.

- *Consistent terminology and abbreviations.* Prepare a list of terms and acceptable abbreviations and use the list diligently, making additions only after careful consideration. Instead of varying between such terms as "Address," "Employee Address," "ADDR.," and "Addr.," stick to one term, such as "Address."

- *Visible space and boundaries for data-entry fields.* Users should be able to see the size of the field and to anticipate whether abbreviations or other trimming strategies will be needed. An appropriate-sized box can show field length in GUIs.

- *Convenient cursor movement.* Provide a simple and visible mechanism for moving the cursor between fields using the keyboard, such as the Tab key or cursor-movement arrows.
- *Error correction for individual characters and entire fields.* Allow use of a backspace key and overtyping to enable the user to make easy repairs or changes to entire fields.
- *Error prevention.* Where possible, prevent users from entering incorrect values. For example, in a field requiring a positive integer, do not allow the user to enter letters, minus signs, or decimal points.
- *Error messages for unacceptable values.* If users enter unacceptable values, the error messages should indicate permissible values of the field; for example, if the zip code is entered as 28K21 or 2380, the message might be "Zip codes should have 5 digits."
- *Immediate feedback.* Immediate feedback about errors is preferable. When feedback can only be provided after the entire form has been submitted, such as when using plain HTML forms, the location of the field needing corrections should be made clearly visible (for example, by displaying the error message in red next to the field, in addition to general instructions at the top of the form).
- *Optional fields clearly marked.* The word "Optional" or other indicators should be visible. Optional fields should follow required fields, whenever possible.
- *Explanatory messages for fields.* If possible, explanatory information about a field or its permissible values should appear in a standard position, such as in a window next to or below the field, whenever the cursor is in the field.
- *Completion signal.* It should be clear to the users what they must do when they are finished filling in the fields. Generally, designers should avoid automatic form submission when the final field is filled in because users may wish to review or alter previous field entries. When the form is very long, multiple Submit buttons can be provided at several places in the form.

These considerations may seem obvious, but often forms designers omit the title or an obvious way to signal completion, or include unnecessary computer file names, strange codes, unintelligible instructions, unintuitive groupings of fields, cluttered layouts, obscure field labels, inconsistent abbreviations or field formats, awkward cursor movement, confusing error-correction procedures, or hostile error messages.

Detailed design rules should reflect local terminology and abbreviations. They should specify field sequences familiar to the users; the width and height of the display device; highlighting features such as reverse video, underscoring, intensity levels, color, and fonts; the cursor-movement keys; and coding of fields.

7.7.2 Format-specific fields

Columns of information require special treatment for data entry and for display. Alphabetic fields are customarily left justified on entry and on display. Numeric fields may be left justified on entry, but then become right justified on display. When possible, avoid entry and display of leftmost zeros in numeric fields. Numeric fields with decimal points should line up on the decimal points.

Pay special attention to such common fields as these:

- *Telephone numbers.* Offer a form to indicate the subfields:

```
Telephone: (_ _ _) _ _ _ - _ _ _ _
```

Be alert to special cases, such as addition of extensions or the need for non-standard formats for international numbers.

- *Social security numbers.* The pattern for U.S. social security numbers should appear on the screen as

```
Social security number: _ _ _ - _ _ - _ _ _ _
```

When the user has typed the first three digits, the cursor should jump to the leftmost position of the two-digit field.

- *Times.* Even though the 24-hour clock is convenient, many people in the United States find it confusing and prefer A.M. or P.M. designations. The form might appear as

```
_ _ : _ _   _ _   (09:45 AM or PM)
```

Seconds may or may not be included, adding to the variety of necessary formats.

- *Dates.* How to specify dates is one of the nastiest problems; no good solution exists. Different formats for dates are appropriate for different tasks, and European rules differ from American rules. An acceptable standard may never emerge. Instructions need to show an example of correct entry; for example:

```
Date: _ _/_ _/_ _ _ _  (04/22/2005 indicates April 22, 2005)
```

For many people, examples such as the following are more comprehensible than abstract descriptions:

```
MM/DD/YYYY
```

Providing a pop-up graphical calendar will reduce the number of errors.

- *Dollar amounts (or other currency).*   The currency sign should appear on the screen, so users enter only the amount. If a large number of whole-dollar amounts is to be entered, users might be presented with a field such as

```
Deposit amount: $_ _ _ _ _.00
```

with the cursor to the left of the decimal point. As the user types numbers, they shift left, calculator style. To enter an occasional cents amount, the user must type the decimal point to reach the 00 field for overtyping (but again, remember that different countries have different conventions for entering numbers).

Using custom direct-manipulation graphical widgets will facilitate data entry and reduce errors. Calendars can be used to enter dates, seating maps help select airplane seats, and menus using photographs might help clarify choices of pizza style. Other considerations in form-fillin design include multiscreen forms, mixed menus and forms, relationship to paper forms, handling of special cases, and integration of a word processor to allow comments to be entered.

7.7.3   Dialog boxes

In modern GUIs, many tasks are interrupted to request users to select options or perform limited data entry. The most common solution is to provide a dialog box. Familiar examples include the Open, Save, Find, Print, and Font (Fig. 7.16) dialog boxes. Dialog boxes can also contain task-specific functions, such as entering the customer's name and address for a car rental; specifying clothing color, size, and fabric for an order-entry system; or selecting colors and textures for a geographic-information system.

Dialog-box design combines menu-selection and form-fillin issues with additional concerns about consistency across hundreds of dialog boxes and relationships with other items on the screen (Galitz, 2002). A guidelines document for dialog boxes can help to ensure appropriate consistency (Box 7.3). Dialog boxes should have meaningful titles to identify them and should have consistent visual properties—for example, centered, mixed uppercase and lowercase, 12-point, black Helvetica font. Dialog boxes are often shaped and sized to fit each

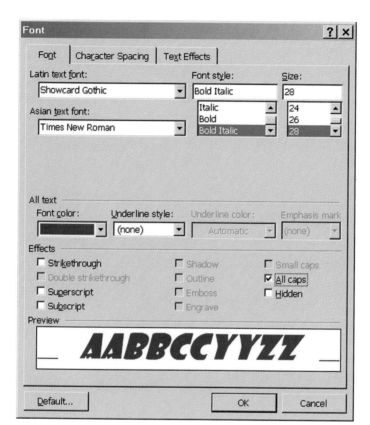

Figure 7.16

A dialog box allows users to select font and style options in Microsoft Word. The preview of a sample bit of text helps users make their selections before they are applied to the document.

situation, but distinctive sizes or aspect ratios may be used to signal errors, confirmations, or components of the application. Within a dialog box, there should be standard margins and visual organization, typically from top-left to bottom-right for languages that read left to right. A grid structure helps to organize the contents, and symmetry can be used to provide order when appropriate. Clustering of related items within a box or separation by horizontal and vertical rules helps users to understand the contents. Emphasis can be added by color, font size, or style of type.

Dialog-box design also involves the relationship of the box with the current contents of the screen. Since dialog boxes usually pop up on top of some portion of the screen, there is a danger that they will obscure relevant information.

Box 7.3

Dialog-box guidelines.

Internal layout: like that of menus and forms
- Meaningful title, consistent style
- Top-left to bottom-right sequencing
- Clustering and emphasis
- Consistent layouts (margins, grid, whitespace, lines, boxes)
- Consistent terminology, fonts, capitalization, justification
- Standard buttons (OK, Cancel)
- Error prevention by direct manipulation

External relationships
- Smooth appearance and disappearance
- Distinguishable but small boundary
- Size small enough to reduce overlap problems
- Display close to appropriate items
- No overlap of required items
- Easy to make disappear
- Clear how to complete/cancel

Therefore, dialog boxes should be as small as is reasonable to minimize the overlap and visual disruption. Dialog boxes should appear near, but not on top of, the related screen items. When a user clicks on a city on a map, the dialog box about the city should appear just next to the click point. The classic annoying example is to have the Find or Spell Check box obscure a relevant part of the text.

Dialog boxes should be distinct enough that users can easily distinguish them from the background, but should not be so harsh as to be visually disruptive. Finally, dialog boxes should disappear easily, with as little visual disruption as possible.

When tasks are complex, multiple dialog boxes may be needed, leading some designers to choose to use a tabbed dialog box, in which two or more protruding tabs in one or several rows indicate the presence of multiple dialog boxes. This technique can be effective, but it carries with it the potential problem of too much fragmentation; users may have a hard time finding what they want underneath the tabs. A smaller number of larger dialog boxes may be advantageous, since users usually prefer doing visual searches to having to remember where to find a desired control.

7.7.4 Novel designs combining menus and direct manipulation

Several refinements of the circular menus combine menu selection with direct-manipulation data entry. For example, early pie menus allowed users to specify both the size and style of a typographic font in one gesture (Hopkins, 1991). The direction selects the font style from a set of possible attributes, and the distance selects the point size from the range of sizes. An increased distance from the center corresponds to an increase in the point size, and visual feedback is provided by dynamically shrinking and swelling a text sample shown in the center as users move the pointer in and out. *Control menus* (Pook et al., 2000) demonstrate a similar technique. When the pointing device reaches a specified threshold, the command is issued and direct manipulation can proceed immediately. *Marking menus* (Tapia and Kurtenbach, 1995) also allow direct manipulation and show that the release of the pointing device can be used as a command-selection mechanism.

Another novel menu type, called a *FlowMenu* (Guimbretière and Winograd, 2000), uses the return to the central rest area after the menu selection to trigger the direct manipulation needed to specify a parameter (Fig. 7.17). Multiple selections and direct manipulations can be chained together without lifting the pointing device, allowing complex menu selections and data entry. These techniques are particularly well adapted to wall displays, as they do not require users to return to a faraway menu bar to initiate the interaction.

Another option, *Toolglass* (Bier et al., 1993), uses two-handed operation to combine menu selection and data entry. Users move their nondominant hand to manipulate a translucent tool palette while their dominant hand selects commands and performs direct-manipulation tasks. For example, to create a colored line, one hand positions the palette's line tool at the starting point, while the other hand clicks through the transparent tool and drags to draw the line. Tool-

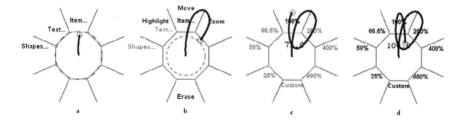

Figure 7.17

To zoom on an object using FlowMenu, users move the cursor or pen from the center to Item... (**a**). A second level of menu appears (Highlight, Move, Zoom), and users can select Zoom (**b**). Moving back to the center brings up a third menu of zoom values (**c**). The appropriate zoom value is selected by moving towards 100% and then back to the center (**d**). Note that the figure explicitly shows the pen track, while in normal use, the pen track is not displayed and the selected object is visible in transparency behind the menu.

glass can be useful for medium-sized displays, where all menus remain within arm's reach and users can easily find their location on the display.

7.8   Audio Menus and Menus for Small Displays

Mobile computing applications rely on small devices users can carry with them. These devices have small screens (perhaps 120×160 pixels) that make most desktop screen designs impractical. They require a radical rethinking of what functionalities should be included and often lead to novel interface and menu designs specially adapted to the device and the application (Bergman, 2000; Weiss, 2002; Lindholm and Keinonen, 2003). This section includes audio menus as well, because they are useful when hands and eyes are busy, such as when users are driving or testing equipment. Audio menus are also important in public-access situations that need to accommodate blind or vision-impaired users, such as information kiosks or voting machines.

7.8.1   Audio menus

With audio menus, instruction prompts and lists of options are spoken to users, who respond by using the keys of a keyboard or touchtone phone, or by speaking. While visual menus have the distinct advantage of persistence, audio menus have to be memorized. Similarly, visual highlighting can confirm users' selections, while audio menus have to provide confirmation dialogs. As the list of options is read to them, users must compare each proposed option with their goal and place it on a scale from no match to perfect match. Different designs either request users to accept or reject each option immediately, or allow users to select at any time while the entire list is being read. A way to repeat the list of options and exit mechanisms must be provided, preferably by detecting users' inaction.

Complex menu structures should be avoided. A simple guideline is to limit the number of choices to three or four to avoid memorization problems, but this rule should be re-evaluated in light of the application. For example, a theater information system will benefit from using a longer list of all the movie titles rather than breaking them into two smaller, arbitrarily grouped menus. Dial-ahead capabilities allow repeat users to skip through the prompts. For example, users of a drugstore telephone menu might remember that they can dial 1 followed by 0 to be connected to the pharmacy immediately, without having to listen to the store's welcome message and the list of options. Many design variations exist (Resnick and Virzi, 1995; Marics and Engelbeck, 1997).

Voice recognition enables users of Interactive Voice Systems (Gardner-Bonneau, 1999) to speak their options instead of hitting letter or number keys.

An early use of voice activation was to emulate keypresses with voice cues (for example, "To hear your options again, press or say nine"). This is useful when users' hands are busy, such as while driving a car, but it leads to longer prompts and longer task-completion times. Other systems use automatic word recognition to match the spoken words or short phrases to one of the available options.

Advanced systems are exploring the use of natural-language analysis to improve voice recognition. One field study compared traditional touchtone menu selection with the natural-language analysis of users' answers to the prompt "Please tell me, briefly, the reason for your call today." Callers could be routed to one of five types of agents. Results suggested that the number of callers routed to the correct agent increased when natural language was used, and that it was preferred by users (Suhm et al., 2002). However, effective natural-speech recognition of even modestly complex requests, such as "Reserve two seats on the first flight tomorrow from New York to Washington," is still a challenge and can lead to errors and frustrating dialogs (see Section 9.4).

To speed interaction, interactive voice systems can offer the option to let users speak while the instruction prompt is read. This *barge-in* technique works well when most users are repeat users who can immediately speak the options they have learned from previous experience. One challenge is to identify novices who will attempt to use commands that are not recognized and switch them to a more directed mode that lists options. To develop successful audio menus, it is critical to know the goals of users and to make the most common tasks easy to perform rapidly.

7.8.2 Menus for small displays

Two distinct application domains exist for devices with small displays: entertainment (for example, games played on Nintendo Game Boys), and information and communication services (for example, calendars, address books, navigation assistants, repair and inventory management systems, or medical devices). Entertainment applications involve long sessions of informal, content-intensive interactions, while the use of information and communication applications consists of repetitive, brief, and highly structured sessions, often conducted under time or environmental pressure. Menus and forms often constitute a major part of these interfaces.

Learnability is a key issue, as there is usually no documentation at hand for the growing number of products that are sometimes called *information appliances*. These products need to be learned in a few minutes or risk being abandoned (Bergman, 2000). Successful designs limit the number of functions to the most essential ones (Box 7.4). They bury other features in less accessible parts of the interface, relegate them to the counterpart desktop application (if one exists), or even eliminate the features all together. An often-mentioned rule of thumb for small devices is "Less is More" (Fig. 7.18). If needed, additional menus might be activated by hardware buttons. For example, on the Palm Pilot a permanent button on the device brings up a pull-down menu bar giving access to advanced functions, such as the beaming of address-book entries to other devices. An "Advanced" or "More" button can also be used to add frequently used items to the existing simpler menus that are used most of the time.

The smaller the screen, the more temporal the interface becomes (all the way to entirely linear audio interfaces when no display is available). Small devices can only present part of the information at a time, and therefore particular attention must be given to how users navigate between menu items in a sequence, levels of the hierarchy, and parts of long forms. Many devices have dedicated navigation keys, providing at least the two keys needed to navigate through sequences, and a Select button. Some small devices use "soft" keys placed next to or below the screen; their onscreen labels can be changed dynamically depending on the context (Fig. 7.19). Soft keys allow designers to provide direct access to the next-most logical command at every step (Lindholm and Keinonen, 2003). Navigation keys also simplify the navigation of forms on larger displays with scroll bars, such as the Palm or Pocket PC devices.

Designing for responsiveness implies ease of launching the most common applications or tasks. This can be achieved by providing hardware buttons. Most personal information devices have dedicated buttons for launching the calendar or the address book; phones have a dedicated button to hang up. Sequencing by frequency of use can be more useful than sequencing by category or alphabetical order, as speed of access to the most commonly used options is critical. Reviewing a list to get a feeling for the natural groupings

Box 7.4

Five design considerations for information appliances (from Michael Mohageg and Annette Wagner in Bergman, 2000).

1. Account for target domain
   Entertainment applications vs. information access and communication vs. assistant devices

2. Dedicated devices mean dedicated user interfaces

3. Allocate functions appropriately
   Consider usage frequency and importance

4. Simplify
   Focus on important functions, relegate others to other platforms

5. Design for responsiveness
   Plan for interruptions, provide continuous feedback

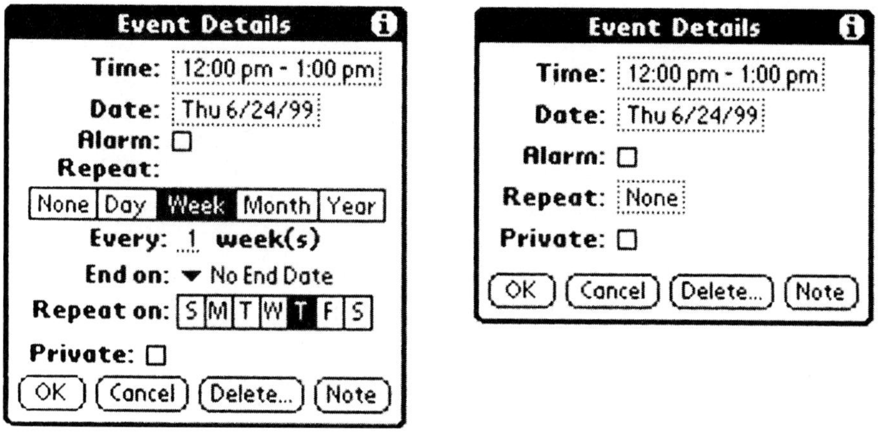

Figure 7.18

Early and revised designs for the Palm to enter a new calendar event. The original design is on the left. The new design on the right simplifies the screen and pushes all the recurrent event controls to a secondary screen, greatly simplifying the most common task. (from Rob Haitani in Bergman, 2000)

becomes impractical on smaller screens. Mobile device designers also need to allow users to deal with interruptions and distractions in their environment. Providing an automatic Save function addresses those issues and simplifies the interface. The dismissal of opened dialog boxes may not be necessary either, as they can always be superceded by other commands or a tap outside the dialog box. This differs greatly from desktop applications, where they often demand more attention. For example, a word processor will require the print dialog box(es) to be closed before an emergency save command can be issued when the phone rings.

Concise writing and careful editing of titles, labels, and instructions will lead to simpler and easier to use interfaces. Every word counts on a small screen, and even unnecessary letters or spaces should be eliminated. Consistency remains important, but clear differentiation of menu types helps users remain oriented when no context can be provided. For example, most Nokia phones use three main styles of screens consistently across products: First-level menus show one item at a time with both an icon and label, second-level menus scroll one by one through lists of items without icons, and option screens are distinct because they show multiple items with only one highlighted. Tiny icons are difficult to design and are rarely used, as they take space and require labels anyway. On the other hand, large color icons have

Figure 7.19

Telephone menus use soft keys to present context-dependent menu items. The convention used here is to consistently place selections on the left side, and back or exit options on the right side. Hard buttons control the connect and disconnect functions. Two dedicated buttons facilitate scrolling through lists. The current position in the list is indicated on the right side of the screen.

been used successfully in car navigation systems because they can be recognized at a glance once they have been learned.

Future applications are likely to use contextual information such as location or proximity to objects to present relevant information. These applications can display most likely menu items on soft keys and suggest default values for data entry. Global Positioning Services (GPS) or Radio Frequency Identification (RFID) tags might facilitate applications such as tourist guides or medicine-cabinet valets (Fano and Gershman, 2002). Precise position information relative to the user's body might also lead to new modes of interaction with menus. For example, users might be able to move the device in front of them to scroll through long lists or pan across maps and diagrams (Yee, 2003).

Practitioner's Summary

Concentrate on organizing the structure and sequence of menus to match the users' tasks, priorities, and environment. Ensure that each menu is a meaningful, task-related unit, and create items that are distinctive and comprehensible. Favor broad and shallow hierarchical menus. If some users make frequent use of the system, then shortcuts, mouse-ahead, or dial-ahead options should be provided. Permit simple traversals to the previously displayed menu and to the main menu. Remember that audio menus and menus for small devices require careful rethinking of what functionalities should be included. For such menus frequency of use becomes a more important criterion for sequencing and grouping of menu items. Pop-up menus using gestures are useful for large wall displays. Consider direct-manipulation graphical widgets to facilitate data entry with form fillin. Such widgets, along with immediate feedback and dynamic help, will help reduce errors and speed data entry.

Be sure to conduct usability tests and to involve human-factors specialists in the design process. When the interface is implemented, collect usage data, error statistics, and subjective reactions to guide refinement. Whenever possible, use software tools to produce and display menus, forms, or dialog boxes, as they reduce implementation time, ensure consistent layout and instructions, and simplify maintenance. At every stage, consider the plasticity of the interface to enable users with differing skill levels and disabilities, as well as speakers of different languages, to succeed.

Researcher's Agenda

Experimental research could help to refine the design guidelines concerning organization and sequencing in single and linear sequences of menus. How can differing communities of users be satisfied with a common organization when their information needs are markedly different? Should users be allowed to tailor the structure of the menus, or is there greater advantage in compelling everyone to use the same structure and terminology? Should a tree structure be preserved even if some redundancy is introduced?

Research opportunities abound, and the quest for better menu-selection strategies for small and large displays continues. Layout strategies, graphic design, selection from long lists, adaptable and adaptive techniques are all excellent candidates for experimentation. Implementers would benefit from advanced software tools to automate creation, management, usage-statistics gathering, and evolutionary refinement. Portability could be enhanced to facilitate transfer across systems, and internationalization could be facilitated by tools to support redesign for multiple national languages.

WORLD WIDE WEB RESOURCES

Information on menu, form-fillin, and dialog-box design including empirical studies and examples of systems. The most interesting experience is scanning the World Wide Web to see how designers have laid out simultaneous or large menus or form fillins in registration or search interfaces.

http://www.aw.com/DTUI

References

Ahlberg, C. and Shneiderman, B., AlphaSlider: A compact and rapid selector, *Proc. CHI '94 Conference: Human Factors in Computing Systems*, ACM, New York (1994), 365–371.

Bederson, B., Fisheye menus, *Proc. User Interface Software Technology*, ACM, New York (2000), 217–225.

Bergman, E., *Information Appliances and Beyond*, Morgan Kaufmann Publishers, San Francisco, CA (2000).

Bier, E., Stone, M., Fishkin, K., Buxton, W., and Baudel, T., A taxonomy of see-through tools, *Proc. CHI '94 Conference: Human Factors in Computing Systems*, ACM, New York (1994), 358–364.

Brown, C. M., *Human-Computer Interface Design Guidelines*, Ablex, Norwood, NJ (1988).

Callahan, J., Hopkins, D., Weiser, M., and Shneiderman, B., An empirical comparison of pie versus linear menus, *Proc. CHI '88 Conference: Human Factors in Computing Systems*, ACM, New York (1988), 95–100.

Card, S. K., User perceptual mechanisms in the search of computer command menus, *Proc. CHI '82 Conference: Human Factors in Computing Systems*, ACM, New York (1982), 190–196.

Ceaparu, I. and Shneiderman, B., Finding governmental statistical data on the web: A Study of Categorically-Organized Links for the FedStats Topics Page, *Journal of the American Society for Information Science and Technology* 55 (2004).

Fano, A. and Gershman, A., The future of business services in the age of ubiquitous computing, *Communications of the ACM*, 45, 12 (December 2002), 83–87.

Galitz, Wilbert O., *The Essential Guide to User Interface Design: An Introduction to GUI Design Principles and Techniques, Second Edition*, John Wiley & Sons, New York (2002).

Gardner-Bonneau, D. J., (Editor). *Human Factors and Voice Interactive Systems*, Kluwer Academic Publishers, Boston, MA (1999).

Greenberg, S. and Witten, I. H., Adaptive personalized interfaces: A question of viability, *Behaviour & Information Technology*, 4, 1 (1985), 31–45.

Guimbretière, F. and Winograd, T.,. FlowMenu: Combining command, text, and parameter entry, *Proc. User Interface Software Technology*, ACM, (2000), 213–216.

Harrison, B. L. and Vicente, K. J., An experimental evaluation of transparent menu usage, *Proc. CHI '96 Conference: Human Factors in Computing Systems*, ACM, New York (1996), 391–398.

Hochheiser, H. and Shneiderman, B., Performance benefits of simultaneous over sequential menus as task complexity increases, *International Journal of Human-Computer Interaction*, 12, 2 (1999), 173–192.

Hopkins, D., The design and implementation of pie menus, *Dr. Dobb's Journal*, 16, 12 (1991), 16–26.

Jacko, J. and Salvendy, G., Hierarchical menu design: Breadth, depth, and task complexity,. *Perceptual and Motor Skills*, 82 (1996), 1187–1201.

Kiger, J. I., The depth/breadth trade-off in the design of menu-driven user interfaces, *International Journal of Man-Machine Studies*, 20 (1984), 201–213.

Koved, L. and Shneiderman, B., Embedded menus: Menu selection in context, *Communications of the ACM*, 29 (1986), 312–318.

Landauer, T. and Nachbar, D., Selection from alphabetic and numeric menu trees using a touch screen: Breadth, depth, and width, *Proc. CHI '85 Conference: Human Factors in Computing Systems*, ACM, New York (1985), 73–78.

Larson, K. and Czerwinski, M., Page design: Implications of memory, structure and scent for information retrieval, *Proc. CHI '98 Conference: Human Factors in Computing Systems*, ACM, New York (1998), 25–32.

Laverson, A., Norman, K., and Shneiderman, B., An evaluation of jump-ahead techniques for frequent menu users, *Behaviour & Information Technology*, 6 (1987), 97–108.

Liebelt, L. S., McDonald, J. E., Stone, J. D., and Karat, J., The effect of organization on learning menu access, *Proc. Human Factors Society, Twenty-Sixth Annual Meeting*, Santa Monica, CA (1982), 546–550.

Lindholm, C. and Keinonen, T., *Mobile Usability: How Nokia Changed the Face of the Mobile Phone*, McGraw-Hill, New York (2003).

Marics, M.A. and Engelbeck, G., Designing voice menu applications for telephones, in Helander, M., Landauer, T., and Prabhu P., (Editors), *Handbook of Human-Computer Interaction*, North-Holland, Amsterdam, The Netherlands (1997) 1085–1102.

McDonald, J. E., Stone, J. D., and Liebelt, L. S., Searching for items in menus: The effects of organization and type of target, *Proc. Human Factors Society, Twenty-Seventh Annual Meeting,* Santa Monica, CA (1983), 834–837.

McGrenere, J., Baecker, R., and Booth, K., Evaluation of a multiple interface design solution for bloated software, *Proc. CHI 2002 Conference: Human Factors in Computing Systems,* ACM, New York (2002), 164–170.

Mitchell, J. and Shneiderman, B., Dynamic versus static menus: An experimental comparison, *ACM SIGCHI Bulletin,* 20, 4 (1989), 33–36.

Norman, K., *The Psychology of Menu Selection: Designing Cognitive Control at the Human/Computer Interface,* Ablex, Norwood, NJ (1991).

Norman, K. L. and Chin, J. P., The effect of tree structure on search in a hierarchical menu selection system, *Behaviour & Information Technology,* 7 (1988), 51–65.

Norman, K. L. and Chin, J. P., The menu metaphor: Food for thought, *Behaviour & Information Technology,* 8, 2 (1989), 125–134.

Pook, S., Lecolinet, E., Vaysseix, G., and Barillot, E., Control menus: Execution and control in a single interactor, *CHI 2000 Extended Abstracts,* ACM, New York (2000), 263–264.

Resnick , P. and Virzi, R. A., Relief from the audio interface blues: expanding the spectrum of menu, list, and form styles, *ACM Transactions on Computer-Human Interaction,* 2, 2 (June 1995), 145–176.

Sears, A. and Shneiderman, B., Split menus: Effectively using selection frequency to organize menus, *ACM Transactions on Computer-Human Interaction,* 1, 1 (1994), 27–51.

Shneiderman, B. (Editor), *Hypertext on Hypertext,* Hyperties disk with 1 Mbyte data and graphics incorporating, *Communications of the ACM,* ACM, New York (July 1988).

Shneiderman, B. and Kearsley, G., *Hypertext Hands-On! An Introduction to a New Way of Organizing and Accessing Information,* Addison-Wesley, Reading, MA (May 1989); book and hypertext disk using Hyperties.

Somberg, B. and Picardi, M. C., Locus of information familiarity effect in the search of computer menus, *Proc. Human Factors Society, Twenty-Seventh Annual Meeting,* Santa Monica, CA (1983), 826–830.

Suhm, B., Bers, J., McCarthy, D., Freeman, B., Getty, D., Godfrey, K., and Peterson, P., A comparative study of speech in the call center: Natural language call routing vs. touch-tone menus, *Proc. CHI 2002 Conference: Human Factors in Computing Systems,* ACM, New York (2002), 283–290

Tapia, M. A. and Kurtenbach, G., Some design refinements and principles on the appearance and behavior of marking menus, *Proc. User Interface Software and Technology '95,* ACM, New York (1995), 189–195.

Teitelbaum, R. C. and Granda, R., The effects of positional constancy on searching menus for information, *Proc. CHI '83 Conference: Human Factors in Computing Systems,* ACM, New York (1983), 150–153.

Wallace, D. F., Anderson, N. S., and Shneiderman, B., Time stress effects on two menu selection systems, *Proc. Human Factors Society, Thirty-First Annual Meeting,* Santa Monica, CA (1987), 727–731.

Weiss, S., *Handheld Usability,* John Wiley & Sons, New York (2002).

Yee, K.-P., Peephole displays: Pen interaction on spatially aware handheld computers, *Proc. CHI 2003 Conference: Human Factors in Computing Systems*, ACM, New York (2003), 1–8

Zaphiris, P., Shneiderman, B., and Norman, K.L., Expandable indexes versus sequential menus for searching hierarchies on the World Wide Web, *Behaviour & Information Technology*, 21, 3 (2002), 201–207.

Zaphiris, P. and Ellis, R.D., Mathematical modeling of age differences in hierarchical information systems, *Proc. ACM 2000 Conference on Universal Usability*, ACM, New York (2000), 157–158.

Command and Natural Languages

I soon felt that the forms of ordinary language were far too
diffuse.... I was not long in deciding that the most favorable
path to pursue was to have recourse to the language of
signs. It then became necessary to contrive a notation which
ought, if possible, to be at once simple and expressive, easily
understood at the commencement, and capable of being
readily retained in the memory.

CHARLES BABBAGE
"On a method of expressing by signs the action of machinery," 1826

8.1 Introduction

The history of written language is rich and varied. Early tally marks and pictographs on cave walls existed for millennia before precise notations for numbers or other concepts appeared. The Egyptian hieroglyphs of 5,000 years ago were a tremendous advance because standard notations facilitated communication across space and time. Eventually languages with a small alphabet and rules of word and sentence formation dominated because of the relative ease of learning, writing, and reading them. In addition to these natural languages, special languages for mathematics, music, and chemistry emerged because they facilitated communication and problem solving. In the twentieth century, novel notations were created for such diverse domains as dance, knitting, higher forms of mathematics, logic, and DNA molecules.

The basic goals of language design are:

- Precision
- Compactness
- Ease in writing and reading
- Completeness
- Speed in learning
- Simplicity to reduce errors
- Ease of retention over time

Higher-level goals include:

- Close correspondence between reality and the notation
- Convenience in carrying out manipulations relevant to users' tasks

- Compatibility with existing notations
- Flexibility to accommodate novice and expert users
- Expressiveness to encourage creativity
- Visual appeal

Constraints on a language include:

- The capacity for human beings to record the notation
- The match between the recording and the display media (for example, clay tablets, paper, printing presses)
- The convenience in speaking (vocalizing)

Successful languages evolve to serve the goals within the constraints.

The printing press was a remarkable stimulus to language development because it made widespread dissemination of written work possible. The computer has been another remarkable stimulus to language development, not only because widespread dissemination through networks is possible, but also because computers are a tool to manipulate languages and because languages are a tool for manipulating computers.

The computer has had only a modest influence on spoken natural languages, compared to its enormous impact as a stimulus to the development of numerous new formal written languages. Early computers were built to perform mathematical computations, so the first programming languages had a strong mathematical flavor. But computers were quickly found to be effective manipulators of logical expressions, business data, graphics, sound, and text. Increasingly, computers are used to operate on the real world: directing robots, issuing money at bank machines, controlling manufacturing, and guiding spacecraft. These newer applications encourage language designers to find convenient notations to direct the computer while preserving the needs of people to use the languages for communication and problem solving.

Therefore, effective computer languages must not only represent the users' tasks and satisfy the human needs for communication, but also be in harmony with mechanisms for recording, manipulating, and displaying these languages on a computer.

Computer programming languages such as FORTRAN, COBOL, ALGOL, PL/I, and Pascal that were developed in the 1960s and early 1970s were designed for use in a noninteractive computer environment. Programmers composed hundreds or thousands of lines of code, carefully checked that code, and then *compiled* or interpreted it by computer to produce a desired result. Incremental programming was one of the design considerations in BASIC and in advanced languages such as LISP, APL, and PROLOG. Programmers in these languages were expected to build small pieces online and to test the pieces interactively. Still, the common goal was to create a large program that was preserved, studied, extended, and modified. The attraction of rapid compilation and execution led to the widespread success of the compact, but sometimes obscure, notation used in C. The pressures for team programming, organizational standards for sharing, and the increased demands for reusability promoted encapsulation and the development of object-oriented programming concepts in languages such as ADA and C++. The demands of network environments and the pursuit of cross-platform tools led to the emergence of Java and C#.

Scripting languages emphasizing screen presentation and mouse control became popular in the late 1980s, with the appearance of HyperCard, Super-Card, ToolBook, and so on. These languages included novel operators, such as ON MOUSEDOWN, BLINK, and IF FIRST CHARACTER OF THE MESSAGE BOX IS 'A'. Java expanded the possibilities for web-oriented screen management, secure network operations, and portability. Scripting languages such as Perl and Python that enabled richer interactive services flourished in the web environment.

Database-query languages for relational databases were developed in the middle to late 1970s; they led to the widely used Structured Query Language, or SQL, which emphasized short segments of code (3 to 20 lines) that could be written at a terminal and executed immediately. The goal of the user was to create a result, rather than a program. A key part of database-query languages and information-retrieval languages was the specification of Boolean operations: AND, OR, and NOT.

Command languages, which originated with operating-systems commands, are distinguished by their immediacy and by their impact on devices or information. Users issue a command and watch what happens. If the result is correct, the next command is issued; if not, some other strategy is adopted. The commands are brief and their existence is transitory. Command histories are sometimes kept and macros are created in some command languages, but the essence of command languages is that they have an ephemeral nature and that they produce an immediate result on some object of interest.

A simple example is World Wide Web addresses, which can be seen as a form of command language. Users come to memorize the structure and to memorize favorite site addresses, even though the typical usage is to click on a link to select an address from a web page or a bookmark list. Web addresses begin with a protocol name (*http, ftp, gopher*, and so on), followed by a colon and two forward slashes, then the server address (which also can include country codes or domain names, such as *gov, edu, mil*, or *org*), and potentially a directory path and file name. For example:

```
http://www.whitehouse.gov/WH/glimpse/top.html
```

Command languages are distinguished from menu-selection systems in that their users must recall notation and initiate action. Menu-selection users view or hear the limited set of menu items; they respond more than initiate. Command-language users are often called on to accomplish remarkable feats of memorization and typing. For example, this Unix command, used to delete blank lines from a file, is not obvious:

```
grep -v ^$ filea > fileb
```

Even worse, to get a printout on unlined paper on a high-volume laser printer, a user at one installation was instructed to type

```
CP TAG DEV E VTSO LOCAL 2 OPTCD=J F=3871 X=GB12
```

When asking about the command, the puzzled user met with a shrug of the shoulders and the equally cryptic comment that "Sometimes, logic doesn't come into play; it's just getting the job done." This approach may have been acceptable in the past, but user communities and their expectations are changing. While there are still millions of users of command languages, the development of new command languages has slowed dramatically due to the emergence of direct-manipulation and menu-selection interfaces.

Command languages should be designed to suit the operations that users will carry out with them (Section 8.2). They may have simple or complex syntaxes and may have only a few operations or thousands. The commands may have a hierarchical structure or may permit concatenation to form variations (Section 8.3). A typical form is a verb followed by a noun object with qualifiers or arguments for the verb or noun—for example, PRINT MYFILE 3 COPIES. Imposing a meaningful structure on the command language can be highly beneficial (Section 8.4), and permitting abbreviations may be useful (Section 8.5). Feedback may be generated for acceptable commands, and error messages (Section 12.2) may result from unacceptable forms or typos. Command-language systems may offer the user brief prompts or may be close to menu-selection systems. As discussed in Section 8.6, natural-language interaction can be considered as a complex form of command language.

8.2   Functionality to Support Users' Tasks

People use computers and command-language systems to accomplish a wide range of tasks, such as text editing, operating-system control, bibliographic retrieval, database manipulation, electronic mail, financial management, airline or hotel reservations, inventory, manufacturing process control, and adventure games.

People will use a computer system if it gives them powers not otherwise available. If the power is attractive enough, people will use a system despite a poor user interface. Therefore, the first step for the designer is to determine the functionality of the system by studying the users' task domain. The outcome is a list of task actions and objects, which is then abstracted into a set of interface actions and objects. These items, in turn, are represented with the low-level interface syntax.

A common design error is to provide excessive numbers of objects and actions, which can overwhelm the user. Excessive objects and actions take more code to maintain, may cause more bugs and slower execution, and require more help screens, error messages, and user manuals (see Chapters 12 and 13). For the user, excess functionality slows learning, increases the chance of error, and adds the confusion of longer manuals, more help screens, and less-specific error messages. On the other hand, insufficient objects or actions may leave the user frustrated, because desired functions may not be supported. For instance, users might have to copy a list with a pen and paper because there is no simple print command or to reorder a list by hand because there is no sort command.

Careful task analysis might result in a table of user communities and tasks, with each entry indicating expected frequency of use. The high-volume tasks should be made easy to carry out. The designer must decide which communities of users are the prime audiences for the system. Users may differ in their position in an organization, their knowledge of computers, or their frequency of system use.

At an early stage, the destructive actions—such as deleting objects or changing formats—should be evaluated carefully to ensure that they are reversible, or at least are protected from accidental invocation. Designers should also identify error conditions and prepare error messages. A transition diagram showing how each command takes the user to another state is a highly beneficial aid to design, as well as to eventual training of users (Fig. 8.1). A diagram that grows too complicated may signal the need for system redesign. Another key feature is the capacity to record histories and review, save, send, search, edit, replay, and annotate them. Finally, help and tutorial features should be provided.

Major considerations for expert users are the possibilities of tailoring the language to suit personal work styles and of creating named macros to permit several operations to be carried out with a single command. Macro facilities allow extensions that the designers did not foresee or that are beneficial to only a small fragment of the user community. A macro facility can be a full programming language that might include specification of arguments, conditionals, iteration, integers, strings, and screen-manipulation primitives, plus library and editing tools. Well-developed macro facilities are one of the strong attractions of command languages.

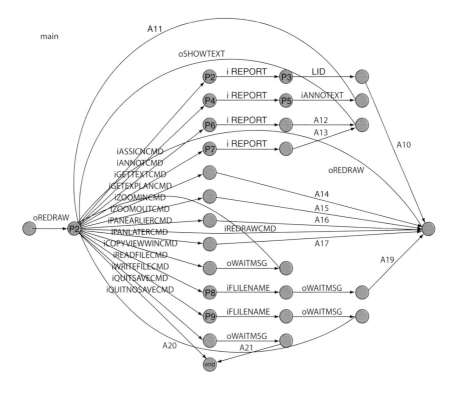

Figure 8.1

Transition diagram indicating user inputs with an "i" and computer outputs with an "o." This relatively simple diagram shows only a portion of the system. Complete transition diagrams may comprise many pages. (Courtesy of Robert J. K. Jacob, Naval Research Laboratory, Washington, D.C.)

8.3   Command-Organization Strategies

Several strategies for command organization have emerged. A unifying interface concept or metaphor aids learning, problem solving, and retention. Electronic-mail enthusiasts conduct lively discussions about the metaphoric merits of such task-related objects as file drawers, folders, documents, memos, notes, letters, or messages. They debate the appropriate interface actions (CREATE, EDIT, COPY, MOVE, DELETE) and the choice of action pairs such as LOAD/SAVE (too much in the computer domain), READ/WRITE (acceptable for letters, but awkward for file drawers), or OPEN/CLOSE (acceptable for folders, but awkward for notes).

Designers often err by choosing a metaphor closer to the computer domain than to the users' task domain. Of course, metaphors can mislead the user, but careful design can reap the benefits while reducing the detriments. Having adopted an interface concept or metaphor for actions and objects, the designer must then choose a strategy for the command syntax. Mixed strategies are possible, but learning, problem solving, and retention may be aided by limitation of complexity. This section presents three options for command organization.

8.3.1   Simple command set

In the first and simplest option, each command is chosen to carry out a single task, and the number of commands matches the number of tasks. When there is only a small number of tasks, this approach can produce a system that is simple to learn and use. Some MUD commands are simple, such as look, go, who, rooms, and quit. When there is a large number of commands, however, there is danger of confusion. The vi editor on Unix systems offers many commands while attempting to keep the number of keystrokes low. The result is complex strategies that employ single letters, shifted single letters, and the CTRL key plus single letters (Fig. 8.2). Furthermore, some commands stand alone, whereas others must be combined, often in irregular patterns.

8.3.2   Commands plus arguments/options

The second option is to follow each command (COPY, DELETE, PRINT) by one or more *arguments* (FILEA, FILEB, FILEC) that indicate objects to be manipulated:

```
COPY FILEA,FILEB
DELETE FILEA
PRINT FILEA,FILEB,FILEC
```

The commands may be separated from the arguments by a blank space or other delimiter, and the arguments may have blanks or delimiters between them (Schneider et al., 1984). Keyword labels for arguments may be helpful to some users; for example,

```
COPY FROM=FILEA TO=FILEB
```

The labels require extra typing and thus increase chances of a typo, but readability is improved and order dependence is eliminated.

Commands may also have *options* (3, HQ, and so on) to indicate special cases. For example,

```
PRINT/3,HQ FILEA
PRINT (3,HQ) FILEA
PRINT FILEA —3,HQ
```

```
VI COMMANDS TO MOVE THE CURSOR

Moving within a window

H          go to home position (upper left)
L          go to last line
M          go to middle line
(CR)       next line (carriage return)
+          next line
-          previous line
CTRL-P     previous line in same column
CTRL-N     next line in same column
(LF)       next line in same column (line feed)

Moving within a line

0          go to start of line
$          go to end of line
(space)    go right one space
CRTL-H     go left one space
h          go left one space
w          forward one word
b          backward one word
e          end (rightmost) character of a word
)          forward one sentence
(          backward one sentence
}          forward one paragraph
{          backward one paragraph
W          blank out a delimited word
B          backwards blank out a delimited word
E          go to the end of a delimited word


Finding a character

fx         find the character x going forward
Fx         find the character x going backward
tx         go up to x going forward
Tx         go up to x going backward


Scrolling the window

CTRL-F     go forward one screen
CTRL-B     go backward one screen
CTRL-D     go forward one half screen
CTRL-U     go backward one half screen
G          go to line
/pat       go to line with pattern forward
pat        go to line with pattern backward
```

Figure 8.2

The profusion of cursor-movement commands in vi enable expert users to get tasks done with just a few actions, but they can overwhelm novice and intermittent users.

may produce three copies of FILEA at the printer in the headquarters building. As the number of options grows, the complexity can become overwhelming and the error messages must be less specific. The arguments also may have options, such as version numbers, privacy keys, or disk addresses.

The number of arguments, of options, and of permissible syntactic forms can grow rapidly. One airline-reservations system uses the following command to check the seat availability on a flight on August 21, from Washington's National Airport (DCA) to New York's LaGuardia Airport (LGA) at about 3:00 P.M.:

```
A0821DCALGA0300P
```

Even with substantial training, error rates can be high with this approach, but frequent users seem to manage and even to appreciate the compact form of this type of command.

The Unix command-language system is widely used, in spite of the complexity of its command formats, which have been criticized severely (Norman, 1981). Here again, users will master complexity to benefit from the rich functionality in a system. Error rates with Unix commands have ranged from 3 to 53% (Hanson et al., 1984). Even common commands have generated high syntactic error rates: 18% for mv and 30% for cp. Still, the complexity has a certain attraction for a portion of the potential user community. Users gain satisfaction in overcoming the difficulties and becoming one of the inner circle (gurus or wizards) who are knowledgeable about system features—command-language machismo.

8.3.3   Hierarchical command structure

In the third option, the set of commands is organized into a tree structure, like a menu tree. The first level might be the command action, the second might be an object argument, and the third might be a destination argument:

Action	Object	Destination
CREATE	File	File
DISPLAY	Process	Local printer
REMOVE	Directory	Screen
COPY		Remote printer
MOVE		

If a hierarchical structure can be found for a set of tasks, it offers a meaningful structure to a large number of commands. In this case, $5 \times 3 \times 4 = 60$ tasks can be carried out with only 5 command names and 1 rule of formation. Another advantage is that a command-menu approach can be developed to aid the novice or intermittent user, as was done in VisiCalc and later in Lotus 1–2–3 and Excel.

8.4   The Benefits of Structure

Human learning, problem solving, and memory are greatly facilitated by meaningful structure. If command languages are well designed, users can recognize the structure and can easily encode it in their semantic-knowledge storage. For example, if users can uniformly edit such objects as characters, words, sentences, paragraphs, chapters, and documents, this meaningful pattern is easy for them to learn, apply, and recall. On the other hand, if they must overtype a character, change a word, revise a sentence, replace a paragraph, substitute a chapter, or alter a document, the challenge and potential for error grow substantially, no matter how elegant the syntax is (Scapin, 1982).

Meaningful structure is beneficial for task concepts, computer concepts, and syntactic details of command languages. Yet many systems fail to provide a meaningful structure. Users of one operating system display information with the LIST, QUERY, HELP, and TYPE commands and move objects with the PRINT, TYPE, SPOOL, SEND, COPY, or MOVE commands. Defaults are inconsistent, four different abbreviations for PRINT and LINECOUNT are required, binary choices vary between YES/NO and ON/OFF, and function-key usage is inconsistent. These flaws emerge from multiple uncoordinated design groups and reflect insufficient attention by the managers, especially as features are added over time.

An explicit list of design conventions in a *guidelines document* can be an aid to designers and managers. Exceptions may be permitted, but only after thoughtful discussions. Users can learn systems that contain inconsistencies, but they do so slowly and with a high chance of making mistakes.

8.4.1   Consistent argument ordering

Several studies have shown that there are benefits associated with using a consistent order for arguments. For example, when presented with commands with inconsistent and consistent argument ordering, users performed significantly faster with the consistent argument ordering (Barnard et al., 1981):

Inconsistent order of arguments	Consistent order of arguments
SEARCH file no,message id	SEARCH message id,file no
TRIM message id,segment size	TRIM message id,segment size
REPLACE message id,code no	REPLACE message id,code no
INVERT group size,message id	INVERT message id,group size

8.4.2   Symbols versus keywords

Evidence that command structure affects performance comes from a comparison of 15 commands in a commercially used symbol-oriented text editor and revised commands that had a more keyword-oriented style (Ledgard et al., 1980). Here are three sample commands:

Symbol editor	**Keyword editor**
FIND:/TOOTH/;−1	BACKWARD TO "TOOTH"
LIST;10	LIST 10 LINES
RS:/KO/,/OK/;*	CHANGE ALL "KO" TO "OK"

Single-letter abbreviations (L;10 or L 10 L) were permitted in both editors, so the number of keystrokes was approximately the same. The results (Table 8.1) for inexperienced, familiar, and experienced users clearly favored the keyword editor, indicating that command-formation rules do make a difference.

8.4.3   Hierarchical structure and congruence

Carroll (1982) altered two design variables to produce four versions of a 16-command language for controlling a robot (Table 8.2). Commands could be hierarchical (verb–object–qualifier) or nonhierarchical (verb only) and congruent (for example, ADVANCE/RETREAT or RIGHT/LEFT) or noncongruent (GO/BACK or TURN/LEFT). Carroll uses *congruent* to refer to meaningful pairs of opposites (*symmetry* might be a better term). Hierarchical structure and congruence have been shown to be advantageous in psycholinguistic experiments. Subjects did best on memory and problem-solving tasks with the congruent forms, and error rates were dramatically lower for the congruent hierarchical forms.

This study assessed performance of new users of a small command language. Congruence helped subjects to remember the natural pairs of concepts and terms. The hierarchical structure enabled subjects to master 16 commands with only one rule of formation and 12 keywords. With a larger command set—say, 60 or 160 commands—the advantage of hierarchical structure should increase, assuming that a hierarchical structure can be found to accommodate the full set of commands. Another conjecture is that retention should be facilitated by the hierarchical structure and congruence.

	Percentage of Task Completed		Percentage of Erroneous Commands	
	Symbol	**Keyword**	**Symbol**	**Keyword**
Inexperienced users	28	42	19.0	11.0
Familiar users	43	62	18.0	6.4
Experienced users	74	84	9.9	5.6

Table 8.1

Effects of revised text-editor commands on three levels of users (Ledgard et al., 1980)

| CONGRUENT | | NONCONGRUENT | |
Hierarchical	Non-hierarchical	Hierarchical	Non-hierarchical
MOVE ROBOT FORWARD	ADVANCE	MOVE ROBOT FORWARD	GO
MOVE ROBOT BACKWARD	RETREAT	CHANGE ROBOT BACKWARD	BACK
MOVE ROBOT RIGHT	RIGHT	CHANGE ROBOT RIGHT	TURN
MOVE ROBOT LEFT	LEFT	MOVE ROBOT LEFT	LEFT
MOVE ROBOT UP	STRAIGHTEN	CHANGE ROBOT UP	UP
MOVE ROBOT DOWN	BEND	MOVE ROBOT DOWN	BEND
MOVE ARM FORWARD	PUSH	CHANGE ARM FORWARD	POKE
MOVE ARM BACKWARD	PULL	MOVE ARM BACKWARD	PULL
MOVE ARM RIGHT	SWING OUT	CHANGE ARM RIGHT	PIVOT
MOVE ARM LEFT	SWING IN	MOVE ARM LEFT	SWEEP
MOVE ARM UP	RAISE	MOVE ARM UP	REACH
MOVE ARM DOWN	LOWER	CHANGE ARM DOWN	DOWN
CHANGE ARM OPEN	RELEASE	CHANGE ARM OPEN	UNHOOK
CHANGE ARM CLOSE	TAKE	MOVE ARM CLOSE	GRAB
CHANGE ARM RIGHT	SCREW	MOVE ARM RIGHT	SCREW
CHANGE ARM LEFT	UNSCREW	CHANGE ARM LEFT	TWIST
Subjective Ratings (1 = Best, 5 = Worst)			
1.86	1.63	1.81	2.73
Test Scores 14.88	14.63	7.25	11.00
Errors 0.50	2.13	4.25	1.63
Omissions 2.00	2.50	4.75	4.15

Table 8.2

Command sets and partial results (Carroll, 1982)

Carroll's study was conducted during a half-day period; with one week of regular use, differences probably would be reduced substantially. However, with intermittent users or with users under stress, the hierarchical congruent form might again prove superior.

In summary, sources of structure that have proved advantageous include these:

- Positional consistency
- Grammatical consistency
- Congruent pairing
- Hierarchical form

In addition, as discussed in Section 8.5, a mixture of meaningfulness, mnemonicity, and distinctiveness is helpful.

8.5 Naming and Abbreviations

In discussing command-language names, Schneider (1984) takes a delightful quote from Shakespeare's *Romeo and Juliet*: "A rose by any other name would smell as sweet." As Schneider points out, the lively debates in design circles suggest that this concept does not apply to command-language names. Indeed, the command names are the most visible part of a system and are likely to provoke complaints from disgruntled users.

Critics (Norman, 1981, for example) focus on the strange names in Unix, such as `mkdir` (make directory), `cd` (change directory), `ls` (list directory), `rm` (remove file), and `pwd` (print working directory). Part of their concern is the inconsistent abbreviation strategies, which may take the first few letters, first few consonants, first and final letter, or first letter of each word in a phrase. Worse still are abbreviations with no perceivable pattern.

8.5.1 Specificity versus generality

Names are important for learning, problem solving, and retention over time. When it contains only a few names, a command set is relatively easy to master; but when it contains hundreds of names, the choice of meaningful, organized sets of names becomes more important. Similar results were found for programming tasks, where variable name choices were less important in small modules with from 10 to 20 names than in longer modules with dozens or hundreds of names.

With larger command sets, the names do make a difference, especially if they support congruence or some other meaningful structure. One naming-rule debate revolves around the question of *specificity versus generality* (Rosenberg, 1982). Specific terms can be more descriptive than general ones are, and if they are more distinctive, they may be more memorable. General terms may be more familiar and therefore easier to accept. Two weeks after a training session with 12 commands, subjects were more likely to recall and recognize the meanings of specific commands than those of general commands (Barnard et al., 1981).

In a paper-and-pencil test, subjects studied one of seven sets of commands (Black and Moran, 1982). Two of the commands—the commands for inserting and deleting text—are shown here in all seven versions:

Infrequent, discriminating words	insert	delete
Frequent, discriminating words	add	remove
Infrequent, nondiscriminating words	amble	perceive
Frequent, nondiscriminating words	walk	view
General words (frequent, nondiscriminating)	alter	correct
Nondiscriminating nonwords (nonsense)	GAC	MIK
Discriminating nonwords (icons)	abc-adbc	abc-ac

The "infrequent, discriminating" command set resulted in faster learning and superior recall than did other command sets. The general words were correlated with the lowest performance. The nonsense words did surprisingly well, supporting the possibility that, with small command sets, distinctive names are helpful even if they are not meaningful.

8.5.2 Abbreviation strategies

Even though command names should be meaningful for human learning, problem solving, and retention, they must satisfy another important criterion: They must be in harmony with the mechanism for expressing the commands to the computer. The traditional and most widely used command-entry mechanism is the keyboard, so commands should use brief and kinesthetically easy codes. Commands requiring SHIFT or CTRL keys, special characters, or difficult-to-type sequences are likely to cause higher error rates. For text editing, when many commands are applied and speed is appreciated, single-letter approaches are attractive. Overall, brevity is a worthy goal, since it can speed entry and reduce error rates. Early word-processor designers pursued this approach, even when mnemonicity was sacrificed, thereby making use more difficult for novice and intermittent users.

In less demanding applications, designers have used longer command abbreviations, hoping that the gains in recognizability will be appreciated over the reduction in keystrokes. Novice users may actually prefer typing the full name of a command to using a shortcut, because they have greater confidence in its success (Landauer, Calotti, and Hartwell, 1983).

The phenomenon of preferring to use the full command name also appeared in our study of bibliographic retrieval with the Library of Congress's SCORPIO system. Novices preferred typing the full name, such as BROWSE or SELECT, rather than the traditional four-letter abbreviations BRWS or SLCT, or the single-letter abbreviations B or S. After five to seven uses of the commands, their confidence increased and they attempted the single-letter abbreviations. A designer of a text adventure game recognized this principle; new users are first instructed to type EAST, WEST, NORTH, or SOUTH to navigate, and then after five full-length commands have been entered the system tells the user about the single-letter abbreviations.

With experience and frequent use, abbreviations become attractive for and even necessary to satisfy the "power" user. Efforts have been made to find optimal abbreviation strategies. Several studies support the notion that abbreviation should be accomplished by a consistent strategy (Ehrenreich and Porcu, 1982; Benbasat and Wand, 1984). Here are six potential strategies:

1. *Simple truncation.* Use the first, second, third, and so on letters of each command. This strategy requires that each command be distinguishable by the leading string of characters. Abbreviations can be all of the same length or of different lengths.

2. *Vowel drop with simple truncation.* Eliminate vowels and use some of what remains. If the first letter is a vowel, it may or may not be retained. H, Y, and W may or may not be considered as vowels for this purpose.

3. *First and final letter.* Since the first and final letters are highly visible, use them; for example, use ST for SORT.

4. *First letter of each word in a phrase.* Use the popular acronym technique, for example, with a hierarchical design plan.

5. *Standard abbreviations from other contexts.* Use familiar abbreviations such as QTY for QUANTITY, XTALK for CROSSTALK (a software package), PRT for PRINT, or BAK for BACKUP.

6. *Phonics.* Focus attention on the sound; for example, use XQT for execute.

8.5.3   Guidelines for using abbreviations

Ehrenreich and Porcu (1982) offer this set of guidelines:

1. A *simple* primary rule should be used to generate abbreviations for most items; a *simple* secondary rule should be used for those items where there is a conflict.

2. Abbreviations generated by the secondary rule should have a marker (for example, an asterisk) incorporated in them.

3. The number of words abbreviated by the secondary rule should be kept to a minimum.

4. Users should be familiar with the rules used to generate abbreviations.

5. Truncation should be used because it is an easy rule for users to comprehend and remember. However, when it produces a large number of identical abbreviations for different words, adjustments must be found.

6. Fixed-length abbreviations should be used in preference to variable-length ones.

7. Abbreviations should not be designed to incorporate endings (ING, ED, S).

8. Unless there is a critical space problem, abbreviations should not be used in messages generated by the computer and read by the user.

Abbreviations are an important part of system design, and they are appreciated by experienced users. Users are more likely to use abbreviations if they are confident in their knowledge of the abbreviations and if the benefit is a savings of more than one to two characters (Benbasat and Wand, 1984).

8.5.4   Command menus and keyboard shortcuts

To relieve the burden of memorization of commands, some designers offer users brief prompts of available commands, in a format called a *command menu.* For example, the text-only web browser called lynx displays this prompt:

```
H)elp O)ptions P)rint G)o M)ain screen Q)uit
       /=search [delete]=history list
```

Experienced users come to know the commands and do not need to read the prompt or the help screens. Intermittent users know the concepts but refer to the prompt to jog their memories and to get help in retaining the syntax for future uses. Novice users do not benefit as much from the prompt and may need to take a training course or consult the online help.

Keyboard shortcuts in most graphical user interfaces become a kind of command menu for experienced users. Windows XP shows the single-letter command shortcut by underscoring a letter in the menu, allowing users to perform all operations with keyboard commands (see Fig. 7.5). With a fast display, command menus blur the boundaries between commands and menus.

Box 8.1

Command-language guidelines.

- Create explicit model of objects and actions.
- Choose meaningful, specific, distinctive names.
- Try to achieve hierarchical structure.
- Provide consistent structure (hierarchy, argument order, action-object).
- Support consistent abbreviation rules (prefer truncation to one letter).
- Offer frequent users the ability to create macros.
- Consider command menus on high-speed displays.
- Limit the number of commands and ways of accomplishing a task.

8.6   Natural Language in Computing

Even before there were computers, people dreamed about creating machines that would be able to process *natural language*. It is a wonderful fantasy, and the success of word-manipulation devices such as word processors, audio recorders, and telephones may give encouragement to some people. However, language is subtle; there are many special cases, contexts are complex, and emotional relationships have a powerful and pervasive effect in human/human communication.

Although there has been progress in machine translation from one natural language to another (for example, Japanese to English), most effective systems require constrained or preprocessed input, or postprocessing of output. Undoubtedly, improvements will continue and constraints will be reduced, but high-quality, reliable translations of complete documents without human intervention seem difficult to attain. Structured texts such as weather reports are translatable; technical papers are marginally translatable; novels or poems are not easily translatable. Still, machine translation software is helpful, for example, in getting quick translations of web pages to extract information and see if the pages are valuable enough to request help from a human translator. Even rough translations may be helpful to language learners and certainly to tourists. Multilingual search engines—in which users may type query keywords in one language and get appropriate search results in many languages—are another interesting case.

Although full comprehension and generation of language seems an inaccessible goal, there are still many ways that computers can be used in dealing with natural language, such as for interaction, queries, database searching, text generation, and adventure games (Allen, 1995). So much research has been invested in natural-language systems that undoubtedly some successes will emerge, but widespread use may not develop because the alternatives may be more appealing. More rapid progress is made when carefully designed experimental tests are used to discover the users, tasks, and interface designs for which natural-language applications are most beneficial (King, 1996; Oviatt, 2000).

8.6.1   Natural-language interaction

Researchers hope to fulfill the *Star Trek* scenario in which computers will respond to commands users issue by speaking (or typing) in natural language. *Natural-language interaction* (NLI) might be defined as the operation of computers by people using a familiar natural language (such as English) to give instructions and receive responses. With NLI, users do not have to learn command syntax or to select from menus. Early attempts at generalized "automatic programming" from natural-language statements have faded, but there are continuing efforts to provide domain-specific assistance.

The problems with NLI lie in not only implementation on the computer, but also desirability for large numbers of users for a wide variety of tasks. Contrary to the common belief, human/human interaction is not necessarily an appropriate model for human operation of computers. Since computers can display information 1,000 times faster than people can enter commands, it seems advantageous to use the computer to display large amounts of information and to allow novice and intermittent users simply to choose among the items. Selection helps to guide the user by making clear what objects and actions are available. For knowledgeable and frequent users, who are thoroughly aware of the available functions, a precise, concise command language is usually preferred.

The scenarios of artificial intelligence (smart machines, intelligent agents, and expert systems) are proving to be mind-limiting distractions that inhibit designers from creating more powerful tools. We believe that the next generation of commercially successful interfaces to support collaboration, visualization, simulation, and teleoperated devices are likely to come from user-centered scenarios, rather than from the machine-centered artificial-intelligence scenarios.

The OAI model may help us to sort out the issues. Most designs for NLI do not provide users with information about available task actions and objects; usually a simple box invites a natural-language statement. The key impediment to NLI is the *habitability* of the user interface—that is, how users can know what objects and actions are appropriate. Visual interfaces provide the cues for the semantics of interaction, but NLI interfaces typically depend on assumed user models. Users who are knowledgeable about their tasks—for example, stock-market brokers who know the objects and buy/sell actions—could place orders by voice or by typing in natural language. However, these users prefer compact command languages because they are more rapid and reliable. NLI designs also do not usually convey information about the interface objects and actions (for example, tree structure of information, implications of a deletion, Boolean operations, or query strategies). NLI designs should relieve users from learning new syntactic rules, since they presumably will accept familiar English-language requests. Therefore, NLI can be effective for intermittent users who are knowledgeable about specific tasks and interface concepts but have difficulty retaining the syntactic details of the interface.

By this analysis, NLI might apply well to checkbook maintenance (Shneiderman, 1980). The users recognize that there is an ascending sequence of integer-numbered checks and that each check has a single payee field, single amount, single date, and one or more signatures. Checks can be issued, voided, searched, and printed. Following this suggestion, Ford (1981) created and tested a textual NLI system for this purpose. Subjects were paid to maintain their checkbook registers by computer using a program that was refined incrementally to account for unanticipated entries. The final system successfully handled 91% of users' requests, such as these:

```
Pay to Safeway on 3/24/86 $29.75.
June 10 $33.00 to Madonna.
Show me all the checks paid to George Bush.
Which checks were written on October 29?
```

Users reported satisfaction with the system and were eager to continue to use it after completing several months of experimentation. This study can be seen as a success for NLI, but 20 years later, such systems are still not succeeding in the marketplace. Instead, direct-manipulation alternatives (for example, Quicken from Intuit) have proven to be more attractive. With these programs, showing a full screen of checkbook entries with blank lines for new entries may allow users to accomplish most tasks without any commands and with minimal typing. Users can search by entering partial information (for example, Britney Spears in the payee field) and then pressing a query key. Direct-manipulation designs guide users, thereby providing a more effective solution to the habitability problem than NLI.

There have been numerous informal tests of NLI systems, but the most famous and controversial is the Loebner Prize, which since 1991 has sponsored an annual contest to choose the system that comes closest to satisfying the Turing Test. The organizers describe the goal as a "computer program whose conversation is indistinguishable from a human's," (http://www.loebner.net/Prizef/loebner-prize.html) and judges rate the performance of the programs in terms of "humanness." In spite of enthusiastic responses from the media, critics complain that the contest "has no clear purpose, that its design prevents any useful outcome."

This controversy reveals the evolution of thinking about and research on natural-language interaction. Early Hollywood imagery, such as HAL in the movie *2001: A Space Odyssey*, and research projects, such as Weizenbaum's ELIZA, emphasized dialog-like interaction through a keyboard and display. This 1960s-era goal is still portrayed in some films, but the research and practical outcomes have been modest. A devoted community of linguistically oriented computer scientists still pursues natural-language work, but little of it is devoted to dialog-like interaction. In part, their work has matured because of a positive shift to rigorous evaluations such as the Text REtrieval Conference (TREC), run since 1992 by the U.S. National Institute for Standards and Technology. Workshops on evaluation and scientific journals such as *Natural Language Engineering* have also promoted focused evaluations with appropriate user groups.

As early studies began to reveal the difficulty with and inappropriateness of human-like natural-language interaction, research shifted to more specific goals. Identifying features in documents, such as personal, place, or corporate names, is a realizable and beneficial goal, even when accuracy is less than perfect. Other goals involved linguistic analysis to determine whether a web page contained an answer to a given question and text summarization to extract the key sentences or phrases that would best represent a web page in a result set.

Empirical studies of natural-language interaction for spreadsheets and airline reservations revealed that compact visual interfaces were much faster and preferred by users. Web services grew rapidly by using visual displays with form fillin and check boxes, while mobile devices flourished with physical buttons and rapid scrolling through meaningful menu choices. An imaginative approach is the AskJeeves web site, which invites natural-language questions but then does keyword extraction to lead to standard web-page result sets.

Some NLI work has turned to automatic speech recognition and speech generation to reduce the barriers to acceptance (see Section 9.4). Some users will benefit from NLI, but it may not be as many as promoters believe. Computer users usually seek predictable responses and are discouraged if they must engage in clarification dialogs. By contrast, visually oriented interactions embracing the notions of direct manipulation (see Chapter 6) make more effective use of the computer's capacity for rapid display and human capacity for rapid visual recognition. In short, pointing and selecting in context is often more attractive than is typing or even speaking an English sentence.

8.6.2 Natural-language queries and question answering

Since general interaction is difficult to support, some designers have pursued a more limited goal of *natural-language queries* (NLQ) against relational databases. The *relational schema* contains attribute names and the database contains attribute values, both of which are helpful in disambiguating queries. A simulated query system was used to compare a subset of the structured SQL database facility to a natural-language system (Small and Weldon, 1983). The SQL simulation resulted in faster performance on a benchmark set of tasks. Similarly, a field trial with a real system, users, and queries pointed to the advantages of SQL over the natural-language alternative (Jarke et al., 1985). Believers in NLQ may claim that more research and system development is needed before that approach can be excluded, but improvements in menus, command languages, and direct manipulation seem equally likely.

Supporters of NLQ can point with some pride at the modest success of the INTELLECT system, which had approximately 400 installations on large mainframe computers during the 1980s. Business executives, sales representatives, and other people used INTELLECT to search databases on a regular basis. Several innovative implementation ideas helped to make INTELLECT appealing. First, the parser used the contents of the database to parse queries; for example, the parser could determine that a query containing "Cleveland" referred to city locations, because Cleveland is an instance in the database. Second, the system administrator could conveniently include guidance for handling domain-specific requests, by indicating fields related to who, what, where, when, why, and how queries. Third, INTELLECT rephrased the users' queries and displayed responses, such as PRINT THE CHECK NUMBERS WITH PAYEE = BRITNEY SPEARS. This structured response served as an educational aid, and users gravitated towards expressions that mimicked the style. Eventually, as users became more knowledgeable, they often used concise, commandlike expressions that they believed would be parsed successfully. Even the promoters of INTELLECT recognized that novice users who were unfamiliar with the task domain would have a difficult time, and that the ideal user might be a knowledgeable intermittent user. However, the system's appeal faded as users turned to other approaches.

A more successful product was Q&A from Symantec, which provided rapid, effective query interpretation and execution on IBM PCs. The package made a positive impression during the late 1980s, but few data were reported about actual usage. The designers cited many instances of happy users of NLQ and found practical applications in the users' daily work, but the popularity of the package seems to have been more closely tied to its word-processor, database, and form-fillin facilities (Church and Rau, 1995). Microsoft's 1999 SQL Server product, called English Query, allowed natural-language database queries, provided a restatement to help users interpret the results, and presented a tabular output (Fig. 8.3) Despite moderate success, INTELLECT, Q&A, English Query, and most other NLQ packages are no longer sold. The dream of NLQ remains alive in some quarters, but commercial applications are rare.

A variant notion is *natural language question answering* (NLQA), in which users prepare fact questions such as "What is the capital of Zambia?" or "Who was the first prime minister of the European Union?" The original challenge was to provide the brief and exact answer, but later systems merely provided a set of web pages in which the users can hunt for the answer. Major difficulties are that user questions often make incorrect assumptions (maybe the European Union has a president, or maybe it should be European Commission) and that many apparently simple ques-

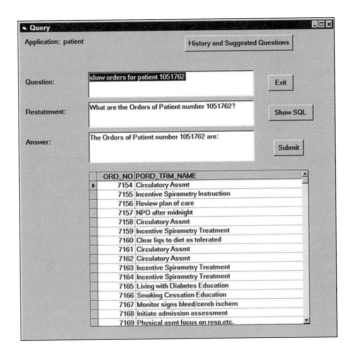

Figure 8.3

Microsoft's 1999 SQL Server product, called English Query, supported a natural-language front end for its database. Users could type a question in English and get the result of a structured database search. In this example, the user has typed a query, the system has responded with a restatement, and then the system has generated the tabular result. (http://www.microsoft.com/mind/0699/equery/Equeryfig03.gif)

tions need much clarification. Even common words such as "year" can have many interpretations (calendar, fiscal, academic, Martian), and similar terms may be used in diverse situations (wages, earnings, salary, income, pay, take-home pay, pay-check). While evaluations are often done with well-formed questions (Voorhees, 2002), users often have ill-formed questions, and they are notoriously unpre-dictable. Habitability remains a problem. Therefore, simple key-phrase queries that yield web-page results are an effective and often more informative solution.

8.6.3   Text-database searching

Text-database searching is a growing application for natural-language enthusiasts who have developed filters and parsers for queries expressed in natural lan-guage (Lewis and Jones, 1996). At one end of the spectrum is the full under-standing of the meaning of a query and fulfillment of the users' information needs. For example, in a legal application ("Find cases of tenants who have sued landlords unsuccessfully for lack of heat"), the system parses the text grammat-ically, provides synonyms from a thesaurus ("renters" for "tenants"), deals with singulars versus plurals, and handles other problems such as misspellings or foreign terms. Then, the analyzer separates the query into standard compo-nents—such as plaintiff, defendant, and cause—and finds all meaningfully related legal citations.

More realistic and typical scenarios are for parsers to eliminate noise words (for example, *the, of,* or *in*), provide stemming (plurals or alternate endings), and produce a relevance-ranked list of documents based on term frequencies. These systems do not deal with negation, broader or narrower terms, and relationships (such as plaintiff sues defendant), but they can be effective with skilled users. A comparative-evaluation contest among information-retrieval programs that use natural-language strategies to select documents from a large collection contin-ues to be extremely successful in promoting rapid progress (Voorhees, 2002). Many of the popular search tools on the World Wide Web (for example, Lycos, Google, AltaVista) use natural-language techniques, such as stemming, rele-vance ranking by word-frequency analysis, latent semantic indexing, and filter-ing of common words.

Another application with textual databases is *extraction*, in which a natural-language parser analyzes the stored text and creates a more structured format, such as a relational database. The advantage is that the parsing can be done once in advance to structure the entire database and to speed searches when users pose relational queries. Legal (Supreme Court decisions or state laws), medical (scientific journal articles or patient histories), and journalistic (Associated Press news stories or *Wall Street Journal* reports) texts have been used. This application is promising because even a modest increase in suitable retrievals is appreciated by users, and incorrect retrievals are tolerated better than are errors in natural-language interaction. Extraction is somewhat easier than the task of writing a natural-language summary of a long document, as summaries must capture the essence of the content and convey it accurately in a compact manner.

A variant task is to make categories of documents based on contents. For example, it would be useful to have an automated analysis of business news stories to separate out mergers, bankruptcies, and initial public offerings for companies in the electronics, pharmaceutical, or oil industries. The categorization task is appealing because a modest rate of errors would be tolerable (Church and Rau, 1995).

8.6.4   Natural-language text generation

Natural-language text generation (NLTG) includes simple tasks, such as the preparation of structured weather reports ("80% chance of light rain in northern suburbs by late Sunday afternoon"), as well as the generation of complex full-length stories with rich character development (Church and Rau, 1995). Generated reports from structured databases can be sent out automatically, while timely spoken reports can be made available over the telephone in multiple languages.

Elaborate applications of NLTG include preparation of reports of medical laboratory or psychological tests. The computer generates not only readable reports ("White-blood-cell count is 12,000"), but also warnings ("This value exceeds the normal range of 3,000 to 8,000 by 50%") or recommendations ("Further examination for systemic infection is recommended"). Still more involved scenarios for NLTG involve the creation of legal contracts, wills, or business proposals.

On the artistic side, computer generation of poems and even novels is a regular discussion point in literary circles. Although computer-generated combinations of randomly selected phrases can be provocative, some hold that they are still ultimately the creative work of the person who chose the set of possible words and decided which of the potential outputs to publish. This position parallels the custom of crediting the human photographer, rather than the camera or the subject matter of a photograph.

8.6.5   Adventure games and instructional systems

Natural-language interaction techniques have enjoyed notable and widespread success in a variety of computer-based adventure games. Users may indicate directions of movement, for example, or type commands such as TAKE ALL OF THE KEYS, OPEN THE GATE, or DROP THE CAGE AND PICK UP THE SWORD. Part of the attraction of using natural-language interaction in this situation is that the system is unpredictable, and some exploration is necessary to discover the proper incantation. However, such games have largely disappeared from the market.

Natural language for instructional tutorials has proven to be successful with some students, especially when the materials and pedagogy have been carefully tested and refined. Providing feedback and guidance in natural language, even in spoken form, can be helpful in encouraging students to stay engaged in the educational process (Di Eugenio, Glass, and Trolio, 2002). Advanced instructional systems have been developed to teach high-school– and college-level topics in areas such as algebra, physics, electronics, programming, and computer literacy (Fig. 8.4). These systems, often based on rich pedagogical theories, guide students through the learning process by presenting challenges and providing feedback in conversational natural language. Careful design and thorough testing has led to successful tools that have been shown to improve learning over comparable classroom experiences. Some of these systems are used by tens of thousands of students. For example, this tutorial dialog in a computer-literacy

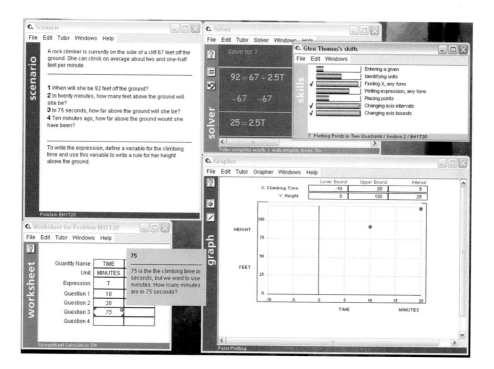

Figure 8.4

Cognitive Tutor software from Carnegie Learning, Inc. has been implemented for algebra, geometry, and related areas of mathematics. It traces student progress in mastering skills and concepts, then assigns individually tuned problems. This screen display shows windows for the scenario, worksheet, graph, solver, and skills. (http://www.carnegielearning.com/products/algebra_1/cog_tutor_software)

course was recorded between an onscreen anthropomorphic character and a college student in the AutoTutor system (Graesser et al., 2001):

> TUTOR-1: Alright, let's go on. You want to take photos and send them over the Internet. Consider this problem. What hardware do you need to take photos and send them over the Internet?
> STUDENT-1: First of all you need to have access to the Internet.
> TUTOR-2: What else?
> STUDENT-2: a camera.
> TUTOR-3: Yeah. For what type of connection do you need a network card?
> STUDENT-3: a network card?
> TUTOR-4: Okay. Now, if you have access to the Internet through a network card then your connection is…
> STUDENT-4: I don't know.
> TUTOR-5: Is direct. Okay. A network card is needed if you have a direction connection to the Internet. Okay. How does the user get hooked up to the Internet?
> STUDENT-5: by a plug.
> TUTOR-6: Once again, a network card is needed if you have a direct connection to the Internet. Okay, what does a modem do?
> STUDENT-6: connects network card and internet.
> TUTOR-7: Okay. Try this. A modem is required when there is …
> STUDENT-5: a connection
> TUTOR-6: a dial up connection.
> …
> TUTOR-30: Let's review. To send your photos on the Internet, you need either a digital camera or a regular camera to take photos. If you use…

Practitioner's Summary

Command languages can be attractive when frequent use of a system is anticipated, users are knowledgeable about the task and interface concepts, screen space is at a premium, response time and display rates are slow, and numerous functions can be combined in a compact expression. Users have to learn the semantics and syntax, but they can initiate, rather than respond, and can rapidly specify actions involving several objects and options. Finally, a complex sequence of commands can be easily specified and stored for future use as a macro.

Designers should begin with a careful task analysis to determine what functions should be provided. Hierarchical strategies and congruent structures facilitate learning, problem solving, and human retention over time. Laying out the full set of commands on a single sheet of paper helps to show the structure to the designer and to the learner. Meaningful specific names aid learning and retention. Compact abbreviations constructed according to consistent rules facilitate retention and rapid performance for frequent users.

Command menus can be effective if rapid response to screen actions can be provided. Natural-language interaction and English-language queries have been implemented, but their effectiveness and advantages are limited, mainly because of habitability issues. Natural-language support has more success in text searching, text generation, extraction, and some instructional systems.

Researcher's Agenda

The benefits of structuring command languages based on hierarchy, congruence, consistency, and mnemonicity have been demonstrated in specific cases, but replication in varied situations should lead to a comprehensive cognitive model of command-language learning and use (Box 8.1). Novel input devices and high-speed, high-resolution displays offer new opportunities—such as command and pop-up menus—for breaking free from the traditional syntax of command languages.

Natural-language interaction still holds promise in certain applications, and empirical tests offer us a good chance to identify the appropriate niches and design strategies.

WORLD WIDE WEB RESOURCES

You'll find some information on command languages and lots of activities on natural-language translation, interaction, queries, and extraction. Many sites let you try natural-language services.

http://www.aw.com/DTUI

References

Allen, James, *Natural Language Understanding, Second Edition*, Addison-Wesley, Reading, MA (1995).

Barnard, P. J., Hammond, N. V., Morton, J., Long, J. B., and Clark, I. A., Consistency and compatibility in human-computer dialogue, *International Journal of Man-Machine Studies*, 15 (1981), 87–134.

Benbasat, Izak and Wand, Yair, Command abbreviation behavior in human-computer interaction, *Communications of the ACM*, 27, 4 (April 1984), 376–383.

Black, J. and Moran, T., Learning and remembering command names, *Proc. Chi '82 Conference: Human Factors in Computing Systems*, ACM, Washington, D.C. (1982), 8–11.

Carroll, John M., Learning, using and designing command paradigms, *Human Learning*, 1, 1 (1982), 31–62.

Church, Kenneth W. and Rau, Lisa F., Commercial applications of natural language processing, *Communications of the ACM*, 38, 11 (November 1995), 71–79.

Di Eugenio, Barbara, Glass, Michael, and Trolio, Michael J., The DIAG experiments: Natural language generation for intelligent tutoring systems, *Proc. International Conference on Natural Language Generation* (2002). Available at http://inlg02.cs.columbia.edu/.

Ehrenreich, S. L. and Porcu, Theodora, Abbreviations for automated systems: Teaching operators and rules, in Badre, Al and Shneiderman, Ben (Editors), *Directions in Human-Computer Interaction*, Ablex, Norwood, NJ (1982), 111–136.

Ford, W. Randolph, *Natural Language Processing by Computer—A New Approach*, Ph.D. Dissertation, Department of Psychology, Johns Hopkins University, Baltimore, MD (1981).

Graesser, Arthur C., VanLehn, Kurt, Rose, Carolyn P., Jordan, Pamela W., and Harter, Derek, Intelligent tutoring systems with conversational dialogue, *AI Magazine*, 22, 4 (Winter 2001), 39–52.

Hanson, Stephen J., Kraut, Robert E., and Farber, James M., Interface design and multivariate analysis of Unix command use, *ACM Transactions on Office Information Systems*, 2, 1 (1984), 42–57.

Hauptmann, Alexander G. and Green, Bert F., A comparison of command, menu-selection and natural language computer programs, *Behaviour & Information Technology*, 2, 2 (1983), 163–178.

Jarke, Matthias, Turner, Jon A., Stohr, Edward A., Vassiliou, Yannis, White, Norman H., and Michielsen, Ken, A field evaluation of natural language for data retrieval, *IEEE Transactions on Software Engineering*, SE–11, 1 (January 1985), 97–113.

King, Margaret, Evaluating natural language processing systems, *Communications of the ACM*, 39, 1 (January 1996), 73–79.

Landauer, T. K., Calotti, K. M., and Hartwell, S., Natural command names and initial learning, *Communications of the ACM*, 26, 7 (July 1983), 495–503.

Ledgard, H., Whiteside, J. A., Singer, A., and Seymour, W., The natural language of interactive systems, *Communications of the ACM*, 23 (1980), 556–563.

Lewis, David and Jones, Karen Sparck, Natural language processing for information retrieval, *Communications of the ACM*, 39, 1 (January 1996), 92–101.

Napier, H. Albert, Lane, David, Batsell, Richard R., and Guadango, Norman S., Impact of a restricted natural language interface on ease of learning and productivity, *Communications of the ACM*, 32, 10 (October 1989), 1190–1198.

Norman, Donald, The trouble with Unix, *Datamation*, 27 (November 1981), 139–150.

Oviatt, Sharon L., Taming speech recognition errors within a multimodal interface, *Communications of the ACM*, 43, 9 (September 2000), 45–51.

Rosenberg, Jarrett, Evaluating the suggestiveness of command names, *Behaviour & Information Technology*, 1 (1982), 371–400.

Scapin, Dominique L., Computer commands labeled by users versus imposed commands and the effect of structuring rules on recall, *Proc. CHI '82 Conference: Human Factors in Computing Systems*, ACM, Washington, D.C. (1982), 17–19.

Schneider, M. L., Hirsh-Pasek, K., and Nudelman, S., An experimental evaluation of delimiters in a command language syntax, *International Journal of Man-Machine Studies*, 20, 6 (June 1984), 521–536.

Shneiderman, Ben, *Software Psychology: Human Factors in Computer and Information Systems*, Little, Brown, Boston, MA (1980).

Small, Duane and Weldon, Linda, An experimental comparison of natural and structured query languages, *Human Factors*, 25 (1983), 253–263.

Voorhees, Ellen M., Overview of TREC 2002, *National Institute of Standards and Technology Special Publication SP 500-251: The Eleventh Text Retrieval Conference* (2002). Available at http://trec.nist.gov/pubs/trec11/papers/OVERVIEW.11.pdf.

Interaction Devices

The wheel is an extension of the foot,

the book is an extension of the eye,

clothing, an extension of the skin,

electric circuitry an extension of the central nervous system.

MARSHALL McLUHAN AND QUENTIN FIORE,

The Medium Is the Message, 1967

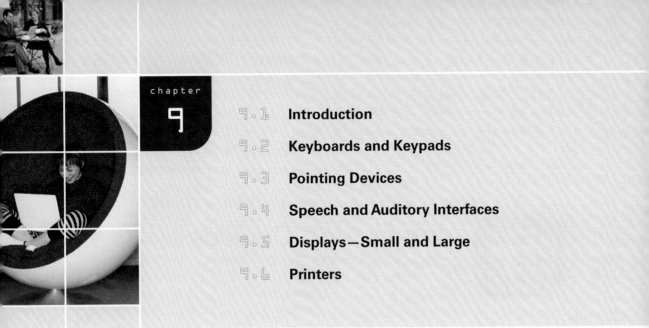

9.1 Introduction

The remarkable progress since 1960 in computer-processor speeds and storage capabilities has been matched by improvements in many input/output devices. Ten-character-per-second Teletypes have been replaced by high-speed mega-pixel graphical displays for output. Although the common Sholes or QWERTY keyboard layout is likely to remain the primary device for text input, novel strategies have emerged to meet the needs of mobile device users. Pointing devices, especially the mouse and touchscreen, free users from keyboards for many tasks. The future of computing is likely to include more gestural input, two-handed input, three-dimensional pointing, voice input/output, wearable devices, and whole-body involvement for some input and output tasks.

Pointing devices have gone through hundreds of refinements to accommodate varied users and to squeeze out further performance improvements. More unusual devices, such as eye-trackers, DataGloves, and haptic or force-feedback devices have been applied for specific niche applications such as telemedicine. Experiments with users with severe disabilities are leading the way with brain-controlled mouse movement, while still more exotic ideas for implanted devices have been raised by some visionaries. Innovative input devices, sensors, and effectors, and integration of computers into the physical environment, open the door to a variety of applications (Card, Mackinlay, and Robertson, 1991; Jacob et al., 1993; Abowd and Mynatt, 2000).

The still-improving speech recognizers have been joined by more mundane but widely used speech store-and-forward technologies with increased emphasis on telephone-based applications and non-speech auditory interfaces.

Color displays are standard for desktops, laptops, and increasingly for handheld devices, but special strategies are needed for large and small displays. Digital cameras with instant viewing on small liquid crystal displays (LCDs) are already a success story, while wall-sized high-resolution displays are opening up new possibilities. Low-cost color printers are widely used, raising further doubts about the idea of the paperless office, while Braille printers open the door to more users and three-dimensional (3D) printers allow the production of custom devices for tangible interfaces.

In addition to the refinement of individual input and output devices, a strong effort has been devoted to multimodal interfaces, which combine several modes of input and output. Initially researchers believed that simultaneous use of multiple modes could improve performance, but these methods have had limited applications. Successful examples of simultaneous multimodal interfaces exist, such as combining voice commands with pointing to apply actions to objects. However, the bigger payoff appears to be in giving users the ability to switch between modes depending on their needs—for example, allowing car drivers to operate their navigation systems by touch actions or voice input and to invoke visual or voice output depending on whether they are at a stop or busy attending to traffic (Oviatt, Darrell, and Flickner, 2004). The development of multimodal interfaces will also benefit users with disabilities who may need video captioning, audio transcriptions, or image descriptions. Progress in multimodal interfaces will contribute to the goal of universal usability.

Another lively research direction, encouraged by the widespread use of mobile devices, is context-aware computing. Mobile devices can use location information from Global Positioning System (GPS) satellites, cell-phone sources, wireless connections, or other sensors. Such information may allow users to receive information about nearby restaurants or gas stations, museum visitors or tourists to access detailed information about their surroundings, or users of tablet computers to connect to the printer located in the room they are in. The provocative applications of context-aware computing may open large markets, although concerns about privacy must be addressed.

This chapter first reviews keyboards and keypads and discusses data-entry techniques for mobile devices (Section 9.2). Section 9.3 describes pointing devices and introduces Fitts's law. The promises and challenges of speech and auditory interfaces are discussed in Section 9.4. Section 9.5 reviews traditional and novel display technologies and design particularities of large and small displays. Finally, printers are discussed in Section 9.6. Examples of possible solutions for users with disabilities are distributed through the chapter.

⎤ . ⊒   **Keyboards and Keypads**

The primary mode of textual data entry is still the keyboard (Fig. 9.1). This much-criticized device is impressive in its success. Hundreds of millions of people use keyboards; although the rate for beginners is generally less than 1 keystroke per second, and the rate for average office workers is 5 keystrokes per second (approximately 50 words per minute), some users achieve speeds of up to 15 keystrokes per second (approximately 150 words per minute). Contemporary keyboards generally permit only one keypress at a time, although dual keypresses are used to produce capitals (SHIFT plus a letter) and special functions (CTRL or ALT plus a letter). It seems that there is potential for higher rates of data entry than is possible with the current computer keyboards. An inspiration might be the piano keyboard, an impressive data-entry device that allows several finger presses at once and is responsive to different pressures and durations.

Figure 9.1

A laptop with a QWERTY keyboard showing the inverted T movement keys at the bottom right and function keys across the top. Users can choose to use one of the two pointing devices: a trackpoint mounted between the G and H keys or the touch-pad below the keyboard, each of which has a corresponding pair of buttons. (http://www.dell.com)

More rapid data entry can be accomplished by chord keyboards that allow several keys to be pressed simultaneously to represent several characters or a word. Courtroom recorders regularly use chord keyboards to enter the full text of spoken arguments, reaching rates of up to 300 words per minute. This feat requires months of training and frequent use to retain the complex pattern of chord presses.

Keyboard size and packaging also influence user satisfaction and usability. Large keyboards with many keys give an impression of professionalism and complexity, but they may threaten novice users. Small keyboards seem lacking in power to some users, but their compact size is an attraction for mobile devices. One-handed keyboards might be useful when users' tasks require simultaneous data entry and manipulation of physical objects (Fig. 9.2). Adjustable keyboards that tilt forward or back, or that split in the middle to reduce stressful ulnar

Figure 9.2

The Handkey Twiddler combines a chord keyboard and a trackpoint pointing device and can be used with one hand. (http://www.handykey.com/)

abduction and pronation, are found helpful by some users (Fig. 9.3). Finally, tiny keyboards on mobile devices, such as the Blackberry and telephone keypads, have become lively domains for innovation, from clever combinations of static and dynamically labeled keys to foldable or virtual keyboards.

9.2.1   Keyboard layouts

The Smithsonian Institution's National Museum of American History in Washington, D.C. has a remarkable exhibit on the development of the typewriter. During the middle of the nineteenth century, hundreds of attempts were made to build typewriters, with a stunning variety of positions for the paper, mechanisms for producing characters, and layouts for the keys. By the 1870s, Christopher Latham Sholes's design was becoming successful—it had a good mechanical design and a clever placement of the letters that slowed down the users enough that key jamming was infrequent. This *QWERTY layout* put frequently used letter pairs far apart, thereby increasing finger travel distances.

Sholes's success led to such widespread standardization that, more than a century later, almost all keyboards use the QWERTY layout or one of its variations developed for other languages (Fig. 9.4). The development of electronic keyboards eliminated the mechanical problems and led many twentieth-century

Figure 9.3

Alternative ergonomic and adjustable keyboards from Kinesis Corporation. (http://www.kinesis-ergo.com/)

inventors to propose alternative layouts to reduce finger travel distances (Montgomery, 1982; Kroemer, 1993). The *Dvorak layout,* developed in the 1920s, supposedly reduces finger travel distances by at least one order of magnitude, thereby increasing the typing rate of expert typists from about 150 words per minute to more than 200 words per minute, while reducing errors.

Acceptance of the Dvorak design has been very limited, despite the dedicated work of devotees. Those people who have tried the keyboard report that it takes about a week of regular typing to make the switch, but most users have been unwilling to invest this much effort. We are thus confronted with an interesting example of how even documented improvements are hard to disseminate because the perceived benefit of change does not outweigh the effort.

A third keyboard layout of some interest is the *ABCDE style,* which has the 26 letters of the alphabet laid out in alphabetical order. The rationale here is that nontypists will find it easier to locate the keys. A few data-entry terminals for numeric and alphabetic codes still use this style, though studies have shown no

Figure 9.4

The reduced-size keyboard of a Franklin Dictionary. Most users type with one finger, or with the thumbs. This French version uses the AZERTY keyboard layout instead of the English QWERTY layout. (http://www.franklin.com/)

advantage for the ABCDE style; users with little QWERTY experience are eager to acquire this expertise and often resent having to use the ABCDE layout.

The placement of the non-alphabetic keys on full-size keyboards has long been a source of controversy, but the now-widespread use of laptop and pocket computers has reduced the debate, as overall size has become more important than consistent placement of the less often used keys such as HOME or INSERT. Number pads are another source of controversy. Telephones have the 1–2–3 keys on the top row, but calculators place the 7–8–9 keys on the top row. Studies have shown a slight advantage for the telephone layout, but most computer keyboards use the calculator layout.

Some researchers have recognized that the wrist and hand placement required for standard keyboards is awkward and have proposed more ergonomic keyboards (Fig. 9.3). Redesigned keyboards that separated the keys for the left and right hands led to lower reported tension, better posture, and higher preference scores (Nakaseko et al., 1985). The two halves of the keyboard used in that study were separated by 9.5 centimeters, had an opening angle of 25 degrees with an inclination of 10 degrees, and offered large areas for forearm/wrist support. However, separated keyboards have the disadvantage that visual scanning is disrupted. Various geometries have been tried with split and tilted keyboards, but empirical verification of benefits in typing speed, accuracy, or reduced repetitive strain injury is elusive.

To address the needs of users with disabilities, designers have reconsidered the typing process entirely. For example, KeyBowl's orbiTouch keyless keyboard replaces the keys with two inverted bowls, on top of which users' hands rest comfortably. The combination of small hand movements and small finger presses on the two bowls selects letters or controls the cursor. No finger or wrist movement is needed, which might be helpful to users with carpal tunnel syndrome or arthritis. Another approach is to rely on pointing devices such as mice, touchpads, or eye-trackers for data entry. Early solutions used large menus of fixed choices, but novel techniques are being explored; an example is Dasher (Fig 9.5), which predicts probable characters and words as users make their selections in a continuous two-dimensional stream of choices (Ward, Blackwell, and MacKay, 2000).

9.2.2   Keys

Modern keyboards with 1/2-inch-square (12-millimeter-square) keys have been refined carefully and tested thoroughly in research laboratories and the marketplace. The keys have slightly concave surfaces for good contact with fingertips, and a matte finish to reduce both reflective glare and the chance of finger slips. The keypresses require a 40- to 125-gram force and a displacement of

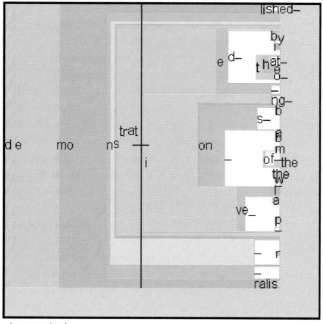

Figure 9.5

A user is writing "demonstration" with Dasher. Dasher predicts probable characters or words and allows selection among alternatives by continuous two-dimensional pointing with a mouse, touchpad, or eye-tracker. After the first letters have been selected, possible word choices are "demolished," demonstrated that", "demonstration," "demonstrative," or "demoralise." The display continuously scrolls to the left, revealing more choices as the cursor is positioned on the chosen character or word. (Ward, Blackwell, and McKay, 2000.)

3 to 5 millimeters. The force and displacement have been shown to produce rapid typing with low error rates while providing suitable feedback to users.

An important element in key design is the profile of force displacement. When the key has been depressed far enough to send a signal, the key gives way and emits a very light click. The tactile and audible feedback is extremely important in touch typing; hence, membrane keyboards that use a nonmoving surface are unacceptable for extensive touch typing. However, such keyboards are durable and therefore acceptable for challenging environments such as fast-food restaurants, factory floors, or amusement parks.

Certain keys, such as the space bar, ENTER key, SHIFT key, or CTRL key, should be larger than others to allow easy, reliable access. Other keys, such as CAPS LOCK and NUM LOCK, should have a clear indication of their state, such as by physical locking in a lowered position or by an embedded light. Key labels should be large enough to read, meaningful, and permanent. Large-print keyboards are available for vision-impaired users. Discrete color coding of keys helps to make a pleasing, informative layout. A further design principle is that the "home" keys—F and J in the QWERTY layout—may have a deeper concavity or a small raised dot to reassure touch typists that their fingers are placed properly.

Many keyboards contain a set of additional *function keys* for special functions or programmed functions. These keys are often labeled F1 . . . F10 but may also have meaningful labels or icons. Users must remember the functions attached to each key in different applications. The use of function keys is now greatly diminished, in favor of key combinations (for example, CTRL-C for Copy). This newer approach has some mnemonic value, keeps hands on the home keys, and reduces the need for extra keys.

A special category of function keys is the *cursor-movement keys*, which have become more important with the increased use of form-fillin and direct-manipulation interfaces. There are usually four keys: up, down, left, and right. Some large keyboards have eight keys to simplify diagonal movements. The placement of the cursor-movement keys is important in facilitating rapid and error-free use. The popular and compact inverted-T arrangement (Fig. 9.1) allows users to place their middle three fingers in a way that reduces hand and finger movement. The cross-arrangement is a good choice for novice users. Additional cursor movements might be performed by the TAB key for larger jumps, the HOME key to go to the top left, or the END key to go to the bottom right of the display. Other application-dependent *accelerators* are also popular, such as CTRL with up, down, left, or right keypresses, to jump a word or a paragraph. Cursor-movement keys can be used to select items in a menu or on a display, but more rapid pointing at displays than can be provided by cursor-movement keys is often desired. In some applications, such as games where users spend hours using the movement keys, designers reassign letter keys as cursor-movement keys to minimize finger motion between the movement keys and other action keys.

Most keys have an *auto-repeat feature*; that is, repetition occurs automatically with continued depression. This feature is widely appreciated and may improve performance, especially if users can control the repetition rate to accommodate their preferences (important for very young users, older adults, or users with motor impairments).

9.2.3 Keyboards and keypads for small devices

Even on laptop computers, keyboards are usually full-size, but some smaller computers and electronic appliances use keyboards of greatly reduced size (Figs. 1.10 and 9.4) or disconnect the keyboard from the main device by using wireless or foldable keyboards (Fig. 9.6). Virtual keyboards are appearing as well, where a projector displays the image of a keyboard on a flat surface and a sensor tracks finger movements (Fig. 9.7). Virtual keyboards permit a variety of

Figure 9.6

Weighing in at less than eight ounces, this full-size Palm keyboard folds into a size just slightly bigger than a Palm device. (http://www.palmone.com)

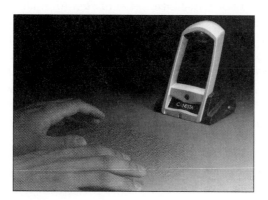

Figure 9.7

The Canesta Keyboard, a virtual projection keyboard. (http://www.canesta.com)

keyboard sizes and easily accommodate international variations. Another innovation is cloth keyboards, being introduced by ElekSen. They can take any shape and be folded easily, but like virtual keyboards, they lack adequate tactile feedback for touch typing.

Mobile-phone functionalities are increasing considerably (messaging, photo capture, web access, and so on) while their size is still shrinking, thereby posing a challenge that results in a rich set of interesting designs. Most devices combine normal static keys with dynamically labeled *softkeys* whose functions are dependent on status and context. Softkeys are usually located immediately below the display (see for example the Select or Exit keys in Fig. 7.19). The phone's number keypad layouts are fairly standard—with rare exceptions such as circular layouts—so user-interface innovations focus mainly on techniques to enter text. MultiTap requires users to hit a number key multiple times to specify a letter and to pause between letters using the same key. *Predictive* techniques, such as T9 by Tegic Communications, use dictionary-based disambiguation and are often preferred for writing text messages. Alternatives include LetterWise, which uses the probabilities of prefixes and facilitates the entry of non-dictionary words, such as a proper nouns, abbreviations, or slang. After training, users could type 20 words per minute with LetterWise compared to 15 words per minute with MultiTap (MacKenzie et al., 2001). New techniques will continue to improve data entry on small keyboards.

Many handheld devices have abandoned keyboards entirely and rely on pointing and drawing devices such as pens and touchscreens for all text entry (MacKenzie and Soukoreff, 2002). Users can tap on virtual keyboards, if the screen is large enough to display a keyboard (Fig. 9.8). In our studies with touch-screen keyboards that were 7 and 25 centimeters wide, users could, with some practice, type from 20 to 30 words per minute, respectively, which is quite acceptable for limited text entry (Sears et al., 1993). Another method is to handwrite on a touch-sensitive surface, typically with a stylus, but character recognition remains error prone. Contextual clues and stroke speed plus direction can enhance recognition rates (Frankish, Hull, and Morgan, 1995), but the most successful gestural data-entry methods involve using simplified and more easily recognizable character sets, such as the unistrokes used by Graffiti on the Palm devices (Fig. 9.9). Recognition is fairly good and most users learn the codes quickly, but the required training can be a hurdle for new and intermittent users.

For some languages, such as Japanese or Chinese, handwriting recognition has the potential to dramatically increase the user population. On the other hand, users with disabilities, older adults, and young children may not have the necessary fine control to use such interfaces on tiny touch-sensitive surfaces. For them, innovations such as EdgeWrite (Wobbrock, Myers, and Kembel, 2003) might be helpful. EdgeWrite relies on the use of a physical border to frame the drawing area and uses a modified character set that can be recognized by identifying the series of corners being hit instead of the pattern of the pen stroke.

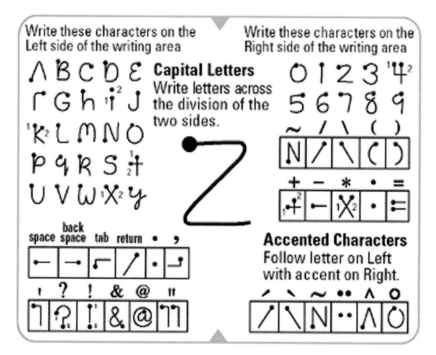

Figure 9.8

A virtual keyboard as it appears on the screen of a Palm device.
(http://www.palmone.com/us/products/input)

Figure 9.9

The Palm Graffiti2 characters.
(http://www.palmone.com/us/products/input/graffiti2_alphabet.pdf)

With this technique, accuracy increased for all users compared to Graffiti, and some users with motor impairments who had been unable to use traditional keyboards or reproduce recognizable Grafitti shapes were able to write with EdgeWrite.

⌐.Ξ   Pointing Devices

With complex information displays such as those found in computer-assisted design tools, drawing tools, or air-traffic–control systems, it is often convenient to point at and select items. This direct-manipulation approach is attractive because the users can avoid learning commands, reduce the chance of typographic errors on a keyboard, and keep their attention on the display. The results are often faster performance, fewer errors, easier learning, and higher satisfaction. Pointing devices are also important for small devices and large wall displays that make keyboards impractical as input devices.

The diversity of tasks, the variety of devices, and the strategies for using them create a rich design space (Card, Mackinlay, and Robertson, 1991; Hinckley, 2003). Physical device attributes (rotation or linear movement), dimensionality of movement (1, 2, 3 ...), and positioning (relative or absolute) are useful ways of categorizing devices, but here we focus on tasks and degree of directness as organizing dimensions.

⌐.Ξ.⅃   Pointing tasks

Pointing devices are useful for six types of interaction tasks (Foley, Wallace, and Chen, 1984):

1. *Select.* Users choose from a set of items. This technique is used for traditional menu selection, identification of a file in a directory, or marking, for example, a part in an automobile design.

2. *Position.* Users choose a point in a one-, two-, three-, or higher-dimensional space. Positioning may be used to create a drawing, to place a new window, or to drag a block of text in a figure.

3. *Orient.* Users choose a direction in a two-, three-, or higher-dimensional space. The direction may simply rotate a symbol on the screen, indicate a direction of motion, or control the operation of a robot arm or other device.

4. *Path.* Users rapidly perform a series of positioning and orientation operations. The path may be realized as a curving line in a drawing program, a character to be recognized, or the instructions for a cloth-cutting or other type of machine.

5. *Quantify.* Users specify a numeric value. The quantify task is usually a one-dimensional selection of integer or real values to set parameters, such as the page number in a document, the velocity of a ship, or the amplitude of a sound.

6. *Text.* Users enter, move, and edit text in a two-dimensional space. The pointing device indicates the location of an insertion, deletion, or change. Beyond the simple manipulation of the text are more elaborate tasks, such as centering, setting margins and font sizes, highlighting (boldface or underscore), and page layout.

It is possible to perform all these tasks with a keyboard by typing numbers or letters to select, integer coordinates to position, a number representing an angle to point, a number to quantify, and cursor-control commands to move about in text. In the past, the keyboard was used to perform all these tasks, but now users employ pointing devices to perform them more rapidly and with fewer errors. For expert users, tasks that are invoked frequently might still be performed with special keys, such as CTRL-C to copy a marked item.

Pointing devices can be grouped into those that offer (1) *direct control* on the screen surface, such as the touchscreen or stylus, and (2) *indirect control* away from the screen surface, such as the mouse, trackball, joystick, graphics tablet, or touchpad. Within each category are many variations, and novel designs emerge frequently (Box 9.1).

9.3.2   Direct-control pointing devices

The *lightpen* was an early device that enabled users to point to a spot on a screen and then press a button to perform a select, position, or other task. The lightpen had several disadvantages: users' arms got tired and their hands obscured part of the screen, users had to remove their hands from the keyboard to pick up the lightpen, and the lightpen was too fragile for public-access environments.

Some of these disadvantages were overcome by the *touchscreen* (Fig. 9.10), which is very robust and does not require picking up an external device; instead, it allows users to make direct-control touches on the screen with a finger (Shneiderman, 1991). Arm fatigue remains a problem, but it can be addressed with good kiosk design by tilting the screen and providing a surface on which to rest the arm. Early touchscreen implementations had problems with imprecise pointing, as the software accepted the touch immediately (the *land-on strategy*), denying users the opportunity to verify the correctness of the selected spot. These early designs were based on physical pressure, impact, or interruption of a grid of infrared beams. Later designs have dramatically improved touchscreens to permit high precision (Sears and Shneiderman, 1991). The resistive, capacitive, or surface acoustic-wave hardware often provide up to 1600 x 1600 sensitivity, and the *lift-off strategy* enables users to point at a single pixel. The lift-off strategy

Box 9.1

Pointing devices.

Direct control devices (easy to learn and use, but hand may obscure display)
- Lightpen
- Touchscreen
- Stylus

Indirect control devices (takes time to learn)
- Mouse
- Trackball
- Joystick
- Trackpoint
- Touchpad
- Graphics tablet

Novel devices and strategies (special purposes)
- Foot controls
- Eye tracking
- 3D trackers
- DataGloves
- Boom Chameleon
- Haptic feedback
- Bimanual input
- Tangible user interfaces
- Digital paper

Criteria for success
- Speed and accuracy
- Efficacy for task
- Learning time
- Cost and reliability
- Size and weight

---

has three steps: users touch the surface, and then see a cursor that they can drag to adjust its position; when they are satisfied, they lift their fingers off the display to activate. The availability of high-precision touchscreens has opened the doors to many applications, such as building-management, banking, medical, and military systems (Sears, Plaisant, and Shneiderman, 1992).

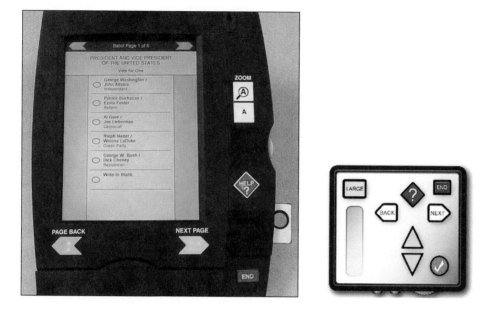

Figure 9.10

Users of this touchscreen voting tablet need only touch any text on screen to have it read to them via headphones. Touching the checkbox marks the vote, with verbal confirmation if headphones are used. Users who are completely blind, or have severe physical disabilities that prevent them from using the touchscreen (even with voice), can use a detachable keypad—with or without voice. Keypad also allows connection of custom switches voter brings with them. (http://www.trace.wisc.edu/)

Touchscreens are often integrated into applications directed at novice users in which the keyboard can be eliminated and touch is the main interface mechanism. Designers of public-access systems value touchscreens because there are no moving parts, and durability in high-use environments is good (the touchscreen is the only input device that has survived at Walt Disney World theme parks). Strategies have been described to provide access to touchscreen systems such as information kiosks or voting systems for people who are vision-impaired or blind, are hard of hearing or deaf, have trouble reading or are unable to read at all, or have physical disabilities (Vanderheiden, 1997, 2004). Multiple-touch touchscreens that allow a single user to use both hands or multiple fingers at once, or allow multiple users to work together on a shared surface, have been slow to emerge but are now becoming available (FingerWorks, MERL DiamondTouch).

Tablet PCs and mobile devices make it natural to point on the LCD surface, which can be held in the arm or hand, placed on a desk, or rested on the lap. The *stylus* is an attractive device because it is familiar and comfortable for users, and users can guide the stylus tip to the desired location while keeping the whole context in view. These advantages, however, must be balanced against the need to pick up and put down the stylus. Most stylus interfaces (also called pen-based interfaces), such as the Palm Pilot, are based on touchscreen technology; users can write with a stylus for more natural handwriting and increased motion control but can also use a finger for quick selection. Like touchscreens, stylus interfaces misbehave when users touch the screen in two or more locations at once. To avoid this problem, devices with large touchable surfaces, such as tablet PCs, might require the use of an active stylus that can be recognized by the touch-sensitive surface.

Popular mobile devices such as the Palm Pilot and Pocket PC created a huge market for stylus devices based on well-designed services such as address books, calendars, or notes (Fig. 1.10). They now include phone and Internet capabilities, allowing direct dialing by selecting a name in an address book with a stylus, or downloading of maps and directions while on the road. Novel menu selection based on gestures (see Chapter 7) and handwriting recognition are competing with pull-down–menu and direct-manipulation strategies as designers strive to create novel and attractive interfaces for this growing market (see Section 9.5.4).

9.3.3   Indirect-control pointing devices

Indirect pointing devices eliminate the hand-fatigue and hand-obscuring-the-screen problems, but they require the hand to locate the device and demand more cognitive processing and hand/eye coordination to bring the onscreen cursor to the desired target.

The *mouse* is appealing because of its low cost and wide availability. The hand rests in a comfortable position, buttons on the mouse are easy to press, long motions can be done rapidly by moving the forearm, and positioning can be done precisely with small finger movements. However, users must grab the mouse to begin work, desk space is consumed, and the mouse wire can be annoying. Other problems are that pickup and replace actions are necessary for long motions and some practice is required to develop skills (usually from 5 to 50 minutes, but sometimes much more for older adults or users with disabilities). The variety of mouse technologies (physical, optical, or acoustic), number of buttons, placement of the sensor, weight, and size indicate that designers and users have yet to settle on one preferred design. Personal preferences and the variety of tasks to be done leave room for lively competition. The mouse may be simple or may incorporate a wheel and additional buttons to facilitate scrolling or web browsing (Fig 9.11). Those additional mouse features can sometimes be programmed to perform common tasks of special-purpose applications, such as adjusting the focus of a microscope and switching its magnification level.

The *trackball* has sometimes been described as an upside-down mouse. It is usually implemented as a rotating ball, 1 to 15 centimeters in diameter, that moves a cursor on the screen as it is moved (Fig. 9.12). The trackball is wear

Figure 9.11

The Apple wireless mouse on the left has only one button, activated by pressing the whole mouse down. The Microsoft Wireless IntelliMouse (shown on the right) includes in between the two buttons a tilt wheel, which can be used to scroll documents, and two thumb buttons for backward and forward Internet browsing.

Figure 9.12

The Logitech marble mouse is really a trackball. (www.logitech.com)

resistant and can be firmly mounted in a desk to allow users to hit the ball vigorously and to make it spin. Trackballs have been embedded in control panels for air-traffic–control or museum information systems, and are also commonly used in video-game controllers.

The *joystick*, whose long history began in aircraft-control devices and early computer games, has dozens of versions with varying stick lengths and thicknesses, displacement forces and distances, anchoring strategies for bases, and placement relative to the keyboard and screen. Joysticks are appealing for tracking purposes (to follow or guide an object on a screen), partly because of the relatively small displacements needed to move a cursor, the ease of direction changes, and the opportunity to combine the joystick with additional buttons, wheels, and triggers (Fig. 9.13).

The *trackpoint* is a small isometric joystick, embedded in keyboards between the letters G and H (Fig. 9.1). It is sensitive to pressure and does not move. It has

Figure 9.13

A Saitek joystick used to control the X-Plane flight simulator. Two-handed operation is possible, and adjustments can be made to accommodate both right- and left-handed users. (http://www.saitek.com, http://www.x-plane.com)

a rubber tip to facilitate finger contact, and with modest practice, users can quickly and accurately use it to control the cursor while keeping their fingers on the keyboard home position. The trackpoint is particularly effective for applications such as word processors that require constant switches between the keyboard and pointing device. Because of their small size, trackpoints can be easily combined with other devices such as chord keyboards (Fig. 9.2) or even mice to facilitate two-dimensional scrolling.

A *touchpad* (a touchable surface of about 5 by 8 centimeters) offers the convenience and precision of a touchscreen while keeping the user's hand off the display surface. Users can make quick movements for long-distance traversals and can gently rock their fingers for precise positioning before lifting off. Often built in below the keyboard (Fig. 9.1), the touchpad can be used with the thumbs while keeping the hands in typing position. The lack of moving parts and the thin profile make touchpads appealing for portable computers.

The *graphics tablet* is a touch-sensitive surface separate from the screen, usually laid flat on the table or in the user's lap. This separation allows for comfortable hand positioning and keeps the users' hands off the screen. The graphics tablet is appealing when users' hands can remain with the device for long periods without switching to a keyboard. Furthermore, the graphics tablet permits a surface even larger than the screen to be covered with printing to indicate available choices, thereby providing guidance to novice users and preserving valuable screen space. Limited data entry can be done with the graphics tablet. The graphics tablet can be operated by placement of a finger, pencil, puck, or stylus, using acoustic, electronic, or contact position sensing. Wireless pens allow a higher freedom that is appreciated by artists using drawing programs (Fig. 9.14).

Among these indirect pointing devices, the mouse has been the greatest success story. Given its rapid high-precision pointing abilities and comfortable hand position, the modest training period is only a small impediment to its use. Most desktop computer systems offer a mouse, but the battle for the laptop continues, with many vendors offering multiple pointing devices on a single machine.

9.3.4 Comparison of pointing devices

Early studies found that direct pointing devices such as a lightpen or touchscreen were often the fastest but the least accurate devices (Haller, Mutschler, and Voss, 1984). Decades of studies have consistently shown the merits of the mouse over alternative devices for speed and accuracy (English, Engelbert, and Berman, 1967; MacKenzie, Tauppinen, and Silfverberg, 2001). The mouse has been found to be faster than the trackpoint, due to tremors in finger motion during fine finger movements (Mithal and Douglas, 1996). Trackballs and touchpads fall somewhere in between. Users' tasks matter when comparing devices. For example, when browsing the World Wide Web, users are constantly

Figure 9.14

A digital painting created by Larry Ravitz using Adobe PhotoShop and a Wacom tablet. The Wacom pressure-sensitive stylus and graphics tablet allow the precise pointing and accurate control that artists need.

involved in both scrolling and pointing—one study showed that a mouse with a finger wheel did not improve user's performance over a standard mouse. However, performance increased with an isometric joystick mounted on a mouse (Zhai, Smith, and Selker, 1997). New accuracy measures for precision pointing tasks (MacKenzie, Tauppinen, and Silfverberg, 2001) that capture fine aspects of movement behavior during a pointing task such as target re-entry or movement variability might provide a better understanding of the benefits and limitations of each device.

The usual belief is that pointing devices are faster than keyboard controls such as cursor-movement keys, but this assertion depends on the task. When a few (2 to 10) targets are on the screen and the cursor can be made to jump from one target to the next, then using the cursor jump keys can be faster than using pointing devices. For short distances and for tasks that mix typing and pointing, cursor keys have also been shown to be faster than and preferred to the mouse.

Joysticks and trackballs are often preferred over mice by users with motor disabilities, as their location remains fixed, they have a small footprint (allowing them to be mounted on wheelchairs), and they can be operated by small residual movements. Touch-sensitive devices are useful when applying force is a problem. In general, designers should attempt to detect inadvertent or uncontrolled movements and smooth out trajectories. Using active target areas that are larger than the button or icon to be selected is effective to shorten selection time and reduce frustration for every user, and in some cases might be all that is needed to render an application usable by many more users.

Pointing devices—especially indirect-control devices such as the mouse—are particularly challenging for users who have vision impairments. With those devices, well-designed cursors of adjustable size and shape can help. Interfaces using direct-control input devices such as touchscreens can more easily be explored and memorized when speech synthesis or sonification is available to describe the display, read menu options, and confirm selections. Alternative keyboard or keypad navigation options should be provided whenever possible. For example, in a touchscreen voting kiosk, arrow keys can navigate through lists of candidates whose names are read and listened to with headphones (Fig. 9.10). Successful examples demonstrate that it is possible to design powerful systems that are truly accessible to the general public, including users with a wide range of disabilities (Vanderheiden, Kelso, and Krueger, 2004).

In summary, much work remains to sort out the role of tasks and individual differences with respect to pointing devices. The touchscreen and trackball are durable in public-access, shop-floor, and laboratory applications. The mouse, trackball, trackpoint, graphics tablet, and touchpad are effective for pixel-level pointing. Pens are appreciated for drawing and handwriting. Cursor jump keys remain attractive when there are a small number of targets. Joysticks are appealing for games or specialized navigation applications. Indirect-control pointing devices require more learning than direct-control devices but offer many useful options.

9.3.5 Fitts's Law

A predictive model of time to point at an object would be a great help to designers of interfaces and pointing devices. Such a predictive model would help to decide the location and size of buttons and other elements when laying out screens and would indicate which pointing devices are best suited to performing common tasks. Fortunately, a model of human hand movement, developed by Paul Fitts (1954), has turned out to be well suited to user interfaces. Fitts noticed that the time for hand movements was dependent on the distance users had to move, D, and the target size, W. Doubling the distance from, say, 10 cm to 20 cm took longer, but not twice as long. Increasing the target size, for example from 1 cm^2 to 2 cm^2, enabled users to point at it more rapidly.

Since the time to start and stop moving is constant, an effective equation for the movement time (*MT*) for a given device, such as a mouse, turns out to be

$$MT = a + b \log_2(D/W + 1)$$

where *a* approximates the start/stop time in seconds for a given device and *b* measures the inherent speed of the device. Both *a* and *b* need to be determined experimentally for each device. For example, if *a* were 300 milliseconds, *b* were 200 msec/bit, *D* were 14 cm, and *W* were 2 cm, then the movement time *MT* would be $300 + 200 \log_2(14/2 + 1)$, which equals 900 milliseconds.

Several versions of Fitts's law are used, but this equation has been demonstrated to provide good predictions in a wide range of situations. The variations are due to differences such as the direction of motion (horizontally or vertically), device weight (heavier devices are harder to move), device grasp, shape of targets, and arm position (on a table or in the air).

MacKenzie (1992) lucidly describes what Fitts's law is, how it has been applied, and refinements for cases such as two-dimensional pointing. In our studies of high-precision touchscreens (Sears and Shneiderman, 1991), we found that, in addition to the gross arm movement predicted by Fitts, there was also a fine-tuning motion of the fingers to move in on small targets such as single pixels. A three-component equation was thus more suited for the precision pointing movement time (*PPMT*):

$$PPMT = a + b \log_2(D/W + 1) + c \log_2 (d / W).$$

The third term, time for fine tuning, increases as the target width, *W*, decreases. This extension to Fitts's law is quite understandable; it suggests that the precision pointing movement time consists of the start/stop time, *a*, a time for gross movement, and a time for fine adjustment. Other studies deal with a greater range of arm motion as well as pointing in three-dimensional space (Zhai, Smith, and Selker, 1996).

Fitts's law is well established for adult users, but it may need refinements for special populations such as young children or older adults. In one recent study, 13 4-year-olds, 13 5-year-olds, and 13 young adults performed point-and-click selection tasks (Hourcade et al., 2001). As expected, age had a significant effect on speed and accuracy (and of course trajectories, as shown in Fig. 9.15). A detailed analysis showed that Fitts's law models children well for the first time they enter the target, but not for the time of final selection.

The open problem remains: How can we design devices that produce smaller constants for the predictive equation? One study has shown that multiscale pointing with zooming (Guiard et al., 2001) works best with two-handed input and a constant zoom speed. Another study looked at crossing-based interfaces, in which targets are merely crossed instead of pointed at. The target-crossing completion time was found to be shorter than or equal to pointing performance

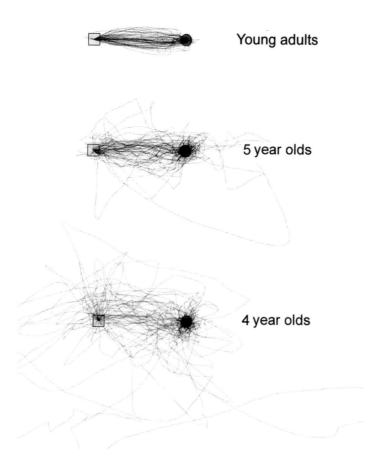

Young adults

5 year olds

4 year olds

Figure 9.15

Tracing the trajectory of the mouse cursor during a repeated target-selection task illustrates the dramatic difference between adults' and children's use of the mouse. (Hourcade et al., 2001)

under the same index of difficulty, and depended on the type of task performed (Accot and Zhai, 2002). The quest for faster selection time continues.

9.3.6 Novel devices

The popularity of pointing devices and the quest for new ways to engage diverse users for diverse tasks has led to provocative innovations. Improving the match between the task and the device and refining the input plus feedback strategies are common themes (Jacob et al., 1994).

Since users' hands might be busy on the keyboard, designers have explored other methods for selection and pointing. *Foot controls* are popular with rock-music performers, organists, dentists, and car drivers, so maybe computer users could benefit from them as well. A foot mouse was tested and was found to take about twice as much time to use as a hand-operated mouse, but benefits in special applications may exist—for example, switches and pedals activated by foot might be effective to specify modes.

Eye-tracking, gaze-detecting controllers use video-camera image recognition of the pupil position to give 1- or 2-degree accuracy. Fixations of 200 to 600 milliseconds are used to make selections. Unfortunately, the "Midas touch problem" intrudes, since every gaze has the potential to activate an unintended command. Combining eye tracking with manual input is one way to address this problem, but eye tracking remains mostly a research tool and a possible aid for users with motor disabilities (Majaranta and Raiha, 2002; Zhai, 2003).

Multiple-degree-of-freedom devices can sense multiple dimensions of spatial position and orientation. Control over three-dimensional objects seems a natural application, but comparisons with other strategies reveal low precision and slow responses (Zhai, 1998). Support for virtual reality (see Chapter 6) is one motivation, but many design, medical, and other tasks may require three-dimensional input or even six degrees of freedom to indicate a position and an orientation. Commercial tracking devices include the Logitech 3Dconnexion SpaceBall and SpaceMouse, the Ascension Bird, and Polhemus's Liberty or Isotrack.

The VPL *DataGlove* appeared in 1987 and attracted serious researchers, game developers, cyberspace adventurers, and virtual-reality devotees (see Section 6.6 and Fig. 9.16). Descendants of the original DataGlove are still often made of sleek black spandex with attached fiber-optic sensors to measure angles of finger joints. The displayed feedback can show the relative placement of each finger; thus, commands such as a closed fist, open hand, index-finger pointing, and thumbs-up gesture can be recognized. Combined with a hand-tracker, complete three-dimensional placement and orientation can be recorded. Devotees claim that the naturalness of gestures will enable use by many keyboard-averse or mouse-phobic users, although users require substantial training to master more than half a dozen gestures. Gestural input with the glove can make special applications possible, such as the recognition of American Sign Language or virtual musical performances.

An alternative to the goggles-and-gloves approach is to allow users to step up to a viewer with handles that can be used to shift vantage points within the range of a mechanical boom (see Fig. 6.20). The display updates to create the illusion that the user is moving in three dimensions, and users have an immersive experience without the heavy and confining head-mounted goggles. The Boom Chameleon project combines a boom with a touchscreen and allows voice and gesture interaction to provide a compelling 3D annotation environment (Tsang et al., 2002). Glove-mounted devices and tethered balls are being refined,

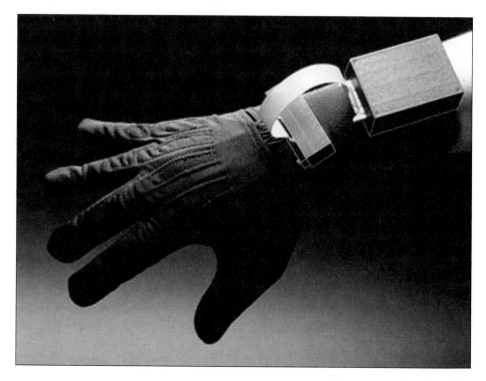

Figure 9.16

The iReality.com wireless DataGlove has 14-sensors that measure finger flexure (2 sensors per finger) as well as the abduction between fingers and the orientation (pitch and roll) of the user's hand. (iREALITY.com)

and other graspable user interfaces seem ripe for exploration (Fitzmaurice, Ishii, and Buxton, 1995).

Pointing devices with *haptic feedback* are an intriguing research direction (Iwata, 2003). Several technologies have been employed to allow users to push a mouse or other device and to feel resistance (for example, as they cross a window boundary) or a hard wall (for example, as they navigate a maze). Three-dimensional versions, such as SensAble Technology's Phantom, are still more intriguing, but compelling commercial applications have yet to emerge. Because sound and vibrations are often a good substitute for haptic feedback, the use of advanced haptic devices remains limited to special-purpose applications (such as training surgeons for heart surgery) while devices using simple vibrations have become mainstream in game controllers.

Bimanual input can facilitate multitasking or compound tasks. A theory of bimanual input (Guiard, 1987) suggests that the nondominant hand sets a frame of reference in which the dominant hand operates in a more precise fashion. A natural application of bimanual operation for desktop applications is that the nondominant hand selects actions (for example, the fill command of a paint program) while the dominant hand precisely selects the objects of the operation (see also Section 7.7.4).

Ubiquitous computing and *tangible user interfaces* (Abowd and Mynatt, 2000; Ishii and Ullmer, 1997) depend on embedding sensing technologies into the environment. For example, active badges can sense when a user enters a room, which can trigger the loading of personal files into the room's computer. The positioning of physical objects can specify modes or trigger actions. Ambient light, sound, or airflow can also be modified to present a small amount of information to users. Entertainment or artistic applications use video cameras or body sensors to track body positions and create enticing user experiences. Early explorations by performance artist Vincent John Vincent led to three-dimensional environments for theatrical exploration such as Mandala, in which performers or amateur users touch images of harps, bells, drums, or cymbals, and the instruments respond. Myron Krueger's artificial realities contain friendly video-projected cartoonlike creatures that playfully crawl on your arm or approach your outstretched hand. Such environments invite participation, and the serious research aspects fade as joyful exploration takes over and you step inside the computer's world (see Section 6.6). StoryRoom is another such application that enables children to actively construct their own interactive environments, using props and magic wands to create stories that other children are invited to experience (Montemayor et al., 2004).

Paper can also be used as an input device. Early applications demonstrated the benefits of capturing annotations on large documents such as blueprints or lab notebooks with video cameras (Mackay et al., 2002). Pens such as the Logitech digital pen with Anoto functionality facilitate interaction, particularly in mobile situations. The pen has a small camera in its tip. It records pen strokes drawn on a special paper printed with a unique pattern which identifies the location of each stroke. The handwriting can then be transferred to a computer or a mobile phone (Fig. 9.17). The ease of learning might help novice users: Paper augmented digital documents can be edited both in digital and paper form (Guimbretière, 2003). We are using digital pens in our research to allow grandparents to share notes and calendar information with distant family members.

Handheld devices can also be used as input devices. For example, CMU's Pebbles project is exploring how mobile devices can be used as input devices to communicate with personal computers, with other mobile devices, or with home appliances, automobiles, or factory equipment (Myers, 2001). Mobile devices can also act as intelligent universal remote controls, potentially empowering all users by reading aloud menu options, translating instructions written in a foreign language, or offering speech recognition when needed. Sensors added to handheld devices can in turn enrich the interaction with the device itself—for example, users may be able to zoom and pan on a map by adjusting the proximity or lateral position of a mobile device in front of them. Tilting the

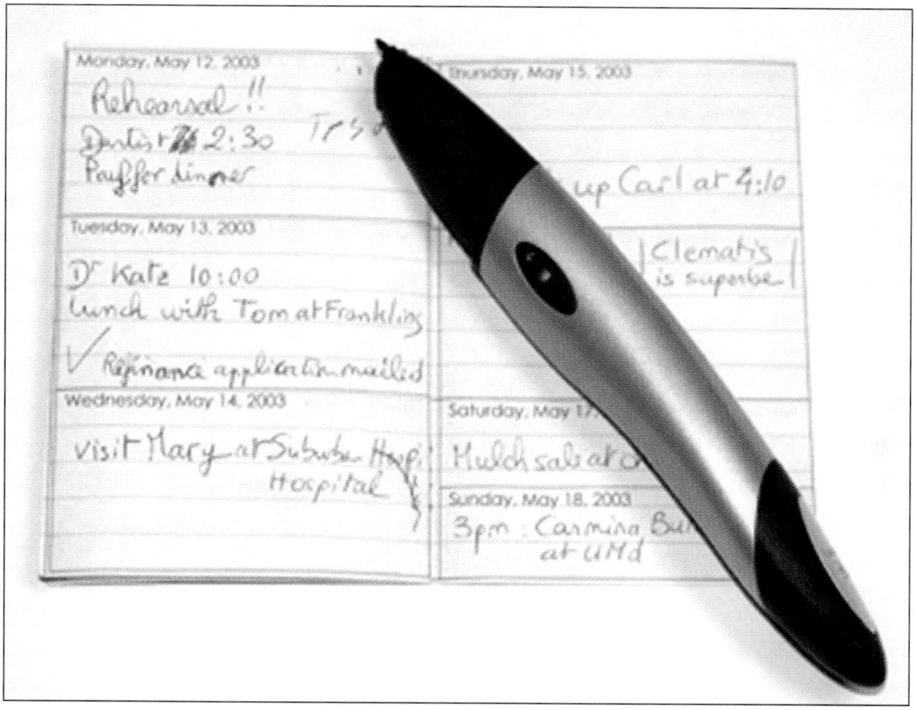

Figure 9.17

A Logitech io digital pen with Anoto functionality records the strokes of ink written on digital paper. When the pen is returned to its base, the data is transferred to the computer. In this example from one of our research projects, calendar information can then be shared with distant family members. (www.logitech.com)

device could scroll through a list of names, and bringing the device near the ear could answer an incoming call (Hinckley et al., 2000).

Another innovative device is Measurand's ShapeTape, which provides bend and twist information along a one meter tape, allowing the shape of the tape to be reconstructed in three dimensions for creating or manipulating curves or for tracking angles of arms and legs in motion capture applications (Grossman et al., 2002).

Devices engineered for particular applications sometimes find unexpected success in other domains. Intel's toy optical microscope, designed for children's exploration, became a huge success as it could help stamp collectors to document their collections and graphic artists to collect abstract patterns (Fig. 9.18). Also, popular game controllers such as the Logitech Wingman Rumble Pad can be reprogrammed to provide haptic feedback about boundary crossings or color intensity to users who cannot see them.

Figure 9.18

Intel's Digital Blue QX3+ Computer Microscope. The QX3 + microscope magnifies anything from 10x all the way to 200x and takes pictures. It allows children to explore the world around them, and applications for stamp collectors, paleontologists, and watch-repair businesses have also taken advantage of this low-cost unconventional input device.

Finally, custom devices can be created from scratch using an endless variety of sensors. Users with motor disabilities can control wheelchairs, home devices, or computer applications using custom-fitted sensors chosen to best match their remaining motor abilities. Switches can be triggered by small head or shoulder movements, a light blow in a tube, the blink of an eye, and even faint myoelectric currents generated when muscles are being tensed.

ꓞ.ꓴ   Speech and Auditory Interfaces

The dream of speaking to computers and having computers speak has lured many researchers and visionaries. Arthur C. Clarke's 1968 fantasy of the HAL 9000 computer in the book and movie *2001: A Space Odyssey* has set the standard for performance of computers in science fiction and for some advanced developers. The reality is more complex and sometimes more surprising than the dream. Hardware designers have made dramatic progress with speech recognition, generation, and processing, but current successes are sobering compared to the science-fiction fantasy (Gardner-Bonneau, 1999; Weinschenk and Barker, 2000; Balentine, Morgan, and Meisel, 2001). Even science-fiction writers have shifted their scenarios, as shown by the reduced use of voice interaction in favor of larger visual displays in Star Trek's *Voyager* or movies such as *Minority Report*.

The vision of computers chatting leisurely with users now seems more of an uninformed fantasy than a desirable reality. Instead, practical applications of speech interaction succeed when they serve users' needs to work rapidly with low cognitive load and low error rates. Even as technical problems are being solved and the recognition algorithms are improving, designers are reluctantly recognizing that voice commanding is more demanding of users' working memory than is hand/eye coordination, and thus may be more disruptive to users while they are carrying out tasks. Speech requires use of limited resources, while hand/eye coordination is processed elsewhere in the brain, enabling a higher level of parallel processing. Planning and problem solving can proceed in parallel with hand/eye coordination, but they are more difficult to accomplish while speaking (Ashcraft, 2001).

Unfortunately, background noise and variations in user speech performance make the challenge of *speech recognition* still greater. By contrast, *speech store and forward* and *speech generation* are satisfyingly predictable, low cost, and widely available because of the telephone's ubiquity and the compactness of speech chips. However, every designer must cope with the three obstacles to speech output: the slow pace of speech output when compared to visual displays, the ephemeral nature of speech, and the difficulty in scanning/searching (Box 9.2). Speech store and forward is a success because the emotional content and prosody in human speech is compelling in voice messaging, museum tours, and instructional contexts.

The benefits to people with certain physical disabilities are rewarding to see, but the general users of office or personal computers are not rushing to implement speech input and output devices. Speech is the bicycle of user-interface design: It is great fun to use and has an important role, but it can carry only a light load. Sober advocates know that it will be tough to replace the automobile, graphical user interfaces.

Speech enthusiasts can claim success in telephony, where digital circuitry has increased the capacity of networks and improved voice quality. Cellular telephones have been a huge success in developed countries and often bring telephone service rapidly to less developed countries. Internet telephony, often called Voice over IP (Internet Protocol), is rising rapidly, giving many users low-cost long-distance service, albeit with lower sound quality. The immediacy and emotional impact of a telephone conversation is a compelling component of human/human communication.

Box 9.2

Speech systems.

Opportunities
- When users have vision impairments
- When the speaker's hands are busy
- When mobility is required
- When the speaker's eyes are occupied
- When harsh or cramped conditions preclude use of a keyboard

Technologies
- Speech store and forward
- Discrete-word recognition
- Continuous-speech recognition
- Voice information systems
- Speech generation

Obstacles to speech recognition
- Increased cognitive load compared to pointing
- Interference from noisy environments
- Unstable recognition across changing users, environments, and time

Obstacles to speech output
- Slow pace of speech output when compared to visual displays
- Ephemeral nature of speech
- Difficulty in scanning/searching

For designers of human/computer interaction systems, speech and audio technologies have at least five variations: discrete-word recognition, continuous-speech recognition, voice information systems, speech generation, and non-speech auditory interfaces. These components can be combined in creative ways: from simple systems that merely play back or generate a message, to complex interactions that accept speech commands, generate speech feedback, provide sonification of scientific data, and allow annotation and editing of stored speech.

A deeper understanding of neurological processing of sounds would be helpful to designers in this field. Why does listening to Mozart symphonies encourage creative work, whereas listening to radio news reports suspends it? Is the linguistic processing needed to absorb a radio news report disruptive, whereas background Mozart is somehow invigorating? Of course, listening to Mozart with the serious intention of a musicologist would be completely absorbing of mental resources. Are there uses of sound or speech and ways of shifting attention that might be less disruptive or even supportive of symbolic processing, analytic reasoning, or graphic designing? Could sound be a more useful component of drawing software than of word processors?

9.4.1 Discrete-word recognition

Discrete-word–recognition devices recognize individual words spoken by a specific person; they can work with 90 to 98% reliability for 100- to 10,000-word or larger vocabularies. *Speaker-dependent training*, in which users repeat the full vocabulary once or twice, is a part of many systems. Such training yields higher accuracy than in *speaker-independent* systems, but the elimination of training expands the scope of commercial applications. Quiet environments, head-mounted microphones, and careful choice of vocabularies improve recognition rates in both cases.

Applications for users with disabilities have enabled paralyzed, bedridden, or injured people to broaden the horizons of their lives. They can control wheelchairs, operate equipment, or use personal computers for a variety of tasks. Similarly, applications for older adults or cognitively or emotionally challenged individuals might allow them to have a greater level of independence, restore lost skills, and regain confidence in their capabilities. Unfortunately, speech impairments are often associated with other disabilities and will greatly limit those benefits.

Telephone-based information services have flourished in recent years, providing weather, sports, stock market, and movie information. Telephone companies offer voice-dialing services, even on cell phones, to allow users simply to say "Call Mom" and be connected. However, difficulties with training for multiple users in a household, user reluctance to use speech commands, and unreliable recognition are apparently slowing acceptance, even in cars, where hands-free operation is a big advantage.

Phone-based recognition of numbers, yes/no answers, and selections from voice menus are successful and increasingly applied. However, full-sentence commands such as "Reserve two seats on the first flight tomorrow from New York to Washington" are just moving from a research challenge to commercial use. Several proposals for structured speech have been made, but even if users learn a limited grammar, such as <action> <object> <qualifier> ("Reserve seats two" "Depart New York tomorrow"), interaction is difficult.

Many advanced development efforts have tested speech recognition in military aircraft, medical operating rooms, training labs, and offices. The results reveal problems with recognition rates even for speaker-dependent training systems, when background sounds change, when users are ill or under stress, and when words in the vocabulary are similar (dime/time or Houston/Austin).

Other applications have been successful when at least one of these conditions exist:

- Speaker's hands are busy.
- Mobility is required.
- Speaker's eyes are occupied.
- Harsh or cramped conditions preclude use of a keyboard (for example, in underwater or rescue operations).

Example applications include systems for aircraft-engine inspectors, who wear wireless microphones as they walk around the engine opening coverplates or adjusting components. They can issue orders, read serial numbers, or retrieve previous maintenance records by using a 35-word vocabulary. Implementers of such challenging applications should consider conducting speaker-dependent training in the task environment.

For common computing applications, when a display is used, speech input has marginal benefits. Studies of users controlling cursor movement by voice confirm slower performance for cursor movement tasks such as button clicking and web browsing (Christian et al., 2000; Sears, Lin, and Karimullah, 2002).

On the other hand, a study of drawing program users showed that allowing users to select one of 19 commands by voice instead of selection from a palette improved performance times by an average of 21% (Pausch and Leatherby, 1991). The advantage seems to have been gained by avoiding the time-consuming and distracting effort of moving the cursor repeatedly from the diagram to the tool palette and back. A replication confirmed this result with word-processing tasks using 18 spoken commands such as "boldface," "down," "italic," "paste," and "undo" (Karl, Pettey, and Shneiderman, 1993). Although overall using voice commands was faster than mouse pointing, mainly due to mouse acquisition time, error rates were higher for voice users in tasks that required high short-term–memory load. This unexpected result was explained by psychologists, who pointed out that short-term memory is sometimes referred to as "acoustic memory." Speaking commands is more demanding of working memory than is performing the hand/eye coordination needed for mouse pointing, which is handled in parallel by other parts of the brain (Ashcraft, 2001).

This phenomenon may explain the slower acceptance of speech interfaces as compared with graphical user interfaces; speaking commands or listening disrupts planning and problem solving more than does selecting actions from a menu with a mouse. This was noted by product evaluators for an IBM dictation package, who wrote that "thought, for many people is very closely linked to language. In keyboarding, users can continue to hone their words while their fingers output an earlier version. In dictation, users may experience more interference between outputting their initial thought and elaborating on it" (Danis et al., 1994).

An important success story for speech recognition is in toys, where dolls and small robots may speak to users and respond to human voice commands. Low-cost speech chips and compact microphones and speakers have enabled designers to include playful systems in high-volume products. Errors often add to the fun and charm of such toys and challenge in games. Proposals for voice-controlled consumer appliances have been made but are yet to be successful.

Current research projects are devoted to improving recognition rates in difficult conditions, eliminating the need for speaker-dependent training, and increasing the vocabularies handled to 100,000 or more words.

Speech recognition for discrete words works well for special-purpose applications, but it does not serve as a general interaction medium. Keyboards, function keys, and pointing devices with direct manipulation are often more rapid, and the actions or commands can be made visible for easy editing. Also, error handling and appropriate feedback with voice input are difficult and slow. However, combinations of voice and direct manipulation may be useful, as indicated by Pausch and Leatherby's study.

9.4.2 Continuous-speech recognition

HAL's ability to understand the astronauts' spoken words and even to read their lips was an appealing fantasy, but the reality is more sobering. Many research projects have pursued *continuous-speech recognition,* and widespread hope for commercially successful products flourished during the dot-com boom. Consumers bought the heavily promoted products, but exaggerated promises led to much disappointment. Speech dictation products work but error rates and error repair are serious problems (Karat et al., 1999; Suhm, Meyers, and Waibel, 1999). In addition, the cognitive burdens of dictation interfere with planning and sentence formation, often reducing the quality of documents when compared with typewritten composition.

A major difficulty for software designers is recognizing the boundaries between spoken words, because normal speech patterns blur the boundaries. Other problems are diverse accents, variable speaking rates, disruptive background noise, and changing emotional intonation. The slips produced by speech-recognition programs make for entertaining sections in product reviews in the trade press. Of course, the most difficult problem is matching the semantic interpretation and contextual understanding that humans apply easily to predict and disambiguate words. This problem was nicely highlighted in one of the few humorous titles of an IBM Technical Report: "How to wreck a nice beach" (a play on "How to recognize speech").

To cope with some of these problems, IBM's speech-dictation system, ViaVoice, is "trained" by users reading standard passages of text (for example, excerpts from *Treasure Island*) for 15 to 30 minutes. Specialized systems for hospital workers (Lai and Vergo, 1997), lawyers, and certain business professionals have become commercial successes, with companies such as Philips producing versions in at least 22 languages. Ironically, technical fields with much jargon are good candidates because of the distinctive nature of the terminology.

Continuous-speech–recognition systems enable users to dictate letters and compose reports verbally for automatic transcription. Review, correction, and revision are usually accomplished with keyboards and displays. Users need practice in dictation and seem to do best with speech input when preparing standard reports. Creative writing and thoughtful articles require full use of the scarce cognitive resources of human working memory. These tasks are often done best with keyboard entry, and some users still prefer the familiarity of pen and paper. Writers can improve their dictation skills with practice, and developers may improve system accuracy, error-correction strategies, and voice-editing methods.

Continuous-speech–recognition systems also enable automatic scanning and retrieval from radio or television programs, court proceedings, lectures, or telephone calls for specific words or topics (Makhoul et al., 2000). These applications can be highly successful and beneficial even when there are errors. Generation of closed-caption text for television programs is also economically advantageous; errors can be irritating, but they are acceptable for most television viewers. The indexing of audio and video archives can also be facilitated by continuous-speech recognition and do not require real-time performance.

Using voice recognition for identification purposes is also a workable feature for security systems. Users are asked to speak a novel phrase, and the system ascertains which of the registered users is speaking. However, ensuring robust performance, coping with users with colds, and dealing with noisy environments are still challenges. Voice graphs are accepted in courtrooms, and they may become useful in security systems.

Although progress has been made by many companies and research groups (Barker, 2003), the following evaluation is still valid: "Comfortable and natural communication in a general setting (no constraints on what you can say and how you say it) is beyond us for now, posing a problem too difficult to solve" (Peacocke and Graf, 1990).

9.4.3   Voice information systems

The appeal of the human voice as a source of information and as a basis for communication is strong. Stored speech is commonly used to provide telephone-based information about tourist sites and government services, and for after-hours messages from organizations. These voice information systems, often called Interactive Voice Response (IVR), can provide good customer service at low cost if proper development methods and metrics are used (Suhm and Peterson, 2002; Gardner-Bonneau, 1999). Voice prompts guide users so they can press keys to check on airline flight departure/arrival times, order drug prescription refills, or reserve theater tickets. The use of speech recognition to short-cut through menu trees can be successful when users know the names of what they seek, such as a city, person, or stock name. However, users become frustrated when the menu structures become complex and deep, or when long voice information segments contain irrelevant information (see Section 7.8). The slow pace of voice output, the ephemeral nature of speech, and the difficulty in scanning/searching remain great challenges, but voice information systems are widely used because they enable services that would otherwise be too expensive; hiring well-trained customer-service representatives available 24 hours a day is not practical for many organizations.

Voice information technologies are also used in popular personal voicemail systems. These telephone-based speech systems enable storing and forwarding of spoken messages with user commands entered with keypads. Users can receive messages, replay messages, reply to the caller, forward messages to other users, delete messages, or archive messages. The automatic elimination of silences and the increase of replay speed, along with frequency shifting to maintain original frequency ranges, can cut listening time in half. Voicemail technology works reliably, is fairly low cost, and is generally liked by users. Problems arise mainly because of the awkwardness of using the 12-key telephone pad for commands, the need to dial in to check whether messages have been left, and the potential for too many "junk" telephone messages because of the ease of broadcasting a message to many people. Some e-mail developers believe that speech recognition for user commands may enable users to gain telephone-based access to their e-mail messages. However, designers are still struggling to find the right balance between guided instruction and user control (Walker et al., 1998). Even if they find good solutions to command input, the three obstacles of voice output (Box 9.2) raise questions about the utility of this application.

Audio recorders are moving toward digital approaches, with small handheld voice note-takers carving out a successful consumer market. Credit-card–sized devices that cost less than $50 can store and randomly access an hour of voice-quality notes. More ambitious handheld devices, such as Apple's iPod, enable users to manage large audio databases and retrieve selected music segments or recorded lecture segments.

Audio tours in museums and audio books have been successful because they allow user control of the pace, while conveying the curator's enthusiasm or author's emotion. Educational psychologists conjecture that, if several senses (sight, touch, hearing) are engaged, then learning can be facilitated. Adding a spoken voice to an instructional system or an online help system may improve the learning process. Adding voice annotation to a document may make it easier for teachers to comment on student papers, or for business executives to leave detailed responses or instructions. But again, the cognitive burdens for speakers, the difficulty in editing voice annotations, and other obstacles (Box 9.2) may mean that adoption will be limited.

९.4.4   Speech generation

Speech generation is a successful technology with widespread application in consumer products and on telephones (Pitt and Edwards, 2003). Inexpensive, compact, reliable systems using digitized speech segments (also called canned speech) have been used in automobile navigation systems ("Turn right onto route M1"), Internet services ("You've got mail"), utility-control rooms ("Danger, temperature rising"), and children's games.

In some cases, the novelty wears off, leading to removal of the speech generation. Talking supermarket checkout machines that read products and prices were found to violate shoppers' sense of privacy about purchases and to be too noisy. Similarly, annoying warnings from cameras ("Too dark—use flash") and automobiles ("Your door is ajar") were replaced with gentler tones and red-light indicators. Spoken warnings in cockpits and control rooms are still used because they are omni-directional and elicit rapid responses. However, even in these environments warnings are sometimes missed, or are in competition with human/human communication.

When algorithms are used to generate the sound (synthesis), the intonation may sound robotlike and distracting. The quality of the sound can be improved when phonemes, words, and phrases from digitized human speech can be smoothly integrated into meaningful sentences. However, for some applications, a computerlike sound may be preferred. For example, the robotlike sounds used in the Atlanta airport subway drew more attention than did a tape recording of a human giving directions.

Applications for the blind are an important success story. Text-to-speech utilities like the built-in Microsoft Windows Narrator can be used to read passages of text in web browsers and word processors. Screen readers like Freedom Scientific's JAWS allow users with visual impairments to productively navigate between windows, select applications, browse graphical interfaces, and of course read text. Such tools rely on textual descriptions being made available for visual elements (labels for icons and image descriptions for graphics). Reading speed is adjustable, to speed up interaction when needed. Book readers are also widely used in libraries. Patrons can place a book on a copierlike device that scans the text and does an acceptable job of reading it. Speech generation for graphical user interfaces and voice browsers for web applications have opened many doors for vision-impaired users. Speech-enabled readers for documents, newspapers, statistical data, and even maps continue to be improved.

Web-based voice applications are also seen as promising by many developers. Standards for voice tagging of web pages (VoiceXML and Speech Application Language Tags, or SALT) and improved software could enable several innovative applications. For example, cell-phone users could access web information through combinations of visual displays and speech-generation output.

Speech generation and digitized speech segments are usually preferable when the messages are simple and short, deal with events in time, and require an immediate response (Michaelis and Wiggins, 1982). Speech becomes advantageous to users when their visual channels are overloaded; when they must be free to move around; or when the environment is too brightly lit, too poorly lit, subject to severe vibration, or otherwise unsuitable for visual displays.

Telephone-based voice information systems may mix digitized speech segments and speech generation to allow appropriate emotional tone and current information presentation. Applications based on keypad selections and limited speech recognition include banking (Fidelity Automated Service Telephone, or FAST), phone directories (British Telecom), and airline schedules (American Airlines Dial-AA-Flight). The ubiquity of telephones makes these services attractive, but an increasing number of users prefer the speed of web-based visual inquiries.

In summary, speech synthesis is technologically feasible. Now, clever designers must find the situations in which it is superior to pre-recorded and digitized human voice messages. Novel applications by way of the telephone, as a supplement to displays, or through embedding in small consumer products all seem attractive.

9.4.5 Non-speech auditory interfaces

In addition to speech, auditory outputs include individual audio tones and more complex information presentation by combinations of sound and music (Rocchesso, Bresin, and Fernstrom, 2003). Research on more sophisticated information presentations often refers to *sonification*, *audiolization*, or *auditory interfaces*. Early Teletypes included a bell tone to alert users that a message was coming or that paper had run out. Later computer systems added a range of tones to indicate warnings or to acknowledge the completion of an action. Keyboards and mobile devices such as digital cameras are built with electronically generated sound feedback. Gaver's SonicFinder (1989) added sound to the Macintosh interface by offering a dragging sound when a file was being dragged, a click when a window boundary was passed, and a thunk when the file was dropped into the trash can for deletion. The effect for most users is a satisfying confirmation of actions; for visually impaired users, the sounds are vital. On the other hand, after a few hours the sounds can become a distraction rather than a contribution, especially in a room with several machines and users.

Sound designers are likely to become more regular participants in new product development, especially for mobile and embedded devices. A useful distinction is between familiar sounds, called *auditory icons*, and created abstract sounds whose meanings must be learned, called *earcons*. Auditory icons, such as a door opening, liquid pouring, or ball bouncing, help reinforce the visual metaphors in a graphical user interface or the product concepts for a toy. Earcons, such as a rising set of tones or a sharp loud sound to draw attention, are effective for mobile devices or in control rooms. Other categories of sound usage include "cartoonified" sounds that exaggerate aspects of familiar sounds, or familiar sounds used in novel ways. Game designers know that sounds can add realism, heighten tension, and engage users in powerful ways.

Clever designers have developed a variety of auditory-interface ideas, such as scroll bars that provide feedback about user actions, maps or charts that provide auditory information, and sonification of tabular data (Brewster, 2002). Beyond presentation of static data, sound can be effective in highlighting data changes and supporting animated changes in presentations. Research continues on auditory methods for emphasizing the distributions of data in information visualization or drawing attention to patterns, outliers, and clusters.

Auditory web browsers for blind users (see Section 1.5.5) or telephonic usage have been developed (Tannen, 1998). Users can hear text and link labels, and then make selections by key entry. Auditory file browsers continue to be refined: each file might have a sound whose frequency is related to its size, and might be assigned an instrument (violin, flute, trumpet). Then, when the directory is opened, each file might play its sound simultaneously or sequentially. Alternatively, files might have sounds associated with their file types, so that users can hear whether there are spreadsheet, graphic, or other text files.

More ambitious auditory interfaces have been proposed in which data are presented as a series of stereophonic or three-dimensional sounds rather than as images (Kramer, 1994; Shinn-Cunningham et al., 1997). The technical problems of generating appropriate three-dimensional "spatial audio" include the measurement of the listener's head-related transfer function (HRTF). Each person's unique head and ear shape and density must be measured to enable algorithms to generate sounds that are perceived as having an origin in space: left-right, up-down, front-back, and near-far. Ambitious goals include giving blind or partially sighted users enough auditory feedback to enable them to follow directions along a busy street or steer a wheelchair through a hospital. Other explorations have included sonification of mass-spectrograph output, allowing operators to hear the differences between a standard and a test sample, or the generation of appealing musical representations of algorithms running on a computer with parallel processors in order to facilitate debugging.

Adding traditional music to user interfaces seems to be an appropriate idea to heighten drama, to relax users, to draw attention, or to set a mood (patriotic marches, romantic sonatas, or gentle waltzes). These approaches have been used in video games and educational packages; they might also be suitable for public-access systems, home-control applications, sales kiosks, bank machines, and other applications.

The potential for novel musical instruments seems especially attractive. With touch-sensitive and haptic devices it is possible to offer appropriate feedback to give musicians an experience similar to a piano keyboard, a drum, or a woodwind or stringed instrument. It is also possible to invent new instruments whose frequencies, amplitudes, and effects are governed by the placement of the touch, as well as by its direction, speed, and acceleration. Music composition using computers expanded as musical-instrument digital-interface (MIDI) hardware and software became widely available at reasonable prices. Newer standards, faster hardware, and innovative user interfaces are now promoting more novel musical instruments (Roads, 1996).

9.5   Displays—Small and Large

The display is the primary source of feedback to users from the computer (Luczak, Cakir, and Cakir, 2002; Helander, 1987). It has many important characteristics, including:

- Physical dimensions (usually the diagonal dimension and depth)
- Resolution (the number of pixels available)
- Number of available colors, color correctness
- Luminance, contrast, and glare
- Power consumption
- Refresh rates (sufficient to allow animation and video)
- Cost
- Reliability

Usage characteristics also distinguish display devices. Portability, privacy, saliency (need to attract attention), ubiquity (likelihood of being able to locate and use the display), and simultaneity (number of simultaneous users) can be used to describe displays (Raghunath and Narayanaswami, 2003). Mobile phones provide displays for portable and private interaction with the device. Ubiquitous television displays allow social interactions between, for example, multiple users controlling characters in video games. Salient information displays found in malls or museums might offer store location information to a single user, or an emotional theatrical experience to dozens of impressed visitors. Whiteboard displays allow collaborators to share information, brainstorm, and make decisions. Immersive displays can transport a user into an imaginary world to learn a new skill.

This section first reviews basic display technologies, then considers the designs of large wall displays and head-mounted displays, followed by displays for mobile devices. It then discusses progress in animation, image, and video technology.

9.5.1   Display technology

For certain applications, *monochrome displays* are adequate and are attractive because of their lower cost. Color displays make video games, educational simulations, computer-assisted design tools, and many other applications more attractive and effective for users (Luczak, Cakir, and Cakir, 2002). There are, nevertheless, some dangers in misusing color and difficulties in ensuring color constancy across devices.

Display technologies include:

- *Raster-scan cathode-ray tubes (CRTs).* These devices are similar to a television monitor, with an electron beam sweeping out lines of dots to form letters and graphics. Early CRT displays were often green because the P39 green phosphor has a long decay time, permitting relatively stable images. CRT sizes (measured diagonally) range from less than 2 inches to more than 30 inches; popular models are in the range of 11 to 17 inches. Once ubiquitous in offices, the bulky CRTs are becoming less and less popular.

- *Liquid-crystal displays (LCDs).* In LCDs, voltage changes influence the polarization of tiny capsules of liquid crystals, turning some spots darker when viewed by reflected light. LCDs are flicker-free. Laptops and handheld computers use LCD displays because of their thin form, light weight, and low electricity consumption. Bright active matrix LCDs with better contrast, improved viewing from oblique angles, and more rapid adaptation to movement have helped LCDs become the leading type of displays. Even desktop users now frequently use flat display panels, as LCD resolutions have moved up from the early 640 x 480 to the now common 1280 x 1024 displays. For a higher cost, higher resolutions such as 3840 x 2400 allow up to 2 double pages to be displayed at a 204-pixels-per-square-inch resolution.

- *Plasma display danels (PDPs).* In PDPs, rows of horizontal wires are slightly separated from vertical wires by small glass-enclosed capsules of neon-based gases. When the horizontal and vertical wires on either side of the capsule receive a high voltage, the gas glows. Like LCDs, plasma displays have a flat profile, but they consume more electricity. They are very bright and visible even from side locations, making them valuable for mounted wall displays of control rooms, public displays, or conference rooms.

- *Light-emitting diodes (LEDs).* In LEDs, certain diodes emit light when a voltage is applied. Early LEDs were mostly red and were used in calculators and watches, but those small devices now use LCDs. Newer LEDs are available in many colors and are being used in large public displays. The curved display used in New York's famous Times Square uses 19 million LEDs to give stock prices, weather information, or news updates with bright graphics. Matrices of miniature LEDs are also used in some head-mounted displays. Manufacturers are actively developing new displays using organic light emitting diodes (OLED). Those durable organic displays are energy efficient and can be laid on flexible plastic or metallic foil leading to new opportunities for wearable or rollable displays.

- *Electronic ink.* New products are appearing that attain paperlike resolution of 80 dots per inch (dpi), with prototypes demonstrating up to 200 dpi. Electronic ink technology uses tiny capsules containing negatively charged black particles and positively changed white particles that can be selectively made visible (Fig. 9.19). Display rates allow some animation but no video displays.

- *Braille displays.* These refreshable displays for blind users provide up 80 cells, each displaying a character. A couple of cells can be mounted on a mouse, and small displays can fit above the keyboard. Prototypes of refreshable graphic displays with up to several thousand pins are being developed.

Health concerns—such as visual fatigue, stress, and radiation exposure—are being addressed by manufacturers and government agencies. Adverse effects

Figure 9.19

E-ink high-resolution portable displays allow readers to adjust distance and orientation, which can improve reading comfort. (www.eink.com)

seem for the most part attributable to the overall work environment more than the visual display units themselves, but research remains active (Luczak, Cakir, and Cakir, 2002).

⁹·5·2   Large displays

The ubiquity of computer displays, from desktops to mobile devices, projectors, and large televisions, lets us envision how integrating all those displays could provide more productive work and play environments. The differentiation might fade in the future, but there are currently three types of large displays. *Informational wall displays* provide shared views to users standing far away from the display, while *interactive wall displays* allow users to walk up to the display and interleave interaction and discussion among participants. Finally, users sitting at their desks can connect *multiple desktop displays* to their computers to have a larger number of windows and documents visible at the same time and within reach of the mouse. Of course, hybrid combinations are possible (Funkhouser and Li, 2000; Guimbretière, Stone, and Winograd, 2001; Swaminathan and Sato, 1997).

Large informational wall displays are effective in control rooms to provide overviews of the system being monitored (Fig. 9.20); details can be retrieved on

Figure 9.20

Multiple high-resolution plasma screens and CRTs are tiled together to present weather, traffic, message sign status, and road conditions information to the operators in the State of Maryland Highway Administration control room. (http://www.chart.state.md.us)

individual consoles. Military command and control operations, utility management, and emergency response are common applications, as large displays help to build situation awareness through a common understanding of the information presented and to facilitate coordination. Wall displays also allow teams of collaborating scientists or decision makers to look at applications that may be running on different computers, locally or remotely, but presented on a single display.

Originally built with matrices of CRTs and made popular in commercial or entertainment settings, wall displays now often use rear-projection techniques. Improved calibration and alignment techniques are leading to seamless tiled displays (Fig. 9.21). When seen from a distance, informational wall displays require bright projectors, but the resolution does not need to be very high—35 dots per inch is sufficient. When users need the close-range interactions of digital whiteboard applications, higher resolution (similar to desktop displays) is required.

Figure 9.21

Users discuss and point at details of the NASA Space Station near the Princeton University wall display. Twenty-four projectors are tiled together to create a seamless image of 6000 x 3000 pixels. (http://www.cs.princeton.edu/omnimedia/)

For interactive wall displays (Fig. 9.22), the traditional desktop interaction techniques, such as indirect-control pointing devices and pull-down menus, become impractical. New techniques are being devised to maintain fluid interaction with freehand sketching or novel menu techniques (see Section 7.7). Even on large interactive group displays, space is limited and designers are exploring new ways to dynamically scale, summarize, and manage the information presented or generated by users on the display.

Simpler digital whiteboard systems such as the SMART Board provide a large touch-sensitive screen on which a computer image is projected. Their functionality is identical to that of the desktop machine, using users' fingers as pointing devices. Colored pens and a digital eraser simulate a traditional whiteboard, augmented with annotation recording and a software keyboard.

Facilitating collaboration between local or remote users (Chapter 10), managing the recording and reuse of brainstorming information, providing new creative tools for artists and performers, or designing new interaction methods

Figure 9.22

Users use a wireless pen to interact with the Stanford Interactive Mural, a 6 x 3.5-foot high-resolution (64 dpi) display used for digital brainstorming. Documents can be brought to the display from different computers or scanners. When moved to the top portion of the screen, documents are scaled down to free some space on the display. (Guimbretière, Stone, and Winograd, 2001)

using mobile devices are examples of challenges and opportunities created by interactive wall displays.

Multiple desktop displays usually employ traditional CRTs or flat panels, which introduce discontinuities in the overall display surface (Fig. 9.23). Those displays can also be of different size or resolution, adding the possibility of misalignments. On the other hand, users can continue interacting with applications in the familiar way, eliminating training as users simply spread windows across displays. Another concern is that multiple desktop displays may require users to rotate their heads or bodies to attend to all displays, and even attentive users might not notice warnings or alarms that are far from their foci of attention. Organized users might assign displays to particular functions (for example, the lefthand display may always show e-mail and calendar applications and the front display always a word processor), but this strategy can be detrimental when the current task would benefit from using the entire display space.

Multiple desktop displays are particularly useful for personal creative applications. For example, creating a Flash application might require a timeline, a stage, graphic-component editors, a scripting-language editor, a directory browser, and a

Figure 9.23

A multiple desktop display with three flat panels.

preview window all open at the same time. Multiple desktop displays might also facilitate side-by-side comparisons of documents, software debugging, and information visualization and analysis. They are usually greatly appreciated by users, and empirical evidence of their benefits is starting to emerge (Czerwinski et al., 2003). Of course, there is a danger that cluttered displays will become more cluttered and that new strategies will be needed to manage them. Also, direct manipulation on large displays can become a challenge because of the distance between objects. Refinements should be made so that the mouse cursor can easily be found and tracked across displays. Rapid focus switching between windows might be facilitated by clicking on small overviews placed at strategic locations on the display. Strategies for automatic window layout and coordination among windows will become critical, but as the cost of displays continues to drop it seems clear that multiple desktop displays or simply larger single displays will become prevalent.

9.5.3   Heads-up and helmet-mounted displays

Personal display technology involves small portable monitors, often made with LCDs in monochrome or color. A *heads-up display* projects information on a partially silvered windscreen of an airplane or car, for example, so that the pilots or drivers can keep their attention focused on the surroundings while receiving computer-generated information.

An alternative, the *helmet- or head-mounted display* (HMD) used in virtual-reality or augmented-reality applications (see Section 6.6 and Fig. 6.16), lets users see information even while turning their heads. In fact, the information that they see may be varied as a function of the direction in which they are looking if the display is equipped with tracking sensors. Different models provide varying levels of visual-field obstruction, audio capabilities, and resolution. For example, the iReality.com CyberEye has an 800 x 600 display and fully obstructed vision. The Private Eye technology uses a line of LEDs and a moving mirror to produce 720 x 280-pixel images in a lightweight and small display that can be mounted on a pair of glasses. This early example of wearable computers focused attention on small portable devices that people could use while moving or accomplishing other tasks, such as jet-engine repair or inventory control, but current technology still requires hardware to be carried in a backpack or users to remain near the base computer.

Attempts to produce 3D displays include vibrating surfaces, holograms, polarized glasses, red/blue glasses, and synchronized shutter glasses (StereoGraphics, eDimensional) that give users a strong sense of 3D stereoscopic vision.

9.5.4   Mobile device displays

The use of mobile devices is becoming widespread in personal and business applications and has the potential to improve medical care, facilitate learning in schools, and contribute to more fulfilling sightseeing experiences (Myers and Beigl, 2003). Medical monitors can alert doctors when a patient's life signs reach a critical level, school children may gather data or solve problems collaboratively using handheld devices, and emergency rescue personnel can evaluate their situation in dangerous environments by using small devices fixed on their suits. Small displays are also finding ways into our homes, with reprogrammable picture frames and other devices, and even onto our bodies, with ever more powerful wristwatches or with jewelry such as the Nokia Medallion that can be personalized with pictures captured with a mobile-phone camera (Fig. 9.24).

Guidelines are slowly emerging from experience with mobile devices (Bergman, 2000; Weiss, 2002). Industry is leading the way by providing useful design case studies (Lindholm, Keinonen, and Kiljander, 2003) and detailed guidelines such as those developed for Palm devices.

With the exception of video games, mobile devices are generally used for brief but routine tasks—for example, dialing a phone, checking appointments, finding a location, or obtaining directions. Therefore, it is critical to optimize the designs for those repetitive tasks, while hiding or eliminating less important functions (see Section 7.8). Whenever possible, data entry should be reduced and complex tasks offloaded to the desktop.

While researchers and developers are steadily increasing the scope of applications for mobile devices, a framework for thinking about the range of actions may be helpful. Whether the application is financial-, medical-, or travel-related, the following five pairs of actions should be considered: (1) *monitor* dynamic information sources and then *alert* when appropriate; (2) *gather* information from many sources and then *spread out* information to many destinations; (3) *participate* in a group and *relate* to individuals; (4) *locate* services or items that are not visible (for example, the nearest gas station) and *identify* objects that are seen

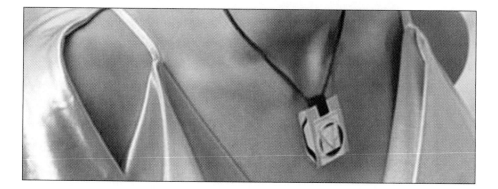

Figure 9.24

Nokia's Medallion (jewelry showing photo of a leaf that was beamed from telephone). (www.nokia.com)

(for example, the name of a person or flower); and (5) *capture* information from local resources and *share* your information with future users.

Most applications for handheld devices are custom designed to take advantage of every pixel available on a particular platform. Designs might also take advantage of zooming to generate animated displays. The calendar application DateLens (Fig. 9.25) allows compact overviews of available meeting times, feedback on conflicting appointments, and quick zooming on specific weeks or dates on small displays of any size, from handheld devices to desktops. DateLens can

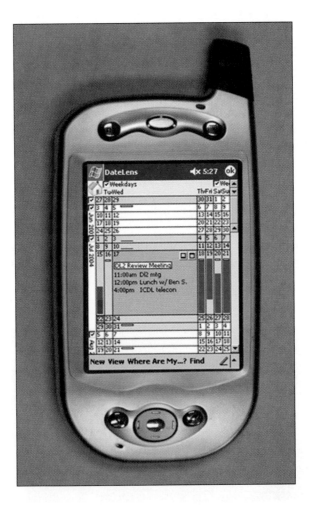

Figure 9.25

DateLens is a calendar interface for mobile devices using a fisheye representation of dates coupled with compact overviews, user control over the visible time period, and integrated search capabilities. (Bederson et al., 2004)

be effective because the layout of overviews by week or month is familiar to users and color-coding or abbreviations can be learned quickly (Bederson et al., 2004).

Poor readability will be an issue in low light or for users with poor eyesight, and users will appreciate the ability to adjust font size. Reading on small screens might also be improved with *rapid serial visual presentation* (RSVP), which presents text dynamically at a constant speed or at a speed adapted to the content. Using RSVP, a 33% improvement was measured in speed of reading for small texts, while no differences were found for long texts (Oquist and Goldstein, 2003).

Some applications, such as web searching and browsing, remain very ineffective on small displays (Jones, Buchanan, and Thimbledy, 2003). Custom redesigns are preferable but not always feasible. There are several approaches for migrating information from full-sized to small displays (MacKay and Watters, 2003). Direct data migration into long scrollable displays might be acceptable for linear reading but makes comparisons within the document difficult. Data modification involves summarizing text or creating smaller pictures. It is effective to provide quick access to all parts of the documents and allow users to request more information. Data suppression can be done by eliminating sections of the document, or selectively sampling words. Finally, compact overviews using visualization techniques (Section 14.5) can provide access to all of the original information.

As mobile devices become information appliances, they may contribute to the goal of bridging the digital divide. These low-cost devices, which are easier to learn, may enable a wider range of people to benefit from information and communication technologies. For users with disabilities, mobile telecommunication devices offer a unique opportunity to design *modality translation services*, as described by a project of the Trace Center at the University of Wisconsin: Remote services can provide instant translation from one presentation mode to another, anywhere and at any time, via mobile devices. This permits text-to-speech, sign-language, international-language, and language-level translation, as well as print recognition and image/video description services. Modality translation could benefit people with disabilities and people who have no disabilities but experience functional limitations when driving their cars, visiting a foreign country, or touring a museum without reading glasses.

9.5.5 Animation, image, and video

Besides improvements in display technology, dramatic progress has recently been made in computer graphics. Dazzling 3D modeling and animations, impressive high-resolution photographs and satellite images, and videos streamed from the World Wide Web are changing the nature of what is being presented on the displays.

Accelerated graphics hardware (available from NVidia or 3Dlab, for example) has led to increasing use of animation and motion pictures. Startling images have been created by George Lucas's Industrial Light and Magic and by Pixar Animated Studios. Many television commercials, station-identification segments, and news-related graphics have been constructed by computer animation. Video games are another source of impressive computer-graphics imagery. Finally, even end users can design creative animations with standard tools such as Flash, or animate 3D creatures with Alice (Conway et al., 2000). The ACM's SIGGRAPH (Special Interest Group on Graphics) has an exciting annual conference with exhibitions of novel graphics devices and applications. The conference proceedings and videotape digest are rich sources of information.

Scientific exploration, government or business archiving, medicine, surveillance, and even personal-life recording are generating immense archives of digital imagery that need to be stored, searched, browsed, and analyzed. Digital photography first became widespread in the news media and photographic agencies, where rapid electronic editing and dissemination are paramount. Professional and amateur photographers warmed up quickly to digital cameras when they became affordable. Downloading to personal computers has been simplified, and sharing albums on the World Wide Web is a popular pursuit. Special hardware and software is being developed to cater to the needs of professionals such as real-estate agents or insurance-claim adjustors who make heavy use of photographs in their reports and need rapid annotation and publishing methods.

The increasing use of images has stimulated the need to be able to scan photos, maps, documents, and handwritten notes. Page-sized scanners with 2,400-points-per-inch resolution are commonly available, and larger scanners with higher resolutions can be had for higher prices. Scanning packages often include optical character recognition (OCR) software that can convert text in printed documents into electronic forms with fairly good recognition reliability, but verification is necessary for demanding applications. Handheld scanners allow the rapid capture of small amounts of text for note taking, and phones equipped with small cameras are an engaging way to capture touching memories or to document work processes.

Digital video is also evolving rapidly. The first generation of interactive video applications was based on videodisk sources provided by producers who have access to interesting visual resources. Producers such as National Geographic (GEO) and the Library of Congress (American Memory) generated videodisks with tens of thousands of still images and hundreds of motion video segments. The 12-inch videodisks could store up to 54,000 still images or 30 minutes of motion video per side. Access time was in the order of a second. In an early application, Abbe Don, a multimedia artist who created "We Make Memories," used a HyperCard stack and a videodisk to display family history as told by herself, her sister, her mother, and her grandmother. In this electronic version of a family photo album, events took on universal themes, and the emotional engagement foretells future applications that deal more with the heart than the head.

CD-ROMs, the successors to videodisks, can store 750 megabytes of textual or numeric data, or approximately 6,000 graphic images, one hour of uncompressed music, or 6 to 72 minutes (depending on effectiveness of compression and the resolution of the images) of motion video. CD-ROMs are being used extensively by libraries and museums to disseminate information about their multimedia collections. *Digital versatile disks* (DVDs) allow the storage of two hours of medium-resolution video, and their use and acceptance has spread quickly.

Since image or video storage can consume many megabytes, efficient and rapid compression and decompression techniques are vital. The *Motion Picture Experts Group* (MPEG) approach has made digital-video Internet servers a workable reality, even for full-length motion pictures. MPEG algorithms can compress one second of full-motion video into about 150 kilobytes, or approximately 5 kilobytes per frame. MPEG algorithms attempt to store only differences across frames, so that stable images are compressed more than active or panning sequences. With sufficient network speed, video can be streamed to users in real time, eliminating the need for local storage of the material. Music compression with standards such as MPEG Audio Layer 3 (MP3) is very effective and is a particularly hot subject of debate as the rapid proliferation of online music-sharing environments (Napster, Gnutella, KazaA) conflicts with publishers' goals and authors' rights. User-interface issues for these audio and video environments are just beginning to be explored. For retrieval-oriented applications, the key question is how to find the desired multimedia document in a library or a segment within a two-hour long document (see Section 14.3).

Computer-based video-conferencing systems allow users to send images over normal telephone lines in compressed data formats in a fraction of a second for low-resolution images and in from 5 to 30 seconds for higher-resolution images. Increasingly available higher-speed lines—such as DSL, cable TV or direct broadcast satellites—are enabling good-quality images and video to be used in a wide range of applications.

As the amount of multimedia materials available to the general public increases steadily, designers and managers need to remain vigilant to address the needs of users with disabilities by providing multiple representations of the information. Video can be close captioned, audio recordings transcribed, and images or photographs supplemented by text descriptions. This information in turn facilitates language translation, indexing, and retrieval of the materials for the benefit of everyone.

9.6 Printers

Even when they have good-quality, high-speed displays, people still have a strong desire for hardcopy printouts. Paper documents can be easily copied, transported, mailed, marked, and stored, and they give a sense of ownership and control. The following are important criteria for printers:

- Speed
- Print quality
- Cost
- Compactness
- Quietness of operation
- Type and size of paper
- Support for special formats
- Reliability

Early computer printers worked at 10 characters per second and did not support graphics. *Thermal printers* (still used in some Fax machines) offered quiet, compact, and inexpensive output on specially coated or plain paper. Personal-computer *dot-matrix printers* have been replaced by *inkjet printers* that offer quieter operation and quality black-and-white or color output on plain paper. When large volumes of printing are needed, systems on mainframe computers with *impact-line printers* have all but vanished in favor of *laser printers* that operate at up to 30,000 lines per minute. Speeds vary from 4 to 40 pages per minute; resolution ranges from 200 to 1,200 dots per inch. Color laser printers or dye-transfer methods bring the satisfaction of bright and sharp color images, but at a higher price, especially when considering the price of ink cartridges.

Plotters enable output of graphs, bar charts, line drawings, and maps on rolls of paper or sheets up to 100 by 150 centimeters. Plotters may have single pens, multiple pens, or inkjets for color output. Other design factors are the precision of small movements, the accuracy in placement of the pens, the speed of pen motion, the repeatability of drawings, and the software support. *Photographic printers* allow the creation of 35-millimeter or larger slides (transparencies) and photographic prints. Software to permit publication-quality typesetting opened the door to *desktop-publishing* ventures that produce elegant business documents, scientific reports, novels, or personal correspondence, and very little printing is done without computer layout.

For blind users *Braille embossers* allow printing of text documents, while *tactile graphics* can be produced by using thermal paper-expansion machines (Fig. 9.26). While the process for producing a raised image is easy, the equipment is expensive, and designing effective tactile graphics is challenging as images have to remain simple and be consistent with Braille labels and symbols.

Finally, *three-dimensional printers* allow custom objects to be printed in three dimensions. They have been used to develop prototypes of new devices, to individually adapt existing devices to users with physical disabilities, and to create custom shapes for tangible interfaces (see Fig. 6.19).

Figure 9.26

A blind student uses a Touch Graphics tactile map mounted on a touchscreen. Audio descriptions provide information about regions of the map. (http://www.touchgraphics.com/)

Practitioner's Summary

Choosing hardware always involves making a compromise between the ideal and the practical. The designer's vision of what an input or output device should be must be tempered by the realities of what is commercially available within the project budget. Devices should be tested in the application domain to verify the manufacturer's claims, and testimonials or suggestions from users should be obtained.

New devices and refinements to old devices appear regularly; device-independent architecture and software permit easy integration of novel devices. Avoid being locked into one device, as the hardware is often the softest part of the system. Also, remember that a successful software idea can become even more successful if reimplementation on other devices is easy to achieve and if cross-modality permits users with disabilities to access the system. Remember Fitts's law to optimize speed of performance and consider two-handed operations.

Keyboard entry is here to stay, but always consider other forms of input when text entry is limited. Selecting rather than typing has many benefits for both novice and frequent users. Direct-pointing devices are faster and more convenient for novices than are indirect-pointing devices, and accurate pointing is possible.

Speech input and output devices are commercially viable and should be applied where appropriate, but take care to ensure that performance is genuinely improved over other interaction strategies. Display technology is moving rapidly, and user expectations are increasing. Higher-resolution and larger displays are becoming prevalent. Resist the temptation to provide too many features on portable devices, and relegate rarely used features and most data entry to the desktop. Provide high-quality hardcopy output.

Researcher's Agenda

Novel text-entry keyboards to speed input and to reduce error rates will have to provide significant benefits to displace the well-entrenched QWERTY design. For the numerous applications that do require extensive text entry, or for mobile devices, many opportunities remain to create special-purpose devices or to redesign the tasks to permit direct-manipulation selection instead of keyboarding. Increasingly, input can be accomplished via conversion or extraction of data from online sources. Another input source is optical character recognition of printed text or of bar codes printed in magazines, on bank statements, in books, or on music recordings.

Research on speech systems could be directed at redesigning the applications to make more effective use of the speech input and output technology. Complete and accurate continuous-speech recognition does not seem attainable, but if users will modify their speaking styles in specific applications, more progress is possible. Another worthy direction is to improve continuous-speech recognition for such tasks as finding a given phrase in a large body of recorded speech, or to combine speech and image recognition for video captioning and describing.

The range of display sizes available has widened enormously, and users need applications that can operate on mobile devices, desktops, and large wall displays. We need to understand how to design plastic or multimodal interfaces that allow users to adapt their interfaces depending on the environment, preferences, and abilities. What are the strategies for increasing productivity with multiple screens? Sensors embedded in the environment and in many mobile devices can provide information about users' locations or activities to enable development of context-aware applications. The benefits may be large, but inconsistent behavior and privacy concerns will have to be addressed before adoption becomes widespread.

Among the most exciting developments will be the increased facility for manipulating video and images. Many possibilities will open with faster image-processing hardware and algorithms and cheaper image input, storage, and output devices. How will people search for images, integrate images with text, or modify images? What level of increased visual literacy will schools expect? How can animation be used as a more common part of computer applications?

WORLD WIDE WEB RESOURCES

Rich resources are available on commercial input devices, especially pointing and handwriting input devices. Commercial packages, software tools, and demonstrations are available for speech generation and recognition. MIDI tools and virtual-reality devices enable serious hobbyists and researchers to create novel experiences for users. Novel strategies and uses for large displays emerge frequently from research and product groups.

http://www.aw.com/DTUI

References

Abowd, G. and Mynatt, E., Charting past, present, and future research in ubiquitous computing, *ACM Transactions on Computer-Human Interaction*, 7, 1 (2000), 29–58.

Accot, J. and Zhai, S., More than dotting the i's—Foundations for crossing-based interfaces, *Proc. CHI '02 Conference: Human Factors in Computing Systems*, ACM Press, New York (2002), 73–80.

Ashcraft, Mark H., *Cognition, Third Edition*, Prentice-Hall, Englewood Cliffs, NJ (2001).

Baggi, D. L., Computer-generated music, *IEEE Computer*, 24, 7 (July 1991), 6–9.

Balentine, B., Morgan, D. P., and Meisel, W. S., *How to Build a Speech Recognition Application: A Style Guide for Telephony Dialogues, Second Edition*, Enterprise Integration Group, San Ramon, CA (2001).

Barker, D., Microsoft Research spawns a new era in speech technology, *PC AI Magazine*, 16, 6 (2003), 17–27.

Bederson, B. B., Clamage, A., Czerwinski, M. P., and Robertson, G. G., DateLens: A fisheye calendar interface for PDAs, *ACM Transactions on Computer-Human Interaction* 11, 1 (2004).

Bergman, E., *Information Appliances and Beyond*, Morgan Kaufmann Publishers, San Francisco, CA (2000).

Brewster, S. A., Non-speech auditory output, in Jacko, J. and Sears, A. (Editors), *Human Computer Interaction Handbook*, Lawrence Erlbaum Associates, Mahwah, NJ (2002), 220–239.

Card, S. K., Mackinlay, J. D., and Robertson, G. G., A morphological analysis of the design space of input devices, *ACM Transactions on Information Systems*, 9, 2 (1991), 99–122.

Christian, K., Kules, B., Shneiderman, B., and Youssef, A., A comparison of voice controlled and mouse controlled web browsing, *Proc. 4th International ACM Conference on Assistive Technologies (ASSETS)*, ACM Press, New York (2000), 72–79.

Conway, M., Audia, S., Burnette, T., Cosgrove, D., and Christiansen, K., Alice: Lessons learned from building a 3D system for novices, *Proc. CHI '00 Conference: Human Factors in Computing Systems*, ACM Press, New York (2000), 486–493.

Czerwinski, M., Smith, G., Regan, T., Meyers, B., Robertson, G., and Starkweather, G., Toward characterizing the productivity benefits of very large displays, in Rauterberg, M. et al. (Editors), *Proc. INTERACT '03*, IOS Press (2003), 9–16.

Danis, C., Comerford, L., Janke, E., Davies, K., DeVries, J., and Bertran, A., StoryWriter: A speech oriented editor, Proc. CHI '94 Conference: *Human Factors in Computing Systems: Conference Companion*, ACM Press, New York (1994), 277–278.

English, W. K., Engelbart, D. C., and Berman, M. L., Display-selection techniques for text manipulation, *IEEE Transactions on Human Factors in Electronics*, HFE–8, 1 (March 1967), 5–15.

Fitts, P. M., The information capacity of the human motor system in controlling amplitude of movement, *Journal of Experimental Psychology*, 47 (1954), 381–391.

Fitzmaurice, G., Ishii, H., and Buxton, W., Laying the foundation for graspable user interfaces, *Proc. CHI '95 Conference: Human Factors in Computing Systems*, ACM Press, New York (1995), 442–449.

Foley, J. D., Wallace, V. L., and Chan, P., The human factors of computer graphics interaction techniques, *IEEE Computer Graphics and Applications*, 4, 11 (November 1984), 13–48.

Frankish, C., Hull, R., and Morgan, P., Recognition accuracy and user acceptance of pen interfaces, *Proc. CHI '95 Conference: Human Factors in Computing Systems*, ACM Press, New York (1995), 503–510.

Funkhouser, T. and Li, K. (Editors), Onto the wall: Large displays, *IEEE Computer Graphics and Applications*, 20, 4 (July/August 2000).

Gardner-Bonneau, Daryle (Editor), *Human Factors and Voice Interactive Systems*, Kluwer Academic Publishers, Boston, MA (1999).

Gaver, W. W., The SonicFinder: An interface that uses auditory icons, *Human-Computer Interaction*, 4, 1 (1989), 67–94.

Grossman, T., Balakrishnan, R., Kurtenbach, G., Fitzmaurice, G. W., Khan, A., and Buxton, W., Creating principal 3D curves with digital tape drawing, *ACM CHI Letters*, 4, 1 (2002), 121–128.

Guiard, Y., Asymmetric division of labor in human skilled bimanual action: The kinematic chain as a model, *Journal of Motor Behavior*, 19, 4 (1987), 486–517.

Guiard, Y., Bourgeois, F., Mottet, D., and Beaudouin-Lafon, M., Beyond the 10-bit barrier: Fitts' law in multi-scale electronic worlds, in *People and Computers XV—Interaction Without Frontiers (Joint Proceedings of HCI 2001 and IHM 2001)*, Springer-Verlag, London, U.K. (2001), 573–587.

Guimbretière, F., Paper augmented digital documents, *Proc. UIST Symposium on User Interface Software & Technology*, ACM Press, New York (2003), 51–60.

Guimbretière, F., Stone, M., and Winograd, T., Fluid interaction with high-resolution wall-size displays, *Proc. UIST 200 Symposium on User Interface Software & Technology*, ACM Press, New York (2001), 21–30.

Haller, R., Mutschler, H., and Voss, M., Comparison of input devices for correction of typing errors in office systems, *Proc. INTERACT '84* (1984), 218–223.

Helander, M. G., Design of visual displays, in Salvendy, G. (Editor), *Handbook of Human Factors*, John Wiley & Sons, New York (1987), 507–548.

Hinckley, K., Input technologies and techniques, in Jacko, J. and Sears, A. (Editors), *The Human-Computer Interaction Handbook*, Laurence Erlbaum Associates, Mahwah, NJ (2003), 151–168.

Hinckley, K., Pierce, J., Sinclair, M., and Horvitz, E., Sensing techniques for mobile interaction, *Proc. UIST 2000 Symposium on User Interface Software & Technology*, CHI Letters, 2, 2 (2000), 91–100.

Hourcade, J.-P., Bederson, B., Druin, A., and Guimbretière, F., Differences in pointng task performance between preschool children and adults using mice, *ACM Transactions on Computer-Human Interaction* (2004).

Ishii, H. and Ullmer, B., Tangible bits: Towards seamless interfaces between people, bits and atoms, *Proc. CHI '97 Conference: Human Factors in Computing Systems*, ACM Press, New York (1997), 234–241.

Iwata, H., Haptic interfaces, in Jacko, J. and Sears, A. (Editors), *The Human-Computer Interaction Handbook*, Laurence Erlbaum Associates, Mahwah, NJ (2003), 206–219.

Jacob, R. J. K., Sibert, L. E., McFarlane, D. C., and Mullen, Jr., M. P., Integrality and separability of input devices, *ACM Transactions on Computer-Human Interaction*, 1, 1 (March 1994), 3–26.

Jones, M., Buchanan, G., and Thimbledy, H., Improving web search on small screen devices. *Interacting with Computers (special issue on HCI with Mobile Devices)*, 15, 4 (2003), 479–496.

Karat, C., Halverson, C., Horn, D. and Karat, J., Patterns of entry and correction in large vocabulary continuous speech recognition systems, *Proc. CHI '99 Conference: Human Factors in Computing Systems*, ACM Press, New York (1999), 568–575.

Karl, L., Pettey, M., and Shneiderman, B., Speech versus mouse commands for word processing applications: An empirical evaluation, *International Journal for Man-Machine Studies*, 39, 4 (1993), 667–687.

Kramer, G. (Editor), *Auditory Display: Sonification, Audification, and Auditory Interfaces*, Addison-Wesley, Reading, MA (1994).

Kroemer, K. H. E., Operation of ternary chorded keys, *International Journal of Human-Computer Interaction*, 5, 3 (1993), 267–288.

Lai, J. and Vergo, J., MedSpeak: Report creation with continuous speech recognition, *Proc. CHI '97 Conference: Human Factors in Computing Systems*, ACM Press, New York (1997), 431–438.

Lindholm, C., Keinonen, T., and Kiljander, H., *Mobile Usability: How Nokia Changed the Face of the Mobile Phone*, McGraw-Hill, New York (2003).

Luczak, H., Roetting, M., and Oehme, O., Visual displays, in Jacko, J. and Sears, A. (Editors), *The Human-Computer Interaction Handbook*, Laurence Erlbaum Associates, Mahwah, NJ (2003), 187–205.

Luczak, H., Cakir, A. E., and Cakir, G. (Editors), *Proc. 6th International Scientific Conference on Work With Display Units, WWDU 2002* (2002).

MacKay, B. and Watters, C., The impact of migration of data to small screens on navigation, *IT & Society*, 1, 3 (2003), 90–101. Available at http://itandsociety.org.

Mackay, W. E., Pothier, G., Letondal, C., Bøegh, K., and Sørensen, H.E. The missing link: Augmenting biology laboratory notebooks, *Proc. UIST '02 Symposium on User Interface Software & Technology*, ACM Press, New York (2002), 41–50.

MacKenzie, S., Fitts' law as a research and design tool in human-computer interaction, *Human-Computer Interaction*, 7 (1992), 91–139.

MacKenzie, S., Kober, H., Smith, D., Jones, T., and Skepner, E., On the move: LetterWise: prefix-based disambiguation for mobile text input, *Proc. UIST 2001 Symposium on User Interface Software & Technology*, ACM Press, New York (2001), 111–120.

MacKenzie, S. and Soukoreff, R. W., Text entry for mobile computing: Models and methods, theory and practice, *Human-Computer Interaction*, 17, 2 (2002), 147–198.

MacKenzie, S., Tauppinen, T., and Silfverberg, M., Accuracy measures for evaluating computer pointing devices, *Proc. CHI '01 Conference: Human Factors in Computing Systems*, ACM Press, New York (2001), 9–16.

Majaranta, P. and Raiha, K.-J., Twenty years of eye typing: Systems and design issues, *Proc. Eye Tracking Research & Applications Symposium (ETRA)* (2002), 15–22.

Makhoul, J., Kubala, F., Leek, T., Liu, D., Long, N., Schwartz, R., and Srivastava, A., Speech and language technologies for audio indexing and retrieval, *Proceedings of the IEEE*, 88, 8 (August 2000), 1338–1352.

Michaelis, P. R. and Wiggins, R. H., A human factors engineer's introduction to speech synthesizers, in Badre, A. and Shneiderman, B. (Editors), *Directions in Human-Computer Interaction*, Ablex, Norwood, NJ (1982), 149–178.

Mithal, A. K. and Douglas, S. A., Differences in movement microstructure of the mouse and the finger-controlled isometric joystick, *Proc. CHI '96 Conference: Human Factors in Computing Systems*, ACM Press, New York (1996), 300–307.

Montemayor, M., Druin, A., Guha, M. L., Farber, A., Chipman, G., Tools for children to create physical interactive StoryRooms, *ACM Computers in Entertainment*, 1, 2 (2004).

Montgomery, E. B., Bringing manual input into the twentieth century, *IEEE Computer*, 15, 3 (March 1982), 11–18.

Myers, B. and Beigl, M., Introduction to the special issue on handheld computing, *IEEE Computer*, 39, 9 (2003), 27–29.

Myers, B., Using hand-held devices and PCs together, *Communications of the ACM*, 44, 11 (November 2001), 34–41.

Nakaseko, M., Grandjean, E., Hunting, W., and Gierer, R., Studies of ergonomically designed alphanumeric keyboards, *Human Factors*, 27, 2 (1985), 175–187.

Oquist, G. and Goldstein, M., Towards an improved readability on mobile devices: Evaluating adaptative rapid serial visual presentation, *Interacting with Computers*, 15, 4 (2003), 539–558.

Oviatt, Sharon, Darrell, Trevor, and Flickner, Myron, Multimodal interfaces that flex, persist, and adapt, *Communications of the ACM*, 47, 1 (January 2004), 30–33.

Pausch, R. and Leatherby, J. H., An empirical study: Adding voice input to a graphical editor, *Journal of the American Voice Input/Output Society*, 9, 2 (July 1991), 55–66.

Peacocke, R. D. and Graf, D. H., An introduction to speech and speaker recognition, *IEEE Computer*, 23, 8 (August 1990), 26–33.

Pitt, I. and Edwards, A., *Design of Speech-based Devices: A Practical Guide*, Springer-Verlag, London, U.K. (2003).

Raghunath, M. and Narayanaswami, C., Fostering a symbiotic handheld environment, *IEEE Computer*, 36, 9 (2003) 57–65.

Roads, C., *The Computer Music Bible*, MIT Press, Cambridge, MA (1996).

Rocchesso, Davide, Bresin, Roberto, and Fernstrom, Mikael, Sounding objects, *IEEE Multimedia*, 10, 2 (April–June 2003), 42–52.

Sears, A., Plaisant, C., and Shneiderman, B., A new era for touchscreen applications: High-precision, dragging, and direct manipulation metaphors, in Hartson, R. H. and Hix, D. (Editors), *Advances in Human-Computer Interaction, Volume 3*, Ablex, Norwood, NJ (1992), 1–33.

Sears, A., Revis, D., Swatski, J., Crittenden, R., and Shneiderman, B., Investigating touchscreen typing: The effect of keyboard size on typing speed, *Behaviour & Information Technology*, 12, 1 (Jan–Feb 1993), 17–22.

Sears, A. and Shneiderman, B., High precision touchscreens: Design strategies and comparison with a mouse, *International Journal of Man-Machine Studies*, 34, 4 (April 1991), 593–613.

Sears, A., Lin, M., and Karimullah, A. S., Speech-based cursor control: Understanding the effects of target size, cursor speed, and command selection, *Universal Access in the Information Society*, 2, 1 (November 2002), 30–43.

Shinn-Cunningham, B. G., Lehnert, H., Kramer, G., Wenzel, E. M., and Durlach, N. I., Auditory displays, in Gilkey, R. and Anderson, T. (Editors), *Binaural and Spatial Hearing in Real and Virtual Environments*, Lawrence Erlbaum Associates, Mahwah, NJ (1997), 611–663.

Shneiderman, B., Touch screens now offer compelling uses, *IEEE Software*, 8, 2 (March 1991), 93–94, 107.

Suhm, B., Meyers, B., and Waibel, A., Empirical and model-based evaluation of multimodal error correction, *Proc. CHI '99 Conference: Human Factors in Computing Systems*, ACM Press, New York (1999), 584–591.

Suhm, B. and Peterson, P., A data-driven methodology for evaluating and optimizing call center IVRs, *International Journal of Speech Technology*, 5, 1 (2002), 23–38.

Swaminathan, K. and Sato, S., Interaction design for large displays, *ACM Interactions*, (January–February 1997), 15–24.

Tannen, Robert S., Breaking the sound barrier: Designing auditory displays for global usability, *Proc. 4th Conference on Human Factors and the Web* (1998). Available at http://www.research.att.com/conf/hfweb.

Tsang, M., Fitzmaurice, G. W., Kurtenbach, G., Khan, A., and Buxton, W. A. S., Boom Chameleon: Simultaneous capture of 3D viewpoint, voice and gesture annotations on a spatially-aware display, *Proc. UIST 2002 Symposium on User Interface Software & Technology, CHI Letters*, 4, 2 (2002), 111–120.

Vanderheiden, G. Cross-disability access to touch screen kiosks and ATMs, *Advances in Human Factors/ Ergonomics, 21A, HCI International Conference* (1997), 417–420

Vanderheiden, G., Kelso, D., and Krueger, M., Extended usability versus accessibility in voting systems, *Proceedings of the RESNA 27th Annual Conference*, Orlando (2004).

Walker, M. A., Fromer, J., Di Fabbrizio, G., Mestel, C., and Hindle, D., What can I say? Evaluating a spoken language interface to email, *Proc. CHI 2002 Conference: Human Factors in Computing Systems*, ACM Press, New York (1998), 582–589.

Ward, D., Blackwell, A., and MacKay, D., Dasher—A data entry interface using continuous gestures and language models, *Proc. UIST 2000 Symposium on User Interface Software & Technology*, ACM Press, New York (2000), 129–137.

Ware, C. and Baxter, C., Bat Brushes: On the uses of six position and orientation parameters in a paint program, *Proc. CHI '89 Conference: Human Factors in Computing Systems*, ACM Press, New York (1989), 155–160.

Weinschenk, S. and Barker, D. T., *Designing Effective Speech Interfaces*, John Wiley & Sons, New York (2000).

Weiser, M., The computer for the twenty-first century, *Scientific American*, 265, 3 (1991) 94–104.

Weiss, S., *Handheld Usability*, John Wiley & Sons, New York (2002).

Wobbrock, J., Myers, B., and Kembel, J., EdgeWrite: A stylus-based text entry method designed for high accuracy and stability of motion, *Proc. UIST '03 Symposium on User Interface Software & Technology*, ACM Press, New York (2003), 61–70.

Wobbrock, J., Myers, B., and Kembel, J., EdgeWrite: A stylus-based text entry method designed for high accuracy and stability of motion, *Proc. UIST '03 Symposium on User Interface Software & Technology*, ACM Press, New York (2003), 61–70.

Zhai, S., User performance in relation to 3D input device design, *Computer Graphics*, 32, 4 (November 1998), 50–54.

Zhai, S., What's in the eyes for attentive input, *Communications of the ACM*, 46, 3 (March 2003), 34–39.

Zhai, S., Smith, B., and Selker, T., Improving browsing performance: A study of four input devices for scrolling and pointing tasks, *Proc. INTERACT '97* (1997), 286–292.

chapter

10 Collaboration

Three helping one another will do as much as six working singly.

SPANISH PROVERB

written in collaboration with Jenny Preece

10.1   Introduction

The introversion and isolation of early computer users has given way to lively online communities of busily interacting teams and bustling crowds of chatty users. The pursuit of human connections has prompted millions of users to join listservers, visit chat rooms, and fill online communities with useful information and supportive responses, peppered with outrageous humor. But, as in most human communities, there is also controversy, anger, slander, and pornography. The World Wide Web has dramatically enriched textual communications with colorful graphics and sometimes too-dazzling Java or Flash animations. The Web is sometimes derided as a playground, but serious work and creative endeavors are enormously facilitated by the easy flow of information it provides. Cell phones and mobile devices have also expanded the possibilities for communication by voice, text messages, digital photos, and videos.

The expanding options for online computing and communication have benefits for everyone. Playful and social personalities enjoy laughing with siblings and surprising their friends halfway around the world. Goal-directed individuals quickly recognize the benefits of electronic collaboration and the potentials for business in the networked global village. The distance to colleagues can now be measured not in miles or kilometers, but rather in intellectual compatibility and responsiveness; a close friend is someone who responds from across an ocean within three minutes at 3:00 A.M. with the rare music file that you long to hear.

The good news is that computing, once seen as alienating and antihuman, is becoming a socially respectable and interpersonally positive force. Enthusiasts hail collaborative interfaces, such as groupware for team processes, health support groups, collaborative virtual environments, and other communal utopias. However, these new media have limitations, and there may be a dark side to the force. Will the speedup in work rates reduce quality, increase burn-out, or undermine loyalty? Can collaborative interfaces be turned into oppressive tools or confrontive environments? Does intimacy survive when participants are remote in time and physical space? Can laughter, hugs, and tears mean the same thing for electronic-dialog partners as for face-to-face partners?

The first steps in understanding the social dimension of technology are to understand its terminology and scope. Although the conferences on *computer-supported cooperative work* have established *CSCW* as a new acronym, the organizers still debate whether that acronym covers *cooperative, collaborative,* and *competitive* work and whether it includes play, family activities, and educational experiences. CSCW researchers focus on designing and evaluating new technologies to support work processes, but some researchers also study social exchanges, learning, games, and entertainment. The implementers and marketers quickly gravitated to *groupware* as a term to describe the team-oriented commercial products (Baecker, 1993; Beaudouin-Lafon, 1999). For educators, the movement towards social-construction theories of learning has been furthered by the World Wide Web and by collaborative classroom tools and techniques (Hiltz, 1992; Hazemi and Hailes, 2001). For consumers, the cell phone is part of the infrastructure for social relationships; giving out your phone number is a step in the direction of personal intimacy and business trust.

Extrapolating current trends leads to the suggestion that most computer-based tasks will become collaborative, just as most work environments have social aspects. When theorists pointed out the situated nature of interaction (see Section 2.4.6), they were drawing attention to the ways in which users were embedded in physical and social environments. But these claims were more than academic abstractions. Leading designers already support users' needs to learn from colleagues, consult with partners, annotate documents received from associates, and present results to managers. These designers also have started to design software that accommodates interruptions from co-workers, deals with privacy, and establishes responsibility. It may be useful to think of collaboration as the motivating force for using computers. Under this way of thinking, direct manipulation of display elements is part of a larger goal, which might be labeled *direct collaboration*. This expansion of scope for interaction designers is why Part II of this book includes collaboration—it is a design requirement for most interfaces.

This chapter begins with an analysis of why people collaborate, then presents a 2 × 2 matrix of collaborative interfaces to support the needs people have. The next three sections cover asynchronous distributed, synchronous distributed, and face-to-face interfaces. Section 10.3 focuses on electronic mail, collaborative interfaces such as newsgroups and listservers, and the more ambitious online and networked communities. Section 10.4 covers synchronous distributed tools such as chat, instant messaging, texting, and video conferencing. Section 10.5 addresses the growing array of face-to-face software for electronic meetings and shared displays.

10.2   Goals of Collaboration

People collaborate because doing so is satisfying or productive. Collaboration can have purely emotionally rewarding purposes or specific task-related goals. It can be sought personally or imposed managerially. It can be a one-time encounter or an enduring partnership. Analyzing these varied situations for collaborative interfaces is facilitated by understanding the processes and strategies of the participants:

- *Focused partnerships* are collaborations between two or three people who need each other to complete a task, such as joint authors of a technical report, two pathologists consulting about a cancer patient's biopsy, programmers debugging a program together, or an astronaut and a ground controller repairing a faulty satellite. The growing set of partnerships involves consumers who may negotiate with a travel agent, stock broker, or customer-support staffer. Often, there are electronic documents or images to "conference over." Partners can use electronic mail, chat, instant messaging (IM), telephone, voice mail, video conferencing, or a combination of these technologies. Newer strategies enable partnering through mobile devices, such as text messaging (texting) or photo exchanging from cell phones.

- *Lecture or demo* formats have one person sharing information with many users at remote sites. The start time and duration are the same for all; questions may be asked by the recipients. No history keeping is required, but a replay capability is helpful for later review and for those who could not attend.

- *Conferences* allow groups whose participants are distributed to communicate at the same time (synchronous) or spread out over time (asynchronous). Many-to-many messaging may be used, and there is typically a record of conversations. Examples include a program committee making plans for an upcoming event or a group of students discussing a set of homework problems. In more directed conferences, a leader or moderator supervises the online discussion to achieve goals within deadlines. New approaches such as blogs (personal diaries that invite outside commenting) and wikis (group editing spaces, usually for coordination) are sometimes replacing conferences.

- *Structured work processes* let people with distinct organizational roles collaborate on some task: a scientific-journal editor arranges online submission, reviewing, revisions, and publication; a health-insurance agency receives, reviews, and reimburses or rejects medical bills; or a university admissions committee registers, reviews, chooses, and informs applicants.

- *Meeting and decision support* can be done in a face-to-face meeting, with each user working at a computer and making simultaneous contributions. Shared and private windows plus large-screen projectors enable simultaneous shared comments that may be anonymous. Anonymity not only encourages shy participants to speak up, but also allows forceful leaders to accept novel suggestions without ego conflicts. Voting can also play a significant role.

- *Electronic commerce* includes customers browsing and comparing prices online, possibly followed by short-term collaborations to inquire about a product before ordering it. It also includes business-to-business negotiations to formulate major sales or contracts. Electronic negotiations can be distributed in time and space, while producing an accurate record and rapid dissemination of results.

- *Teledemocracy* allows small organizations, professional groups, and city, state, or national governments to conduct online town-hall meetings, to expose officials to comments from constituents, or to produce consensus through online conferences, debates, and votes.

- *Online communities* are groups of people who may be widely distributed geographically and across different time zones. These people come online to discuss, share information or support, socialize, or play games. Communities that focus on shared interests, such as health concerns or a hobby, are often referred to as *communities of interest* (CoIs). Communities whose focus is professional are known as *communities of practice* (CoPs). Communities whose members are located in the same geographical region are known as *networked communities*; these people usually meet face-to-face as well as virtually.

- *Collaboratories* are novel organizational forms for groups of scientists or other professionals to work together across time and space, possibly sharing expensive equipment such as telescopes or orbiting sensor platforms. These groups share interests, but may compete for resources.

- *Telepresence* enables remote participants to have experiences that are almost as good as being physically co-present. Telepresence is supported by immersive 3D virtual environments, which often involve users donning electronic devices (DataGloves, goggles), wearing special clothing, or entering an environment containing electronic sensors so that they can manipulate objects and communicate with each other in 3D space (see Section 6.6).

This list is just a starting point—there are undoubtedly other collaborative processes and strategies, such as for entertainment, multiperson games, challenging contests, theatrical experiences, or playful social encounters. The potential market for innovative software tools is large; however, designing for collaboration is a challenge because of the numerous and subtle questions of etiquette, trust, and responsibility. The challenge is increased by the need to account for anxiety, deceit, desire for dominance, and abusive behavior.

This variety of collaborative processes and strategies begs the question, how can we make sense of such a mix? The traditional way to decompose collaborative interfaces is by a time/space matrix (Ellis, Gibbs, and Rein, 1991):

	Same Time	*Different Times*
Same Place	synchronous local (face-to-face) (control rooms, meeting rooms, desk/wall projections, art/building installations)	asynchronous local (equipment logs, team scheduling, group calendars)
Different Places	synchronous distributed (chat, texting, instant messaging, video/audio conferencing)	asynchronous distributed (e-mail, newsgroups, listservers, discussion boards, conferences, blogs, wikis, online and networked communities)

This descriptive model focuses on two critical dimensions, and guides designers and users. However, as collaboration strategies become more sophisticated, many designers combine interfaces from two or more cells in this matrix. For example, many online community environments offer combinations of e-mail, bulletin boards, chat, and instant messaging for flexibility in discussions; some also have voting and group decision-support tools for orderliness in decision making. Choosing which software to include depends on the users' needs.

Research in collaborative interfaces is often more complicated than in single-user interfaces. The multiplicity of users makes it difficult to conduct controlled experiments, and the flood of data from multiple users defies orderly analysis. Studies of small-group psychology, industrial and organizational behavior, sociology, and anthropology provide useful research paradigms, but many researchers must invent their own methodologies. Participant reports and ethnographic observations are appealing because they emphasize the colorful raw data from human discourse. Reflective case studies of groupware tools provide well-reasoned analyses to guide improvement and adoption, but the most compelling indicator of success for many organizations is the willingness of users to continue using a software tool.

Collaborative interfaces are maturing, but the determinants of success are still not clear. Why is electronic mail so widely used, while video conferencing is limited to mostly corporate meetings? Why are cell phones intensely popular worldwide, while immersive environments remain a research topic? Understanding the causes of failures in work-oriented groupware, such as disparities between who does the work and who gets the benefit, could lead to refinements. Other potential problems that must be overcome are threats to existing political power structures and insufficient critical mass of users who have convenient access. More subtle problems involve violation of social taboos and resistance to change (Grudin, 1994). Successful designers will be those who find ways to accommodate strongly held community values and create acceptable social norms.

Arguments over measures of success complicate any evaluation. Whereas some people cite the high utilization of electronic mail, others question whether electronic mail aids or hinders job-related productivity (Jackson, Dawson, and Wilson, 2003). The number of participants registered in a discussion board, the number of messages posted, and the regularity of return visits are automatable metrics that can be viewed as indicators of success. Subjective measures obtainable by surveys and ethnographic observation include how satisfied participants are with the discussions and whether they feel a sense of belonging to the community. These individual measures need to be supplemented by community measures of the ambience (empathic or hostile), thread depth, and goal achievement (Smith, 2002). For business managers, cost/benefit analyses are also important (Millen et al., 2002). Video conferencing may initially reduce travel expenses, but it can encourage collaboration and familiarity with more distant partners. However, eventually these relationships may lead to increasing costs and possibly more travel as a desire for face-to-face meetings grows. In educational environments, improved outcomes can be measured by comparison of scores on final exams, but when students work collaboratively in networked environments they are often learning new skills that cannot be measured quantitatively. Too many educators ignore these collaboration skills, which are needed in the workplace, where teamwork and effective communication are essential.

For all the talk about how communication technologies are once again bringing about the "death of distance," distance really does matter for many activities and relationships (Olson and Olson, 2000). Physically close partnerships have the advantage of serendipitous encounters for lightweight exchanges, plus the facile capacity to confer easily over documents, maps, diagrams, or objects. Co-location also facilitates awareness of a partner's gaze and body language and enhances trust-building eye contact; for more personal encounters, electronic hugs are still no match for the real thing. Wide-angle, high-resolution, and low-latency video technologies can't yet match the richness of being there. Another often-overlooked factor is that there is something profound about the shared risk accepted by those who participate in face-to-face encounters. The willingness to separate oneself from familiar surroundings and possibly even expose oneself to physical harm, especially if arduous travel is required, raises the status of a meeting among all partners and can increase the commitment to making a constructive outcome.

Collaboration and discussion are a natural part of democratic processes, so online campaigning, organizing, and consensus building are becoming required skills for politicians. Electronic mail to public officials and online town-hall meetings are already possible, but electronic parliaments with committee cau-cusing, deal making, and voting are slower to emerge. Utopian visionaries sug-gest increased and constructive participation in democratic processes, but other people warn about the dangers of uninformed citizens influencing legislation and of harmful speedups that reduce thoughtful deliberation.

10 · 3   Asynchronous Distributed Interfaces: Different Place, Different Time

Close collaboration across time and space is one of the gifts of technology. Durable messages transmitted electronically enable collaboration. For many users, electronic mail has become as much a way of life as the telephone; for oth-ers it is the starting point for using computers. Electronic mail is widely appreci-ated because of its simple, personal, and prompt service, enabling communication between business partners or family members and friends. It is excellent for clearly conveying facts such as phone numbers or flight times and convenient because cutting and pasting from/to other documents is easy. On the other hand, for complex negotiations or extended discussions, it can be too loosely structured (endless chatting with no leader, chaotic processes that don't lead to a decision), overwhelming (hundreds of messages per day can be diffi-cult to absorb), and frustrating when it comes to locating relevant messages. In addition, late joiners to an e-mail discussion will find it hard to catch up on ear-lier comments. To remedy these problems, structured methods for electronic conferencing and various discussion-group methods have emerged (Hiltz and Turoff, 1998).

10 · 3 · 1   Electronic mail

The atomic unit of collaboration for electronic-mail users is the message; the FROM party sends a message to the TO party. Electronic-mail systems (Fig. 10.1) share the notion that one person can send a message to another person or a list of people. Messages usually are delivered in seconds or minutes; replying is easy and rapid, but recipients retain control of the pace of interaction by decid-ing how long to wait before replying.

Electronic-mail messages typically contain text, but graphics, spreadsheets, sounds, animations, and other structured objects can be included as part of the message or attached as separate documents. However, for users with slow dial-up lines, these additions can cause minutes of frustrating delays and raise costs as they download. Downloading long messages, graphics, and photos can be a problem on mobile devices too. In spite of the capacity of images and animation

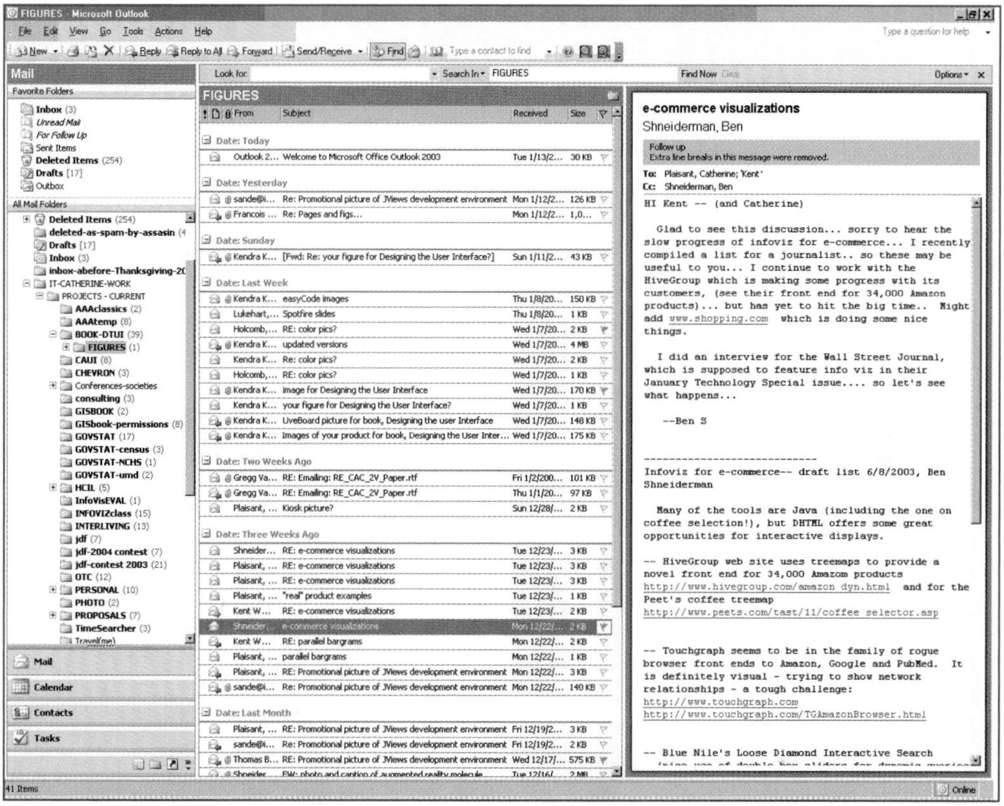

Figure 10.1

Electronic-mail interface for Microsoft Outlook 2003, showing the content of a folder selected in a hierarchy of folders, and the content of an e-mail message. This is also a good example of coordinated windows and effective use of display space.

to enhance presentations or add a personal touch, many users strongly prefer plain text messages because, in addition to rapid downloading, they can be scanned swiftly, searched conveniently, and edited easily. Of course, some images contain essential information such as diagrams or maps, so users may be willing to wait for and pay for these.

Most electronic-mail systems provide fields for FROM (sender), TO (list of recipients), CC (list of copy recipients), DATE, and SUBJECT. Users can specify that copies of certain messages will be sent to colleagues or assistants, and filters allow users to specify that they do not want to receive notices from a given sender or about a certain subject. Additional tools for filtering, searching, and archiving in commercial electronic-mail packages (for example, Microsoft Outlook, Lotus Notes, FirstClass, and Eudora) enable users to manage incoming and previously received electronic mail. However, better tools are still needed for high-volume users who receive hundreds of messages each day. Spam— unwanted, unsolicited advertisements, personal solicitations, and pornographic invitations—seriously annoys and frustrates many users. Internet services such as America Online (AOL), T-Online, and Starpower provide steadily improving filtering tools, but for many users spam dramatically undermines their satisfaction in using e-mail. In 2003, AOL reported that 80% of the e-mail that entered its system was spam that was suppressed by filters.

Many web services offer their own e-mail programs, sometimes for free, such as Microsoft's Hotmail and Yahoo! Mail (Fig. 10.2). Web-based e-mail services

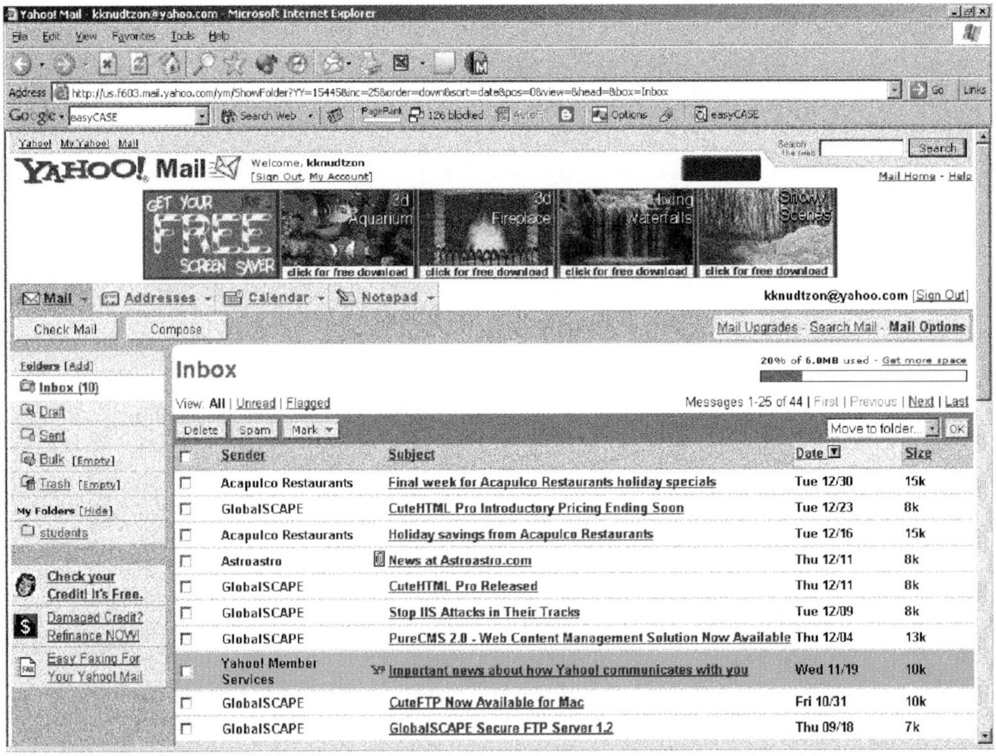

Figure 10.2

Web-based e-mail through Yahoo! showing Inbox.

have become increasingly popular because they provide easy access from anywhere in the world via any computer equipped with a web browser. Electronic mail is also available on some specialized mobile devices, such as the RIM Blackberry (Fig. 10.3), and is offered by many cell-phone service providers (Fig. 10.4). These services are likely to increase in scope, making e-mail and text messages universally accessible via small mobile devices.

In the U.S., more than half the population uses e-mail at work, at home, or via public-access terminals. Internet cafes are springing up all over the world, sometimes in the most unlikely places. A traveler from Tibet recently reported that getting access to e-mail was easier and cheaper than getting a shower. She paid $0.50 for one hour of fast e-mail access, while a shower cost $1.00 for a few minutes. However, making e-mail truly universal will require greater simplicity, faster training, more effective filtering, and lower-cost hardware and network services (Anderson et al., 1995).

Online directories and the ease with which e-mail addresses can be found on the Web are good facilitators, since it is necessary to know a person's electronic-mail

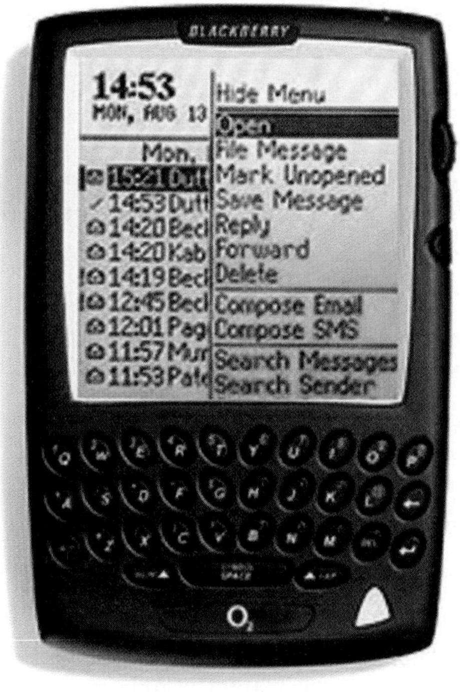

Figure 10.3

E-mail on a Blackberry. (www.blackberry.com)

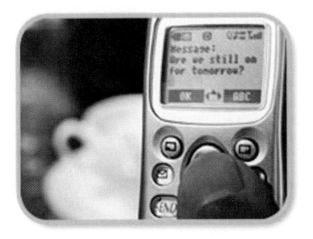

Figure 10.4

E-mail message on a cell phone. (www.iialert.com)

address before sending a message. Such online directories often include the capacity to create new group lists, so that large groups can be reached easily. The dangers and frustrations of spam remain, though, and even noble ideas of collaboration can be undermined by users who fail to be polite, nuisances who persistently disrupt, electronic snoopers who do not respect privacy, or calculating opportunists who abuse their privileges.

10.3.2   Newsgroups, listservers, discussion boards, conferences, blogs, and wikis

Electronic mail is a great way to get started in electronic communication, but its basic features need extension to serve the needs of groups. When groups want more structured discussions, they need tools to organize, archive, and search the discussion history. One popular strategy is the *USENET newsgroups,* in which thousands of topics are listed. Newsgroup users initiate action by selecting a newsgroup and reading as many previous notes and related comments as they wish (Fig. 10.5). Global searches of all newsgroups is an option by way of web search engines, such as Google. Newsgroups are organized into hierarchies to help users to find topics of interest. Carefully specified naming conventions also help. Four well-known categories are `alt` (alternative discussions), `comp` (computers), `rec` (recreational interests), and `soc` (social discussions). The naming conventions for newsgroups support this organization further by including the category in the name. For example, `comp.sware` would be a newsgroup about

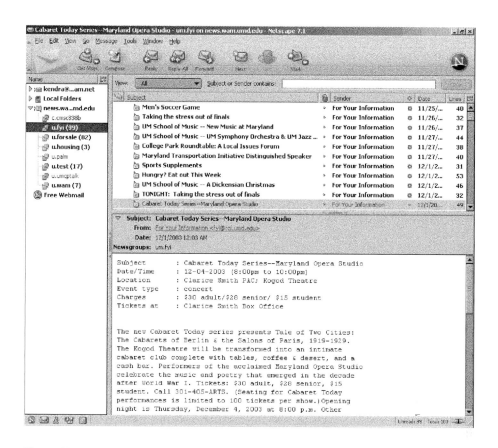

Figure 10.5

News reader system for Netscape Navigator, showing a news server list, a list of "fyi" announcements, and the text of one announcement.

software in the comp hierarchy. Typically, the past few weeks of notes are maintained on the user's Internet Service Provider's (ISP) server machine in chronological order. ISPs have different regulations to determine the number of messages that they store and the length of time messages are maintained for users. Often the amount of storage available is the deciding factor.

A second popular community structure is the *listserver,* to which individuals must subscribe to receive electronic-mail notices. Listserv is a popular example of listserver software. Listservers can be moderated by a leader who keeps out irrelevant messages, or they can be unmoderated, simply acting as a mail reflector that sends out copies of received electronic-mail notes to all subscribers. Users can opt to receive these messages as they trickle through one by one, or choose to have them collected into long messages known as *digests.* Receiving messages individually makes replying to a single user straightforward, whereas it is cumbersome to extract a message from a digest of dozens of messages. Either way, keeping track of how messages relate to each other can be a problem, particularly when they get mixed in with regular e-mail. Many high-volume users try to get around the problem by setting filters to catch messages from different sources. Getting flooded with listserver electronic-mail notes can be a burden, so the decision to subscribe is sometimes a serious commitment. Listservers keep lists of subscribers and searchable archives of notes. L-Soft, a major supplier of free and professional versions of listserver software, claims to support more than 115,000,000 subscribers to over 300,000 listservers.

A third popular form of community structure is the web-based *discussion board*, which evolved from the older dial-in *bulletin boards*. The basic advantage of discussion boards is that the messages can be re-ordered chronologically, by author, or by topic, but some modern newsgroup and listserver interfaces now provide such support. Each message has a short one-line heading and an arbitrarily long body. Messages may contain a question or an answer, an offer to buy or sell, an offer of support, interesting news, a joke, or a "flame" (abusive criticism). Topic *threads* starting with the initial question and then listing all the responses make it easier to follow the progress of a discussion (Fig. 10.6 and Fig. 13.6). Two basic types of messages can be sent: those that launch a new discussion topic, and those that reply to an existing message. To send a reply, users simply click a reply button on the existing message and complete the template that is presented. To initiate a new topic, users specify a subject heading that clearly describes the contents of the message. Cryptic headings are discouraged because other readers cannot see at a glance what topics are covered. The date of posting is usually shown with the user's user name.

Many web-based discussion boards now support graphical attachments, links to web sites, private discussion areas, improved message archiving and searching, e-mail notification about new messages, and powerful tools for managing and moderating discussions. Esthetic features that may enhance the experience include colorful backgrounds that complement the graphic design of the site, graphics, emoticons to signal mood, topic icons to indicate the type of topic, and personal pictures. Commercially produced discussion-board systems such as Discus or Webcrossing typically offer a range of management tools that are sold in differentially priced packages, as well as freeware versions. Robust software on powerful servers supports service to large numbers of participants, provides archival backup, and ensures security, privacy, and protection against viruses and hackers.

Enabling users to search message archives by subject, date, and sender and to view archives in various ways (threaded by date, reverse threaded, by sender) extends the usability of the discussion board. Allowing users to represent themselves with pictures or icons or to link to their home pages increases a sense of presence (the impression that one is actually talking to another human being)

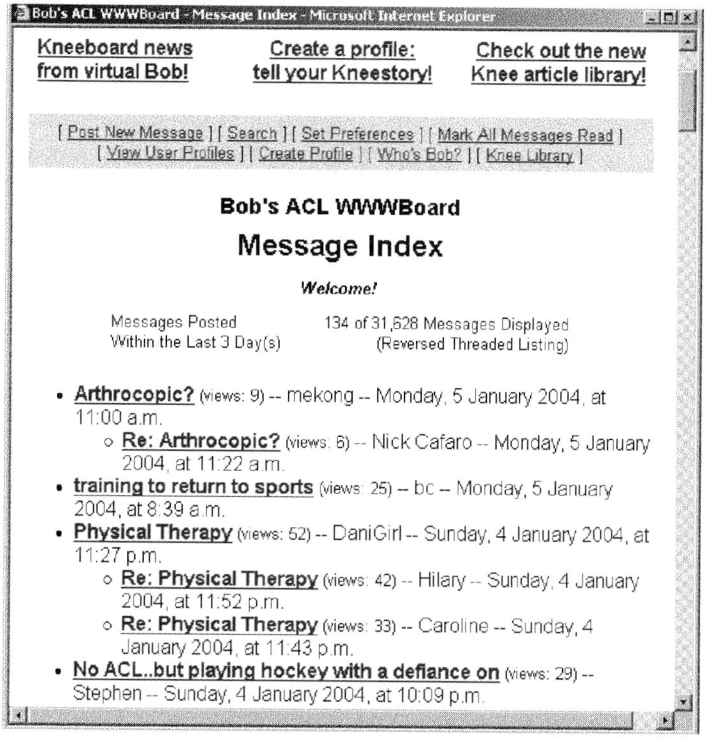

Figure 10.6

Bob's ACL Kneeboard, a threaded discussion board for people who have suffered tears of the anterior cruciate ligaments in their knees. (factotem.org)

and helps users to identify each other. *Emoticons,* known as *smilies* (for example, ☺ ☹), can ease tension by signaling the sender's emotional state in an otherwise textual environment devoid of smiles, laughing, and other body language.

Access to discussion boards may be open or restricted to members who must register and be approved. Restricting membership helps to deter people who are not interested in the topic and troublemakers. It also helps to ensure that discussions stay on topic. Membership-only discussion boards may have only tens or hundreds of participants, whereas open boards may be visited by thousands of people each day.

In large discussion boards, most users read and do not post; they are silent members who are known as *lurkers.* Some researchers estimate that lurkers outnumber posters by as much as 100 to 1, but in some discussion boards—particularly in patient support communities—the ratios are much lower (Nonnecke and Preece, 2000). Whether lurking is a problem depends on the goals of the discussion and the number of people who participate. In a small discussion board where most of the members lurk, the feeling of lively discussion dissipates. In a large discussion board, large numbers of lurkers may be attractive to those who wish to stand out and influence the group. Some participants and moderators like to spark discussion by asking provocative questions or making bold statements. At other times, they may ask active posters to take their discussions offline or to start a separate group, so as to keep the volume of messages low and of interest to the entire group.

Thousands of newsgroups, listserver groups, and discussion-board groups have emerged around the world, administered by devoted moderators. These Gertude Steins of electronic salons keep the discussion moving and on-topic, while filtering out malicious or unsavory messages. Indeed, groups without such dedicated moderators usually do not survive; nurturing the group through all stages of its growth is usually a requirement for success.

Newsgroups, listservers, and discussion boards can be found for most computer-related issues and for many other topics, including movies, kayaking, rap music, folk dancing, health problems, and restaurants. Practical information exchange is common for diverse groups such as cancer researchers, NASA scientists, users with disabilities, and human-computer interaction researchers.

While groups can carry out their business using newsgroups, listservers, and discussion boards, additional features are often provided in *online conferencing* tools. These organized asynchronous conferences are usually moderated, meaning that a conference leader invites participants, poses an issue or theme, and keeps the discussion going if a question is unanswered or if some participants fail to sign on for a few days. Web-based implementations enable a wide range of people to participate. Conferences usually have voting features to allow consensus formation or decision making over a period of hours or days. Organized online conferences often have a schedule to follow with the goal of completing their work or making a decision by a certain date. Additional tools include online directories, document archives, schedules, organization charts, and management policies.

A typical online conference might support a product-planning group in which members propose possible products to develop by the time of an annual industry exposition and then vote to stipulate their choices. Thoughtful discussions within a conference are facilitated because asynchronous communications systems allow time for participants to consider their positions judiciously, consult other materials such as market surveys, discuss issues with colleagues, and review competitors' offerings. Then participants can phrase their contributions carefully, without the pressure to make an immediate comment that is inherent in a telephone call, in a face-to-face meeting, or when using synchronous communications software (see Section 10.4). There is a powerful advantage of 24-hour availability, so users can participate when it is convenient for them. Skeptics who argue for immediacy and high-bandwidth video conferencing should consider the advantages of a slower pace for many personalities and for those for whom writing a well-formed sentence is a challenge.

Web-logs or *blogs* and *wikis* are new forms of social software that started to become popular around 2001. Both types of software support the democratic philosophy that underpins the Web—namely, that anyone should be able to make their opinions widely available to others without having to cross the hurdles of editorial boards and censorship that govern traditional print, TV, and radio. Blogs are open electronic documents or diaries that are "owned" by their creators, but readers can contribute comments. Blogs can focus on any topic; popular themes include politics, music, popular literature, travels, film critiques, and personal diaries. Blog software, provided by Blogger.com and others, makes it easy for the blog owners to tell their stories and then allows readers to add comments (Fig. 10.7). The software provides templates for readers to add pictures and provide links. The success of one's blog is judged according to how many people visit, link to it, and discuss it—in other words, by the attention that it gets from other bloggers.

Figure 10.7

Blogger.com home page. A list of the user's blogs is on the right. New public blogs on the left can be browsed. (www.blogger.com)

Wikis are collaborative web pages that are open for anyone to add or revise content, unless they are limited to members who must supply a password. Wikis are used for discussing a variety of topics, but they are particularly popular with project teams, who like to discuss and record innovative ideas, plan meetings, and develop agendas on the team wiki. *Wikipedia* is a collaborative encyclopedia developed by people from over 40 countries. This amazing venture demonstrates the power of collaboration. Anyone can add to an existing topic or start a new one. Contributors are asked to be respectful to others when editing or adding to their work. An archive of previous pages also helps to ensure that valuable work can be recovered. Surprisingly, this wiki gets less abusive postings than many USENET newsgroups and discussion boards. Maybe its openness makes sabotage less attractive.

Another format for social discussion includes online magazines, newsletters, and journals, which are proliferating with audiences growing rapidly. *Darwin*, *Salon*, and *Slate* seek broad audiences, while specialized newsletters are emerging in every discipline. Often, they are paid for by advertising, but some charge subscription fees. Respected authors or hired staff may initiate a topic with an informative or opinionated essay, often designed to provoke discussion. Hundreds of online newspapers complement printed editions, but newer online-only newspapers, often for narrow audiences, are popping up daily on the Web. They are all exploring how to engage readers in productive and, if possible, profitable ways. Similarly, some scientific journals are available in electronic-only form, with mechanisms to encourage discussion.

10.3.3   Online and networked communities

Online and networked communities have become talk-show topics, with social commentators celebrating or warning about their transformational power. Online communities are topically focused and geographically dispersed; they exist for AIDS patients, archaeologists, and agronomists (Preece, 2000; Kim, 2000). Networked communities are geographically confined, such as the ones in Seattle, Washington, Blacksburg, Virginia, Milan, Italy, and Singapore (Schuler, 1996; Cohill and Kavanaugh, 2000). Online and networked community members may use all the software discussed above and then add other features, such as information resources, community histories, bibliographies, and photo archives.

Howard Rheingold's (1993) popular book tells charming and touching stories of collaboration and support in the San Francisco–based WELL. However, a more troubling picture emerges when clinical psychologists analyze network addictions and deconstruct manufactured cyber-identities (Turkle, 1995). The positive side is the facilitation of communication among like-minded people who have shared interests. Patient support communities have been particularly successful for bringing together those with similar medical problems; patients with rare diseases and those who are house-bound or who live in isolated rural areas are pleased to be able to share their stories and problems and get support. Similarly, online communities are bringing together people from across the world whose access to high-bandwidth communication is limited. As low-cost mobile devices become more pervasive, this trend will continue. The negative side is that online community participants may have less commitment than do those that attend to face-to-face meetings of hobby clubs, neighborhood groups, and parent/teacher associations. Some early studies suggested that active participants on the Internet withdrew from other social contacts and felt more alienated, but later studies have shown more positive outcomes (Kraut et al., 1998; Kraut et al., 2002; Robinson and Nie, 2002).

Community members have a shared goal, identity, or common interest and participate electronically on a continuing basis. Some communities have strict rules on membership, and some members have an intense devotion to their online communities. This generates a sometimes remarkable willingness to trust and assist other community members, leading to what sociologists call "generalized reciprocity"—helping others in the belief that someday someone will help you. In health support communities the help is often in the form of information about treatments or physicians, but a striking aspect to any reader of these discussions is the high level of empathic support conveyed among participants (Preece, 1999). Postings can reveal personal fears about surgery and generate supportive comments such as "Don't worry, I've been through it and you'll do fine" or "Just hang in there—you are not alone" and requests to "Let the group know how your surgery turns out—we're cheering for you."

Developing successful online and networked communities is not easy, as revealed by the thousands of electronic ghost towns without any participants. Good interfaces are just one factor in determining success. Attention to and support for social interaction as the community grows are equally important. The skill, energy, and nurturing attention of community leaders and moderators are often the determining factors in a thriving community. Successful communities tend to have a clearly stated purpose, well-defined membership, and explicit policies to guide behavior (Preece, 2000). For example, Bob's ACL Kneeboard (Fig. 10.6) is for people who have suffered tears of the anterior cruciate ligaments in their knees and are facing decisions about surgical methods. This online community was started 10 years ago by Bob, whose medical history, with explicit pictures of surgery on both his knees, tells his story. Members return year after year to help recent sufferers with their decisions, provide information about new surgical practices, and offer emotional support for their pain and difficult choices.

Community policies must deal with rude behavior, off-topic comments, and commercial notices. Some communities have a written policy document enforced by moderators, while others establish norms of behavior that are upheld by members. Principles of freedom of speech should have extension in the online world, but there are novel dangers of disruptive behaviors, illegal activities, and invasion of privacy. Some online communities have been criticized for spreading racist or otherwise harmful material, so the challenge is to preserve valued freedoms and rights while minimizing harm. Each online community has to decide how to interpret such policies, just as each town and state must decide on local rules.

The user interfaces for online communities tend to be simple to accommodate the large number of users with low-speed dial-in access. The intrigue lies in the complexity of the conversations, especially in spirited replies and debates. As usage increases, the moderator must decide whether to split the community into more focused groups to avoid overwhelming participants with thousands of new messages. Ensuring that the communities remain interesting and consistent is a challenge; if a group of physics researchers who are discussing current theories is visited by students asking beginner-level questions, the experts will want the moderator to steer the students to other discussion boards or communities. An alternative is for the researchers to move their discussion to a new online community web site.

Within corporations, universities, or government agencies, communities may be established for topics such as corporate direction, new technologies, or product development. These specialist groups are often referred to as *Communities of Practice* (CoPs), to acknowledge their professional orientation (Wenger, 1998). Understanding how to make CoPs thriving places for discussion can be a challenge. How can management motivate employees to spend time on helping colleagues, when they may be in competition for a promotion? One school of thought is that automated tools can be used to mine the content of old discussions for nuggets of knowledge that are relevant to a current problem—a hot topic among knowledge-management professionals. However, skeptics suggest that it may be more effective to designate individuals and develop processes for compiling, summarizing, and classifying organizational knowledge so as to facilitate future retrieval. Communities of inquiry are promoted in educational circles as web-based conferences to promote discussions using these stages of action: (1) ask, (2) investigate, (3) create, (4) discuss, and (5) reflect (Bruce and Easley, 2000).

Online communities have become common for distance education courses and as supplements to face-to-face classes, because they can stimulate lively educational experiences. Widespread adoption of educational environments such as WebCT, Blackboard, and FirstClass demonstrate the efficacy of an online format for college courses, complete with homework assignments, projects, tests, and final examinations. Instructors find the constant flow of messages to be a rewarding challenge, and students are generally satisfied with the experience. The essence of the virtual classroom is an environment to facilitate collaborative learning, often with team projects. For distance education students, the increased ability to be in constant communication with other learners is an obvious benefit. But even for campus-based courses, the technology provides a means for a rich, collaborative learning environment that exceeds the traditional classroom in its ability to connect students and make course materials available on an around-the-clock basis (Hiltz, 1992; Hazemi and Hailes, 2001). The University of Phoenix and the British Open University are impressive examples of how interactive technologies are being employed to serve educational needs.

Some online communities support thousands of contributors to important projects such as the Linux operating system. The phenomenal growth of this open-source movement and its remarkable impact demonstrate how effective geographically dispersed online communities can be. Hundreds of thousands of programmers also feel devotion to the Slashdot community, whose lively discussions of technical topics often receive hundreds of comments per hour. Millions of people participate in eBay to buy or sell products, generating feelings of shared experiences that are the hallmark of a community. Sellers strongly identify with their colleagues and collaborate to pressure eBay management for new policies. The reputation manager (Feedback Forum) enables purchasers to record comments on sellers, such as these typically complimentary notes: "Everything works. Quick shipment. thank you. Peace. A+ seller. Item exactly as described, fast shipping, smooth transaction. A++++++++++. I'm very satisfied A++++." And these are just the first steps. Creative entrepreneurs and visionary political organizers are still exploring novel networked approaches for business development and consensus seeking.

For scientists who need to collaborate at a distance, discussing ideas, viewing objects, and sharing data and other resources, *collaboratories*—laboratories without walls—provide new opportunities (Finholt and Olson, 1997; Olson et al., 2001). Geographically dispersed teams, for example, can benefit from sharing costs for and being able to access remote instruments for space or environmental research. Collaboratories can employ all forms of collaborative interfaces, but the asynchronous technologies seem to be most valuable. Collaboratories are also social structures that promote collaboration among groups with complementary skills, accelerate dissemination of novel results, and facilitate learning by students or new researchers. Standard data formats facilitate sharing that leads to multiple analyses, and well-maintained archives reduce redundant experimentation.

10.4   Synchronous Distributed Interfaces: Different Place, Same Time

The dream of being in two places at one time became partially realized with modern technologies such as the telephone and television. Now, distributed applications such as *group editing* and *synchronous online conferencing* further enrich the possibilities. Early systems like the GRoup Outline Viewing Editor (GROVE) enabled multiple users at different locations to edit the same document simultaneously, while coordination was accomplished by voice communication (Ellis, Gibbs, and Rein, 1991).

Modern collaborative interfaces are increasingly flexible, allowing distributed groups to work together at the same time by using chat, instant messaging (IM), or texting. Collaborators desiring the richer experience of the human voice can use audio or video conferencing. For each form of collaboration, users can elect to see the same document, slide show, or web page. Software developers can give demonstrations of new interfaces at multiple sites to dozens of people while talking on a conference call. Physicians in hospitals hundreds of miles apart can all view electronic versions of X-rays, MRIs, and body scans so that they can pool their knowledge about treatments for rare forms of cancer and other ailments.

Another example is sharing of information for applications such as telephone calls to airline-reservation agents. When agents have located a set of possible flights, it would be convenient to show customers rather than to read the list. Customers could then make their selections and have an electronic copy to save, print, or include in other documents. This technology already exists for numerous web-based airline-ticketing sites. Some of the most innovative commercial developments are for interactive games that permit two or more people to participate simultaneously in poker, chess, or complex fantasy games such as Sony's EverQuest. These games offer 3D graphics and animations that engage players as they try to outwit each other; enthusiastic users eagerly acquire high-speed Internet connections, powerful game-playing machines, and special input devices such as paddles with numerous buttons.

10.4.1   Chat, instant messaging, and texting

Even simple synchronous exchanges of text messages among groups of 2 to 20 participants can be exciting. Internet Relay Chat (IRC) programs and specialized software such as that available from Activeworlds.com (Fig. 6.12) have *chat* windows as well as graphical interfaces. Brief greetings and short comments are typical of fast-moving chat environments, where participants must type quickly and hope that their comments appear on the screen near to the ones that they answer. There is little time to reflect. In Activeworlds, users can explore one of the 3D worlds listed in the lefthand window by moving their avatars (graphic characters that represent users instead of a login name) around the screen using the touch pad, cursor keys, or joystick. They can move close to other characters and interact with them or simply tour the environment. The menu of viewing options at the top of the screen also allows users to look up or down, turn around, and jump or wave to express their emotions. Activeworlds has paying customers who develop environments for education with informative posters and for businesses with product displays that include price lists.

However, users can tire of navigating through the graphical worlds, so they often spend more time on the textual chat. This begs the question, what is the added value that avatars and 3D graphics bring to such environments? If avatars are moving around, social proximity can facilitate discussion, since users will know who else is participating. Avatars are an essential feature for many games, but they may be less important for other topics or groups with a stable set of participants. Once past the initial rapid exchange during greetings, text users can conduct useful business meetings, support lively social club-houses, and offer sincere care for those in need.

Another aspect of chat environments is that they allow participants to take on new personalities, underscored by engaging names such as Gypsy, Larry Lightning, or Really Rosie. The social chatter can be light, provocative, or intimidating. Unfortunately, some chat participants turn into wisecracking *flamers* more intent on a putdown than a conversation, and with a tendency to violent or obscene language. Even worse, chat rooms, like the real world, can be environments for deception, illicit invitations, and various forms of entrapment. Children and parents, as well as unsuspecting business people, need to take precautions.

Chat rooms are also used in elaborate MUD (for Multi-User Dungeons or Dimensions systems) and MOOs (a form of Object Oriented MUDs) that offer another kind of fantasy environment. Participants take on novel identities while on quests to explore other facets of their own personas that they may not otherwise wish to reveal (Turkle, 1995). According to a web MUD page: "You can walk around, chat with other characters, explore dangerous monster-infested areas, solve puzzles, and even create your very own rooms, descriptions and items." Variations of these systems are inspiring new approaches for students to learn geometry, creative writing, history, and other subjects (Bruckman, 2002). A virtual university to promote peer learning can have buildings for students to discuss subject areas, libraries with information resources, and commons areas for socializing. Skeptics worry, though, that the emphasis is on social encounters, rather than information or skill acquisition.

Instant messaging is a popular alternative to open chat rooms, in part because membership can be tightly controlled. IM is ideal for quick exchanges between close friends, family members, or small groups who are readily available at their desktop or laptop computers. AOL, Microsoft, and Yahoo! have created IM systems that have hundreds of millions of subscribers.

Users launch IM programs by clicking on a small icon on the desktop, in a toolbar, or in an applications list. This opens a window which shows, on the right, the buddy lists that have been created (Fig. 10.8). Each buddy list contains the names of the participants in that community. A chat window, similar to that found in chat systems, contains the conversation, and new messages can be typed in the lower pane. Conversations can involve two or more people. Typically IM communities contain fewer than 20 people, but they may be larger. Membership is usually restricted to groups whose members know each other and want to be in regular contact. For example, students from Thailand studying in the U.S. may share one IM community, as well as another with Thai

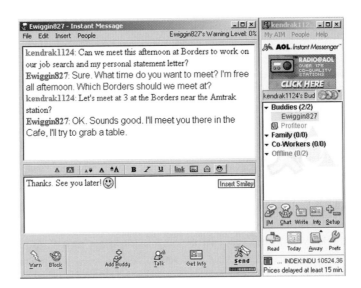

Figure 10.8

AOL's instant messaging interface, showing the history of messages exchanged with a friend selected from the list of buddies, and a message being composed.

friends across the U.S. and friends back home. Much of the motivation is to enable users to track each other's movements and to chat. It's comforting to know when friends come online, how their work is progressing, whether they are sick or well, and so on. IM is used in a similar way to text messaging. It's all about knowing which friends are where, and when; it can also be an inexpensive way to have long-distance conversations.

Most IM systems include features such as emoticons, the ability to send photographs and other files, and a wide variety of sounds and backgrounds. Research into novel ways for users to identify each other indicates that sound may have a role (Issacs et al., 2002); an office manager might be represented by a high-pitched "ping," peers by the "doh, rei, me" musical scale, and a partner or husband by the first three bars of their favorite tune. Comments, like those typical of chats, are short and concise. Groups in which members know each other delight in developing standard phrases (for example, LOL for "laughing out loud" or IMHO for "in my humble opinion") and cryptic shorthand ways to communicate using symbols and characters (for example, "me4u", "cu@1", "☺2cu"). Teenagers are particularly adept and creative users of such shorthand, especially when texting on their cell phones. Researchers report that teenagers

(Grinter and Palen, 2002) and office workers (George, 2002; Herbsleb et al., 2002) are the largest user groups of IM.

Security and privacy are essential for all IM users, although needs may differ. For example, office workers may not want their colleagues and bosses to read their communications. However, the popular assumption that workplace instant messaging is only for idle chatter has been shown to be wrong (Isaacs, Walendowski, and Ranganathan, 2002). According to this study, productive work was carried out by the frequent IM users, who mainly used it to discuss a broad range of topics with colleagues via many fast-paced interactions per day, each with many short turns and much threading and multitasking. Users rarely switched from IM to another medium when the conversations got complex. Only 28% of conversations were simple interactions, and only 31% were about scheduling or coordination. Still, evidence that serious work can be accomplished does not take away from the capacity for IM's informal, flexible style to also support the lightweight exchanges that contribute to awareness of what colleagues, family, or friends are doing and where they are (Nardi, Whittaker, and Bradner, 2000).

Texting (also known as *Short Messaging Systems*, or SMS) via cell phones has also become an extremely popular means of communication. The mobile nature of cell-phone texting allows for lively but private exchanges, but texting is also used to send messages to be read later, or simple alerts. Europeans and Asians have been especially quick to adopt texting, in part because cell-phone usage is high in these areas and texting costs are low.

Cell-phone texting is changing the world by empowering those who cannot afford more expensive devices, and for whom public kiosks and Internet cafes are too limiting. Fishermen in India are using their cell phones to check out the best prices before deciding where to come ashore (Rheingold, 2002). Activists in Indonesia sent text messages to marshal their supporters in the demonstrations that brought down the Suharto government in Indonesia. Similarly, demonstrators against the International Monetary Fund (IMF) and World Bank meeting tried to out-smart the police as they worked to minimize the impact of the demonstrators; plans on both sides changed by the minute, with details going out via cell phone. Texting is also changing our everyday behavior. People can now easily check in with each other to report where they are, what they are doing, and what they intend to do next. A typical text on the D.C. Metro goes like this: "hi, I'm at Cleveland Park be at restaurant 7.20."

10.4.2 Audio and video conferencing

Audio and video conferencing are steadily growing commercial successes for when synchronous communication is needed to organize a special event, deal with tense negotiations, or build trust among new contacts. Standard telephones anywhere in the world can be used to dial into an audio-conferencing system. At the other end of the spectrum, specialized video-conferencing rooms with high-resolution multi-camera setups that must be reserved by appointment give these events greater significance. The convenience of *desktop videoconferencing* (DTVC), which permits users to have access to their papers and computer systems during the conference, had already been recognized by the mid-1990s (Bly, Harrison, and Irwin, 1993; Isaacs et al., 1995; Isaacs, Tang, and Morris, 1996). Video conferencing from home is viable too, enabling grandparents to have regular video visits with grandchildren. The hardware, network, and software architectures that support synchronous video conferencing with multimedia capabilities have dramatically improved. However, users must still deal with the problems of delays, sharing, synchronization of actions, narrow field of view, and poorly transmitted social cues such as gaze and changes in body language, which are essential for effective turn taking and reading the moods of remote participants (Olson and Olson, 2003).

The move from research prototypes to widely used DTVC systems happened as costs dropped, adequate bandwidth became available, and interfaces improved. Cornell University's CU-SeeMe system put the concept on the map by offering free software that ran on most personal computers with no special hardware and ordinary video cameras. The low-resolution (320×240) grayscale images were transmitted via the Internet at whatever frame rates were possible. The images were often jerky, but this pioneering project paved the way for the use of Internet video transmissions for personal conferences, professional work, and distance learning. Today, Microsoft's meeting software captures the promise of these earlier systems by providing individuals or groups with up to four video-conferencing windows; the program runs on most computers. In Microsoft's NetMeeting or Live Meeting (Fig. 10.9), the video window is small; participants can see one another, though detailed facial expressions are hard to discern. Similar services are also available from Yahoo!

The Polycom, Sony, Tandberg, and VTEL video-conferencing platforms provide increasingly high-quality services on telephone lines, the Internet, local-area networks, and leased lines (Fig. 10.10). Once users have had the pleasure of seeing one another on video, done the required hand waving, and adjusted their lighting, cameras, hair, and clothes, it is time to get down to business. Some meetings are simple discussions that replace face-to-face visits; the improvement over the telephone is the capacity to assess facial-expression and body-language cues for enthusiasm, disinterest, or anger. Many professional meetings include conferencing over some object of interest, such as a document, map, or photo. Developers emphasize the need for convenient turn taking and document sharing by using terms such as *smooth, lightweight,* or *seamless integration.*

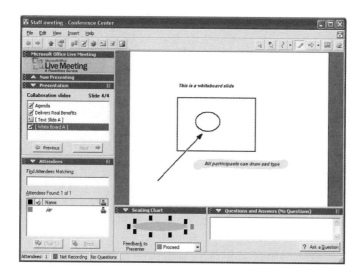

Figure 10.9

Using Microsoft Office Live Meeting, participants can show PowerPoint slide shows and use highlighters or pointers when going through slides. The whiteboard feature allows quick sketching of ideas during meetings.

These same requirements are needed for the growing family market. Grandparents love interacting with grandchildren via video conferencing—they speak about their experiences in glowing terms and schedule regular meetings. Likewise, some parents who must travel make a ritual of after-dinner or bedtime video conferences with their kids to keep in touch.

Controlled experimentation on performance with different media has guided designers in shaping this technology over the years. Chapanis's classic studies (1975) and more recent work confirm that a voice channel is an important component for discussion of what participants see on a shared display. In one comparison, a shared workspace on a computer display was used by four participants. The three treatments were workspace-alone (no audio or video), workspace with audio alone, and workspace with audio and video. Significant differences were found for the meeting-scheduling task, which took almost twice as long with the workspace-alone treatment as it did with the two other treatments. This result reinforces the importance of having a clear voice channel for coordination while users are looking at the objects of interest. One important finding was that for many tasks audio had the greatest impact on performance

Figure 10.10

The Polycom Executive provides high-quality video conferencing.
(www.polycom.com)

even though users expressed desire for video (Sellen, 1994; Finn, Sellen, and Wilbur, 1997). In applications in which users conference over an object (for example, an architect's model), though, having a video or rapidly updated shared visual display is beneficial (Ishii, Kobayashi, and Arita, 1994; Kraut, Gergle, and Fussell, 2002).

Instead of a scheduled video conference, some researchers believe that continuously available video windows, tunnels, or spaces would enable an enriched form of communication that supported opportunistic collaborations and informal awareness. These continuous video connections from public spaces such as kitchens or hallways could enable colleagues to see who is at work and ask the casual questions that might lead to closer ties. Some test subjects appreciated these opportunities, but others found them intrusive, distracting, or violating of their privacy (Jancke et al., 2001). Video connections from individual offices might enable participants to access the resources of their office environments while affording a chance for communication and emotional contact, but again the intrusion of such systems is often seen as an annoyance (Olson and Olson, 2000).

Whether audio or video conferencing is more appealing than chat, IM, and texting or more effective than asynchronous textual discussion are also important questions. The answers depend on the goals of the communication task and the task environment. First-time meetings may be improved by a video conference if a face-to-face meeting is not possible, whereas reflective discussion may be better supported by a bulletin board, a wiki, or e-mail.

Electronic classrooms balance the inclusion of new technologies with the exploration of new teaching and learning styles. At the University of Toronto, the ePresence project gives distant learners increased opportunities for participation during the lectures and the capacity to review later. Webcasting allows remote viewers to see and hear the lecturer, and students can have private chats during and after the lectures (Baecker, Moore, and Zijdemans, 2003). The Georgia Tech eClass project emphasized capturing videos of lecturers and their presentations so students could review them or make up missed classes (Abowd, 1999). Microsoft's exploration of distance learning included video presentations and studied four student discussion channels: text chat, audio conferencing, video conferencing, and face-to-face. Text chat faired poorly, while both conferencing methods were effective in supporting learning; audio conferencing produced the highest satisfaction. Face-to-face discussions among participants were significantly longer than mediated discussions (Cadiz et al., 2000).

10.5   Face-to-Face Interfaces: Same Place, Same Time

Teams of people often work together in the same room and use complex shared technology. Pilot and copilot collaboration in airplanes has been designed carefully with shared instruments and displays. Coordination among air-traffic controllers has a long history that has been studied thoroughly (Wiener and Nagel, 1988). Stock-market traders and commodity-market brokers view complex displays, receive orders from customers, and engage in rapid face-to-face collaboration or negotiations to achieve a deal. Brainstorming and design teams often work closely together and have special needs because of the rapid exchanges, frequent updates, and the necessity for accurate recordings of events and outcomes. Even the familiar classroom lecture has changed as some professors give up chalk and present their notes as slide shows via projectors.

10.5.1   Electronic meeting rooms, control rooms, and public spaces

Ordinary business meetings are rapidly integrating computer technology, because so many participants arrive with relevant information already on their laptops or networks. However, computer presentations in business meetings can interfere with communication by reducing eye contact and turning a lively dialog into a boring monologue in a darkened room. The first challenge is to understand the role of technology in supporting information transfer, while preserving the trust-building and motivational aspects of face-to-face encounters. The second challenge is to recognize the appropriate role of shared control of computing and presentation tools so that participants can be more active, while preserving the leadership role of the meeting organizer.

In business meetings, structured social processes for brainstorming, voting, and ranking can produce highly productive outcomes. The University of Arizona was a pioneer in developing the social process, the physical environment, and the software tools that continue to be marketed by GroupSystems (Fig. 10.11). These environments promise to "reduce or eliminate the dysfunctions of the group interaction so that a group reaches or exceeds its task potential" (Valacich, Dennis, and Nunamaker, 1991). By allowing anonymous submission of suggestions and ranking of proposals, the authors introduced a wider range of possibilities; also, ideas were valued on their merits, independently of their "originators" (Fig. 10.12). Because ego investments and conflicts were reduced, groups seemed to be more open to novel suggestions. With this approach, well-trained facilitators with backgrounds in social dynamics consult with the team leader to plan the decision session and to write the problem state-

Figure 10.11

Semicircular classroom with 24 personal computers built into the desks at the University of Arizona. (www.groupsystems.com)

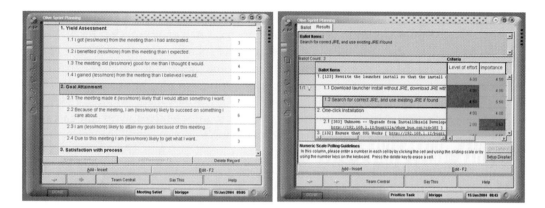

Figure 10.12

Sample screens from Group Systems's Cognito meeting software. An online survey is shown on the left, and the results of a vote are shown on the right. (www.groupsystems.com)

ment. In a typical task, 45 minutes of brainstorming by 15 to 20 people can produce hundreds of lines of suggestions for questions such as "How can we increase sales?" or "What are the key issues in technological support for group work?" Then, items can be filtered, clustered into similar groups, and presented to participants for refinement and ranking. Afterward, a printout and electronic-file version of the entire session is immediately available.

Numerous studies of electronic meeting systems with thousands of users have demonstrated and explored the benefits (Nunamaker et al., 1991):

- Parallel communication promotes broader input into the meeting process and reduces the chance that a few people dominate the meeting.
- Anonymity mitigates evaluation apprehension and conformance pressure, so issues are discussed more candidly.
- The group memory constructed by participants enables them to pause and reflect on information and on opinions of others during the meeting, and serves as a permanent record of what occurred.
- Process structure helps to focus the group on key issues and discourages digressions and unproductive behaviors.
- Task support and structure provide information and approaches to analyze that information.

Even informal processes can be facilitated by shared workspaces in which multiple participants can add their contributions by projecting their displays for the group to see or by cutting and pasting from their materials to the group display.

For example, three architects' proposals or three business plans might be shown on a common display to facilitate comparison. Another approach is for managers to arrive at a meeting and offer copies of slides for all to annotate and take home.

Several shared-workspace designs exist. The pioneering Capture Lab at Electronic Data Systems contains an oval desk with eight Macintosh computers built into the desk to preserve the business-meeting atmosphere (Mantei, 1988). The large display in front of the desk is visible to all attendees, who can each take control of the large screen by pressing a button on a machine. At Xerox PARC, the research system Colab led to the wall-display product called LiveBoard, on which users can see the current list of topics or proposals and can point to, edit, move, or add to them under the policy sometimes called WYSIWIS (what you see is what I see) (Stefik et al., 1987). Newer devices, such as Mimio's simple, cheap sensors tied to special pen holders, allow participants to get electronic copies of what is written on the large whiteboard in front of the group. Smart Technologies Inc.'s SMART Board allows interaction with fingers or pens, locally or remotely (Fig. 10.13).

Expensive control rooms for electric utilities, chemical plants, and transportation networks often have large wall displays so all participants have a shared situation awareness. Similarly, military war rooms and NASA space-flight operations centers enable rapid collaboration among participants often in stress-

Figure 10.13

Children using the SMART Board electronic whiteboard from Smart Technologies Inc. to annotate a diagram in the classroom (left) and compose a story across distributed locations (right). (www.smarttech.com/)

ful conditions. Researchers are developing high-resolution interactive wall displays for smaller groups to conduct brainstorming or design sessions (Guimbretière, Stone, and Winograd, 2001; see also Section 9.5.2).

Interaction in *public spaces* with wall displays may be through personal computers, mobile devices, or special input devices (Streitz et al., 1999; Prante, Magerkuth, and Streitz, 2002). The advantage of a shared public space is that everyone sees the same display and can work communally to produce a joint and recorded result. The disadvantages are that coordination may be complex and technology distractions can interfere with communication—seamlessness is a nice idea, but it's hard to deliver. Some technologies support less goal-directed activities, such as keeping colleagues informed about your whereabouts or a project's status. The Notification Collage allows participants to post information to a large public display in a common area or to secondary displays in private offices. The casual nature of the display facilitates information sharing and promotes awareness of what others are doing (Greenberg and Rounding, 2001). Posting public notices about events or personal photos makes for a lively environment.

Sharing photos is a growing topic for collaborative interfaces. Personal collections made public on the Web and sent as e-mail attachments are the most common approaches, but some innovative approaches are appearing. Projections on living-room walls emulate the traditional slide shows of family pictures, but newer approaches include projections on tables with shared capabilities for manipulating the layout of photos. Another idea is to mount a computer display in an elegant photo frame, which is connected to the Internet. Then parents can upload a changing set of photos of children for grandparents to view on a rotating basis.

Other forms of notification or awareness include reports and alerts about the weather, stock prices, production processes, or equipment status. This can be accomplished by small computer windows that display current information or by audio tones that draw attention to changes. Innovative products from Ambient Technologies include softly glowing colored lights to gently signal changes. Various forms of sculpture, mobiles, light shows, or even changing odors have been suggested to provide minimally intrusive awareness information to users of public spaces. Public spaces are also becoming the objects of creative explorations. Hallways of buildings, foyers of hotels, and museum galleries are beginning to glow with more than advertising signs and hanging pictures. Projected images, large displays, and spatial sound installations can reflect the work tempo or changes in the weather. The goal may be to calm users or make them aware of outside conditions. Lobbies may offer multimedia presentations about the organization, celebrate historic figures, or make an artistic statement in sound and light. Designers may strive to create emotional responses that calm or excite, intrigue or offend—public art pieces are hard to categorize, but they can serve as innovative uses of technology or provocative commentaries on modern life (Halkia and Local, 2003; see Fig 10.14).

Figure 10.14

Modulor II is a time-dependent architectural work of art in which participants create new patterns daily by collaboratively weaving colored strings through an interactive labyrinth of luminous poles. (Halkia and Local, 2003.)

10.5.2   Electronic classrooms

The potential for a groupware-mediated paradigm shift in education evokes passion from devotees, but there is ample reason for skepticism and resistance. By giving each student a keyboard and simple software, it is possible to create an inviting environment for conversation, comparison, or brainstorming. For example, each student can respond to a professor's question by typing a line of text that is shown immediately, with the author's name, on every student's display. With 10 to 50 people typing, new comments may appear a few times per second, and lively (if sometimes confusing) conversations ensue. The academic developers note that

> It seems slightly ironic that the computer, which for twenty-five years has been perceived as anti-human, a tool of control and suppression of human instinct and intuition, has really humanized my job . . . Freed of having to be the cardboard figure at the front of the classroom, I became a person

again, with foibles, feelings and fantasies. As a group, we were more democratic and open with each other than any other writing class I'd had (Bruce,
Peyton, and Batson, 1992).

At the University of Maryland, teaching/learning theaters were built with 40
seats and 20 personal computers to explore face-to-face collaboration methods
(Fig. 10.15). Hundreds of faculty members who used the electronic classrooms
for semester-long courses explored novel teaching and learning styles to create
more engaging experiences for students. While traditional lectures with or without discussion remain common, electronic-classroom technologies can enliven
lectures while enabling active individual learning, small-group collaborative
learning, and entire-class collaborative learning. Most faculty acknowledge
spending more preparation time to use the electronic classrooms, especially in
their first semesters, but one wrote that it was "well worthwhile in terms of
greater learning efficiency" (Shneiderman et al., 1998).

The assumption that improved lectures was the main goal changed as more
faculty tried out the teaching/learning theaters. Faculty who had used paper-
based collaborations appreciated the smoothness of showing student work—
paragraphs from essays, poems, computer programs, statistical results, web
pages, and so on—to the whole class. Faculty who had not used these methods
still appreciated the ease and liveliness of an anonymous electronic brainstorming session. The transformational breakthrough was in opening the learning
process by rapidly showing many students' work to the entire class. Doing so at
first generates student and faculty anxiety, but quickly becomes normal. Seeing
and critiquing exemplary and ordinary work by fellow students provides feedback that inspires better work on subsequent tasks.

Figure 10.15

The AT&T Teaching/Learning Theater at the University of Maryland has 20 high-
resolution displays built into custom desks with seats for 40 students.
(http://www.oit.umd.edu)

Small-group collaborative-learning experiences include having pairs of students work together at a machine on a time-limited task (Fig. 10.13). Pairs often learn better than individuals, because they can discuss their problems, learn from each other, and split their roles into problem solver and computer operator. With paired teams, the variance of completion time for tasks is reduced compared to individual use, and fewer students get stuck in completing a task. Futhermore, verbalization of problems has often been demonstrated to be advantageous during learning and is an important job skill to acquire for modern team-oriented organizations.

Innovative approaches with larger teams include simulated hostage negotiations with terrorist airplane hijackers in a course on conflict resolution, and business trade negotiations in a United Nations format for a course on commercial Spanish. Teams work to analyze situations, to develop position statements online, and to communicate their positions to their adversaries over the network. In an introductory programming course, 10 teams wrote components and sent them through the network to the lead team, who combined the pieces into a 173-line program, all in 25 minutes. The class performed a walkthrough of the code using the large-screen display, and quickly identified bugs.

Some faculty find that adapting to the electronic-classroom environment changes their styles so much that they teach differently even in traditional classrooms. Other faculty vow that they will never teach in a traditional classroom again. Most faculty users want to continue teaching in these electronic classrooms and discover that more than their teaching styles change—their attitudes about the goals of teaching and about the content of the courses often shift as well. Many faculty develop higher expectations for student projects. Some become evangelists within their disciplines for the importance of teamwork and its accompanying communications skills.

On the negative side, a math professor who used the computers only to do occasional demonstrations returned to teaching in a traditional classroom, where he had much more blackboard space. Some reluctant instructors express resistance to changing their teaching styles and anticipate having to make a large effort to use the electronic classrooms. Students are generally positive and often enthusiastic: "Everyone should have a chance to be in here at least once…Great tech. Great education technique…Even though there were a few humps to get over at the beginning—it was well worth the effort (and money)."

The business case for technology-rich classrooms is more difficult to make than for distance education (Baecker, Moore, and Zijdemans, 2003; Abowd, 1999; Cadiz et al., 2000). However, as computer projectors in classrooms become as common as chalkboards, faculty notes migrate to slide presentations, and students begin to carry laptops and mobile devices, it seems likely that educational experiences will become more interactive and collaborative.

Practitioner's Summary

Computing has become a social process. Networks and telephone lines have opened up broad possibilities for collaboration. Electronic mail has made it easy to reach out and touch someone, or thousands of someones. Newsgroups, conferences, online communities, instant messaging, and texting have enabled users to be in closer communication. Coordination within projects or between organizations is facilitated by text, graphic, voice, and video exchanges. Even face-to-face meetings are getting a facelift with new tools for electronic meetings and with teaching/learning theaters. Conferencing methods and collaborative document production will change as bandwidth increases and video capabilities are refined. Electronic meeting rooms and teaching/learning theaters are costly, but they are so attractive that many organizations are likely to spend heavily on these technologies during the next decade. The introspective and isolated style of past computer use has given way to a lively social environment where training has to include *netiquette* (network etiquette) and cautions about flame wars. Collaboration tools will continue to improve and spread. However, as there are in all new technologies, there will be failures and surprising discoveries that will guide the next generation of designers (Box 10.1). Thorough testing of new applications is necessary before widespread dissemination.

Researcher's Agenda

The opportunities for new products and for refinements of existing products seem great. Even basic products such as electronic mail could be improved dramatically by inclusion of advanced features such as online directories, filtering, and archiving tools, as well as by universal usability features such as improved tutorials, better explanations, and convenient assistance.

There are grand opportunities for research on user-interface designs for collaborative interfaces, but the larger and more difficult research problems lie in studying their organizational and societal impacts. Research evidence shows that collaborative interfaces increase the breadth of participation, allowing marginalized individuals greater participation. But even the basic question of their impact on productivity or decision making does not have a clear answer. How will home life and work be changed? Will the ease of contact with distant partners reduce loyalty to companies, neighborhoods, and families? Will trust and responsibility increase because of electronic archives or decrease because of the disembodied nature of electronic communications? Will patients, consumers,

Box 10.1

Questions for consideration. The novelty and diversity of computer-supported cooperative work means that clear guidelines have not emerged, but these sobering questions might help designers and managers.

Computer-supported cooperative work questions

- How would facilitating communication improve or harm teamwork?
- Where does the community of users stand on centralization versus decentralization?
- What pressures exist for conformity versus individuality?
- How is privacy compromised or protected?
- What are the sources of friction among participants?
- Is there protection from hostile, aggressive, or malicious behavior?
- Will there be sufficient equipment to support convenient access for all participants?
- What network delays are expected and tolerable?
- What is the user's level of technological sophistication or resistance?
- Who is most likely to be threatened by computer-supported cooperative work?
- How will high-level management participate?
- Which jobs may have to be redefined?
- Whose status will rise or fall?
- What are the additional costs or projected savings?
- Is there an adequate phase-in plan with sufficient training?
- Will there be consultants and adequate assistance in the early phases?
- Is there enough flexibility to handle exceptional cases and special needs (users with disabilities)?
- What international, national, and organizational standards must be considered?
- How will success be evaluated?

and students be more informed, more misinformed, or more argumentative? Some of the attraction for researchers in computer-supported collaborative work stems from the vast uncharted territory: theories are sparse, controlled studies are difficult to arrange, data analysis is daunting, and predictive models are rare.

WORLD WIDE WEB RESOURCES

Computer-supported cooperative work is naturally a part of the World Wide Web, and novel tools are springing up on many web sites. You can try various chat services, download special-purpose software, or shop for conferencing tools (video, audio, or text-based). Evaluations are also available online.

http://www.aw.com/DTUI

References

Abowd, G. D., Classroom 2000: An experiment with the instrumentation of a living educational environment, *IBM Systems Journal*, 38, 4 (1999), 508–530.

Anderson, Robert H., Bikson, Tora K., Law, Sally Ann, and Mitchell, Bridger M., *Universal Access to Email: Feasibility and Societal Implications*, RAND, Santa Monica, CA (1995). Available at http://www.rand.org.

Badner, E. and Mark, G., Why distance matters: Effects on cooperation, persuasion and deception, *Proc. CSCW 2002 Conference: Computer-Supported Cooperative Work*, ACM Press, New York (2002), 226–235.

Baecker, Ron, *Readings in Groupware and Computer-Supported Cooperative Work: Assisting Human-Human Collaboration*, Morgan Kaufmann Publishers, San Francisco, CA (1993).

Baecker, Ron, Moore, Gale, and Zijdemans, Anita, Reinventing the lecture: Webcasting made interactive, *Proc. Human-Computer Interaction International 2003: Volume 1, Theory and Practice*, Lawrence Erlbaum Associates, Mahwah, NJ (2003), 896–900.

Beaudouin-Lafon, Michel, *Computer Supported Co-operative Work Trends in Software*, John Wiley & Sons, New York (1999).

Bly, Sara A., Harrison, Steve R., and Irwin, Susan, MediaSpaces: Bringing people together in a video, audio, and computing environment, *Communications of the ACM*, 36, 1 (January 1993), 28–47.

Bruce, B. C. and Easley, Jr., J. A., Emerging communities of practice: Collaboration and communication in action research, *Educational Action Research*, 8 (2000), 243–259.

Bruce, Bertram, Peyton, Joy, and Batson, Trent, *Network-Based Classrooms*, Cambridge University Press, Cambridge, U.K. (1992).

Bruckman, Amy, The future of e-learning communities, *Communications of the ACM*, 45, 4 (April 2002), 60–63.

Cadiz, J., Balachandran, A., Sanocki, E., Gupta, A., Grudin, J., and Jancke, G., Distance learning through distributed collaborative video viewing, *Proc. CSCW 2000 Conference: Computer-Supported Cooperative Work*, ACM Press, New York (2000), 135–144.

Chapanis, Alphonse, Interactive human communication, *Scientific American*, 232, 3 (March 1975), 36–42.

Cohill, A. M. and Kavanaugh, A. L., *Community Networks: Lessons from Blacksburg, Virginia, Second Edition*, Artech House, Cambridge, MA (2000).

Ellis, C. A., Gibbs, S. J., and Rein, G. L., Groupware: Some issues and experiences, *Communications of the ACM*, 34, 1 (January 1991), 680–689.

Finholt, T. A. and Olson, G. M., From laboratories to collaboratories: A new organizational form for scientific collaboration, *Psychological Science*, 8 (1997), 28–36.

Finn, K., Sellen, A., and Wilbur, S. (Editors), *Video-mediated Communication*, Lawrence Erlbaum Associates, Hillsdale, NJ (1997).

George, T., Communication gap: Tech-savvy young people bring their own ways of communicating to the workplace, and employees old and young need to adapt, *Information Week* (October 21, 2002), 81–82.

Greenberg, Saul and Rounding, Michael, The notification collage: Posting information to public and personal displays, *Proc. CHI 2001 Conference: Human Factors in Computing Systems*, ACM Press, New York (2001), 515–521.

Greenberg, Saul, Hayne, Stephen, and Rada, Roy (Editors), *Groupware for Real Time Drawing: A Designer's Guide*, McGraw-Hill, New York (1995).

Grinter, R. and Palen, L., Instant messaging in teen life, *Proc. CSCW 2002 Conference: Computer-Supported Cooperative Work*, ACM Press, New York (2002), 21–30.

Grudin, Jonathan, Groupware and social dynamics: Eight challenges for developers, *Communications of the ACM*, 37, 1 (January 1994), 93–105.

Guimbretière, Francois, Stone, Maureen, and Winograd, Terry, Fluid interaction with high-resolution wall-size displays, *Proc. UIST 2001 Symposium on User Interface Software & Technology*, ACM Press, New York (2001), 21–30.

Halkia, Matina and Local, Gary, Building the brief: Action and audience in augmented reality, *Proc. Human-Computer Interaction International 2003: Volume 4, Universal Access in HCI*, Lawrence Erlbaum Associates, Mahwah, NJ (2003), 389–393.

Hazemi, Reza and Hailes, Stephen, *The Digital University: Building a Learning Community*, Springer-Verlag, London, U.K. (2001).

Herbsleb, J., Atkins, D., Boyer, D., Handel, M., and Finholt, T. Introducing instant messaging and chat in the workplace, *Proc. CHI 2002 Conference: Human Factors in Computing Systems*, ACM Press, New York (2002), 171–178.

Hiltz, S. R., *The Virtual Classroom*, Ablex, Norwood, NJ (1992).

Hiltz, S. R. and Turoff, M., *The Network Nation: Human Communication via Computer.* Addison-Wesley, Reading, MA (1978, revised edition 1998).

Isaacs, Ellen, Morris, Trevor, Rodriguez, Thomas K., and Tang, John C., A comparison of face-to-face and distributed presentations, *Proc. CHI '95 Conference: Human Factors in Computing Systems*, ACM Press, New York (1995), 354–361.

Isaacs, Ellen, Tang, John C., and Morris, Trevor, Piazza: A desktop environment supporting impromptu and planned interactions, *Proc. CSCW '96 Conference: Computer-Supported Cooperative Work*, ACM Press, New York (1996), 325–333.

Isaacs, E., Walendowski, A., Whittaker, S., Schiano, D. J., and Kamm, C., The character, functions, and styles of instant messaging in the workplace, *Proc. CSCW 2002 Conference: Computer-Supported Cooperative Work*, ACM Press, New York (2002).

Isaacs, E., Walendowski, A., and Ranganathan, D., Hubbub: A sound-enhanced mobile instant messenger that supports awareness and opportunistic interactions, *Proc. CHI 2002 Conference: Human Factors in Computing Systems*, ACM Press, New York (2002), 179–186.

Ishii, H., Kobayashi, M., and Arita, K., Iterative design of seamless collaboration media: From TeamWorkStation to ClearBoard, *Communications of the ACM*, 37, 8 (1994), 83–97.

Jackson, W. J., Dawson, R., and Wilson, D., Understanding email interaction increases organizational productivity, *Communications of the ACM*, 46, 8 (2003), 80–84.

Jancke, G., Venolia, G., Grudin, J., Cadiz, J., and Gupta, A., Linking public spaces: Technical and social issues, *Proc. CHI 2001 Conference: Human Factors in Computing Systems*, ACM Press, New York (2001), 530–537.

Kim, Amy Jo, *Community Building on the Web*, Peachpit Press, Berkeley, CA (2000).

Kraut, Robert, E., Gergle, Darren, and Fussell, Susan, R., The use of visual information in shared visual spaces: Informing the development of visual co-presence, *Proc. CSCW 2002 Conference: Computer-Supported Cooperative Work*, ACM Press, New York (2002), 31–40.

Kraut, R., Lundmark, V., Patterson, M., Kiesler, S., Mukopadhyay, T., and Scherlis, W., Internet paradox: A social technology that reduces social involvement and psychological well-being? *American Psychologist*, 53 (1998), 1017–1031.

Kraut, R., Kiesler, S., Boneva, B., Cummings, J., Helgeson, V., and Crawford, A., Internet paradox revisited, *Journal of Social Issues*, 58, 1 (2002), 49–74.

Mantei, M., Capturing the capture lab concepts: A case study in the design of computer supported meeting environments, *Proc. CSCW '88 Conference: Computer-Supported Cooperative Work*, ACM Press, New York (1988), 257–270.

Millen, D. R., Fontaine, M. A., and Muller, M. J., Understanding the benefit and costs of communities of practice, *Communications of the ACM* 45, 4 (April 2002), 69–75.

Nardi, B., Whittaker, S., and Bradner, E., Interaction and outeraction: Instant messaging in action, *Proc. CSCW 2000 Conference: Computer-Supported Cooperative Work*, ACM Press, New York (2000), 79–88.

Nonnecke, B. and Preece, J., Lurker demographics: Counting the silent, *Proc. CHI 2000 Conference: Human Factors in Computing Systems*, ACM Press, New York (2000), 73–80.

Nunamaker, J. F., Dennis, Alan R., Valacich, Joseph S., Vogel, Douglas R., and George, Joey F., Electronic meeting systems to support group work, *Communications of the ACM*, 34, 7 (July 1991), 40–61.

Olson, G. M., Atkins, D., Clauer, R., Weymouth, T., Prackash, A., Finholt, T., Jahanian, F., and Rasmussen, C., Technology to support distributed team science: The first phase of the upper atmosphere research collaboratory (UARC), in Olson, G. M., Malone, T., and Smith, J. (Editors) *Coordination Theory and Collaboration Technology*, Lawrence Erlbaum Associates, Hillsdale, NJ (2001), 761–783.

Olson, J. S. and Olson, G. M., Groupware and computer-supported cooperative work, in Jacko, J. A. and Sears, A. (Editors), *The Human-Computer Interaction Handbook: Fundamentals, Evolving Technologies, and Emerging Applications*, Lawrence Erlbaum Associates, Mahwah, NJ (2003), 583–595.

Olson, J. S. and Olson, G. M., Distance matters, *Human-Computer Interaction*, 15, 2/3 (2000), 139–178.

Prante, Thorsten, Magerkurth, Carsten, and Streitz, Norbert, Developing CSCW tools for ideas finding—Empirical results and implications for design, *Proc. CSCW 2002 Conference: Computer-Supported Cooperative Work*, ACM Press, New York (2002), 106–115.

Preece, Jenny, Empathic communities: Balancing emotional and factual communications, *Interacting with Computers* 12, 1 (1999), 63–77.

Preece, Jenny, *Online Communities: Designing Usability and Supporting Sociability*, John Wiley & Sons, New York (2000).

Rheingold, Howard, *The Virtual Community: Homesteading on the Electronic Frontier*, Addison-Wesley, Reading, MA (1993).

Rheingold, Howard, *Smart Mobs: The Next Social Revolution*, Perseus Publishing, New York (2002).

Robinson, John and Nie, Norman, Introduction to IT & Society, Issue 1: Sociability, *IT and Society: A Web Journal Studying How Technology Affects Society* 1, 1 (Summer 2002). Available at http://itandsociety.org.

Roseman, Mark and Greenberg, Saul, TeamRooms: Network places for collaboration, *Proc. CSCW '96 Conference: Computer-Supported Cooperative Work*, ACM Press, New York (1996), 325–333.

Schuler, Doug, *New Community Networks: Wired for Change*, Addison-Wesley, Reading, MA (1996).

Sellen, Abigail J., Remote conversations: The effects of mediating talk with technology, *Human-Computer Interaction*, 10, 4 (1994), 401–444.

Shneiderman, B., Borkowski, E., Alavi, M., and Norman, K., Emergent patterns of teaching/learning in electronic classrooms, *Educational Technology Research & Development*, 46, 4 (1998), 23–42.

Smith, M., Tools for navigating large social cyberspaces, *Communications of the ACM* 45, 4 (April 2002), 51–55.

Stefik, M., Bobrow, D. G., Foster, G., Lanning, S., and Tartar, D., WYSIWIS revised: Early experiences with multiuser interfaces, *ACM Transactions on Office Information Systems*, 5, 2 (April 1987), 147–186.

Streitz, N., Geisler, J., Holmer, T., Konomi, S., Muller-Tomfelde, C., Reischl, W., Rexroth, P., Seitz, P., and Steinmetz, S., I-LAND: An interactive landscape for creativity and innovation, *Proc. CHI '99 Conference: Human Factors in Computing Systems*, ACM Press, New York (1999), 120–127.

Turkle, Sherry, *Life on the Screen: Identity in the Age of the Internet*, Simon and Schuster, New York (1995).

Valacich, J. S., Dennis, A. R., and Nunamaker, Jr., J. F., Electronic meeting support: The GroupSystems concept, *International Journal of Man-Machine Studies*, 34, 2 (1991), 261–282.

Wenger, E., *Communities of Practice: Learning, Meaning and Identity*, Cambridge University Press, Cambridge, U.K. (1998).

Wiener, Earl L. and Nagel, David C. (Editors), *Human Factors in Aviation*, Academic Press, New York (1988).

PART

IV

Design Issues

chapter

Quality of Service

Stimulation is the indispensable requisite for pleasure in
an experience, and the feeling of bare time is the least
stimulating experience we can have.

WILLIAM JAMES
Principles of Psychology, Volume I, 1890

Nothing can be more useful to a man than a determination
not to be hurried.

HENRY DAVID THOREAU
Journal

11.1   Introduction

In the 1960s, user perception of computer speed was determined by response time for mathematical computations, program compilations, or database searches. Then, as time-shared systems emerged, contention for the scarce computational resources led to more complex reasons for delays. With the emergence of the World Wide Web, user expectations for expanded services grew, along with still more complex explanations of delays. Users now have to understand the size differences between text and graphics pages to appreciate the huge variations in server loads, and to tolerate network congestion. They also have to understand the multiple sources of dropped connections, unavailable web sites, and network outages. This complex set of concerns is usually discussed under the term *Quality of Service*.

Concern over Quality of Service stems from a basic human value: Time is precious. When externally imposed delays impede progress on a task, many people become frustrated, annoyed, and eventually angry. Lengthy or unexpected system response times and slow display rates produce these reactions in computer users, leading to frequent errors and low satisfaction. Some users accept the situation with a shrug of their shoulders, but most users prefer to work more quickly than the computer allows.

Discussions of Quality of Service must also take into account a second basic human value: Harmful mistakes should be avoided. However, balancing rapid performance with low error rates sometimes means that the pace of work must slow. If users work too quickly, they may learn less, read with lower comprehension, commit more data-entry errors, and make more incorrect decisions. Stress can build in these situations, especially if it is hard to recover from errors, or if the errors destroy data, damage equipment, or imperil human life (for example, in air-traffic–control or medical systems) (Emurian, 1991; Kohlisch and Kuhmann, 1997).

A third Quality of Service value is to reduce user frustration. With long delays, users may become frustrated enough to make mistakes or give up working. Delays are often a cause of frustration, but there are others, such as crashes that destroy data, software bugs that produce incorrect results, and poor designs that lead to user confusion. Networked environments generate further frustrations: unreliable service providers, dropped lines, e-mail spam, and malicious viruses.

Quality of Service discussions usually focus on the decisions to be made by network designers and operators. This is appropriate, because their decisions have a profound influence on many users. They also have the tools and knowledge to be helpful, and increasingly they must adhere to legal and regulatory controls. For interface designers and builders, there is also a set of design decisions that dramatically influence the user experience. For example, they can optimize web pages to reduce byte counts and numbers of files, or provide previews of materials available in digital libraries or archives to help reduce the number of queries and accesses to the network (see Fig. 11.1 and Section 14.2). In addition, users may have the opportunity to choose from fast or slow services and from viewing low-resolution versus high-resolution images. Users need guidance to understand the implications of their choices and help them to accommodate varying levels of Quality of Service. For users, the main experience of Quality of Service is the computer system's *response time*, so we'll deal with those issues first, before addressing application crashes, unreliable network service, and malicious threats.

Section 11.2 begins by discussing a model of response-time impacts, reviewing short-term human memory, and identifying the sources of human error. Section 11.3 focuses on the role of users' expectations and attitudes in shaping their subjective reactions to the Quality of Service. Section 11.4 deals with productivity as a function of response time, and Section 11.5 reviews the research on the influence of variable response times. Section 11.6 examines the severity of frustrating experiences, including spam and viruses.

11.2   Models of Response-Time Impacts

Response time is defined as the number of seconds it takes from the moment users initiate an action (usually by pressing an ENTER key or mouse button) until the computer begins to present results on the display, printer, loudspeaker, or mobile device. When the response is completed, users begin formulating the next action. The *user think time* is the number of seconds during which users

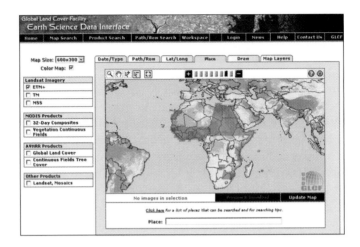

Figure 11.1

The University of Maryland Global Land Cover Facility's online search page indicates where data is available in red on a zoomable map. Users looking for data in Africa can thus tell where to focus their searches, which will allow them to find what they need with fewer queries and network accesses. (glcf.umiacs.umd.edu)

think before initiating the next action. In this simple stages of action model, users (1) initiate, (2) wait for the computer to respond, (3) watch while the results appear, (4) think for a while, and initiate again (Fig. 11.2).

In a more realistic model (Fig. 11.3), users plan while interpreting results, while typing/clicking, and while the computer is generating results or retrieving information across the network. Most people will use whatever time they have to plan ahead; thus, precise measurements of user think time are difficult to obtain. The computer's response is usually more precisely defined and measurable, but there are problems here as well. Some interfaces respond with distracting messages, informative feedback, or a simple prompt immediately after an action is initiated, but actual results may not appear for a few seconds. For example, users may drag a file to a network printer icon using direct manipulation, but then it may take many seconds for confirmation that the printer has been activated or for a dialog box to report that the printer is offline. Delays of more than 160 milliseconds while dragging the icon are noticed and become annoying, but users have come to accept delays for responses from networked devices.

Designers who specify response times and network managers who seek to provide high Quality of Service have to consider the complex interaction of technical feasibility, costs, task complexity, user expectations, speed of task performance,

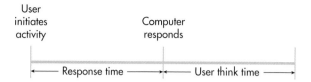

Figure 11.2

Simple stages of action model of system response time and user think time.

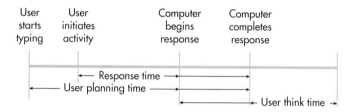

Figure 11.3

Model of system response time, user planning time, and user think time. This model is more realistic than the one in Fig. 11.2.

error rates, and error-handling procedures. Decisions about these variables are further complicated by the influence of users' personality differences, fatigue, familiarity with computers, experience with the task, and motivation (Bouch, Kuchinsky, and Bhatti, 2000; King, 2003).

Although some people are content with slower responses for some tasks, the overwhelming majority prefer rapid interactions. Overall productivity depends not only on the speed of the interface, but also on the rate of human error and the ease of recovery from those errors. Lengthy (longer than 15-second) response times are generally detrimental to productivity, increasing error rates and decreasing satisfaction. More rapid (less than 1-second) interactions are generally preferred and can increase productivity, but they may also increase error rates for complex tasks. The high cost of providing rapid response times and the loss from increased errors must be evaluated in the choice of an optimum pace.

For alphanumeric displays, the *display rate* is the speed, in *characters per second* (cps), at which characters appear for users to read. The rate may be limited to 120 cps by inexpensive modems or noisy communications lines, so the display may take a few seconds to fill. Many mobile devices receive text messages at this slow rate, but since messages are short and displays are small, users are satisfied. In demanding web applications on desktop machines, the faster display rate is usually limited by network transmission speed or server performance. Portions of images or fragments of a page may appear with interspersed delays of several seconds.

Display rates for graphics are measured in bytes per second; a typical home user has a 56-kilobits-per-second (Kbps) modem. Since there are 8 bits/byte and noisy lines reduce performance, dial-up users receive 4–7 kilobytes (KB) per second. At that rate, a page of text might load in a few seconds, but a 100-KB image may take 30 seconds or more to load—a long delay. Some e-mail attachments (such as photos or documents) or file downloads (such as programs or videos) may take minutes or even hours to complete, especially with slower modems. Faster communications lines with advanced network connections (such as Asynchronous Transfer Mode, or ATM), satellite connections, or cable modems significantly reduce download times, but these are not available to all users.

Reading textual information from a screen is more difficult than reading from a book (see Chapter 13). If the display rate can be made so fast that the screen appears to fill instantly (beyond the speed at which someone might feel compelled to keep up), users seem to relax, to pace themselves, and to work productively. Since users often scan a web page looking for highlights or links, rather than reading the full text, it is useful to display text first, leaving space for the graphical elements that are slower to display. Since graphics files can be more than a megabyte in size, user control over image quality and size should be possible.

Consumer demand is a key factor in promoting rapid performance. Many desktop and laptop computers still take several minutes to start, but cell phones, mobile devices, and games are designed to start in seconds. If market competition is insufficient to produce change, consumer pressure on software and hardware makers will be needed to force changes that result in more rapid computer starts. Web sites often distinguish themselves with rapid performance, an attribute that surfers expect from Google or Yahoo! and buyers demand at Amazon.com or eBay (Morris and Turner, 2001; King, 2003).

A cognitive model of human performance that accounts for the experimental results in response time would be useful in making predictions, designing interfaces, and formulating management policies. A complete predictive model that accounts for all the variables may never be realized, but even fragments of such a model are useful to designers.

Robert B. Miller's review (1968) presented a lucid analysis of response-time issues and a list of 17 situations in which preferred response times might differ. Much has changed since his paper was written, but the principles of closure, short-term memory limitations, and chunking still apply. Any cognitive model must emerge from an understanding of these human problem-solving abilities and information-processing capabilities. A central issue is the limitation of *short-term memory* capacity, as outlined in George Miller's (1956) classic paper, "The magical number seven, plus or minus two." Miller identified the limited capacities people have for absorbing information. People can rapidly recognize approximately 7 (this value was contested by later researchers, but it serves as a good estimate) *chunks* of information at a time and can hold those chunks in short-term memory for 15 to 30 seconds. The size of a chunk of information depends on the person's familiarity with the material.

For example, most people can look at 7 binary digits for a few seconds and then recall the digits correctly from memory within 15 seconds. However, performing a distracting task during those 15 seconds, such as reciting a poem, erases the binary digits. Of course, if people concentrate on remembering the binary digits and succeed in transferring them to long-term memory, then they can retain the binary digits for much longer periods. Most Americans can also probably remember seven decimal digits, seven alphabetic characters, seven English words, or even seven familiar advertising slogans. Although these items have increasing complexity, they are still treated as single chunks. However, Americans might not succeed in remembering seven Russian letters, Chinese pictograms, or Polish sayings. Knowledge and experience govern the size of a chunk and the ease of remembering for each individual.

People use short-term memory in conjunction with *working memory* for processing information and for problem solving. Short-term memory processes perceptual input, whereas working memory is used to generate and implement solutions. If many facts and decisions are necessary to solve a problem, then short-term and working memory may become overloaded. People learn to cope with complex problems by developing higher-level concepts that bring together several lower-level concepts into a single chunk. Novices at any task tend to work with smaller chunks until they can cluster concepts into larger chunks. Experts rapidly decompose a complex task into a sequence of smaller tasks that they are confident about accomplishing.

This chunking phenomenon was demonstrated in a study of experienced keypunch operators who typed data records organized into numeric, alphanumeric, and English word fields (Neal, 1977). The median time between keystrokes was 0.2 seconds, but it rose to more than 0.3 seconds at field boundaries and 0.9 seconds at record boundaries.

Short-term and working memory are highly volatile; disruptions cause loss of information, and delays can require that the memory be refreshed. Visual distractions or noisy environments also interfere with cognitive processing. Furthermore, anxiety apparently reduces the size of the available memory, since the person's attention is partially absorbed in concerns that are beyond the realm of the problem-solving task.

If people are able to construct a solution to a problem in spite of interference, they must still record or implement the solution. If they can implement the solution immediately, they can proceed quickly through their work. On the other hand, if they must record the solution in long-term memory, on paper, or on a complex device, the chances for error increase and the pace of work slows.

Multiplying two four-digit numbers in your head is difficult because the intermediate results cannot be maintained in working memory and must be transferred to long-term memory. Controlling nuclear reactors or air traffic is a challenge in part because these tasks often require integration of information (in short-term and working memory) from several sources, as well as maintenance of awareness of the complete situation. In attending to newly arriving information, operators may be distracted and may lose the contents of their short-term or working memory.

When using an interactive computer system, users may formulate plans and then have to wait while they execute each step in the plan. If a step produces an unexpected result or if the delays are long, then users may forget part of the plan or be forced to review the plan continually. This model leads to the conjecture that, for a given user and task, there is a preferred response time. Long response times lead to wasted effort and more errors, because the solution plan must be reviewed repeatedly. On the other hand, short response times may generate a faster pace in which solution plans are prepared hastily and incompletely. More data from a variety of situations and users would clarify these conjectures.

As response times grow longer, users may become more anxious because the penalty for an error increases. As the difficulty in handling an error increases, users' anxiety levels increase, further slowing performance and increasing errors. However, as response times grow shorter and display rates increase, users tend to pick up the pace of the interface and may fail to fully comprehend the presented material, may generate incorrect solution plans, and may make more execution errors. The speed/accuracy tradeoff that is a harsh reality in so many domains is also apparent in interface usage. A related factor is performance in paced versus unpaced tasks. In paced tasks, the computer forces decisions within a fixed time period, thereby adding pressure and forcing a decision to be made. Such high-stress interfaces may be appropriate with trained users in life-critical situations or in manufacturing, where high productivity is a requirement. However, errors, poor-quality work, and operator burn-out are serious concerns. In unpaced tasks, users decide when to respond and can take their time to work at a more relaxed pace or make a careful decision.

Car driving may offer a useful analogy. Although higher speed limits are attractive to many drivers because they lead to faster completion of trips, they also lead to higher accident rates. Since automobile accidents have dreadful consequences, we accept speed limits. When incorrect use of computer systems can lead to damage to life, property, or data, should not speed limits be provided?

Another lesson from driving is the importance of progress indicators. Drivers want to know how far it is to their destination and what progress they are making by seeing the declining number of miles on road signs. Similarly, computer users want to know how long it will take for a web page to load or a file directory scan to be completed (Fig. 11.4). Users given graphical dynamic progress indicators rather than static ("Please wait"), blinking, or numeric (number of seconds left) messages report higher satisfaction and shorter perceived elapsed times to completion (Meyer et al., 1996).

Users may achieve rapid task performance, low error rates, and high satisfaction if the following criteria are met:

- Users have adequate knowledge of the objects and actions necessary for the problem-solving task.
- The solution plan can be carried out without delays.
- Distractions are eliminated.
- User anxiety is low.
- There is feedback about progress towards the solution.
- Errors can be avoided or, if they occur, can be handled easily.

These conditions for optimum problem solving, with acceptable cost and technical feasibility, are the basic constraints on design. However, other conjectures may play a role in choosing the optimum interaction speed:

- Novices may exhibit better performance with somewhat slower response times.
- Novices prefer to work at speeds slower than those chosen by knowledgeable, frequent users.
- When there is little penalty for an error, users prefer to work more quickly.
- When the task is familiar and easily comprehended, users prefer more rapid action.
- If users have experienced rapid performance previously, they will expect and demand it in future situations.

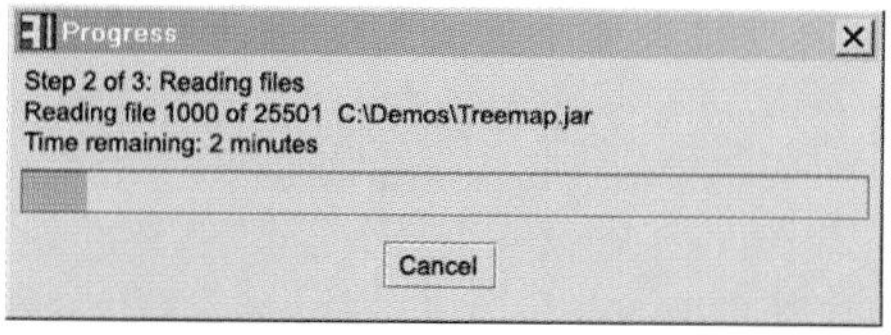

Figure 11.4

Dynamic progress indicators reassure users that the process is underway. Providing time estimates is best, but when that information is difficult to calculate other progress indicators—such as the name of the file or the file count—can be updated at regular intervals.

These informal conjectures need to be qualified and verified. Then, a more rigorous cognitive model needs to be developed to accommodate the great diversity in human work styles and in computer-use situations. Practitioners can conduct field tests to measure productivity, error rates, and satisfaction as a function of response times in their application areas.

Researchers are extending models of productivity to accommodate the realities of work and home environments. These situated action models now include tempting distractions and unavoidable interruptions, such as arriving e-mail messages, pop-up instant messages, phone calls, and requests from fellow workers or family members. Enabling users to easily limit or block interruptions is becoming necessary. Another useful functionality is to provide users with feedback about the amount of time spent on various tasks and a log of how they handled interruptions. Personal, organizational, and cultural differences will have to be accommodated, because of variations in the necessity to accept interruptions from managers or family members.

The experiments described in the following sections are tiles in the mosaic of human performance with computers, but many more tiles are necessary before the fragments can form a complete image. Some guidelines have emerged for designers and information-system managers, but local testing and continuous monitoring of performance and satisfaction are still necessary. The remarkable adaptability of computer users means that researchers and practitioners will have to be alert to novel conditions that require revisions of these guidelines.

11.3   Expectations and Attitudes

How long will users wait for the computer to respond before they become annoyed? This simple question has provoked much discussion and several experiments. There is no simple answer to the question, and more importantly, it may be the wrong question to ask. More refined questions focus on users' needs: Will users more happily wait for a valued document than an undesired advertisement?

Related design issues may clarify the question of acceptable response time. For example, how long should users have to wait before they hear a dial tone on a telephone or see a picture on the television? If the cost is not excessive, the frequently mentioned two-second limit (Miller, 1968) seems appropriate for many tasks. In some situations, however, users expect responses within 0.1 second, such as when turning the wheel of a car; pressing a key on a keyboard, piano, or telephone; dragging an icon; or scrolling through a list on a cell phone. Two-second delays in these cases might be unsettling, because users have adapted a working style and expectations based on responses within a fraction of a second.

In other situations, users are accustomed to longer response times, such as waiting 30 seconds for a red traffic light to turn green, two days for a letter to arrive, or a month for flowers to grow.

The first factor influencing acceptable response time is that people have established expectations based on their past experiences of the time required to complete a given task. If a task is completed more quickly than expected, people will be pleased; but if the task is completed much more quickly than expected, they may become concerned that something is wrong. Similarly, if a task is completed much more slowly than expected, users become concerned or frustrated. Even though people can detect 8% changes in a 2- or 4-second response time (Miller, 1968), users apparently do not become concerned until the change is much greater.

Two installers of networked computer systems reported a problem concerning user expectations with new systems. The first users are delighted, because the response time is short when the load is light. As the load builds, however, these first users become unhappy because the response time deteriorates. At the same time, the users who join later may be satisfied with what they perceive as normal response times. Both installers devised a *response-time choke* by which they could slow down the system when the load was light. This surprising policy makes the response time uniform over time and across users, thus reducing complaints.

Network managers have similar problems with varying response times as new equipment is added or as large projects begin or complete their work. The variation in response time can be disruptive to users who have developed expectations and working styles based on a specific response time. There are also periods within each day when the response time is short, such as at lunchtime, or when it is long, such as midmorning or late afternoon. Some users rush to complete a task when response times are short, and as a result they may make more errors. Some workers refuse to work when the response time is slow relative to their expectations. One subject in a study of web shopping commented "You get a bit spoiled… once you are used to the quickness, then you want it all the time" (Bouch, Kuchinsky, and Bhatti, 2000).

An important design issue is the issue of rapid start-up. Users are annoyed if they have to wait several minutes for a laptop or a digital camera to be ready for usage, and consequently fast starts are a strong distinguishing feature in consumer electronics. A related issue is the tradeoff between rapid start-up and rapid usage. For example, it may take several minutes to download a Java or other web application, but then performance is rapid for most actions. An alternative design might speed the start-up, but the cost could be occasional delays during usage.

A second factor influencing response-time expectations is the individual's tolerance for delays. Novice computer users may be willing to wait much longer than are experienced users. In short, there are large variations in what individuals consider acceptable waiting time. These variations are influenced by many factors, such as personality, cost, age, mood, cultural context, time of day, noise, and perceived pressure to complete work. The laid-back web surfer may enjoy chatting with friends while pages appear, but the anxious deadline-fighting journalist may start banging on desks or keys in a vain attempt to push the computer along.

Other factors influencing response-time expectations are the task complexity and the users' familiarity with the task. For simple, repetitive tasks that require little problem solving, users want to perform rapidly and are annoyed by delays of more than a few tenths of a second. For complex problems, users can plan ahead during longer response times and will perform well even as response time grows. Users are highly adaptive and can change their working styles to accommodate different response times. This factor was found in early studies of batch-programming environments and in recent studies of interactive-system usage. If delays are long, whenever possible users will seek alternate strategies that reduce the number of interactions. They will fill in the long delays by performing other tasks, daydreaming, or planning ahead in their work. But even if diversions are available, dissatisfaction grows with longer response times.

An increasing number of tasks place high demands on rapid system performance; examples are user-controlled three-dimensional animations, flight simulations, graphic design, and dynamic queries for information visualization. In these applications, users are continuously adjusting the input controls, and they expect changes to appear with no perceived delay—that is, within less than 100 milliseconds. Similarly, some tasks (for example, video conferencing, Voice over IP telephony, and streaming multimedia) require rapid performance to ensure high Quality of Service, because intermittent delays cause jumpy images and broken sound patterns that seriously disrupt users. Promoters of these services see the need for ever faster and higher capacity networks.

The expanded audiences and novel tasks on the World Wide Web have brought new considerations into Quality of Service. Since e-commerce shoppers are deeply concerned with trust, credibility, and privacy, researchers have begun to study interactions with time delay. The range of response times is highly varied across web sites (Huberman, 2001; see Fig. 11.5), and site managers are regularly compelled to decide on what level of resource expenditure is appropriate to reduce response times for users. Studies have found that as the response times increase, users find web-page content less interesting (Ramsay, Barbesi, and Preece, 1998) and lower in quality (Jacko, Sears, and Borella, 2000). Long response times may even have a negative influence on user perceptions of the companies who provide the web sites (Bouch, Kuchinsky, and Bhatti, 2000). One web-shopping study participant who believed that successful companies have the resources to build high-performance web sites remarked that "This is the way the consumer sees the company… it should look good, it should be fast."

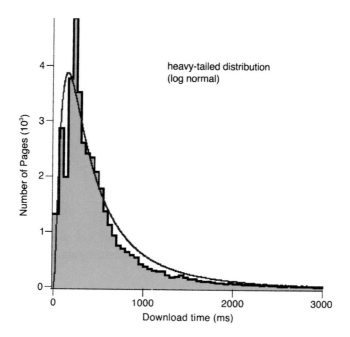

Figure 11.5

Distribution of response times for 40,000 randomly selected web pages, showing a log normal distribution. Half the pages were delivered in under half a second, but the long tail shows the variability. (Huberman, 2001).

In summary, three primary factors influence users' expectations and attitudes regarding response time:

1. Previous experiences
2. Individual personality differences
3. Task differences

Experimental results show interesting patterns of behavior for specific backgrounds, individuals, and tasks, but it is difficult to distill a simple set of conclusions. Several experiments attempted to identify acceptable waiting times by allowing participants to press a key if they thought that the waiting time was too long. Participants who could shorten the response time in future interactions took advantage of that feature as they became more experienced. They forced response times for frequent actions down to well below one second. It seems appealing to offer users a choice in the pace of the interaction. Video-game designers recognize the role of user-controlled pace setting and the increased challenge from fast pacing. One the other hand, older adults and users with disabilities may appreciate being able to slow the pace of interaction. Differing desires also open opportunities to charge premiums for faster service; for example, many World Wide Web users are willing to pay extra for faster network performance.

In summary, three conjectures emerge:

1. Individual differences are large and users are adaptive. They will work faster as they gain experience and will change their working strategies as response times change. It may be useful to allow people to set their own pace of interaction.

2. For repetitive tasks, users prefer and will work more rapidly with short response times.

3. For complex tasks, users can adapt to working with slow response times with no loss of productivity, but their dissatisfaction increases as response times lengthen.

11.4   User Productivity

Shorter system response times usually lead to higher productivity, but in some situations users who receive long system response times can find clever shortcuts or ways to do concurrent processing to reduce the effort and time to accomplish a task. Working too quickly, though, may lead to errors that reduce productivity.

In computing, just as in driving, there is no general rule about whether the high-speed highway or the slower, clever shortcut is better. The designer must survey each situation carefully to make the optimal choice. The choice is not critical for the occasional excursion, but it becomes worthy of investigation when the frequency is great. When computers are used in high-volume situations, more effort can be expended in discovering the proper response time for a given task and set of users. It should not be surprising that a new study must be conducted when the tasks and users change, just as a new route evaluation must be done for each trip.

The nature of the task has a strong influence on whether changes in response time alter user productivity. A *repetitive control task* involves monitoring a display and issuing actions in response to changes in the display. Although the operator may be trying to understand the underlying process, the basic activities are to respond to a change in the display, to issue commands, and then to see whether the commands produce the desired effect. When there is a choice among actions, the problem becomes more interesting and the operator tries to pick the optimal action in each situation. With shorter system response times, the operator picks up the pace of the system and works more quickly, but decisions on actions may be less than optimal. On the other hand, with short response times, the penalty for a poor choice may be small because it may be easy to try another action. In fact, operators may learn to use the interface more quickly with short system response times because they can explore alternatives more easily.

In one study of a control task involving multiparameter optimization, the goal was to force "a displayed graph to lie wholly within a defined acceptance region" (Goodman and Spence, 1981). Operators could adjust five parameters by using lightpen touches, thus altering the shape of the graph. There were response times of 0.16, 0.72, or 1.49 seconds. The participants worked at each of the three response times in this repeated-measures experiment. The solution times and the total user think time were the same for the 0.16- and 0.72-second treatments. The 1.49-second treatment led to a 50% increase in solution time and to a modest increase in user think time. In this case, reducing the response time to less than one second was beneficial in terms of human productivity.

In a study of a data-entry task, users adopted one of three strategies, depending on the response time (Teal and Rudnicky, 1992). With response times under one second, users worked automatically without checking whether the system was ready for the next data value. This behavior resulted in numerous anticipation errors, in which the users typed data values before the system could accept those values. With response times above two seconds, users monitored the display carefully to make sure that the prompt appeared before they typed. In the middle ground of one to two seconds, users paced themselves and waited an appropriate amount of time before attempting to enter data values.

When complex problem solving is required and many approaches to the solution are possible, users will adapt their work styles to the response time. A demonstration of this effect emerged from an early study using four experienced participants doing complex matrix manipulations (Grossberg, Wiesen, and Yntema, 1976). The response-time means were set at 1, 4, 16, and 64 seconds for commands that generated output or an error message. Nonoutput commands were simply accepted by the interface. The remarkable outcome of this study was that the time to solution was invariant with respect to response time! When working with 64-second delays, participants used substantially fewer output commands and also fewer total commands. Apparently, with long response times, participants thought more carefully about the problem solution, since there were also longer intervals between commands. Although the number of participants was small, the results strongly support the notion that, if possible, users will change their work habits as the response time changes. As the cost in time of an error or an unnecessary output command rose, participants made fewer errors and issued fewer commands. These results were closely tied to the study's complex, intellectually demanding task, for which there were several solutions.

Productivity with statistical problem-solving tasks was also found to be constant despite response-time changes over the range of 0.1 to 5.0 seconds (Martin and Corl, 1986). The same study with regular users found linear productivity gains for simple data-entry tasks. The simpler and more habitual the task was, the greater the productivity benefit of a short response time was.

Barber and Lucas (1983) studied professional circuit-layout clerks who assigned telephone equipment in response to service requests. For this complex task, the lowest error rate occurred with a 12-second response time (Fig. 11.6). With shorter response times, the workers made hasty decisions; with longer response times, the frustration of waiting burdened short-term memory. The number of productive transactions (total minus errors) increased almost linearly with reductions in response time, and subjective preference was consistently in favor of the shorter response time.

In summary, users pick up the pace of the interface, and they consistently prefer a faster pace. Error rates at shorter response times increase with the cognitive complexity of the tasks. Each task appears to have an optimal pace—response times that are shorter or longer than this pace lead to increased errors. If error damage can be large and recovery is difficult, users should slow themselves down and make careful decisions.

11.5   Variability in Response Time

People are willing to pay substantial amounts of money to reduce the variability in their lives. The entire insurance industry is based on the reduction of present

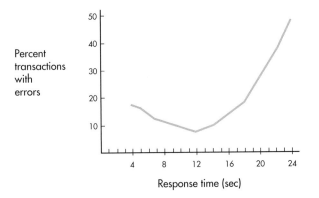

Figure 11.6

Error rates as a function of response time for a complex telephone-circuit–layout task by Barber and Lucas (1983). Although error rates were lowest with long response times (12 seconds), productivity increased with shorter times because the system could detect errors and thus users could rapidly correct them.

pleasures, through the payment of premiums, to reduce the severity of potential future losses. Most people appreciate predictable behavior that lessens the anxiety of contemplating unpleasant surprises.

When using computers, users cannot see into the machines to gain reassurance that their actions are being executed properly, but the response time can provide a clue. If users come to expect a response time of 3 seconds for a common action, they may become apprehensive if this action takes 0.5 or 15 seconds. Such extreme variation is unsettling and should be prevented or acknowledged by the interface, with some indicator for an unusually fast response or a progress report for an unusually slow response.

The more difficult issue is the effect of modest variations in response time. As discussed earlier, Miller (1968) raised this issue and reported that 75% of participants tested could perceive 8% variations in time for periods in the interval of 2 to 4 seconds. These results prompted some designers to suggest restrictive rules for variability of response time. Since it may not be technically feasible to provide a fixed short response time (such as one second) for all actions, several researchers have suggested that the time be fixed for classes of actions. Many actions could have a fixed response time of less than 1 second, other actions could take 4 seconds, and still other actions could take 12 seconds.

Experimental results suggest that modest variations in response time do not severely affect performance. Users are apparently capable of adapting to varying situations, although some of them may become frustrated when performing certain tasks. Goodman and Spence (1982) measured performance changes as a result of response-time variation in a problem-solving situation (a similar situation was used in their earlier experiment, described in Section 11.4). They found no significant performance changes as the variability was increased. The time to solution and the profile of command use were unchanged. As the variability increased, participants took advantage of fast responses by entering subsequent commands immediately, balancing the time lost in waiting for slower responses. Similar results were found by other researchers.

The physiological effect of response time is an important issue for stressful, long-duration tasks such as air-traffic control, but it is also a concern for office workers and sales personnel. While no dramatic differences have been found between constant and variable response-time treatments, statistically significantly higher error rates, higher systolic blood pressure, and more pronounced pain symptoms were found repeatedly with shorter response times (Kohlisch and Kuhmann, 1997). Similarly, a study of database queries compared an 8-second constant response time to a variable response time ranging from 1 to 30 seconds (mean 8 seconds) (Emurian, 1991). Although diastolic blood pressure and masseter (jaw-muscle) tension did increase when compared to resting baseline values, there were no significant differences in these physiological measures between constant and variable treatments.

In summary, modest variations in response time (plus or minus 50% of the mean) appear to be tolerable and to have little effect on performance. Frustration emerges only if delays are unusually long (at least twice the anticipated time). Similarly, anxiety about an erroneous command may emerge only if the response time is unusually short—say, less than one-quarter of the anticipated time. But even with extreme changes, users appear to be adaptable enough to complete their tasks.

It may be useful to slow down unexpected fast responses to avoid surprising users. This proposal is controversial, but it would affect only a small fraction of user interactions. Certainly, designers should also make a serious effort to avoid extremely slow responses, or, if responses must be slow, should give users information to indicate progress towards the goal. One graphics interface displays a large clock ticking backwards; the output appears only when the clock has ticked down to zero. Likewise, many printing and downloading programs display the page numbers to indicate progress and to confirm that the computer is at work productively on the appropriate document.

11.6   Frustrating Experiences

Quality of Service is usually defined in terms of network performance, but another perspective is to think about the quality of user experiences. Many technology promoters argue that the quality of user experiences with computers has been improving over the past four decades, pointing to the steadily increasing chip and network speeds and hard-drive capacities. However, critics believe frustration from interface complexity, network disruptions, and malicious interference has grown. Recent research has begun to document and understand the sources of user frustration with contemporary user interfaces.

User surveys elicit strong responses that convey unsatisfactory experiences in the general population. A British study of 1,255 office workers by a major computer manufacturer found that nearly half of the respondents felt frustrated or stressed by the amount of time it takes to solve problems. In an American survey of 6,000 computer users, the average amount of wasted time was estimated as 5.1 hours per week.

Replacing these possibly exaggerated impressions with more reliable data is a serious challenge. Self-reports and observations from more than 100 users doing their own work for an average of 2.5 hours each produced disturbing results: 46 to 53% of the users' time was seen as being wasted (Ceaparu et al., 2004). Frequent complaints included dropped network connections, application crashes, long system response times, and confusing error messages, but no individual cause contributed more than 9%. The major sources of problems were the popular applications for web browsing, e-mail, and word processing. Recommendations for reducing frustration include interface redesign, software quality improvement, and network reliability increases. Other recommendations focus on what users can do through increased learning, careful use of services, and self-control of their attitudes.

Infrastructure improvements to server capacity, network speed, and modem reliability will improve user experiences, but the continuing growth of Internet usage means there will be problems for many years to come. Poor Quality of Service is a still greater difficulty in emerging markets and developing nations, where infrastructure reliability remains a problem.

Since user training can have a profound influence on reducing frustrating experiences, efforts to improve education through schools and workplaces could improve user experiences. Improved educational programs and refined user interfaces are likely to have the largest effect on poorly educated users, whose difficulties in using Internet services undermine efforts to provide e-learning, e-commerce, and e-government services.

Networked services, especially e-mail, are among the most valued benefits of information and communications technologies. However, e-mail has become the source of frustrating spam (spam is the pejorative term given to unwanted, unsolicited e-mail, including advertisements, personal solicitations, and pornographic invitations). Some of these messages come from major corporations who make an effort to focus their e-mail on current customers, but much spam comes from small companies and individuals who take advantage of the low cost of e-mail to send blanket notices to huge lists of unfiltered e-mail addresses. Anti-spam legislation is being passed in many nations, but the Internet's international reach and open policies limit the success of legal controls. Many network providers intercept e-mail from known spam sources, which account for 80% of all e-mails, but users still complain of too much spam. User-controlled spam filters also help, but the complexity of installation and user controls undermines many users' willingness to use these tools. Furthermore, the increasingly clever spam senders rapidly change their messages to bypass existing filters. Similarly, distributors of pop-up advertisements refine their schemes to account for changing technology and to bypass user-protection strategies. A consumer uprising could pressure software developers, network providers, and government agencies to deal more directly with these annoying problems. Some spam senders and advertisers claim freedom of speech in their right to send spam or ads, but most users wish to see some limitation on the right to send bulk e-mails or unsolicited pop-up ads.

Another frustrating problem for users is the prevalence of malicious viruses that, once installed on a machine, can destroy data, disrupt usage, or produce a cancerous spread of the virus to everyone on the user's e-mail contact list. Viruses are created by malevolent programmers who want to spread havoc, usually by e-mail attachments. Unsuspecting recipients may get an infected e-mail from a known correspondent, but the absence of a meaningful subject line or message is often a clue that the e-mail contains a virus. Deceptive messages that mention previous e-mails or make appealing invitations complicate user decisions, but safety-conscious users will not open attachments unless they expect a document or photo and get an appropriate message from the sender. Before anti-virus software became effective, the famed ILOVEYOU virus contaminated millions of personal computers worldwide; it cost an estimated $10.2 billion to recover from the damage. Most network service providers offer virus filters that stop known viruses, but professional programmers must make weekly or even daily revisions to anti-virus software (suppliers include McAfee and Symantec) to keep up with the increasingly sophisticated virus developers. Since e-mail is the source of so many threats, developers of e-mail software must take more initiatives to protect users.

Practitioner's Summary

The Quality of Service is a growing concern for users and providers on networks, computers, and mobile devices. Rapid system response times and display rates are necessary, because these factors are determinants of user productivity, error rates, working style, and satisfaction (Box 11.1). In most situations, shorter response times (less than one second) lead to higher productivity. For mouse actions, multimedia performances, and interactive animations, even faster performance is necessary (less than 0.1 second). Satisfaction generally increases as the response time decreases, but there may be a danger from stress induced by a rapid pace. As users pick up the pace of the system, they may make more errors. If these errors are detected and corrected easily, then productivity will generally increase. However, if errors are hard to detect or are excessively costly, then a moderate pace may be most beneficial.

Designers can determine the optimal response time for a specific application and user community by measuring productivity, errors, and the cost of providing short response times. Managers must be alert to changes in work style as the pace quickens; productivity is measured by correctly completed tasks rather than by interactions per hour. Novices may prefer a slower pace of interaction. Modest variations around the mean response time are acceptable, but large variations (less than one-quarter of the mean or more than twice the mean) should be accompanied by informative messages. An alternative approach for overly rapid responses is to slow them down and thus to avoid the need for explanatory messages.

A continuing concern is the frustration level of the increasingly diverse set of computer users (Box 11.2). Application crashes, confusing error messages, and network disruptions are a problem that could be addressed by improved interface and software design. Malicious spreaders of spam and viruses are a serious threat to expanding the community of Internet users.

Box 11.1

Response-time guidelines.

- Users prefer shorter response times.
- Longer response times (> 15 seconds) are disruptive.
- Users change usage profiles with response time.
- Shorter response time leads to shorter user think time.
- A faster pace may increase productivity, but it may also increase error rates.
- Error-recovery ease and time influence optimal response time.
- Response time should be appropriate to the task:
  - Typing, cursor motion, mouse selection: 50–150 milliseconds
  - Simple, frequent tasks: 1 second
  - Common tasks: 2–4 seconds
  - Complex tasks: 8–12 seconds
- Users should be advised of long delays.
- Strive to have rapid start-ups.
- Modest variability in response time is acceptable.
- Unexpected delays may be disruptive.
- Offer users a choice in the pace of interaction.
- Empirical tests can help to set suitable response times.

Box 11.2

Reducing user frustration.

- Increase server capacity, network speed, and modem reliability.
- Improve user training, online help, and online tutorials.
- Redesign instructions and error messages.
- Protect against spam, viruses, and pop-up advertisements.
- Organize consumer protection groups.
- Increase research on user frustration.
- Catalyze public discussion to raise awareness.

Researcher's Agenda

The increased understanding of Quality of Service issues is balanced by the richness of new technologies and applications. The taxonomy of issues provides a framework for research, but a finer taxonomy of tasks, of relevant cognitive-style differences, and of applications is needed. Next, a refined theory of problem-solving and consumer behavior is necessary if we are to generate useful design hypotheses.

The interesting result of a U-shaped error curve for a complex task, with the lowest error rate at a 12-second response time (Barber and Lucas, 1983), invites further work. It would be productive to study error rates as a function of response time for a range of tasks and users. Another goal is to accommodate the real-world interruptions that disrupt planning, interfere with decision making, and reduce productivity.

It is understandable that error rates vary with response times, but how else are users' work styles or consumers' expectations affected? Can users be encouraged to be more careful in their decisions by merely lengthening response times and degrading Quality of Service? Does the profile of actions shift to a smaller set of more familiar actions as the response time shortens?

Many other questions are worthy of investigation. When technical feasibility prevents short responses, can users be satisfied by diversionary tasks, or are progress reports sufficient? Do warnings of long responses or apologies relieve anxiety or simply further frustrate users?

Methods for assessing user frustration levels are controversial. Time diaries may be more reliable than retrospective surveys, but how could automated logging and observational techniques be made more effective? More importantly, how could software developers and network providers construct reliable monthly reports to gauge improvements in Quality of Service and reductions in user frustration?

WORLD WIDE WEB RESOURCES

Response-time issues have a modest presence on the Net, although the issue of long network delays gets discussed frequently. User frustration is a lively topic, and many web sites point out flawed interfaces and related frustrating experiences. The New Computing web site suggests ways to help bring about change.

http://www.aw.com/DTUI

References

Barber, R. E. and Lucas, H. C., System response time, operator productivity and job satisfaction, *Communications of the ACM*, 26, 11 (November 1983), 972–986.

Bouch, Anna, Kuchinsky, Allen, and Bhatti, Nina, Quality is in the eye of the beholder: Meeting user requirements for Internet quality of service, *Proc. CHI 2000 Conference: Human Factors in Computing Systems*, ACM, New York (2000), 297–304.

Ceaparu, I., Lazar, J., Bessiere, K., Robinson, J., and Shneiderman, B., Determining causes and severity of end-user frustration, *International Journal of Human-Computer Interaction* (2004).

Emurian, Henry H., Physiological responses during data retrieval: Consideration of constant and variable system response times, *Computers and Human Behavior*, 7 (1991), 291–310.

Goodman, T. J., and Spence, R., The effect of computer system response time variability on interactive graphical problem solving, *IEEE Transactions on Systems, Man, and Cybernetics*, 11, 3 (March 1981), 207–216.

Goodman, Tom and Spence, Robert, The effects of potentiometer dimensionality, system response time, and time of day on interactive graphical problem solving, *Human Factors*, 24, 4 (1982), 437–456.

Grossberg, Mitchell, Wiesen, Raymond A., and Yntema, Douwe B., An experiment on problem solving with delayed computer responses, *IEEE Transactions on Systems, Man, and Cybernetics*, 6, 3 (March 1976), 219–222.

Huberman, Bernardo A., *The Laws of the Web: Patterns in the Ecology of Information*, MIT Press, Cambridge, MA (2001).

Jacko, J., Sears, A., and Borella, M., The effect of network delay and media on user perceptions of web resources, *Behaviour & Information Technology*, 19, 6 (2000), 427–439.

King, Andrew B., *Speed Up Your Site: Web Site Optimization*, New Riders, Indianapolis, IN (2003).

Kohlisch, Olaf and Kuhmann, Werner, System response time and readiness for task execution—The optimum duration of inter-task delays, *Ergonomics*, 40, 3 (1997), 265–280.

Martin, G. L. and Corl, K. G., System response time effects on user productivity, *Behaviour & Information Technology*, 5, 1 (1986), 3–13.

Meyer, Joachim, Shinar, David, Bitan, Yuval, and Leiser, David, Duration estimates and users' preferences in human-computer interaction, *Ergonomics*, 39, 1 (1996), 46–60.

Miller, G. A., The magical number seven, plus or minus two: Some limits on our capacity for processing information, *Psychological Science*, 63 (1956), 81–97.

Miller, Robert B., Response time in man-computer conversational transactions, *Proc. AFIPS Spring Joint Computer Conference*, 33, AFIPS Press, Montvale, NJ (1968), 267–277.

Morris, Michael G. and Turner, Jason M., Assessing users' subjective quality of experience with the World Wide Web: An exploratory examination of temporal changes in technology acceptance, *International Journal of Human-Computer Studies*, 54 (2001), 877–901.

Neal, Alan S., Time interval between keystrokes, records, and fields in data entry with skilled operators, *Human Factors*, 19, 2 (1977), 163–170.

Ramsay, Judith, Barbesi, Alessandro, and Preece, Jenny, A psychological investigation of long retrieval times on the World Wide Web, *Interacting with Computers*, 10 (1998), 77–86.

Teal, Steven L. and Rudnicky, Alexander I., A performance model of system delay and user strategy selection, *Proc. CHI '92 Conference: Human Factors in Computing Systems*, ACM, New York (1992), 295–305.

chapter

12

Balancing Function and Fashion

Words are sometimes sensitive instruments of precision
with which delicate operations may be performed and swift,
elusive truths may be touched.

HELEN MERRELL LYND
On Shame and the Search for Identity

12 . 1   Introduction

Interface design has yet to match the high art of architecture or trendiness of clothing design. However, we can anticipate that, as the audience for computers expands, competition over design will heighten. Early automobiles were purely functional and Henry Ford could joke about customers getting any color as long as it was black, but modern car designers have learned to balance function and fashion. This chapter deals with five design matters that are functional issues with many human-factors criteria but that also leave room for varying styles to suit a variety of customers. They are error messages, nonanthropomorphic design, display design, window design, and color.

User experiences with computer-system prompts, explanations, error diagnostics, and warnings play a critical role in influencing acceptance of software systems. The wording of messages is especially important in systems designed for novice users; experts also benefit from improved messages (Section 12.2). Messages are sometimes meant to be conversational, as modeled by human–human communication, but this strategy has its limits because people are different from computers and computers are different from people. This fact may be obvious, but a section on nonanthropomorphic design seems necessary to steer designers towards comprehensible, predictable, and controllable interfaces (Section 12.3).

Another opportunity for design improvements lies in the layout of information on a display. Cluttered displays may overwhelm even knowledgeable users, but with only modest effort we can create well-organized, information-abundant layouts that reduce search time and increase subjective satisfaction (Section 12.4).

Window management has become standardized, but an understanding of the motivations for multiple-window coordination could lead to improvements and to novel proposals, such as the personal role manager (Section 12.5).

Large, fast, high-resolution color displays offer many possibilities and challenges for designers. Guidelines for color design are useful, but experienced designers know that repeated testing is needed to ensure success (Section 12.6).

Recognition of the creative challenge of balancing function and fashion might be furthered by having designers put their names and photos on a title or credits page, just as authors do in a book. Such acknowledgment is common in games and in some educational software, and it seems appropriate for all software. Credits provide recognition for good work and identify the people responsible. Having their names in lights may also encourage designers to work even harder, since their identities will be public.

12.2   Error Messages

Normal prompts, advisory messages, and system responses to user actions may influence user perceptions, but the phrasing of error messages and diagnostic warnings is critical. Since errors occur because of lack of knowledge, incorrect understanding, or inadvertent slips, users are likely to be confused, to feel inadequate, and to be anxious. Error messages with an imperious tone that condemns users can heighten anxiety, making it more difficult to correct the error and increasing the chances of further errors. Messages that are too generic, such as WHAT? or SYNTAXERROR, or that are too obscure, such as FACRJCT 004004400400 or 0C7, offer little assistance to most users.

These concerns are especially important with respect to novices, whose lack of knowledge and confidence amplifies the stress that can lead to a frustrating sequence of failures. The discouraging effects of a bad experience in using a computer are not easily overcome by a few good experiences. In some cases, interfaces are remembered more for what happens when things go wrong than for when things go right. Although these concerns apply most forcefully to novice computer users, experienced users also suffer. Experts in one interface or part of an interface are still novices in many situations.

Improving the error messages is one of the easiest and most effective ways to improve an existing interface. If the software can capture the frequency of errors, then designers can focus on fixing the most important messages. Error-frequency distributions also enable interface designers and maintainers to revise error-handling procedures, to improve documentation and training manuals, to alter online help, or even to change the permissible actions. The complete set of messages should be reviewed by peers and managers, tested empirically, and included in user manuals.

Specificity, constructive guidance, positive tone, user-centered style, and appropriate physical format are recommended as the bases for preparing error messages (Box 12.1). These guidelines are especially important when the users are novices, but they can benefit experts as well. The phrasing and contents of error messages can significantly affect user performance and satisfaction.

12.2.1   Specificity

Messages that are too general make it difficult for the novice to know what has gone wrong. Simple and condemning messages are frustrating because they provide neither enough information about what has gone wrong nor the knowledge to set things right. The right amount of specificity therefore is important.

Poor: SYNTAX ERROR
Better: Unmatched left parenthesis

Poor: ILLEGAL ENTRY
Better: Type first letter: <u>S</u>end, <u>R</u>ead, or <u>D</u>rop

Poor: INVALID DATA
Better: Days range from 1 to 31

Poor: BAD FILE NAME
Better: The file C:\demo\data.txt.txt was not found

Box 12.1

Error-message guidelines for the end product and for the development process. These guidelines are derived from practical experience and empirical data.

Product
- Be as specific and precise as possible.
- Be constructive: Indicate what the user needs to do.
- Use a positive tone: Avoid condemnation.
- Choose user-centered phrasing.
- Consider multiple levels of messages.
- Maintain consistent grammatical forms, terminology, and abbreviations.
- Maintain consistent visual format and placement.

Process
- Increase attention to message design.
- Establish quality control.
- Develop guidelines.
- Carry out usability tests.
- Record the frequency of occurrence for each message.

One interface for hotel checkin required the desk clerk to enter a 40- to 45-character string containing the name, room number, credit-card information, and so on. If the clerk made a data-entry error, the only message was INVALID INPUT. YOU MUST RETYPE THE ENTIRE RECORD. This led to frustration for users and delays for irritated guests. Interactive systems should be designed to minimize input errors by proper form-fillin strategies (see Chapter 7); when an error occurs, the users should have to repair only the incorrect part.

Interfaces that offer an error-code number leading to a paragraph-long explanation in a manual are also annoying because the manual may not be available, or consulting it may be disruptive and time-consuming. In most cases, interface developers can no longer hide behind the claim that printing meaningful messages consumes too many system resources.

12.2.2   Constructive guidance and positive tone

Rather than condemning users for what they have done wrong, messages should, where possible, indicate what users need to do to set things right:

> **Poor:** Run-Time error '-2147469 (800405)': Method 'Private Profile String' of object 'System' failed.
> **Better:** Virtual memory space consumed. Close some programs and retry.
>
> **Poor:** Resource Conflict Bus: 00 Device: 03 Function: 01
> **Better:** Remove your compact flash card and restart.
>
> **Poor:** Network connection refused.
> **Better:** Your password was not recognized. Please retype.
>
> **Poor:** Bad date.
> **Better:** Drop-off date must come after pickup date.

Unnecessarily hostile messages using violent terminology can disturb nontechnical users. An interactive legal-citation–searching system uses this message: FATAL ERROR, RUN ABORTED. An early operating system threatened many users with CATASTROPHIC ERROR; LOGGED WITH OPERATOR. There is no excuse for these hostile messages; they can easily be rewritten to provide more information about what happened and what must be done to set things right. Where possible, be constructive and positive. Such negative words as ILLEGAL, ERROR, INVALID, or BAD should be eliminated or used infrequently.

It may be difficult for the software writer to create a program that accurately determines the user's intention, so the advice "be constructive" is often difficult to apply. Some designers argue for automatic error correction, but the disadvantage is that users may fail to learn proper syntax and may become dependent on alterations that the system makes. Another approach is to inform users of the possible alternatives and to let them decide. A preferred strategy is to prevent errors from occurring (see Section 2.3.5).

12.2.3   User-centered phrasing

The term *user-centered* suggests that the user controls the interface—initiating more than responding. Designers partially convey this feel by avoiding a negative and condemning tone in messages and by being courteous to the user.

Brevity is a virtue, but users should be allowed to control the kind of information provided. For example, if the standard message is just one line, by keying a ? in a command-language interface, users should be able to obtain a few lines of explanation. ?? might yield a set of examples, and ??? might produce explanations of the examples and a complete description. A graphical user interface can provide a progression of ScreenTips, a special HELP button to provide context-sensitive explanations, and extensive online user manuals.

Some telephone companies, long used to dealing with nontechnical users, offer this tolerant message: "We're sorry, but we were unable to complete your call as dialed. Please hang up, check your number, or consult the operator for assistance." They take the blame and offer constructive guidance for what to do. A thoughtless programmer might have generated a harsher message: "Illegal telephone number. Call aborted. Error number 583-2R6.9. Consult your user manual for further information."

12.2.4   Appropriate physical format

Most users prefer and find it easier to read mixed uppercase and lowercase messages. Uppercase-only messages should be reserved for brief, serious warnings. Messages that begin with a lengthy and mysterious code number serve only to remind the user that the designers were insensitive to the users' real needs. If code numbers are needed at all, they might be enclosed in parentheses at the end of a message.

There is disagreement about the optimal placement of messages in a display. One school of thought argues that the messages should be placed on the display near where the problem has arisen. A second opinion is that the messages clutter the display and should be placed in a consistent position on the bottom of the display. The third approach is to display a dialog box near to, but not obscuring the relevant problem.

Some applications ring a bell or sound a tone when an error has occurred. This alarm can be useful if the operator might otherwise miss the error, but it can be embarrassing if other people are in the room and is potentially annoying even if the operator is alone.

Designers must walk a narrow path between calling attention to a problem and avoiding embarrassment to users. Considering the wide range of experience and temperament in users, maybe the best solution is to offer users control over the alternatives—this approach coordinates well with the user-centered principle.

12.2.5   Development of effective messages

The designer's intuition can be supplemented by simple, fast, and inexpensive design studies with actual users and several alternative messages. If the project goal is to serve novice users, then ample effort must be dedicated to designing, testing, and implementing the user interface. This commitment must extend to the earliest design stages so that interfaces can be modified in a way that contributes to the production of specific error messages. Messages should be evaluated by several people and tested with suitable participants. Messages should appear in user manuals and be given high visibility. Records should be kept on the frequency of occurrence of each error. Frequent errors should lead to software modifications that provide better error handling, to improved training, and to revisions in user manuals and online help.

Users may remember the one time when they had difficulties with a computer system rather than the 20 times when everything went well. Their strong reactions to problems in using computer systems come in part from the anxiety and lack of knowledge that novice users have. This reaction may be exacerbated by a poorly designed, excessively complex interface; by a poor manual or training experience; or by hostile, vague, or irritating messages. Improving the messages will not turn a bad interface into a good one, but it can play a significant role in improving users' performance and attitudes.

Experimental studies support the contention that improving messages can upgrade performance and result in greater job satisfaction. They have led to the following recommendations for system developers (Box 12.1):

1. *Increase attention to message design.* The wording of messages should be considered carefully. Technical writers or copy editors can be consulted about the choice of words and phrasing to improve both clarity and consistency.

2. *Establish quality control.* Messages should be approved by an appropriate quality-control committee consisting of programmers, users, and human-factors specialists. Changes or additions should be monitored and recorded.

3. *Develop guidelines.* Be as specific and precise as possible. Writing good messages—like writing good poems, essays, or advertisements—requires experience, practice, and sensitivity to how the reader will react. It is a skill that can be acquired and refined by programmers and designers who are intent on serving the user. However, perfection is impossible, and humility is the mark of the true professional.

4. *Carry out usability tests* System messages should be subjected to a usability test with an appropriate user community to determine whether they are comprehensible. The test could range from a rigorous experiment with realistic situations (for life-critical or high-reliability systems) to an informal reading and review by interested users (for personal computing or noncritical applications). Complex interactive systems that involve thousands of users are never really complete until they are obsolete. Under these conditions, the most effective designs emerge from iterative testing and evolutionary refinement (Chapter 4).

5. *Record the frequency of occurrence for each message.* Frequency counts should be collected for each error condition whenever possible, particularly during usability tests. If possible, the users' actions should be captured for more detailed study. If you know where users run into difficulties, you can then revise the error messages, improve the training, modify the manual, or change the interface. The error rate per 1,000 actions should be used as a metric of interface quality and a gauge of how improvements affect performance. An error-counting option is useful for internal systems and can be a marketing feature for software products.

Improved messages will be of the greatest benefit to novice users, but regular users and experienced professionals will also benefit. As examples of excellence proliferate, complex, obscure, and harsh interfaces will seem increasingly out of place. The crude environments of the past will be replaced gradually by interfaces designed with the users in mind. Resistance to such a transition should not be allowed to impede progress towards the goal of serving the growing user community.

12.3   Nonanthropomorphic Design

There is a great temptation to have computers "talk" as though they were people. It is a primitive urge that designers often follow, and that children and many adults accept without hesitation (Nass et al., 1995; Reeves and Nass, 1996). Children accept human-like references and qualities for almost any object, from Humpty Dumpty to Tootle the Train. Adults reserve the *anthropomorphic* references for objects of special attraction, such as cars, ships, or computers.

The words and graphics in user interfaces can make important differences in people's perceptions, emotional reactions, and motivations. Attributions of intelligence, autonomy, free will, or knowledge to computers are appealing to some people, but to others such characterizations may be seen as deceptive, confusing, and misleading. The suggestion that computers can think, know, or understand may give users an erroneous model of how computers work and what the machines' capacities are. Ultimately, the deception becomes apparent, and users may feel poorly treated. Martin (1995/96) carefully traces the media impact of the 1946 ENIAC announcements: "Readers were given hyperbole designed to raise their expectations about the use of the new electronic brains.... This engendered premature enthusiasm, which then led to disillusionment and distrust of computers on the part of the public when the new technology did not live up to these expectations."

A second reason for using nonanthropomorphic phrasing is to clarify the differences between people and computers. Relationships with people are different from relationships with computers. Users operate and control computers, but they respect the unique identity and autonomy of individuals. Furthermore, users and designers must accept responsibility for misuse of computers, rather than blaming the machines for errors. It is worrisome that, in one study, 24 of 29 computer-science students believed that computers can have intentions or be independent decision makers, and 6 consistently held computers morally responsible for errors (Friedman, 1995).

A third motivation is that, although an anthropomorphic interface may be attractive to some people, it can be distracting or produce anxiety for others. Some people express anxiety about using computers and believe that computers "make you feel dumb." Presenting the computer through the specific functions it offers may be a stronger stimulus to user acceptance than is promoting the fantasy that the computer is a friend, parent, or partner. As users become engaged, the computer becomes transparent, and they can concentrate on their writing, problem solving, or exploration. At the end, they have the experience of accomplishment and mastery, rather than the feeling that some magical machine has done their job for them. Anthropomorphic interfaces may distract users from their tasks and waste their time as they consider how to please or be socially appropriate to the onscreen character.

Individual differences in the desire for internal locus of control are important, but there may be an overall advantage to clearly distinguishing human abilities from computer powers for most tasks and users (Shneiderman, 1995). On the other hand, there are persistent advocates of creating anthropomorphic interfaces, often called virtual humans, lifelike autonomous agents, and embodied conversational agents (Cassell et al., 2000; Graesser et al., 2001; Gratch et al., 2002). An early provocative scenario was Apple's 1987 video, *The Knowledge Navigator*, which showed a preppie bow-tied young male agent carrying out tasks for an environmental researcher. Some futurists celebrated this vision, but skeptics scorned the scenario as a deception; most viewers, meanwhile, seemed mildly amused.

Advocates of anthropomorphic interfaces assume that human–human communication is an appropriate model for human operation of computers. It may be a useful starting point, but some designers pursue the human-imitation approach long after it becomes counterproductive. Mature technology has managed to overcome the *obstacle of animism,* which has been a trap for technologists for centuries (Mumford, 1934); a visit to the Museum of Automata in York, England, reveals the ancient sources and persistent fantasies of animated dolls and robotic toys.

Historical precedents of failed anthropomorphic bank tellers such as Tillie the Teller, Harvey Wallbanker, and BOB (Bank of Baltimore) and of abandoned talking automobiles and soda machines do not seem to register on some designers. The bigger-than-life-sized Postal Buddy was supposed to be cute and friendly while providing several useful automated services, but users rejected this pseudo–postal clerk after the project had incurred costs of over $1 billion. The web-based news reader Ananova was heralded as the future of computing, but it has fallen into disuse (Fig. 12.1). Advocates of anthropomorphic interfaces suggest that they may be most useful as teachers, salespeople, therapists, or entertainment figures.

Figure 12.1

Ananova's carefully crafted contemporary face and hair styling (left) was heavily promoted as the future of web-based news. Ananova's lips moved in correspondence with the text being read, but this character fell from favor rapidly. Microsoft's Clippit (right) was an energetic character designed to be cartoon-like, but it was seen as more annoying than helpful by most users. (www.ananova.com)

In early studies with a text-based computer-assisted instruction task, participants felt less responsible for their performance when interacting with an anthropomorphic interface. In a later study, a text-only display was compared with displays that showed a stern face and a neutral talking face (Walker, Sproull, and Subramani, 1994). The authors concluded that "incautiously adding human characteristics like face, voice, and facial expressions could make the experience for users worse rather than better." The designers generated the talking faces by texture mapping an image onto a geometric wire frame model to produce a 512×320–pixel face. The lip movements were synchronized with the voice-generation algorithm; the stern expression was produced by contraction of the corrugator muscles in the underlying physical model to pull the inner eyebrows in and down. The experienced users rated the text-only version as statistically significantly more likable, friendly, comfortable, and happy than the talking faces, and as less stiff and less sad. Participants also found the questions clearer and were more willing to continue with the text-only versions. Evidence in favor of the faces was that participants in the face treatments produced fewer invalid answers and wrote lengthier commentaries, especially with the stern face. In a follow-up study to assess willingness to cooperate, participants "kept their promises as much with a text-only computer as with a person"; however, they were more willing to deceive when the interface was more human-like (Kiesler, Sproull, and Waters, 1996).

In another study, a more elaborate computer-generated face (16 muscles and 10 parameters controlling 500 polygons) was compared with a three-dimensional arrow in guiding user attention to moves in a card game (Takeuchi and Naito, 1995). Although the face was appreciated as being "entertaining," the arrow was seen as "useful." The authors noted that participants "tend to try to interpret facial displays and head behaviors," which prevented them from concentrating fully on the game and led to fewer wins than participants had in the arrow treatments.

Animated characters that range from cartoon-like to realistic have been embedded in many interfaces, but evidence is growing that they increase anxiety and reduce performance, especially for users with an external locus of control. Many people are more anxious when someone is observing their work, so it is understandable that computer users might be troubled by animated characters that monitor their performance. This was found in a study with an animated character that appeared to be taking notes on users' work and making screen copies. Participants with an external locus of control had elevated anxiety and were less accurate in their tasks (Reeves and Rickenberg, 2000).

One specific design controversy is over the use of first-person pronouns in an interface. Advocates believe it makes the interaction friendly, but such interfaces may be counterproductive because they can deceive, mislead, and confuse users. It may seem cute on the first encounter to be greeted by "I am SOPHIE, the sophisticated teacher, and I will teach you to spell correctly." By the second session, however, this approach strikes many people as silly; by the third session, it can be an annoying distraction from the task. The alternative for the interface designer is to focus on the user and to use third-person singular pronouns or to avoid pronouns altogether. Improved messages may also suggest a higher level of user control. For example:

Poor: I will begin the lesson when you press RETURN.
Better: You can begin the lesson by pressing RETURN.
Better: To begin the lesson, press RETURN.

The *you* form seems preferable for introductions; however, once the session is underway, reducing the number of pronouns and words avoids distractions from the task. A travel-reservation task was carried out by student participants with a simulated natural-language interface using the *I, you,* or *neutral* styles, called *anthropomorphic, fluent,* and *telegraphic* by the authors (Brennan and Ohaeri, 1994). Users' messages mimicked the style of the messages they received, leading to lengthier user inputs and longer task-completion times in the anthropomorphic treatment. Users did not attribute greater intelligence to the anthropomorphic computer.

The issue of pronoun usage reappears in the design of interactive voice-response telephone interfaces, especially if speech recognition is employed. Advocates argue that greetings from a rental-car reservation service, for example, might be more appealing if they simulate a human operator: "Welcome to Thrifty Car Rentals. I'm Emily, let me help you reserve your car. In what city will you need a car?" While most users won't care about the phrasing, opponents claim that this deception does annoy and worry some users, and that the expedient solution of deleting the chatty second sentence produces higher customer satisfaction.

Some designers of children's educational software believe that it is appropriate and acceptable to have a fantasy character, such as a teddy bear or busy beaver, serve as a guide through a lesson. A cartoon character can be drawn on the screen and possibly animated, adding visual appeal, speaking to users in an encouraging style, and pointing to relevant items on the display. Successful educational software packages such as Reader Rabbit and some empirical research (Moreno et al., 2001; Graesser et al., 2001; see also Sections 2.3.6 and 8.6) provide support for this position.

Unfortunately, cartoon characters were not successful in BOB, a heavily promoted but short-lived home-computing product from Microsoft. Users could choose from a variety of onscreen characters who spoke in cartoon bubbles with phrases such as: "What a team we are," "Good job so far, Ben," and "What shall we do next, Ben?" This style might be acceptable in children's games and educational software, but it is probably not acceptable for adults in the workplace.

Interfaces should neither compliment nor condemn users, just provide comprehensible feedback so users can move forward in achieving their goals. However, anthropomorphic characters will not necessarily succeed here either. Microsoft's ill-fated Clippit character (a lively paper-clip cartoon character) was designed to provide helpful suggestions for users (Fig. 12.1). It amused some but annoyed many, and it was soon removed. Defenders of anthropomorphic interfaces found many reasons to explain Clippit's rejection, primarily its disruptive interference with users. Others believe that successful anthropomorphic interfaces require socially appropriate emotional expressions, as well as well-timed head movements, nods, blinks, and eye contact.

An alternative instructional design approach that seems acceptable to many users is to present the human author of a lesson or software package. The audio or video of the author can speak to users, much as television news announcers speak to viewers. Instead of making the computer into a person, designers can show identifiable and appropriate human guides (Section 13.6.3). For example, the Secretary-General might record a video welcome for visitors to a web site about the United Nations, or Bill Gates might provide greetings for new users of Windows.

Once past these introductions, several styles are possible. One is a continuation of the guided-tour metaphor, in which the respected personality introduces segments but allows users to control the pace, to repeat segments, and to decide when they are ready to move on. A variant of this approach creates an interview-like experience in which users read from a set of three prompts and issue spoken commands to get pre-recorded video segments by noted figures such as Senator John Glenn or biologist Joshua Lederberg (Harless et al., 2003). This approach works for museum tours, tutorials on software, and certain educational lectures.

Another strategy is to support user control by showing an overview of the modules from which users can choose. Users decide how much time to spend visiting parts of museums, browsing a timeline with details of events, or jumping between articles in a hyperlinked encyclopedia. These overviews give users a sense of the magnitude of information available and allow them to see their progress in covering the topics. Overviews also support users' needs for closure, give them the satisfaction of completely touring the contents, and offer a comprehensible environment with predictable actions that foster a comforting sense of control. Furthermore, they support the need for replicability of actions (to revisit an appealing or confusing module, or to show it to a colleague) and reversibility (to back up or return to a known landmark). While in games users may enjoy the challenge of confusion, hidden controls, and unpredictability, this is not the case in most applications; rather, designers must strive to make their products comprehensible and predictable. A summary of nonanthropomorphic guidelines appears in Box 12.2.

Box 12.2

Guidelines for avoiding anthropomorphism and building appealing interfaces.

Nonanthropomorphic guidelines

- Be cautious in presenting computers as people, either with synthesized or cartoon characters
- Design comprehensible, predictable, and user-controlled interfaces.
- Use appropriate humans for audio or video introductions or guides.
- Use cartoon characters in games or children's software, but usually not elsewhere.
- Provide user-centered overviews for orientation and closure.
- Do not use "I" when the computer responds to human actions.
- Use "you" to guide users, or just state facts.

12.4   Display Design

For most interactive systems, the displays are a key component to successful designs, and are the source of many lively arguments. Dense or cluttered displays can provoke anger, and inconsistent formats can inhibit performance. The complexity of this issue is suggested by the 162 guidelines for data display offered by Smith and Mosier (1986). This diligent effort (see Box 12.3 for examples) represents progress over the vague guidelines given in earlier reviews. Display design will always have elements of art and require invention, but perceptual principles are becoming clearer and theoretical foundations are emerging (Kosslyn, 1994; Tullis, 1997; Galitz, 2003). Innovative information visualizations with user interfaces to support dynamic control are a rapidly emerging theme (Section 14.5).

Designers should begin, as always, with a thorough knowledge of the users' tasks, free from the constraints of display size or available fonts. Effective display designs must provide all the necessary data in the proper sequence to carry out the task. Meaningful groupings of items (with labels suitable to the users' knowledge), consistent sequences of groups, and orderly formats all support task performance. Groups can be surrounded by blank spaces or boxes. Alternatively, related items can be indicated by highlighting, background shading, color, or special fonts. Within a group, orderly formats can be accomplished by left or right justification, alignment on decimal points for numbers, or markers to decompose lengthy fields.

Graphic designers have produced principles suited to print formats, and they are now adapting these principles for display design. Mullet and Sano (1995) offer thoughtful advice with examples of good and bad design in commercial

Box 12.3

Samples of the 162 data-display guidelines from Smith and Mosier (1986).

- Ensure that any data that a user needs, at any step in a transaction sequence, are available for display.
- Display data to users in directly usable forms; do not require that users convert displayed data.
- Maintain a consistent format, for any particular type of data display, from one display to another.
- Use short, simple sentences.
- Use affirmative statements, rather than negative statements.
- Adopt a logical principle by which to order lists; where no other principle applies, order lists alphabetically.
- Ensure that labels are sufficiently close to their data fields to indicate association, yet are separated from their data fields by at least one space.
- Left-justify columns of alphabetic data to permit rapid scanning.
- Label each page in multipaged displays to show its relation to the others.
- Begin every display with a title or header, describing briefly the contents or purpose of the display; leave at least one blank line between the title and the body of the display.
- For size coding, make larger symbols be at least 1.5 times the height of the next-smaller symbol.
- Consider color coding for applications in which users must distinguish rapidly among several categories of data, particularly when the data items are dispersed on the display.
- When you use blink coding, make the blink rate 2 to 5 Hz, with a minimum duty cycle (ON interval) of 50%.
- For a large table that exceeds the capacity of one display frame, ensure that users can see column headings and row labels in all displayed sections of the table.
- Provide a means for users (or a system administrator) to make necessary changes to display functions, if data-display requirements may change (as is often the case).

systems. They propose six categories of principles that reveal the complexity of the designer's task:

1. *Elegance and simplicity:* Unity, refinement, and fitness
2. *Scale, contrast, and proportion:* Clarity, harmony, activity, and restraint
3. *Organization and visual structure:* Grouping, hierarchy, relationship, and balance

4. *Module and program:* Focus, flexibility, and consistent application

5. *Image and representation:* Immediacy, generality, cohesiveness, and characterization

6. *Style:* Distinctiveness, integrity, comprehensiveness, and appropriateness

This section deals with some of these issues, offering empirical support for concepts where available.

12.4.1   Field layout

Exploration with a variety of layouts can be a helpful process. These design alternatives should be developed directly on a display screen. An employee record with information about a spouse and children could be displayed crudely as follows:

> **Poor:** `TAYLOR,SUSAN034787331WILLIAM TAYLOR`
> `THOMAS10291974ANN08211977ALEXANDRA09081972`

This record may contain the necessary information for a task, but extracting the information will be slow and error prone. As a first step at improving the format, blanks and separate lines can distinguish fields:

> **Better:** `TAYLOR, SUSAN 034787331     WILLIAM TAYLOR`
> `THOMAS     10291974`
> `ANN        08211977`
> `ALEXANDRA  09081972`

The children's names can be listed in chronological order, with alignment of the dates. Familiar separators for the dates and the employee's social security number also aid recognition:

> **Better:** `TAYLOR, SUSAN 034-78-7331     WILLIAM TAYLOR`
> `ALEXANDRA  09-08-1972`
> `THOMAS     10-29-1974`
> `ANN        08-21-1977`

The reversed order of "last name, first name" for the employee may be desired to highlight the lexicographic ordering in a long file. However, the "first name, last name" order for the spouse is usually more readable. Consistency seems important, so a compromise might be made:

> **Better:** `SUSAN TAYLOR 034-78-7331     WILLIAM TAYLOR`
> `ALEXANDRA  09-08-1972`
> `THOMAS     10-29-1974`
> `ANN        08-21-1977`

For frequent users, this format may be acceptable, since labels have a cluttering effect. For most users, however, labels will be helpful:

```
Better: Employee:  SUSAN TAYLOR
        Social Security Number: 034-78-7331
        Spouse:    WILLIAM TAYLOR
        Children:  Names        Birthdates
                   ALEXANDRA    09-08-1972
                   THOMAS       10-29-1974
                   ANN          08-21-1977
```

Mixed upper- and lowercase letters have been used for the labels to distinguish them from the record information, but the coding might be switched to use boldface and mixed upper- and lowercase for the contents. The lengthy label for social security number might also be abbreviated if the users are knowledgeable. Indenting the information about children might help to convey the grouping of these repeating fields:

```
Better: Employee:  Susan Taylor SSN: 034-78-7331
        Spouse:    William Taylor
        Children:  Names        Birthdates
                   Alexandra    09-08-1972
                   Thomas       10-29-1974
                   Ann          08-21-1977
```

Finally, if boxes are available, then an orderly pattern is sometimes more appealing (although it may consume more screen space):

```
Better: ┌────────────────────────────────────────────┐
        │Employee:  Susan Taylor SSN: 034-78-7331    │
        │Spouse:    William Taylor                   │
        └────────────────────────────────────────────┘

        ┌────────────────────────────────────────────┐
        │Children:  Names        Birthdates          │
        │           Alexandra    09-08-1972          │
        │           Thomas       10-29-1974          │
        │           Ann          08-21-1977          │
        └────────────────────────────────────────────┘
```

For an international audience, the date format would need to be clarified (Month-Day-Year) and the SSN abbreviation kept spelled out. Even in this simple example, the possibilities are numerous. In any situation, a variety of designs should be explored. Further improvements could be made with other coding strategies, such as background shading, color, and graphic icons. An experienced graphic designer can be a great benefit to the design team. Pilot testing with prospective users can yield subjective satisfaction scores, objective times to complete tasks, and error rates for a variety of proposed formats.

12.4.2   Empirical results

Guidelines for display design were an early topic in human–computer interaction research because of the importance of displays in control-room and life-critical applications (see Section 2.3). As technology evolved from 80-column-by-24-line alphanumeric monochrome displays to 20-inch graphical color displays, new empirically validated guidelines became necessary. Then, web-based markup languages and the need to accommodate older adults and users with disabilities provided further design challenges. User control of font size, window size, and brightness meant designers had to ensure that the information architecture could be understood, even as some display elements changed. Now, as small-, wall-, and mall-sized displays have opened further possibilities, there again is renewed interest in display design.

Early studies with alphanumeric displays laid the foundation for design guidelines and predictive metrics. These studies clearly demonstrated the benefits of eliminating unnecessary information, grouping related information, and emphasizing information relevant to required tasks. Simple changes could cut task performance times almost in half.

A NASA study with space-shuttle displays demonstrated that improving the data labels, clustering related information, using appropriate indentation and underlining, aligning numeric values, and eliminating extraneous characters could improve performance (Burns, Warren, and Rudisill, 1986). Task times were reduced by 31% and error rates by 28% for technical and clerical employees at NASA and Lockheed who were unfamiliar with either version. Experts with the existing interface did not perform statistically significantly faster with the improved displays, but they did perform significantly more accurately. A follow-up study validated the benefit of the redesign and showed that appropriate highlighting further reduced search times (Donner et al., 1991).

Expert users can deal with dense displays and may prefer these displays because they are familiar with the format and they must initiate fewer actions. Performance times are likely to be shorter with fewer but denser displays than with more numerous but sparse displays. This improvement will be especially marked if tasks require comparison of information across displays. Systems for stock-market data, air-traffic control, and airline reservations are examples of successful applications that have dense packing, multiple displays, limited labels, and highly coded fields.

In a study of nurses, laboratory reports of blood tests were shown in the standard commercial format of three screens, in a compressed two-screen version, and in a densely packed one-screen version (Staggers, 1993). Search times dropped by half (approximately) over the five trial blocks for novice and experienced nurses, demonstrating a strong learning effect. The dramatic performance result was that search times were longest with the three-screen version (9.4 seconds per task) and shortest with the densely packed one-screen version (5.3 seconds per task) (Fig 12.2). The high cost of switching windows and of reorienting to the new

Low Density Screen

```
Patient Laboratory Inquiry     Large University Medical Center      Pg 1 of 3

Robinson, Christopher  #XXX-20-4627  Unit: 5E, 5133D  M/13  Ph:301-XXX-5885

         <CBC>       Result      Normal   Range         Units
        ------------------------------------------------------------
11/20   Wbc          5.0          4.8  -    10.8         th/cumm
22:55   Rbc          4.78         4.7  -     6.1         m/cumm
        Hgb         12.8         14.0  -    18.0         g/dL
        Hct         37.9         42.0  -    52.0         %
        Plt        163.0        130.0  -   400.0         th/cumm
        Mcv         88.5         82.0  -   101.0         fL
        Mch         30.6         27.0  -    34.0         picogms
        Mchc        34.6         32.0  -    36.0         g/dL
        Rdw         14.5         11.5  -    14.5         %
        Mpv          9.3          7.4  -    10.4         fL
        Key:  * = abnormal
            PgDn for more


Patient Laboratory Inquiry     Large University Medical Center      Pg 2 of 3

Robinson, Christopher  #XXX-20-4627  Unit: 5E, 5133D  M/13  Ph:301-XXX-5885

         <DIFF>      Result      Normal   Range         Unit
        ------------------------------------------------------------
11/20   Segs         35           34  - 75             %
22:55   Bands         5            0  -  9             %
        Lymphs       33           10  - 49             %
        Monos        33            2  - 14             %
        Eosino        5            0  -  8             %

        Baso          2            0  -  2             %
        Atyplymph    20            0  -  0             %
        Meta          0            0  -  0             %
        Myleo         0            0  -  0             %
        Platelets(estimated)                    adeq
        Key:  * = Abnormal
            PgDn for more


Patient Laboratory Inquiry     Large University Medical Center      Pg 3 of 3

Robinson, Christopher  #XXX-20-4627  Unit: 5E, 5133D  M/13  Ph:301-XXX-5885
11/20    22:55

<MORPHOLOGY     Macrocytosis  1+   Basophilic Stippling 1+   Toxic Gran Occ
Hypochromia 1+ Polychromasia 1+   Target Cells         3+   Normocytic  No
Key: * = Abnormal     Priority:  Routine         Acc#: 122045-015212
Ordered by: Holland, Daniel on 10/22/91, 10:00    Ord#: 900928-HH1131
   Personal Data  -  PRIVACY ACT OF 1974  (PL  93-579)
       End of report
```

Figure 12.2

In a study with 110 nurses, results showed an average task time of 9.4 seconds with the low-density version, versus 5.3 seconds with the high-density version. (Staggers, 1993.)

High Density Screen

```
Patient Laboratory Inquiry         Large University Medical Center        Pg 1 of 1
─────────────────────────────────────────────────────────────────────────────────
Robinson, Christopher   #XXX-20-4627  Unit: 5E, 5133D  M/13  Ph:301-XXX-5885
─────────────────────────────────────────────────────────────────────────────────
         <CBC>  Result   Normal Range    Units     <DIFF>     Result Norm Range  Unit
         -----------------------------------------------------------------------------
10/23    Wbc     5.0     4.8 -  10.8    th/cumm    Segs        40    34 - 74    %
0600     Rbc     4.78    4.7 -   6.1    m/cumm     Bands        5     0 -  9    %
         Hgb    15.1    14.0 -  18.0    g/dL       Lymphs      33    10 - 49    %
         Hct    47.9    42.0 -  52.0     %         Monos       10     2 - 14    %
         Plt   163.0   130.0 - 400.0    th/cumm    Eosino       5     0 -  8    %
         Mcv    88.5    82.0 - 101.0    fL         Baso         2     2 -  2    %
         Mch    30.6    27.0 -  34.0    picogms    Atyplymph    0     0 -  0    %
         Mchc   34.6    32.0 -  36.0    g/dL       Meta         0     0 -  0    %
         Rdw    14.5    11.5 -  14.5     %         Myelo        0     0 -  0    %
         Mpv     8.3     7.4 -  10.4    fL                    Plt   (estm)     adeq
<MORPHOLOGY       Macrocytosis  1+    Basophilic Stippling  1+    Toxic Gran Occ
Hypochromia 1+  Polychromasia 1+    Target Cells          3+    Normocytic  No
─────────────────────────────────────────────────────────────────────────────────
Key: * = Abnormal Priority:  Routine      Acc#: 122045-015212
  Ordered by:  Holland, Daniel on 10/22/91, 10:00    Ord#: 900928-HH1131
     Personal Data  -  PRIVACY ACT OF 1974  (PL  93-579)
```

Figure 12.2

(continued)

material appears to be far more destructive of concentration than scanning dense displays. Accuracy and subjective satisfaction were not significantly different across the three versions.

Increased understanding of human visual scanning based on eye-tracking studies has led to a growing understanding of basic perceptual and cognitive principles. One set of web-oriented guidelines encourages designers to "Visually chunk related elements through the use of space, graphical boundaries, or similarities in lightness, color, or orientation. Ensure that the graphical treatment of elements in a display is consistent and predictable" (Williams, 2000).

Every guidelines document implores designers to preserve consistent location, structure, and terminology across displays. Supportive evidence for consistent location comes from an early study of inexperienced computer users of a menu interface (Teitelbaum and Granda, 1983). The positions of the title, page number, topic heading, instruction line, and entry area were varied across displays for half of the participants, whereas the other half saw constant positions. Mean response time to questions about these items for participants in the varying condition was 2.54 seconds, but it was only 1.47 seconds for those seeing constant positions. A student project with experienced computer users showed similar benefits from consistent placement, size, and color of buttons in graphical user interfaces. Even stronger benefits came from consistent button labels. Consistency and quality in web-page contents were also demonstrated to be beneficial in information-gathering tasks (Ozok and Salvendy, 2003).

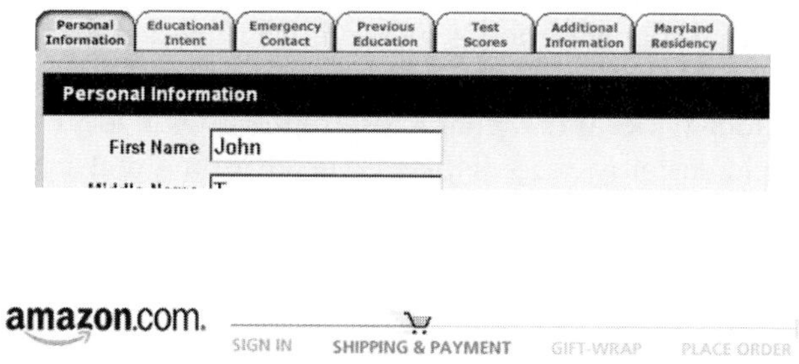

Figure 12.3

Users should be given a sense of how far they have gone within a sequence of displays and of what remains to be done.

Sequences of displays should be similar throughout the system for similar tasks, but exceptions will certainly occur. Within a sequence, users should be offered some sense of how far they have come and how far they have to go to reach the end (Fig. 12.3). It should be possible to go backwards in a sequence to correct errors, to review decisions, or to try alternatives.

12.4.3   Display-complexity metrics

Although knowledge of the users' tasks and abilities is the key to designing effective screen displays, objective and automatable metrics of screen complexity are attractive aids. After a thorough review of the literature, Tullis (1997) developed four task-independent metrics for alphanumeric displays:

1. *Overall density.* The number of filled character spaces as a percentage of total spaces available.
2. *Local density.* The average number of filled character spaces in a five-degree visual angle around each character, expressed as a percentage of available spaces in the circle and weighted by distance from the character.
3. *Grouping.* (1) The number of groups of "connected" characters, where a connection is any pair of characters separated by less than twice the mean of the distances between each character and its nearest neighbor; and (2) the average visual angle subtended by groups and weighted by the number of characters in the group.
4. *Layout complexity.* The complexity, as defined in information theory, of the distribution of horizontal and vertical distances of each label and data item from a standard point on the display.

The argument for local density emerges from studies of visual perception indicating that concentration is focused in a five-degree visual angle. At normal viewing distances from displays, this area translates into a circle approximately 15 characters wide and 7 characters high. Lower local and overall densities should yield easier-to-read displays. The grouping metric was designed to yield an objective, automatable value that assesses the number of clusters of fields on a display. Typically, clusters are formed by characters that are separated by no more than one intervening space horizontally and that are on adjacent lines. Layout complexity measures the variety of shapes that confront the user on a display. Neat blocks of fields that start in the same column will have a lower layout complexity. These metrics do not account for coding techniques, uppercase versus lowercase characters, continuous text, graphics, or multidisplay issues.

To test user preferences and the effects of structural formats on user performance, Bell Laboratories employees did motel- and airline-information retrieval tasks on 520 different displays in a variety of formats (Tullis, 1997; see Fig. 12.4). Performance times and subjective evaluations were collected to generate predictive equations, which were validated in a second study. Correlations between predicted and actual values were 0.80 for search times and 0.79 for subjective ratings.

This impressive result is encouraging; however, the metrics require a computer program to do the computations on the alphanumeric-only displays, and they do not include coding techniques, user-experience levels, or multidisplay considerations. Tullis is cautious in interpreting the results and emphasizes that displays that optimize search times do not necessarily optimize subjective ratings. Grouping of items led to fast performance, but high subjective ratings were linked to low local density and low layout complexity. A simple interpretation of these results is that effective display designs contain a middle number of groups (6 to 15) that are neatly laid out, surrounded by blanks, and similarly structured. This conclusion is a satisfying confirmation of a principle that seems intuitively obvious when stated but has not emerged explicitly in the numerous guidelines documents.

Revised metrics were needed to suit graphical user interfaces with variable font sizes, the capacity to draw boxes to clarify groupings, richer possibilities for highlighting and indentation, and frequent use of buttons. In a study with 16 versions of display layouts, the search time doubled when going from the best to the worst designs (Parush, Nadir, and Shtub, 1998; Fig. 12.5). The strongest distinguishing attributes were the clear groupings provided by drawing boxes and the orderly alignment of similar items. Support for using layouts in which related information was grouped came from a study that found benefits for users when the cognitive load on working memory was large. Accuracy increased when related items were grouped, thus reducing the scanning needed to locate distant items (Vincow and Wickens, 1993).

Web-based designs were dramatically different, because the broader consumer-oriented audience appreciated colorful graphics and many site designers employed eye-catching photos. The race was on to create cool

```
To: Atlanta, GA

    Departs   Arrives    Flight

Asheville, NC          First: $92.57   Coach: $66.85
    7:20a     8:05a      PI 299
   10:10a    10:55a      PI 203
    4:20p     5:00p      PI 259

Austin, TX             First: $263.00  Coach: $221.00
    8:15a    11:15a      EA 530
    8:40a    11:39a      DL 212
    2:00p     5:00p      DL 348
    7:15p    11:26p      DL 1654

Baltimore, MD          First: $209.00  Coach: $167.00
    7:00a     8:35a      DL 1767
    7:50a     9:32a      EA 631
    8:45a    10:20a      DL 1610
   11:15a    12:35p      EA 147
    1:35p     3:10p      DL 1731
    2:35p     4:16p      EA 141
```

```
To: Knoxville, TN
Atlanta, GA  Dp: 9:28a  Ar: 10:10a  Flt: DL 1704  1st: 97.00  Coach: 86.00
Atlanta, GA  Dp: 12:28p  Ar: 1:10p  Flt: DL 152  1st: 97.00  Coach: 86.00
Atlanta, GA  Dp: 4:58p  Ar: 5:40p  Flt: DL 418  1st: 97.00  Coach: 86.00
Atlanta, GA  Dp: 7:41p  Ar: 8:25p  Flt: DL 1126  1st: 97.00  Coach: 86.00
Chicago, Ill.  Dp: 1:45p  Ar: 5:39p  Flt: AL 58  1st: 190.00  Coach: 161.00
Chicago, Ill.  Dp: 6:30p  Ar: 9:35p  Flt: DL 675  1st: 190.00  Coach: 161.00
Chicago, Ill.  Dp: 6:50p  Ar: 9:55p  Flt: RC 398  1st: 190.00  Coach: 161.00
Cincinnati, OH  Dp: 12:05p  Ar: 1:10p  Flt: FW 453  1st: 118.00  Coach: 66.85
Cincinnati, OH  Dp: 5:25p  Ar: 6:30p  Flt: FW 455  1st: 118.00  Coach: 66.85
Dallas, TX  Dp: 5:55p  Ar: 9:56p  Flt: AL 360  1st: 365.00  Coach: 215.00
Dayton, OH  Dp: 11:20a  Ar: 1:10p  Flt: FW 453  1st: 189.00  Coach: 108.00
Dayton, OH  Dp: 4:40  Ar: 6:30p  Flt: FW 455  1st: 189.00  Coach: 108.00
Detroit, Mich.  Dp: 9:10a  Ar: 1:10p  Flt: FW 453  1st: 183.00  Coach: 106.00
Detroit, Mich.  Dp: 2:35p  Ar: 6:30p  Flt: FW 455  1st: 183.00  Coach: 106.00
```

Figure 12.4

Two versions of screens from the first experiment by Tullis (1997): a structured format (top) that leads to superior performance and preference, and an unstructured format (bottom). The results of this experiment led to predictive equations.

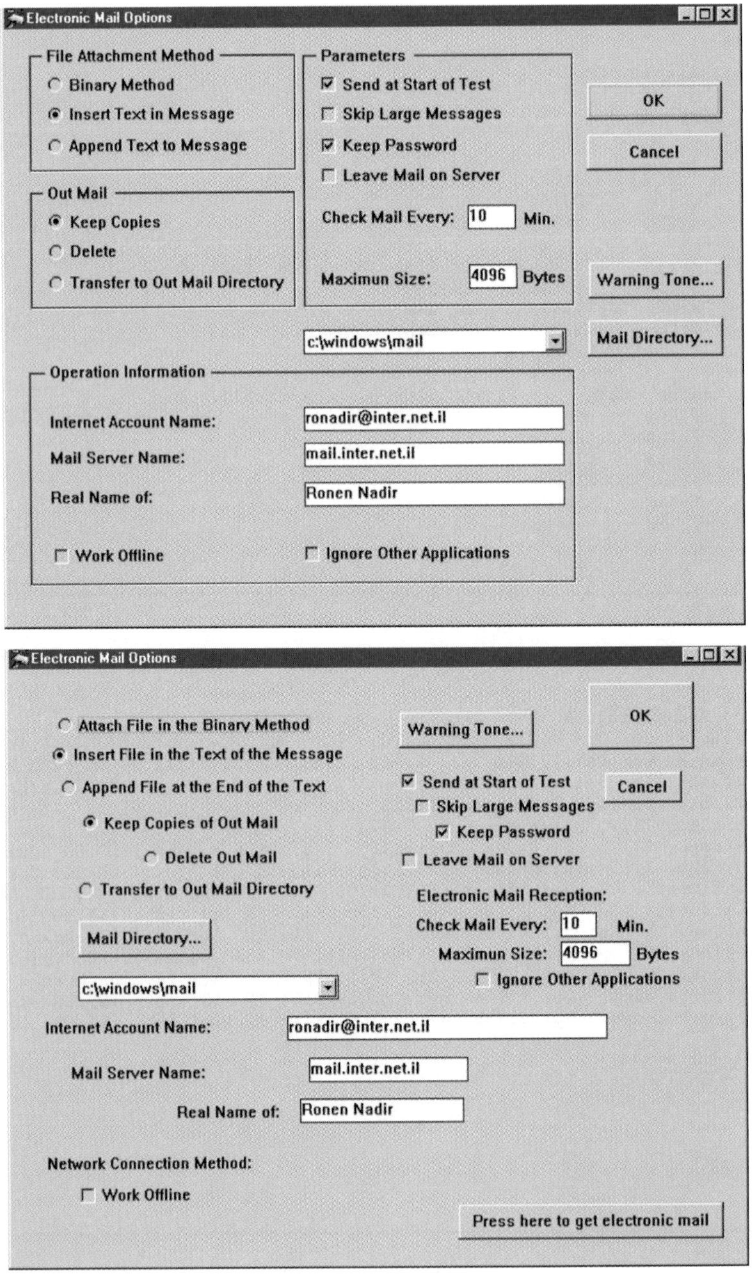

Figure 12.5

Two of the 16 display layouts studied: the best version (top) shows good alignment and grouping; the worst version (bottom) shows chaotic organization and uncertain groupings. (Parush, Nadir, and Shtub, 1998.)

designs, hot images, and attention-grabbing layouts. User preferences became crucial, especially if market researchers could demonstrate that site visitors stayed longer and bought more products at visually compelling web sites. The downside of graphics was the download times, which were significantly slower, especially for dial-up users with slow modems.

In an attempt to quantify design-feature impacts on preference, researchers correlated Webby Award–winning pages with 141 layout metrics (Ivory and Hearst, 2002). The results are complex, showing interactions among types and sizes of web pages. Some of the easily applicable results were that high preferences could be expected if large pages had columnar organization, animated graphical ads were limited, average link text was kept to two to three words, sans-serif fonts were used, and varied colors were used to highlight text as well as headings. These results could also lead to conjectures about the design goals that support high preference—for example, comprehensibility, predictability, familiarity, visual appeal, and relevant content.

A more accurate prediction of user performance is likely to come with metrics that integrate task frequencies and sequences. Sears (1993) developed a task-dependent metric called *layout appropriateness* to assess whether the spatial layout is in harmony with the users' tasks (Fig. 12.6). If users can accomplish frequent tasks by moving through a display in a top-to-bottom pattern, then faster performance is likely, compared to that with a layout that requires numerous jumps around widely separated parts of the display. Layout appropriateness is a widget-level metric that deals with buttons, boxes, and lists. Designers specify the sequences of selections that users make and the frequencies for each sequence. Then, the given layout of widgets is evaluated by how well it matches the tasks. An optimal layout that minimizes visual scanning can be produced, but since it may violate user expectations about positions of fields, the designers must make the final layout decisions.

12.5 Window Design

Most computer users must consult documents, forms, e-mails, web pages, and more to complete their tasks. For example, a travel agent jumps from reviewing a client's e-mail request to viewing the proposed itinerary to reviewing calendars and flight schedules to choosing seat assignments and to selecting hotels. Even with large desktop displays, there is a limit to how many documents can be displayed simultaneously. Designers have long struggled with strategies to offer users sufficient information and flexibility to accomplish their tasks while reducing window-housekeeping actions and minimizing distracting clutter. If users' tasks are well understood and regular, then there is a good chance that an effective *multiple-window display* strategy can be developed. The travel agent

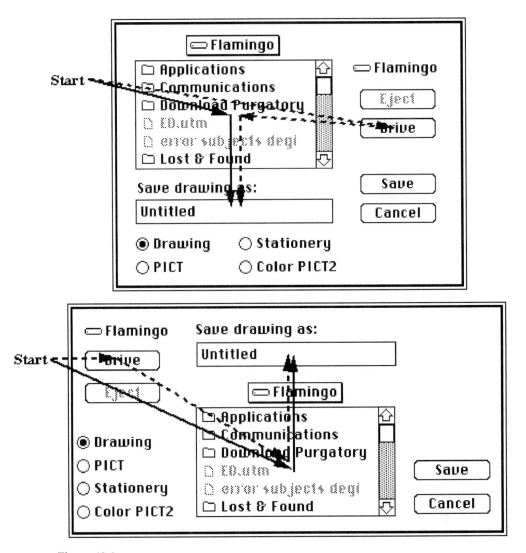

Figure 12.6

Layout appropriateness can help designers to analyze and redesign dialog boxes. Here, the existing dialog box (top) was redesigned based on frequencies of action sequences (bottom). The solid line represents the most frequent sequence of actions; the dashed line represents the second most frequent sequence of actions. (Sears, 1993.)

might start a client-itinerary window, review flight segments from a schedule window, and drag selected flight segments to the itinerary window. Windows labeled "Calendar," "Seat Selection," "Food Preferences," and "Hotels" might appear as needed, and then the charge-card information window would appear to complete the transaction.

If window-housekeeping actions can be reduced, users can complete their tasks more rapidly, and probably with fewer mistakes. The visual nature of window use has led many designers to apply a direct-manipulation strategy (see Chapter 6) to window actions. To stretch, move, and scroll a window, users can point at appropriate icons on the window border and simply click on the mouse button and drag. Since the dynamics of windows have a strong effect on user perceptions, the animations for transitions (zooming boxes, repainting when a window is opened or closed, blinking outlines, or highlighting during dragging) must be designed carefully.

Window design evolved rapidly in the 1980s, from influential designs at Xerox PARC to innovative syntheses by Apple for the Macintosh (see Fig. 1.1) and finally Microsoft's modest refinements into the highly successful Windows series (1.0, 2.0, 3.1, 95, 98, 2000, NT, ME, and XP) (see Fig. 1.3). Overlapping, draggable, resizable windows on a broad desktop have become the standard for most users. Advanced users who work on multiple tasks can switch among collections of windows called workspaces or rooms. Each workspace holds several windows whose states are saved, allowing easy resumption of activity. Much progress has been made, but there is still an opportunity to reduce dramatically the housekeeping chores with individual windows and to provide task-related multiple-window coordination.

12.5.1   Coordinating multiple windows

Designers may break through to the next generation of window managers by developing coordinated windows, in which windows appear, change contents, and close as a direct result of user actions in the task domain. For example, in medical insurance–claims processing, when the agent retrieves information about a client, such fields as the client's address, telephone number, and membership number should appear on the display. Simultaneously, and with no additional commands, the client's medical history might appear in a second window, and the record of previous claims might appear in a third window. A fourth window might contain a form for the agent to complete to indicate payment or exceptions. Scrolling the medical-history window might produce a synchronized scroll of the previous-claims window to show related information. When the claim is completed, all window contents should be saved and all the windows should be closed. Such sequences of actions can be established by designers, or by users with end-user programming tools.

Similarly, for web browsing, job-hunting users should be able to select the five most interesting position-description links and open them all with a single click. Then, it should be possible to explore all of them synchronously to compare the job details, location, or salary, by selecting one scroll action. When one position is selected, it should fill the screen, and the other four should close automatically.

Coordination is a task concept that describes how information objects change based on user actions. A careful study of user tasks can lead to task-specific coordinations based on sequences of actions. The especially interesting case of work with large images such as maps, circuit diagrams, or magazine layouts is covered in the next section. Other important coordinations that might be supported by interface developers include:

- *Synchronized scrolling.* A simple coordination is synchronized scrolling, in which the scroll bar of one window is coupled to another scroll bar, and action on one scroll bar causes the other to scroll the associated window contents in parallel. This technique is useful for comparing two versions of a program or document. Synchronization might be on a line-for-line basis, on a proportional basis, or keyed to matching tokens in the two windows.

- *Hierarchical browsing.* Coordinated windows can be used to support hierarchical browsing. For example, if one window contains a book's table of contents, selection of a chapter title by a pointing device should lead to the display, in an adjoining window, of the chapter contents. Hierarchical browsing was nicely integrated in Windows Explorer to allow users to browse hierarchical directories, in Outlook to browse folders of e-mails (Fig. 10.1), and in many other applications (Fig. 12.7).

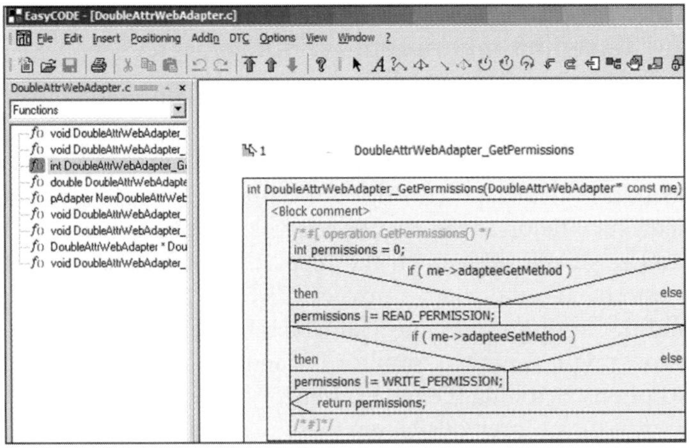

Figure 12.7

Hierarchical browsing in the XperCASE tool (now called EasyCASE with EasyCODE). The specification is on the left. As users click on components (DoubleAttrWebAdapter), the detail view in a Nassi-Shneiderman Chart appears on the right.

- *Opening/closing of dependent windows.* An option on opening a window might be to simultaneously open dependent windows in a nearby and convenient location. For example, when users are browsing a program, if they open a main procedure, the dependent set of procedures could open up automatically (Fig. 12.8). Conversely, in filling in a form, users might get a dialog box with a choice of preferences. That dialog box might lead the user to activate a pop-up or error-message window, which in turn might lead to an invocation of the help window. After the user indicates the desired choice in the dialog box, it would be convenient to have automatic closing of all the windows (Fig 12.9).

- *Saving/opening of window state.* A natural extension of saving a document or a set of preferences is to save the current state of the display, with all the windows and their contents. This feature might be implemented by the simple addition of a "Save screen as..." menu item to the "File" menu of actions. This action would create a new icon representing the current state; clicking on the icon would reproduce that state. This feature is a simple version of the rooms approach (Henderson and Card, 1986).

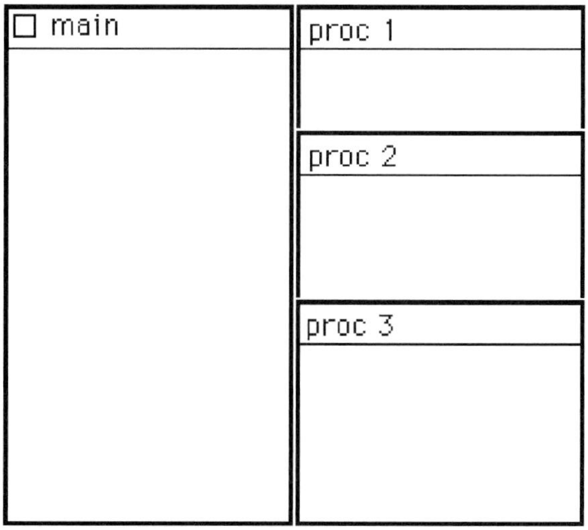

Figure 12.8

Dependent windows. When such windows open, several other windows may open automatically. In this example, the main procedure of a program has been opened, and the dependent procedures 1, 2, and 3 have been opened and placed at convenient locations. Connecting lines, shading, or decoration on the frame might indicate the parent and child relationships.

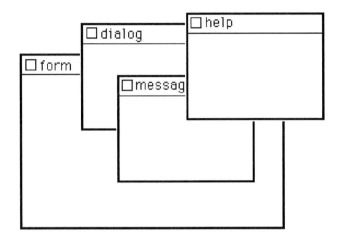

Figure 12.9

Dependent windows. When such windows close, other windows may close too. Here, all four windows will be closed automatically when the parent window, "form", is closed. Lines, shading, or border decorations may indicate families of windows, with special marks to indicate parents and children.

12.5.2 Image browsing

A two-dimensional cousin of hierarchical browsing enables users to work with large maps, circuit diagrams, magazine layouts, photos, or artwork. Users see an overview in one window and the details in a second window. They can move a field-of-view box in the overview to adjust the detail-view content. Similarly, if users pan in the detail view, the field-of-view box should move in the overview. Well-designed coordinated windows have matching aspect ratios in the field-of-view box and the detail view, and a change to the shape of either produces a corresponding change in the other.

The magnification from the overview to the detail view is called the *zoom factor*. When the zoom factors are between 5 and 30, the coordinated overview and detail view pair are effective; for larger zoom factors, however, an additional intermediate view is needed. For example, if an overview shows a map of France, then a detail view showing the Paris region is effective. However, if the overview were of the entire world, intermediate views of Europe and France would preserve orientation (Fig. 12.10).

Side-by-side placement of overview and detail views is the most common layout, since it allows users to see the big picture and the details at the same time. Some systems provide a single view, either zooming smoothly to move in on a selected point (Bederson and Hollan, 1994) or simply replacing the overview with the detail view. This zoom-and-replace approach is simple to

GLOBAL VIEW   INTERMEDIATE VIEWS   DETAIL VIEW

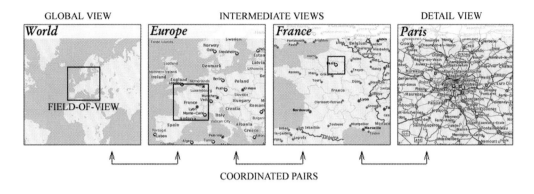

COORDINATED PAIRS

Figure 12.10

Global and intermediate views, which provide overviews for the detail view of Paris. Movements of the field-of-view boxes change the content in the detail view. (Plaisant, Carr, and Shneiderman, 1995.)

implement and gives the maximal screen space for each view, but it denies the users the chance to see the overview and detail view at the same time. A variation is to have the detail view overlap the overview, but it may obscure key items. Semantic zooming, in which objects change the way they are represented depending on their magnification, might help users see an overview by rapidly zooming in and out (Hornbaeck, Plaisant, and Bederson, 2002).

Attempts to provide detail views (focus) and overviews (context) without obscuring anything have motivated interest in *fisheye views* (Sarkar and Brown 1994; Bartram et al., 1995). The focus area (or areas) is magnified to show detail, while preserving the context, all in a single display (Fig. 12.11). This distortion-based approach is visually appealing, even compelling, but the continually changing magnified area may be disorienting, and the zoom factor in published examples rarely exceeds 5.

The design for image browsers should be governed by the users' tasks, which can be classified as follows (Plaisant, Carr, and Shneiderman, 1995):

- *Image generation.* Paint or construct a large image or diagram.
- *Open-ended exploration.* Browse to gain an understanding of the map or image.
- *Diagnostics.* Scan for flaws in an entire circuit diagram, medical image, or newspaper layout.
- *Navigation.* Have knowledge of the overview, but need to pursue details along a highway or vein.
- *Monitoring.* Watch the overview and, when a problem occurs, zoom in on details.

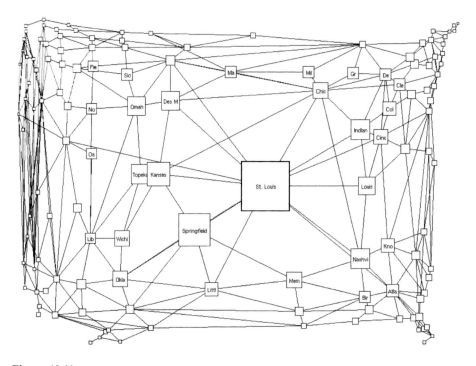

Figure 12.11

Fisheye view of U.S. cities, with the focus on St. Louis. The context is preserved, although the distortions can be disorienting. (Sarkar and Brown, 1994.)

Within these high-level tasks, users carry out many low-level actions, such as moving the focus (jumping from city to city on a map), comparing (viewing two harbors at the same time to compare their facilities, or viewing matching regions in X-ray images of left and right lungs), traversing (following a vein to look for blockages), or marking locations to return to them at a later time.

12.5.3   Personal role management

Window coordination facilitates handling of larger images and tasks that have been too complex to deal with in the past. However, there are other potent opportunities to improve window management. The current graphical user interfaces offer a desktop with applications represented as icons and documents organized into folders, but refinements to this approach are possible.

A natural progression is towards a *role-centered* design, which emphasizes the users' tasks rather than the applications and documents. While computer-supported cooperative work (Chapter 10) is aimed at coordination of several people performing a common task, by contrast, a role-centered design could substantially improve support for individuals in managing their multiple roles. Each role brings these individuals in contact with different people for carrying out a hierarchy of tasks following an independent schedule. A *personal role manager*, instead of a window manager, could improve performance and reduce distraction while the user is working in a given role, and could facilitate shifting of attention from one role to another (Plaisant and Shneiderman, 1995).

In a personal role manager, each role has a *vision statement* (a document that describes responsibilities and goals) that is established by the user or manager. The explicitness of the vision can simplify the training and integration of new personnel into the organization and can facilitate the temporary covering of employees' responsibilities (during vacations or parental leave, for example). Each role also has a *set of people*, a *task hierarchy*, a *schedule*, and a *set of documents*. In addition, web bookmarks and recent documents are maintained for each role.

Screen management is one of the key functions of the personal role manager. All roles should be visible, but the current focus of attention may occupy most of the screen. As users shift attention to a second role, the current one shrinks and the second one grows to fill the screen. Users can simultaneously enlarge two roles if there are interactions between them.

For example, a professor may have roles such as teacher of courses, advisor to graduate students, member of the recruiting committee, principal investigator of grants, author of technical reports, and liaison to industry. In the teacher role, the professor's vision statement might include the intention to make lectures and assignments available via the Web to facilitate a large undergraduate course. Files might include homework assignments, bibliography, course outline, and so on. The task hierarchy might begin with tasks such as choosing a textbook and end with administering the final exam. The subtasks for administering the final exam might include preparing the exam, reserving a room, proctoring the exam, and grading the exam. The set of people includes the students, teaching assistants, bookstore manager, registrar, and colleagues teaching other sections of the course. The schedule would begin with deadlines for submitting the book order to the bookstore manager and end with turning in the final grades to the registrar.

The personal role manager could simplify and accelerate the performance of common coordination tasks, in the same way that graphical user interfaces simplify file-management tasks. The requirements for a personal role manager include these:

- Support a *unified framework* for information organization according to users' roles.
- Provide a *visual, spatial layout* that matches tasks.
- Support *multiwindow actions* for fast arrangement of information.

- Support *information access* with partial knowledge of an information item's nominal, spatial, temporal, and visual attributes and its relationships to other pieces of information.
- Allow *fast switching* and *resumption* of roles.
- Free users' *cognitive resources* to work on *task-domain actions,* rather than making users concentrate on interface-domain actions.
- Use *screen space* efficiently and productively for tasks.

12.6   Color

Color displays are attractive to users and can often improve task performance, but the danger of misuse is high. Color can

- Soothe or strike the eye
- Add accents to an uninteresting display
- Facilitate subtle discriminations in complex displays
- Emphasize the logical organization of information
- Draw attention to warnings
- Evoke strong emotional reactions of joy, excitement, fear, or anger

The principles developed by graphic artists for using color in books, magazines, highway signs, and other print media have been adapted for user interfaces (Thorell and Smith, 1990; Travis, 1991; Marcus, 1992; Shubin, Falck, and Johansen, 1996). Programmers and interactive-systems designers are learning how to create effective computer displays and to avoid pitfalls (Salomon, 1990; Galitz, 2003; Brewer, Hatchard, and Harrower, 2003).

There is no doubt that color makes video games more attractive to users, conveys more information on power-plant or process-control diagrams, and is necessary for realistic images of people, scenery, or three-dimensional objects (Foley et al., 1997; Weinman, 2002). These applications require color. However, greater controversy exists about the benefits of color for alphanumeric displays, spreadsheets, graphs, and user-interface components.

No simple set of rules governs use of color, but these guidelines are a starting point for designers:

- *Use color conservatively.* Many programmers and novice designers are eager to use color to brighten up their displays, but the results are often counterproductive. One home-information system displayed the seven letters of its name in large letters, each with a different color. At a distance, the display appeared inviting and eye catching; up close, however, it was difficult to read.

Instead of showing meaningful relationships, inappropriately colored fields mislead users into searching for relationships that do not exist. Using a different color for each of 12 items in a menu produces an overwhelming effect. Using 4 colors (such as red, blue, green, and yellow) for the 12 items will still mislead users into thinking that all the similarly colored items are related. An appropriate strategy might be to show all the menu items in one color, the title in a second color, the instructions in a third color, and error messages in a fourth color, but even this strategy can be overwhelming if the colors are too visually striking. A safe approach is always to use black letters on a white background, with italics or bold for emphasis, and to reserve color for special highlighting.

- *Limit the number of colors.* Many design guides suggest limiting the number of colors in a single display to four, with a limit of seven colors in the entire sequence of displays. Experienced users may be able to benefit from a larger number of color codes, but for novice users too many color codes can cause confusion.

- *Recognize the power of color as a coding technique.* Color speeds recognition for many tasks. For example, in an accounting application, if data lines with accounts overdue more than 30 days are coded in red, they will be readily visible among the nonoverdue accounts coded in green. In air-traffic control, high-flying planes might be coded differently from low-flying planes to facilitate recognition. In programming workstations, keywords are color-coded differently from variables.

- *Ensure that color coding supports the task.* Be aware that using color as a coding technique can inhibit performance of tasks that go against the grain of the coding scheme. If, in the above accounting application with color coding by days overdue, the task is now to locate accounts with balances of more than $55, the existing coding scheme may inhibit performance on the second task. Also, in the programming application, the color coding of recent additions may make it more difficult to read the entire program. Designers should attempt to make a close linkage between the users' tasks and the color coding, and offer users control where possible.

- *Have color coding appear with minimal user effort.* In general, the color coding should not have to be assigned by users each time they perform a task, but rather should appear automatically. For example, when users click on a web link to start the task of checking for overdue accounts, the color coding is set automatically. When the users click on the task of locating accounts with balances of more than $55, the new color-coding scheme should appear automatically.

- *Place color coding under user control.* When appropriate, the users should be able to turn off color coding. For example, if a spelling checker highlights possibly misspelled words in red, then the user should be able to accept or change the spelling and to turn off the coding. The presence of the highly visible red coding is a distraction from reading the text for comprehension.

- *Design for monochrome first.* The primary goal of a display designer should be to lay out the contents in a logical pattern. Related fields can be shown by contiguity or by similar structural patterns; for example, successive employee records may have the same indentation pattern. Related fields can also be grouped by a box drawn around the group. Unrelated fields can be kept separate by blank space—at least one blank line vertically or three blank characters horizontally. It may be advantageous to design for monochrome rather than relying on color, because color displays may not be universally available.

- *Consider the needs of color-deficient users.* One important aspect to consider is readability of colors by users with color blindness (either red/green confusion, the most common case, or total color blindness). Color impairment is a very common condition that should not be overlooked (Rosenthal and Phillips, 1997; Olson and Brewer, 1997). Approximately eight percent of males and less than one percent of females in North America and Europe have some permanent color deficiency in their vision. Many others have temporary deficiencies due to illness or medications. They may, for example, confuse some shades of orange or red with green, or not see a red dot on a black background. Designers can easily address this problem by limiting the use of color, using double encoding when appropriate (that is, by using symbols that vary in both shape and color or location and color), providing alternative color palettes to choose from, or allowing users to customize the colors themselves. For example, the SmartMoney Map-of-the-Market (Fig. 14.22) provides two choices of color schemes: red/green and blue/yellow. Various tools, such as Vischeck, are available to both simulate color vision impairments and optimize graphics for some of the various forms of color impairment that exist. ColorBrewer offers guidelines on color schemes that work for those with color-vision impairment. Black on white or white on black will work well for most users.

- *Use color to help in formatting.* In densely packed displays where space is at a premium, similar colors can be used to group related items. For example, in a police dispatcher's tabular display of assignments, the police cars on emergency calls might be coded in red, and the police cars on routine calls might be coded in green. Then, when a new emergency arises, it would be relatively easy to identify the cars on routine calls and to assign one to the emergency. Dissimilar colors can be used to distinguish physically close but logically distinct fields. In a block-structured programming language, designers could show the nesting levels by coding the statements in a progression of colors—for example, dark green, light green, yellow, light orange, dark orange, red, and so on.

- *Be consistent in color coding.* Use the same color-coding rules throughout the system. If some error messages are displayed in red, then make sure that every error message appears in red; a change to yellow may be interpreted as a change in the importance of the message. If colors are used differently by several designers of the same system, users will hesitate as they attempt to assign meaning to the color changes.

- *Be alert to common expectations about color codes.* Designers need to speak to users to determine what color codes are applied in the task domain. From automobile-driving experience, red is commonly considered to indicate stop or danger, yellow is a warning, and green is all clear or go. In investment circles, red is a financial loss and black is a gain. For chemical engineers, red is hot and blue is cold. For map makers, blue means water, green means forests, and yellow means deserts. These differing conventions can cause problems for designers. Designers might consider using red to signal that an engine is warmed up and ready, but users might understand the red coding as an indication of danger. A red light is often used to indicate that power is on for electrical equipment, but some users are made anxious by this decision since red has a strong association with danger or stopping. When appropriate, indicate the color-code interpretations on the display or in a help panel.

- *Be alert to problems with color pairings.* If saturated (pure) red and blue appear on a display at the same time, it may be difficult for users to absorb the information. Red and blue are on the opposite ends of the spectrum, and the muscles surrounding the human eye will be strained by attempts to produce a sharp focus for both colors simultaneously. The blue will appear to recede and the red will appear to come forward. Blue text on a red background would present an especially difficult challenge for users to read. Similarly, other combinations (yellow on purple, magenta on green) will appear to be garish and difficult to read. Too little contrast also is a problem: Imagine yellow letters on a white background or brown letters on a black background. A test of 24 color combinations found that error rates ranged from approximately 1 to 4 errors per 1,000 characters read (Pace, 1984). Black on light blue and blue on white were two color schemes associated with low error rates in both tasks, and magenta on green and green on white were two color schemes associated with high error rates. Tests with other monitors and tasks will be required to reach a general conclusion about the most effective color pairs. On each color monitor, colors appear differently, so careful tests with various text and background colors are necessary.

- *Use color changes to indicate status changes.* For automobile speedometers with digital readouts and a wireless receiver of the driving speed limits, it might be helpful to change from green numbers below the speed limit to red above the speed limit to act as a warning. Similarly, in an oil refinery, pressure indicators might change color as the value went above or below acceptable limits. In this way, color acts as an attention-getting method. This technique is potentially valuable when there are hundreds of values displayed continuously.

- *Use color in graphic displays for greater information density.* In graphs with multiple plots, color can be helpful in showing which line segments form the full graph. The usual strategies for differentiating lines in black-on-white graphs—such as dotted lines, thicker lines, and dashed lines—are not as effective as using separate colors for each line. Architectural plans benefit from color coding of electrical, telephone, hot-water, cold-water, and natural-gas lines. Similarly, maps can have greater information density when color coding is used.

Color displays are becoming nearly universal, even in mobile devices, and designers usually make heavy use of color in interface designs. There are undoubtedly benefits of increased user satisfaction and often increased performance, but there are also real dangers in misusing color. Care should be taken to make appropriate designs and to conduct thorough evaluations (Box 12.4).

Practitioner's Summary

The wording of system messages may have an effect on performance and attitudes, especially for novices, whose anxiety and lack of knowledge put them at a disadvantage. Designers might make improvements by merely using more specific diagnostic messages, offering constructive guidance rather than focusing on failures, employing user-centered phrasing, choosing a suitable physical format, and avoiding vague terminology or numeric codes.

When giving instructions, focus on the user and the user's tasks. In most applications, avoid anthropomorphic phrasing and use the *you* form to guide the novice user. Avoid judging the user. Simple statements of status are more succinct and usually are more effective.

Pay careful attention to display design, and develop a local set of guidelines for all designers. Use spacing, indentation, columnar formats, and field labels to organize the display for users. Denser displays, but fewer of them, may be advantageous. Color can improve some displays and can lead to more rapid task performance with higher satisfaction, but improper use of color can mislead and slow users.

Organizations can benefit from careful study of display-design guidelines documents and from the creation of their own sets of guidelines tailored to local needs (see Section 3.2.1). These documents should also include lists of local terminology and abbreviations. Consistency and thorough testing are critical.

Box 12.4

Guidelines that highlight the complex potential benefits and dangers of using color coding.

Guidelines for using color

- Use color conservatively: Limit the number and amount of colors.
- Recognize the power of color to speed or slow tasks.
- Ensure that color coding supports the task.
- Make color coding appear with minimal user effort.
- Keep color coding under user control.
- Design for monochrome first.
- Consider the needs of color-deficient users.
- Use color to help in formatting.
- Be consistent in color coding.
- Be alert to common expectations about color codes.
- Be alert to problems with color pairings.
- Use color changes to indicate status changes.
- Use color in graphic displays for greater information density.

Benefits of using color

- Various colors are soothing or striking to the eye.
- Color can improve an uninteresting display.
- Color facilitates subtle discriminations in complex displays.
- A color code can emphasize the logical organization of information.
- Certain colors can draw attention to warnings.
- Color coding can evoke more emotional reactions of joy, excitement, fear, or anger.

Dangers of using color

- Color pairings may cause problems.
- Color fidelity may degrade on other hardware.
- Printing or conversion to other media may be a problem.

Researcher's Agenda

Experimental testing could refine the error-message guidelines proposed here and could identify the sources of user anxiety or confusion. Message placement, highlighting techniques, and multiple-level message strategies are candidates for exploration. Improved analysis of sequences of user actions to provide more effective messages automatically would be useful. Since anthropomorphic designs are rarely successful, believers in human-like agents should conduct empirical studies.

There is a great need for testing to validate data-display and color-design guidelines. Basic understanding and cognitive models of visual perception of displays would be a dramatic contribution. Do users follow a scanning pattern from the top left? Do users whose natural language reads from right to left or users from different cultures scan displays differently? Does use of whitespace around or boxing of items facilitate comprehension and speed interpretation? When is a single dense display preferable to two sparse displays? How does color coding reorganize the pattern of scanning?

Window-management strategies have become standardized, but there are opportunities for innovation with large and multiple displays, novel applications that require multiple-window coordination, and innovative work-management strategies such as personal role managers.

WORLD WIDE WEB RESOURCES

Usage guidelines for color are nicely done on the World Wide Web, with some empirical results, but the most informative and enjoyable experience is simply browsing through the lively and colorful web sites. Styles and fashions come and go quickly, so save the examples you like best.

http://www.aw.com/DTUI

References

Bartram, Lyn, Ho, Albert, Dill, John, and Henigman, Frank, The continuous zoom: A constrained fisheye technique for viewing and navigating large information spaces, *Proc. UIST '95 Symposium on User Interface Software & Technology*, ACM, New York (1995), 207–215.

Bederson, B. and Hollan, J. D., Pad++: A zooming graphical interface for exploring alternate interface physics, *Proc. UIST '94, Symposium on User Interface Software & Technology*, ACM, New York (1994), 17–26.

Brennan, Susan E. and Ohaeri, Justina O., Effects of message style on users' attributions towards agents, *Proc. CHI '94 Conference: Human Factors in Computing Systems, Conference Companion*, ACM, New York (1994), 281–282.

Brewer, Cynthia A., Hatchard, Geoffrey W., and Harrower, Mark A., ColorBrewer in print: A catalog of color schemes for maps, *Cartography and Geographic Information Science*, 30, 1 (2003), 5–32.

Burns, Michael J., Warren, Dianne L., and Rudisill, Marianne, Formatting space-related displays to optimize expert and nonexpert user performance, *Proc. CHI '86 Conference: Human Factors in Computing Systems*, ACM, New York (1986), 274–280.

Cassell, Justine, Sullivan, Joseph, Prevost, Scott, and Churchill, Elizabeth, *Embodied Conversational Agents*, MIT Press, Cambridge, MA (2000).

Donner, Kimberly A., McKay, Tim, O'Brien, Kevin M., and Rudisill, Marianne, Display format and highlighting validity effects on search performance using complex visual displays, *Proc. Human Factors Society—Thirty-Fifth Annual Meeting*, Santa Monica, CA (1991), 374–378.

Foley, James D., van Dam, Andries, Feiner, Steven K., and Hughes, John F., *Computer Graphics: Principles and Practice, Second Edition*, Addison-Wesley, Reading, MA (1997).

Friedman, Batya, "It's the computer's fault"—Reasoning about computers as moral agents, *Proc. CHI '95 Conference: Human Factors in Computing Systems, Conference Companion*, ACM, New York (1995), 226–227.

Galitz, Wilbert O., *The Essential Guide to User Interface Design: An Introduction to GUI Design Principles and Techniques, Second Edition*, John Wiley & Sons, New York (2003).

Graesser, Arthur C., VanLehn, Kurt, Rose, Carolyn P., Jordan, Pamela W., and Harter, Derek, Intelligent tutoring systems with conversational dialogue, *AI Magazine*, 22, 4 (Winter 2001), 39–52.

Gratch, J., Rickel, J., Andre, E., Badler, N., Cassell, J., and Petajan, E., Creating interactive virtual humans: Some assembly required, *IEEE Intelligent Systems*, 17, 4 (2002), 54–63.

Harless, William G., Zier, Marcia A., Harless, Michael G., and Duncan, Robert C., Virtual conversations: An interface to knowledge, *IEEE Computer Graphics and Applications*, 23, 5 (September–October 2003), 46–53.

Henderson, Austin and Card, Stuart K., Rooms: The use of multiple virtual workspaces to reduce space contention in a window-based graphical user interface, *ACM Transactions on Graphics*, 5, 3 (1986), 211–243.

Hornbaek, K., Bederson, B. B., and Plaisant, C., Navigation patterns and usability of zoomable user interfaces with and without an overview, *ACM Transactions on Computer-Human Interaction 9*, 4 (December 2002), 362–389.

Ivory, M. Y. and Hearst, M. A., Statistical profiles of highly-rated web site interfaces, *Proc. CHI 2002 Conference: Human Factors in Computing Systems*, ACM, New York (2002), 367–374.

Kiesler, Sara, Sproull, Lee, and Waters, Keith, A prisoner's dilemma experiment on cooperation with people and human-like computers, *Journal of Personality and Social Psychology*, 70, 1 (1996), 47–65.

Kosslyn, S. M., *Elements of Graphic Design*, W. H. Freeman and Co., New York (1994).

Mahajan, R. and Shneiderman, B., Visual and textual consistency checking tools for graphical user interfaces, *IEEE Transactions on Software Engineering*, 23 (1997), 722–735.

Marcus, Aaron, *Graphic Design for Electronic Documents and User Interfaces*, ACM, New York (1992).

Martin, Dianne, ENIAC: Press conference that shook the world, *IEEE Technology and Society Magazine*, 14, 4 (Winter 1995/96), 3–10.

Moreno, R., Mayer, R. E., Spires, H., and Lester, J., The case for social agency in computer-based teaching: Do students learn more deeply when they interact with animated pedagogical agents? *Cognition and Instruction*, 19 (2001), 177–213.

Mullet, Kevin and Sano, Darrell, *Designing Visual Interfaces: Communication Oriented Techniques*, Sunsoft Press, Englewood Cliffs, NJ (1995).

Mumford, Lewis, *Technics and Civilization*, Harcourt Brace and World, New York (1934), 31–36.

Nass, Clifford, Lombard, Matthew, Henriksen, Lisa, and Steuer, Jonathan, Anthropocentrism and computers, *Behaviour & Information Technology*, 14, 4 (1995), 229–238.

Olson, J. and Brewer, C. A., An evaluation of color selections to accommodate map users with color-vision impairments, *Annals of the Association of American Geographers*, 87, 1 (1997), 103–134

Ozok, A. Ant and Salvendy, Gavriel, The effect of language inconsistency on performance and satisfaction in using the Web: Results from four experiments, *Behaviour & Information Technology*, 22, 3 (2003), 155–163.

Pace, Bruce J., Color combinations and contrast reversals on visual display units, *Proc. Human Factors Society—Twenty-Eighth Annual Meeting*, Santa Monica, CA (1984), 326–330.

Parush, A., Nadir, R., and Shtub, A., Evaluating the layout of graphical user interface screens: Validation of a numerical computerized model, *International Journal of Human-Computer Interaction*, 10, 4 (1998), 343–360.

Plaisant, Catherine, Carr, David, and Shneiderman, Ben, Image browsers: Taxonomy and design guidelines, *IEEE Software*, 12, 2 (March 1995), 21–32.

Plaisant, Catherine and Shneiderman, Ben, Organization overviews and role management: Inspiration for future desktop environments, *Proc. IEEE Fourth Workshop on Enabling Technologies: Infrastructure for Collaborative Enterprises*, IEEE Press, Los Alamitos, CA (April 1995), 14–22.

Reeves, Byron and Nass, Clifford, *The Media Equation: How People Treat Computers, Television, and New Media Like Real People and Places*, Cambridge University Press, Cambridge, U.K. (1996).

Reeves, B. and Rickenberg, R., The effects of animated characters on anxiety, task performance, and evaluations of user interfaces, *Proc. CHI 2000 Conference: Human Factors in Computing Systems*, ACM, New York (2000), 49–56.

Rosenthal, O. and Phillips, R., *Coping with Color-Blindness*, Avery Publishing Group, New York (1997).

Salomon, Gitta, New uses for color, in Laurel, Brenda (Editor), *The Art of Human-Computer Interface Design*, Addison-Wesley, Reading, MA (1990), 269–278.

Sarkar, Manojit and Brown, Marc H., Graphical fisheye views, *Communications of the ACM*, 37, 12 (July 1994), 73–84.

Sears, Andrew, Layout appropriateness: Guiding user interface design with simple task descriptions, *IEEE Transactions on Software Engineering*, 19, 7 (1993), 707–719.

Shneiderman, Ben, Looking for the bright side of agents, *ACM Interactions*, 2, 1 (January 1995), 13–15.

Shubin, Hal, Falck, Deborah, and Johansen, Ati Gropius, Exploring color in interface design, *ACM Interactions*, 3, 4 (August 1996), 36–48.

Smith, Sid L. and Mosier, Jane N., *Guidelines for Designing User Interface Software*, Report ESD-TR–86–278, Electronic Systems Division, MITRE Corporation, Bedford, MA (1986). Available from National Technical Information Service, Springfield, VA.

Staggers, Nancy, Impact of screen density on clinical nurses' computer task performance and subjective screen satisfaction, *International Journal of Man-Machine Studies*, 39, 5 (November 1993), 775–792.

Takeuchi, Akikazu and Naito, Taketo, Situated facial displays: Towards social interaction, *Proc. CHI '95 Conference: Human Factors in Computing Systems*, ACM, New York (1995), 450–455.

Teitelbaum, Richard C., and Granda, Richard F., The effects of positional constancy on searching menus for information, *Proc. CHI '83 Conference: Human Factors in Computing Systems*, ACM, New York (1983), 150–153.

Thorell, L. G. and Smith, W. J., *Using Computer Color Effectively*, Prentice-Hall, Englewood Cliffs, NJ (1990).

Travis, David S., *Effective Color Displays: Theory and Practice*, Academic Press, New York (1991).

Tufte, Edward, *Envisioning Information*, Graphics Press, Cheshire, CT (1990).

Tullis, T. S., An evaluation of alphanumeric, graphic and color information displays, *Human Factors*, 23 (1981), 541–550.

Tullis, T. S., Screen design, in Helander, M., Landauer, T. K., and Prabhu, P. (Editors), *Handbook of Human-Computer Interaction, Second Edition*, Elsevier, Amsterdam, The Netherlands (1997), 377–411.

Vincow, Michelle A. and Wickens, Christopher, Spatial layout of displayed information: Three steps toward developing quantitative models, *Proc. Human Factors Society—Thirty-Seventh Annual Meeting*, Santa Monica, CA (1993), 348–352.

Walker, Janet H., Sproull, Lee, and Subramani, R., Using a human face in an interface, *Proc. CHI '94 Conference: Human Factors in Computing Systems*, ACM, New York (1994), 85–91.

Weinman, Lynda, *Designing Web Graphics, Fourth Edition*, New Riders, Indianapolis, IN (2002).

Williams, T. R., Guidelines for the display of information on the Web, *Technical Communication* 47, 3 (2000), 383–396.

User Manuals, Online Help, and Tutorials

What is really important in education is…that the mind is matured, that energy is aroused.

SOREN KIERKEGAARD
Either/Or, Volume II

13 . 1   Introduction

Standardization and improvements in user interfaces have made computer applications easier to use, but using new interfaces is still a challenge. First-time computer users struggle to understand basic interface objects and actions as well as their tasks. For experienced users, learning advanced features and understanding novel task domains takes commitment and concentration. Many users learn from another person who knows the interface; others learn by trial and error. The user manuals, online help, and tutorials are typically ignored, but when users get stuck in trying to complete their tasks, these resources can be useful.

Learning anything new is a challenge. Although challenges can be joyous and satisfying, when it comes to learning about computer systems, many people experience anxiety, frustration, and disappointment. Much of the difficulty flows directly from the poor design of the menus, displays, or instructions—which leads to errors and confusion—or simply from users' inability to easily determine what to do next. As the goal of providing universal usability becomes more prominent, online help services are increasingly necessary to bridge the gap between what users know and what they need to know.

Empirical studies show that well-written and well-designed user manuals, on paper or online, can be effective (Carroll, 1998; Hackos and Stevens, 1997; Horton, 1994). Modern interactive systems are expected to provide online help, online manuals, and interactive tutorials to serve user needs for training and reference. In fact, as displays appear in cars, phones, cameras, public kiosks, and elsewhere, ubiquitous online help should be the norm.

Even though increasing attention is being paid to improving user-interface design, the complexity and diversity of interactive applications are also growing. There will always be a need for supplemental materials that aid users, in both paper and online forms. Some of the many forms of traditional paper user manuals are:

- *Installation manual* with step-by-step instructions to set up an application
- *Brief getting-started notes* to enable eager first-time users to try out features
- *Introductory tutorial* to explain common features
- *Thorough tutorial* that covers typical and advanced tasks
- *Detailed reference manual* with all features covered
- *Quick reference card* with a concise presentation of the syntax
- *Conversion manual* that introduces the features of the system to users who are knowledgeable about a similar system or previous versions of the same system

There are also diverse ways of providing guidance to users online (Box 13.1). Most forms of paper manuals now exist online, but popular variations include:

- *Online manual.* An electronic form of comprehensive paper manuals that cover the interface features. Online manuals make the text more readily available, searchable, and up-to-date, but they may be difficult to read, annotate, and absorb.
- *Online help.* Brief descriptions of specific topics to help users cope when problems arise. Online help can provide indexes of terms, keyword searches, step-by-step guidance, and access to complementary web information.
- *Context-sensitive help.* User-controlled interactive help, ranging from simple balloon help explaining objects to system-initiated assistants that monitor users' activities and provide relevant information.
- *Online tutorial.* An online training environment that uses electronic media to teach novices by explaining objects and actions through textual descriptions, graphical imagery, and interface screen grabs. The scope of the tutorial can vary greatly, from brief two-minute introductions to week-long computer-based training courses.
- *Animated demonstration.* Appealing animated graphics presented as a slide show, series of screen captures, or well-produced video engage users and show the actual interface, often with verbal explanations.
- *Guides.* Audio or video recordings of authoritative personalities or animated characters who provide introductions or focused segments that cover key topics.

Box 13.1

Taxonomy of user manuals, online help, and tutorials.

Domain covered by help system
- Description of interface objects and actions (syntactic)
- Sequences of actions to accomplish tasks (semantic)
- Task-domain–specific knowledge (pragmatic)

Degree of integration in the interface (from less to more integrated)
- Online manual and tutorial: independent interface, even possibly developed by a different company
- Online help: integrated into the interface, separate window usually invoked from a "help" button
- Context-sensitive help: a) user-controlled—depends on where the user points (pop-up box, balloon, ScreenTip, or sticky note) b) system initiated—the system makes suggestions and sometimes takes action
- Animated demonstrations and guides: usually integrated into the interface

Time of intervention
- Before starting (manual and tutorial)
- At the beginning of the interaction (getting started, animated demonstration)
- During the task (context sensitive, either user- or system-initiated help)
- After failure (help button, FAQs)
- When the user returns the next time (startup tips)

Media
- Text (paragraphs of text, with a list of steps)
- Graphics (screen prints can illustrate explanations)
- Voice recording
- Video recording of someone using the interface
- Animation
- Record and replay of the interface itself in action, with or without annotations
- Simulation environments for computer-based training

Extensibility
- Closed system
- Users can add more information (annotations, synonyms, or translations)

Other methods of providing help are based on archives of user questions or dialogs among users:

- *FAQs* (Frequently Asked Questions) prepared by developers to answer common questions and kept up to date, usually on the Web.
- *Online communities, newsgroups, listservers, e-mail, chat, and instant messaging* to get answers to specific questions from peer users.

Users' goals are a good way to classify paper and online materials, as shown by this chart (extended from Duffy, Palmer, and Mehlenbacher, 1992):

User's Goal	Example of Delivery Medium	
	Paper	*Online*
I want to *buy* it	Sales brochure, fact sheet	Animated demonstration
I want to *learn* it	Tutorial	Manual, tutorial, guide, animated demonstration
I want to *use* it	User manual	Manual, help, context-sensitive help
I want to *solve* a problem	FAQ	Help, FAQ, online community

Other forms of instruction include classroom instruction, personal training and assistance, telephone consultation, video, and audio recordings. These forms are not discussed here, but many of the same instructional-design principles apply. Another important approach is personal human help from a telephone-accessible help desk. This can be a valuable asset for users, but it is an expensive one for providers.

This chapter starts by reviewing the benefits of paper versus online manuals (Section 13.2), then summarizes the results of user studies that have compared reading on paper and on computer displays (Section 13.3). Section 13.4 discusses the shaping of the contents of manuals, followed by specific approaches for online manuals and help (Section 13.5). Next, tutorials, demonstrations, and guides (Section 13.6) and online communities for user assistance (Section 13.7) are reviewed. The chapter closes with a brief section on the development process for user manuals (Section 13.8).

13.2 Paper Versus Online Manuals

There are many reasons to have online manuals. The positive reasons for doing so include:

- *Physical advantages*
  - Information is available whenever the information appliance or computer is available. There is no need to locate the correct manual (an activity that

could cause a minor disruption if the proper manual is close by, or a major disruption if the manual must be retrieved from another building or person). The harsh reality is that many users lose their paper manuals or do not keep them current with new versions of the software.

- Users do not need to allocate physical workspace to opening up manuals. Paper manuals can be clumsy to use and can clutter a workspace.
- Information can be electronically updated rapidly and at low cost. Electronic dissemination of revisions ensures that out-of-date material cannot be retrieved inadvertently.

- *Navigation features*
  - Specific information necessary for a task can be located rapidly if the online manuals offer indexes, tables of contents, lists of figures, glossaries, and lists of keyboard shortcuts.
  - Searching for one page in hundreds can usually be done much more quickly on a computer than in a paper manual.
  - Linking within texts can guide readers to related materials; linking to external materials such as dictionaries, encyclopedias, translations, and web resources can facilitate understanding.

- *Interactive services*
  - Readers can bookmark and annotate the text (Fig. 13.1) and send text and annotations by e-mail.
  - Authors can use graphics, sound, color, and animations that may be helpful in explaining complex actions and creating an engaging experience for users (Fig. 13.2).
  - Readers can turn to newsgroups, listservers, online communities, e-mail, chat, and instant messaging for further help from other users.
  - Blind users (or busy users on the move) can use screen readers and listen to instructions.

- *Economic advantages*
  - Online manuals are cheaper to duplicate and distribute than paper manuals.

However, these advantages can be compromised by potentially serious negative side effects:

- Displays may not be as readable as paper manuals (see Section 13.3).
- Each display may contain substantially less information than a sheet of paper. The display resolution is also lower than that for paper, which is especially important when pictures or graphics are used.

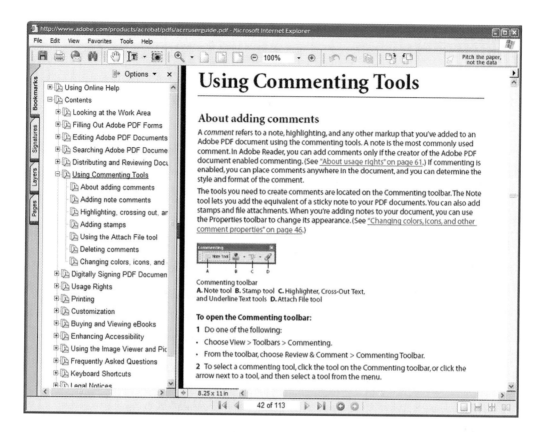

Figure 13.1

The user manual for Adobe Reader 6.0 is a linear PDF document that can be printed or read online. Tabs provide access to an expandable table of contents, page thumbnails, or bookmarks. Users can click on links to related sections, zoom, add comments, search, and more. (www.adobe.com)

- The user interface of online help systems may be novel and confusing to novices. By contrast, most people are thoroughly familiar with the "user interface" of paper manuals.
- The extra mental effort required for navigating through many screens may interfere with concentration and learning, and annotation can be difficult.
- Splitting the display between work and help or tutorial windows reduces the space for work displays. If users must switch to a separate help or tutorial application, the burden on short-term memory can be large. Users may lose

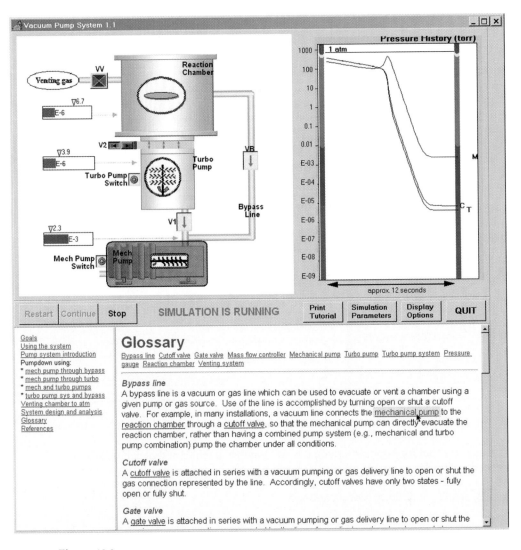

Figure 13.2

In the EquipSim learning system, when the cursor hovers over the glossary term "Mechanical pump", the corresponding component is highlighted and animated in the pump system diagram. (www.isr.umd.edu/CELS/)

the context of their work and have difficulty remembering what they read in the online manual. Large displays provide a potential resolution for this problem for desktop applications (see Section 9.5).

- Small devices such as cell phones do not have enough display space to provide online help. They usually have to rely on paper manuals or separate web-based online manuals and tutorials.

The current trend is to provide most documentation online, except for small mobile-device applications. For high-end systems the cost of printing manuals is not an issue, so customers appreciate also having the paper user manuals. For low-end desktop applications, paper user manuals can be made available at extra cost. A lively market for training books testifies to the appeal of high-quality instructional materials.

13.3   Reading from Paper Versus from Displays

The technology of printing text on paper has been evolving for more than 500 years. The paper surface and color, the typeface, character width, letter sharpness, text contrast with the paper, width of the text column, size of margins, spacing between lines, and even room lighting all have been explored in efforts to produce the most appealing and readable format.

In the last 50 years, the cathode ray tube (CRT), often called the *visual display unit* (VDU) or *tube* (VDT), became the alternate medium for presenting text (Hansen and Haas, 1988; Oborne and Holton, 1988; Creed, Dennis, and Newstead, 1988; Horton, 1994; Schilit, Golovchinsky, and Price, 1998). Early concerns about CRT radiation or other health hazards have lessened as manufacturers, labor unions, and government agencies have funded major research in this area. The increasingly popular liquid crystal displays (LCDs) not only eliminate concerns about radiation, but their compact designs consume less physical space. Since the cost of LCDs continues to decline, current systems increasingly use them.

Visual fatigue and stress from reading computer displays are problems, but these conditions respond well to rest, frequent breaks, and task diversity. But even if users aren't aware of visual fatigue or stress, their capacity to work with displays may be below their capacity to work with paper manuals.

Numerous studies have found 15 to 30% slower task times for comprehension or proofreading of text on computer displays, compared to on paper. The potential disadvantages of reading from displays include these:

- *Fonts* may be poor, especially on low-resolution displays. The dots composing the letters may be so large that each is visible, making users expend effort to recognize characters. Monospace (fixed-width) fonts, lack of appropriate kerning (for example, adjustments to bring "V" and "A" closer together), inappropriate interletter and interline spacing, and inappropriate colors may all complicate recognition.

- *Low contrast* between the characters and the background and *fuzzy character boundaries* also can cause trouble.

- *Emitted light* from displays may be more difficult to read by than reflected light from paper; glare may be greater, *flicker* can be a problem, and the *curved display surface* may be troubling.

- *Small displays* require frequent *page turning*; issuing the page-turning commands is disruptive, and the page turns are unsettling, especially if they are slow and visually distracting.
- *Reading distance* is easily adjustable for paper, while most displays are *fixed* in place, and display *placement* may be too high for comfortable reading (optometrists suggest reading be done with the eyes in a downward-looking direction). The "near quintad" (Grant, 1990) are the five ways eyes adjust to seeing close items: *accommodation* (lens-shape change), *convergence* (looking towards the center), *meiosis* (pupillary contraction), *excyclotorsion* (rotation), and *depression of gaze* (looking down). Users of tablet computers and mobile devices often hold their displays in a lower position than desktop displays, to facilitate reading.
- *Layout and formatting* can be problems—for example, improper margins, inappropriate line widths (35 to 55 characters is recommended), or awkward justification (left justification and ragged right are recommended). Multicolumn layouts may require constant scrolling up and down. Page breaks may be distracting and waste space.
- *Reduced hand and body motion* with fixed-position displays, as compared to paper, may be more fatiguing.
- *Unfamiliarity of displays* and the *anxiety* of navigating the text can increase stress.

The fascinating history of this issue goes back at least to Hansen and associates (1978), who found that students who were asked to take examinations on paper and on computer displays took almost twice as long online. Much of the increased time could be attributed to system delays, poor software design, and slower output rates, but the authors could not account for 37% of the longer time online. They conjectured that this additional time could be attributed to uncertainty about how to control the display, what the system would do, and what the system had done.

Similarly, a series of studies of proofreading tasks found that subjects worked faster and more accurately with paper documents rather than displays. However, a later series of studies with improved displays led to much smaller differences, suggesting that the key issue was poor display resolution (Gould et al., 1987).

The problem was resolved when researchers demonstrated no difference between reading text on displays versus on paper, if enough variables were controlled. Oborne and Holton (1988) believe that earlier studies may have been flawed by lack of control and comparing low-resolution displays to high-quality print. In their comprehension studies, there were no statistically significant differences between displays and photographs of displays. They controlled for position, distance to retina, line length, layout, and illumination. When the resolution of the display matches that of the hard copy, there is no difference in reading speed or perceived image quality (Jorna, 1991). However, since most computer displays do not yet have the resolution of paper, it is still easier to read from paper when lengthy texts must be read.

These empirical studies isolated the issues and led to a clear message for designers: High-resolution and larger displays are recommended if users are to read large amounts of material online. Related studies clarify that short response times, fast display rates, black text on white background, and page-sized displays are important considerations if displayed text is meant to replace paper documents. Some general applications, such as Microsoft Word 2003, provide a dedicated reading mode that limits the number of controls and increases the space available for the text. Also, dynamic pagination can take into account the display size to facilitate paging through the document instead of scrolling.

The interest in reading from displays has increased as mobile devices, specialized electronic book platforms (Fig. 9.19), and web-based libraries have grown more common. The capacity to download the morning newspaper onto a pocket-sized computer to read while standing in a crowded subway or to carry a full city guide on such a device while touring are strong attractions. Similarly, large online libraries of books available for free, such as the Gutenberg archives or the International Children's Digital Library (Fig. 1.16), or for pay, as offered by numerous publishers, promote efforts to improve the reading experience. The U.S. National Academy of Sciences, which makes more than a thousand of its books available for free online in a convenient format, has found that this service promotes sales of their paper books. Scientific journal publishers are evolving to satisfy the intense demand for online access to articles, while struggling to ensure a way to recover their costs. They are moving towards subscription-based access to augmented documents with linked references or citation-export facilities. Publishers of newspapers, such as *The Wall Street Journal* and *Le Monde* are experimenting with a balance of free access and paid subscriptions to find a profitable way to address the needs of different users.

Plasticity of documents is becoming a requirement. Documentation designers have to structure their materials so that they can be read on small, medium, and large displays and at different font sizes to accommodate vision-impaired users. Markups of the text (for example, XML-based markups) can support the automatic generation of paper and online versions, tables of contents, diverse indexes, enhanced search capabilities, shortened versions for quick scanning, and links for further details. Advanced features could include automatic conversion to foreign languages, tools for annotation, bookmarks, capacity to have the text read out loud, and highlights for different classes of readers.

13.4   Shaping the Content of the Manuals

Traditionally, training and reference materials for computer systems were paper manuals. Writing these manuals was often left to the most junior member of the development team as a low-effort task at the end of the project. As a result, the manuals were often poorly written, were not suited to the background of the users, were delayed or incomplete, and were tested inadequately. By now, managers recognize that designers often lack sensitivity to user needs, that system developers might not be good writers, and that it takes time and skill to write effective manuals. They have also learned that testing and revisions must be done before widespread dissemination and that system success is closely coupled to documentation quality. Early experiments have made a strong case for the effect of the quality of writing on user success. The benefits of well-designed manuals include shorter learning times, better user performance, increased user satisfaction, and fewer calls for support (Spencer and Yates, 1995; Allwood and Kalen, 1997). After listing 20 studies concluding the advantage of either paper or online documentation over the other, Horton (1994) concludes that "good online documentation is better than poor paper documentation and good paper documentation is better than poor online documentation."

13.4.1   Towards minimal manuals

Thinking-aloud studies (see Section 4.3) of subjects who were learning word processors have revealed the enormous difficulties that most novices have and the strategies that they adopt to overcome those difficulties (Carroll and Mack, 1984). Learners are actively engaged in trying to make the system work, to read portions of the manual, to understand the displays, to explore the functions of keys, and to overcome the many problems that they encounter. The "active user paradox" (Carroll and Rosson, 1987) states that users' eagerness to conduct meaningful activities often stops them from spending time "just" learning, and therefore their skills remain mediocre. Learners apparently prefer trying out actions on the computer, rather than reading lengthy manuals. They want to perform meaningful, familiar tasks immediately and to see the results for themselves. They apply real-world knowledge, experience with other interfaces, and frequent guesswork. The image of the new user patiently reading through and absorbing the contents of a manual is rare in reality.

These observations led to the design of *minimal manuals* that anchor the tool in the task domain, encourage active involvement with hands-on experience as soon as possible, promote *guided exploration* of system features, and support error recognition and recovery. The key principles of user-manual design (Box 13.2) have been refined over time, described in detail, and validated in practice (van der Meij and Carroll, 1995; Carroll, 1998).

Results of field trials and of dozens of empirical studies demonstrate that with improved manuals, learning time can be reduced substantially and user satisfaction can be increased (van der Meij and Lazonder, 1993; Stieren, 1998). Users benefit from seeing typical queries that demonstrate the syntax and serve as templates for other queries. In fact, complete *sample tasks* and *interaction sessions* are extremely helpful in giving a portrait of the interface features and inter-

Box 13.2

User-manual guidelines based on practice and empirical studies (mostly based on Carroll, 1998).

Choose an action-oriented approach.
- Provide an immediate opportunity to act.
- Encourage and support exploration and innovation.
- Respect the integrity of the user's activity.
- Show numerous examples.

Let users' tasks guide organization.
- Select or design instructional activities that are real tasks.
- Present task concepts before interface objects and actions.
- Create components of instructions that reflect the task structure.

Support error recognition and recovery.
- Prevent mistakes whenever possible.
- Provide error information when actions are error prone or correction is difficult.
- Provide error information that supports detection, diagnosis, and correction.
- Provide on-the-spot error information.

Support reading to do, study, and locate.
- Be brief; don't spell out everything.
- Provide a table of contents, index, and glossary.
- Keep the writing style clean and simple.
- Provide closure for chapters.

action style (Fig. 13.3). Many users will work through these sessions to verify their understanding, to gain a sense of competence, and to see whether the interface and the manual match.

Visual aspects are helpful to readers, especially with highly visual direct-manipulation interfaces and graphical user interfaces. Viewing numerous well-chosen screen prints that demonstrate typical uses enables users to develop an understanding and a *predictive model* of the interface. Often, users will mimic the examples in the manual during their first trials of the software. Figures containing complex data structures, transition diagrams, and menus can improve performance dramatically by giving users access to systems models created by designers.

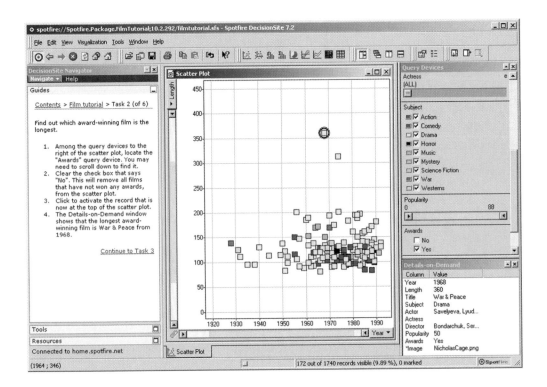

Figure 13.3

The discovery tool Spotfire provides examples guiding users while they learn to use the interface. Here, a sample dataset about films was loaded in the tool, and users use step-by-step instructions to find out "which award-winning film is the longest." (www.spotfire.com)

Of course, every good manual should have a *table of contents* and an *index*. *Glossaries* can be helpful for clarifying technical terms. *Appendices* with error messages are recommended.

Whether to give *credit* to authors and designers is a lively and frequently debated issue. Advocates encourage giving credit in the manuals to honor good work, to encourage contributor responsibility for doing an excellent job, and to build the users' trust. Responsibility and trust are increased because the contributors are willing to have their names listed publicly. Having the writers' and designers' names in the manuals makes software fit in with other creative human endeavors, such as books, films, and music, in which contributors are acknowledged, even if there are dozens of them. Opponents say that it is sometimes difficult to identify who contributed what or that unwelcome telephone calls might be received by contributors.

13.4.2   Use of the OAI model to design manuals

The object-action interface (OAI) model (Section 2.5) offers insight into the learning process and thus provides guidance to instructional-materials designers. If users have only partial knowledge of the task objects and actions (Fig. 13.4), then training in the task is the first step. For a task such as letter writing, users must learn about address blocks, salutations, content, and signatures. Once users know the hierarchy of objects from the high-level down to the atomic and recognize the range of their high-level intentions down to their specific action steps (Fig. 13.5), they are equipped to learn about the interface representations. The instructional materials should start with familiar objects and actions in the letter-writing task, link these concepts to the high-level interface objects and actions (Fig. 13.6), and then show the syntax needed to accomplish each task. Knowledgeable users who understand the task and interface (see Fig. 2.6) can move on to expert levels of usage with shortcuts that speed performance.

Some users are complete novices, while others are knowledgeable about the task (letter writing or word processing) but must learn a new tool (word processor).

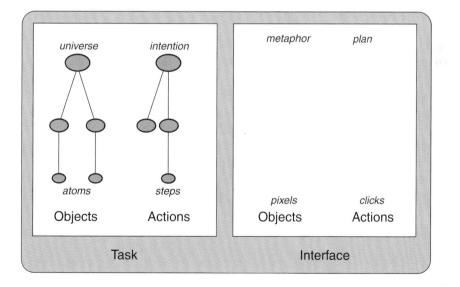

Figure 13.4

A representation of users who know some of the task objects and actions but know nothing about the interface. A deeper knowledge of task objects and actions will give them a framework for learning about the interface.

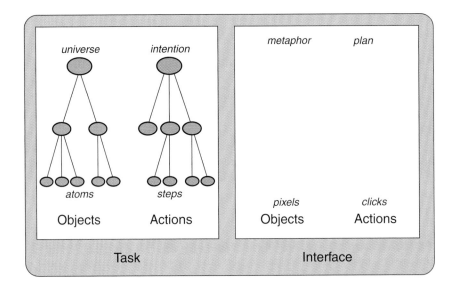

Figure 13.5

A representation of users who know the task adequately but do not know the interface. Educational materials for this community should explain the interface objects and actions, starting with plans.

These users need a presentation that shows the relationship between the metaphors and plans they know and the new ones—these metaphors and plans are becoming increasingly standard across word processors, but the dialog boxes, clicks, and keystrokes may vary. Finally, some users will have learned the task and interface objects and actions but be unable to recall details of how to convert their plans into specific actions. These three scenarios demonstrate the need for three popular forms of paper manuals: the *introductory tutorial,* the *conversion manual,* and the *quick reference* (cheat sheet).

The OAI model can also help researchers to map the current levels of knowledge in learning systems. For example, users who are learning about database-management systems for U.S. Congressional voting patterns might have some knowledge about the database and its manipulation, the query-language concepts, and the syntax needed. These users would benefit from seeing typical queries that demonstrate the syntax and serve as templates for other queries. In fact, complete sample tasks and interaction sessions are extremely helpful in giving a portrait of the interface features and interaction style. Many users will work through these sessions to verify their understanding, to gain a sense of competence in using the interface, and to see whether the interface and the manual match. Another helpful guide to using a system is an overall *flow diagram* of activity (Fig. 13.7). Such visual

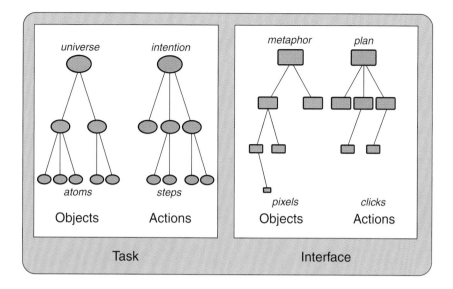

Figure 13.6

A representation of users who are knowledgeable about the task and high-level interface aspects and need to learn only the specific visual representations and syntactic details. For example, someone who knows about writing scientific articles and is familiar with at least one word processor will find it relatively easy to acquire the low-level objects and actions in another word processor.

overviews provide a map that orients users to the transitions from one activity to another. Similarly, if the interface uses a complex model of data objects, an overview diagram may help users to appreciate the details.

13.4.3   Organization and writing style

Designing instructional materials is a challenging endeavor. The author must be knowledgeable about the technical content; sensitive to the background, reading level, and intellectual ability of the reader; and skilled in writing lucid prose. Assuming that the author has acquired the technical content, the primary job in creating a manual is to understand the readers and the tasks that they must perform.

A precise statement of the *instructional objectives* (Mager, 1997) is an invaluable guide to the author and the reader. The sequencing of the instructional content should be governed by the reader's current knowledge and ultimate objectives. Precise rules are hard to identify, but the author should attempt to present concepts in a logical sequence in increasing order of difficulty, to ensure that each concept is used in subsequent sections, to avoid forward references,

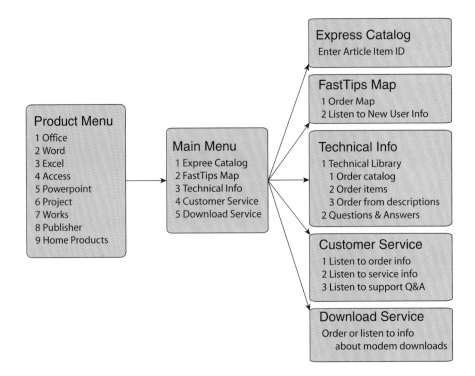

Figure 13.7

A transition diagram can be a helpful aid for users. This FastTips map, adapted from an early version of the Microsoft Support Network, gives telephone callers an overview and therefore capability to move rapidly within the support service. Users identify relevant articles, which are faxed to them.

and to construct sections that contain approximately equal amounts of new material. In addition to these structural requirements, the manual should have sufficient examples and complete sample sessions.

Within a section that presents a concept, the author should begin with the reason for covering the concept, describe the concept in task-domain semantic terms, then show the computer-related semantic concepts, and, finally, offer the syntax.

The choice of words and their phrasing is as important as the overall structure. A poorly written sentence mars a well-designed manual, just as an incorrect note mars a beautifully composed sonata. *The Elements of Style* (Strunk, White, and Angell, 2000) and *Writing Well* (Zinsser, 1998)—two classic books on writing—are valuable resources. Style guides for organizations represent worthy attempts at ensuring consistency and high quality. Of course, no set of guidelines can turn a mediocre writer into a great writer. Writing is a highly creative act; effective writers are national treasures.

Writing style should match users' reading ability. Subjects of a study on learning performance and reading ability (Roemer and Chapanis, 1982) used a tutorial written at the fifth-, tenth-, or fifteenth-grade reading level. Higher reading ability led to significant reductions in the completion time and number of errors and to higher scores on a concepts test. Increased complexity of the writing style did not lead to significant differences on the performance variables, and subjective preferences significantly favored the fifth-grade version. Subjects could overcome the complex writing style, but the authors conclude, "the most sensible approach in designing computer dialogue is to use the simplest language."

13.5   Online Manuals and Help

Although paper manuals often yield faster learning (Hertzum and Frokjaer, 1996), the online environment opens the door to a variety of helpful facilities (Roesler and McLellan, 1995) that might not be practical in printed form (Section 13.2). Studies have confirmed that well-designed online documentation can be very effective (Cohill and Williges, 1982; Magers, 1983). In spite of improvements, however, most users avoid user manuals and prefer to learn interface features by exploration (Rieman, 1996). Even when problems arise, many users are reluctant to consult written documentation. Hence, designers have begun to explore new ways to provide help besides traditional user manuals.

Kearsley (1988) offers examples of online help with empirical data about usage, and these guidelines:

- Make the help system easy to access and easy to return from.
- Make online help as specific as possible.
- Collect data to determine what help is needed.
- Give users as much control as possible over the help system.
- Supply different help for different types of users.
- Make help messages accurate and complete.
- Do not use help to compensate for poor interface design.

Standard formats such as WinHelp and Windows HTML Help have stimulated development of a growing number of software tools, such as RoboHelp and helpMATIC Pro. These tools facilitate coordination among teams of authors in creating interactive online help in multiple formats for multiple platforms.

13.5.1   Online manuals

Most manufacturers now put their user documentation online. The low production and shipping costs of CD-ROMs first encouraged hardware suppliers to produce online manuals that were exact images of the paper manuals. Apple put its six-volume *Inside Macintosh* series for developers onto a single CD-ROM with scanned images and hypertext links (Bechtel, 1990). Another Apple (1993) innovation was to create a CD-ROM guide for interface designers with more than a hundred animations of poor, good, and better designs. Modern designs assume that online manuals or web-based manuals will be available, usually with standard browsing interfaces to reduce learning effort. For mobile devices, small displays limit the possibilities, but providing helpful instructions on the device to complement printed user manuals should still be a priority.

Although they are often generated from the same source document (usually an XML document), online manuals now tend to differ from paper manuals in many ways. Online manuals can benefit from all the physical advantages, navigation features, and interactive services mentioned in Section 13.2. On the other hand, paper manuals have traditionally housed supplementary local information that is often written in margins or included on slips of paper stuck in at the appropriate pages. Online manuals that allow for local annotations, synonyms, or translations have enhanced value. Additional desirable services include bookmarking and automatic history keeping that allows backtracking. Designers will be most effective when they design online manuals to fit the electronic medium and take advantage of text highlighting, color, sound, animation, and especially string search with relevance feedback.

A vital feature for online manuals is a properly designed table of contents that can remain visible to the side of the page of text. Selection of a chapter or other entry in the table of contents should immediately produce the appropriate page on the display (Fig. 13.1). Use of expanding or contracting tables of contents (Egan et al., 1989) or multiple panes to show several levels at once can be beneficial (Chimera and Shneiderman, 1994).

13.5.2   Online help

Online help that offers concise descriptions of the interface objects and actions is probably most effective for intermittent knowledgeable users; it is likely to be less useful for novices who have more need for tutorial training. The traditional approach is to have users type or select a help-menu item and to display a list of alphabetically arranged topics for which there is a paragraph or more of helpful information that users can read. This method can work, but it is often frustrating for those users who are not sure of the correct term for the task they wish to accomplish. They may see several familiar terms (search, query, select, browse, find, reveal, display, info, or view) but not know which one to select. Worse still, there may not be a single command that accomplishes the task, and there is usually little information about how to assemble actions to perform tasks, such as converting graphics into a different format.

Sometimes simple lists—for example, of *keyboard shortcuts, menu items*, or *mouse shortcuts*—can provide the necessary information. Each item in the list might have an accompanying feature description. However, many designers recognize that such lists can be overwhelming and that users usually want guidance for accomplishing their specific intended tasks (for example, printing on envelopes).

Users expect to be able to search through the full text of online documentation. In one approach, an expanding and contracting table of contents was combined with string-search capabilities and relevance feedback indicating the number of "hits" on the table-of-contents listing (Egan et al., 1989). A series of three empirical studies showed the effects of several improvements to the online documentation and compared it with the paper version. Use of the electronic version was advantageous, especially when the search queries contained words that were in the document headings or text. Browsing strategies were found to be most effective, but search by keywords proved to be a useful complement (Hertzum and Frokjaer, 1996).

The online help and support center in Microsoft Windows XP offers many ways of finding relevant articles, called *topics*. Users can browse an organized table of contents that lists the topics hierarchically or search the text of the articles (Fig. 13.8). Finally, Microsoft's Answer Wizard approach allows users to type requests using natural-language statements; the program then selects the relevant keywords and offers a list of topics organized into categories. For example, typing "Tell me how to print addresses on envelopes" produces:

What do you want to do?

Create and print an envelope
Print envelopes by merging an address list

This example shows a successful response from the natural-language system, but the quality of the responses varies greatly in typical usage situations. Users may not type in appropriate terms, and they often have difficulty understanding the instructions.

13.5.3 Context-sensitive help

The ability to provide context-sensitive information is a powerful advantage of online help systems. The simplest way to take context into account is to monitor the cursor location and provide helpful information about the object under the cursor. This form of user-controlled interactive object help is readily understandable to users and even fun to use. Another approach is to provide system-initiated help, often called "intelligent help," that tries to make use of the interaction history, a model of the user population, and a representation of their tasks to make assumptions about what users need.

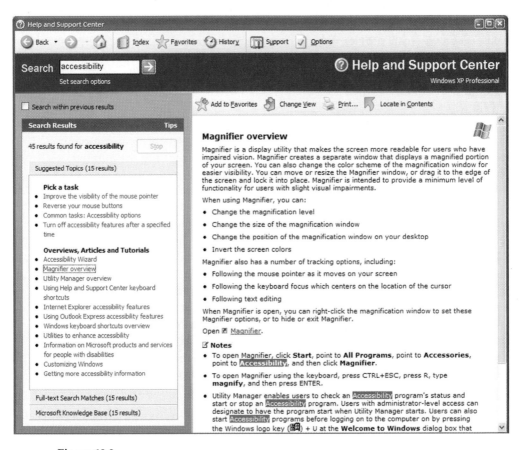

Figure 13.8

The Microsoft Windows XP Help and Support Center provides multiple ways to navigate to the pages of information. Here, a search for "accessibility" returns a list of tasks, articles, and tutorials. Commands (such as the opening of the Magnifier) can be activated within the help pages.

User-controlled, interactive object help   A simple approach to context-sensitive help is based on the interactive widgets in the interface. Users position the cursor on a widget (or other visible interface object) and then press a help key or remain still for a couple of seconds to produce information about the object on which the cursor is resting. In a common version of this technique, users simply move the cursor to the desired location and hover over the object, causing a small pop-up box (often called *a tool tip, ScreenTip,* or *balloon help*) to appear with an explanation of that object (Fig. 13.9). A variant consists in turning on all the balloons at once, so that users can see all the explanations simultaneously. Another approach is to dedicate a portion of the display to help, which is updated automatically as users hover over or select interface widgets (Fig. 13.10).

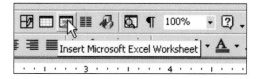

Figure 13.9

In Microsoft Office, when users hover over an icon, a ScreenTip appears that explains the command represented by the icon, providing help at the widget level.

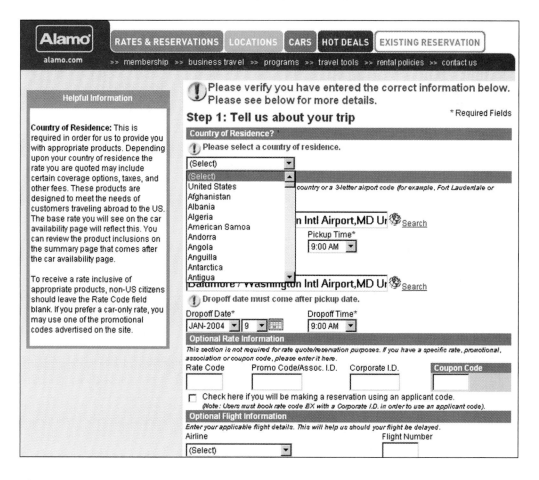

Figure 13.10

To rent a car, users fill in a form with information about their trips. As they click on a field (here, the "country of residence" menu), context-sensitive, detailed help information appears on the left part of the screen, explaining why the information is needed. Comments colored in red on the form indicate missing or incorrectly entered information and provide directions to correct the data—for example, "Dropoff date must come after pickup date." Notes in italics give brief directions and explain why the data is needed. (www.alamo.com)

User-controlled help can also be used for objects more complex than widgets, such as control panels or forms (Fig. 13.11).

System-initiated help By keeping track of user actions, some researchers believe that they can provide effective system guidance, such as suggesting that users should redefine their margins since they are indenting every line. Research in computer-based intelligent user interfaces has seen mixed results (Hook, 2000). Early on, a simulated "intelligent help" system was tested with eight users doing business tasks such as printing a mailing list (Carroll and Aaronson, 1988). The researchers prepared messages for expected error conditions, but they found

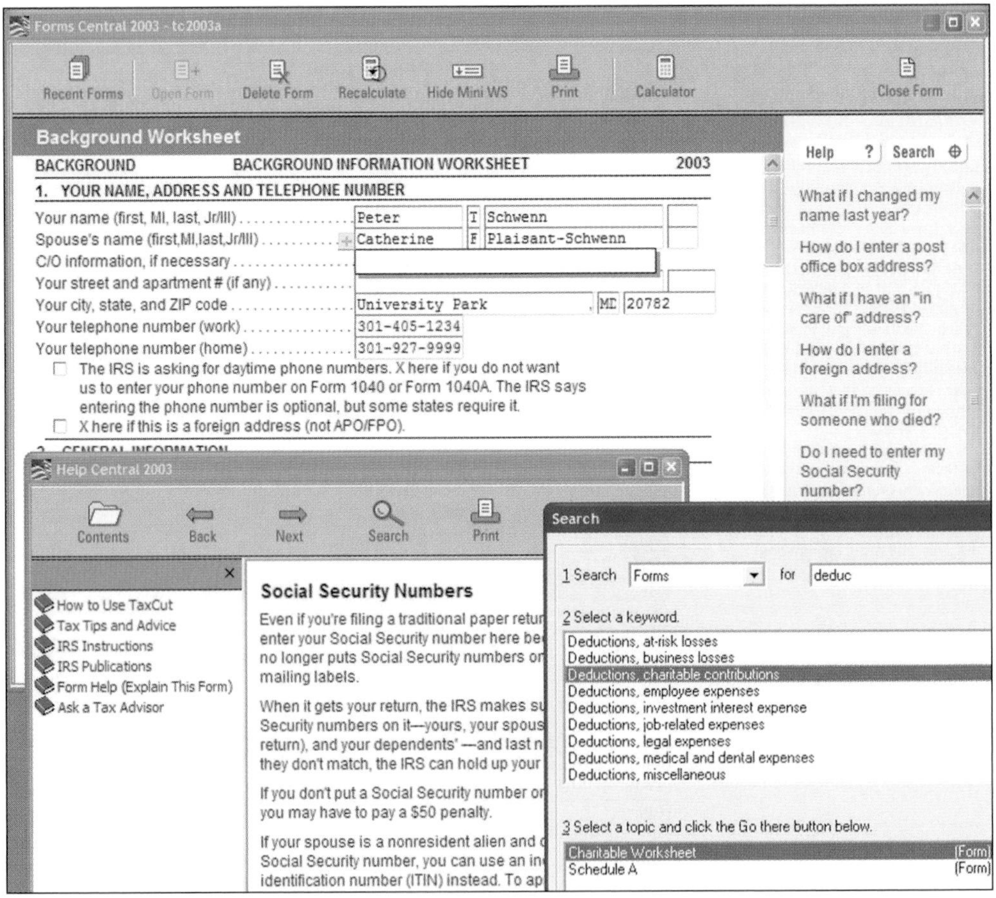

Figure 13.11

Taxcut helps users file their tax documents. Frequently asked questions are listed next to each form or worksheet. Clicking on the question "Do I need to enter my Social Security Number?" opens the corresponding help page. A keyword search is also available. (www.taxcut.com)

that "people are incredibly creative in generating errors and misconceptions, and incredibly fast." The results, even with a simulated system, were mixed; the authors concluded, "Development of intelligent help systems faces serious usability challenges." A system-initiated help system has been implemented in the Smalltalk programming environment, where cartoon-like gurus appear on the display and offer audio commentaries with animated demonstrations of the graphical user interface (Alpert, Singley, and Carroll, 1995). The designers considered many of the problems of anthropomorphic help, such as user initiation, pacing, and user control of remediation; unfortunately, however, no empirical evidence of the efficacy of the help system is available.

Intelligent help systems that provide system-initiated support have generally failed. The most infamous example illustrating the problems of this approach is Microsoft's Office Assistant (or "Clippit"), which has created much controversy (Shroyer, 2000). One of its functions was that as soon as users typed "Dear ...", Clippit popped up and offered assistance in formatting a letter (Fig. 13.12).

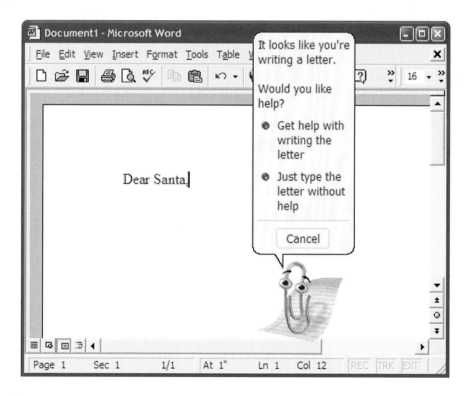

Figure 13. 12

Clippit the Office Assistant guesses that a letter is being written and offers help to prepare a standard letter in Word 2000.

Many users considered the paper clip so intrusive that they immediately turned it off.

Hybrid approaches   More recently, intelligent help advocates have promoted a mixed-initiative approach in which initiative is shared between the user and system (Horvitz, 1999) and an advice-giving approach (Lieberman, 2001). For example, Letizia (Lieberman, 1997) gives advice and suggestions to users browsing the Web, but its focus is on web-site suggestions rather than interface training. A Telephone Triage Assistant for junior nurses received good feedback during usability testing (Mao and Leung, 2003). The content of the advice window was unpredictable but rather unobtrusive, and it did not interfere with users' tasks. This approach requires dedicating a large portion of the display to the help information, but it keeps users in control of the amount and timing of the advice they receive, making this technique an effective hybrid of online help and tutorial approaches.

13.6   Online Tutorials, Demonstrations, and Guides

An online tutorial is an interactive training environment in which users can view explanatory descriptions of user-interface objects and actions, often tied to realistic task scenarios. There are many approaches to the use of electronic media to teach users how to master an interface. Depending on the complexity of the interface and the amount of time users are ready to spend absorbing the tutorial materials, they might be served well by an extensive computer-based training module, an animated demonstration of features, or a recorded welcome message by a familiar person. The challenge often is to prepare materials that will satisfy users who want a three-minute introduction as well as those who need a one-hour in-depth treatment. This section reviews a range of online possibilities, from textual and graphical tutorials to animated demonstrations and guides.

A more ambitious approach to training is based on a complex model of learning patterns tied to carefully designed educational tutorials that guide users and correct their mistakes. These have demonstrated impressive outcomes, but the success stories are based on years of development, testing, and refinement. The successful designs provide clear challenges, helpful tools, and excellent feedback (see Section 8.6.5). They do not depend on natural-language interaction, but rather provide users with a clear context in which to work and control their learning experience.

13.6.1   Online tutorials

One introductory tutorial for the Adobe PhotoShop package displays the exact steps users must make, and then shows the actions being carried out using a recorded demonstration. Users just keep pressing the space-bar key to speed through the demonstration. Some users find this guided approach attractive; others are put off by the restrictive sequencing that prevents errors and exploration. In contrast, Adobe's PhotoDeluxe includes an online tutorial that leads users through the multiple steps needed for graphical image manipulation (Fig. 13.13).

The opportunity for carrying out *practice tasks* as part of online tutorials is one of their greatest strengths. Getting users to be active is one of the key tenets of the minimal-manual approach, and it applies especially well to online tutorials. One study of hands-on practice methods for learning software compared free exploration, exercises, and a combined format consisting of an exercise followed by free exploration. The type of practice did not affect the performance of the low-experience subjects, but the performance of high-experience subjects significantly improved when they were trained using exercises (Wiedenbeck and Zila, 1997).

Creators of interactive tutorials must address the usual questions of instructional design and also the novelty of the computer environment. A library of common tasks for users to practice is a great help. Sample documents for word processors, slides for presentation software, and maps for geographic-information systems help users to experience the applications. Repeated testing and refinement is highly recommended for tutorials.

One attractive variant is the start-up tip: Each time users start the interface, they get a pop-up box displaying a brief explanation of a feature. Some systems monitor user behavior and show start-up tips only for features that are not used by this particular user.

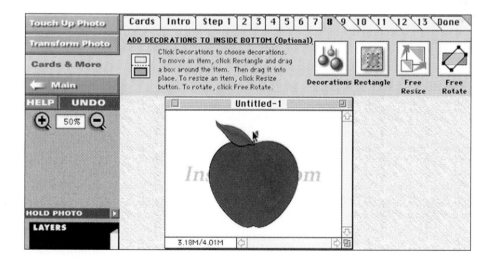

Figure 13.13

Adobe's PhotoDeluxe includes an online tutorial that leads users through the multiple steps needed for graphical image manipulation.

13.6.2   Animated demonstrations

Animated demonstrations have become a modern high-tech art form. Manufacturers originally designed them mostly to attract potential users of software or hardware by showing off system features using the best animations, color graphics, sound, and information presentation that advertising agencies can produce. Those demonstrations focus on building a positive product image. More recently, demonstrations have become a standard technique to train users as they work. The focus is on demonstrating step-by-step procedures and explaining the results of the actions. Automatic pacing or manual control satisfies hands-off or hands-on users, respectively. Additional control to allow users to stop, replay, or skip parts adds to the acceptability.

An animated demonstration can be prepared as a slide show, a screen-capture animation, or a video recording of a person using the device. A slide show might be appropriate for form-fillin or menu-based interfaces, but animation is preferable to demonstrate direct-manipulation interactions such as drag-and-drop operations, zoom boxes, or dynamic-query sliders. A screen-capture animation is easy to produce with standard tools such as Camtasia. These recordings can then be saved, possibly annotated or narrated, and then replayed automatically by users. In our own explorations, we found that users appreciated the recorded voice explanations, which make the demonstrations livelier and lead to more compact demonstrations; however, providing scripts and subtitles is necessary to address the needs of users with disabilities. Also, a video recording of a person using the interface can help clarify how special hardware is to be used—for example, to demonstrate the two-handed operation of a drawing system or the unfolding of a telephone keyboard accessory.

Animated demonstrations have been shown to be more effective at conveying the purpose and use of a tool than static explanations (Baecker, Small, and Mander, 1991; Sukaviriya and Foley, 1990). Users have also been shown to be faster and more accurate to perform tasks after being shown animated demonstrations rather than textual explanations. Surprisingly, however, the time and error effect was reversed after a week, showing limitations to the benefits of using animations as teaching tools (Palmiter and Elkerton, 1991). The authors suggest reinforcing the animations (which were nonsegmented—that is, in one continuous execution) with textual explanations. Segmenting the animations may also help comprehension and retention. Other studies show that the benefits of animations for learners may not be clear, but that users usually enjoy this presentation style (Payne, Chesworth, and Hill, 1992; Harrison, 1995).

Integrating the help facility by building overlays with *sticky notes* (short instructions that look like PostIt notes) proved to be effective in our PhotoFinder kiosk (Fig. 13.14), in which tasks such as searching for or annotating a photo could be demonstrated by a sequence of three to five sticky notes (Shneiderman et al., 2002). The sticky-note approach was also useful to help users get started

Figure 13.14

In PhotoFinder, sticky notes give the four main steps to annotate photos and provide a menu of tasks for which more help is available. (www.cs.umd.edu/hcil/photofinder)

with dynamic queries for map software (Kang, Plaisant, and Shneiderman, 2003). Dynamap's multilayered design allows novices to start with a simple interface consisting of only a map in Level 1 (Fig. 13.15) and to move up to Level 2 or Level 3 when they are ready, adding dynamic-query filters and a scatter plot, respectively. Because of the multilayered interface design, the number of sticky notes needed at any level is small. "Show me" demonstrations can be launched from the sticky notes, all from within the live interface itself. A greater level of integration in the application permits users to alternate between watching a demonstration and trying other steps by themselves.

Computer-game designers deserve credit for advancing the art of the animated demonstration, with lively introductions that show samples of how the game is played. With public kiosk games, the motivation is clear: getting users to put their money in the machine. Demonstrations have to explain the game and make it seem appealing and challenging, all within 30 seconds.

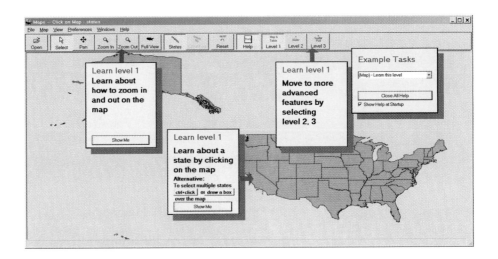

Figure 13.15

Dynamap is a multilayered interface with three levels. Level 1, shown here, consists only of a map. Sticky notes introduce the main functions and example tasks. The "show me" buttons initiate animated demonstrations that activate the interface itself. Users can advance step by step through the demonstration or execute the commands themselves, following the directions. A sticky note also points to the buttons allowing users to move to levels 2 and 3.

13.6.3   Guides

Audio and video recordings of *human guides*, such as the marketing manager for the software, a famous personality related to the content, or a cartoon character for children, can lead users through a body of knowledge. A pioneering effort was the GUIDES 3.0 project, in which a Native American chief, a settler wife, and a cavalryman appear as small photographs on the display to guide readers through the materials by offering their points of view on the settling of the American West (Oren et al., 1990). When selected, the guides tell their stories through video sequences. In addition, a modern woman is available in TV format to help guide the readers through using the system. This approach does not anthropomorphize the computer, but rather makes the computer a medium of communication, much as a book enables an author to speak to readers by way of the printed page. For games and children's software, a cartoon character has been shown to be equally helpful and appealing as a real person.

Introductions to online services such as CompuServe or America Online, web sites such as the Library of Congress, and Bill Gates' CD-ROM book *The Road Ahead* (1995) welcome new users and offer guidance about which features to begin using. Audio tours of art galleries have also become popular at many museums. An informed and engaging curator such as J. Carter Brown can lead visitors through the National Gallery of Art in Washington, D.C., but users can control the pace and replay sections. The well-designed CD-ROM *A Passion for Art* has several authoritative guides explaining the software, discussing history, and exploring the impressionist art in the Barnes collection (Corbis, 1995); a still photo or a video of the speaker is accompanied by spoken text to guide users through the software and the collection.

Audio or video lectures may be recorded for playback on the computer or on a separate system. Video Professor has become a successful company selling such introductions for dozens of popular software programs. These videos are tutorials, meant to be viewed from beginning to end, rather than a way of getting help when problems emerge.

13.7   Online Communities for User Assistance

Instead of natural-language conversations with computers to get help, interaction with other people online is proving to be effective. This communal approach may employ e-mail, chat, or instant messaging for question asking and responses (Eveland et al., 1994; Ackerman, 1994; Ackerman and Palen, 1996). Questions can be sent to a designated help desk or staff person, or posted on a discussion board (see Fig. 13.16 and Section 10.3.2). Responses can be received in seconds or, more typically, minutes or hours, but the downside is that users must publicly expose their lack of knowledge and risk getting incorrect advice. In one simple but positive example, a broadcast message produced the answer to a user's query in 42 seconds:

```
Time: 18:57:10
From: <azir>
  after i change a list to a group, how long before I can use it?
Time: 18:57:52
From: starlight on a moonless night <clee>
  you can use it immediately
```

The communal broadcast approach is increasingly appealing because of the low cost to software maintenance organizations and help-desk staff. Many respondents get a sense of satisfaction from being able to help others and demonstrate their abilities. Some are motivated to achieve prominence within a community in the hope of gaining consulting contracts. Microsoft has made an ambitious effort to use online communities to provide assistance for professionals and novices (Smith, 2002). They reward active contributors with a Most Valuable Professional citation on the web site, thereby steering consulting opportunities to

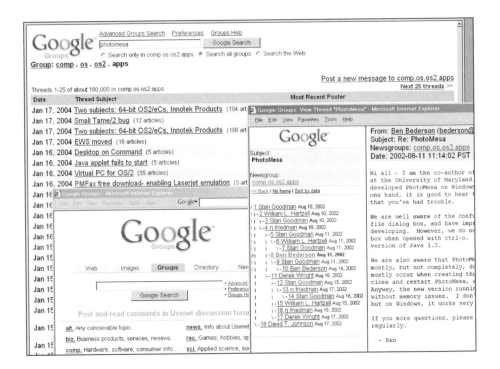

Figure 13.16

Using Google Groups, users can post questions on discussion boards and get answers from other users. A search for "photomesa" in comp.os.os2.apps finds a thread of 18 messages discussing this photo browser. Each group has a list of threads, and a directory helps users find the most appropriate group.

these active contributors. Microsoft's web site describes it as "a worldwide award and recognition program that strives to identify amazing individuals in technical communities around the globe who share a passion for technology and the spirit of community."

Purchasers of more expensive software expect and may pay for dedicated help-desk services, which promise e-mail or chat responses within hours or minutes. They may also pay for telephone-based customer service to get personalized help. Government agencies are often required to provide help to citizens, especially at tax-filing time, but these personal services can be costly to provide.

To prevent basic questions from tying up staff resources, managers of help desks often record common questions and answers into files of FAQs. This enables newcomers to browse typical problems discussed in the past.

13.8   The Development Process

Recognizing the difference between a good and a bad user manual is necessary for producing a successful manual on time and within a reasonable budget. Production of a manual, like any project, must be managed properly, staffed with suitable personnel, and monitored with appropriate milestones (Box 13.3).

Getting started early is invaluable. If the manual-writing process begins before the implementation, there will be adequate time for review, testing, and refinement. Furthermore, the user manual can act as a more complete and comprehensible alternative to the formal specification for the software. Implementers may miss or misunderstand some of the design requirements when reading a formal specification; a well-written user manual may clarify the design. The manual writer becomes an effective critic, reviewer, or question asker who can stimulate the implementation team. Early development of the manual enables pilot testing of the software's learnability even before the interface is built. In the months before the software is completed, the manual may be the best way to convey the designers' intentions to potential customers and users, as well as to implementers and project managers.

Informal walkthroughs with users are usually an enlightening experience for software designers and manual writers. Potential users are asked to read through the manual and to describe aloud what they are seeing and learning. Field trials with moderate numbers of users constitute a further process for identifying problems with the user manual and the software. Field trials can range in scope from half an hour with half a dozen people to several months with thousands of users. One effective and simple strategy is for field-trial users to mark up the manual while they are using it. They can thus rapidly indicate typos, misleading information, and confusing sections.

Software and the accompanying manuals are rarely truly completed. Rather, they go into a continuous process of evolutionary refinement. Each version eliminates known errors, adds refinements, and extends the functionality. If the

Box 13.3

Development process guidelines.

- Seek professional writers and copy writers.
- Prepare user manuals early (before implementation).
- Review drafts thoroughly.
- Field test early editions.
- Provide a feedback mechanism for readers.
- Revise to reflect changes regularly.

users can communicate with the manual writers, then there is a greater chance of rapid improvement. When possible, keeping logs of the use of help materials and help-desk calls will determine which part of the system needs modification.

Practitioner's Summary

Paper user manuals, online help, and tutorials can determine the success or failure of a software product, mobile device, or web service. Sufficient personnel, money, and time should be assigned to these support materials. Paper user manuals and online help should be developed before the implementation to help the development team to define the interface and to allow adequate time for testing. Both paper user manuals and online help should be tailored to specific user communities and to accomplishment of specific goals (for example, offer task instruction or describe interface objects and actions). Instructional examples should be realistic, encourage active exploration with exercises, use consistent terminology, and support error recognition and recovery. Animated demonstrations should be used when possible. Online guides can lend a human touch if they contain presentations by real humans or appropriate animated characters. Social interaction through newsgroups, listservers, online communities, e-mail, chat, and instant messaging provides powerful low-cost support mechanisms. Where possible, explore a multilayer user interface that promotes graceful evolution as user skills increase.

Researcher's Agenda

The main advantage of online materials is the potential for rapid retrieval and traversal, but little is known about how to offer this advantage conveniently without overwhelming novice users. Cognitive models of how animated, integrated demos facilitate learning need refinement to guide designers. Users' navigation of online help systems should be recorded and studied, so that we can gain a better understanding of what characterizes effective help strategies. Better strategies for integrating help directly in the user interface are needed. Multilayered designs in which users can select their level of expertise seem helpful, but further testing and refinement are necessary.

References

Ackerman, Mark S., Augmenting the organizational memory: A field study of Answer Garden, *Proc. CSCW '94 Conference: Computer-Supported Cooperative Work*, ACM, New York (1994), 243–252.

Ackerman, Mark S. and Palen, Leysia, The Zephyr help instance: Promoting ongoing activity in a CSCW system, *Proc. CHI '96 Conference: Human Factors in Computing Systems*, ACM, New York (1996), 268–275.

Allwood, C. M. and Kalen, T., Evaluating and improving the usability of a user manual, *Behaviour & Information Technology*, 16, 1 (January–February 1997), 43–57.

Alpert, Sherman R., Singley, Mark K., and Carroll, John M., Multiple multimodal mentors: Delivering computer-based instruction via specialized anthropomorphic advisors, *Behaviour & Information Technology*, 14, 2 (1995), 69–79.

Baecker, Ronald, Small, Ian, and Mander, Richard, Bringing icons to life, *Proc. CHI '91 Conference: Human Factors in Computing Systems*, ACM, New York (1991), 1–6.

Bechtel, Brian, Inside Macintosh as hypertext, in Rizk, A., Streitz, N., and Andre, J. (Editors), *Hypertext: Concepts, Systems and Applications*, Cambridge University Press, Cambridge, U.K. (1990), 312–323.

Brockmann, R. John, *Writing Better Computer User Documentation: From Paper to Hypertext, Version 2.0*, John Wiley & Sons, New York (1990).

Carroll, J. M., *Minimalism Beyond the Nurnberg Funnel*, MIT Press, Cambridge, MA (1998).

Carroll, John M. and Aaronson, Amy P., Learning by doing with simulated intelligent help, *Communications of the ACM*, 31, 9 (September 1988), 1064–1079.

Carroll, J. M. and Mack, R. L., Learning to use a word processor: By doing, by thinking, and by knowing, in Thomas, J. C., and Schneider, M. (Editors), *Human Factors in Computing Systems*, Ablex, Norwood, NJ (1984), 13–51.

Carroll, J. M., Rosson, M. B., Paradox of the active user, in Carroll, J. M. (Editor), *Interfacing Thought*: *Cognitive Aspects of Human-Computer Interaction*, MIT Press, Cambridge, MA (1987) 80–111.

Chimera, R. and Shneiderman, B., Evaluating three user interfaces for browsing tables of contents, *ACM Transactions on Information Systems*, 12, 4 (October 1994), 383–406.

Cohill, A. M. and Williges, R. C., Computer-augmented retrieval of HELP information for novice users, *Proc. Human Factors Society—Twenty-Sixth Annual Meeting*, Human Factors Society, Santa Monica, CA (1982), 79–82.

Corbis Publishing, *A Passion for Art*, Bellevue, WA (1995).

Creed, A., Dennis, I., and Newstead, S., Effects of display format on proof-reading on VDUs, *Behaviour & Information Technology*, 7, 4 (1988), 467–478.

Duffy, Thomas, Palmer, James, and Mehlenbacher, Brad, *Online Help Systems: Theory and Practice*, Ablex, Norwood, NJ (1992).

Egan, Dennis E., Remde, Joel R., Gomez, Louis M., Landauer, Thomas K., Eberhardt, Jennifer, and Lochbum, Carol C., Formative design-evaluation of SuperBook, *ACM Transactions on Information Systems*, 7, 1 (January 1989), 30–57.

Eveland, J. D., Blanchard, A., Brown, W., and Mattocks, J., The role of "help networks" in facilitating use of CSCW tools, *Proc. CSCW '94 Conference: Computer-Supported Cooperative Work*, ACM, New York (1994), 265–274.

Gates, Bill, *The Road Ahead*, Viking Penguin, New York (1995).

Gould, J., Alfaro, L., Finn, R., Haupt, B., and Minuto, A., Reading from CRT displays can be as fast as reading from paper, *Human Factors*, 29, 5 (1987), 497–517.

Grant, Allan, Homo quintadus, computers and ROOMS (repetitive ocular orthopedic motion stress), *Optometry and Vision Science*, 67, 4 (1990), 297–305.

Hackos, J. T., *Managing Your Documentation Projects,* John Wiley & Sons, New York (1994).

Hackos, J. T. and Stevens, D.M., *Standards for Online Communication,* John Wiley & Sons, New York (1997).

Hansen, Wilfred J., Doring, Richard, and Whitlock, Lawrence R., Why an examination was slower on-line than on paper, *International Journal of Man-Machine Studies,* 10 (1978), 507–519.

Hansen, Wilfred J. and Haas, Christine, Reading and writing with computers: A framework for explaining differences in performance, *Communications of the ACM,* 31, 9 (1988), 1080–1089.

Harrison, Susan M., A comparison of still, animated, or non-illustrated on-line help with written or spoken instructions in a graphic user interface, *Proc. CHI '95 Conference: Human Factors in Computing Systems,* ACM, New York (1995), 82–89.

Hegner, Stephen J., McKevitt, Paul, Norvig, Peter, and Wilensky, Robert L., *Intelligent Help Systems for UNIX,* Kluwer Academic Publishers, Boston, MA (2001).

Hertzum, Morten and Frokjaer, Erik, Browsing and querying in online documentation: A study of user interfaces and the interaction process, *ACM Transactions on Computer-Human Interaction,* 3, 2 (June 1996), 136–161.

Hook, K., Steps to take before intelligent user interfaces become real, *Interacting with Computers,* 12, 4 (2000), 409–426.

Horton, William K., *Designing and Writing Online Documentation: Hypermedia for Self-Supporting Products,* John Wiley & Sons, New York (1994).

Horvitz, E., Principles of mixed-initiative user interfaces, *Proc. CHI '99 Conference: Human Factors in Computing Systems,* ACM, New York (1999), 159–166.

Jorna, Gerard C., Image quality determines differences in reading performance and perceived image quality with CRT and hard-copy displays, *Proc. Human Factors Society—Thirty-Fifth Annual Meeting,* Human Factors Society, Santa Monica, CA (1991), 1432–1436.

Kang, H., Plaisant, C., and Shneiderman, B., New approaches to help users get started with visual interfaces: Multi-layered interfaces and Integrated Initial Guidance, *Proc. Digital Government Research Conference,* Boston, MA (May 2003), 141–146.

Kearsley, Greg, *Online Help Systems: Design and Implementation,* Ablex, Norwood, NJ (1988).

Lieberman, H., Interfaces that give and take advice, in *Human-Computer Interaction for the New Millennium,* ACM Press/Addison-Wesley, Boston, MA (2001), 475–485.

Lieberman, H., Autonomous interface agents, *Proc. CHI '97 Conference: Human Factors in Computing Systems,* ACM, New York (1997), 67–74.

Mager, Robert F., *Preparing Instructional Objectives: A Critical Tool in the Development of Effective Instruction,* Center for Effective Performance, Atlanta, GA (1997).

Magers, Celeste S., An experimental evaluation of on-line HELP for non-programmers, *Proc. CHI '83 Conference: Human Factors in Computing Systems,* ACM, New York (1983), 277–281.

Mao, J.-Y. and Leung, Y. W., Exploring the potential of unobtrusive proactive task support, *Interacting with Computers* 15, 2, (2003), 265–288.

McGrenere, Joanna, Baecker, Ronald M., and Booth, Kellogg S., An evaluation of a multiple interface design solution for bloated software, *Proc. CHI 2002 Conference: Human Factors in Computing Systems,* ACM, New York (2002), 163–170.

Oborne, David J. and Holton, Doreen, Reading from screen versus paper: There is no difference, *International Journal of Man-Machine Studies*, 28 (1988), 1–9.

Oren, Tim, Salomon, Gitta, Kreitman, Kristee, and Don, Abbe, Guides: Characterizing the interface, in Laurel, Brenda (Editor), *The Art of Human-Computer Interface Design*, Addison-Wesley, Reading, MA (1990), 367–381.

Palmiter, Susan and Elkerton, Jay, An evaluation of animated demonstrations for learning computer-based tasks, *Proc. CHI '91 Conference: Human Factors in Computing Systems*, ACM, New York (1991), 257–263.

Payne, S. J., Chesworth, L., and Hill, E., Animated demonstrations for exploratory learners, *Interacting with Computers*, 4 (1992), 3–22.

Rieman, John, A field study of exploratory learning strategies, *ACM Transactions on Computer-Human Interaction*, 3, 3 (September 1996), 189–218.

Roemer, Joan M. and Chapanis, Alphonse, Learning performance and attitudes as a function of the reading grade level of a computer-presented tutorial, *Proc. CHI '82 Conference: Human Factors in Computing Systems*, ACM, Washington, DC (1982), 239–244.

Roesler, A. W. and McLellan, S. G., What help do users need? Taxonomies for on-line information needs and access methods, *Proc. CHI '95 Conference: Human Factors in Computing Systems*, ACM, New York (1995), 437–441.

Schilit, Bill N., Golovchinsky, Gene, and Price, Morgan N., Beyond paper: Supporting active reading with free form digital ink annotations reading and writing, *Proc. CHI '98 Conference: Human Factors in Computing Systems*, ACM, New York (1998), 249–256.

Shneiderman, B., Kang, H., Kules, B., Plaisant, C., Rose, A., and Rucheir, R., A photo history of SIGCHI: Evolution of design from personal to public, *ACM Interactions*, 9, 3 (May 2002), 17–23.

Shroyer, R., Actual readers versus implied readers: Role conflicts in Office 97, *Technical Communication*, 47, 2 (2000), 238–240.

Smith, Marc, Supporting community and building social capital: Tools for navigating large social cyberspaces, *Communications of the ACM*, 45, 4 (2002), 51–55.

Spencer, C. J. and Yates, D. K., A good user's guide means fewer support calls and lower support costs, *Technical Communication*, 42, 1 (1995), 52.

Stieren C., The zen of minimalism, *Proc. 16th Annual International Conference on Computer Documentation* (September 1998), 103–112.

Strunk, Jr., William, White, E. B., and Angell, Roger, *The Elements of Style, Fourth Edition*, Allyn & Bacon, New York (2000).

Sukaviriya, Piyawadee "Noi" and Foley, James D., Coupling a UI framework with automatic generation of context-sensitive animated help, *Proc. UIST '90 Symposium on User Interface Software & Technology*, ACM, New York (1990), 152–166.

van der Meij, Hans and Carroll, John M., Principles and heuristics in designing minimalist instruction, *Technical Communication* (Second Quarter 1995), 243–261.

van der Meij, Hans and Lazonder, Ard W., Assessment of the minimalist approach to computer user documentation, *Interacting with Computers*, 5, 4 (1993), 355–370.

Wiedenbeck, S. and Zila, P. L., Hands-on practice in learning to use software: A comparison of exercise, exploration, and combined formats, *ACM Transactions on Computer-Human Interaction*, 4, 2 (June 1997), 169–196.

Zinsser, William, *Writing Well*, *Sixth Edition*, Harper Reference, New York (1998).

14

Information Search and Visualization

The real voyage of discovery consists not in seeking new
landscapes but in having new eyes.

MARCEL PROUST

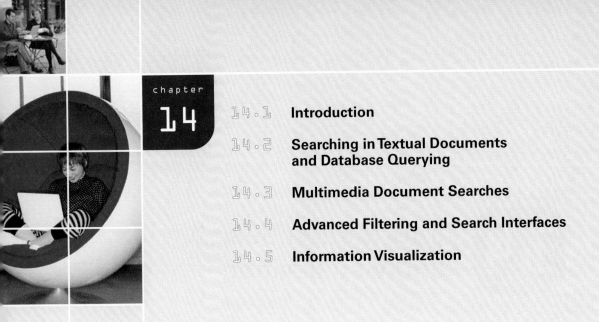

14.1   Introduction

Information exploration should be a joyous experience, but many commentators talk of information overload and anxiety (Wurman, 1989). However, there is promising evidence that the next generation of digital libraries and databases will enable convenient exploration of growing information spaces by a wider range of users. User-interface designers are inventing more powerful search and visualization methods, while offering smoother integration of technology with task (Hearst, 1999).

The terminology swirl in this domain is especially colorful. The older terms *information retrieval* (often applied to bibliographic and textual document systems) and *database management* (often applied to more structured relational database systems with orderly attributes and sort keys) are being pushed aside by newer notions of *information gathering, seeking, filtering,* or *visualization.* Computer scientists now focus on the huge volumes of available data and talk about *data mining* from *data warehouses* and *data marts,* while visionaries talk about *knowledge networks* or *semantic webs.* The distinctions are subtle; the common goals range from finding a narrow set of items in a large collection that satisfy a well-understood information need (a *known-item search*) to making sense of information or discovering unexpected patterns within the collection (Marchionini, 1995).

Exploring information collections becomes increasingly difficult as the volume and diversity grows. A page of information is easy to explore, but when the source of information is the size of a book, or a library, or even larger, it may be difficult to locate known items or to browse to gain an overview. The strategies to focus and narrow are well understood by librarians and information-search specialists, and now these strategies are being implemented for widespread use.

The computer is a powerful tool for searching, but older user interfaces have been a hurdle for novice users (complex commands, Boolean operators, unwieldy concepts) and challenging for experts (difficulty in repeating searches across multiple databases, weak methods for discovering where to narrow broad searches, poor integration with other tools). This chapter reviews interfaces appropriate for first-time or intermittent versus frequent computer users, and also for task novices versus experts. Improvements on traditional text and multimedia searching seem possible as a new generation of visualization strategies for query formulation and information presentation emerges.

Designers are just discovering how to use rapid processors and high-resolution color displays to present large amounts of information in orderly and user-controlled ways. Perceptual psychologists, statisticians, and graphic designers offer valuable guidance about presenting static information (Bertin, 1983; Cleveland, 1993; Tufte, 1983, 1997; Wilkinson, 1999), but the opportunity for dynamic displays takes user-interface designers well beyond current wisdom.

The object-action interface (OAI) model (see Fig. 2.6) helps by separating task concepts (do you think of your organization as a hierarchy or a matrix?) from interface concepts (is your hierarchy best represented as an outline, a node-link diagram, or a treemap?). The OAI model also separates high-level interface issues (is an overview diagram necessary for navigation?) from low-level interface issues (will color or size coding be used to represent salary levels?).

First-time users of an information-exploration system (whether they have little or much task knowledge) often struggle to understand what they see on the display while keeping in mind their information needs. They will be distracted if they have to learn complex query languages or elaborate shape-coding rules. They need the low cognitive burdens of simple keyword searches, menu and direct-manipulation designs, and simple visual-coding rules. As users gain experience with the interface, they can request additional features by adjusting control panels or seeing previews and overviews of the information available. Knowledgeable and frequent users want a wide range of search tools with many options that allow them to compose, save, replay, and revise increasingly elaborate query plans.

To facilitate discussion, we need to define a few terms. *Task objects*, such as Leonardo's notebooks or sports-video segments from the Olympics, are represented by *interface objects* in structured relational databases, textual document libraries, or multimedia document libraries. A *structured relational database* consists of *relations* and a *schema* to describe the relations. Relations have *items* (usually called *tuples* or *records*), and each item has multiple *attributes* (often called *fields*), which each have *attribute values*. In the relational model, items form an unordered set (although one attribute can contain sequencing information or be a unique key to identify or sort the other items), and attributes are *atomic*.

A *textual document library* consists of a set of *collections* (typically up to a few hundred collections per library) plus some *descriptive attributes* or *metadata* about the library (for example, name, location, owner). Each collection has a *name*, plus some descriptive attributes about the collection (for example, location, media type, curator, donor, dates, geographic coverage) and a set of items (typically 10 to 100,000 items per collection). Items in a collection may vary greatly, but usually a superset of attributes exists that covers all the items. Attributes may be blank, have single values, have multiple values, or be lengthy texts. A collection is owned by a single library, and an item belongs to a single collection, although exceptions are possible. A *multimedia document library* consists of collections of documents that can contain images, scanned documents, sound, video, animations, datasets, and so on. *Digital libraries* are generally sets of carefully selected and cataloged collections, while *digital archives* tend to be more loosely organized. *Directories* hold metadata about the items in a library and point users to the appropriate locations (for example, the NASA Global Change Master Directory simply helps scientists locate datasets in NASA's archives).

Task actions are decomposed into *browsing* or *searching* and are represented by *interface actions* such as scrolling, zooming, joining, or linking. Users begin by formulating their information needs in the task domain. Tasks can range from specific fact finding, where there is a single readily identifiable outcome, to more extended fact finding with uncertain but replicable outcomes. Relatively unstructured tasks include exploration of the availability of information on a topic, open-ended browsing of known collections, and complex analysis of problems.

- Specific fact finding (known-item search)
  - Find the e-mail address of Hilary Clinton.
  - Find the highest-resolution LANDSAT image of College Park at noon on May 26, 2004.
- Extended fact finding
  - What other books are by the author of *Jurassic Park*?
  - How do Maryland and Virginia counties compare on the Consumer Price Index in 2003?
- Exploration of availability
  - What genealogical information is available at the National Archives?
  - Is there new work on voice recognition in the ACM digital library?
- Open-ended browsing and problem analysis
  - Does the Mathew Brady Civil War photo collection show the role of women in that war?
  - Is there promising new research on fibromyalgia that might help my patient?

Once users have clarified their information needs, the first step in satisfying those needs is to decide where to search. The conversion of information needs, stated in task-domain terminology, to interface actions is a large cognitive step.

Once this is done, users can express these actions in a query language or via a series of mouse selections.

Supplemental *finding aids* can help users to clarify and pursue their information needs. Examples include tables of contents or indexes in books, descriptive introductions, and subject classifications. Careful understanding of previous and potential search requests, and of the task analysis, can improve search results by allowing the system to offer hot-topic lists and useful classification schemes. For example, the U.S. Congressional Research Service has a list of approximately 80 hot topics covering current bills before Congress and has 5,000 terms in its Legislative Indexing Vocabulary. The National Library of Medicine maintains the Medical Subject Headings (MeSH), with 14,000 items in a 7-level hierarchy, and the Gene Ontology Database has 15,000 genes organized in a 19-level hierarchy, with many genes appearing at multiple nodes.

Additional *preview and overview surrogates* for items and collections can be created to facilitate browsing (Greene et al., 2000). Graphical overviews indicate scope, size, or structure and help gauge the relevance of collections. Previews consisting of samples entice users and help them define productive queries.

Section 14.2 presents full text search and database query strategies and introduces a five-phase search framework. Section 14.3 reviews the special case of multimedia documents, and Section 14.4 covers advanced search and filter interfaces. In Section 14.5, a taxonomy of information visualization and exploration, based on data types and user tasks, helps to organize the presentation of research and commercial tools.

14.2   Searching in Textual Documents and Database Querying

The way users conduct searches has gone through dramatic changes over the past decade. Once reserved for search experts who had mastered cryptic languages, searching vast computer archives is now fully feasible for children preparing school reports, patients looking for possible medical treatments, or researchers looking for up-to-date results and experts to consult.

General World Wide Web search engines have greatly improved their performance by making use of statistical rankings and the information latent in the Web's hyperlink structure. For example, the search engine Google (Fig. 1.12) implements a link-based ranking measure called PageRank (Brin and Page, 1998), to compute a query-independent score for each document, taking into consideration the importance of the pages that point to a given page. Because of the diversity of users, providing simple user interfaces to get started is important—Google starts with a simple search interface and offers advanced and specialized search interfaces as needed, including human-generated directory interfaces. Thanks to the redundancy of information on the Web, results almost always return some relevant documents, and they allow users to find answers by following hyperlinks. For example, to find an expert on information retrieval, users might first find papers on that topic, leading to identifying a major journal publication, the editors of the journal, and their personal web pages. However, empirical evaluation of the current algorithms shows that the quality of the relevant documents retrieved still needs to be improved (Amento, Terveen, and Hill, 2000).

Database searches have become widespread as the general public turns to the World Wide Web to reserve travel packages, shop for groceries, or search digital libraries of children's books. Specialized databases also help lawyers find relevant court cases or scientists locate the scientific data they need. The Structured Query Language (SQL) has become a widespread standard for searching such structured relational database systems and often remains the underlying query mechanism hidden under a more accessible front end. Using SQL, expert users can write queries that specify matches on attribute values, such as author, date of publication, language, or publisher. Each document has values for the attributes, and database-management methods enable rapid retrieval even with millions of documents. For example, an SQL-like command might be:

```
SELECT DOCUMENT#
FROM JOURNAL-DB
WHERE    (DATE >= 2001 AND DATE <= 2003)
    AND  (LANGUAGE = ENGLISH OR FRENCH)
    AND  (PUBLISHER = ASIST OR HFES OR ACM)
```

SQL has powerful features, but using it requires training (2 to 20 hours), and even then users make frequent errors for many classes of queries (Welty, 1985; see also Chapter 8).

Natural-language queries (for example, "please list the documents that deal with ...") are meant to be appealing, but the computer's capacity for processing such natural-language queries is too often limited to eliminating frequent terms or commands and searching for remaining words, leading to frustration for users (Section 8.6). Research continues on this topic.

Form-fillin queries (Section 7.7) have substantially simplified query formulation while still allowing some Boolean combinations to be made available (usually a conjunction of disjuncts, or ORs, within attributes with ANDs between attributes). A more powerful approach that extends the form-fillin idea is *query-by-example*, in which users enter attribute values and some keywords in relational table templates. This approach has influenced modern systems but is no longer a major interface.

Finding a way to provide powerful search capabilities without overwhelming novice users remains a challenge, usually addressed by providing both simple and advanced search interfaces (Fig. 14.1). The simple search allows users to

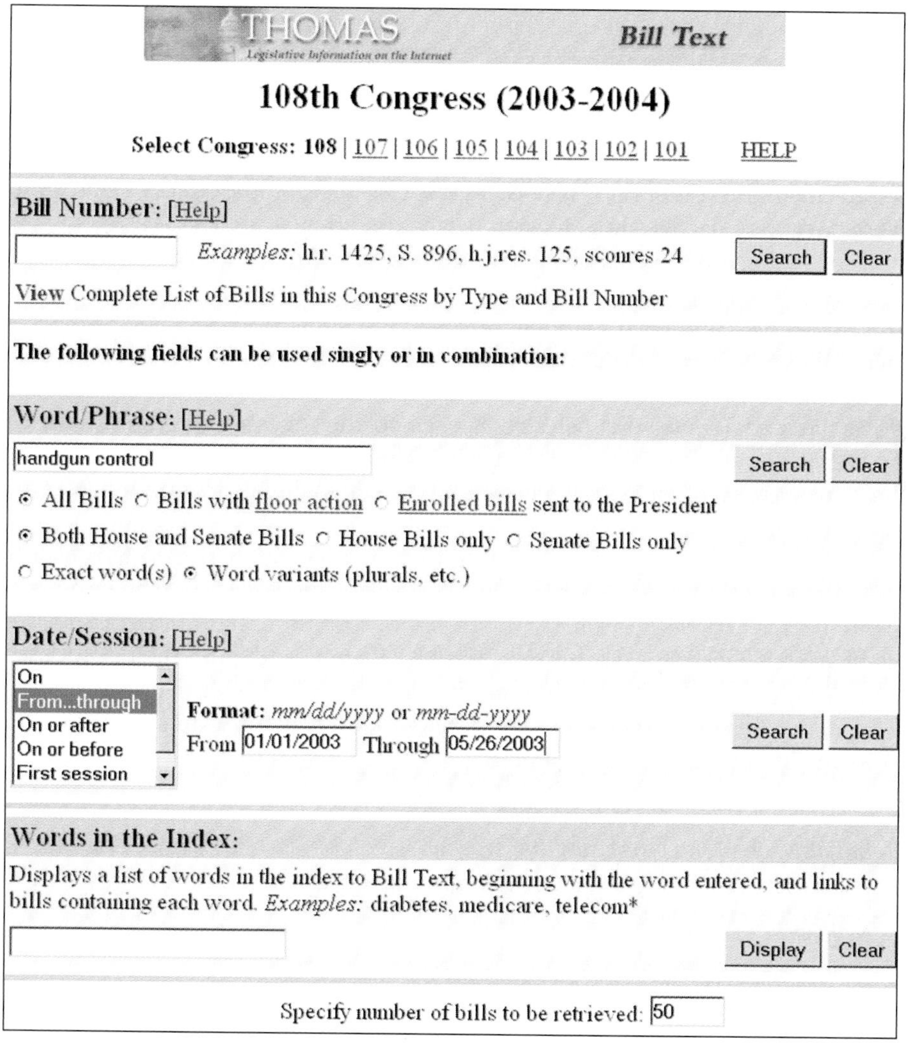

THOMAS
Legislative Information on the Internet
Bill Text

108th Congress (2003-2004)

Select Congress: 108 | 107 | 106 | 105 | 104 | 103 | 102 | 101   HELP

Bill Number: [Help]

           Examples: h.r. 1425, S. 896, h.j.res. 125, sconres 24   [Search] [Clear]

View Complete List of Bills in this Congress by Type and Bill Number

The following fields can be used singly or in combination:

Word/Phrase: [Help]

handgun control   [Search] [Clear]

  ⦿ All Bills ○ Bills with floor action ○ Enrolled bills sent to the President

  ⦿ Both House and Senate Bills ○ House Bills only ○ Senate Bills only

  ○ Exact word(s) ⦿ Word variants (plurals, etc.)

Date/Session: [Help]

On
From...through   **Format:** *mm/dd/yyyy* or *mm-dd-yyyy*
On or after
On or before   From 01/01/2003   Through 05/26/2003   [Search] [Clear]
First session

Words in the Index:

Displays a list of words in the index to Bill Text, beginning with the word entered, and links to bills containing each word. *Examples:* diabetes, medicare, telecom*

                                      [Display] [Clear]

            Specify number of bills to be retrieved: 50

Figure 14.1

An advanced search interface at the U.S. Library of Congress's web site helps users find bills (that is, proposed legislation) that were debated in Congress during current or past years. Controls are available to select the scope of the search and allow variants. Examples and help buttons are provided. (www.loc.gov/thomas)

specify phrases that are searched in all the fields, while the advanced search allows users to specify more precise terms. This is a good example of a successful multilayered interface.

Unfortunately, interfaces often either hide important aspects of the search (by poor design or to protect proprietary relevance-ranking schemes) or make the advanced query specification so difficult that they discourage use. Evidence from empirical studies shows that users perform better and have higher subjective satisfaction when they can view and control the search (Koenemann and Belkin, 1996), but the lack of consistency between search interfaces means that users have to rediscover how to search each time they search in a different system. An analogy to the evolution of automobile user interfaces might clarify the need for standardization of search interfaces. Early competitors offered a profusion of controls, and each manufacturer had a distinct design. Some designs—such as having a brake pedal that was far from the gas pedal—were dangerous. Furthermore, if you were accustomed to driving a car with the brake to the left of the gas pedal, and your neighbor's car had the reverse design, it might be risky to trade cars. It took half a century to achieve good design and appropriate consistency in automobiles; let's hope that we can make the transition faster for text-search user interfaces.

The success of a search service often depends on the degree to which user frustration and confusion are reduced. A *five-phase framework* may help to coordinate design practices to satisfy the needs of first-time, intermittent, and frequent users who are accessing a variety of textual and multimedia libraries (extending the ideas in Shneiderman, Byrd, and Croft, 1997). This framework (Box 14.1) gives great freedom to designers to offer features in an orderly and consistent manner. The phases are:

1. *Formulation:* expressing the search
2. *Initiation of action:* launching the search
3. *Review of results:* reading messages and outcomes
4. *Refinement:* formulating the next step
5. *Use:* compiling or disseminating insight

The formulation phase includes identifying the *source* of the information, the *fields* for limiting the source, the *phrases,* and the *variants.* Even if technically and economically feasible, searching all libraries or collections in a library is not always the preferred approach. Users often prefer to limit the sources to a specific library or a specific collection in a library. Users may also limit their searches to specific fields (for example, to the title or abstract of a scientific article), and the sources might be further restricted by structured fields such as year of publication, volume number, or language).

In textual databases, users typically seek items that contain meaningful phrases (Civil War, Environmental Protection Agency, carbon monoxide), and multiple entry fields should be provided to allow for multiple phrases. Searches on phrases

Box 14.1

Five-phase framework to clarify user interfaces for textual search.

1. *Formulation*
   - Provide access to the appropriate sources in libraries and collections.
   - Use *fields* for limiting the source: structured fields such as year, media, or language, and text fields such as titles or abstracts of documents.
   - Recognize *phrases* to allow entry of names, such as George Washington or Environmental Protection Agency, and concepts, such as abortion rights reform or gallium arsenide.
   - Permit *variants* to allow relaxation of search constraints, such as case sensitivity, stemming, partial matches, phonetic variations, abbreviations, or synonyms from a thesaurus.
   - Control the size of the result set.

2. *Initiation of action*
   - Include *explicit actions* initiated by buttons with consistent labels (such as "Search"), locations, sizes, and colors.
   - Include *implicit actions* initiated by changes to a parameter of the formulation phase that immediately produce a new set of search results.

3. *Review of results*
   - Present explanatory messages.
   - View an overview of the results and previews of items.
   - Manipulate visualizations.
   - Adjust the size of the result set and which fields are displayed.
   - Change the sequencing (alphabetical, chronological, relevance ranked, and so on).
   - Explore clustering (by attribute value, topics, and so on).
   - Examine selected items.

4. *Refinement*
   - Use meaningful messages to guide users in progressive refinement; for example, if the two words in a phrase are not found near each other, then offer easy selection of individual words or variants.
   - Make changing of search parameters convenient.
   - Explore relevance feedback.

5. *Use*
   - Allow queries, the setting of each parameter, and results to be saved and annotated, sent by e-mail, or used as input to other programs, such as visualization or statistical tools.

have proved to be more accurate than are searches on words. Phrases also facilitate searching on names (for example, a search on George Washington should not turn up George Bush or Washington,D.C.). Since some relevant items may be missed by a phrase approach, though, users should have the option to expand a search by breaking the phrases into separate words. If Boolean operations, proximity restrictions, or other combining strategies are specifiable, then users should also be able to express them. Users or service providers should also have control over stop lists (common words, single letters, obscenities).

When users are unsure of the exact value of the field (subject term, or spelling or capitalization of a name), they may need to relax the search constraints by allowing variants to be accepted. In structured databases, the variants may include a wider range on a numeric attribute. In a textual-document search, interfaces should allow user control over variant capitalization (case sensitivity), stemmed versions (the keyword teach retrieves variant suffixes such as teacher, teaching, or teaches), partial matches (the keyword biology retrieves sociobiology and astrobiology), phonetic variants from soundex methods (the keyword Johnson retrieves Jonson, Jansen, and Johnsson), synonyms (the keyword cancer retrieves malignant neoplasm), abbreviations (the keyword IBM retrieves International Business Machines, and vice versa), and broader or narrower terms from a thesaurus (the keyphrase New England retrieves Vermont, Maine, Rhode Island, New Hampshire, Massachusetts, and Connecticut).

The second phase is the *initiation of action,* which may be explicit or implicit. Most current systems have a search button for explicit initiation, or for delayed or regularly scheduled initiation. The button label, size, and color should be consistent across versions. An appealing alternative is *implicit initiation,* in which each change to a component of the formulation phase immediately produces a new set of search results (Fig. 14.2). *Dynamic queries*—in which users adjust query widgets to produce continuous updates—have proved to be effective and satisfying. They require adequate screen space and rapid processing, but their advantages are great (see Section 14.4).

The third phase is the *review of results,* in which users read messages, view textual lists, or manipulate visualizations. Previews consisting of samples or summaries help users select a subset of the results for use and can help them define more productive queries as they learn about the contents of the collections. Translations may also be proposed. Users should be given control over the size of the result set, which fields are displayed, how results are sequenced (alphabetical, chronological, or relevance ranked; see Fig. 1.13), and how results are clustered (by attribute value, by topics). One strategy, used by Vivisimo (Fig. 14.3) and Grokker, involves automatic clustering and naming of the clusters. Studies show that clustering according to more established and meaningful hierarchies, such as the Open Directory Project, might be effective (Dumais, Cutrell, and Chen, 2001).

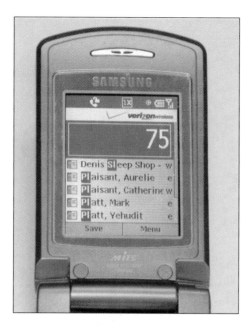

Figure 14.2

As users press keys on a SmartPhone keypad, the digits are shown and a search is implicitly initiated to display the list of names in the address book that match the series of keys pressed.

The fourth phase is *refinement*. Search interfaces should provide meaningful messages to explain search outcomes and to support progressive refinement. For example, users could be encouraged to provide fewer terms to allow partial matches. If two words in a search phrase are not found proximally, then feedback should be given about the occurrence of the words individually. Corrections can be proposed; for example, asking "Did you mean Fibromyalgia?" when the keyword was misspelled. If multiple phrases are input, then items containing all phrases should be shown first and identified, followed by items containing subsets; if no documents are found with all phrases, that failure should be indicated. There is a fairly elaborate decision tree (maybe 60 to 100 branches) of search outcomes and messages that needs to be specified. Another aspect of feedback is that, as searches are made, the system should keep track of them in a *search history* to allow review and reuse of earlier searches (Komlodi, 2002). Progressive refinement, in which the results of a search are refined by changing the search parameters, should be convenient.

The final phase, *use* of the results, is where the payoff comes. Results can be merged and saved, disseminated by electronic mail, or used as input to other programs—for example, for visualization or statistical tools.

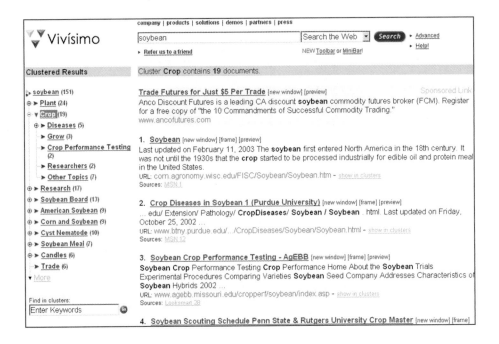

Figure 14.3

A search for "soybean" in Vivisimo automatically clusters the results in a hierarchy of about 50 clusters. Each one can be reviewed individually. One challenge in making clustering effective is to generate representative cluster names. (vivisimo.com)

The five-phase framework can be applied by designers to make the search process more visible, comprehensible, and controllable by users. This approach is in harmony with the general move towards direct manipulation, in which the state of the system is made visible and is placed under user control. Novices may not want to see all the components of the five phases initially, but if they are unhappy with the search results, they should be able to view the settings and change their queries easily.

14.3   Multimedia Document Searches

Interfaces to structured databases and textual-document libraries are good and getting better, but search interfaces in multimedia-document libraries are still in their early stages of development. Most systems used to locate images, videos, sound, or animation depend on descriptive documents or metadata searches to locate the items. For example, searches in photo libraries can be done by date, photographer, medium, location, or text in captions, but without captioning and costly human annotation, finding a photo of a particular ribbon-cutting ceremony or horse race is very difficult. Nevertheless, even if completely automatic recognition is not possible, it is useful to have computers perform some filtering. As technology simplifies the creation and use of multimedia documents, multimedia-document search interfaces will have to rely on the integration of powerful annotation and indexing tools, improved search algorithms to filter the collections, and effective browsing techniques for viewing the results.

- *Image search.* Finding images of things such as the Statue of Liberty is a substantial challenge for image-analysis researchers, who describe this task as *query by image content* (QBIC). Lady Liberty's distinctive profile might be identifiable if the orientation, lens focal length, and lighting were held constant, but the general problem is difficult in large and diverse collections of photos. Two promising approaches are to search for distinctive features, such as the torch or the seven spikes in the crown, or to search for distinctive colors, such as red, white, and blue to look for an American flag. Of course, separating out the British, French, and other flags is not easy. More success is attainable with restricted collections, such as of glass vases or blood cells, for which users can draw a desired profile and retrieve items with matching features. For smaller collections of personal photos, it is important to provide effective browsing and lightweight annotation mechanisms such as, for example, PhotoMesa (Fig. 14.4), PhotoFinder (Fig. 13.14), or Adobe Photoshop Album.

- *Map search.* Computer-generated maps are increasingly available online. Locating a map by latitude and longitude is the structured-database solution, but searching by features is now possible because geographical information systems preserve the structural aspects and the multiple layers in maps (Dykes, MacEachren, and Kraak, 2004). For example, users might specify a search for all port cities with a population greater than 1 million and an airport within 10 miles. Applications for mobile devices might allow users to locate Italian restaurants within two hundred yards of any station on a given subway line.

- *Design or diagram search.* Some computer-assisted design packages offer users limited search capabilities within a single design or across design collections. Finding red circles inside blue squares may help in some cases, but more elaborate strategies, such as for finding engine designs with pistons smaller than 6 centimeters, could prove more beneficial. Document-structure recognition and search tools already exist that allow searching, for example, for newspaper front pages with headlines that span the front page and no advertisements (Doermann, 1998).

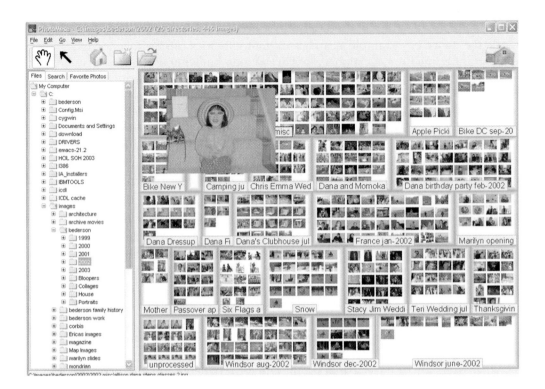

Figure 14.4

PhotoMesa is a zoomable image browser. Users can browse multiple directories of images (here, personal photos), without having to describe the photos with meta-data. Smooth animation between thumbnails of increasing resolution and the full-size photographs provides an enticing experience. PhotoMesa can also be used to browse the results of image searches. (www.photomesa.com)

- *Sound search.* Music-information retrieval (MIR) systems can now use audio input, where users can query with musical content (Hu and Dannenberg, 2002). Users can sing or play a theme, hook, or riff from the desired piece of music, and the system returns the most similar items. It is even becoming possible to recognize individual performers, such as "find Caruso" (Wakefield and Bartsch, 2003). Finding a spoken word or phrase in databases of telephone conversations is still difficult, but it is becoming possible, even on a speaker-independent basis (see Section 9.4).

- *Video search.* Searching a video or film involves more than simply searching through each of the frames. The video should be segmented into scenes or cuts and allow scene skipping. Gaining an overview of a two-hour video by a timeline of scenes enables better understanding, editing, and selection. The Informedia project is an example library of digital video (Fig. 14.5). It uses a variety of visual features (for example, color, faces, or text superimpositions) as well as textual features such as speech-to-text transcripts to make a large volume of digital video retrievable (Wactlar et al., 1999).

- *Animation search.* Animation authoring tools are becoming prevalent with the success of Flash, so it might become possible to specify searches for certain kinds of animation, such as spinning globes or morphing faces.

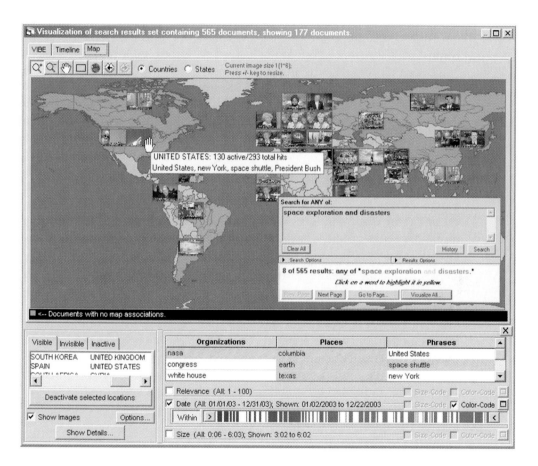

Figure 14.5

Informedia allows users to search archives of digital videos. A search for "space exploration and disaster" returned 565 news video clips. Users can choose among several views of the results (here, a map to show the origins of some of the results). A click on the United States updates the timeline to show the distribution of the videos over time. One of the challenges is to provide adequate previews of the videos. (www.informedia.cs.cmu.edu)

14.4   Advanced Filtering and Search Interfaces

Users have highly varied needs for advanced filtering features (Hearst, 1999). This section reviews a few alternatives to the form-fillin query interface.

- *Filtering with complex Boolean queries.* Commercial information-retrieval systems such as DIALOG and FirstSearch permit complex Boolean expressions with parentheses, but their widespread adoption has been inhibited by their difficulty of use. Numerous proposals have been put forward to reduce the burden of specifying complex Boolean expressions (Reisner, 1988). Part of the confusion stems from informal English usage. For example, a query such as "List all employees who live in New York and Boston" usually would result in an empty list, because the "and" would be interpreted as an intersection; only employees who live in both cities would qualify! In English, "and" usually expands the options; in Boolean expressions, AND is used to narrow a set to the intersection of two others. Similarly, in the English "I'd like Russian or Italian salad dressing," the "or" is exclusive, indicating that you want one or the other but not both; in Boolean expressions, however, an OR is inclusive, and is used to expand a set. The desire for *full Boolean expressions,* including nested parentheses and NOT operators, has led to novel metaphors for query specification. Venn diagrams, decision tables, and metaphors of water flowing through a series of filters have been used, but these representations become clumsy as query complexity increases.

- *Automatic filtering.* Another form of filtering is to apply a user-constructed set of keywords to dynamically generated information, such as incoming electronic-mail messages, newspaper stories, or scientific journal articles (Belkin and Croft, 1992). Users create and store their profiles, which are evaluated each time that a new document appears. Users can be notified by electronic mail that a relevant document has appeared, or the results can be simply collected into a file until users seek them out. These approaches are a modern version of a traditional information-retrieval strategy called *selective dissemination of information* (SDI), which was used in the earliest days of magnetic-tape distribution of document collections.

- *Dynamic queries.* The dynamic-queries approach of adjusting numeric range sliders, alphasliders for names or categories, or buttons for small sets of categories is appealing to many users for many tasks (Shneiderman, 1994). Dynamic queries might be called *direct-manipulation queries,* since they share the same concepts of visual display of actions (the sliders or buttons) and objects (the query results in the task-domain display); the use of rapid, incremental, and reversible actions; and the immediate display of feedback (less than 100 milliseconds). Additional benefits are the prevention of syntax errors and an encouragement of exploration. A subset of Boolean queries are possible

(ORs between attribute values and ANDs between attributes). The early Dynamic HomeFinder (Fig. 14.6) used dynamic queries for finding homes for sale; it helped users explore trends as well as answer specific questions (Williamson and Shneiderman, 1992).

Searching in online databases can also be done with dynamic queries (Fig. 14.7). To preserve the 100-millisecond reaction time of dynamic queries, data must be downloaded to and kept in the memory of the user's computer, which becomes problematic when the data are very large. *Query previews* (Doan et al., 1999) address this issue by first providing an interactive overview of the data available. This overview allows users to gain useful information about the distribution of the data available over a few selected attributes and to rapidly

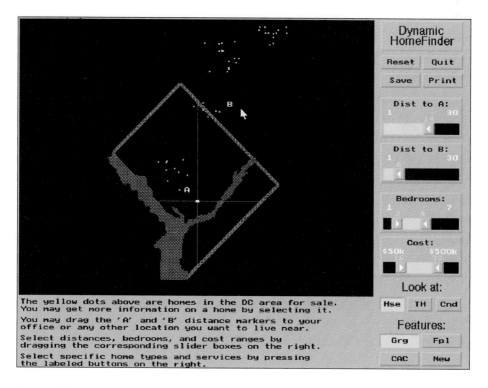

Figure 14.6

The Dynamic HomeFinder, an early application of dynamic queries. Homes for sale in the Washington, D.C. area were shown as 1,100 points of light. As users moved the sliders, the screen was updated immediately to show the points matching the current query. By clicking on any point, users could get a detailed description. A and B represent places of work. (Williamson and Shneiderman, 1992.)

eliminate undesired items (Fig. 14.8). After rough selections have been made, the metadata of the remaining items can be downloaded for refinement of the query. While the form-fillin interfaces often lead users to waste time posing queries that have zero-hit or mega-hit result sets, a user study showed that query previews made performance 1.6 to 2.1 times faster and led to higher subjective satisfaction (Tanin et al., 2000).

- *Faceted metadata search.* This type of search interface integrates category browsing with keyword searching, as demonstrated in Flamenco (Yee et al., 2003; Fig. 14.9). This interface makes use of hierarchical faceted metadata presented as simultaneous menus (Section 7.4.1), and dynamically generated numerical query previews. It allows users to navigate explicitly along multiple conceptual dimensions that describe the images and to progressively narrow or expand the scope of the query while browsing images. In the example of architectural photo browsing, users can look for photos of modern homes,

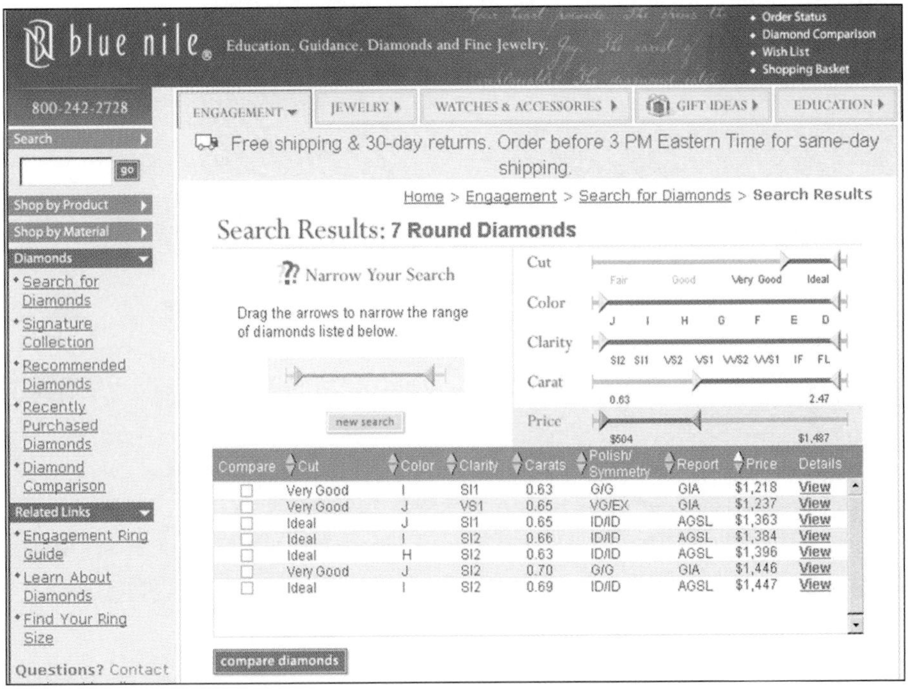

Figure 14.7

Blue Nile uses dynamic queries to narrow down the results of searches. Here, the double-sided sliders were adjusted to show only lower-priced diamonds with very good cut and high carat ratings. (www.bluenile.com)

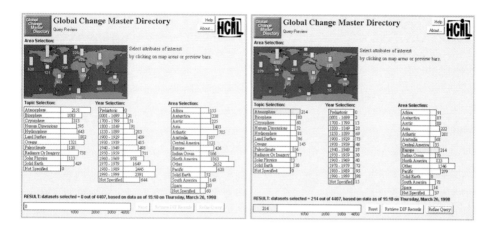

Figure 14.8

Query previews can assist users of online search services to evaluate the availability of data before submitting a query. In this early prototype for NASA's Global Change Master Directory users can first see the distribution of data available by topic, year, and geographical area (left). As they click on Atmosphere and then on Europe, the bars are updated within 10 milliseconds to reflect the distribution of the remaining datasets (right). When they are satisfied with their selections they can submit the query, or they can refine the search in the remaining subset with other attributes. (www.cs.umd.edu/hcil/eosdis)

narrow on front doors, narrow further on homes located in Virginia, then widen the query to show windows and doors, then switch to homes in Maryland, all the while staying in the flow and focusing their attention on the images. Many search interfaces are now using selection in multiple menus as their primary search interfaces, but they often only allow refinements in one menu at a time—for example, in Epicurious (Fig. 7.9) or the International Children's Digital Library (Fig. 1.16)—as opposed to simultaneous menus, such as in Shopping.com (Fig. 7.12).

- *Collaborative filtering.* This social form of filtering allows groups of users to combine their evaluations to help one another find interesting items in large collections (Riedl, Konstan, and Vrooman, 2002). Each user rates items in terms of their interest. Then, the system can suggest unread items that are close to users' interests, as determined by matches with other people's interests. This method can also be applied to movies, music, restaurants, and so on. For example, if you rate six restaurants highly, the algorithms will provide you with other restaurants that were rated highly by people who liked your six

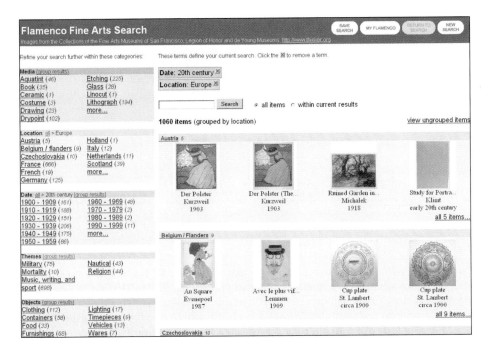

Figure 14.9

Flamenco is an example of faceted metadata search. Facets include Media, Location, Date, Theme, and so on. Two attribute values are selected (Date=20th century and Location=Europe), with results grouped by locations. The image previews are updated immediately as constraints are added or removed (another example of implicit query initiation). Clicking on a group heading such as "Belgium/Flanders" refines the query into that category, while clicking on "All" dates relaxes the date constraint. (bailando.sims.berkeley.edu/flamenco.html)

restaurants. This strategy has an inherent appeal, and dozens of such systems have been built for organizational databases, news files, music groups, and World Wide Web pages.

- *Multilingual searches.* In some cases users want to be able to search collections of multilingual documents. Current web search engines merely provide rudimentary translation tools, but prototypes of multilingual information systems allow users to select appropriate dictionaries, restrict keyword translations, and use more powerful translation systems to carefully identify documents that justify the cost of high-quality professional translation (Hovy et al., 2001; Oard et al., 2004).

- *Visual searches.* The specification of query fields can sometimes be simplified by using specialized visual representations of the possible values (Figs. 7.10 and 7.11). For example, selecting dates on calendars or using a plane layout to select among available seats is useful. For vacationers seeking tourist information about Marseilles who do not know its location, a scrolling alphabetical list is needed; but when a map of France or Europe is displayed it becomes possible to point rapidly at hundreds of other locations, allowing the selection of other Mediterranean cities without having to know their names. When there are no natural graphical representations of the choices, information-visualization techniques can be used. For example, a treemap can be used to represent a product catalog (Fig. 14.10). Visual search interfaces provide context and help users refine their needs. They are attractive and can reduce error

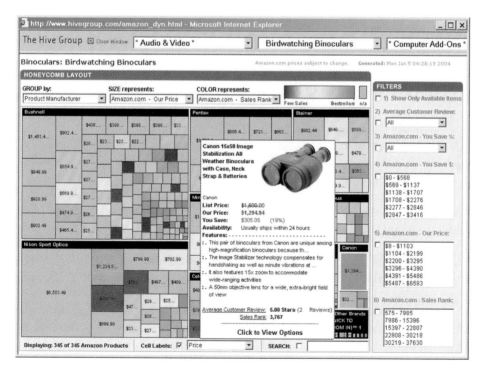

Figure 14.10

Using The Hive Group's treemap users can select "birdwatching binoculars" in the "audio and video" catalog of Amazon.com products and see an overview of 345 binoculars grouped by manufacturer. Each box corresponds to a pair of binoculars and the size of the box is proportional to its price. Green boxes are best-sellers, gray indicates unavailability. Users can also filter the results using the menus on the right. (www.hivegroup.com)

messages such as "data out of range" while providing information about data availability and a feeling of thoroughness to users.

There is much in common between visual search interfaces and browsing interfaces that use combinations of menus (see Section 7.4). Enhanced with implicit initiation and immediate feedback, visual search interfaces can become powerful dynamic-query interfaces, while the addition of abstract data previews and overviews transforms visual search interfaces into potent information-visualization and exploration tools that help users explore the data visually before any search is even specified.

14.5   Information Visualization

> Grasping the whole is a gigantic theme. Arguably, intellectual history's most important. Ant-vision is humanity's usual fate; but seeing the whole is every thinking person's aspiration.
>
> David Gelernter
> *Mirror Worlds*, 1992

The success of direct-manipulation interfaces was a first step towards using the power of computers in a more visual or graphic manner. A picture is often said to be worth a thousand words, and for some tasks, a visual presentation—such as a map or photograph—is dramatically easier to use or comprehend than is a textual description or a spoken report. As processor speeds and display resolution increase, designers are discovering how to present and manipulate large amounts of information in compact and user-controlled ways. We can now argue that an interface is worth a thousand pictures. Information visualization can be defined as the use of interactive visual representations of *abstract* data to amplify cognition (Card, Mackinlay, and Shneiderman, 1999; Spence, 2001; Bederson and Shneiderman, 2003; Ware, 2004). The abstract characteristic of the data is what distinguishes information visualization from scientific visualization. For scientific visualization, three dimensions are necessary, because typical questions involve continuous variables, volumes, and surfaces (inside/outside, left/right, and above/below). However, for information visualization, typical questions involve more categorical variables and the discovery of patterns, trends, clusters, outliers, and gaps in data such as stock prices, patient records, or social relationships (Chen, 1999; 2003; Card, 2002; Borner and Chen, 2003).

Information-visualization researchers aim to provide compact graphical presentations and user interfaces for interactively manipulating large numbers of items (10^2–10^6), possibly extracted from far larger datasets. Sometimes called visual data mining, it uses the enormous visual bandwidth and the remarkable human perceptual system to enable users to make discoveries, make decisions, or propose explanations about patterns, groups of items, or individual items. Information visualization allows users to answer questions they didn't know they had.

Humans have remarkable perceptual abilities that are greatly underutilized in most current interface designs. Users can scan, recognize, and recall images rapidly, and can detect subtle changes in size, color, shape, movement, or texture. The core information presented in graphical user interfaces has remained largely text oriented (even if enhanced with attractive icons and elegant illustrations), so as more visual approaches are explored, appealing new opportunities are emerging. Perceptual psychologists, statisticians, and graphic designers (Tufte, 1983; 1997) offer valuable advice about presenting static information, but advances in processor speed, design tools, and dynamic displays take user-interface designers well beyond current wisdom.

As the field evolves, research prototypes are now finding their way into commercial products. However, information-visualization designers must understand the principles that will help them cross the chasm to wider success. They must get past the infatuation with novelty and integrate visualization tools into solutions for realistic business problems. This means that they will have to facilitate the importation of data from many sources, cope with large volumes of data, and enable users to integrate other tools, such as those for data mining. Then when users form hypotheses about relationships and spot interesting patterns, they will need to be able to save, send, print, and share these insights with others through well-integrated coordination interfaces.

Many users resist visual approaches and are satisfied with potent textual approaches, such as multiple menus and numerical query previews in faceted metadata searches. Their resistance may be appropriate, since these textual tools use compact presentations that are rich with meaningful information and comfortably familiar. Successful information-visualization tools have to be more than "cool"; they have to provide measurable benefits for realistic tasks. They also have to be built to satisfy universal-usability principles of working on a variety of platforms, display sizes, and network bandwidths, while enabling access for users with disabilities and users speaking differing languages.

As information visualization matures, guidelines, principles, and theories will emerge for this area. Among them will probably be this widely cited principle, usually known as the *visual-information-seeking mantra*:

> Overview first, zoom and filter, then details on demand
> Overview first, zoom and filter, then details on demand
> Overview first, zoom and filter, then details on demand

Overview first, zoom and filter, then details on demand

Overview first, zoom and filter, then details on demand

Overview first, zoom and filter, then details on demand

Overview first, zoom and filter, then details on demand

The repetition suggests how often the principle has been applied and the recursive nature of the exploration process. Information-visualization researchers and commercial developers may be able to sort out the numerous tools and identify new opportunities by using a *data type by task taxonomy* (Box 14.2). As in the case of searches, users are viewing collections of items, where items have multiple attributes. The data type by task taxonomy includes seven basic data types and seven basic tasks. The basic data types are one-, two-, three-, or multidimensional, followed by three more structured data types: temporal, tree, and network. This simplification is useful to describe the visualizations that have been developed and to characterize the classes of problems that users encounter. For example, with temporal data users deal with events and intervals, and their questions are concerned with before, after, or during. With tree-structured data, users deal with labels on internal nodes and values at leaf nodes, and their questions are about paths, levels, and subtrees. The seven basic tasks are: overview, zoom, filter, details-on-demand, relate, history, and extract. Our discussion begins with the seven data types, followed by the seven tasks.

14.5.1   1D linear data

Linear data types are one-dimensional; they include program source code, textual documents, dictionaries, and alphabetical lists of names, all of which can be organized in a sequential manner. For program source code, the substantial compressions of one pixel per character produce compact displays of tens of thousands of lines of program source code on a single display (Fig. 14.11) (Eick, 1998; Stasko et al., 1998). The attributes, such as the date of most recent modification or the author name, may be used for color-coding. Interface-design issues include what colors, sizes, and layout to use, and what overview, scrolling, or selection methods to provide for users. User tasks might be to find the number of items, to see items having certain attributes (for example, program lines that were changed from the previous version), to see the most common words in Chapter 3 of *Alice in Wonderland* (Fig. 14.12 on page 585), or to see an item with all its attributes.

14.5.2   2D map data

Planar data include geographic maps, floorplans, and newspaper layouts. Each item in the collection covers some part of the total area and may or may not be rectangular. Each item has task-domain attributes, such as name, owner, and value, and interface-domain features, such as size, color, and opacity. Many systems

Box 14.2

Data type by task taxonomy to identify visualization data types and the tasks that need to be supported.

Data Types

1D Linear	Document Lens, SeeSoft, Information Mural, TextArc
2D Map	Geographic information systems, ESRI ArcInfo, ThemeView, newspaper layout, self-organizing maps
3D World	Desktops, WebBook, VRML, Web3D, architecture, computer-assisted design, medicine, molecules
Multidimensional	Parallel coordinates, scattergram matrices, hierarchical clustering, prosection matrices, Visage, Table Lens, InfoZoom
Temporal	Perspective Wall, exploratory sequential data analysis (ESDA), Project Managers, LifeLines, TimeSearcher
Tree	Outliners, Superbook, Degree-of-Interest Trees Cone/Cam Trees, Hyperbolic, SpaceTree, treemaps
Network	NetMap, netViz, SemNet, SeeNet, Butterfly

Tasks

Overview	Gain an overview of the entire collection.
Zoom	Zoom in on items of interest.
Filter	Filter out uninteresting items.
Details-on-demand	Select an item or group and get details when needed.
Relate	View relationships among items.
History	Keep a history of actions to support undo, replay, and progressive refinement.
Extract	Allow extraction of subcollections and of the query parameters.

adopt a multiple-layer approach to dealing with map data, but each layer is two-dimensional. User tasks are to find adjacent items, regions containing items, and paths between items, and to perform the seven basic tasks. Examples include geographic information systems (see Fig. 6.4), which are a large research and commercial domain (Dykes, MacEachren, and Kraak, 2004). Information-visualization researchers have used spatial displays of document collections organized proximally by term co-occurrences, such as ThemeView (Wise et al., 1995; see Fig. 14.13).

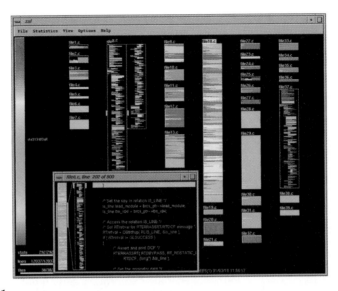

Figure 14.11

SeeSoft shows computer program with 4,000 lines of code. The newest lines are in red; the oldest are in blue. The smaller browser window shows a code overview and detail window (Eick, 1998).

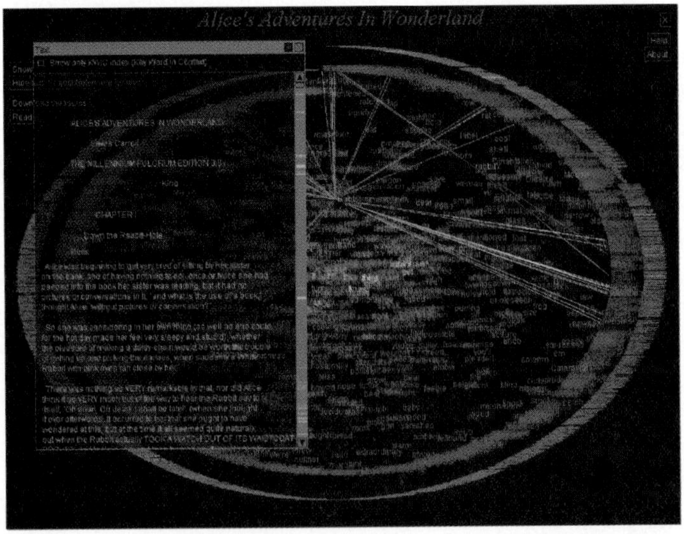

Figure 14.12

The entire text of *Alice in Wonderland* is arranged in an arc, stepping clockwise, starting at 12:00. Lines are drawn around the outside, words around the inside. Words that appear more often are brighter. Here, "Rabbit" is highlighted in the arc and an overlay full-text window. Lines containing "Rabbit" are drawn in green around the arc, in the text window, and even in the scroll bar. (http://www.textarc.org)

Such displays seem useful to give users an overview of the collection, but they may not necessarily be as useful as a textual representations to find documents, because relevance is difficult to judge without reading some text (Hearst, 1999).

14.5.3   3D world data

Real-world objects such as molecules, the human body, and buildings have volume and complex relationships with other items. Computer-assisted medical imaging, architectural drawing, mechanical design, chemical structure modeling, and scientific simulations are built to handle these complex three-dimensional relationships. Users' tasks typically deal with continuous variables such as temperature or density. Results are often presented as volumes and surfaces, and users focus on relationships of left/right, above/below, and inside/outside. In three-dimensional applications, users must cope with their position and orientation when viewing the objects and must handle the potential problems of *occlusion* and *navigation*. Solutions using enhanced 3D techniques, such as overviews, landmarks, teleportation, multiple views, and tangible user interfaces (Fig. 6.19), are finding their way into research prototypes and commercial systems (Section 6.4). Successes include medical imagery from sonograms that helps doctors in planning surgery and architectural walkthroughs or flythroughs that give home buyers an idea of what a finished building will look like.

Examples of three-dimensional computer graphics and computer-assisted design tools are numerous, but information-visualization work in three dimensions is still controversial. Some virtual-environment researchers and business

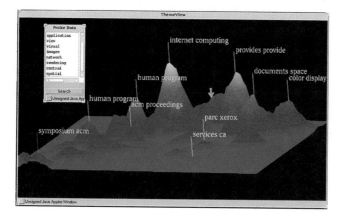

Figure 14.13

ThemeView (formerly ThemeScape) shows a three-dimensional map representing the results of a search in a large corpus of documents. Proximity indicates similarity of the topics, while height reflects the number of documents and frequency of terms. Commercial applications exist from OmniViz, Inc.

graphics producers have sought to present information in three-dimensional structures, but these designs seem to require more navigation steps and to make the results harder to interpret (see Section 6.4).

14.5.4   Multidimensional data

Most relational- and statistical-database contents can be conveniently manipulated as multidimensional data, in which items with n attributes become points in an *n-dimensional space.* The interface representation may be a dynamic two-dimensional scattergram, with each additional dimension controlled by a slider (Ahlberg and Shneiderman, 1994). Buttons can be used for attribute values when the cardinality is small—say, less than 10. Tasks include finding patterns, such as correlations among pairs of variables, clusters, gaps, and outliers. Multidimensional data can also be represented by a three-dimensional scattergram, but disorientation (especially if the user's point of view is from inside the cluster of points) and occlusion (especially if close points are represented as being larger) can be problems. The early HomeFinder (Fig. 14.6) and FilmFinder developed dynamic queries on zoomable, color-coded, user-controlled scattergrams of multidimensional data and laid the basis for the commercial product Spotfire (Figs. 13.3 and 14.14). Parallel coordinate plots are one of the few truly compact multidimensional techniques (Inselberg, 1997; see Fig. 14.18). Each parallel vertical axis represents a dimension, and each item becomes a line connecting values in each dimension. Training and practice are particularly helpful to become a "multidimensional detective." Other techniques include matrices that combine series of small bivariate representations (MacEachren et al., 2003; see Fig. 14.15) and the commercial products Table Lens (Fig. 14.16), which uses a spreadsheet metaphor, and InfoZoom (Fig. 14.17), which uses a zoomable table of content showing the distribution of values for each dimension and allowing progressive filtering of the data by clicking on those values. Finally, an increasingly common approach to looking at multidimensional data is to use *hierarchical* or *k-means* clustering algorithms to identify similar items. Hierarchical clustering identifies close pairs of items and forms ever-larger clusters until every point is included in a cluster (Fig. 14.18). K-means clustering starts by users specifying how many clusters to create, then the algorithm places every item into the most appropriate cluster. Surprising relationships and interesting outliers can be identified by these techniques.

14.5.5   Temporal data

Time series are very common (for example, electrocardiograms, stock market prices, or weather data) and merit a data type that is separate from one-dimensional data (Silva and Catarci, 2000). The distinctions of *temporal data* are that items (events) have a start and finish time, and that items may overlap. Frequent tasks include

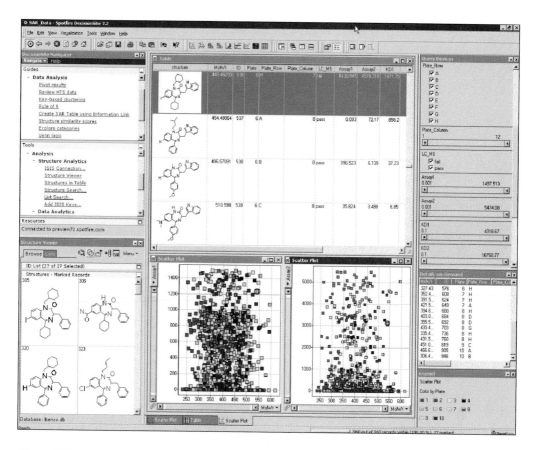

Figure 14.14

To gain insights into compound activity, chemists can use Spotfire to explore this dataset of 960 molecules. The coordinated tables and scatterplots can be filtered using query sliders. Details about individual molecules are shown in the detail-on-demand window. The online decision site provides access to help, data-analysis tools, and repositories of results. An external molecule-structure viewing tool has also been invoked. (www.spotfire.com)

finding all events before, after, or during some time period or moment, and in some cases comparing periodical phenomena, plus the seven basic tasks. Many project-management tools exist; novel visualizations of time include the Perspective Wall (Robertson, Card, and Mackinlay, 1993) and LifeLines (Plaisant et al., 1998; see Fig. 14.19). Temporal-data visualization components are included in applications for editing video data, composing music, or preparing animations such as Flash, and they are appearing in search interfaces (Fig. 14.5). Space-time data have been a focus of great attention in geovisualization (Andrienko, Andrienko, and Gatalsky, 2003). TimeSearcher combines multiple time series, such as stock-market prices over time,

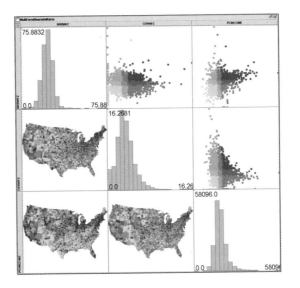

Figure 14.15

A multiform bivariate matrix allows users to look at multiple coordinated views of the data. Here, three variables are being studied: cervical cancer rates, breast cancer rates, and income. Single variables are views with histograms, while choropleth maps and scatterplots are paired to show bivariate relationships. The multiform bivariate matrix is a component of the GeoVISTA Studio open source toolkit. (www.geovista.psu.edu)

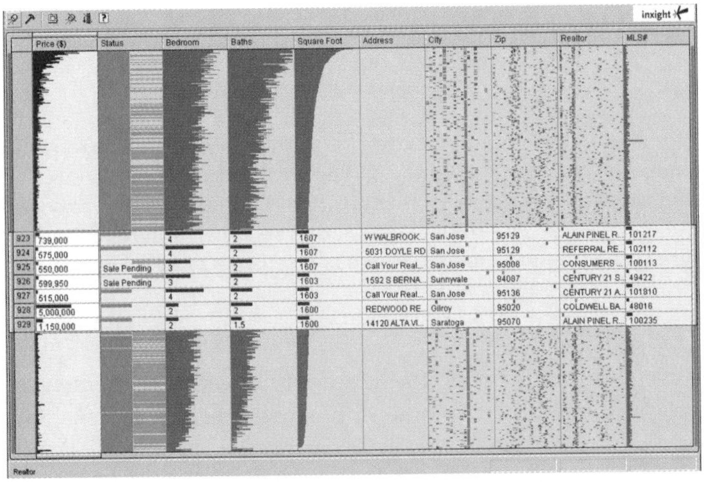

Figure 14.16

Table Lens provides a spreadsheet-like view of table data—here, a listing of houses for sale. The houses were ordered using the "Square Foot" attribute, which reveals that price is mostly related to the square footage, with some exceptions that are easy to spot in the Price column. The fisheye effect reveals details about the houses. (www.inxight.com)

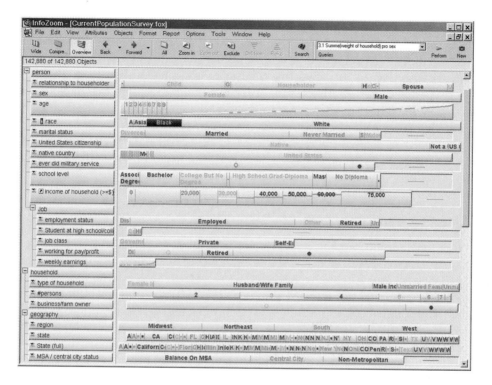

Figure 14.17

InfoZoom's overview shows the distribution of the values of a hierarchy of attributes. The data shown here is a table of 142,880 household types, based on the U.S. Census Population Survey. One can see that most household types are headed by a white married person born in the U.S. Here, the race attribute "black" was selected, and color indicates the relative representation of those household types in each category (green is over-representation and red is under-representation). By clicking on attribute values, users can filter the data, updating all distributions, until the individual data item can be seen. (www.humanit.com)

or other linear data series, such as temperature in an oil-well bore hole. Users draw boxes on the display to specify combinations of ranges, and TimeSearcher shows series whose data all fall within the range (Hochheiser and Shneiderman, 2004).

14.5.6   Tree data

Hierarchies or tree structures are collections of items, in which each item (except the root) has a link to one parent item. Items and the links between parent and child can have multiple attributes. The basic tasks can be applied to items and links, and tasks related to structural properties become interesting—for example, for a company organizational chart, is it a deep or shallow hierarchy, and how many employees does each manager supervise? Interface representations of trees can employ the outline style of indented labels used in tables of contents or the Windows file explorer, or a node-and-link diagram such as the Degree-of-Interest Tree (Fig. 14.20), SpaceTree (Plaisant, Grosjean, and Bederson, 2002), or the hyperbolic browser (Fig. 14.21). A space-filling approach, treemaps, show arbitrary-sized trees in a fixed rectangular space (Shneiderman, 2004; Bederson, Shneiderman, and Wattenberg, 2002). The treemap approach has been applied successfully to many applications, from stock-market data visualization (Fig. 14.22) to oil-production monitoring and searching in electronic product catalogs (Fig. 14.10).

14.5.7   Network data

When relationships among items cannot be captured conveniently with a tree structure, items are linked to an arbitrary number of other items in a network (Fig. 14.23 on page 596). Although many special cases of networks exist (acyclic, lattices, rooted versus unrooted, directed versus undirected), it is convenient to consider them all as one data type. In addition to performing the basic tasks applied to items and links, network users often want to know about the shortest or least costly paths connecting two items or traversing the entire network. Interface representations include node-and-link diagrams (but layout algorithms are often so complex that user interaction is limited when large networks are shown) and matrices of items with each cell representing a potential link and its attribute values.

Network visualization is an old but still imperfect art, because of the complexity of relationships and user tasks (Herman, Melançon, and Marshall, 2000). Specialized visualizations can be designed to be more effective for a given task and there are a number of useful geographical applications (Dykes, MacEachren, and Kraak, 2004). New interest in this topic has been spawned by attempts to visualize the World Wide Web (Dodge and Kitchin, 2001; see Fig. 14.24).

The seven data types reflect an abstraction of the reality. There are many variations on these themes (two-and-one-half or four-dimensional data, multitrees, and many prototypes use combinations of these data types). The second framework for analyzing information visualizations covers seven basic tasks that users typically perform:

14.5.8   Overview task

Users can gain an overview of the entire collection. Overview strategies include zoomed-out views of each data type that allow users to see the entire collection plus an adjoining detail view. The overview might contain a movable field-of-view box with which users control the contents of the detail view, allowing zoom factors of 3 to 30. Replication of this strategy with intermediate views

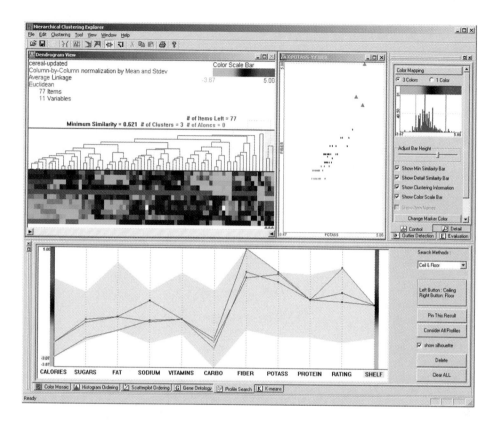

Figure 14.18

The Hierarchical Clustering Explorer allows users to explore high-dimensional data-sets to find similar items. In this example, 11 characteristics of 77 breakfast cereals are shown by a red-green mosaic with red for high values and green for low values. HCE clusters the cereals that are similar, as shown by the dendogram in the top left. The rightmost cluster has been selected and highlighted in yellow. It contains three cereals that have high fiber and high potassium, as shown by the bright red in the 7th and 8th rows. Those three cereals are also highlighted as triangles in the scatterplot (upper right), and as the only three remaining lines in the parallel coordinate display (bottom). This technique has been applied to gene expression data-sets containing more than 30,000 genes and 100 characteristics. (www.cs.umd.edu/hcil/hce)

enables users to reach larger zoom factors (Fig. 12.10). Another popular approach is the fisheye strategy, whose distortion magnifies one or more areas of the display (Fig. 12.11), but geometric zoom factors have to be limited to about five or different levels of representations must be used for the context to

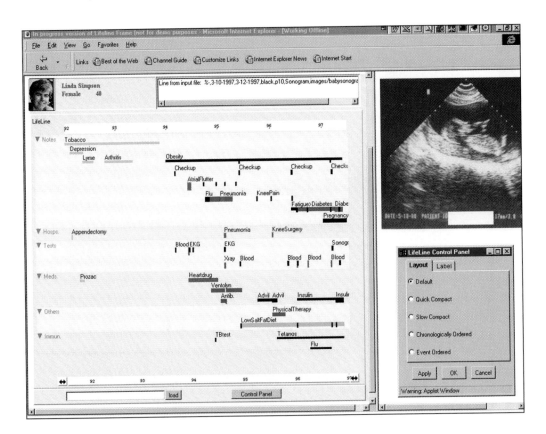

Figure 14.19

LifeLines present a summary of personal records, here a medical record, on a zoomable timeline. LifeLines show multiple facets of the record, such as doctors' notes, hospitalizations, or tests, and they use line thickness and color to map data attributes such as severity or drug dosage. A LifeLine acts as a giant menu—users click on events to display related information. (www.cs.umd.edu/hcil/lifelines)

be usable (Figs. 14.16 and 14.20). Since most query-language facilities make it difficult to gain an overview of a collection, the provision of adequate overview strategies is a useful criterion to judge such interfaces.

14.5.9 Zoom task

Users can zoom in on items of interest. Users typically have an interest in some portion of a collection, and they need tools to enable them to control the zoom focus and the zoom factor. Smooth zooming helps users to preserve their sense of position and context. Users can zoom on one dimension at a time by moving the

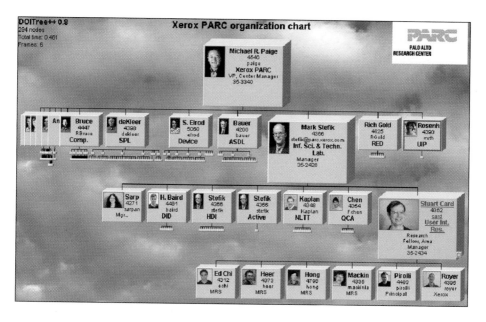

Figure 14.20

An organization chart is represented with a Degree-of-Interest Tree. The sizes of the 341 nodes are determined dynamically to provide focus and context with a fisheye view that always fits within the boundary of the display. Users click on nodes to change the focus. Here, the focus is on Stuart Card. (Card and Nation, 2002)

zoom bar controls or by adjusting the size of the field-of-view box. A satisfying way to zoom in is to point to a location and to issue a zooming command, usually by holding down a mouse button. Jazz and its successor Piccolo are popular user-interface toolkits (Bederson, Meyer, and Good, 2000) that allow programmers to quickly create zooming environments. Zooming is particularly important in applications for small displays (Fig. 9.25).

14.5.10 Filter task

Users can filter out uninteresting items. Dynamic queries applied to the items in the collection constitute one of the key ideas in information visualization (Shneiderman, 1994). When users control the contents of the display, they can quickly focus on their interests by eliminating unwanted items. Sliders, buttons, or other control widgets coupled with rapid (less than 100 milliseconds) display update is the goal, even when there are tens of thousands of displayed items. Similarly, brushing and linking techniques allow users to dynamically highlight items of interest across displays.

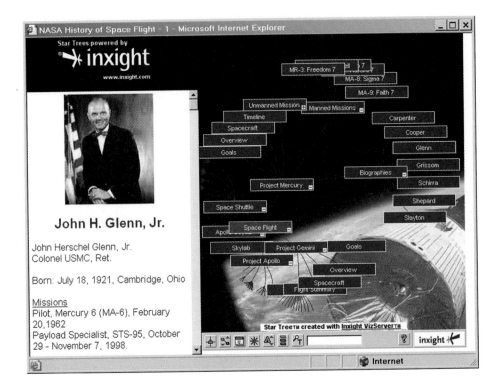

Figure 14.21

A hyperbolic tree browser that allows 10 to 30 nodes near the center to be seen clearly; branches are reduced gradually as they get closer to the periphery. This display technique guarantees that large trees can be accommodated in a fixed screen size. As the focus is shifted among nodes, the display updates smoothly, producing a satisfying animation. Landmarks or other features can be introduced to reduce the disorienting effect of movement. (www.inxight.com)

14.5.11   Details-on-demand task

Users can select an item or group to get details. Once a collection has been trimmed to a few dozen items, it should be easy to browse the details about the group or individual items. The usual approach is to simply click on an item and review details in a separate or pop-up window. In Spotfire (Figs. 13.3 and 14.14), the details-on-demand window can contain HTML text with links to further information.

14.5.12   Relate task

Users can relate items or groups within the collection. The attraction of visual displays, when compared to textual displays, is that they make use of the

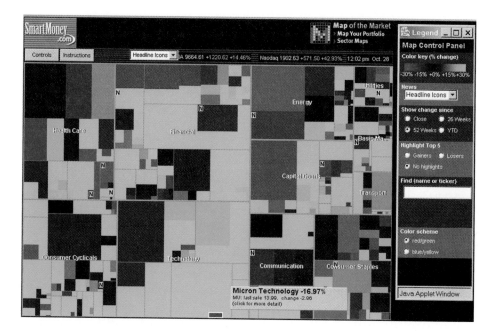

Figure 14.22

The Map of the Market uses a treemap. Rectangles each represent a stock and are organized by industry groups. The rectangle size is proportional to the market capitalization and the color indicates the percentage gain or loss for the given time period, showing at a glance that most stocks went up on this particular day, with some exceptions. The "N" icon signifies and links to a news story. A menu of time periods is available, as well as two color schemes to address the needs of users with color deficiencies. (www.smartmoney.com)

remarkable human perceptual ability for visual information. Within visual displays, there are opportunities for showing relationships by proximity, by containment, by connected lines, or by color coding. Highlighting techniques can be used to draw attention to certain items in a field of thousands of items. Pointing to a visual display can allow rapid selection, and feedback is apparent. The eye, the hand, and the mind seem to work smoothly and rapidly as users perform actions on visual displays. In LifeLines (Fig. 14.19), for example, users can click on a medication and see the related visit notes or test results. Designing user-interface actions to specify which relationship is to be manifested is still a challenge. In Spotfire, details-on-demand window users can select an attribute, such as a film's director, and cause the director alphaslider to be reset to the director's name, thereby displaying only films by that director in a query-by-example style of interaction. Users may also want to combine multiple visualization techniques that are tightly coupled. Tools are being developed to allow users to specify what

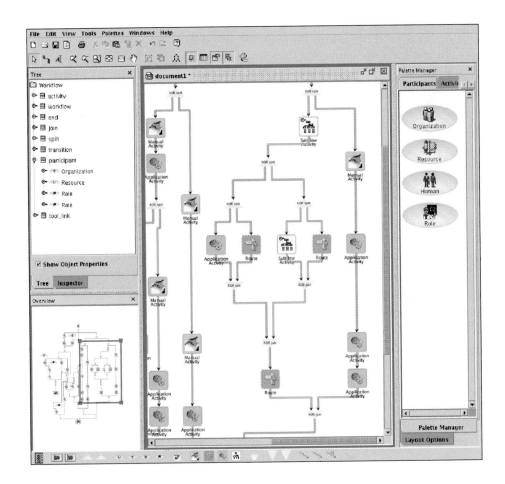

Figure 14.23

Using ILOG JViews, designers can create a workflow network model by adding and linking objects and activities, then developers can connect the display to the underlying software. The lower-left window's overview becomes important for large networks. (www.ilog.com)

visualizations they need and how the interaction between the visualizations should be controlled (North, Conklin, and Saini, 2002).

14.5.13 History task

Users can keep a history of actions to support undo, replay, and progressive refinement. It is rare that a single user action produces the desired outcome.

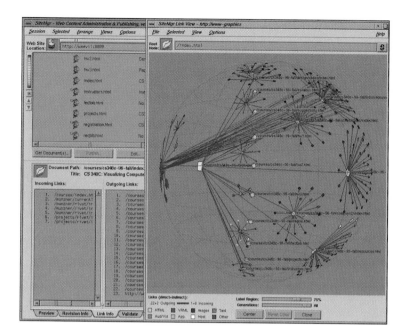

Figure 14.24

H3 shows the hyperlink structure of a web site in a three-dimensional ball. Users can navigate by rotating the structure or moving the focus to any node. Usage logs can be played back to see visitors' paths in the context of the network of possibilities. (Munzner, 1997)

Information exploration is inherently a process with many steps, so keeping the history of actions and allowing users to retrace their steps is important. However, most products fail to deal adequately with this requirement. Designers would do well to model information-retrieval systems, which typically preserve the sequence of searches so that these searches can be combined or refined.

14.5.14   Extract task

Users can allow extraction of subcollections and of the query parameters. Once users have obtained the item or set of items that they desire, it is useful for them to be able to extract that set and to save it, send it by electronic mail, or insert it into a statistical or presentation package. They may also want to publish that data for others to view with a simplified version of the visualization tool.

⊥4.5.⊥5 Challenges for information visualization

The data type by task taxonomy helps organize our understanding of the range of problems, but there are still many challenges that information-visualization researchers need to face to create successful tools:

- *Import data.* Deciding on how to organize input data to achieve a desired result often takes more thought and work than expected. Then, getting data into the correct format, filtering out incorrect items, normalizing attribute values, and coping with missing data can be burdensome tasks.

- *Combine visual representations with textual labels.* Visual representations are potent, but meaningful textual labels have an important role. Labels should be visible without overwhelming the display or confusing users. Mapmakers have long wrestled with this problem, and their work offers valuable lessons. Often, user-controlled approaches such as ScreenTips and excentric labels can help (Fig. 14.25). (Fekete and Plaisant, 1999)

- *See related information.* Additional information is often needed to make meaningful judgments. Patent lawyers want to see related patents, other filings by the same people, or recent filings by competing companies. Genomics researchers want to see how clusters of genes work in harmony during the phases of cellular processes, and then view similar genes in the Gene Ontology or read research papers on relevant biological pathways. The pursuit of meaning during discovery requires rapid access to rich sources of related information.

- *View large volumes of data.* A general challenge to information visualization is the handling of large volumes of data. Many innovative prototypes can only deal with a few thousand items, or have difficulties maintaining real-time interactivity when dealing with larger numbers of items. Dynamic visualizations showing millions of items (Fig. 14.26) demonstrate that information visualization is not yet close to reaching the limits of human visual abilities, and user-controlled aggregation mechanisms will push the envelope even further (Keim, 2001). Larger displays (Section 9.5.2) can help because additional pixels enable users to see more details, while maintaining a reasonable overview.

- *Integrate data mining.* Information visualization and data mining originated from two separate lines of research. Information-visualization researchers believe in the importance of letting users' visual systems lead them to hypothesis making, while data-mining researchers believe that statistical algorithms and machine learning can be relied on to find interesting patterns. Sometimes consumer purchasing patterns stand out when properly visualized, such as spikes in demand before snowstorms or correlations between beer and pretzel purchases. However, statistical tests can be helpful in finding more subtle trends in consumer desires or demographic linkages for product purchases.

Increasingly, researchers are combining those two approaches (Fayyad, Grinstein, and Wierse, 2001). Statistical summaries are appealing for their objective nature, but they can hide outliers or discontinuities (like freezing or boiling points). On other hand, data mining might point users to more interesting parts

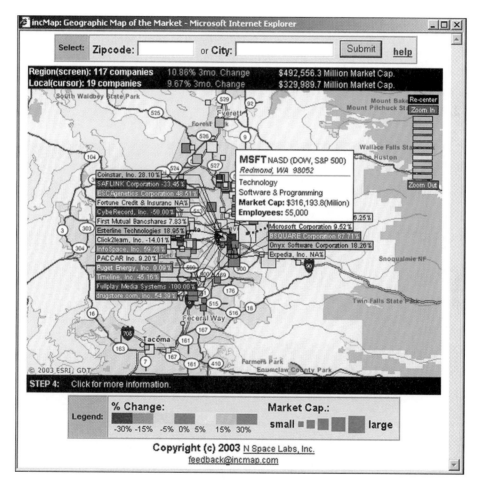

Figure 14.25

Dynamic labeling of items is still a challenge. Here, excentric labels in incMap show the labels of all the items inside the circle, revealing hidden items and allowing their selection. (www.incmap.com)

of the data which could be visually inspected. For example, Spotfire's viewtip highlights pairs of variables that show strong linear correlations.

- *Collaborate with others.* Discovery is a complex process that depends on knowing what to look for, verifying assumptions by collaboration with others, noticing anomalies, and convincing others of the significance of a finding. Since support for social processes is critical to information visualization, software tools should make it easy to record the current state and send it to colleagues or post it to a web site with annotations and data (see Chapter 10).

- *Achieve universal usability.* Making visualization tools accessible to diverse users regardless of their backgrounds, technical disadvantages, or personal disabilities is necessary when the tools are to be used by the public, but it remains a huge challenge for designers (Plaisant, 2004). For example, visually impaired users

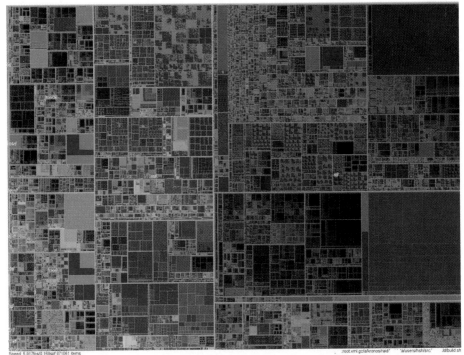

Figure 14.26

A treemap displaying a million files from a large file system, without aggregation. Careful examination of the high-resolution display reveals patterns, and special algorithms preserve the interactivity of the rich overviews and filtering tools. (Fekete and Plaisant, 2002.) (www.cs.umd.edu/hcil/millionvis)

may need to use text-based alternatives to the visual display; a good example is provided by the National Cancer Institute's cancer atlas (http://www3.cancer.gov/atlasplus/). Encouraging results have been found with the sonification of graphs, scatterplots, and tables, and in the future, spatial sound might help sonify more complex data representations (see Section 9.4.5). Tactile displays (Fig. 9.26) are still low resolution, but they may be useful when augmented with audio descriptions. Unfortunately, they are not widely available. Users with color deficiencies can be provided with alternative palettes or tools to customize the colors. For example, Smartmoney's Map-of-the-Market (Fig. 14.22) provides two choices of color: red/green and blue/yellow. ColorBrewer and VisCheck offer guidelines on color schemes that work for those with color vision impairment.

Another concern is that, for web-based users, designers must work with the limitations of slow connections. However, clever solutions are often possible. The Java prototype for DynaMap, a map-based dynamic-query interface for government statistics, loaded and ran quickly enough on standard PCs and broadband connections, but it took minutes to download with a 56-Kbps modem and could not maintain the interactivity needed for dynamic queries (100-millisecond updates) on low-end PCs. A new algorithm led to download times 5 to 10 times shorter (often counted in seconds instead of minutes for modem users) while keeping the needed interactivity (Zhao, Plaisant, and Shneiderman, 2003).

Practitioner's Summary

Improved user interfaces to digital libraries and multimedia databases have spawned appealing new products. Flexible queries against complex text, sound, graphics, image, and video databases are emerging. Novel graphical and direct-manipulation approaches to query formulation and information visualization are now possible. Information visualization is moving out of research laboratories with a growing number of commercial products (such as those from Spotfire, Inxight, and HumanIT), additions to statistical packages (SPSS/SigmaPlot, SAS/GRAPH, and DataDesk), and commercial development environments (ILOG). Many other resources are available to designers and developers, such as XmdvTool, Xgobi, Common GIS, GeoVISTA studio, the Indiana University InfoVis Repository, Jean-Daniel Fekete's InfoVis Toolkit and the University of Maryland Piccolo toolkit for zooming user interfaces. New products need to provide smooth integration with existing software and to support the full task list: overview, zoom, filter, details-on-demand, relate, history, and extract. These products will be attractive because they will present information rapidly and allow user-controlled exploration. If they are to be fully effective, they will require advanced data structures, high-resolution color displays, fast data retrieval, and novel forms of user training. Careful testing should be conducted to go beyond the desire for "cool" interfaces and to implement designs that have demonstrated benefits for realistic tasks.

WORLD WIDE WEB RESOURCES

Information-visualization tools are growing more effective for a wider range of tasks, and commercial tools are now available. Search services such as Google or the Library of Congress digital libraries provide always-improving access to the World Wide Web. Other information-retrieval topics, such as collaborative filtering, multimedia search and retrieval, and indexing methods are also covered.

http://www.aw.com/DTUI

Researcher's Agenda

Although the computer contributes to the information explosion, it is potentially also the magic lens for finding, sorting, filtering, and presenting the relevant items. The need to search in complex structured documents, graphics, images, and sound or video files presents grand opportunities for the design of advanced user interfaces. Powerful search engines will be able to find the needles in the haystacks and the forests beyond the trees. The novel information-exploration tools—such as dynamic queries, treemaps, zoomable user interfaces, hierarchical faceted metadata interfaces, and parallel coordinates—are but a few of the inventions that will have to be tamed and validated by user-interface researchers. A better integration with perceptual psychology (understanding preattentive processes and the impact of varied coding or highlighting techniques) and with business decision making (identifying tasks and procedures that occur in realistic situations) is needed, as are theoretical foundations and practical benchmarks for choosing among the diverse emerging visualization techniques. Information exploration can result in complex interfaces that might be overwhelming for novice users, and novel demonstration or training methods might be useful. Empirical studies will help to sort out the specific situations in which visualization is most helpful. Finally, software toolkits for building visualizations will facilitate the exploration process.

References

Ahlberg, C. and Shneiderman, B., Visual information seeking: Tight coupling of dynamic query filters with starfield displays, *Proc. CHI '94 Conference: Human Factors in Computing Systems*, ACM, New York (1994), 313–321 and color plates.

Amento, B., Terveen, L., and Hill, W., Does "authority" mean quality? Predicting expert quality ratings of web documents, *Proc. ACM SIGIR 2000 Conference*, ACM, New York (2000), 296–303.

Andrienko, N., Andrienko, G., and Gatalsky, P., Exploratory spatio-temporal visualization: An analytical review, *Journal of Visual Languages and Computing*, 14, 6 (2003), 503–541.

Bederson, B. B., PhotoMesa: A zoomable image browser using quantum treemaps and bubblemaps, *Proc. UIST 2001 Symposium on User Interface Software & Technology*, ACM CHI Letters, 3, 2 (2001), 71–80.

Bederson, B. B., Meyer, J., and Good, L., Jazz: An extensible zoomable user interface graphics toolkit in Java, *Proc. UIST 2000 Symposium on User Interface Software & Technology*, ACM CHI Letters, 2, 2 (2000), 171–180.

Bederson, B. B. and Shneiderman, B., *The Craft of Information Visualization: Readings and Reflections*, Morgan Kaufmann Publishers, San Francisco, CA (2003).

Bederson, B. B., Shneiderman, B., and Wattenberg, M., Ordered and quantum treemaps: Making effective use of 2D space to display hierarchies, *ACM Transactions on Graphics*, 21, 4 (October 2002), 833–854.

Belkin, N. J. and Croft, B. W., Information filtering and information retrieval: Two sides of the same coin?, *Communications of the ACM*, 35, 12 (1992), 29–38.

Bertin, J., *Semiology of Graphics*, University of Wisconsin Press, Madison, WI (1983).

Borner, B. and Chen C. (Editors), *Visual Interfaces to Digital Libraries: Motivation, Utilization, and Socio-Technical Challenges* (Lecture Notes in Computer Science, 2539), Springer-Verlag, London, U.K. (2003).

Brin S. and Page L., The anatomy of a largescale hypertextual web search engine, *Proc. Seventh International World Wide Web Conference* (1998), 107–117.

Card, S., Mackinlay, J., and Shneiderman, B., *Readings in Information Visualization: Using Vision to Think*, Morgan Kaufmann Publishers, San Francisco, CA (1999).

Card, S., Information visualization, in Jacko, J. and Sears, A. (Editors), *The Human-Computer Interaction Handbook*, Lawrence Erlbaum Associates, Mahwah, NJ (2002), 544–582.

Card, S. and Nation, D., Degree-of-interest trees: A component of attention-reactive user interface, *Proc. Advanced Visual Interface '02* (2002), 231–245.

Chen, C., *Information Visualisation and Virtual Environments*, Springer-Verlag, Berlin, Germany (1999).

Chen, C., *Mapping Scientific Frontiers: The Quest for Knowledge Visualisation*, Springer-Verlag, Berlin, Germany (2003).

Cleveland, W., *Visualizing Data*, Hobart Press, Summit, NJ (1993).

Doan, K., Plaisant, C., Shneiderman, B., and Bruns, T., Interface and data architecture for query preview in networked information systems, *ACM Transactions on Information Systems*, 17, 3 (1999), 320–341.

Dodge, M. and Kitchin, R., *Atlas of Cyberspace*, Addison-Wesley, Reading, MA (2001).

Doermann, D., The indexing and retrieval of document images: A survey, *Computer Vision and Image Understanding*, 70, 3 (1998), 287–298.

Dumais, S., Cutrell, E., and Chen, H., Optimizing search by showing results in context, *Proc. CHI 2001 Conference: Human Factors in Computing Systems* (2001), 277–284.

Dykes, J., MacEachren A. M., and Kraak, M. J. (Editors), *Exploring Geovisualization*, Elsevier, Amsterdam, The Netherlands (2004).

Eick, Stephen, Maintenance of large systems, in Stasko, John, Domingue, John, Brown, Marc H., and Price, Blaine A. (Editors), *Software Visualization: Programming as a Multimedia Experience*, MIT Press, Cambridge, MA (1998), 315–328.

Fayyad, U., Grinstein, G., and Wierse, A., *Information Visualization in Data Mining and Knowledge Discovery*, Morgan Kaufmann Publishers, San Francisco, CA (2001).

Fekete, J.-D. and Plaisant, C., Excentric labeling: Dynamic neighborhood labeling for data visualization, *Proc. CHI '99 Conference: Human Factors in Computing Systems*, ACM, New York (1999), 512–519.

Fekete, J.-D. and Plaisant, C., Interactive information visualization of a million items, *Proc. IEEE Symposium on Information Visualization* (2002), 117–124.

Friendly, M., Mosaic displays for multi-way contingency tables, *Journal of the American Statistical Association*, 89 (1994), 190–200.

Greene, S., Marchionini, G., Plaisant, C., and Shneiderman, B., Previews and overviews in digital libraries: Designing surrogates to support visual information-seeking, *Journal of the American Society for Information Science*, 51, 3 (March 2000), 380–393.

Hearst, M., User interfaces and visualization, in Baeza-Yates, Ricardo and Ribeiro-Neto, Berthier (Editors), *Modern Information Retrieval*, Addison-Wesley, Reading, MA (1999).

Herman, I., Melançon, G., and Marshall, M. S., Graph visualization and navigation in information visualization: A survey, *IEEE Transactions on Visualization and Computer Graphics*, 6, 1 (2000), 24–43.

Hochheiser, H. and Shneiderman, B., Dynamic query tools for time series data sets: Timebox widgets for interactive exploration, *Information Visualization*, 3, 1 (2004, 1–18).

Hornbaek, K., Bederson, B. B., and Plaisant, C., Navigation patterns and usability of zoomable user interfaces with and without an overview, *ACM Transactions on Computer-Human Interaction*, 9, 4 (2002), 362–389.

Hovy, E. H., Ide, N., Frederking, R.E., Mariani, J., and Zampolli, A. (Editors), *Multilingual Information Management*, Giardini Editori e Stampatori, Pisa, Italy and Kluwer Academic Publishers, Dordecht, The Netherlands (2001).

Hu, N. and Dannenberg, R., Music digital libraries: A comparison of melodic database retrieval techniques using sung queries, *Proc. 2nd ACM/IEEE-CS Joint Conference on Digital Libraries* (2002), 301–307.

Inselberg, A., Multidimensional detective, *Proc. IEEE Symposium on Information Visualization* (October 1997), 100–107.

Keim, D. A., Visual exploration of large data sets, *Communications of the ACM*, 44, 8 (August 2001), 38–44.

Koenemann, J. and Belkin, N., A case for interaction: A study of interactive information retrieval behavior and effectiveness, *Proc. CHI '96 Conference: Human Factors in Computing Systems*, ACM, New York (1996), 205–212.

Komlodi, A., The role of interaction histories in mental model building and knowledge sharing in the legal domain, *I-KNOW '02 2nd International Conference on Knowledge Management, Journal of Universal Computer Science*, 8, 5 (2002), 557–566.

MacEachren, A., Dai, X., Hardisty, F., Guo, D., and Lengerich, G., Exploring high-D spaces with multiform matrices and small multiples, *Proc. IEEE Symposium on Information Visualization* (2003), 31–38.

Marchionini, Gary, *Information Seeking in Electronic Environments*, Cambridge University Press, Cambridge, U.K. (1995).

Munzner, T., Drawing Large Graphs with H3Viewer and Site Manager, Lecture Notes in Computer Science series, *Proceedings for the Symposium on Graph Drawing, GD '98*, Montreal, Canada (1998).

North, C., Conklin, N., and Saini, V., Visualization schemas for flexible information visualization, *Proc. IEEE Symposium on Information Visualization* (2002), 15–22.

Oard, D. W., Gonzalo, J., Sanderson, M., Lopez-Ostenero, F., and Wang, J., Interactive cross-language document selection, *Information Retrieval*, special issue on results from the Cross-Language Evaluation Forum (2004).

Pirolli, P., Schank, P., Hearst, M., and Diehl, C., Scatter/gather browsing communicates the topic structure of a very large text collection, *Proc. CHI '96 Conference: Human Factors in Computing Systems*, ACM, New York (1996), 213–220.

Plaisant, C., Information visualization and the challenge of universal access, in Dynes, J., MacEachren, A. M., and Kraak, M. J. (Editors), *Exploring Geovisualization*, Elsevier, Amsterdam, The Netherlands (2004).

Plaisant, C., Mushlin, R., Snyder, A., Li, J., Heller, D., and Shneiderman, B., LifeLines: Using visualization to enhance navigation and analysis of patient records, *American Medical Informatics Association Annual Fall Symposium*, AMIA, Bethesda, MD (1998), 76–80.

Plaisant, C., Grosjean, J., and Bederson, B. B. SpaceTree: Supporting exploration in large node link tree, design evolution and empirical evaluation, *Proc. IEEE Symposium on Information Visualization* (2002), 57–64.

Reisner, P., Query languages, in Helander, M. (Editor), *Handbook of Human-Computer Interaction*, North-Holland, Amsterdam, The Netherlands (1988), 257–280.

Riedl, J., Konstan, J., and Vrooman, E., *Word of Mouse: The Marketing Power of Collaborative Filtering*, Warner Business Books, New York (2002).

Robertson, George G., Card, Stuart K., and Mackinlay, Jock D., Information visualization using 3-D interactive animation, *Communications of the ACM*, 36, 4 (April 1993), 56–71.

Shneiderman, B., Dynamic queries for visual information seeking, *IEEE Software*, 11, 6 (1994), 70–77.

Shneiderman, B., Byrd, D., and Croft, B., Clarifying search: A user-interface framework for text searches, *D-LIB Magazine of Digital Library Research* (January 1997). Available at http://www.dlib.org/.

Shneiderman, B., Treemaps for space-constrained visualization of hierarchies, (2004). Available at http://www.cs.umd.edu/hcil/treemap-history.

Silva, S. F., and Catarci, T., Visualization of linear time-oriented data: A survey, *Proc. First International Conference on Web Information Systems Engineering (WISE '00)*, IEEE Computer Society (2000), 310–319.

Spence, R., *Information Visualisation*, Addison-Wesley, Reading, MA (2001).

Stasko, John, Domingue, John, Brown, Marc H., and Price, Blaine A. (Editors), *Software Visualization: Programming as a Multimedia Experience*, MIT Press, Cambridge, MA (1998).

Tanin, E., Lotem, A., Haddadin, I., Shneiderman, B., Plaisant, C., and Slaughter, L., Facilitating network data exploration with query previews: A study of user performance and preference, *Behaviour & Information Technology*, 19, 6 (2000), 393–403.

Tufte, E., *The Visual Display of Quantitative Information*, Graphics Press, Cheshire, CT (1983).

Tufte, E., *Visual Explanations*, Graphics Press, Cheshire, CT (1997).

Wactlar, H. D., Christel, M. G., Yihong G., and Hauptmann, A. G., Lessons learned from building a terabyte digital video library, *IEEE Computer*, 32, 2 (1999), 66–73.

Wakefield, G. and Bartsch, M., Where's Caruso? Singer identification by listener and machine, *Cambridge Music Processing Colloquium 2003* (2003).

Ware, Colin, *Information Visualization: Perception for Design: Second Edition*, Morgan Kaufmann Publishers, San Francisco, CA (2004).

Welty, C., Correcting user errors in SQL, *International Journal of Man-Machine Studies*, 22 (1985), 463–477.

Wilkinson, L., *The Grammar of Graphics (Statistics and Computing)*, Springer-Verlag, New York (1999).

Williamson, C. and Shneiderman, B., The dynamic HomeFinder: Evaluating dynamic queries in a real-estate information exploration system, *Proc. ACM SIGIR '92 Conference*, ACM, New York (1992), 338–346.

Wise, J. A., Thomas, J., Pennock, K., Lantrip, D., Pottier, M., Schur, A., and Crow, V., Visualizing the non-visual: Spatial analysis and interaction with information from text documents, *Proc. IEEE Symposium on Information Visualization*, IEEE Computer Press, Los Alamitos, CA (1995), 51–58.

Wurman, Richard Saul, *Information Anxiety*, Doubleday, New York (1989).

Yee, K.-P., Swearingen, K., Li, K., and Hearst, M., Faceted metadata for image search and browsing, *Proc. CHI 2003 Conference: Human Factors in Computing Systems*, ACM, New York (2003), 401–408.

Zhao, H., Plaisant, C., and Shneiderman, B., Improving accessibility and usability of geo-referenced statistical data, *Proc. 2003 National Conference on Digital Government Research* (2003), 147–152 (available at www.dgrc.org).

Afterword

Societal and Individual Impact of User Interfaces

The machine itself makes no demands and holds out no promises: it is the human spirit that makes demands and keeps promises. In order to reconquer the machine and subdue it to human purposes, one must first understand it and assimilate it. So far we have embraced the machine without fully understanding it.

LEWIS MUMFORD
Technics and Civilization, 1934

A.1   Future Interfaces

Human-computer interaction (HCI) researchers and usability professionals can reflect proudly on a quarter century of accomplishments such as menu systems, graphical user interfaces, the World Wide Web, online communities, information visualization, mobile devices, and much more. User interfaces are not perfect, but they have facilitated progress in many fields such as medical care, education, management, science, and engineering. They have also spawned consumer success stories in e-commerce, family photography with digital cameras, and entertainment with games.

The Afterword considers future directions (Section A.1) and cautions about some potential dangers (Section A.2). It then takes a reflective, historical perspective on how we think about ourselves as being different from our technologies (Section A.3).

The natural question that journalists ask of HCI researchers is what is the next big thing? One popular school of thought claims that future innovations emerge from advanced technology development. Leaders of this view believe that advances will come by developing new devices, especially those that are ubiquitous and pervasive, suggesting that they are everywhere, cheap, and small. A second theme is that these new devices will be wearable, mobile, personal, and portable, suggesting that they can be carried by users at all times. The third theme is that these new devices will be embedded, context aware, and ambient, suggesting that they are built into our surroundings and thereby making them invisible but available when needed and responsive to user needs. Finally, some of these new devices are labeled as perceptive and multimodal, suggesting that they perceive user status and needs and allow interaction by visual, aural, tactile, haptic, gestural, and other stimuli. The members of this school have generated clever innovations such as tiny medical sensors that monitor health, hidden detectors that protect from dangers, and entertainment devices that enrich experiences. Technology development is a fertile source of new ideas, but the tasks supported by many of these proposed devices are often described vaguely.

Another school of thought, universal usability, suggests that the focus of the next quarter century will be on spreading the early successes to a broader community of users. Students of this view believe that they can enable every person to benefit from information and communication technologies. Advocates of universal usability claim that this principle can stimulate innovative advances. Progress toward universal usability is measured by the steadily increasing percentage of the population that has convenient, low-cost access to computer and Internet services.

There are still many forgotten users, especially low-income citizens in every country and most residents of developing nations. E-mail, Web sites, and many services can be reshaped to accommodate weak writers and readers, while helping to improve their skills. Job training and hunting can be organized to serve those people with poor employment skills and transient lifestyles. Services such as voting, motor vehicle registration, or crime reporting can be enhanced if universal usability is assumed. Designers can begin by improving interfaces for common tasks and then provide training and help methods so that using a computer is a satisfying opportunity, rather than a frustrating challenge. Evolutionary learning with multilayer interfaces would allow first-time users to succeed with common tasks and provide a growth path to more complex features.

Tailoring of interfaces for diverse populations can be accomplished by extending and improving control panels to allow users to specify easily their national language, units of measurement, skill level, and more. Portability to nonstandard hardware, accommodation of varying screen sizes or modem speeds, and design for physically challenged and older adult users should be common practices. Support for increased plasticity of information and services is technologically possible. Convenient semantic tagging of items enables software designers to reformat presentations to adjust to users' needs.

A third school of thought claims that those attending to individual and societal needs will generate technological innovations more often. They believe that satisfying human needs with predictable, controllable technology that empowers users will lead to societal advancement. Students of this view are most likely to discuss values, privacy, trust, empathy, and responsibility. Several opportunities seem ready for rapid progress, such as terror prevention and response, international development, medical informatics, e-commerce, government services, and creativity support tools.

A1.1   Terror Prevention and Response

The aftermath of the terrorist attacks in New York City and Washington, D.C. on September 11, 2001 created many new needs for protective technologies. Some of these are tied to detecting terrorist activities in time to stop them, whereas others are intended to help first responders to cope with attacks. Ambitious efforts to collect extensive records from every citizen have the serious risk of violating privacy and increasing discrimination. Worse still such efforts may be ineffective means to prevent terrorism. Alternatives are to focus analysts' attention on specific threats with data such as visa applications, financial transfers among identified individuals, purchases of restricted materials, and hospital emergency room admissions. Biometric identification could be a valuable tool in reducing terrorist attacks and other criminal activity, but implementation and privacy problems must be addressed. Positive approaches are to increase understanding of other cultures, history, and languages.

A1.2 International Development

In communities where adequate housing, sanitation, and food are still problems, information and communications technologies are not primary needs, but they can be helpful as part of an overall development plan. Community-networking technologies that are used in financially secure cities such as Singapore and Seattle are being adapted to mountainous Nepal, urban Rio de Janeiro, or rural Botswana. Multilingual designs and citizen participation will accelerate education and adoption. International efforts to create a global information society and promote development are coordinated by United Nations agencies, regional alliances, and many smaller nongovernmental organizations.

A1.3 Medical Informatics

The scientific exploration of genomics requires intense computer support to understand biological pathways that govern cell processes. As researchers improve their understanding, new treatments will emerge, even for severe diseases such as cancer. Medical care by physicians and nurses will also improve as interfaces enable refined diagnoses and treatment plans, as well as the basic record keeping necessary for hospitals and clinics. Patients will become more informed from Web sites and online community discussion. Home medical devices will become important components of health monitoring and personal health care, but standard data formats and interfaces are necessary.

A1.4 E-commerce

Shopping was heralded as the major application of the World Wide Web, but the dot-com crash of 2000 stalled or slowed many efforts. Still the growing use of the World Wide Web for buying books, airline tickets, and an increasing array of products should continue. Universal usability will expand markets, designers will fashion convenient Web sites, and trust management strategies will reduce fraud. The convenience of information gathering for product and price comparison facilitates commerce.

A1.5   Government Services

Citizen access will continue to improve for services such as motor vehicle registration, business licenses, tax information, park and recreation facilities, and much more. Local, state, and national services will grow over time as universal usability expands the number of users.

A1.6   Creativity Support Tools

Technology has always been a part of creative endeavors in music, art, science, and engineering. Now user interfaces are enabling a higher degree of information discovery through information visualization and easier consultation through collaboration technologies. Advanced composition tools, simulations, and history-keeping permit rapid exploration of alternatives. The potential is for users to be more creative more of the time.

Undoubtedly, other opportunities and unexpected developments in human-computer interaction research will occur. Another way to gain ideas about future directions is to assess the serious problems that plague users (see the next section).

A.2   Ten Plagues of the Information Age

The real question before us lies here: Do these instruments further life and enhance its values, or not?

Mumford
Technics and Civilization, 1934

It would be naïve to assume that widespread use of computers brings only benefits. There are legitimate reasons to worry that increased dissemination of computers might lead to a variety of personal, organizational, political, or social oppressions. People who fear computers have good reason for their concerns. The disruption from unwanted e-mail (spam), malicious viruses, pornography, and other annoyances must be addressed if we desire to increase the beneficial uses of information and communication technologies. Designers have an

opportunity and a responsibility to be alert to the dangers and to make thoughtful decisions about reducing them. The following is a personal list of potential
and real dangers from use of information and communication technologies:

1. *Anxiety*

   Many people avoid the computer or use it with great anxiety; they experience *computer shock, web worry,* or *network neurosis.* Their anxieties include
   fear of breaking the machine, worry over losing control of the computer,
   trepidation about appearing foolish or incompetent ("computers make you
   feel so dumb"), or more general concern about facing something new. These
   anxieties are real, should be acknowledged rather than dismissed, and can
   often be overcome with positive experiences. Can we build improved user
   interfaces that will reduce the high level of anxiety experienced by many
   users?

2. *Alienation*

   As people spend more time using computers, they may become less connected to other people. Computer users as a group are more introverted than
   others, and increased time with the computer may increase their isolation.
   The dedicated game player who rarely communicates with another person is
   an extreme case, but what happens to the emotional relationships of a person
   who spends two hours per day dealing with e-mail instead of chatting with
   colleagues or family members (Kraut et al., 1998; Kraut et al., 2002; Robinson
   and Nie, 2002)? Can we build user interfaces that encourage more constructive human social interaction?

3. *Information-poor minority*

   Although some utopian visionaries believe that computers will eliminate
   the distinctions between rich and poor or will right social injustices, often
   computers are just another way in which the disadvantaged are disadvantaged (Friedman and Nissenbaum, 1996; NTIA, 2000). Those people who are
   without computer skills may have a new reason for not succeeding in school
   or not getting a job. The well-documented digital divide can be overcome if
   we recognize it and make commitments to bridging it by offering appropriate access, training, support, and services. Can we build user interfaces that
   empower low-skilled workers to perform at the level of experts? Can we
   arrange training and education for every able member of society?

4. *Impotence of the individual*

   Large organizations can become impersonal because the cost of handling
   special cases is great. Individuals who are frustrated in trying to receive personal treatment and attention may vent their anger at the organization, the
   personnel they encounter, or the technology that limits rather than enables.
   People who have tried to find out the current status of their social security

accounts or have banks explain accounting discrepancies are aware of the problems, especially if they have language or hearing deficits, or other physical or cognitive handicaps. How can we design so that individuals will feel more empowered and self-actualized?

5. *Bewildering complexity and speed*

   The tax, welfare, and insurance regulations developed by computer-based bureaucracies are so complex and fast changing that it is extremely difficult for individuals to make informed choices. Even knowledgeable computer users are often overwhelmed by the torrent of new software packages, mobile devices, and Web services, each with hundreds of features and options. Speed dominates, and more features are seen as preferable. Simplicity is a simple, but too often ignored, principle. Stern adherence to basic principles of design may be the only path to a safer, more sane, simpler, and slower world where human concerns predominate.

6. *Organizational fragility*

   As organizations come to depend on more complex technology, they can become fragile. When breakdowns or virus attacks occur, they can propagate rapidly and halt the work of many people. With computer-based airline services, telephone switching, or electricity grids, failures can mean rapid and widespread shutdowns of service. Since networks can cause concentration of expertise, a small number of people can disrupt a large organization. Can developers anticipate the dangers and produce robust designs?

7. *Invasion of privacy*

   The widely reported threat of invasion of privacy is worrisome because the concentration of information and the existence of powerful retrieval systems make it possible to violate the privacy of many people easily and rapidly. Of course, well-designed computer systems have the potential of becoming more secure than paper systems if managers are dedicated to privacy protection. Airline, telephone, bank, medical, legal, and employment records can reveal much about an individual if confidentiality is compromised. Can managers seek policies and systems that increase rather than reduce the protection of privacy in a computer-based organization?

8. *Unemployment and displacement*

   As automation spreads, productivity and overall employment may increase, but some jobs may become less valued or eliminated. Retraining can help some employees, but others will have difficulty changing lifetime patterns of work. Displacement may happen to low-paid clerks or highly paid typesetters whose work is automated, as well as to the bank vice-president whose mortgage-loan decisions are now made by an expert system. Can employers develop labor policies that ensure retraining and guarantee jobs?

9. *Lack of professional responsibility*

   Faceless organizations may respond impersonally to, and deny responsibility for, problems. The complexity of technology and organizations provides ample opportunities for employees to pass the blame on to others or to the computer: "Sorry, the computer won't let us loan you the library book without your machine-readable card." Will users of medical diagnostic or defense-related user interfaces be able to escape responsibility for decisions? Will computer displays become more trusted than a person's word or a professional's judgment? Complex and confusing user interfaces enable users and designers to blame the machine, but with improved designs, users and designers will give and accept responsibility and credit where it is due.

10. *Deteriorating image of people*

   With the presence of *intelligent terminals, smart machines,* and *expert systems,* it seems that the machines have indeed *taken over* human abilities. These misleading phrases not only generate anxiety about computers, but also may undermine the image that we have of people and their abilities. Some behavioral psychologists suggest that we are little more than machines; some artificial intelligence workers believe that the automation of many human abilities is within reach. The rich diversity of human skills, the generative or creative nature of daily life, the emotional or passionate side of human endeavor, and the idiosyncratic imagination of each child seem lost or undervalued. Rather than be impressed by smart machines, accept the misguided pursuit of the Turing test, or focus on computational skills in people, the authors believe that we should recognize how designs that empower users will increase their appreciation of the richness and diversity of unique human abilities.

Undoubtedly, more plagues and problems exist. Each situation is a small warning for the designer. Each design is an opportunity to apply computers in positive, constructive ways that avoid these dangers.

There is no sure vaccine for preventing the ten plagues. Even well-intentioned designers can inadvertently spread them, but alert, dedicated designers whose consciousness is raised can reduce the dangers. The strategies for preventing the plagues and reducing their effects include the following:

- *Human-centered participatory design.* Concentrate attention on the users and tasks they must accomplish. Make users the center of attention, include them in the design process, and build feelings of competence, mastery, clarity, and predictability. Construct well-organized menu trees, present specific and constructive instructions and messages, develop comprehensible displays, offer informative feedback, enable easy error handling, ensure appropriate response time, and produce comprehensible learning materials.

- *Organizational support.* Beyond the interface design, the organization must also support the users. Apply participatory design and elicit frequent evaluation and feedback from users. Techniques include personal interviews, focus groups, online surveys, paper questionnaires, online communities, online consultants, and suggestion boxes.

- *Job design.* European labor unions have been active in setting rules for computer users to prevent the exhaustion, stress, or burnout caused by an *electronic sweatshop.* Rules might be set to limit hours of use, guarantee rest periods, facilitate job rotation, and support education. Similarly, negotiated measures of productivity or error rates can help reward exemplary workers and guide training. Monitoring or metering of work must be done cautiously, but both managers and employees can be beneficiaries of a thoughtful plan.

- *Education.* The complexity of modern life and user interfaces makes education critical. Schools and colleges, as well as employers, all play a role in training. Special attention should be paid to continuing education, on-the-job training, and teacher education.

- *Feedback and rewards.* User communities can be more than passive observers. They can ensure that system failures are reported, that design improvements are conveyed to managers and designers, and that manuals and online aids are reviewed. Similarly, excellence should be acknowledged by awards within organizations and through public presentations. Professional societies in computing might promote awards, similar to the awards of the American Institute of Architects, the Pulitzer Prize Committee, or the Academy of Motion Picture Producers.

- *Public consciousness raising.* Informed consumers of personal computers and users of commercial systems can benefit the entire community. Professional societies such as the ACM and IEEE and user groups can play a key role through public relations, consumer education, and professional standards of ethics.

- *Legislation.* Much progress has been made with legislation concerning privacy, right of access to information, and computer crime, but more work remains. Cautious steps toward regulation, work rules, and standardization can be highly beneficial. Dangers of restrictive legislation do exist, but thoughtful legal protection will stimulate development and prevent abuses.

- *Advanced research.* Individuals, organizations, and governments can support research to develop novel ideas, minimize the dangers, and spread the advantages of interactive systems. Theories of user cognitive behavior, individual differences, acquisition of skills, visual perception, and organizational change would be helpful in guiding designers and implementers.

A.3   Overcoming the Obstacle of Animism

> Unlike machines, human minds can create ideas. We need ideas to guide us to progress, as well as tools to implement them. . . . Computers don't contain "brains" any more than stereos contain musical instruments. . . . Machines only manipulate numbers; people connect them to meaning.
>
> *Penzias*, 1989

The emergence of user interfaces is a fundamental historical advance. Such upheavals are neither all good nor all bad, but rather are an amalgam of many individual designer decisions about how a technology is applied. The metaphors, images, and names chosen for user interfaces play a key role in the designers' and the users' perceptions. It is not surprising that many computer-user interface designers still mimic human or animal forms. The first attempts at flight imitated birds, and the first designs for microphones followed the shape of the human ear. Such primitive visions may be useful starting points, but success comes most rapidly to people who move beyond these fantasies. Except for amusement, the goal is never to mimic the human form, but rather is to provide effective service to the users in accomplishing their tasks.

Lewis Mumford, in his classic book, *Technics and Civilization* (1934), characterized the problem of "dissociation of the animate and the mechanical" as the "obstacle of animism." He described Leonardo da Vinci's attempt to reproduce the motion of birds' wings, then Ader's batlike airplane (as late as 1897), and Branca's steam engine in the form of a human head and torso. Mumford wrote: "The most ineffective kind of machine is the realistic mechanical imitation of a man or another animal . . . for thousands of years animism has stood in the way of . . . development."

Choosing human or animal forms as the inspiration for some projects is understandable, but significant advances will come more quickly if we recognize the goals that serve human needs and the inherent attributes of the technology that is employed. Hand-held calculators do not follow human forms, but serve effectively for doing arithmetic. Designers of championship chess-playing programs no longer imitate human strategies. Vision-systems researchers realized the advantages of radar or sonar range finders and retreated from using humanlike stereo depth-perception cues.

Robots provide an informative case study. Beyond stone idols and voodoo dolls, we can trace modern robots back to the devices built by Pierre Jacquet-Droz, a Swiss watchmaker, from 1768 to 1774. The first child-size mechanical robot, called the Scribe, could be programmed to write any message up to 40 characters long. It had commands to change lines, skip a space, or dip the quill in the inkwell. The second, called the Draughtsman, had a repertoire of four pencil sketches: a boy, a dog, Louis XV of France, and a pair of portraits. The third robot, the Musician, performed five songs on a working pipe organ and could operate for 1.5 hours on one winding. These robots made their creators famous and wealthy, since they were in great demand at the courts of the kings and in public showings. Eventually, however, printing presses became more effective than the Scribe and the Draughtsman, and tape players and phonographs were superior to the Musician.

Robots of the 1950s included electronic components and a metallic skin, but their designs were also strongly influenced by the human form. Robot arms were of the same dimension as human arms and the hands had five fingers. Designers of modern robots have finally overcome the obstacle of animism and now construct arms whose dimensions are appropriate for the steel and plastic technology and for the tasks. Two fingers are more common than five on robot hands, and the hands can often rotate more than 270 degrees. Where appropriate, fingers have been replaced by rubber suction cups with vacuum pumps to pick up parts.

The banking machine offers a simple example of the evolution from anthropomorphic imagery to a service orientation. Early user interfaces had such names as Tillie the Teller or Harvey Wallbanker and were programmed with such phrases as, "How can I help you?" These deceptive images rapidly gave way to a focus on the computer technology, with such names as the Electronic Teller, CompuCash, Cashmatic, or CompuBank. Over time, the emphasis has moved toward the service provided to the user: CashFlow, Money Exchange, 24-Hour Money Machine, All-Night Banker, and Money Mover.

The computer revolution will be judged not by the complexity or power of technology, but rather by the service to human needs. By focusing on users, researchers and designers will generate powerful yet simple user interfaces that permit users to accomplish their tasks. These tools will enable short learning times, rapid performance, and low error rates. Putting users' needs first will lead to more appropriate choices of user interface features, giving them a greater sense of mastery and control, as well as the satisfaction of achievement. At the same time, users will feel increased responsibility for their actions and may be more motivated to learn about the tasks and the interactive user interface.

Sharpening the boundaries between people and computers will lead to a clearer recognition of computer powers and human reasoning (Weizenbaum, 1976; Winograd and Flores, 1986). Rapid progress will occur when designers accept that human–human communication is a poor model for human–computer interaction. People are different from computers, and human operation of computers is vastly different from human relationships. Vital factors that distinguish human behavior include the diversity of skills and background across individuals; the creativity, imagination, and inventiveness incorporated in daily actions; the emotional involvement in every act; the desire for social contact; and the power of intention.

Ignoring these primitive but enduring aspects of humanity leads to inappropriate technology and hollow experiences. Embracing these aspects can bring about powerful tools, joy in learning, the capacity to realize goals, a sense of accomplishment, and increased social interaction.

Although designers may be attracted to the goal of making impressive and autonomous machines that perform tasks as well as humans do, realizing this goal will not provide what most users want. We believe that users want to have a sense of their own accomplishment, rather than to admire a smart robot, intelligent agent, or expert system. Users want to be empowered by technology to apply their knowledge and experience to make judgments that lead to improved job performance and greater personal satisfaction.

Some examples may help us clarify this issue. Doctors do not want a machine that does medical diagnosis; rather, they want a machine that enables them to make a more accurate, reliable diagnosis; obtain relevant references to scientific papers or clinical trials; gather consultative support rapidly; and record that support accurately. Similarly, air-traffic or manufacturing controllers do not want a machine that automatically does their job; rather they want one that increases their productivity, reduces their error rates, and enables them to handle special cases or emergencies effectively. We believe that an increase in personal responsibility will result in improved service.

Practitioner's Summary

Successful interactive user interfaces will bring ample rewards to the designers, but widespread use of effective tools is only the means to reach higher goals. A user interface is more than a technological artifact—Interactive systems, especially when linked by computer networks, create human social systems. As Marshall McLuhan pointed out, "The medium is the message," and therefore each interactive user interface is a message from the designer to the user. That message has often been a harsh one, with the underlying implication that the designer does not care about the user. Nasty error messages are obvious manifestations; complex menus, cluttered screens, and confusing dialog boxes are also sentences in the harsh message.

Most designers want to send a more kind and caring message. Designers, implementers, and researchers are learning to send warmer greetings to the users with effective and well-tested user interfaces. The message of quality is compelling to the recipients and can instill good feelings, appreciation for the designer, and the desire to excel in one's own work. The capacity for excellent systems to instill compassion and connection was noted by Sterling (1974) at the end of his guidelines for information systems: "In the long run what may be important is the *texture* of a system. By texture we mean the *quality* the system has to evoke in users and participants a feeling that the system increases the kinship among people."

At first, it may seem surprising that information and communication technologies can instill a kinship among people, but every technology has the potential to engage people in cooperative efforts. Each designer can play a role—not only that of fighting for the users, but also that of nurturing, serving, and caring for them.

Researcher's Agenda

High-level goals might include world peace, excellent health care, adequate nutrition, accessible education, improved communication, freedom of expression, support for creative exploration, safe transportation, and socially constructive entertainment. Computer technology can help us attain these high-level goals if we clearly state measurable objectives, obtain participation of professionals, and design effective human–computer interfaces. Design considerations include adequate attention to individual differences among users; support of social and organizational structures; design for reliability and safety; provision of access by older adults, physically challenged, or illiterate users; and appropriate user-controlled adaptation.

The goals for new devices, universal usability, and creativity support contain enough ambitious research projects for a generation. Terror prevention and response, international development, medical informatics, e-commerce, and government services are the most appealing candidates for early research, because the impact of changes could be so large. If we are to provide novel services to diverse users, we need effective theories and rigorous empirical research to achieve ease of learning, rapid performance, low error rates, and good retention over time, while preserving high subjective satisfaction.

WORLD WIDE WEB RESOURCES

Organizations dealing with ethics, social impact, and public policy are doing their best to make computing and information services as helpful as possible. Ways for you to become an activist are also included.

http://www.aw.com/DTUI

References

Friedman, Batya and Nissenbaum, Helen, Bias in computer systems, *ACM Transactions on Information Systems*, 14, 3 (July 1966), 330–347.

Kraut, R., Lundmark, V., Patterson, M., Kiesler, S., Mukopadhyay, T., and Scherlis, W., Internet paradox: A social technology that reduces social involvement and psychological well-being? *American Psychologist*, 53 (1998), 1017–1031.

Kraut, R., Kiesler, S., Boneva, B., Cummings, J., Helgeson, V., and Crawford, A., Internet paradox revisited, *Journal of Social Issues, 58*, 1 (2002), 49–74.

Mumford, Lewis, *Technics and Civilization*, Harcourt Brace and World, New York (1934).

National Telecommunications and Information Administration, U. S. Dept. of Commerce, Falling Through the Net: Toward Digital Inclusion, Washington, DC (October 2000), http://www.ntia.doc.gov/ntiahome/fttn00/contents00.html. Accessed on January 20, 2004.

Norman, Don, *The Psychology of Everyday Things*, Basic Books, New York (1988).

Penzias, Arno, *Ideas and Information*, Simon and Schuster, New York (1989).

Robinson, John and Nie, Norman, Introduction to IT & Society, Issue 1: Sociability, *IT and Society: A Web Journal Studying How Technology Affects Society*, 1, 1 (Summer 2002). Available at http://itandsociety.org.

Shneiderman, B., Universal usability: Pushing human-computer interaction research to empower every citizen, *Communications of the ACM*, 43, 5 (2000), 84–91.

Sterling, T. D., Guidelines for humanizing computerized information systems: A report from Stanley House, *Communications of the ACM*, 17, 11 (November 1974), 609–613.

Weizenbaum, Joseph, *Computer Power and Human Reason*, W. H. Freeman, San Francisco, CA (1976).

Winograd, Terry and Flores, Fernando, *Understanding Computers and Cognition: A New Foundation for Design*, Ablex, Norwood, NJ (1986).

Name Index

A

Abowd, Gregory D., 53, 208, 346, 372, 401, 437, 444, 447
Abraham, D., 103
Accot, J., 369, 401
Ackerman, Mark S., 551, 554, 555
Adler, Paul S., 55
Ahlberg, C., 275, 310, 586, 603
Ahlstrom, Vicki, 49
Alavi, M., 450
Alexander, Christopher, 93, 102
Alfaro, L., 555
Allen, James, 332, 342
Allison, R. S., 261, 356
Allwood, C. M., 532, 555
Alpert, Sherman R., 545, 555
Amento, B., 564, 603
Anderson, Ben, 262, 419
Anderson, J. R., 91, 103
Anderson, N. S., 312
Anderson, Robert H., 447
Andre, E., 104, 517
Andrienko, G., 587, 603
Andrienko, N., 587, 603
Angell, Roger, 538, 557
Apperley, M. D., 231, 263
Arita, K., 436, 449
Ark, Wendy, 245, 260
Arnheim, Rudolf, 232, 236, 260
Ashcraft, Mark H., 27, 52, 375, 378, 401
Ashley, Maryle, 46
Atkins, D., 448, 449
Audia, S., 402

B

Badler, N., 104, 517
Badner, E., 447
Badre, Albert, 55
Baecker, Ronald M., 56, 69, 105, 289, 312, 411, 437, 444, 447, 548, 555, 556
Baggi, D. L., 402
Bailey, Robert W., 26, 49, 52, 69, 103, 104
Balachandran, A., 447
Balakrishnan, R., 403
Balentine, B., 375, 402
Bandlow, A., 36, 45
Barber, R. E., 468, 475
Barbesi, Alessandro, 464, 475
Barfield, W., 254, 260, 261

Barillot, E., 312
Barker, D., 227, 375, 380, 402
Barker, D. T., 406
Barnard, P. J., 325, 328, 342
Bartram, Lyn, 507, 516
Bartsch, M., 572, 606
Bass, Len, 192, 208
Batsell, Richard R., 343
Batson, 443, 447
Baudel, T., 310
Bauer, Malcom L., 103
Baumeister, L., 91, 102
Bawa, Joanna, 57
Baxter, C., 406
Beale, Russell, 53, 208
Beaudouin-Lafon, Michel, 53, 403, 411, 447
Bechtel, Brian, 540, 555
Bederson, Ben B., 22, 45, 46, 198, 208, 275, 310, 394, 402, 403, 506, 507, 516, 580, 590, 593, 603, 604, 605
Begh, K., 404
Beigl, 393, 405
Belkin, N. J., 566, 574, 603, 605
Benbasat, Izak, 227, 260, 329, 330, 342
Benford, Steve, 251, 257, 260
Bentley, R., 123, 134
Benyon, D., 52
Bergman, Eric, 56, 306, 307, 310, 393, 402
Berman, M. L., 365, 402
Berners-Lee, Tim, 80, 103
Bers, J., 312
Bertin, J., 561, 603
Bertran, A., 402
Bessiere, K., 475
Beyer, Hugh, 53, 118, 135
Bhatti, Nina, 457, 463, 464, 475
Bias, Randolph, 56, 113, 135
Bier, E., 293, 303, 310
Bikson, Tora K., 447
Billinghurst, Mark, 263
Billings, Charles E., 80, 103
Bitan, Yuval, 475
Black, J., 328, 342
Blackmon, M. H., 142, 170
Blackwell, A., 352, 353, 406
Blanchard, A., 555
Blenkhorn, 32, 45
Bly, Sara A., 447
Bobrow, D. G., 450

Subject Index

Acknowledgments

Figure	Source
1.1	These materials have been reproduced with the permission of eBay Inc. COPYRIGHT © EBAY INC. ALL RIGHTS RESERVED
1.2	linux.slashdot.org
1.4	*The New York Times* Online, www.nytimes.com
1.5	www.amazon.com
1.6	AOL screenshots © 2004 America Online, Inc. Used with permission
1.8	Used by permission of Orbitz
1.9	THUG is a trademark of Activision Publishing. Tony Hawk is a registered trademark of Tony Hawk. Used with permission from Activision Publishing, Inc. © 2003
1.10	Photos courtesy of PalmOne, Apple Computer, Inc. All rights reserved., and Blackberry
1.11	www.yahoo.com
1.12	www.google.com
1.13	www.google.com
1.14	Illustration courtesy of Kimberly Clauer and Christopher Marston
1.15	Copyright © Leapfrog Enterprises, Inc. Used with Permission
1.16	Photo by John T. Consoli/University of Maryland
1.17	StarLogo, MIT Media Lab, Cambridge, MA
2.4	Used with permission of Bonnie E. John, HCI Institute, School of Computer Science, Carnegie Mellon University, Pittsburgh, PA.
3.2	Courtesy of International Business Machines Corporation unauthorized use not permitted. http://www.ibm.com/easy
3.3	Photos by Catherine Plaisant, and University of Baltimore, KidsTeam (Nancy Kaplan)
3.4	Illustration contributed by Allison Druin, University of Maryland, 2004
4.1	Indiana University School of Library and Information Science (photo by Margaret B. Swan)
4.2	Indiana University School of Library and Information Science (photo by Margaret B. Swan)
4.3	Lab-in-a-Box System at UserWorks, Inc., as supplied by Norm Wilcox Associates
5.6	Illustration courtesy of Nicolas Gaudron
5.10	ILOG Jviews is a product of ILOG S.A © 2004. All rights reserved.
5.11	© 2003 Copyright National Instruments Corporation. LabVIEW™ and National Instruments™ are trademarks and trade names of National Instruments Corporation.

Figure	Source
6.2	Printed with permission of Lotus Development Corporation, Cambridge, MA
6.4	Graphic Image Courtesy of ESRI
6.9	Artwork provided by www.smarthome.com
6.12	ActiveWorlds Inc. www.activeworlds.com
6.13	http://everquest.station.sony.com/
6.14	Screen shot(s) reprinted by permission from Microsoft Corporation
6.15	VA Medical Center—Milwaukee
6.16	Image courtesy: www.5DT.com
6.17	Electronic Visualization Laboratory, University of Illinois at Chicago, drawn by Milana Huang
6.18	© 1995 IEEE
6.19	photo by A. Olson, TSRI copyright 2003
7.6	Image courtesy of Don Hopkins and Maxis: The Sims
7.7	Ben Bederson, University of Maryland
7.8	Peapod, LLC 9933 Woods Dr. Skokie, IL 60093
7.9	www.epicurious.com
7.10	www.alamo.com
7.11	Peapod, LLC 9933 Woods Dr. Skokie, IL 60093
7.12	www.shopping.com
7.13	www.lycos.com
7.14	Screen shot(s) reprinted by permission from Microsoft Corporation
7.15	www.alamo.com
7.17	Illustration courtesy of Francois Guimbretière
7.18	Bergman, E., *Information Appliances and Beyond*, Morgan Kaufmann Publishers, San Francisco (2000)
8.3	Screen shot(s) reprinted by permission from Microsoft Corporation
8.4	Carnegie Learning, Inc.
9.2	Handkey Corp., www.handkey.com
9.3	Courtesy of Kinesis Corp., www.kinesis.com
9.5	Associate, Inference Group, Cavendish Laboratory, University of Cambridge, UK
9.6	PalmOne
9.7	Canesta Keyboard™
9.8	PalmSource
9.9	PalmSource
9.10	Courtesy of Trace R & D Center, University of Wisconsin-Madison, trace.wisc.edu
9.11a	Copyright © 2004 Apple Computer, Inc. All rights reserved.
9.11b	Screen shot(s) reprinted by permission from Microsoft Corporation
9.12	Logitech
9.14	Photograph courtesy of Larry Rativz, Takoma Park, MD
9.15	Image courtesy of Jean-Pablo Hourcade
9.16	iReality.com, Inc.
9.18	QX3™ Microscope.© 2002 Digital Blue™ and Prime Entertainment Inc., www.playdigitalblue.com.All Rights Reserved.

Figure	Source
9.19	Image courtesy of Philips
9.20	Maryland State Highway Administration
9.21	Princeton University, Immersive Media Systems
9.22	Illustration courtesy of Francois Guimbretière
9.23	www.DONZ.com
9.24	Nokia
9.25	Windsor Interfaces, Inc. www.datelens.com
9.26	Touch Graphics Company, USA, 2004
10.2	www.yahoo.com
10.3	Blackberry
10.4	www.iialert.com
10.5	Netscape
10.6	Bob's ACL WWWBoard
10.7	www.blogger.com
10.8	AOL screenshots © 2004 America Online, Inc. Used with permission
10.9	Screen shot(s) reprinted by permission from Microsoft Corporation
10.10	Polycom
10.11	Used with permission from groupsystems.com
10.12a	Used with permission from groupsystems.com
10.12b	Used with permission from groupsystems.com
10.13a	Smart Technologies, Inc.
10.13b	Smart Technologies, Inc.
10.14	Halkia, M., Local, G., *Building the Brief: Action and Audience in Augmented Reality*. In: Stephanidis, C., (Ed), *Universal Access in HCI: Inclusive Design in the Information Society*, v.4 . Lawrence Erlbaum Associates: London 2003 pp. 389–393 (figure 3 is on page 392).
10.15	Office of Information Technology, University of Maryland
11.1	Global Land Cover Facility at the University of Maryland Institute for Advanced Computer Studies
11.5	Huberman, Bernardo A., *The Laws of the Web: Patterns in the Ecology of Information*, MIT Press, Cambridge MA (2001).
12.1a	www.ananova.com
12.1b	Screen shot(s) reprinted by permission from Microsoft Corporation
12.3a	University of Maryland
12.3b	www.amazon.com
12.5	Parush, A., Nadir, R., and Shtub, A (1998), Evaluating the layout of graphical user interface screens: Validation of a numerical computerized model, *International Journal of Human-Computer Interaction*, 10(4), 343–360.
12.7	Please contact for any further questions: h.weber@easycode.de
13.1	Adobe Systems, Inc.
13.2	The Institute for Systems Research, University of Maryland
13.3	www.spotfire.com
13.8	Screen shot(s) reprinted by permission from Microsoft Corporation
13.10	www.alamo.com
13.11	www.taxcut.com

Figure	Source
13.12	Screen shot(s) reprinted by permission from Microsoft Corporation
13.13	Adobe Systems, Inc.
13.16	www.google.com
14.3	http://vivisimo.com/
14.4	Ben Bederson, University of Maryland
14.5	Informedia Digital Video Library. News Images copyright CNN; Used with Permission
14.6	Christopher Williamson, Ben Shneiderman: The Dynamic HomeFinder: Evaluating Dynamic Queries in a Real-Estate Information Exploration System. *SIGIR 1992:* 338–346
14.7	www.bluenile.com
14.8	Global Change Master Directory, University of Maryland
14.9	Courtesty of Marti Hearst
14.10	The Hive Group
14.11	Used with permission of AT&T Bell Labs, Naperville, IL
14.12	TextArc (http://textarc.org) by W. Bradford Paley, © 2002–2004
14.13	Pacific Northwest National Laboratory
14.15	www.spotfire.com
14.16	GeoVISTA *Studio* open source toolkit courtesy of Alan MacEachren and Xiping Dai, www.geovista.psu.edu
14.17	Inxight Software Inc., www.inxight.com
14.18	Courtesy of Fraunhofer FIT and humanIT
14.20	Courtesy PARC
14.21	Inxight Software Inc., www.inxight.com
14.22	SmartMoney.com
14.23	ILOG Jviews is a product of ILOG S.A © 2004. All rights reserved.
14.24	Drawing Large Graphs with H3Viewer and Site Manager, Tamara Munzner, Lecture Notes in Computer Science series, *Proceedings for the Symposium on Graph Drawing, GD '98,* Montreal, Canada, August 1998.
14.25	Douglas B. Shore, N Space Labs, Inc.
14.26	Fekete and Plaisant, 2002

About the Authors

Ben Shneiderman is a Professor in the Department of Computer Science, Founding Director (1983–2000) of the Human-Computer Interaction Laboratory (http://www.cs.umd.edu/hcil), and Member of the Institute for Advanced Computer Studies and the Institute for Systems Research, all at the University of Maryland at College Park. He is a Fellow of the ACM and AAAS and received the ACM CHI (Computer Human Interaction) Lifetime Achievement Award. His books, research papers, and frequent lectures have made him an international leader in this emerging discipline. For relaxation he likes biking, hiking, skiing, and travel.

Catherine Plaisant is Associate Research Scientist at the Human-Computer Interaction Laboratory of the University of Maryland Institute for Advanced Computer Studies. She earned a Doctorat d'Ingénieur degree in France in 1982 and has been conducting research in the field of human-computer interaction since then. In 1987, she joined Professor Shneiderman at the University of Maryland, where she has worked with students and members of the lab, throughout the growth of the field of human-computer interaction. Her research contributions range from focused interaction techniques to innovative visualizations validated with user studies to practical applications developed with industrial partners.